THE SCIENCE OF SACRED THEOLOGY

The Science
of
Sacred Theology

BOOKS 1–4
Complete in one volume

EMMANUEL DORONZO, O.M.I.
Introduction by
Matthew K. Minerd, Ph.D.

AROUCA
PRESS

Originally published as *The Science of Sacred Theology*
for Teachers in four separate volumes
by Notre Dame Institute Press (Middleburg,
Virginia) in 1974 & 1976.

NIHIL OBSTAT
Rev. Msgr. Eugene Kevane, Ph.D
Censor deputatus

IMPRIMATUR
✠ Most Rev. John T. Russell, D.D.
February 7, 1973
Richmond, Virginia

ISBN: 978-1-990685-29-3 (pbk)
ISBN: 978-1-990685-30-9 (hc)

Arouca Press
PO Box 55003
Bridgeport PO
Waterloo, ON N2J 3G0
Canada
www.aroucapress.com
Send inquiries to info@aroucapress.com

CONTENTS

INTRODUCTION by Matthew K. Minerd   xi

BOOK 1: INTRODUCTION TO THEOLOGY   1
   Preface   3
   1 What is Theology?   5
   2 Possibility, Usefulness and Necessity of Theology   7
   3 Theology as a Science   10
   4 Properties of Theology   16
   5 Functions of Theology   22
   6 Methods of Theology   26
   7 Division of Theology   30
   8 History of Theology   33

   Glossary   43
   Analytical Index   52
   Bibliography   55

BOOK 2: REVELATION   57
   Introduction   59

PART I: *General Notions on Revelation*   63
   1 Nature of Revelation   65
   2 Possibility of Revelation   69
   3 Fittingness and Necessity of Revelation   74
   4 The Nature or Rational Credibility
      of Revelation   77
   5 Necessity or Rational Credibility of Revelation   79
   6 The Natural Genesis of the Credibility
      of Revelation   83
   7 Criteria of the Credibility of Revelation   85

PART II: *The Fact of Revelation*   87
   8 Christ's Testimony About His Mission As
      Herald of God's Revelation   89
   9 Subjective Criteria of the Fact of Revelation   92
   10 Objective Intrinsic Criteria of the
      Fact of Revelation   100

11 Objective Extrinsic Criteria of the Fact of
 Revelation. Physical Miracles 118
12 Objective Extrinsic Criteria of the Fact
 of Revelation. Prophecies 138
13 Conclusion 153

 Glossary 155
 Analytical Index 159
 Bibliography 164

BOOK 3: THE CHANNELS OF REVELATION 165
 Introduction 167

PART I: *The Three Channels of Revelation* 169
 1 Scripture, The Written Deposit of Revelation 171
 2 Tradition, The Living Deposit of Revelation 178
 3 The Magisterium, Organ of Revelation 197

PART II: *The Theological Contents of the*
 Channels of Revelation 203
 4 Dogma 205
 5 Theological Conclusion 216
 6 Theological Notes and Censures 223

 Glossary 229
 Analytical Index 233
 Bibliography 237

BOOK 4: THE CHURCH 239
 Introduction 241
 1 Institution and Purpose of the Church 247
 2 The Intimate Nature of the Church 255
 3 The Exterior Structure of the Church 271
 4 The Threefold Power of the Church 282
 5 Peter's Primacy 300
 6 The Primacy of the Roman Pontiff 312
 7 The Nature of the Primacy of the
  Roman Pontiff 331
 8 Infallibility of the Roman Pontiff 337
 9 Divine Origin of the Episcopacy 359
 10 Collegial Nature of the Episcopacy 369
 11 Monarchical Form of the Episcopacy 381

12 The Threefold Degree of the Power of Orders,
     Episcopate, Presbyterate, and Diaconate   387
13 The Members of the Church   410
14 The Laity   421
15 The Properties of the Church   431
16 The Marks of the Church, Showing the
     Trueness of the Catholic Church   439
17 Activity of the Church in the World   445

Glossary   456
Analytical Index   468
Bibliography   482

INTRODUCTION

Emmanuel Doronzo

A FORGOTTEN GIANT OF AMERICAN THOMISTIC THEOLOGY

MATTHEW K. MINERD, PH.D.
Ss. Cyril and Methodius Byzantine Catholic Seminary

OURS IS AN AGE OF SURPRISING CONTRADIC-tions. The broader culture of the developed West seems to be on the inclining slope of a kind of forgetfulness of its past. Whether in intellectual culture, political and social customs, or even religious institutions and memory, our present-day bonds to our inherited past seem to be matters of little importance. The transhumanist man of tomorrow would appear to be the goal of our greatest endeavors. It is the future, not the past that beckons. On the other hand, certain quarters are marked by a growing awareness of the ways in which modernity in general and, in particular, the past century have robbed the West of much of its patrimony. Even if some figures in this latter vein are inflected toward a kind of kneejerk antiquarianism, many younger scholars, thinkers, and men and women of good will merely understand the sound wisdom of Edmund Burke: "People will not look forward to posterity, who never look backward to their ancestors."[1]

Among such ancestors whose memory is being recovered, thanks to the labors of Arouca Press, we can now most happily number Fr. Emmanuel Doronzo, O. M. I. A native of the city of Barletta in South-Eastern Italy, a graduate of the Gregorianum and the Angelicum (where he was a student of the great Thomist master, Fr. Reginald Garrigou-Lagrange), Fr. Doronzo taught for decades in Europe and the United States, first in Turin, Italy, then at the scholasticate of the Oblates of Mary in San Antonio, Texas, and finally at the Catholic University of America. He was

---

1 Edmund Burke, *Reflections on the Revolution in France* (Cambridge: W. P. Grant, 1836), 42.

a two-time recipient of the Catholic Theological Society of America's Cardinal Spellman Award, receiving it, along with several other recipients, in 1947 (the first year this award was conferred) as well as a second time in 1951. And he served as a consultator for the American pre-conciliar theological commission for the Second Vatican Council, doing so alongside then-Bishop John Wright, Bishop James Griffiths, Msgr. Joseph Clifford Fenton, and Capuchin Fr. Dominic Unger.[2]

Fr. Doronzo's primary specialization and publishing work was devoted to sacramental theology. From 1945 to 1963, in addition to several scholarly articles in Latin and English, he published over 11,000 pages in closely documented texts devoted to the seven sacraments. Although these volumes could be (and, by some, were) classified among the genre referred to as "manuals," it is likely better to think of them as scholarly monographs written in Latin, in the scholastic style of questions and articles, presenting the state of the art concerning the topics treated therein. Published over the course of a twenty-year period in Milwaukee by Bruce, the tomes are an impressive array of dogmatic treatises on the seven sacraments. Chronologically, these works are:[3]

- *Tractatus dogmatici de baptismo et confimatione* (1945): 453 pages
- *Tractatus dogmaticus de sacramentis in genere* (1946): 595 pages
- *Tractus dogmaticus de eucharistia* (1947–8): Vol. 1, *De sacramento*, 860 pages; Vol. 2, *De sacrificio*, 486 pages
- *Tractatus dogmaticus de poenitentia* (1949–1953), Vol. 1, *De sacramento et virtute*, 560 pages; vol. 2, *De contritione et confessione*, 1044 pages; vol. 3, *De satisfactione et absolutione*, 742 pages; vol. 4, *De causis extrinsecis*, 1208 pages
- *Tractatus dogmaticus de extrema unctione* (1954–5): Vol. 1, *De causis intrinsicis*, 634 pages; Vol. 2, *De causis extrinsecis*, 881 pages

---

2 For a brief account concerning Fr. Doronzo, see Raymond Cooney et al., "Americans Preparing Vatican II," *Dominicana* 47, no. 2: 155–178 (here 161). This is the only place I have found Fr. Doronzo referred to with the title "Msgr." I will continue to use "Fr.," though a book concerning the details of his life deserves to be written in full, based on archival material from the O. M. I. archives as well as those of The Catholic University of America.

3 I have opted, following the general approach of the reviewers in *The Thomist*, to include his very excellent indices in the page counts. Likewise, in line with the *Thomist*'s approach, I have included his introductory pages in the total. All of the introductions are very brief.

- *Tractatus de ordine* (1957–1962): Vol. 1, *De institutione*, 1014 pages; Vol. 2 *De institutione et de materia et forma*, 912 pages; *De causis extrinsicis*, 868 pages
- *Theologia dogmaticus de matrimonio* (1964): Vol. 1, *De institutione, essentia, et fine*, 973 pages; Vol. 2 not completed

In his introduction to the first volume of Fr. Doronzo's *De poenitentia*, his former professor, Fr. Reginald Garrigou-Lagrange, warmly recalls Doronzo as a "dear" and "most excellent" (*optimus*) student, who "fixed his mind upon the higher principles [of theological topics under discussion]."[4] And as he remarks in a review of Fr. Doronzo's works on the sacraments in general, Baptism, Confirmation, and the Eucharist: "He is not guilty of the shortcoming that we can see in those who are more concerned with conclusions to be drawn rather than with principles."[5] Anyone who is familiar with Fr. Garrigou-Lagrange's works knows of his repeated emphasis on the need to focus on principles rather than mere material erudition. Yet the Dominican master also notes in his aforementioned introduction Fr. Doronzo's expertise in positive theology, the details of speculative theology, as well as the practical applications of sacramental dogmatics. And who cannot help but admire a Thomist who "sets forth, with great clarity, the Church's teaching, according to the interpretation given by St. Thomas and his best commentators: Cajetan, John of St. Thomas, [Jean-Baptiste] Gonet, and the Carmelites of Salamanca."[6]

Fr. Joseph Clifford Fenton, long-time editor of the *American Ecclesiastical Review* and conciliar peritus to Cardinal Alfredo Ottaviani at the Second Vatican Council, remarked in 1951 (long before the full completion of all of Doronzo's labors) that the sacramental theologian's works were arguably to be numbered among "the most important theological works ever issued by American Scholars."[7] In his 1952 review of the second volume of *De poenitentia*, Fr. William Le Saint, S. J., light-heartedly remarked

---

4   See Reginald Garrigou-Lagrange, "Praefatio" in Emmanuel Doronzo, *De Poenitentia*, vol. 1 *De sacramento et virtute* (Milwaukee: Bruce, 1949), vii–viii (here, vii).
5   Reginald Garrigou-Lagrange, "Review of Emmanuel Doronzo, *De sacramentis in genere, De Baptismo et confirmation*, and *De Eucharistia*," *Angelicum* 24, no. 4 (October–December, 1947): 297–298 (here 297).
6   Ibid.
7   Joseph Clifford Fenton, "America's Two Theological Associations," *The American Ecclesiastical Review* 125 (July–December, 1951): 449–458 (here, 457).

that perhaps one day just as the Irish say that a man is a liar if he says he has read all the miracles of St. Kevin, so too one may render the same judgment of the man "who claims to have read all that Fr. Doronzo has written on the sacraments." He continues his praise in no faint words: "It is remarkable that he writes so much; it is more remarkable that he writes so much so well." And as he closes his review, he remarks, "It may be said with assurance that every theologian who wants the most complete, modern account of the sacrament of penance, published in any country and written in any language, needs this book."[8]

Such is a repeated refrain in the review literature. In reference to his over 1,400 pages devoted to the sacrament of the anointing of the sick, we find a reviewer commenting that his volumes are "a peerless achievement in the history of sacramental theology," drawing particular attention to his lengthy chapter on the effects of the sacrament, which the reviewer refers to as a "tour de force," going on to state, "Nowhere in modern theological literature will one find a more accurate and fully speculative discussion of the sevenfold effect which theological tradition has assigned to this sacrament."[9] Another reviewer comments on the same work: "A statement concerning the previous volumes [by Fr. Doronzo] bears reaffirmation: the student of theology who is not acquainted with this comprehensive treatment of Extreme Unction denies himself the full breadth of view of the subject; the professor of sacramental theology will find among modern manuals no more satisfying a source-book."[10] And it is noted that in contrast to many manuals of that time, Fr. Doronzo always keeps the dogmatic consideration of the sacraments *in themselves* central, though he also is sensitive to moral and canonical questions related to the sacraments.[11] Similar remarks are repeated

---

8 William Le Saint, "Review of De poenitentia, vol. 2, by Emmanuel Doronzo, O. M. I.," *Theological Studies* 13, no. 3 (1952): 445–447.

9 Patrick J. Sullivan, "Review of De extrema unctione, vol. 2, by Emmanuel Doronzo, O. M. I.," *Theological Studies* 17, no. 2 (May, 1956): 260–262.

10 Nicholas Halligan, "Review of De extrema unctione by Emmanuel Doronzo, O. M. I.," *The Thomist* 20, no. 2 (January 1957): 103–106 (here, 103).

11 See "Brief Notice Concerning De Poenitentia, 4 vols. by Emmanuel Doronzo," *The Thomist* 17, no. 1 (1954): 120–121. In this, we see evidence that Fr. Doronzo was well aware of the intimate union that binds together dogmatic theology and the other branches of theology, an outlook that he would have imbibed from Fr. Garrigou-Lagrange, who—long before even someone like Fr. Pinckaers (who

over and over concerning all of his treatises on the Sacraments.

In his more general dogmatic works, Fr. Doronzo likewise bears witness to his erudition, both in the history of theology as well as concerning many contemporary debates. As a pedagogical aid to the contemporary reader of his day (and ours), he published a translation of the *Dizionario di teologia dommatica* by Pietro Parente, Antonio Piolanti, and Salvatore Garofalo.[12] However, more impressive are his two volumes in Dogmatic Theology, *Theologia Dogmatica*, totaling over 2,000 pages.[13] The text was originally intended to be a four-volume series to be used in Latin Catholic seminary formation.[14] The first two volumes contain his discussions of the nature of theology, the question of the extrinsic credibility of revelation and its distinction from the supernatural assent of faith, an excellent and clear discussion of the treatise *De locis theologicis* on theological sources, the treatment of God as One and Three, the theology of creation and the causation of grace, and finally, the dogmatic theology of grace itself. How unfortunate it is that his final two volumes, devoted to Christology, Mariology, and Ecclesiology (vol. 3), and to the Sacraments and the Last Things (vol. 4), were never published!

These Latin dogmatics volumes, founded on his massive erudition, were the source for the abbreviated, though profound, texts gathered together in the present volume. They were published by the Notre Dame Pontifical Catechetical Institute founded by

---

is most often credited with this emphasis, at least among contemporary Thomists)—repeatedly critiques the somewhat empty casuistic excesses of a morality that is detached from its dogmatic roots. Obviously, too, Fr. Doronzo would have been reinforced in this insight by many of the discussions undertaken on this subject in the 1940s–1960s.

12   See Pietro Parente and Antonio Piolanti, and Salvatore Garofalo, *Dictionary of Dogmatic Theology*, trans. Emmanuel Doronzo (Milwaukee: Bruce, 1951).

13   See Emmanuel Doronzo, *Theologia dogmatica*, 2 vols. (Washington, DC: The Catholic University of America Press, 1966 and 1968). For a full discussion of Fr. Doronzo's own understanding of the unity and division of theology, accompanied by significant awareness of contemporary discussions concerning this matter, see *Theologia dogmatica*, vol. 1, p. 85–92.

14   See C. McAuliffe, "Short Notice for *Theologia Dogmatica* by Emmanuel Doronzo," *Theological Studies* 28, no. 3 (1967): 630–631; L. Ciappi, "Review of *Theologia Dogmatica*, 2 vols, by Emmanuel Doronzo," *Angelicum* 50 (1973): 106–108. This use in seminary formation doubtless was one of the reasons for adopting the somewhat problematic division between dogmatic theology and, for example, moral theology. On the unity of theology, see ST I, q. 1, a. 3 and 7, as well as the various classical and modern Thomistic commentaries on these articles.

Msgr. Eugene Kevane, the dean of the school of education at the Catholic University of America during the period of upheaval raised by the moral-theological dissent of certain members of the faculty of theology in the late 1960s.[15]

Although one Dominican reviewer lamented that the texts were marked by the Latin style of the original, he appreciatively noted their usefulness, especially Doronzo's introduction to theology and the "channels of revelation" (the portion devoted to topics falling to the traditional theological treatise De locis theologicis).[16] In line with his era, the reviewer was less sanguine concerning the text on revelation, though in fact, the astute reader will see how it is that Fr. Doronzo here summarizes with great clarity the "border-land" of faith and reason, a task that is utterly necessary lest theological reflection fall either into rationalism or fideism. All four volumes gathered here are, however, more than merely useful. They are crystal-clear waters flowing with the best of Thomistic theology on these topics.

Of greatest interest, however, among the texts gathered here is his fourth volume on the Church. Marked by the same clarity as the first three texts, nonetheless this fourth work is more technical and filled with the contemporary theological erudition that can be found in Fr. Doronzo's other books. It would seem that this volume, the longest of the four, was a shortened form of the dogmatic treatise on the Church that he had originally intended to write. In it, we find an incredibly well-informed Thomist writing after the promulgation of the Vatican II declarations concerning the Church. If ever there were an example of a "hermeneutic of continuity" it is found here. This volume alone is a rich and organized ecclesiological synthesis. Even if it is inflected toward a certain kind of Roman theological stamp (which I cannot, as an Eastern Catholic, wholly gloss over), nonetheless, Fr. Doronzo's synthesis is peerless among English-language works of ecclesiology. It makes one wonder: what would life today be like if American Catholic theology had remained at his caliber, rather

---

15 For an account of Fr. Kevane's involvement in defense of Catholic orthodox during the Curran affair, see Peter M. Mitchell, The Coup at Catholic University: The 1968 Revolution in American Catholic Education (San Francisco: Ignatius Press, 2015), 103–117. Concerning his founding of the Notre Dame Institute, see ibid., 103n8.
16 See P. McCarroll, "Review of The Science of Sacred Theology for Teachers, vols. 1–3," The Thomist 39, no. 1 (January 1975): 180.

than in the ersatz forms it assumed in far too many quarters in the later 60s, 1970s, and 1980s?

It is striking — and somewhat sobering concerning the state of things — that few theologians know Fr. Doronzo's name, much less the quality of his work.[17] Obviously, as an Eastern Catholic, I have hopes for more than a mere repetition of the Latin theology of the past. However, precisely as one who desires a true and penetrating *intellectus fidei* to be present and operative in the Church, I profoundly hope for the day when Latin Catholics will draw from the *nova* and the *vetera*, learning from true past experts before declaring themselves to be such in the midst of the novel concerns of contemporary scholarly debates, many of which will fall into the desuetude that befalls all structures that do not plunge down their foundation to solid and established ground. In almost every review of Fr. Doronzo's labors, his interlocutors noted points where they disagreed with him. However, across the board, they all marveled at his erudition and sound exposition of theology, at once truly "speculative," while also striving to found itself on the *loci theologici*, the positive-theological sources of speculative-theological labors. How desirable it would be if theological culture could take for granted today a full understanding of the topics in the sacraments and general dogmatics as we find them in Fr. Doronzo. Slightly expanding the words of a dear old Thomist, for whom I have the greatest of affection: "If we won't listen to 'secondary sources' like Cajetan, Poinsot [John of St. Thomas], Garrigou-Lagrange, Maritain, and Simon," as well as Emmanuel Doronzo, "Why should anyone listen to secondary sources like us?"[18] Today, at least, we can most joyfully salute this first stage of recovery, thanks to the tireless work of Arouca Press. Let us read and listen![19]

---

17 A few specialists clearly do, as their monographs attest. However, that is insufficient to the massive erudition of this great theologian.

18 John C. Cahalan, "Thomism's Conceptual Structure and Modern Science," in *Facts are Stubborn Things: Thomistic Perspectives on the Philosophies of Nature and Science*, ed. Matthew K. Minerd (Washington, DC: American Maritain Association, 2021), 40–68 (here 66).

19 Some time ago, Mr. Mitchell Kengor and Mr. Caleb Hood made me aware of some biographical details concerning Fr. Doronzo, of whom I knew solely through his works, upon which I had providentially stumbled once upon a time. I thank them for forwarding me this information, cited above. Also, I owe gratitude to several friends who provided editorial remarks that helped to shape elements of this brief introduction.

BOOK 1
Introduction to Theology

PREFACE

IN HIS REPROBATION OF THE THEOLOGICAL IRE-
nicism and relativism, which began to creep among Catholic writers several years ago under the fallacious name of "The
New Theology," and which seems to make progress in these
days, Pope Pius XII declared: "It would be extremely imprudent
to neglect or throw away or deprive of their proper value, the
many so important things which have been thought, formulated
and polished, with increasing accuracy, in order to express the
truths of faith. It is a process that has required several centuries of labor, carried out by men of uncommon skill and holiness,
under the vigilance of the sacred Magisterium and the light and
guidance of the Holy Spirit. To substitute for such concepts
conjectural notions and the vague fluid formulas of a new philosophy, which like flowers of the field blossom today and wilt
tomorrow, would also be harmful to dogma itself. Dogma would
become like a reed shaken by the wind. Contempt for the expressions and notions commonly used by scholastic theologians leads
to a weakening of so-called speculative theology, which, as they
claim [namely, the defenders of the new opinions], lacks true
certitude, inasmuch as it is grounded on theological reasoning."[1]

The Second Vatican Council, far from opening the door to such
neo-modernism (as some dare to claim) directs us to the "Common Doctor" of the Church as the norm of theological research.
"In order to illustrate the mysteries of salvation as thoroughly as
possible," the Council states, "students should learn to penetrate
them more deeply by means of speculative procedure, under the
guidance of St. Thomas."[2]

And again, speaking in general about Catholic schools of higher
learning, the Council declares that they should conduct a deeper
search into contemporary problems and their harmonization with
supernatural truth, "following in the footsteps of the Doctors of
the Church, above all of St. Thomas Aquinas."[3]

Pope Paul VI renews this same commendation even more

---

1 Encyclical *Humani generis*, AAS 42 (1950) 567.
2 Decree on Priestly Formation, no. 16 (Oct. 28, 1965).
3 Declaration on Christian Education, no. (Oct. 28, 1965).

3

explicitly and urgently. "Those to whom the teaching function has been entrusted," he says, "should reverently listen to the voice of the Doctors of the Church, among whom Saint Thomas holds the principal place. For the angelic Doctor's genius is so powerful, his love for truth so sincere, his wisdom so great in investigating and illustrating sublime truths, and gathering them into a fitting bond of unity, that his doctrine is the most efficacious instrument not only for safeguarding the foundations of the Faith, but also for reaping the fruits of sounds progress in a profitable and sure manner."[4]

Bearing in mind such urgent recommendations on the part of the Magisterium, we believe it useful to publish this short treatise, Thomistic in character, as an introduction to Sacred Theology. This we do in the hope that teachers may derive some fruit from it, and hand this fruit on to others. We beg indulgence if the matter may appear hard to unaccustomed eyes, for its very nature does not allow for easy presentation or light reading.

We agree, of course, that even theology, in organizing its various treaties and in treating of its various questions, needs some kind of *aggiornamento* or adaptation to modern mentality and temperament. But we are also convinced that theological science itself, in its nature, specific functions and proper methods as described in this work, cannot be changed, just as man himself amid the variety of seasonal conditions may well change his clothing but can never change his skin. The severe warning of Pius XII still stands against those who "dare to go so far as to question seriously whether theology and its method, as carried on in the schools with the approval of ecclesiastical authority, should not only be improved, but completely changed."[5]

---

4 Allocution delivered at the Pontifical Gregorian University, AAS 56 (1964) 365.
5 Encyclical *Humani generis*, AAS 42 (1950) 564.

1

What is Theology?

THE WORD "THEOLOGY" DERIVES FROM THE TWO
Greek nouns, "theós" (God) and "lógos" (word, speech, discourse).
Hence theology in general is a discourse about God. In this sense
the word was used originally by pagan writers, as Plato[6], Aristotle[7], and Cicero[8].

Later on the fathers of the Church began to use it as early as
the third century; thus a word foreign to Scripture was introduced
into ecclesiastical literature. Eusebius of Caesarea (†340) gave the
title "Ecclesiastical Theology" to one of his works. Toward the
end of the fifth century, pseudo-Dionysius the Areopagite wrote
a work entitled "Mystical Theology."

In the patristic literature, however, the word "theology" has
only a generic meaning, that of any discourse about God, whether
given in a scientific way, or in a pastoral and instructional manner,
as in the kerygmatic or homiletic forms of discourse. The medieval theologian, beginning with Abelard (†1142), narrowed the
meaning of the word, confining it to a "scientific discourse about
God." It was with this meaning that they gave their great scientific
and systematic works the title of "Summae Theologiae." In his
"Summa Theologiae" St. Thomas (†1274) distinguished further
between natural theology and supernatural theology.[9] Natural or
philosophical theology, now called theodicy, considers God only
under the light of reason, while supernatural theology now called
simply theology, treats of God under the light of revelation. Since
that time, this distinction has become classic and is in common
usage among theologians.

Thus the general notion of theology in ecclesiastical literature
can be described as the *entire reasoning process of our mind about revelation*, that is, about those divine truths which have been directly

---

6 *Republic* II. 379.
7 *Metaphysics* III. 4; VI. 1.
8 *The nature of the Gods* III. 21.
9 I-II, q. 1, a. 1, ad. 2.

manifested to us by God. This is what St. Anselm of Canterbury (†1109) expressed synthetically in his famous aphorism: "Faith seeking understanding."[10]

---

10 *Proslogion*, prologue.

2

Possibility, Usefulness and Necessity of Theology

GIVEN THE FACT OF SUPERNATURAL REVELATION, which we know from faith and which is also shown from reason in the apologetical treatise on revelation, we must admit the *possibility of theology*, that is of some reasoning process of our mind about the truths which have been revealed. This process consists in further expressing something true, objective and stable about those truths, and inferring from them logical conclusions, beyond what is simply and without reasoning understood and admitted through faith alone.

This possibility has been questioned recently and even denied by some Catholic theologians, basing their views on a kind of theological relativism and pleading for the introduction of a "new theology." Speculative theology, they claim, has a merely relative value and can only furnish mere probabilities or hypotheses, since it uses analogical concepts, which do not necessarily correspond to objective reality. Besides, any philosophical system can contribute to such probabilities and hypotheses, and indeed the philosophical systems of different ages ought to make this contribution. Thus theology should result from a legitimate and fruitful contact of eternal revealed truth with the actual culture and formation of the human intellect in the given circumstances of history.[11]

But the denial of the possibility of theology on the basis of such historical relativism leads necessarily to the denial of the

---

11   This opinion was patronized, among others, by N. D. Chenu, "Position de la théologie," *Revue des sciences philosophiques et théologiques* 24 (1935) 232–257; L. Charlier, *Essai sur le problème théologique*, Thuillies 1938; J. M. Le Blond, "L'analogie de la vérité," *Recherches de science religieuse* 34 (1947) 129–141; H. Bouillard, "Notions concillaires et analogie de la vérité," *Recherches de science religieuse* 35 (1948) 251–270; H. De Lubac, *Corpus Mysticum. L'Eucharistie et l'Eglise au moyen âge* (éd. 2, Paris 1949) 248–277; cf. also *Recherches de science religieuse* 35 (1948) 130–160; 36 (1949) 80–121. See the criticism of this opinion by M. Labourdette, "La théologie et ses sources," *Revue thomiste* 46 (1946) 353–371, and by R. Garrigou-Lagrange, "La nouvelle théologie où va-t-elle?," *Angelicum* 33 (1946) 126–145.

possibility of revelation itself. For revelation too is expressed by means of analogical concepts, as when we say that God is the Father or the Son, that in God there are three persons, that God speaks to men through revelation, that grace is a participation in the divine nature, and so on. No one can deny that these concepts — father, son, person, speech, nature — have an objective and certain value when used to express revealed truths, otherwise we give up revelation itself and we face pure Modernism. Therefore, we must conclude that also the analogical concepts, by which discursive reason inquires into these revealed truths and draws further conclusions from them, have an objective and certain value.

The truth of this position receives strong confirmation from the Church's Magisterium in the encyclical *Humani generis*.[12]

The great usefulness and relative necessity of theology is shown clearly by the following three considerations.

First, theology in its generic sense of a reasoning process about revelation, meets a physical need and native disposition of our mind. For it is connatural to man to inquire and to reason about an object which he possesses in his mind, and to draw conclusions from principles that he holds. Therefore, just as philosophical science is born from principles known through revelation and believed by faith, it is connatural to us to fashion and develop a sort of theological science.[13]

Secondly, theology is required by faith itself. For, as St. Augustine puts it, "Through this science ... faith ... is begotten, nourished, defended, and strengthened."[14]

Through theology, faith is begotten in unbelievers by way of exterior persuasion, inasmuch as it presents to them the "preambles of faith," that is, those natural truths about God which are necessarily presupposed by faith. Such are, for example, the existence of God and his providence. Through theology faith is also nourished in Christians. For it gives them a clearer and deeper understanding of the mysteries of the faith, of their mutual

---

12 See AAS 42 (1950) 565–574; quoted above, in the Preface.
13 Scripture itself not only transmits to us truths to be believed, in the form of an assertion, but frequently uses also the discourse of reason to illustrate them or to infer one from another. Thus Christ, from the words of Ps. 109:1 ("The Lord said to my Lord ... ") infers his own Divinity (Matt. 19:6). St. Paul, from the resurrection of Christ, who is the head of the Mystical Body, infers the resurrection of his members, that is of the faithful (1 Cor. 15:20).
14 *De Trinitate* 24.1, ML 42.1037.

connection and of their harmonious agreement with the truths of natural reason. Furthermore, theology defends the Catholic faith. This it does against exterior adversaries, by repulsing their scoffing and exposing their sophistry. Even more importantly, it does so against harmful tendencies within the mind of the faithful, since without solid theological science, human nature slides down easily into superficiality, sentimentalism, and arbitrary views in the interpreting of Scripture, in preaching the word of God, and in the spiritual direction of souls.

Finally, theology strengthens faith in two ways. Subjectively it adds the light of reason, by which faith becomes also a "reasonable submission"[15] of our mind to God. Objectively it contributes to the growth of faith itself, inasmuch as through the work and labor of theologians, the infallible definitions of the Magisterium normally are prepared.

Thirdly, philosophy itself is helped and to some extent perfected by theology, just as nature is perfected by grace and reason by revelation. This is especially evident in the higher branches of philosophy, namely theodicy and ethics, which deal with God and morality. For, since theology is based directly on revelation, it shares to some degree in the same moral necessity that the human intellect has of the direct word of God, in order to acquire suitably the right knowledge of those same truths about God which can be reached through natural reason.

Pope Pius XII in his encyclical "Humani generis" declares: "Divine revelation must be called morally necessary for the suitable knowledge of those religious and moral truths which are not of themselves beyond the power of human reason, so that, even in the present condition of mankind they may be reached by all men promptly, firmly, and without any admixture of error."[16] In this the Holy Father is repeating the teaching of St. Thomas and of the First Vatican Council.[17]

---

15   Rom. 12.1. Such is the sense given to this text by theologians and by the Vatican Council I (Sess. 3, chap. 3 on faith, Denz. 3008).
16   AAS 42 (1950) 562.
17   See St. Thomas, *Summa Theologiae*, I, q. 1, a. 1.

3

Theology as a Science

WE SAID ABOVE THAT THEOLOGY CONSIDERED IN its generic sense is a reasoning process of our mind about the truths of revelation. We shall now analyze the intrinsic nature of this process, that is, the specific notion of theology. This can be summarized briefly and fittingly in the following definition: *Theology is the science about God under the light of revelation.* This definition is made up of two elements which must be given a full and adequate explanation. The first element is the proper scientific nature of theology as an act or process of the human mind; the second is the proper object of theology, namely God himself under the light of revelation.

1. THEOLOGY IS A TRUE SCIENCE

By a true science we understand, "the certain and evident knowledge of an object through its proper causes."

If knowledge is not certain, it is merely opinion. If it is certain but not evident, it is called faith. Thus opinion and faith are both distinguished from science properly so-called. Furthermore, to constitute a science, it is not sufficient simply to have a certain and evident knowledge; it must also be knowledge of an object through its proper causes. Thus if I say, "The human soul is immortal," I express merely a simple knowledge of the immortality of the soul. If, however, I add, "The human soul is immortal, because it is spiritual," I have a scientific knowledge of the immortality of the soul, because I know it through its cause, that is, as an effect of its proper cause, which is spirituality, for without spirituality there can be no immortality.

Such scientific knowledge consists really in a reasoning process, in which the cause is expressed by principles, and the effect by a conclusion. In other words, it consists in inferring a conclusion (the effect) from principles (the cause).

In summary, therefore, three elements are required for a true science, namely: first, it must be the knowledge of an object through its cause, by a discursive process moving from principles to conclusions; second, it must be certain; third, it must be evident. We now proceed to show that these three essential requirements are actually found in the theology.

Theology is indeed a *discursive process*, in which the mind moves from some principles or truths, known through revelation and held by faith, to infer real conclusions, that is, new truths, not explicitly contained in the former. For example, from the revealed truth of the presence of two natures in Christ, theology infers the presence of two wills, human and divine, in the same person of Christ.

Theology is moreover *certain* knowledge because it is based upon and proceeds from the principles of faith. Therefore it shares in their absolute certitude.

Theology is also an *evident* knowledge, because it shares likewise in the intrinsic evidence of its principles. In other words, it necessarily infers its conclusions from revealed principles which are objectively evident in themselves, and will also be subjectively evident to us in the beatific vision, although they are not evident to us in our present state of simple faith. Seen from this point of view, theology exhibits a certain imperfection, for it is a *science subalternate* to the knowledge which we will have in the higher science of beatific vision, in which its principles are immediately evident.

Music offers an example which may help to understand this better. Music is a science subalternate to arithmetic, in which the laws and principles of musical rhythm become immediately evident. Thus a musician who is not at the same time a mathematician has only mediate evidence of his principles, and in his present state he must receive them from the mathematician through an act of natural faith.

2. THE OBJECT OF THEOLOGY IS GOD, UNDER THE LIGHT OF REVELATION

The expression "God under the light of revelation" includes the material object, the formal object, and the formal light of the science of theology. These three are technical terms in any science, and must be analyzed carefully for accuracy and precise understanding.

The *material object* of a science is the concrete being or reality which is under consideration. In the case of theology, this is God himself, understood both in his nature as the principal material object, and in his effects, namely creatures, which are the secondary material object. The reason for this extension of the material object of theology is the fact that every cause is found in its effects and extends itself to them.

The *formal* object of a science is the particular aspect under which the material object is considered. In the case of theology, the particular aspect under which God is considered is the concept of *Deity*. This means that God is studied by theology formally as God, that is according to those inner attributes which are properly and exclusively divine, such as the mystery of the Holy Trinity and of our participation in this mystery through sanctifying grace.

The other attributes to God which are common to creatures, such as being, truth, power, intelligence and will, belong only to the material object of theology. They are the formal object of philosophy itself, that is, of that branch of metaphysics which is called theodicy.

The *formal light* of a science is that property which makes the formal object itself adequate to our intellect, that is, able to be reached by our intellect. This is nothing else but the proper immateriality of the object, which makes the object intelligible, and for this reason it is called light. Hence, in the case of theology, its formal light is the supreme immateriality of Deity, made proportionate to our intellect by means of revelation, and for this reason it is called the light of revelation.

Now we are in a position to state the total object of theology. It is God and all created things in their relation to God as to their cause. However, God is considered formally as Deity, that is, in his intimate nature, under the light of revelation, that is, according to his supreme immateriality and intelligibility as manifested to us by revelation.

This can be illustrated by using the example of the act of *ocular vision*. Here the material object is a *body, concrete with quantity*. The formal object is *color*, which is primarily and directly reached by the eye when it sees a quantified body. The formal light under which color is reached by the eye is the *sensible light*, understood, however, as that degree of immateriality which is found in color and which makes color visible, namely, adjusted to the power of sight.

A further example can be given from the field of philosophy. In the science of *metaphysics*, the material object is *being*. The formal object is *being as such*, that is, the pure and simple concept of being; hence metaphysics is the science of being, formally as being. The formal light is the natural *light of reason*, understood as that high degree of immateriality which is proper to being as being. It is called the light of reason because the human intellect is by itself adequate and adjusted to reach such an object.

Some theologians have proposed supernatural reality other than Deity as the formal object of theology. In particular, they have proposed Christ, understood as "the whole Christ," both physically and mystically — in other words, Christ and the Church together. This opinion suggested by a few writers in the Middle Ages, has been taken up again in our time and advocated insistently by several writers.[18]

This view does not stand precise theological analysis, for the following reasons.

First of all, the formal object of a science must be such that it can explain all the other objects which that same science considers. In other words, it must be implicit in all the other objects, embracing them all and reducible to no one of them. These requirements fit only the concept of Deity, which is found both in God himself as his intimate nature, and in all other things as their efficient and final cause.

All other objects or concepts, as Church, Christ, the whole Christ, are not found in God himself, and cannot explain the attributes of God, for he is prior to them. The very concept of Christ, as such, is not contained in the divine attributes nor in the inner life of God. Neither does the concept of Christ explain these attributes since they are prior to it, in other words, the Incarnation is subsequent to the inner life of God. Nor does the fact that Christ includes divinity itself change the case. For one part of him, that

---

18 St. Thomas mentions and refutes this and other opinions advanced in the Middle Ages (*Summa Theol.* I, q. 1, a. 7; *In.* 1 *Sent.* Prolog., q. 1, a. 4). In recent years the opinion about "the whole Christ" was again proposed, especially by E. Mersch, "Le Christ mystique, centre de la théologie comme science," *Nouvelle revue théologique* 61 (1934) 449–475; "L'object de la théologie et le 'Christus totus'," *Recherches de science religieuse* 26 (1936) 129–157; A. Stolz, *Introductio in sacram theologiam* (Friburgi Br. 1941) 71; C. Colombo, "La metodologia e la sistematica teologica," *Problemi e orientamenti di teologia dommatica* 1 (Milano 1957) 47.

is his humanity, has its own explanation only in the divinity, as in its cause. Nor does Christ's divinity, as identified with the person of the Word and communicated to his human nature, explain the other two persons of the Trinity, nor even the procession of the Word from the Father, for this also precedes the Incarnation.

Furthermore, since theology proceeds from the truths of faith and from revealed principles, it must necessarily have the same formal object as faith and revelation themselves. But the formal object of faith and revelation is the concept of Deity, on whose sole authority the revealed truths are believed. Therefore, the formal object of theology is also the concept of Deity, from which ultimately all theological conclusions derive.

St. Paul himself seems to suggest this when he says: "all things are yours, and you are Christ's, and Christ is God's."[19] Therefore we must conclude with St. Thomas: "In sacred science all things are considered under the aspect of God, either because they are God himself, or because they are referred to God as to their principle and end."[20]

The aforementioned theologians seem to confuse science with action, theology with the practice of preaching and the activities of Christian life. In such practical activities, the center and primary object is without doubt Christ himself, because he in his humanity is for us the means and the way to God. The same apostle St. Paul recognizes this as well: "For I have not judged myself to know anything among you, except Jesus Christ and him crucified."[21] But from this it does not follow that Christ, as such, is the primary and formal object of theological science, since the community of Christ and the very mystery of the Incarnation find their reason and explanation in the higher mystery of the Trinity and in the intimate nature of Deity.

The same practical purpose, as well as the man-centered ideas and tendencies of our time, have led other recent authors to place the formal object of theology in man himself. Thus they define theology *as the science of salvation*. This opinion is not really new; it simply receives new inspiration and force from the present times. St. Thomas himself points this error out and refutes it, saying:

---

19 1 Cor. 3:23.
20 *Summa Theologiae*, I, q. 1, a. 7.
21 1 Cor. 2:2.

"Some doctors, focusing their attention on the things that are treated in this science rather than on the formal aspect under which they are considered, assign as its proper object the work of reparation [that is of man's salvation, rather than God himself]."[22] In these brief words St. Thomas pinpoints the irrelevant character of this opinion.

As a matter of fact, everyone admits that theology is the science of revelation, that is, of the supernatural revealed truths as distinct from philosophy, which is the science of reason and natural truths. Hence theology is principally and formally the science of the primary revealed truth, which is not man, even as to his salvation, nor Christ himself as to his saving mission, but God alone in his intimate mysteries, shared by man through the Savior.

Thus several modern theologians, in their hasty practical purposes and tendencies, have been slipping, first, from pure theology into nothing but Christology, and then further down from Christology itself into a kind of supernatural anthropology. This in its turn is likely to be changed, through the same logical process of descent, into a sort of supernatural cosmology, dealing with the salvation or supernatural renovation of this world. When this takes place, theologians are bound to waver and wander, gradually losing sight of God, under the deceptive brilliancy of the world.

---

22 *Summa Theologiae*, I, q. 1, a, 7.

4

Properties of Theology

THEOLOGICAL SCIENCE IS ENDOWED WITH FIVE essential properties which show its distinctive features and its higher rank in comparison with the natural philosophical sciences. These properties are: supernatural character, specific unity, speculative-practical character, superior dignity, and sapiential nature. We shall discuss and analyze each one briefly.

1. THE SUPERNATURAL CHARACTER OF THEOLOGY

Speaking of supernaturality in a broad sense, it is self-evident that theology is supernatural in character on account of its intimate connection with supernatural principles and a supernatural object, namely, faith and Deity.

But a further question is debated among theologians, whether theology is properly and strictly a supernatural science. The reason for doubt arises from the fact that theology is a discourse of natural reason, although it proceeds from the supernatural principles of faith. Hence some theologians hold that it is simply a natural science. On the other hand, theology truly proceeds from those supernatural principles and it is specified by a supernatural object, namely Deity, although it makes use of the discourse of natural reason. Hence there are theologians who hold it to be simply a supernatural science.

There is, however, a third and better opinion, which in view of the reason advanced by the other two, takes a middle course, as follows. Theology is both a natural and a supernatural science, under different aspects. It is *formally and essentially natural*, because it consists in a process of natural reason and furthermore it is an acquired, not an infused, habit of the mind. (It should be noted that no supernatural habit can be acquired, but is necessarily infused into the soul by God, as for example faith, sanctifying grace, charity, hope, and so on.) But theology is also *radically and modally supernatural* because it proceeds from the supernatural principles.

It does not, of course, proceed from supernatural principles in the line of efficiency and vitality, as if it were a habit produced by the habit or act of faith, but only in the objective line of intelligibility, inasmuch as those principles are the reason why we give our assent to the theological conclusions. Nor does it matter that the object of theology is essentially supernatural, that is, Deity itself. For Deity is the object of theology in a different way than it is the object of faith, namely, not simply and formally as such, without qualification. It is the object of theology as undergoing a discourse of reason, that is, as known through a discourse of natural reason, proceeding from revealed principles. Hence Deity, while it specifies theology under this aspect, does not communicate to it its own intrinsic supernatural character.

Nevertheless, because it is rooted and grounded in the supernatural principles of faith, theology is so essentially dependent upon faith that it cannot exist without it; hence it cannot exist in a pagan or in a heretic. For the same reason, despite the rational character of its procedure, theology is entirely homogeneous with faith, in its proper object, that is, in the truths logically derived from the principles of faith. This is why St. Thomas defines theology as "an impression of the divine science [in our mind]"[23] and likewise St. Anselm of Canterbury describes it as "faith seeking understanding."[24]

2. THE SPECIFIC UNITY OF THEOLOGY

This means that theology, in all its various parts and treatises, is one single science. It is not, therefore, a collection of several sciences specifically distinct from each other. Nor is it a science in a generic sense, which would be divided into several species, as is the case with philosophy.

This property of theology follows from the specific and indivisible unity of its formal object, the concept of Deity, which is constantly and equally considered in all the parts and treatises of this science. In fact such treatises may be given the following formal titles: On the One God; On the Trinity in God; On God creating and elevating; On God sanctifying through grace; On God incarnate; On the Mother of God; On the Church, the

---

23 *Summa Theologiae*, I, q. 1, a. 3, ad. 2.
24 *Proslogion*, prologue.

sheepfold of God; On the sacraments, sanctifying instruments of God; On God the Rewarder, or the Last Things. This is the reason why the division of theology into its various parts or treatises is not an essential division, that is, a division into specifically distinct treatises. It is only an accidental division, that is, into integrative or complementary parts which make up one total and single science. This is true not only of the treatises just mentioned, but also of other parts in which theology is usually divided, as systematic and positive parts and speculative and practical parts (see the general division below, pp. 30–32).

3. THE SPECULATIVE-PRACTICAL CHARACTER OF THEOLOGY

This means that theology unifies into one single science both speculative and practical matters. In this it differs from the philosophy, which is divided into two specifically different kinds of science, the speculative and the practical, for example, metaphysics and ethics.

This property of theology follows from the unity and universality of its specific object, that is, from the fact that theology deals with revealed truth, which involves both speculative concepts and human acts to be performed, and considers all of them under one specific and indivisible formal object, which is Deity itself.

Because the principal material object of theology is God, we can say that this science is more speculative than practical. In fact, theology on the one hand deals more directly with divine truths than with human acts, and on the other hand it considers these acts in their relationship to the ultimate end, which consists essentially in the beatific vision, that is, in an act of the speculative order.[25]

However, the speculative and the practical orders, taken formally and in themselves, imply two specific and irreducible differences within the genus of intelligible objects, as is clear in philosophy. Hence it is more accurate to say that theology is at once speculative and practical, not formally and specifically, but only eminently. This means that it unifies both formalities in the eminence of a higher object, namely the Deity itself, in which this distraction and opposition between the speculative

---

25 *Summa Theologiae*, I, q. 1, a. 4.

and the practical orders vanishes. For such is the case with faith itself, and with the infinite knowledge of God himself whose perfection is shared by theology.[26]

It goes without saying that this property of theology is extremely significant for catechists and teachers of religion. The more they do their teaching under the theological light rather than through a philosophical pattern, the easier it will be for them to bring the students to reduce the truths they learn to practice in the activities of their life. The dichotomy between doctrine and life, always a real possibility in the all-too-human mode of philosophy, disappears the more the teacher draws upon theological wisdom.

4. THE SUPERIOR DIGNITY OF THEOLOGY

By this we mean that theology is placed on a higher level than any of the other human sciences, including philosophy with its lofty natural wisdom called metaphysics.[27] This property follows from three considerations.

First, it is a corollary of the three properties which we have touched upon so far — its supernatural character, its specific unity, and the fact that it is both speculative and practical. No other science has such characteristics.

Secondly, from the eminence of its formal object, the Deity itself, which is very intimate essence of the Supreme Being, transcending all the concepts of human reason. The objects of all the other sciences fall within the ambit of human reason: they consist either in some definite created being, or at best, as in metaphysics alone, in the abstract concept of being as such. Metaphysics, indeed, reaches God himself, but only as being and according to his external attributes which are common also to creatures.

Thirdly, from its certitude, which is absolute. The reason for this is the fact that theology is grounded in the absolute certitude of its revealed principles, and through these in the certitude of God's own knowledge, who is Truth itself.

26　It is evident that one and the same faith deals both orders, namely truths to be understood and things to be done. See *Summa Theologiae*, p. II-II, q. 9, a. 3. In another place, St. Thomas states: "God knows both himself and the things that he does by one and the same kind of knowledge" (*ibid.*, I, q. 1, a. 4; see also q. 14, a. 16).
27　Cf. *Summa Theologiae*, I, q. 1, a. 5; II-II, q. 4, a. 8; M. Philipon, "La théologie, science supreme de la vie humaine," *Revue thomiste* (1935) 387–421; B. Baudoux, "Philosophia ancilla theologiae," *Antonianum* 12 (1937) 293–326.

This last consideration regards theological science taken objectively and in itself, but it does not necessarily apply to theology as it stands in the human subject who theologizes. As we noted above (p. 11), theology is only a subalternate science, based upon faith and drawing its principles from faith. Hence, so long as the subject who theologizes is still here on earth far from the beatific vision, his theology will lack immediate evidence of its principles. In this relative and subjective sense, theology has an imperfection in comparison with the other sciences, especially metaphysics. Moreover, since certitude is founded in evidence, such lack of immediate evidence will produce also a certain imperfection in the very certitude of theology — again not considered objectively (for as we noted above, its certitude is objectively absolute), but on the part of the subject. For he can undergo doubt or hesitation in his theologizing, as well as in his faith, on which theology depends.

5. THE SAPIENTIAL CHARACTER OF THEOLOGY

Theology is not only a true science (see above, pp. 10–11), but also wisdom, that is, science brought to its highest level — the summit of science. Moreover, as St. Thomas says, theology is "the greatest human wisdom on earth, not only in one or the other order, but absolutely."[28]

While science in general is knowledge of an object through its causes, wisdom is knowledge of that same object through its ultimate or proper causes.[29] In this broad sense every philosophical science, and for that matter also mathematics and natural philosophy, is a wisdom. A science can be wisdom either relatively, that is, in a particular order, or simply, and absolutely, that is, in every order. In the first sense, mathematics is wisdom in the order

---

28 *Summa Theologiae*, I, q. 1, a. 6.
29 See Aristotle, *Metaphysics* I. 1, 2 and 12; II. 7. By knowledge through ultimate or proper causes we understand the knowledge of the essence of some object, which is obtained through an argument "propter quid" (which is always "a priori"). For example when we say: "God is eternal because he is immutable," immutable is the proper and immediate cause of his eternity, and hence its ultimate cause, the root and intelligible ground of his eternity. On the other hand, an argument called, "quia," does not lead to knowledge of this type of immediate cause, it leads only to the knowledge of the existence of the object, and if it is an argument "a priori," it leads only to the knowledge of a remote cause of the object, not its immediate cause. For example when we say: "God is eternal because he is all-perfect," the immediate cause of God's eternity is not his all-perfection, but that particular perfection which we call his immutability.

of reality as quantified, and natural philosophy in the order of reality as subject to changes. In the second sense metaphysics is wisdom in the universal order of being as such, and hence the supreme wisdom among natural philosophical sciences.

Theology is not only true wisdom, like mathematics and natural philosophy, nor only wisdom simply and absolutely, like metaphysics; it also the supreme human wisdom, that is, knowledge through the ultimate or proper causes in every order and at every level, since it stands above the level of natural reason. This follows from the universality and superiority of its formal object, which is Deity, that is God not simply as being or even as the Supreme Being, but God formally as God, the highest Cause of the universe, considered according to the deepest concept of his intimate essence.

SCHEMATIC DIVISION OF THEOLOGICAL AND PHILOSOPHICAL SCIENCES:

Theology: the science of Deity under supernatural light.

> Theology of God himself: under an infinite light: infinite wisdom.
>
> Theology of the Blessed: under the light of beatific vision: supreme created wisdom.
>
> *Theology of the wayfarer: under the light of revelation or faith: supreme wisdom on earth.*

Philosophy: the science of being under the natural light of reason.

> Metaphysics in the broad sense: the science of being, as being.
>
>> Metaphysics in the strict sense: the science of being, as real (which reaches its apex in theodicy, the science of the uncreated being): absolute and supreme wisdom among the natural sciences.
>>
>> Logic: the science of being, as existing only the mind (being of reason).
>
> Mathematics: the science of being as quantified.
>
>> Arithmetic: the science of discrete (or numerical) quantity.
>>
>> Geometry: the science of continuous (or extended) quantity.
>
> Physics or natural philosophy: the science of being, as changeable (subject to change).
>
>> Psychology: the science of living changeable being (within which ethics may be located).
>>
>> Cosmology: the science of non-living changeable being.

5

Functions of Theology

THE FUNCTIONS OF THEOLOGY, THAT IS, THE duties it discharges and the purpose it achieves, must be determined according to its double aspect, as a science and as wisdom.

1. THE FUNCTIONS OF THEOLOGY AS A SCIENCE

The proper function of theology, formally as a science, is to deduce conclusions from the principles of faith with certitude, by means of syllogisms properly so-called. Through such syllogisms new and formal truths are inferred which were contained only virtually in the principle, while improper or expository syllogisms consist only in mere explanations of the principles.

This work of inference by the use of proper syllogisms is the fundamental function of theology. Without it, it would not be a true science, nor consequently a wisdom, which is the summit of science itself — just as there is no roof without the construction of the lower portions of a house.

It follows that the mere consideration, study, explanation, or defense of the principles of faith is not properly theology, but mere informal thought or reasoning about revelation. To be theology, it must be a scientific reasoning about revelation.

2. THE FUNCTIONS OF THEOLOGY AS WISDOM

The general function of wisdom is "judging and ordering."[30]

Theology performs this double function in several ways, both with regard to its own principles, by explaining and defending them and with regard to the philosophical and natural sciences below it, by surveying them and their principles, and by using them in its own service.

As regards its own principles, theology judges and orders in five ways.

First, it proves their *extrinsic credibility* through evident criteria, consisting in miracles and prophecies. For instance, it shows the

---

30 *Summa Theologiae*, I, q. 1, a. 6; I-II, q. 57, a. 2, corp. and ad 1.

credibility of the Divinity of Christ from the miracles performed by him as the Lord and Master of things. This is the apologetical function of theology.

Secondly, theology *argues about the principles themselves,* not indeed to prove them directly (for no science proves its own principles; it presupposes them as true), but only indirectly, by reducing a denial of them to absurdity, or by what is called the argument "ad hominem," which consists in inferring one truth, denied by the adversary, from another truth, which he admits. For example, against the Jews, theological wisdom argues from the authority of the Old Testament, or from both Testaments. Likewise, from the admission of the resurrection of Christ, theological wisdom concludes to our own resurrection. St. Paul himself uses this argument in 1 Cor. 15, 17.

Thirdly, theology *explains its own principles,* in three ways. It determines their direct and immediate meaning more clearly; for instance, by expressing them with more suitable and precise formulas. It expounds their immediate virtual content through merely expository syllogisms. Especially it illustrates one truth through comparison with another; for example, the mystery of the elevation and fall of man in Adam with the mystery of our reparation in Christ, the mystery of the Eucharist, with the mystery of the Incarnation, the mystery of the Church with the mystery of Christ. This last method, usually called *"analogy of faith"* (mutual agreement between the different truths of faith), is the most excellent function of theology as wisdom.[31]

Fourthly, theological wisdom *strengthens reason.* It does this in two ways. First, by proposing merely probable arguments, or *reasons of fittingness,* as an extrinsic persuasion of the incomprehensible mysteries; such are, among others, the various reasons that are usually brought forward to clarify the supreme mysteries of the Trinity and the Incarnation.[32] The other way is by showing the various *similitudes* with the mysteries that are found especially

---

31   Cf. Ch. Journet, *Introduction á la théologie* (Paris 1947) 100–102; B. M. Xiberta, "La 'analogia fidei' como procedimiento de técnica teológica," *XI Semana española de teologia* (Madrid 1952) 321–336.

32   The value of the argument from fittingness is emphasized by ST. Thomas, *Summa Theologiae,* I, q. 32, a. 1, ad. 2; R. Garrigou-Lagrange, *De Deo Trino et Creatore)* Taurine 1943) 67; Ch. Journet, *Introduction á la théologie* (Paris 1947) 103–114; M. Flick, "Il valore dell'argomento di convenienza," *Problemi scelti di teologia contemporanea* (Roma 1954) 57–62.

in material and sensible things; for human reason usually draws its concepts from sensible things and rises from visible likeness to the understanding of invisible realities.

Fifthly, theology in its sapiential function *defends its own principles*, refuting the objections of the adversaries of faith by means of the natural principles of metaphysics or the art of logic. For these are the common heritage of human reason, and if they are used rightly, they can show that whatever is objected against faith is false and impossible, or at least does not follow necessarily. Indeed, since faith rests upon infallible divine truth, nothing opposing it can ever be demonstrated.[33]

As regards the natural sciences, it is evident that theology cannot prove their principles, since it proceeds under a different kind of light of revelation. In this particular point, therefore, theology yields to metaphysics, which as the supreme natural wisdom, demonstrates, judges, and synthesizes within its proper field the principles of all the other natural sciences. Nevertheless, theology, as a wisdom superior to metaphysics itself, perform its proper function of "judging and ordering" with respect to all the other sciences, including metaphysics itself.[34]

It accomplishes this sapiential function in the following three ways:

First, it passes judgement on them, insofar as it condemns as false whatever is found in them that is contrary to its own theological principles or conclusions; for truth cannot be opposed to truth.

Secondly, it makes use of these inferior sciences, as it were like handmaids. It borrows their principles for its own reasoning process, as is clear especially in the case of the principles of metaphysics (for example, the principles of contradiction and causality), without which no theological reasoning is possible. It makes use also of the demonstrations and conclusions of these lower philosophical and natural sciences, as is obvious especially regarding ethics and theodicy, which are incorporated respectively into moral theology and speculative theology.

Thirdly, theology, while judging and using these sciences, *elevates and perfects them*, just as faith perfects reason. As the First Vatican Council states, "faith frees and guards reason from error

---

33 *Summa Theologiae*, I, q. 1, a. 8.
34 Ibid., a. 6.

and furnishes it with a more ample knowledge,"[35] which is true also of theology, the daughter of faith. This is conspicuously evident in the questions on God's existence as constituent principles of created being; on creation; on the immortality of the human soul. It becomes also generally clear if we make a careful comparative study of the theodicy and ethics of Aristotle, the greatest among pagan philosophers, and Christian theodicy and ethics, especially as expounded by St. Thomas, the greatest among theologians and Christian philosophers.

---

35 Session 3, chapter 4.

6

Methods of Theology

THE WORD "METHOD" DERIVES FROM THE TWO
Greek words, "metá ," meaning after; and "odós," meaning way.
Thus a method, literally, is a "way of going after something." It
comes to mean, therefore, a certain definite and systematic manner of inquiry.

In theological science, method can be divided as follows,
reflecting a logical process as well as the historical forms it has
taken through the ages.

Expository (or kerygmatic, homiletic, catechetical): used by the
Apostles and the Fathers.
Argumentative
Polemical (or apologetical): used especially by the second
century Fathers, called the Apologists.
Doctrinal: developed especially since the Middle Ages.
Positive (or historical in a broader sense): developed par-
ticularly since the 16th century.
Systematic (or theological, scholastic): the classic form of
theology since the Middle Ages.
Inductive: that is, proceeding from the particular to
the universal.
Deductive: proceeding from the universal to the
particular.

From what has been said above, in the explanation of the various functions of theology, it is evident that theology, *formally as
a science*, allows but one method, that is, the *systematic and deductive*. This follows from the fact that the only specific function of
theology as a science is to infer conclusions from its principles.

If theology is considered *formally as wisdom*, however, that is,
as extended to further functions, then it necessarily takes up
other methods in its rational process, especially with regard to
the explanation and defense of its own principles. Thus, according to the various functions, it becomes inductive, or positive, or

polemical. It takes up the *inductive* method, when it uses probable arguments and similitudes of created beings to lead us, by the way of extrinsic persuasion, to a better understanding of the lofty mysteries of faith. It uses a *positive* method, when it explains its own principles, by determining their true meaning and formulating their expression in a scientific manner, by making their virtual content explicit through expository syllogisms, and by comparing the various mysteries of faith with each other in order to illustrate and clarify them. Finally, it uses a *polemical* method when it shows the extrinsic credibility of its principles, that is the mysteries of faith, when it defends them against adversaries by arguing "ad hominem" and refuting their objections; and when it judges the falsehood contained in the principles and conclusions of the natural sciences, if they are opposed to its own principles and conclusions.

A NOTE ON THE SO-CALLED POSITIVE THEOLOGY

Positive theology (from the Latin "ponere," meaning to place in position or set up) has a comparatively recent origin. Its importance and need have grown rapidly, and its nature and its object have been discussed widely in recent years. The explanation of its nature, which follows, is generally admitted. Our purpose is to show its distinctive characteristics, and to make clear how it differs from systematic theology. Its historical origin will be shown below (p. 39).

As regards its immediate object positive theology is not concerned with conclusions, but only with the revealed principles in themselves. Hence it goes directly to the channels of revelation — Scripture, Tradition, and the Magisterium —, in order to grasp and determine the precise meaning of the revealed truths. As such it can be called a "science of documents," and hence it is commonly divided into three parts, reflecting the three channels or the three kinds of documents, biblical, patristic, and symbolic theology.

Regarding its *method*, positive theology excludes the argumentative — dialectical form, namely, the scientific form, in its stricter sense. This means that it does not use philosophy, nor proper or illative syllogisms, nor the classic order and division of questions, as is the case in systematic theology. Instead, it adopts an expository and historical form, in the broader sense of "historical," In other words, it uses a scientific non-dialectical form, and hence an exegetical, critical, literary, philological, and strictly historical form. However positive theology does not proceed in a purely historical manner, for a theologian is not a historian, whether he is dealing with systematic or positive theology. A pure historian is concerned only with the rational exegesis of what the document immediately before him appears to record and to report. The positive theologian, on the contrary, proceeds in a manner that is truly theological, that is, in close dependence upon revelation and upon the Magisterium, so as to be able to grasp the proper and intimate meaning of a revealed truth, in the frame and in the spirit of all the others. It is clear, therefore, that positive theology is completely distinct from the purely historical and critical auxiliary disciplines of theological science, such as exegesis, patrology, Church history, and the history of dogmas.

Thus rightly understood, positive theology is truly a part of the science of sacred theology, under its sapiential aspect. It is not, of course, a theological science specifically distinct from systematic theology; for, as we have shown above, theology as a whole is one single specific science. Nor is it properly an integrating part of theology, as if it would combine with systematic theology as an equal and separate part of one total theological science (in the way speculative and moral theology make up one systematic theology). It is, therefore, a complementary or extensive part (a "potential part," in technical terms), inasmuch as it brings a necessary element to the perfection of theological science, and expounds the inner power of this science, under its aspect of wisdom. For, in whatever way positive theology is understood or further determined, it is after all to be reduced to a more accurate explanation and a fuller understanding of the principles of theological science. This function belongs to theology itself under its formal aspect of wisdom.

This positive function is not to be exercised separately from the other systematic function, but it must be intimately joined to it in the treatment of the individual theological questions themselves. Separation of these two functions would be harmful to both of them. For, on the one hand, systematic theology, unduly separated from the vital font of its revealed principles, would be in danger of quickly drying up and perishing, or of wandering vainly through subtle and empty questions and dialectical exercises. On the other hand, positive theology itself, violently torn from the solid support of rational principles and from its proper purpose of nourishing the very processes of theological reasoning, would lapse into a mere historical discipline, foreign to the nature of theology, or it would settle down, idle and sterile, within the enclosure of a mere simple faith; for, as St. Thomas warns, "if a teacher settles a question by sheer authority, his pupil will be convinced that it is so, but he will acquire no science or understanding and he will go away empty."[36]

---

36 Quodl. 4, a. 18.

7
Division of Theology

THE THEOLOGICAL DIVISION OF THEOLOGY, AS
that of any science, is to be drawn from its object, as well as from
its properties and its method, which are themselves rooted in
and derived from the object. Since the formal object of theology,
namely Deity in itself, is one and indivisible, no division can be
drawn from it, otherwise theology would not be one single specific
science but several sciences, like philosophy.

Hence there remain only three possible ways of dividing
theology.

The first and principal division can be taken *from the material
object*, that is, God, as the primary object, and created things, as
the secondary object. Thus theology is divided, as into integrating parts, into various particular treatises, for example, on the
One God, on the Trinity, on God creating and elevating, on the
Incarnate Word, etc.

The second division can be drawn *from a property* of this science. Thus theology is divided into speculative and practical
(dogmatic and moral theology), as its integrating parts. For, as
has been explained above (p. 18f.), speculative and practical are
two formally distinct objects, although unified in the eminence
of theology and its object.

The third division is taken *from the variety of method* used in the
scientific investigation. Thus theology is divided into systematic
and positive theology, as its complementary parts.

St. Thomas in his *Summa Theologiae* adopts only the first division, that is, according to the material object. However, he logically and subtly incorporates into it also the second division of
dogmatic and moral theology.

Outline of St. Thomas' division[37]

> On God, *as in himself*, or, as it were, formally (in modern terms: On God Triune): 1st part, qq. 2–43.
> On God, *as the cause of things.*
>> As the *efficient cause* (On God Creating and Elevating): 1st part, qq. 44–119.
>> As the *final cause* (of the rational creature): that is, on the rational *movement of man* toward God: 2nd and 3rd parts, plus Supplement.
>>> On such *movement in itself* (the entire Moral Theology): 2nd part, subdivided into 1st–2nd, qq. 1–89 (Special Moral Theology).
>>> On the *path* of this movement (that is, about Christ, the Incarnate Word, and his extension through the sacrament, qq. 1–68.
>>> On *the term* of this movement (that is, the Last Things): Supplement, qq. 69–99.

This division, very simple and very logical indeed, can be completed as below, according to the way theology is now treated and extended, by the addition of positive and fundamental theology, as well as by a different distribution and designation of the various treatises.[38]

Theology

> *Positive*, about the principles of the theology or revealed truths, considered with a *historical or non-dialetical method*,
>> *Biblical*. It considers these principles in the deposit of Scripture (It is to be distinguished from mere exegesis and from the biblical history.)
>> *Patristic*. It considers the same principles in the deposit of Tradition (It is to be distinguished from history of dogmas.)
>> *Symbolic* (so called from the Symbols of faith proposed by

---

37 Cf. G. lafont, *Structures et méthode dans la Somme Théologique de Saint Thomas d'Aquin*, Paris 1960; *Initiation* théologique (par un groupe de théologiens) 1 (Paris 1952) 377–393, where the entire division of the *Summa Theologiae* is shown down to the particular questions.
38 Cf. G. Rabeau, *Introduction á l'étude de la théologie* (Paris 1926), 3me partie; Ch. Journet, *Introduction á la théologie* (Paris 1947) 143–153, 200–203; B. Xiberta, *Introductio in Sacram Theologiam* (Matriti 1949) 192–197, 344–349.

the Magisterium). It considers those principles in the pronouncements of the Magisterium, organ of revelation (it is to be distinguished from Church history and history of Dogmas.)

Systematic, about both principles of theology and the conclusions thereof, considered with an *argumentative and dialectical method*, and gathered into a scientific unity which can be called a system. This principal part of theology is divided according to the *object*, as follows:

Fundamental (or general), on revelation generically considered:

On revelation itself (Apologetics).

On the channels of revelation (or, more extensively, On the Theological *Loci*).

Formal (or special). On the individual revealed truths.

Speculative (or dogmatic). On speculative truths.

On God.

According to his essence (On the One God).

According to his persons (On Trinity).

On man, and the other creatures (On God Creating and Elevating).

On God-Man, Christ, and the other mysteries immediately depending on him (On the Incarnate Word, the Blessed Virgin, Grace of Christ, Church of Christ, Sacraments of Christ, the Last Things through Christ).

Practical. On practical truths, or things to be done according to revelation.

Moral. On practical truths and principles, inasmuch as they regulate human acts in themselves, that is in their interior aspect, as the subject of morality and sanctity. To this part of theology are reduced *Pastoral theology and Ascetic-Mystical theology.*

Canonical. On practical truths and principles, inasmuch as they regulate human acts in their exterior and social aspect, or as they become the object of ecclesiastical law. To this part of theology can be reduced *Liturgy,* as the object of ecclesiastical law in matters of cult, although, under a higher and more theological aspect, it belongs also to the aforesaid patristic and symbolic positive theology.

8
History of Theology[39]

THE SCIENCE OF SACRED THEOLOGY, TAKEN IN
the stricter sense of scientific and systematic process of reasoning
about revelation, emerged, into full view during the Middle Ages,
more exactly in the 12th century; it began to flourish at that time
in the Catholic schools of Western Christendom. But, taken in a
broader sense of any process of reasoning about revealed truths,
theology had its beginning in the early patristic age, and has continued developing and making progress up to the modern time.
Hence the history of theology can be divided into three periods;
ancient, from the 2nd to the 11th centuries; medieval, from the
12th to the 16th centuries, more exactly up to the Council of
Trent; and modern, from the 16th to the 20th centuries. The
very recent years of the 20th century are excluded, as not yet
belonging to history.

Comparing these three periods from the viewpoint of both the
object considered and the method applied, they manifest altogether a striking diversity and a successive progress of the sacred
science. In the first period, the object under consideration consists
rather in the principles of theology, or the revealed truths taken
in themselves, and the method used is mainly expository. In the
second period the object of study becomes rather the conclusions inferred from those principles and the method is eminently
systematic. In the third period, an increasing attempt is made at
giving a proportionate treatment to both objects, that is, principles and conclusions, joining to the medieval systematic method
a positive scientific one, and leaving aside the expository method
of early times of the Church as not properly scientific.

---

39   Cf. M. Grabmann, *Die Geschichte der katholischen Theologie*, Freiburg 1 Br. 1933;
L. Allevi, *Disegno di storia della teologia catolica*, Torino 1939; M-J. Congar, "Théologie," *Dictionnaire de théologie catholique* 10-1 (Paris 1946) 346–447; A *History
of Theology*, New York 1968; J.-J. De Santo-Tomas, "De la théologie patristique á
la théologie scolastique," *Revue thomiste* 58 (1958) 709–773; *Bilan de la théologie
du XXe siècle*, 2 tomes, Tournai-Paris 1970–1971.

1. THE ANCIENT PERIOD, FROM THE 2ND TO THE 11TH CENTURIES

This period includes the strictly *patristic age*, from the 2nd to the 8th century, up to and including St. John Damascene, and the *late-patristic extension*, from the 9th to the 11th century, up to and including St. Anselm of Canterbury. It shows a discursive consideration of the *principles of theology* or revealed truths, as derived directly from revelation and as seen in their mutual relationships, as well as in their immediate virtualities or conclusions. However, theology in these times does not extend such conclusions any further with the aid of profound philosophical notions and principles. Consequently, the *method is rather expository*, confining itself mainly to the explanation of the text of revelation. However, the very apologetical purpose, which quite early succeeded to the mere instructional and catechetical one, that is the necessity of protecting the revealed truths against the attacks of pagan philosophers (2nd century) and from the infiltration of heresies (3rd to 5th centuries), as well as the contact itself with pagan philosophy (gnostic and especially neo-platonic), occasioned among the early Fathers the first elaboration of a Christian philosophy, the first mingling of philosophy with revelation and, as it were, the rise of a rudimental theological science.

The founders of this science were, almost at the same time but independently, *Origen* (about 185–254) in the East, and *Tertullian* (about 160–222) in the West, inasmuch as they gave the start to a twofold manner of reasoning, of quite different mentality and inclination, namely the eastern and the western theology.

Eastern theology began to take shape in the third century by reason of the contact of the Fathers with gnostic and neoplatonic philosophy in the *Alexandrian School*, and later in the fourth and fifth centuries rapidly developed in the same region during the conflict against the two great heresies of Arianism and Nestorianism. In that same school flourished at the beginning of the third century *Origen* († about 254), who in his main work *On Principles* displays a sort of theological summa, placing the neo-platonic philosophy itself at the service of revelation. Likewise the other *Antiochian School* ,which began to develop at the same time, although opposed to the Alexandrian as to its mode of interpreting Scripture, proceeded in the same manner and with the same speed in the theological investigation of revealed truths, as is shown in the various works on Trinity, Divinity of the Word and Incarnation, produced in the twin schools. In the later part of the patristic age, two doctors must be noted for their stricter theological character. The first *pseudo-Dionysius the Areopagite* (an unknown writer about the end of the fifth century), in his works (*On the Divine Names, On Mystical Theology, On the Heavenly Hierarchy, On the Ecclesiastical Hierarchy*) adopted and theologically elaborated the neo-platonic philosophy. The other *St. John Damascene* (†749; the last of the Eastern Fathers), in his work *Dialectics* offers a sort of philosophical introduction, following in the footsteps of Aristotle and Porphyry; in the work *On Heresies* he attempts a theological introduction; and in his major synthesis *On the Orthodox Faith* he approaches and explains theological matter itself, on God, creation, Incarnation, sacraments. Both pseudo-Dionysius and St. John Damascene had decisive influence on the medieval theology of the West.

Western theology began to develop toward the end of the second century in the apologetical, dogmatic and polemical works of *Tertullian* († about 222; *Apologetics, On the Prescription of Heretics, Against Marcion, On Baptism, On the Soul*). It progressed at a slower pace, due in part to the lack, or lesser repercussion, of the aforesaid heresies in the West. It has also a different character than the eastern theology, namely a practical, juridical, dialectic, and psychological character, according to the Roman mentality and culture. This diversity is manifest in the treatment and interpretation of the mysteries of faith, especially Trinity and Incarnation. This theology reached its peak in *St. Augustine* (354–430), who unified into a higher synthesis the theological developments of both the Western and the Eastern Fathers, so that he can be called the forefather of theology, from whom the medieval theologians themselves drew the substance of their speculation. His principal theological works are *On the Trinity, City of God*, and *On the True Religion* (apologetical work); however, in all the other works, both moral and polemical (*Enchiridion, On Christian Doctrine*, and various writings against Manichaeism, Donatism and Pelagianism), elements of theological science and of the highest speculation are found widely spread and unexpectedly offered.

The Patristic age in the West comes to a close with *St. Isidore of Seville* (†636), who in his various works (*Sentences, Etymologies,*

Differences, On the Order of Creatures, On Catholic Faith), diligently gathered and expounded in an orderly manner the theological doctrine of the preceding Fathers, especially of St. Augustine.

In the following late-patristic age (9th to 11th centuries) theological science suffered a relative decline, together with the general culture. The reasons for this were the schism steadily progressing in the east, which brought with it theological sterility, and the harshness of social conditions in the West, due to the barbarian invasions and to the slow ripening of a new civilization. Among outstanding but not original writers, as Alcuin, Paschasius Radbertus, and Ratramnus, under a theological and scientific viewpoint particular mention is to be made of John Scotus Eriugena (ninth century; from Scotland or Ireland; master in the palace of Charles the Bald, king of France). He translated into Latin the works of pseudo-Dionysius the Areopagite, and in his treatise *On the Division of Nature*, he gathered the entire theological knowledge on God and creatures, bringing forth an audacious synthesis, based on platonic philosophy, which although mingled with several errors and ambiguities, was the first attempt at introducing scientific speculation into theology. At the very end of this age, *St. Anselm of Canterbury* (1034–1109; Italian by birth, abbot of the Bec monastery in France, archbishop of Canterbury in England) wrote his conspicuous works *Monologion* (on the essence of God and on Trinity), *Proslogion* (on the existence and attributes of God; here he utters the famous aphorism: "Faith seeking understanding" and proposes the well known *a priori* argument for the existence of God), and *Cur Deus Homo* (on the Incarnation), in which he opens a new method of theological speculation, introducing dialectical reasoning and thus paving the way to scholastic theology.

2. THE MEDIEVAL PERIOD, FROM THE 12TH TO THE 16TH CENTURIES, UP TO THE COUNCIL OF TRENT

This period includes the strictly scholastic age (12th–13th centuries) and the late-scholastic (14th–16th centuries). The primary object of theology is no longer the principles of this science in themselves and in their immediate implication, but the *theological conclusions*, derived from such principles and established with the aid of philosophical notions and principles. Consequently, the method itself is no longer expository but *systematic*, proceeding with a scientific ordering of all those things which the philosophical reasoning process finds about revelation.

In the strictly scholastic age (12th and 13th centuries),[40] systematic theology began to develop in France in the twofold school of Saint Victor and of Abelard, both originating from the older school of Laon (1120–1135) and both later mingled in the Lombardian school, as in a synthesis of doctrines and tendencies. The principal theologian of the first school is *Hugh of Saint Victor* (1100–1141), a man of mystic character, whose principal theological work is *On the Sacraments of Christian Faith*; probably he is also the author of another outstanding work of the same school by the title *Summa of Sentences*. The other school was founded by *Peter Abelard* (1079–1142), man of liberal tendencies, whose principal theological work is *Introduction to Theology* (All other theological doctrines of Abelard are expounded by his disciple Herman in the *Epitome of Christian Theology*.) notwithstanding several false or ambiguous doctrines, which met with ecclesiastical condemnation (cf. Denzinger, nos. 721–739), the great merit of Abelard was the fact that he first introduced the philosophy of Aristotle into theology (commenting some of the Philosopher's works in his *Dialectics)* and moreover he fashioned the method of scholastic disputation in his work *Sic et Non* (*Yes and No*). About the middle of the same century *Peter Lombard* (†1160; called "The Master of Sentences," or simply "The Master"; originally from Lombardy in Italy; professor and later archbishop in Paris), unified all the theological developments of the preceding schools in his famous work *Four Books of Sentences* (about the year 1150), which became the classical work in the schools up to the sixteenth century, when it was supplanted by the Theological Summa of St. Thomas.

In the course of the 13th century systematic theology reached its peak and showed the perfect expression of its form in the various *Commentaries on the Sentences* of Peter Lombard and in the *Theological Summas*. The principal authors of such works are: *Alexander of Hales* (1180–1245), Franciscan, "Irrefragable Doctor," *Glossa on the Four Books of Sentences. St. Bonaventure* (1221–1274),

---

40   Cf. M. Grabman, *Die Geschichte der scholastischen Methode*, 2 vols., Freiburg i. Br. 1909–1911; M.-D. Chenu, *La Théologie comme science au XIIe siècle*, èd. 3, Paris 1957; H. Cloes, "La systèmatisation théologique pendant la première moitiè du XIIe siècle," *Ephemerides theologicae Lovanienses* 34 (1958) 277–329.

Franciscan, "Seraphic Doctor," *Commentaries on the Four Books of Sentences*. St. *Albert the Great* (1206–1280), Dominican, "Universal Doctor," promoter of Aristotelian philosophy, teacher of St. *Thomas Aquinas* (1225–1274), Dominican, "Angelic Doctor" for the purity and loftiness of his doctrine, and "Common Doctor" for the Church, as declared by Pius XI, the supreme and probably charismatic mind in the world of theology, *Commentaries on the Four Books of Sentences* (1254–1256), *Summa contra Gentiles* (1258–1260), *Summa Theologiae* (1267–1273).

The late-scholastic age (14th to 16th centuries, up to the Council of Trent) gave rise to two major schools, called thomistic and scotistic from the name of their patrons, which divided the theological battlefield up to the present day. Notwithstanding the undisputed brilliancy and genius of several theologians, these schools show evident signs of downfall and senility in classical theology, namely, the servile way of swearing on the authority of the Master ("iurare in verba Magistri"), a lesser purity of form and concepts, undue multiplication of particular and useless questions, exaggerated subtlety in distinctions and abuse of dialectic sophistry.

In the *Thomistic School*, prevalently Dominican, which hinges on the doctrines of St. Thomas Aquinas and boasts of its fidelity to this Master, the principal or better known theologians are: *John Capreolus* (Jean Chevrier; †1444), called "Prince of Thomists" because of his faithful explanation of the text of St. Thomas and his effective defense of Aquinas, *Defense of the Theology of St. Thomas Aquinas*. *Ferrariensis* (Francis Sylvester, or Ferrara; †1528), *Commentary on the Summa Contra Gentiles* (reproduced in the Leonine edition of the works of St. Thomas). *Cajetanus* (Thomas de Vio, of Gatea; †1534), called "Leader of Thomists," probably the supreme genius produced by this school, the first to comment directly on the *Summa Theologiae* of St. Thomas, *Commentaries on the Summa Theologiae* (reproduced by Leo XIII in the aforementioned edition of the works of St. Thomas). *Francis of Vitoria* (†1546), founder of the flourishing Dominican school at Salamanca and the first to introduce the *Summa Theologiae* of St. Thomas into schools, *Relectiones theologicae*. *Melchior Cano* (†1560), Vitoria's disciple and successor at Salamanca, tridentine theologian, author of the famous treatise *On Theological Loci* which paved the way to modern fundamental and positive theologies.

The *Scotistic School*, integrally Franciscan, hinges directly on the doctrines of *John Duns Scotus* (1266–1308), Franciscan, "Subtle Doctor," author of a twofold *Commentary on the Four Books of Sentences* (called of Oxford and of Paris), from whom it inherited a peculiar kind of Aristotelianism combined with Augustinianism, and a marked theological voluntarism, frequently opposed to the doctrines of St. Thomas. The principal theologians in this school are: *Peter Auriol* († about 1322), "Eloquent Doctor," disciple of Scotus and defender of his doctrines. *Francis of Meyronnes* (†1325), "Acute Doctor of Abstractions." *John of Bassolis* (†1347), disciple of Scotus. *Peter of Aquila* (†1348), called "Little Scotus," author of a faithful *Compendium* of Scotus' doctrines. *Francis Lychetis* (†1516), author of a *Commentary* on Scotus' works.

3. THE MODERN PERIOD, FROM THE 16TH TO THE 20TH CENTURIES

This period shows a revival and a renewal of theology, due to the particular impulse given by the Council of Trent to the ecclesiastical disciplines. In this period an increasing attempt is made at giving proportionate treatment to *both objects of theology*, namely principles and conclusions, as well as completing the medieval systematic method with the addition of the scientific *positive method*. Hence the rise of the so-called positive theology and of the classical distinction of theology into positive and systematic (cf. above, pp. 26–31).

This *positive theology* began to develop under the adverse pressure of Humanism and Protestantism, which appealed only to the deposit of revelation and simply discarded systematic theology. Hence the Catholic theologians were forced to revert directly to the same deposit. Already Melchior Cano (†1560) in his work *On Theological Loci* had laid the general foundation of this positive theology; but its immediate founders and propagators were in the 17th century *Dionysius Petau* (†1652; *Theological Dogmas*); John Morin (†1659; *Commentary on the Discipline in Administration of the Sacrament of Penance; On sacred Ordinations of the Church*); and *Louis Thomassin* (†1695; *Theological Dogmas*). Thereafter this theology entered more and more into the tracts of dogmatic theologians and into the explanation of the individual questions, thus integrating systematic theology into a harmonious doctrinal balance.

To this development the recent Magisterium itself has given an efficacious impulse.[41]

Furthermore, in this period theological science as a whole, including its systematic part, underwent several changes which can be termed a rupture, both with regard to the theological schools, to the scientific disciples themselves, and to the manner of presenting the doctrine.

As regards the *theological schools*, a third one was now born by the name of *Suaresian School* (so called from its principal doctor, Suarez), which represents a rupture or breaking off from the Thomistic School itself, with a tinge of theological eclecticism. In fact, while generally opposed to the scotistic doctrines, it withdraws also from pure Thomism in some important questions, as on divine foreknowledge, predestination and grace. These were the occasion of long, bitter and fruitless controversies (called "De Auxiliis," that is, on grace as supernatural help). As regards the *scientific disciplines*, which formerly were treated as a single organized unit, theology was broken down into various separated parts, bearing the features of many distinct sciences (polemic, historical, dogmatic, moral, ascetical, mystic), so that several doctors became specialists rather than simply theologians. This contributed indeed to the breadth of erudition, but was detrimental to depth of knowledge and hence to the progress of solid and true theological science. As regards the *manner of presenting the doctrine*, independent theological courses took the place at first of the customary commentaries on the works of the masters (Peter Lombard, St. Thomas, Scotus); later came the production of separated tracts (On the One God, On Trinity, On Incarnation, etc.); and these in their turn were finally shortened and gathered into the form of manuals for the schools.

In the *Thomistic School* the more prominent theologians are: *Dominic Bañez* (†1604), disciple of Melchior Cano at Salamanca, bitter adversary of Molina during the controversy on grace mentioned above. *John of St. Thomas* (†1644), author of both a *Philosophical* and a *Theological Course*, clear and faithful interpreter of St. Thomas and rightly numbered among the greatest

---

41   Cf. Pius X, Encyclical "Pascendi," AAS 40 (1907) 640 f; Pius XI, Epist. "Officiorum" 1922, and Constit. "Deus scientiarum Dominus" 1931, AAS 14 (1922) 455 f; 23 (1931) 253; Pius XII, Encyclical "Humani generis" AAS 42 (1950) 568f.

thomists (alongside Capreolus, Ferrariensis and Cajetanus). J.-B. Gonet (†1681), author of the *Shield of Thomistic Theology*. R. Billuart (†1757), author of the well-known *Summa of Saint Thomas Adapted to the Modern Customs of Academies*, which has served as a model and basis for many recent theological tracts and manuals. Several other great theologians, outside the Dominican order, belong to the same school, particularly the *Salamanticenses* (Carmelite professors at Salamanca), authors of the extensive and profound *Theological Course* (edited from 1630 to 1701), and the *Salisburgenses* (Benedictine professors at Salzburg), authors of *Thomistic Scholastic Theology of Salzburg* (about the end of 17th century). Among recent writers or neo-thomists, both in and out the Dominican order, the better known are Zigliara, Satoli, Pégues, Janssens, Lèpicier, Mattiussi, Hugon, Garrigou-Lagrange, and, at least partially, Billot.

In the *Scotistic School* there flourished, particularly in the dogmatic field as distinct from the moral: *Michael Medina* (†1578), author of the work *On the continence of sacred men*. *Anthony Hickey* (†1641), author of a *Commentary* on the work of Scotus. *Bartholomew Mastrius* (†1678), defender of Scotus in his *Theological Disputations*. *Claude Frassen* (1711) author of the work *Scotus Academic*, outstanding in erudition and clarity. *Jerome of Montefortino* (†1728), who in his *Theological Summa of J.D. Scotus* expounds and arranges the entire doctrine of Scotus according to the plan of St. Thomas' *Summa Theologiae*, into parts, questions and articles.

In the *Suaresian School* (named after Suárez, not as the first in the time but as the principal doctor) the more prominent or better known theologians are: *Francis Toledo* (†1596), who published a clear *Interpretation of the Theological Summa of Saint Thomas* and introduced Thomism into the Roman College of the Society of Jesus. *Louis Molina* (†1600), famous for his work *Concordia*, which stirred up the controversy on grace. *Gabriel Vasquez* (†1604), author of an original and critical *Commentary on the Summa Theologiae of St. Thomas*. *Francis Suárez* (†1617), called, "Eminent Doctor" by the Roman Pontiffs, the greatest theologian of the Society of Jesus, a most prolific writer but of eclectic tendencies, who produced an ample commentary on almost the entire *Summa Theologiae* of St. Thomas. *St. Robert Bellarmine* (†1621), Doctor of the Church, in dogmatic matters not particularly original but greatest in his *Controversies of the Christian Faith Against the Heretics of This Time*. Leonard Lessius (†1623), author of the works *On Efficacious Grace* and *On Divine perfections and Manners*. John De Lugo (†1660), a more argumentative than solid author of the works *On Divine Faith, On the Incarnation, On the Eucharist, On Penance*. Among more recent theologians, all of the Society of Jesus, the better known are Perrone, Palmieri, Franzelin, C. Mazzella, Ch. Pesch, Billot, Galtier, D'Alès.

About the present state and condition of theology, particularly after the Second World War, there is nothing to be said here, as it does not yet belong to history. This applies to the eruption of a "new theology," based on irenicism and relativism (already singled out and rejected by Pius XII in the encyclical "Humani generis," 1950), to the kind of neo-modernism, which is creeping into some theological circles after Vatican Council II, and to the new forms, for which the authentic theology itself seems to be searching with adventurous steps and uncertain future.[42]

---

42 Cf. the general bibliography, section B, given at the beginning of the treatise.

GLOSSARY OF TECHNICAL WORDS
Occurring in This Treatise

Analogy, derived from the Greek word "análogos," means similarity. Both in philosophy and theology, it is used to signify similarity between two concepts, contrary to univocity which means identity of two concepts. Thus if I say: Christ is the Son of God, Francis is the son of Michael, and Peter is the son of Joseph, the concept of sonship is similar (or analogous), but not just the same (or univocal) in Christ and in Francis or Peter, while it is just the same in Francis and Peter in relation to their fathers. All concepts common to God and creatures (as being, good, intelligent, father, son, etc.) are necessarily analogous; if they were univocal, creatures would be specifically the same as God, just as two men are specifically the same.

An analogous concept can be either *proper or merely metaphorical*. It is proper, if the thing expressed by it is found in both subjects of which it is predicated, as sonship is found in Christ and in Francis in the above example, or as being, goodness, intelligence, etc., are found both in God and in man. It is merely metaphorical if the thing expressed by it is found only in one subject on account of some similarity with it; for instance, if I say: Christ is a lion (the lion of Juda, according to Scripture) or Francis is a fox, the concept of lion or fox is found only in the two brutes and it is metaphorically attributed to Christ or Francis by reason of similarity, that is because Christ is strong, as a lion is strong, and Francis is sly, as a fox is sly.

"Analogy of faith" is an expression used by theologians and the Magisterium to signify the mutual agreement which exists necessarily between the various truths of our faith, so that one cannot contradict the others. Hence it becomes also the basis of an important theological argument, which deduces or illustrates one truth from another. For instance, from the truth of the perpetual virginity of Mary we deduce that the words "brother" or "sister" of Christ in the Gospel cannot be taken in the strict sense, but only in the sense of a relative of Christ.

Apologetics is derived from the Greek word "apologia," meaning defense (from "apó," after, and "lógos," speech). In recent years it has become the name of that branch of theology which deals with the defense of faith or of revelation in general. If it deals only with the defense of a particular revealed truth, as the Trinity or Incarnation, it is called more properly apology. Even the English word "apology" or "to apologize" has the basic sense of defending or excusing oneself. The derived theological expressions "apologetic function, or method, or Father (more simply apologist)" have the same sense of defense of the revealed truths.

A priori," "A posteriori" are classical expressions used to qualify the syllogistic or demonstrative form of our rational process. "*A priori*" means a deductive process by which we deduce an effect from its cause. For instance: Christ is God (cause), therefore he is all-powerful (effect). "*A posteriori*" means the contrary inductive process by which we deduce the cause from its effect; for instance: Christ is all powerful, therefore he is God; or, Christ was born, therefore he is a man; or, the world is finite and mutable, therefore there exists an infinite and immutable Being who made it.

The "a priori" argument is called "propter quid" ("on account of which"), if it assigns the proper and ultimate cause; for example: God is immutable, therefore he is eternal (immutability is the proper and ultimate cause of eternity). It is called an argument "*quia*" ("consequent to which"), if it assigns only a proximate or general cause of the effect; for example: God is all-perfect, or infinite, therefore he is eternal (the proper cause of eternity is not infinite perfection, but immutability, which is included in the infinite perfection).

Cause — Casuality. Generically, cause is that on which the very nature of something depends. There are *four causes*, two intrinsic, called *formal cause and material cause*, and two extrinsic, called *efficient cause and final cause*.

The first two causes make up the very essence of a thing, if, however, it is a material being, necessarily composed of matter and form, which are in a relationship of determining element (form) and determined element (matter). Those spiritual natures that are simple, as God and angels, have no formal and material causes; they are simply an act or simple reality, which may be called "form" in a broader sense.

The last two causes have an exterior influence on the nature of a thing. The *efficient cause* produces its existence (or puts it into existence), while the *final cause* specifies its essence or nature and also conditions its existence. Thus, man, whose nature is composed of matter and form, that is, of body and soul, is created by God (primary efficient cause) and generated by parents (secondary efficient cause), for the purpose of living and progressing (proximate final cause) in order to reach God himself (from who he came) thus entering into an eternal state of beatitude, consisting in the beatific vision of God (ultimate final cause).

Moreover, the final cause is divided in *proximate* and *ultimate*, as in the example just given. The efficient cause is divided in *primary* cause (which is God alone in every created action and effect) and *secondary* cause (the creatures). This secondary cause can be either a *principal cause*, that is, acting by its own power (as the parents in generation, or the writer of a letter, or a smith forging his metal), or an *instrumental cause*, that is, acting by the power of another actually communicated to it (as the pen of a writer or the hammer of a smith).

Certitude is a state of mind, opposed to opinion, implying a firm assent to some truth, which is based on the evidence of an object. Such evidence can be either *immediate*, when it flows from the direct knowledge of the object, or mediate, when it is based on the evidence of an authoritative testimony about the object. In this second case, we have the certitude of faith.

The mediate certitude of faith is divided, according to the quality of the witness, into *human* (or natural) and *divine* (or supernatural), which is based on the testimony and authority of God himself.

The immediate or objective certitude is threefold according to its foundation. *Metaphysical* or absolute certitude is based on metaphysical laws, that is, on the very nature of things and hence allows no exception whatsoever. For instance, God exists, man is contingent and mortal, everything has its sufficient reason, etc. (This applies not only to metaphysical but also to mathematical objects or truths.) *Physical or moral* certitude is only hypothetical, because it is based on physical or moral laws, which admit no exceptions only if a certain condition is fulfilled. For instance, according to the physical law of gravity, it is certain that a stone will fall, providing no extrinsic cause prevents it from falling, and, according to the moral law, which governs the moral actions and inclinations of men, it is certain that a mother will not kill her son, unless an unusual perversion makes her withdraw from such law.

The certitude of divine and *supernatural faith* (as well as that of theology and theological conclusions based on faith) is also *absolute*, by reason of the infallibility of the testimony of God, and in this sense it is to be reduced to metaphysical certitude.

Channels of revelation. The *source* of revelation is the Gospel itself, that is, the teaching of Christ and of the apostles. The *channels*, through which such source is transmitted to us, are *Scripture, Tradition*, and the *Magisterium;* but the first two channels, Scripture and Tradition, are also a *deposit* (one or two deposits, under various considerations), in which revelation has been placed, while the Magisterium is only the *organ* of revelation, the channel bringing revelation from the deposit to us. The three channels are also called the *rule of faith;* but the deposit is only the *remote rule* while the Magisterium is the *proximate rule*, because we are not obliged to believe a truth contained in the deposit unless it has been proposed to us, one way or the other, by the infallible definition of the Magisterium.

Conclusion, theological is that which is drawn from revealed principle and constitutes the proper object and function of theology. There are two kinds of theological conclusion or syllogism. One is a *proper and illative conclusion*, which contains a totally new concept, other than that contained in the revealed principles; for instance, Christ has a human will because he is a man. The other is an *improper and expository conclusion* which contains a mere explanation or analysis of the revealed truth; for instance, Christ has a soul, or he is rational, because he is a man. The first type of conclusion constitutes theology formally as a science; the second type belongs to theology as wisdom. Even the first type of conclusion implies an absolute certitude, otherwise they would be mere theological probable opinions.

Deity means God considered in his most intimate essence, or according to what makes God to be God and distinguishes him from creatures. Hence, Deity is something different from and beyond all those divine attributes which are in some way common to creatures, such as being, one, true, good, intelligent, willing, potent, acting, etc. All such attributes are really found also in creatures, although in God they are in an infinite manner proper to God, and, in this sense of infinity, they are proper to God.

This essence, rather than being, unity, truth, goodness, intelligence, will, power, is *something above being, unity, truth, etc.*, which founds and explains all such attributes in an infinite and simple way. *That something is what we call Deity.*

God, according to the aforesaid common attributes can be known through natural reason and is the proper object of *theodicy*, the highest part of Metaphysics. But God as Deity can be known only through a supernatural light of beatific vision or faith, and he is also the proper object of *theology*, which proceeds from the principles of faith.

Essence is a word frequently used in theology, as well as in philosophy, to designate the proper nature of something, its constituent and distinctive element, that which makes it such and distinguishes it from all other things (thus the essence of man is rational animal, the essence of a brute is irrational animal). The essence of a thing is called also nature and substance. But there is a shade of meaning or a distinction of concepts between these three words. Properly, the same thing is called *essence* in relation to existence (thus essence and existence are the two constituent parts of every created being); it is called *nature* in relation to its acts or operations, which proceed from the essence; it is called *substance* in relation to the accidents, which are placed in the essence as in a subject or a support.

In that sense we talk of essential parts, essential properties, essential division, things essentially supernatural, etc.

In God, as considered by philosophy or theodicy, we distinguish his *physical essence*, that is, the aggregate of all his perfections and attributes with their infinite character, and his *metaphysical essence*, that is, the one fundamental attribute which is the root and the reason for all the others. This is, according to the Thomistic opinion, the Subsisting Being, the "esse subsistens," in which there is no distinction between essence and existence. However, the real and proper nature of God is not even such metaphysical essence, which is only the dominant note among the divine attributes common to creatures, but it is that mysterious and sovereign reality which transcends all human concepts and which under the name of *Deity* (see this entry) is the proper object of faith and of theology.

Faith. We must carefully distinguish the meaning of several expressions occurring here and there in theology, which are intimately connected with the concept of faith.

Faith itself is taken either subjectively, for the infused virtue through which we assent to the revelation of God, or objectively for the revealed truths we believe.

Preambles of faith are those truths about God which we can know through the natural reason without revelation (as the existence of God and his providence); they are called preambles because they prepare for faith. *Foundations of faith* are the revealed truths themselves, or generically revelation. *Principles of faith* are the same truths which become also principles, properly so-called, of theological science. *Truths of faith* is another name for the same. *Articles of faith* are more strictly the fundamental truths of faith, as those contained in the Creed or Symbol of faith. *Formula of faith* is a definite expression of the truths of faith, as the various *Symbols of faith.*

Rule of faith is the threefold channel, that is, Scripture, Tradition, and the Magisterium, as explained above. *Dogma of faith*, or simply *dogma*, is a truth revealed by God (placed in the deposit of Scripture and Tradition) and infallibly proposed by the Magisterium, which is the proximate rule of faith. *Dogmatic formula* is the expression of a dogma, which can be of various kinds.

Fathers of the Church. The generic concept of Father of the Church is connected with that of generation. Hence a Father of the Church is one who helped to bring to maturity the adolescent Church or to generate the faith in others at the beginning of the Church. *Four qualifications* are required to be a Father of the Church. First, *sanctity* by reason of the intimate connection between Christian life and Christian doctrine. Second, *orthodox doctrine* (as a whole, notwithstanding a particular or material error); hence, some outstanding doctors, as Tertullian and Origen, are not strictly Fathers of the Church on account of various important errors. Third, *antiquity*, corresponding to the beginnings of the Church. This means the first five centuries, up to St. Gregory the Great, †604; however this period is usually extended to the eighth century in order to include such outstanding writers as St. Isidore of Seville and St. John Damascene. Fourth, *ecclesiastical approbation*, because the Magisterium alone is qualified to judge on the orthodoxy of a writer; this approbation need not be individual or explicit; a general or implicit approbation is sufficient.

All the other doctors, who lack one or another of these requisites, particularly orthodoxy or antiquity, are called strictly and merely *ecclesiastical writers.*

Several of the Fathers (20 of them, among others Athanasius, Basil, Gregory Nazianzen, Chrysostom in the East, and Ambrose, Augustine, Jerome, Gregory the Great in the West) received also a special approbation of the Magisterium through the official title of *Doctors of the Church.* But also several theologians (12 of them, first in time Thomas Aquinas and Bonaventure, last in the present time women, Teresa of Avila and Catherine of Siena) have received the same title, based on a special doctrinal contribution to the cause of faith.

"Loci theologici" are the places where theologians find the bases and the principles for their scientific investigations. The principal "loci" are the same three channels of revelation mentioned above under the proper entry, that is *Scripture, Tradition*, and the *Magisterium*; the first two are "loci" or places which contain revelation, the last is a place which only proposes revelation. To these three can be reduced other "loci," that is *the believing Church* (the faithful as a whole body), the *Fathers*, and the *theologians*, who are part of Tradition. Also *natural reason* and the authority of philosophers can be accounted as foreign or borderline "loci," inasmuch as they may confirm some revealed truth.

Magisterium is the teaching authority in the Church, which is proper to the Pope and the bishops (even individually). It is the right and duty of authoritatively proposing revealed truth. It is divided into ordinary and extraordinary. The *ordinary Magisterium* is carried out in a common manner of teaching by the official pastors (Pope and bishops) or by others under their direction, through preaching, allocutions, pastoral letters, catechetical instructions. The *extraordinary* or solemn declaration of the supreme authority (Pope, or bishops acting as a body with the Pope). Both kinds of Magisterium are either infallible or not infallible, depending upon their intention (thus Vatican I proposed its teaching infallibly, Vatican II not infallibly). The infallible definition made by the Pope alone has received the special name of definition *ex cathedra*, by reason of its peculiar character of solemnity.

As we noticed in the preceding entries, the Magisterium is the *organ of revelation*, the *proximate rule of faith*, and the third theological "locus."

Notes and censures, theological. By this expression, often occurring in theology, is meant the qualification given to a proposition or doctrine as to its agreement (note) or disagreement (censure) with a revealed truth proposed by the Magisterium.

The principal censures, often assigned by the Magisterium itself, are the following five: 1) *Heretical*, that is a proposition or doctrine directly opposed to a truth of faith (for instance: Christ is not a man); the opposite note is: *de fide*. 2) *Erroneous*, that is, a proposition directly opposed not to faith itself but to a doctrine necessarily following from faith (for instance: Christ does not have a human heart); the opposite note is: *theology certain, or Catholic doctrine.* 3) *Temerarious*, that is, a proposition which has no sufficient foundation or is opposed to the common and firm opinion of the theologians (for instance: St. John the Baptist had the privilege of an immaculate conception like the Blessed Virgin); the opposite note is: *highly probable, or morally certain.* 4) *Ill-sounding*, that is, a proposition lacking correct expression which may lead to an error about faith (for instance: In God there are three relative essences; which may lead to believe that there are three Gods); the opposite note is: *correct-sounding.* 5) *Offensive to pious ears*, that is, a proposition expressing a truth without the reverence due to holy things (for instance, calling

St. Peter a perjurer or St. Paul a persecutor of the Church); the opposite note is: *fitting to piety.*

Object of a science, or rather of every knowing faculty, is roughly speaking the subject matter, the whole thing which is dealt with in a science or by a faculty. But we must distinguish three ascending degrees in it, in the manner of getting in touch, as it were, with the knowing faculty; in other words there are three manners of considering the same total object, and hence three kinds of object. The first is called *material object,* that is, the concrete being or reality under consideration; for instance, the concrete quantitative body which I see with my eyes. The second is called *formal object,* that is, the particular aspect or quality which is considered or reached by a faculty or a science in that material object; for instance, the color which the eyes see in the body and without which the body could not be seen. The third may be called the *formal light* (or a more formal object; as a matter of fact philosophers call it formal object "quo," that is, "through which"). This is more difficult to understand and the very name "light" may be misleading. The light under which an object is reached is nothing else than its own immateriality, which makes an object knowable or proportioned to the knowing faculty (for knowledge consists precisely in abstracting or separating an object from material conditions) and which for this reason is called light. Thus the formal light under which the eyes see the color of a body is the sensible light, meaning by that, the proper immateriality of color which makes the color visible, that is, adequate and adjusted to the eyes.

In the case of *theology* its material object is God and his divine works; the formal object, which is directly considered in God himself, is his intimate nature called the *Deity;* the formal light is the light of revelation, that is, the high and pure immateriality of this nature, which becomes adjusted to our intellect by an action of God revealing, and for this reason is called *the light of revelation.*

Revelation, which etymologically means the removal of a veil, in theology is taken in two ways, namely, for the action of God manifesting his mysteries to men (*active revelation*), and for its effect in man (*passive revelation*). This effect is twofold, that is, the presentation of an object or truth to the intellect (*objective revelation*) and a supernatural light infused in the intellect to make it able to understand such an object (*subjective revelation*).

When we speak of source, channel, deposit, organ or principles of revelation, revelation is taken objectively, for the revealed truth. In this sense revelation is both *the principle and the formal light of theology.* It is also the proper object of that introductory part of theology which is called Apologetics.

Supernatural means anything above nature. It can be taken either in a relative sense, and thus whatever is natural to a being is supernatural to a lower being (as speech, which is natural to man, is supernatural to a brute), or in an *absolute and theological sense*, and thus it is defined: *that which is above all created things, as to their nature, their power, and their exigencies.*

This is twofold. Either it is *essentially supernatural*, if the essence of the thing itself is supernatural (such are the intimate mysteries of God, as Trinity and Incarnation, and their participation is us, through revelation, grace, and glory). Or it is only *modally supernatural*, if the essence of the thing is natural, but it is produced in a supernatural manner, that is, in a manner in which no power of created things can do it. Examples are what we call miracles of the physical order, as resurrection, healing of incurable diseases, etc.

The principles of theology (revealed truths), its formal object (Deity) and its formal light (revelation), are essentially supernatural, and in this sense theology is fundamentally supernatural. But the science of theology itself, as a habit of the mind, is not formally supernatural, because it is essentially based on a process of natural reason and it is an acquired habit, while no supernatural habit can be acquired, but must be simply infused by God.

Theology strictly so-called is a science about God, considered in his intimate essence, or inner attributes, which we call Deity (see this entry). If God is considered in his external attributes, that is, those perfections that are common to him and to creatures, such knowledge or science is called properly theodicy (or natural theology) which is the highest part of metaphysics.

With the word and the concept of theology are connected three technical expressions, namely "theological conclusions," "theological loci," and "theological notes and censures," of which we spoke above in the corresponding entries.

Tradition is derived from the Latin word "trader," meaning to hand over or on. As a theological term, it means the handing on of revelation or of the things preached by Christ and the apostles. It can be taken in two senses. First, in an active sense (*active Tradition*), that is, for all the means through which revelation is transmitted, which are the inspired books themselves (Scripture), the Magisterium, the writings of the Fathers and other doctors, liturgy, canonical laws, etc. Second, in an objective sense (*objective Tradition*), that is, for the object or truths handed on.

This objective Tradition again can be taken in two senses. First, in an integral sense (*integral Tradition*), that is, for all the truths which are handed over through whatever means, and therefore also for the truths that are contained in Scripture. Second, in a partial sense (*partial or constitutive Tradition*), that is, only for those truths that are not contained in Scripture (at least not sufficiently), but only the other aforementioned means of transmission (such are the list of the books of Scripture, their divine inspiration, and other truths and usages).

Among such means of transmission, the writings of the Fathers of the Church and other ecclesiastical writers (see entry: Fathers of the Church) are an outstanding and certain element for knowing the traditional truths, and for this reason the *argument from Tradition* in theology refers mainly to the doctrine of the Fathers.

As has been said in the preceding entries ("Channels," "Loci"), Tradition is a *deposit* of revelation, a *remote rule of faith*, and a theological "locus."

Vision, beatific, is the immediate vision of God, in his infinite essence and as it were face to face. On the part of our intellect, this act supposes a supernatural light, called *light of glory*, which elevates the intellect and makes it able to see God intuitively. This kind of act constitutes essentially what we call heaven, beatitude, eternity.

Beatific vision is at once the supernatural and ultimate *end of man, the fulfillment of our state of grace*, which is called the seed of glory because it will blossom into a full vision and love of God (replacing faith, hope and other virtues presently needed), and the *ultimate resolution of theology*, whose revealed principles are immediately evident only in the beatific vision.

ANALYTICAL INDEX

Abelard (Peter) gave a scientific meaning to the word "theology," 1, and introduced Aristotelian philosophy and the method of scholastic disputation, 37f.

Analogy has an objective value in expressing revealed as well as theological truths, 7f.

"Analogy of faith," that is, the mutual agreement between the various truths of faith, is the base of an outstanding theological argument, 23.

Anselm of Canterbury (St.) is the author of the famous aphorism which describes theology as "faith seeking understanding," 6, 17, 36. He closes the ancient and opens the scholastic period of the theological investigation, 34, 36f.

Apologetics, as method, 26f.; as science, 23, 33; as means used by the Fathers of the Church, 25, 34, 35

Augustine (St.) brought the patristic theological investigation to its apex and hence he can be called the forefather of the theological science, 35. His famous expression about theology "begetting and nourishing faith," 8

Certitude of the theological science is absolute, but only objectively, not necessarily subjectively, 11, 19–20

Christ is not the proper and principal object of the theological science, but only of the practical preaching and of Christian life, 13–15

Conclusion, theological, is twofold, namely proper and improper; *see Syllogism.* Drawing proper conclusions from revealed principles, is the object, function and method of theology, formally as a science, 11, 16., 22, 26., 33f., 36–37

Damascene (St. John) closes the patristic age in the East and has a particular importance in patristic theological thought, 34, 35

Deity. *See God*

Dionysius (pseudo-) *the Areopagite* used the word "theology" as the title of one of his works, 5, 35, and adopted neoplatonic philosophy in his theological investigation, 35

Division of theology, which can be made in several ways, 30, has first been arranged in logical manner by St. Thomas, 31, and further extended by modern theologians, 31–32

Faith requires a "reasonable submission" (Romans 12:1) of our mind, 9; it is protected and nourished by theology, 9, and in its turn perfects reason and philosophy, 9. *See Revelation. Science. Theology*

Fathers (The) of the Church brought into use the word "theology," 5. Patristic theology, as a part of positive theology investigates the revealed truths in the works of the Fathers, 28, 31. Development of theological investigation in the patristic age, 33–36

Fittingness (Reasons of), as a valuable theological argument, 23

God is the principal material object of theology, 12, 30, 31, 32, and, if considered as Deity or in his intimate essence, he is also the formal object of this science, 12, 13, 19

Immateriality, or abstraction from material conditions, is the immediate root of intelligibility, 12f.

Magisterium (The) of the Church approves traditional and Thomistic theology against foreign infiltration, (preface), 3. It teaches moral necessity of revelation, 9. It gives impulse to positive theology, 39. Its pronouncements are the object of symbolic positive theology, 27, 31–32

Metaphysics, as to its formal object, namely being as being, 12, 13, 19, 21, and its comparison with the other natural sciences, 30. It is the highest wisdom among natural sciences, 19f., 23. Comparison with theology, as to its object, 13, 21, the evidence of its principles, 19, and its sapiential nature, 19f. Theology uses it as a handmaid, 23f.

Method, as to its notion, 26, division, 26, and application in the historical development of theology, 33f., 37

Origen is the founder of theological investigation in the eastern patristic age, 34. *See Tertullian*

Object of a science, as to its notion and division, 12, 21. *See Science. Theology*

Philosophy, as to its division, 21, comparison with theology, 9, 17, 20–21, and influence in theological patristic thought, 34, 35, 36f. *See Metaphysics. Science. Theology*

Platonism (Neo-) had its influence in the rise and development of theological investigation in the patristic age, 34, 35, 36

Positive theology, as to its proper object and its difference from systematic theology, 27–29, its division, 28, 30f., and its historical development, 39

Practical and speculative are two concepts formally and philosophically distinct, which, however, mingle in the higher object of theology, 18

Reason is perfected by revelation and theology, 9f., 24. *See Philosophy. Faith Science. Theology*

Revelation furnished the principles of theology, 11, 14, 15, and it is also its formal light, 12f., 21. How does theology deal with its own revealed principles, 22f. *See Faith. Theology*

Science, as to its proper nature, 10f., its difference from wisdom, 20, and its general division, 21. Notion of sub-alternate science, 11, 20. Natural sciences are used and perfected by theology, 23f. *See Metaphysics. Philosophy. Syllogism. Theology*

Scripture, as the object of positive theology, 28, 30f.

Speculative. *See Practical and speculative*

Supernatural character of theology, 16f.

Syllogism is twofold, namely proper (or illative) and improper (or expository), 11, 22, 23, 27, 37. *See Origen*

Theodicy is specifically different from theology, 5, 12. *See Metaphysics. Theology*

Theology. Use of this word by the Fathers and theologians, 1. Historical development of theology, 33–34. Its general and scientific definition, 5f., 10. Theology is a true science, 10f., different from theodicy, 5, 12, having as its proper object not Christ, nor man's salvation, but God himself, 12–15. It is a supernatural science, not essentially, but fundamentally, 16f. its principles are objectively, not subjectively, evident and certain, 11, 19. It unifies practical and speculative matters in its higher object, 17. It is the highest human wisdom on earth, 19–21. It has different character, functions, and method, when dealing as a science or as wisdom, 19f., 22, 26f. It uses and perfects natural sciences, 24f. The so-called "new theology," as to its general tendencies, (see preface and bibliography at the beginning of this treatise), 42, and as to its opinion about the scientific nature of theology, 7f., and the proper object of this science, 12–15

Thomas Aquinas (St.) is the supreme, and probably charismatic, mind in the world of theology, 38. His doctrine is commended by the Magisterium (see preface). Division of theology into natural and supernatural, 5. Supernatural theology is properly described as "an impression of the divine science [in our mind]," 16. Only God is the principal object of theology, 13, 14, 15. Theology is the supreme wisdom on earth, 19. Positive theology is of itself insufficient without the systematic, 29. Logical division of theology, 30

Tradition. *See Fathers of the Church*

Vision, beatific, is the ultimate resolution of theology, inasmuch as it contains the immediate evidence of the theological principles, 11, 19, 21

Wisdom is the apex of science, 19f. Metaphysics is the supreme wisdom among natural sciences, and theology is the supreme wisdom among all sciences on earth, 19–21. The proper function of any wisdom is "judging and ordering," 22, which function is performed by theology in several important ways, 22–25. *See Metaphysics. Science. Theology*

BIBLIOGRAPHY

SECTION A: BASIC WRITINGS

Berti, C. M., *Methodologiae theologiae elementa*, Romae 1955.

Beumer, J., *Theologie als Glaubensverständnis*, Würzburg 1953.

Bilz, J., *Einführung in die Theologie*, Freiburg 1935.

Camps, G. M., *Bases de una metodología teológica*, Montserat 1954.

Colombo, C., "La metodologia e la sistemazione teologica," Problemi e orientamenti di teologia dommatica 1 (Milano 1957) 1–47.

Congar, Y., *La foi et la théologie*, Tournai 1962.

Doronzo, E., *Theologia Dogmatica* (Washington, D. C. 1966) 1–92.

Fabro, C., "Semantica teologica e Filosofia contemporanea," Asprenas 15 (1968) 7–26.

Gardeil, A., *Le donné révélé et la théologie*, éd. 2, Paris 1932.

González, E., *Manual de introducción a la teologica*, Salamanca 1959.

Journet Ch., *Introduction á la théologie*, Paris 1947.

Kolping, A., *Einführung in die katholische Theologie*, Münster 1960.

Latourelle, R., *Theology: Science of Salvation* (transl. from the French), New York 1970.

Rabeau, R., *Introduction á l'étude de la théologie*, Paris 1926.

Touilleux, P., *Introduction á la théologie*, Paris 1967.

Wyser, P., *Theologie als Wissenschaft*, Salzburg-Leipzig 1938.

Xiberta, B. M., *Introductio in S. Theologiam*, Matriti 1949.

SECTION B: DISCUSSIONS, OF MIXED CHARACTER, ON AGGIORNAMENTO IN THEOLOGY

Adnés, P., La théologie catholique, Paris, 1967.

Aubert, R., "Les mouvements théologiques dans l'Eglise catholique durant le dernier quart de siècle." La foi et le temps 2 (1969) 125–152.

Auricchio, J., *The Future of Theology*, New York 1970.

Avenir de la théologie (collective work), Paris 1968.

Balthasar, H. U. von, *Cordula ou l'épreuve decisive*, Paris 1968.

Comblin, J., *Vers une théologie de l'action*, Paris 1964.

Congar, Y., *Situation et tâches présentes de la théologie*, Paris 1967.

Contributo al rinnovamento degli studi teologici, Venegono 1967.

Denis, H., *Where is Theology Going?* (trans. T. Du Bois), Glen Rock, N. J. 1968.

Dondeyne, A., *La foi écoute le monde*, Paris 1964.

Dumont, C., "De trois dimensions retrouvées en théologie: eschatologie-orthopraxie-herméneutique," Nouvelle revue théologique 92 no. 6 (1970) 561–591.

Flick, M., Alszeghy, Z., *Metodologia per una teologia dello sviluppo*, Brescia 1970.

Flick, M., Alszeghy, Z., *Fondamenti di una antropologia teologica*, Firenze 1970.

Gesché, A., "Vrai et faux changement en théologie," Collectanea Mechliniensia 53 (1968) 303–333.

Kasper, W., Renouveau de la méthode théologique (traduit de l'allemand par A. Liefoogue), Paris 1968.

Latourelle, R., Theology: Science of Salvation (transl. from the French), New York 1970.

"Linguaggio teologico oggi," Civiltá cattolica 120 (1969) 1, pp. 271–275.

Maritain, J., The Peasant of the Garonne: An Old Layman Questions Himself about the Present Time (trans. M. Cuddihy and E. Hughes), New York 1968.

Moltmann, J., Perspektiven der Theologie, Mainz-München 1968; Religion, Revolution and the Future, New York 1969.

Parente, P., Itinerario teologico ieri e oggi, Firenze 1968.

Projections: Shaping an American Theology for the Future (eds. Th. F. O'Meara and D. M. Weisser), Garden City 1970.

Rahner, K., Theology of Renewal, New York 1965.

Rossel, J., "From a Theology of Crisis to Theology of Revolution?," Ecumenical Review 21 (1969) 204–215.

Rust, E. C., Evolutionary Philosophies and Contemporary Theology, Philadelphia 1969.

Sesboüé, B., "Autorité du Magistére et vie de foi ecclésiale," Nouvelle revue théologique 93 (1971) 337–362.

Sontag, F., The Future of Theology, Philadelphia 1969.

Teologia del rinnovamento. Mete, problem e prospettive della teologica contemporanea, Assisi 1969.

Teologia (La) dopo il Vaticano II (ed. J. M. Miller), Brescia 1967.

Théologie d'aujourd'hui et de demain (collective work), Paris 1967.

Theology of Renewal, 1: Renewal of Religious Thought; 2: Renewal of Religious Structures, Montreal (Canada) 1968.

Theology in Revolution (ed. George Devine), New York 1970.

Tihon, P., "J. A. T. Robinson et la recherché d'un style théologique pour notre temps," Nouvelle revue théologique 91 (1968) 149–168.

Waelkens, R., Catholicisme et requétes contemporaines, Bruxelles 1965.

Weiland, J. S., La nouvelle théologie, Bruges 1969.

Zumstein, J., "Théologie et philosophie. Quel doit étre aujourd'hui le róle de la réflexion philosophique en théologie," Revue de théologie et de philosophie 18 (1968) 389–401.

BOOK 2
Revelation

INTRODUCTION

THE SUBJECT MATTER OF THIS TREATISE IS REV-
elation generically considered, without particular reference to the
individual revealed truths. As shown in the preceding treatise on
Introduction to Theology (p. 10f.) revelation is both the formal reason of theology as a whole, that is, the light under which God and
the other objects are considered, and its proper principle, inasmuch as it is revelation which proposes those truths from which,
as from true principles, theology draws its conclusions. Under
both aspects, revelation is the foundation of theology. Hence this
treatise is rightly called *Fundamental Theology.*

Revelation, precisely because it is the principle of theology,
cannot be directly proved by this science, for no science proves
its own principles. Each science supposes its principles as certain and evident from other sources, either through reason or
through faith. Theology holds its principles through faith. However, theological science, being also wisdom, indeed the supreme
wisdom on earth, can and must direct its attention in a scientific
manner to its own revealed principles. It must not only explain
and present them by way of persuasion, but also defend them,
by proving with certainty their extrinsic credibility, namely that
it is fitting to believe them through supernatural faith, because
Christ's testimony of the fact of revelation is absolutely truthful, being warranted and endorsed by God himself through his
miraculous intervention. Hence this treatise is also essentially
apologetic and can be rightly called with the combined name of
Apologetic Fundamental Theology.[1]

This leads us to its proper *definition*, expressing its nature and
object: it is *the scientific demonstration of the extrinsic credibility of
revelation, through evident criteria, under the light of natural reason.*

---

1 *Apologetics* (from the Greek "apologhia," a speech in defense, from "apó," after,
and "lègo," I speak) means generically a defense. The word is often used in Scripture in the sense of self-defense (Act 22:1; 25:16; 1 Cor. 9:3; 2 Cor. 7:11; 2 Tim.
4:16; 1 Pet. 3:15) and at least once in the sense of defense of a thing, namely of the
Gospel itself (Phil. 1:7, 16: "In the defense and confirmation of the gospel ... I am
appointed for the defense of the gospel." Theologians usually distinguish between
apology and *apologetics*, meaning by the first the defense of a particular truth (as
Trinity, Incarnation, etc.), and by the second, the defense of revelation as a whole.
Hence this treatise is commonly called Apologetics.

It is a true scientific demonstration, not as a science standing by itself, but as a mere *integrating part of the single science of theology,* considered as wisdom, as we just noted. Hence, it does not matter that it proceeds under the light of natural reason while theology must proceed under the light of revelation, precisely because it is merely an extension of theological science, taking over the light of reason to its own service for the purpose of explaining and defending its supernatural principles.

Its *material* object is revelation, theoretically considered in its general notions; its *formal object* is the fact of revelation, shown as credible through evident criteria; its *formal reason,* or the light under which it proceeds, is the light of reason, because its purpose is to prove the credibility or knowability of revelation in a rational manner, that is, from philosophical and historical principles. For it is impossible to prove revelation by revelation itself without making a vicious circle; however, since it is a question of a mere extensive function of theology itself, the light of reason here must proceed under the direction of the light of revelation.

Hence the whole scientific process of Apologetics consists in attributing the concept of credibility to revelation (more precisely to the fact of revelation) by means of evident criteria, so that such criteria are like principles from which the following conclusion is drawn: Revelation (the fact of revelation) is credible. Such a process can be briefly reduced to the following general syllogism: That which is endorsed by evident extrinsic criteria, is evidently credible. But revelation (namely that God has really talked to men, according to Christ's testimony) is endorsed by evident criteria, that is by the miraculous intervention of God. Therefore revelation is credible.[2]

---

2   Do not, however think that in this manner the act of faith itself about revelation is resolved into such a syllogism, or that the evidence of faith itself is resolved into this rational evidence of credibility, for this is only an extrinsic credibility of the fact of revelation, which cannot generate faith but only dispose to it. In fact, in the genesis of the act of supernatural faith we find the following three steps. First, there must be *the intrinsic evidence of the given testimony and of the authority or competence (Knowledge and veracity) of the witness* (namely, that Christ, a man of wisdom and veracity, testified that God has spoken). Second, there follows *the extrinsic evidence of credibility about the fact of revelation,* that is, about the objective truth of Christ's testimony (namely, that it is true and credible that God has spoken, as Christ testified, and that this is shown by evident criteria). Finally, there comes *supernatural faith itself,* with its own intrinsic evidence and certitude, founded only on the testimony of God revealing, and elicited under the movement of grace;

From the aforesaid object we logically draw the *division of this treatise* into two parts. In the *first part* we shall consider *revelation* in its *general notions* (material object), that is, its nature and properties, among which is found credibility; and this amounts to the question of the essence of revelation. (Theoretical Apologetics). In the *second part* we shall deal with *the fact of revelation*, shown through evident criteria or motives of credibility (formal object); and this amounts to the question of the existence of revelation (Practical Apologetics).

---

however, this faith, which is a purely infused gift of God, does not follow if the will of man refuses to comply with the aforesaid extrinsic evidence of credibility and resists the movement of the grace of God, tending to the infusion of faith (see below, footnote 25 and p. 154).

PART I

General Notions on Revelation
(THEORETICAL APOLOGETICS)

IN THE FOLLOWING SEVEN CHAPTERS WE CON-
sider revelation as to its nature (chap. 1), its possibility (chap. 2),
fittingness and necessity (chap. 3), and especially its credibility
or knowability. This latter is more important for our apologetical
purpose and hence requires a careful explanation of its nature
(chap. 4), possibility (chap. 5), genesis (chap. 6), and criteria
(chap. 7).

1

Nature of Revelation

THE CATHOLIC NOTION OF REVELATION, AS PRO-
posed by the Magisterium itself with its foundation in Scripture,
can be described as a *direct action of God, which through words and
deeds, manifests to men things and truths known only to him.*

In the *New Testament* this manifestation of God is expressed by
three words: revelation, manifestation, and speech.

Revelation (in Greek "apokálupsis," the English apocalypsis,
from "apó," back "kaléo," I call) indicates a manifestation of
supernatural truth (Rom. 16:25; Eph. 1:17; Luke 2:32), or an
extraordinary manifestation through visions (Apoc. 1:1; Gal.
1:12; Eph. 3:3; 1 Cor. 14:6, 26; 2 Cor. 12:1, 7), or the second
advent of Christ (1 Cor. 1:7; 2 Thess. 1:7; 1 Pet. 1:13).

Manifestation (in Greek "fanérosis," from "faneróo," I manifest, I make visible; remotely from "fáino," I bring light, I make
appear, hence "epifánia,": the English epiphany) indicates the
first advent of Christ (1 John 1:2; 3:5, 8; Tit. 3:16; Heb. 9:26;
1 Pet. 1:20), as well as his second advent (Col. 3:4; 1 Pet. 5:4;
1 John 2:28; 3:2).

Speech (in Greek "lálema," talk) indicates a speech of God to
man, both by spoken words (Heb. 1:1f.[3]; 2.2) and by written
words (Heb. 2:5; 6:9; 2 Pet. 3:16); the same meaning is brought
out by the kindred word *oracle* (in Greek "lóghion," from "légo," I
tell, I speak), which is used to indicate the prophecies of the Old
Testament (Acts 7:38; Rom. 3:2).

The *Magisterium* gives us the Catholic notion of revelation in
both Vatican Councils, which deals directly with this subject. *Vatican I,* speaking of the "supernatural way [in which God chose]
to reveal himself and the eternal decrees of his will to mankind,"

---

3 Particular value has to be given to Heb. 1.1f., which refers to all prophetical
revelations of the O. T. as to a speech of God: "God, who at sundry times and in
divers manners spoke in times past to the fathers by the prophets, last of all in these
days has spoken to us by his Son." In the O. T. itself the various manifestations
of God to the prophets are called "speech" or "word:" (Ps. 84:9; Isa. 50:4; Osee.
1:1; Joel 1:1; Jonas 1:1; Mich. 1:1; Soph. 1:1; Agg. 1:1; Zach. 1:1; Mal. 1:1, etc.)

sees it expressed in the words of St. Paul, Heb. 1:1f. about God speaking to men through the prophets and through Christ[4] (Sess, 3, chap. 2, Denz. 3044). Here revelation is presented *only as speech*. *Vatican II* extends the concept of revelation so as to include both *speech* and *deeds*: "[God's] plan of revelation is realized by *deeds* and *words*, intrinsically connected, so that the deeds, wrought by God in the history of salvation, declare and strengthen the doctrine and the things signified by the words, while the words proclaim the deeds and clarify the mystery contained in them" (Constitution on Divine Revelation, no. 2).

In this extension there is no essential addition, but only a further explanation of the concept of speech, which can be expressed formally and primarily by words and equivalently also by deeds, having, however, their value of sign and expression of the mind by the words themselves. Also a man can be said to talk, or to manifest his mind, both by words and by deeds (that is, by signs other than words), provided the meaning of his deeds has been previously declared by his words, otherwise the mere deeds would not carry a clear and certain sense and would not sufficiently manifest the object and the intention of the mind. As St. Augustine puts it, "Among men words have obtained the leading role in the realm of signification" (*On Christian Doctrine* 2.2.3); applying this principle to the sacraments, particularly to baptism, the holy Doctor says: "If the word is missing, the water is nothing but water. If on the contrary the word is joined to the material element, there will be a sacrament, which becomes in itself a visible word" (*On John*, tract. 80, no. 3). We may say, likewise, in God's revelation or manifestation of his mind, if we remove the words, the deeds are mute deeds; but if we add the words to the deeds, then we have revelation in the deeds themselves, which take up the value of living and practical words.[5]

---

4 See preceding footnote.
5 Hence some authors (as Latourelle, Léonard, Quinn, mentioned above, p. iv, v) exaggerate when they say that the Council, by mentioning the deeds as means of revelation, has changed the traditional concept of revelation, given by the first Vatican Council itself. Some go so far as to define revelation generically as God's communication to man or as God's manifestation; in the first case the infusion of sanctifying grace would be a revelation, in the second case any supernatural instinct, or inspiration (as in the writers of the Holy Scripture), or assistance of the Holy Spirit (as that given to the Magisterium), would be revelation. Is not all this an effect and a cause of theological confusions?

Hence supernatural revelation consists *essentially and formally in a speech of God* to man, secondarily also in deeds inasmuch as these manifest and confirm in a practical way the words themselves. Such a concept of speech attributed to God is not improper or merely metaphorical, but proper, although analogical.[6] For speech consists essentially in manifesting one's own thought to another, as from person to person; nor does it matter in which way it is done, whether through a merely sensible sign or through a purely intellectual means, that is, by the infusion of the intelligible species in the mind of another. This can be done also by God, and in both ways. Moreover, in the act of revelation of a supernatural object, *besides the mere presentation of the object* (either through sensible or intellectual means), God must and can infuse some *supernatural light* in the intellect itself, to make it able to understand such an object. Hence God's revelation is a more proper and more perfect speech than that of man, since it communicates to man the thoughts of God in two ways, that is, both objectively and subjectively.

These two elements of revelation or speech of God can be separated, so that God would offer to a man only the presentation of the object without the supernatural light to understand it, or vice versa. However, in such cases there would be no revelation properly so called, that is real speech of God, but only an inferior kind of manifestation of God; in the first case there would be only a *prophetic instinct* (cf. *Summa Theol.*, II-II, q. 173, a. 2), like in the vision given to Pharaoh and interpreted later by Joseph (Gen. 41:14–32) or in the words uttered by Caiaphas about the death of Christ and interpreted by St. John (John 11:51). In the second case there would be either a higher *prophetic instinct*, as was given to the aforementioned Joseph and John, or an *inspiration* (that is a supernatural movement to write what God wants a man to write, so that the writing is properly attributed to God, as principal

---

6 Not every *analogical* concept is metaphorical. It can be purely *metaphorical* or improper, as when we say: This food is healthy, or Peter is a lion (both concepts of good and lion are purely metaphorical). It can be also *proper*, that is, expressing something which is formally and properly in the subject; thus, when we say: God is being, intelligent and volitional, and likewise, man is being, intelligent and volitional, these three perfections (being, intelligence and will) are predicated properly of both God and man, because they are found in both formally, although not in the same way, but proportionally, and hence analogically.

author), as happened to the various writers of Holy scripture, or a mere supernatural *assistance* (by which a writer or a speaker is merely preserved from error), as happens to the Church magisterium when defining infallibly truths of natural lights or helps, bestowed by God to man, namely revelation, prophetic instinct, inspiration, and assistance of the Holy Spirit.

2

Possibility of Revelation

AS SHOWN ABOVE, REVELATION IMPLIES TWO
elements, one objective, the presentation of a supernatural object
to human intellect, and the other subjective, the infusion of a
supernatural light in the intellect by which it is made proportioned to the understanding of such an object. Both of these elements presuppose the existence of a supernatural order in God
which manifests itself in them. Hence the possibility of revelation
is not shown unless we show first the existence of supernatural order, and then the possibility of proposing it as an object
understandable by a human intellect, and of infusing in the same
intellect a light above reason, making it able to understand such
an object. Since these two things are supernatural, that is, above
all created nature and its powers, we can bring forth no direct and
positive proof, but only indirect or probable arguments, such as
are sufficient to the apologetical purpose of refuting the negation
of Rationalists on those two points.[7]

The *existence of a supernatural order* or order of mysteries[8]
(which is *de fide* from Vatican Council I, sess. 3, can. 1 on faith and
reason) cannot be directly proved, since the object is essentially

---

7 *Rationalism*, from its general and common principle of the complete autonomy
of natural reason, draws the conclusion that these is no supernatural order, that
is, an order of things and truths above reason. This is the teaching of pure *Positive
Rationalism*, either materialistic (as that of E. Haeckel), or idealistic (as that of
Hegel), both of which deny the very existence of God, identifying him with the
world. A form of apparently mitigated Rationalism teaches that, even if there were
a supernatural order, the human intellect would not in any way be able to know it,
and therefore its revelation would be impossible. This is the *Agnostic Rationalism*,
which denies directly not the existence of God, but the possibility of knowing him
and the objective value of the principles of reason leading to knowledge of him.
The reason for this agnosticism would be either the pure phenomenal nature of our
ideas (Agnostic Empirical Rationalism of H. Spencer, A. Comte, and W. James), or
their purely subjective value (Agnostic Idealistic Rationalism, founded by E. Kant).
This agnostic rationalism, under both forms, was adopted within the Church by
Modernism. Modernism denies that human reason can reach beyond phenomena
and know with certainty even the existence of God.
8 *Supernatural*, in a proper and absolute sense, is that which is above all created
nature, as to the essence of the created nature or at least as to its powers and exigencies. It is divided into *essentially or intrinsically supernatural* (or as to its intrinsic

supernatural. It can be derived indirectly, however, from the very existence of God, as a personal being, distinct from the world. For, what is proper to God (his nature and inner attributes) is higher than the proper object of our intellect and is in no way manifested by this lower object; hence it cannot be naturally reached by our intellect and constitutes an order above reason, that is a supernatural order. Indeed, the proper and formal object of our intellect is not God himself but a created being, that is being as limited and determined by sensible nature. Otherwise our intellect would be equal to the intellect of God, as being specified by the same object, and even would be identified with it which is idealistic pantheism. Now, in this kind of created being God is indeed manifested and known in some way, as a cause in its effect, and therefore according to the attributes that are common to him and the creatures (as being, one, good, intelligence, will, power). But God cannot be manifested and known as to what is proper to him and is not found in the creatures, for no effect contains adequately the nature and power of its proper cause. Hence, this intimate reality of God in himself, which cannot be known by our intellect through its proper and formal object of created being, constitutes an order above reason, that is a supernatural order.

---

causes), which surpasses both the essence of all created nature and its powers and the exigencies (such are Deity, Trinity, Incarnation, glory, grace); and *modally or extrinsically supernatural* (or as to its extrinsic causes) which surpasses only the powers and exigencies, not the essence, of created nature, and therefore consists in something which is essentially natural, but cannot be produced by any natural cause (such are most of those things that are called miracles, as glorification of the body, resurrection, the knowledge of the secrets of hearts, the gift of languages.) At present we are dealing only with the essentially or intrinsically supernatural.

Mystery (in Greek "mustérion," from "muo," I close) etymologically means something closed, and, by evolution of speech, something closed to knowledge, that is secret; the word was used especially to designate religious truths and rites, as being most secret and unknown. It is divided into *natural* mystery, which can be known without God's revelation, and *supernatural mystery*, which cannot be known without supernatural revelation. This is subdivided into mystery in a *broad sense*, that which, after its revelation by God, is perfectly understood both as to its existence and its nature (such are divine decrees about natural facts, for instance about future happenings which we cannot foresee) and mystery in the *strict sense*, which even after revelation (at least the revelation we have in this life, through the obscure light of faith), is not perfectly known, for we know by faith only its existence and have only an obscure analogical concept of its essence, so that it still remains a mystery as to its intimate nature (such are Deity, trinity, Incarnation, glory, grace). At present we are dealing especially with mysteries in the strict sense, which are at the same time essentially supernatural, so that the supernatural order is perfectly equivalent to the order of mysteries.

The possibility of revelation to man of this supernatural order (which is *de fide* from Vatican I, sess.3, can. 2–3 on revelation) cannot be reasonably denied. On the contrary, it can be sufficiently shown, not indeed through certain and evident proofs, but at least by the aid of persuasive and probable arguments.

The possibility of proposing a truth of this supernatural order, as an object understandable by the human intellect, lies in the objective and ontological value of our analogical concepts. Indeed, most of the concepts by which we express higher natural truths themselves and with which we deal in our natural sciences, including metaphysics and its higher part theodicy (as the concepts of being, cause, end, relation, substance, accident, and God himself as the supreme Being — true, good, and omnipotent) are analogical concepts. No one can deny objective and ontological value to them, without rejecting the objective value of our entire knowledge. Therefore there is no reason why a higher truth of the supernatural order could not likewise be expressed with similar analogical concepts, having their objective and ontological value, and hence carrying to the human intellect a proper, although analogical, understanding of a supernatural reality. For example, when divine paternity or filiation is revealed, it is not repugnant that the concept of paternity or filiation, drawn from creatures, signifies properly, although analogically, something pertaining to the intimate essence of God. [9]

The possibility of infusing in the human intellect a light above the light of reason, to make it able to understand this supernatural object analogically expressed, cannot be rejected through any *a priori* reason, as from the impossibility of conceiving such a light or of putting it in the light of the intellect itself, and hence doubling up the intellectual light or mingling the two lights in a hybrid and contradictory being, at once natural and supernatural. For, if a supernatural order is granted, there is no reason to deny that God can communicate it to a creature in the manner of light or intelligibility, just as by creation he communicates his natural infinite science to a finite human intellect. Such supernatural light (as that of faith or beatific vision) is not received in the light of reason as a distinct intellectual power, but as a sort of habit or disposition which elevates the natural intellectual power so that

---

9 As shown in footnote 6 an analogical concept can be also proper and formal.

it can elicit a higher intellectual act. Hence the two lights do not make up a contradictory being, because natural and supernatural are not opposed as being and non-being, but as imperfect being and perfect being, constituting two lines specifically distinct. On this account they can be in the same subject, as one perfecting the other.

Besides, such possibility can be shown positively by a threefold persuasive and probable reason. *The first reason* is the existence of the so-called *obediential potency*[10] in every created being in relation to God, that is, of an inner transcendental reference to God and dependence upon him, as the universal cause of being as such. On account of this potency, it does not seem impossible for God to work in any creature whatever is being, provided it is not in contradiction with the nature of an individual creature (cf. *Summa Theol.*, III, q. 11, a. 1).[11] Therefore it is not impossible for God to infuse in the human intellect a supernatural light, since, as has been shown, this is not in contradiction with the natural light of the human intellect. *The second reason* is the radical *capacity of our intellect for knowing any being.* For, although the proper and specific object of the human intellect, formally as human, is only a determined kind of being, that is being as found in the sensible nature, nevertheless the extensive object, generically as intellect, is being as such, in all its breadth. Hence it does not seem impossible that the human intellect be so changed and elevated by a supernatural light as to be able to extend its act to a higher object beyond its specific object (cf. *Summa Theol.*, p.1, q.13, a.4, ad 3). *The third reason* is a kind of *natural desire of knowing God in himself,* according to his inner essence, which spontaneously arises in anyone who through the light of reason knows the existence of God and his natural attributes.[12] This

---

10 About the origin and the nature of the concept of obediential potency, see L. B. Gillon, in *Revue thomiste* 47 (1947) 304–310, and G. Cala Ulloa, in *Sapienza* 5 (1952) 242–256.

11 Thus by no power whatsoever can it happen that a rock, remaining a rock, would have feeling and sensation; or a brute, remaining a brute, would reason; or a corporeal eye, remaining such, would have an intellectual vision or knowledge; or a man, as finite being, would understand as God understands, in an infinite manner.

12 Cf. *Summa Theol.* I, q. 1, a. 1; I-II, q. 3, a. 8; *Summa Contra Gentiles* 3.50. On this desire much has been written in recent years, especially on the occasion of the controversy about the absolute supernaturality of the elevation of man. See P. A. Ciappa, *Partecipazione e desiderio natural di vedere Dio in S. Tommaso d' Aquino,*

desire, being natural and spontaneous, although inefficacious and conditional ("I would wish, if it were possible, to know the inner essence of God") and as such absolutely capable of frustration, cannot be simply vain and void, that is tending to an impossible object, for nature does not tend to emptiness and impossibility (cf. *Summa Theol.*, I, q. 12, a. 1).

Verona 1969; L. B. Gillon, in *Angelicum* 26 (1949) 3–30, 115–142; L. Malevez in *Nouvelle revue théologique* 69 (1947) 1–31; 75 (1953) 561–586, 673–689; W. R. O'Connor. *The Eternal Quest. The Teaching of St. Thomas Aquinas on the Natural Desire for God*, New York 1947; L. Roy, in *Sciences ecclesiastiques* 1 (1948) 110–142; B. Stoeckle, in *Trierer Theologische Zeitschrift* 72 (1963) 1–22.

3

Fittingness and Necessity of Revelation

THE MERE POSSIBILITY OF REVELATION DOES NOT necessarily prove its fittingness and much less its necessity. It even seems that supernatural revelation is highly unsuitable and harmful to human reason, depriving it of its autonomy by a submission to an exterior rule and extrinsic authority. it seems to propose to it an object different from its proper object, which cannot be assimilated, like a stone in the stomach. It seems to provide it with a light not proportioned to its natural powers and tendencies, just as if the eyes of the night owl or a bat were placed before the bright sunlight. Moreover, granting the fittingness of revelation, there is no sufficient basis for its necessity, because man with his reason is naturally complete in his own order and needs no exterior help or complement whatsoever. Such are the objections of Rationalism.

The *fittingness* of revelation (defined by Vatican Council I, sess. 3, can. 2 on revelation) is shown by the fact that through it human reason is perfected with an additional light and object, and its knowledge carried to a higher level. However, by this supplement of knowledge and perfection, natural reason is in no way disturbed or displaced in the normal functions of its proper inferior sphere; for, as we have shown above (p. 71), no mixture of the two natural and supernatural lights is made, nor does the supernatural light usurp or hinder the rights and the activities of natural reason, but it exercises its proper intellectual activity in a distinct and higher sphere, seeking nothing else from the human intellect but the necessary support or the natural base for its own operation, and a "reasonable submission" to its higher truths.[13] Besides, notwithstanding

---

13 Such is the sense usually given by theologians to Rom. 12:1: "*Rationabile obsequium vestrum*" (Vulgate version). However, the immediate exegetical sense is (reasonable worship or service," consisting in a holy life, befitting rational beings, as is shown by the Greek original "loghikén latréian;" and such is the sense usually given in the vernacular translations. In other passages St. Paul speaks of "obedience

the distinction and mutual respect of the two lights, their community and partnership in the same intellect is profitable to both, as it fosters mutual help, so that for the aforesaid support and submission which the light of revelation receives from the light of reason, it abundantly repays the same light by freeing and protecting it from error and by providing it with manifold knowledge, even in its own rational sphere, as we shall see below.

The *necessity* of revelation for the knowledge of *supernatural truths* is self-evident, since such truths are above the proper object of human reason. Hence, in the hypothesis that God elevates man to a supernatural end, as *de facto* happened, it follows necessarily, by a strict and physical necessity,[14] that he has to reveal this end to man and all the essential truths connected with it, so that man may direct to it his intention and his actions. For nothing is willed unless it is known and he who proposes an end will also provide the means without which such end cannot be reached (cf. *Summa Theol.*, I, q. 1, a. 1).

Furthermore, the fittingness and necessity of revelation extends beyond its proper object and reaches also natural truths themselves (as Vatican Council I teaches, sess. 3, can. 2 and chap. 2 on revelation), although in a different manner and at a lower level, since such truths are the proper object of natural reason.

Its *fittingness* for the knowledge of natural truths is shown by the limited perfection of our intellect, subject to the deception of

---

to faith" (Rom. 1:5; 16:26; cf. 2 Cor. 10:5 f). to which can be reduced also the reasonable worship of Rom. 12:1.

Vatican Council I (Sess. 3, chap. 3 on faith) uses Rom. 12:1 speaking of the "obedience of faith, fitting reason," but it is not clear whether the sense is "reasonable obedience to faith" or "reasonable obedience by faith" (that is, in which faith itself consists); this second sense seems more probable, if we have to explain the expression by another occurring in the same context (at the beginning of the same chapter), which reads: "Man is obliged to give to God revealing a full obedience of the intellect and the will by his faith." However, the reasonable character of the obedience of the act of faith is explained by the Council through the criteria knowable by reason and thus we revert to the sense given by the theologians to the Pauline "rational obedience," used by the Council.

14 Necessity of finality (arising from a final cause or end, that is the necessity of means in relation to an end) is called *physical or strict necessity*, if without certain means an end can in no way be reached, and corresponds to physical inability (thus food is strictly necessary for corporal life). It is called *moral necessity*, if without certain means an end cannot be suitably reached, that is, without great difficulty, and corresponds to moral inability (thus a horse or a car, and in modern life an automobile or train or plane, is morally necessary for a journey). Cf. *Summa Theol.* I, q. 82, a. 1.

the senses and to the influence of the will and its passions, which are often sources of error. This is especially true in the area of religion and morality. Therefore, to be taught by God, infallible Truth, concerning the very things which human reason can know with its own limited and fallible light, is highly perfective of reason itself, because on the one hand it receives an infallible confirmation of its own right doctrines and on the other hand it is preserved from easy deception and error.[15] Moreover, as regards specifically moral and religious natural truths, the fittingness of revelation is so great that it grows into a true *moral necessity*,[16] in the sense that without revelation such truths cannot be suitably known by men, that is *quickly, readily, certainly, and universally,* as they should be known, since on them the end of man's salvation is totally dependent.[17] This is strikingly confirmed by the history of pagan peoples, on whom the light of revelation did not shine and who professed many grave errors in religious and moral matters, as is shown in the very best of Greek and Roman civilization, as well as in the great philosophers, Plato and Aristotle themselves.[18]

---

15 In the preceding treatise on *Introduction to Theology* (p. 24) we have shown how theological science, which is the daughter of revelation, elevates and perfects the natural sciences.

16 See footnote 14 about the notion of moral necessity.

17 See the admirable passage of St. Thomas (*Summa Theol.* I, q. 1, a. 1; cf. II-II, q. 2, a. 4; C. Gent. 1.4; *De veritate*, q. 14, a. 10), repeated and adapted by both Vatican I (Sess. 3, chap. 2 on revelation) and Vatican II (Constitution, On Divine Revelation, no. 6).

18 See below, footnote 40.

4

The Nature or Rational Credibility of Revelation[19]

SO FAR WE HAVE CONSIDERED REVELATION IN itself. In this and the following chapters we shall deal with the apologetical problem of the rational knowability or credibility of revelation. The problem amounts to this: if actually there is a revelation from God, can we know with certainty, through our natural reason and before we give supernatural assent of faith to the revealed truths, that such revelation has really been made, and how can we know it? What are the proofs, the means, the criteria by which we can be certain of that fact?

Such rational knowability of revelation is also called its extrinsic or rational credibility, if we consider it, as we do in this apologetical treatise, in its connection with the subsequent supernatural act of faith; for, if revelation is naturally knowable or able to be ascertained, it is also credible, that is suitable to believed supernaturally. In this credibility lies the rational extrinsic foundation of the supernatural faith.[20] In the present chapter we shall consider only the nature of this credibility, leaving for the following three chapters the explanation of its possibility, genesis, and criteria.

The rational credibility of revelation is the aptitude of revealed truths to be believed with supernatural faith (that is, on the authority of God revealing), resulting from its extrinsic evidence, namely, from the rational evidence of the very fact of God's testimony.

The aptness of this definition is shown by the analysis of the concept of credibility in general, as applicable also to things which we know from faith on human testimony. For, there are two ways of certainly and evidently knowing something, that is, either through the immediate and intrinsic evidence of the object itself, directly manifesting to the intellect its own intelligibility

---

19   Cf. A. Gardeil, "Crédibilité," *Dictionnaire de théologie catholique* 3-2 (Paris 1907) 2201–2215; *La crédiblité et l'Apologétique*. Paris 1908; E. Hugueny, in *Revue thomiste* 17 (1909) 275–298; C. M. Lagae, ibid. 18 (1910) 478–489, 612–641.
20   See footnote 2 and pp. 19f., 106f.

(called evidence of truth), or through a mediate and extrinsic evidence, resulting in the object from the evidence of the fact of a given testimony and of the authority (knowledge and truthfulness) of the witness. This is called evidence of credibility, by which an object becomes apt to be believed, that is, held with certitude through an act of faith. Now this concept of credibility also fits revelation. For, if we can rationally show through evident signs that God spoke to man (the fact of testimony or revelation), that same God whose knowledge and truthfulness need to be proved, it follows that the truths testified or revealed by God are rationally credible, that is, extrinsically evident and suitable for being believed with a supernatural faith, based on the authority of God revealing.

5

Necessity or Rational
Credibility of Revelation

A QUESTION SOMEWHAT DEBATED AMONG THEO-
logians is whether credibility of revelation is absolutely necessary
to faith; that is, whether, in order to be able to elicit the act of
supernatural faith (and hence to receive the infused habit of faith
by God), a man must first acquire a rational evidence and a true
objective certitude[21] of the fact of revelation, namely that God
has really spoken. This necessity has been denied or doubted by
some recent theologians, on the ground of an alleged moral impossibility for some people (as the uneducated and the children), to
acquire, prior to faith itself, such rational evidence and objective
certitude of the fact of revelation. Hence they hold, as sufficient,
some kind of imperfect certitude, which is not a true objective
certitude, but only a high probability, that is, according to different expressions, an imperfect moral certitude, a practical certitude
(sufficient to act prudently in the ordinary circumstances of life),
a respective certitude (that is, relative to some classes of people,
as the uneducated and the children), a subjective certitude.[22]

---

21 Certitude is divided into merely *subjective* (that is, not founded in the evidence of
the object, but in purely subjective motives) and *objective or formal* (founded in the
evidence of the object, immediate or mediate through faith). This is subdivided into
absolute or metaphysical certitude, which is founded in the very nature of things and
hence admits no exception whatsoever, and *conditional certitude*, which is founded in
physical or moral laws and hence admits no exception only on the supposition that
some conditions are kept, which could however be lacking and hence allow exceptions.
If this certitude is founded in physical laws, it is called *physical certitude* (thus it is
certain that a stone will fall, provided the law of gravity is not counter-balanced
by an extrinsic agent); and if it is founded in moral laws, it is called *moral certitude*
(thus it is certain that a mother will not kill her child, unless by an unusual perversion she withdraws from those laws that rule the moral actions and inclinations of
men). Below certitude is found *probability*, which can be so great as to amount to a
practical certitude (without ever reaching the strength and the nature of a proper
certitude) and in moral matters is called *imperfect or practical moral certitude*, as being
a sufficient rule for moral and prudent actions, since a strict certitude cannot be
obtained in the ordinary circumstances of life.
22 Thus particularly J. H. Newman, *A Grammar of Assent* (new edition by Fr. Har-
rold, London 1947) 312, who speaks of "an accumulation of various probabilities";

By far the more common opinion of theologians, however, closely following in the steps of the Magisterium itself,[23] teaches that *true and objective rational certitude of the fact of revelation is always and in all subjects required* for the eliciting the act of supernatural faith, although a physical certitude is not required, but a moral (even vulgar or common) certitude is sufficient. This teaching excludes, however, any inferior degree of persuasion (as the so-called imperfect, or practical, or respective certitude), which does not reach the minimum requisite for a true moral certitude.

The necessity of a true and objective rational certitude of the fact of revelation is shown by the general concept of faith, whether human or divine. Any faith is a state of firm assent, in which the intellect rests without positive fear of erring; but such a state of firmness cannot exist without a rational and objective certitude, founded in the evidence of the object, obtained mediately and extrinsically through the testimony of a witness.[24] If this objective evidence of the existence of the authoritative testimony is necessary for the genesis of any faith, even of the human faith which can be discontinued and revoked by reason of a subsequently detected incompetence of the witness, *a fortiori* it is necessary for the genesis of divine faith, which is absolutely infallible and irrevocable, being founded on the infallible testimony of God who can neither deceive nor be deceived. Hence no other kind of intellectual persuasion, below true certitude about the fact of revelation, is sufficient for the genesis of divine faith, enabling one to elicit the act of divine faith.

By *genesis of divine faith* we do not mean the direct production of this faith in the intellect by the preceding judgement of evident

---

S. Harent (in *Dict. Théol. Cath.* 6-1, col. 219–231); *Lercher-Schlagenhaufen* and *Nicolau* (in their theological manuals, where they discuss revelation), who speak of respective certitude; *P. Rousselot* (followed by several of his disciples), "Les yeux de la foi," *Recherches de science religeuse* 1 (1910) 241–259, 444–475, who even denies that reason prior to faith and independently from faith can elicit any certain and sufficient judgement about the fact of revelation, which would be solicited afterwards with the help of grace, that is, under the light of faith itself ("les yeux de la foi").

23 Cf. Gregory XVI, condemning the Fideism of Bautin (Denz. 2753–56); Pius IX, encycl. "Qui pluribus" (Denz. 2778–80), and in his condemnation of the Fideism of Bonnety (Denz. 2813); Vatican Council I (Sess. 3, cans. 3–4 and chap.3 on faith); Pius X (Decree "Lamentabili," prop. 25, Denz. 3425).

24 To St. Augustine it is evident that "no one believes something, unless he first thinks that he has to believe" (*On the Predestination of Saints* 2.5, ML 44.962).

credibility, as happens *de facto* in human faith, otherwise we would resolve supernatural faith into natural reason, as to its proper and immediate cause. We only mean that the natural judgment of credibility is the necessary, although extrinsic, prerequisite to the act of divine faith, without which faith cannot be generated in the human mind by its proper cause which is essentially above reason, that is, the supernatural authority of God revealing.[25]

Hence the act of faith has a twofold resolution. One is intrinsic and objective, wholly related to the object, resting on the sole authority of God revealing, belonging exclusively to the supernatural sphere, without any foundation or connection with the judgment of natural reason (hence: "I believe this particular truth simply because God has revealed it"). The other resolution is extrinsic and subjective, wholly related to the subject and resting on the rational judgment of evident credibility, as a necessary prerequisite to the supernatural act of faith and to its intrinsic and objective resolution. In this judgment of credibility, the authority of God revealing, or the action of revelation, is reached not in its essentially supernatural essence, but only in its exterior aspect, as something supernatural *in its mode*, that is, as a miraculous divine intervention. In this subjective sense we can rightly say that the act of divine faith is extrinsically resolved into an act of rational evidence, that is, in the evident credibility of the fact of revelation, inasmuch as this is only extrinsically and modally supernatural, that is miraculous.

The *sufficiency of moral certitude* about the fact of revelation is based on two reasons.

First, this kind of certitude is the only one available to everyone. The physical certitude was available only to those first Christians who physically heard the preaching of Christ and of the apostles and saw their miracles. All other Christians, to whom the knowledge of their preaching and miracles came through the testimony of others, have only a moral certitude of the fact of revelation, based on the testimony of others and on that moral law according to which a worthy witness does not lie. Only a few can now acquire a physical certitude from a careful and scientific examination of

---

25 We noted above (footnote 2, see also p. 154) that, even after this necessary foundation is laid, faith is not necessarily born, unless the will of man corresponds to the movement of the grace of God, tending to the infusion of faith.

those miracles of a higher moral order which permanently remain in the revealed religion and are in some way visible to all, as is the Church itself by reason of its universality, sanctity, fruitfulness, unity and stability (see below, pp. 107–110).

Secondly, the supernatural act of faith does not demand from the natural reason more than a rational and prudential foundation, that is a firm and prudent judgment on the credibility of the fact of revelation. But, in order to act rationally and prudently, even in very serious matters, with firm and prudent trust in someone's testimony, a moral certitude is sufficient, thus in civil courts moral certitude, based on the testimony of upright men, is judged sufficient to infer even capital punishment.

For the same reason, it is not necessary for everyone to have a moral scientific certitude of the fact of revelation; *a vulgar or common certitude is sufficient*. For, on the one hand this is the only one available to many people who are unable to inquire scientifically into the criteria or proofs of that fact, and on the other hand such certitude, based on common knowledge and evidence, is amply sufficient for acting firmly and prudently in natural affairs and decisions, even of serious character. However, it must be a true and objective moral certitude and not a mere probability, no matter how great and how practical (as is the so-called practical, or respective, or subjective certitude, mentioned above, p. 80), which is not really sufficient even for natural affairs and decisions. Such common certitude is generally found also in illiterate people and in children. However, the simple and sufficient judgment of evident credibility, which these prudently make on the immediate testimony of learned people or parents, does not lean exclusively on such testimony, but through that it joins the true motives of credibility, confusedly grasped, that is, either the many historical miracles which are told to them or that great and ever-living miracle of the Church itself, to which they belong and in which they know so many wonderful things are contained and manifested.

6

The Natural Genesis of the
Credibility of Revelation

NATURAL REASON ITSELF IS PHYSICALLY AND
morally able to elicit the judgment of evident credibility of
the fact of revelation, without the help of supernatural grace,
although such help is usually granted.[26]

Indeed, the fact of revelation, although essentially supernatural
in itself, is only modally supernatural in its exterior signs, such
as miracles. Hence under this aspect it is essentially natural and
falls under the proper object of natural reason, namely, being as
found in sensible nature. Thus a miracle is perfectly knowable
by natural reason, both as to its historical truth, that is, as a fact
truly miraculous or above natural powers and hence a direct work
of God.[27] This is the reason why even devils, obviously without
any help of grace but compelled by the evidence of exterior signs,
elicit a judgment of evident credibility, cause of a kind of natural faith. St. James points this out in his epistle, saying: "You

---

26 This statement is questioned, without sufficient reason, by a few theologians.
Thus the aforementioned *Rousselot* (p. 80) denies the very physical ability of human
reason for eliciting such a judgment, even with the aid of grace and after the infusion of faith. F. Taymans (in *Nouvelle revue théologique* [1951] 14–16) and J. B. Alfaro
(*Adnotationes in tractatum de virtutibus theologicis* [Rome 1956] 169–176, 197–202,
234–268) grant the physical power, but deny the moral ability for eliciting such
a judgment without the aid of grace.

27 *Vatican Council* I, speaking of the preparation to faith, distinguishes between
"internal helps of the Holy Spirit" (grace) and "external arguments of revelation,
that is, divine deeds, primarily miracles and prophecies, which, because they clearly
show the omnipotence and infinite science of God, are evident signs of divine
revelation, *suitable to every man's intelligence*" (Sess. 3, chap. 3). Such an opposition
between internal helps and exterior evident signs suitable to the intelligence of
everyone, suggests quite clearly that interior grace (or grace properly so called) is
not necessary to the actual intelligence of the signs of revelation.

The same meaning must be given to the following parallel text of *Vatican Council
II*: "In order to elicit the act of faith, the grace of God and the internal helps of
the Holy spirit must precede and assist, moving and converting the heart to God,
opening the eyes of the mind, and giving to everyone sweetness in assenting to an
believing the truth" (Dogmatic Constitution on Divine Revelation, no. 5). In this
text "the grace of God," as distinguished from the internal helps of God, means
grace in a broader sense, that is, exterior help, such as miracles and prophecies.

believe in the one God, that is creditable enough, but the demons have the same belief, and they tremble with fear" (2:19; on the manifestation of this kind of faith in the devils, see Matt. 8:24; Mark 1:2; Acts 16:17; 19:15).

However, since this judgment of credibility is directed to dispose a man to the genesis of supernatural faith, it is becoming to divine providence to help with supernatural grace to make such a judgment easier, by inclining the mind and will of man to the consideration and ready acceptance of the motives of credibility, and even in some exceptional cases by directly, and hence miraculously, supplying the motives of credibility themselves, which perhaps were not sufficiently proposed to some individuals through the ordinary natural ways. As regards children and illiterate men, who have already received the infused habit of faith in their baptism, this faith is already present in the subject, and connaturally inclines them to form the judgement of credibility of the fact of revelation, the foundation of their faith. For, as St. Thomas keenly puts it, "the light of faith makes one see the things that are believed" (*Summa Theol.*, II-II, q. 1, a. 4, ad. 3; cf. a. 5, ad 1; q. 2, a. 9, ad. 3).

7

Criteria of the Credibility of Revelation

THE AFOREMENTIONED JUDGMENT OF EVIDENT credibility is based on objective signs or motives or criteria, through which the fact of revelation becomes manifest and hence credible or apt to be believed with a supernatural faith.[28] In this criterion three things are required; first, that it be something historically certain (its *historical truth*); second, that it involve a direct and miraculous intervention of God (its *philosophical truth*); third, that it be clearly connected with revelation, that is, made and directed to the purpose of showing the fact of revelation, namely that God has spoken (its *relative truth*).

Since the historical truth and the relative truth can be easily ascertained, *the whole strength and importance of these criteria lie in their philosophical truth*, that is, in the fact that they involve a miraculous effect, which alone is a certain sign of the intervention of God. In this sense there is only one criterion, miracle itself, which is found in all other criteria, classified below, inasmuch as they show more or less clearly their miraculous character. However, since Christian revelation is a mediate and public revelation, to be transmitted to others, its criteria must be not only miraculous, but *exterior and sensible as well*, otherwise its divine origin would not be manifest to others. Hence, the miraculous revelation, given immediately and interiorly to prophets and apostles by God and certified personally to them through a miraculous and interior sign, does not become a criterion for Christian public revelation, unless it is also shown through a sensible sign, that is through a new miraculous intervention of God perceptible by the senses, which would certify for us that such men are speaking as God's legates.

---

28   They are called either *signs* (marks), because they lead to the knowledge of the facts of revelation; or *motives* of credibility, because they move to faith; or, more aptly under our apologetical viewpoint, *criteria* of revelation (from the Greek "krinein," to discern), because, as distinctive signs, they lead us properly to discern or distinguish revelation from other facts.

These criteria can be *divided* as follows:

Subjective, which are found within man (such as a satisfying experience of spiritual peace and joy; the fulfillment of the higher tendencies and aspirations of human nature).
Objective, which are found outside man.
    Intrinsic to revealed truth itself (such as sublimity of doctrine and its wonderful fruits in the life of Christians).
    Extrinsic to revealed truth (physical miracles and prophecies).

This division follows both a logical order, as is self-evident, and an order of value and importance, which gradually grows in descending direction, down to the physical miracles and prophecies, which are "The Criteria" by antonomasia, as will be shown below (pp. 118ff.).

PART II

The Fact of Revelation
(PRACTICAL APOLOGIES)

IN THE PRECEDING PART, WHICH WE CALLED "Theoretical Apologetics," we have discussed the general notions of revelation and credibility, showing that a true and supernatural revelation of God, if any has come to pass, can be known with certainty and made evidently credible to man. In this second part, which can be called "Practical Apologetics," we deal with the fact of revelation itself, endeavoring to show, with suitable criteria or proofs, that revelation has in fact been made, namely, that God really has spoken to mankind.

Since what we claim to be God's revelation is contained principally in Christ's testimony,[29] first entrusted to the apostles and then faithfully kept and constantly transmitted by the Church, before expounding the various criteria or the miraculous interventions of God which prove such testimony to be true, it is fitting to give, in a first introductory chapter (chap. 8), a brief and general summary of this revelation, which in its breadth is sufficiently known from the Bible itself and particularly from the Gospel.

The subsequent four chapters will show the character and value of the various criteria, following the division just given above, that is, of the subjective criteria (chap. 9), of the objective intrinsic criteria (chap. 10), and of the objective extrinsic criteria, divided into physical miracles (chap. 11) and prophecies (chap. 12). We will end our apologetical treatise with a Conclusion about the obligation of believing the revelation made by God and the genesis of the supernatural act of faith (chap. 13).

---

29   From time to time, even the question of the historical Jesus is brought up. Cf. F. M. Braun, *Oú en est le probléme de Jésus*, Bruxelles 1932; J. G. H. Hoffmann, *Les vies de Jésus et le Jésus de l'histoire*, Paris 1947; M. Goguel, *Jésus* (2nd ed., Paris 1950) 39–80, 132–140; I. De la Potterie, "Come impostare oggi il problema del Gesú storico?," *Civiltà cattolica* 120 (1969) 2, pp. 447–463; Ch. Anderson, *The Historical Jesus: A Continuing Quest*, Grand Rapids 1972.

8

Christ's Testimony About His Mission As Herald of God's Revelation[30]

THE MISSION IS IMPLICIT *IN THE VERY DIGNITY OF Messiah*,[31] which Christ claims for himself. Christ calls himself and is called by others Messiah, the Messiah whom the prophets had announced and the Jews were expecting. To John the Baptist's disciples inquiring of him: "Are you he who is to come, or shall we look for another," he answers in the affirmative to the first part of the inquiry, referring them to the miracles he is working. He implicitly approves Andrew's statement to Peter his brother: "We have found the Messiah" (John 1:41). To the Samaritan woman who was talking of the expected Messiah, Christ says directly: "I who speak with you am he" (John 4:26); he emphatically approves Peter's confession: "You are the Christ [that is, the Messiah]" (Matt. 16:15–17); to the Jews murmuring against him, he says: "If you believed Moses you would believe me also, for he wrote of me [Deut. 18:15, 18]" (John 5:46). To Caiaphas asking him with the solemnity of a religious judge: "I adjure you by the living God that you tell us whether you are the Christ, the son of God," Jesus simply answered: "You have said it" (Matt. 26:63ff.); he

---

30 Christ's testimony about his Divinity is not directly considered here, as being rather one of the objects of the revelation of God. For our apologetical purpose it is sufficient to show that Christ testified to the fact of revelation, saying that God has spoken to man, and that he himself is the speaker for God, the herald of God's revelation. Once granted the Divinity of Christ, which is dogmatically more important, it follows that Christ is not only the speaker for God and the herald of revelation, but is God himself speaking and revealing.

31 The title *Messiah* (from the Aramaic "Mesiah" and the Hebrew "Màsiah," anointed, translated into Greek as "Kristós," anointed) in the Greek version of the Old Testament, is rendered constantly by the name "Kristos" (Christ); in the New Testament it occurs only twice, with the Greek word "Kristós" as an explanation: John 1:41: "We have found the Messiah (which interpreted is Christ)"; 4:25: "I know that Messiah is coming (who is called Christ)." The corresponding title "Kristós," as a proper name, occurs very frequently, often coupled with the name Jesus, "Jesus Christ" (Matt. 1:1; John 17:3; Acts 5:42; Rom. 1:1, 4, 6, 8).

allows others (as Peter and Caiaphas, above) to call him Christ, which is the same as Messiah; he calls himself Christ (Matt. 23:10: "One only is your master, the Christ"; John 17:3: "That they may know you, the only true God, and him whom you have sent, Jesus Christ"; cf. Matt. 22:42). The very title "Christ," simply the translation of the title "Messiah," occurring very often in Scripture as the proper name of Jesus,[32] testifies to his messianic mission.

The biblical concept of Messiah, as was expressed by the prophets themselves and kept in the Jewish tradition, implied the threefold function of king, priest, and *prophet or teacher from God, herald of God's revelation.* Moses prophesied: "A prophet like me will the Lord, your God, raise up for you from among your own kinsmen; to him you shall listen ... And the Lord said to me: ... I will raise up for them a prophet like you from among their kinsmen, and will put my words into his mouth; he shall tell them all that I command him" (Deut. 18:15, 18; cf. John 5:46; Acts 3:22). Isaias described this magisterial function of the future Messiah in the following prophecy: "The spirit of the Lord is upon me, because the Lord has anointed me. He has sent me to preach to the meek, to heal the contrite of heart, and to preach a release to the captives and deliverance to them that are shut up, to proclaim the acceptable year of the Lord and the day of vengeance of our God" (Is. 61:1f.). Christ applied this prophecy to himself, saying to the Jews in the synagogue at Nazareth: "Today this Scripture has been fulfilled in your hearing" (Luke 4:18–21).

The persuasion of the common people is simply expressed in the words of the Samaritan woman to Christ: "I know that Messiah is coming (who is called Christ), and when he comes he will tell us all things," Christ applied the full meaning of this himself, saying: "I who speak with you am he" (John 4:25ff.).

Christ exercised de facto the proper magisterial function of Messiah by communicating to men, as legate of God, divine revelation about truths to be believed and precepts to be observed. St. John in the prologue of his gospel calls Christ "the true light that enlightens every man who comes into the world" (1:9). At the age of twelve, as a future teacher, he is "in the temple, sitting in the midst of teachers, listening to them and asking them questions; and all who were listening to him were amazed at his understanding

---

32 See preceding footnote.

and his answers" (Luke 2:46f.). At the start of his public life he applied to himself the prophecy of Isaias, quoted above, and "from that time...[he] began to preach, and to say: 'Repent, for the kingdom of heaven is at hand'" (Matt. 4:17), and "they were astonished at his teaching, for his word was with authority" (Luke 4:32; cf. Matt. 7:29).

Christ declared that he was preaching *not on his own initiative, but as sent by God* to spread the "gospel," to inaugurate "the kingdom of God." For example: Luke 4:43: "*I must proclaim the kingdom of God, for this is why I have been sent*"; John 18:37: "*This is why I was born and why I have come into the world, to bear witness to the truth*"; Luke 4:18–21: "*The Spirit of the Lord is upon me...to bring good news to the poor he has sent me...*, to proclaim the acceptable year of the Lord and the day of recompense... Today this Scripture has been fulfilled in your hearing"; John 12:49ff.: "*I have not spoken in my own authority, but he who sent me, the Father, has commanded me what I should say, and what I should declare. And I know that his commandment is everlasting life. The things, therefore, that I speak, I speak as the Father has bidden me.*"

The object of Christ's testimony, which we call God's revelation, is described as the "gospel" (in Greek "euanghélion," "good news," from "éu," well, and "anghelia," news); and the "kingdom of God." It consists generically in the "knowledge of the mysteries of the kingdom of heaven" (Matt. 13:11), of those things that are known only by the Father and the Son and are revealed by them to whom they choose (Matt. 11:25–27), things pertaining to "everlasting life" (John 12:50). It consists particularly in a well-defined and specific body of supernatural truths and precepts, which are individually indicated and explained in the Gospel through the mouth of Christ himself, expounded in the epistles of the apostles, and divulged through the ages by the Church founded by Christ for this purpose. To this Church Christ gave the command to perpetuate his preaching and hand over his testimony of God's revelation through the ages; Matt. 24:14: "And this gospel of the kingdom shall be preached in the whole world, for a witness to all nations: and then will come the end"; 28.18: "Go, therefore, and make disciples of all nations..., teaching them to observe all that I have commanded you; and behold I am with you all days, even unto the consummation of the world."

9

Subjective Criteria of
the Fact of Revelation

BY SUBJECTIVE CRITERIA WE MEAN THE PROOFS
that are derived directly from the subject, namely, found within
man himself. These criteria can be expressed and determined in
several ways and considered under different aspects, but they all
amount generically to a *fulfillment of the various human aspirations*,
both intellectual and moral, which arise in the individual man and
in the collectivity, such as individual longing for interior peace
and joy, universal aspiration for truth, religion, morality, virtue,
justice, stability of family and society. We shall consider first the
existence of such a fulfillment of human aspirations through revelation or Christian religion, and then its apologetical value, that is,
whether it is an evident sign or criterion of the fact of revelation,
the supernatural origin of this religion.

1. CHRISTIAN REVELATION GREATLY SATISFIES AND
FULFILLS ALL HUMAN ASPIRATION, IN BOTH THE
INTELLECTUAL AND THE MORAL ORDER[33]

The individual aspirations or deepest longings of every man for
*peace and joy of mind, for human dignity, for personal liberty, for
freedom of conscience* or religious freedom, are safeguarded and

---

[33] This fact is denied by *Rationalism*, which rejects the fittingness (even the possibility itself) of revelation, as being harmful to human reason (see above, pp. 5, 11).
Against it *Pius IX* declares that "faith is the teacher of life, the guide of salvation,
the expeller of all vices, the fecund parent and nurse of virtues..., the one who
'preached peace, announced good things' (Isa. 52:7) to all" (Encycl. "Qui pluribus," 1846, Denz. 2779). *Vatican Council I* attributes to the Church "inexhaustible
fruitfulness in all good things" (Sess. 3, chap. 3, on faith), adding that the Church
"far from opposing the culture of human arts and sciences, aids and promotes it in
many ways" (Chap. 4, Denz. 3013, 3019).
More recent documents of the Magisterium, particularly those of social character,
show how aptly the Christian revelation meets the weighty problems of present
age, both individual and social. Thus *Leo XIII*, Encycl. "Divini illius Magistri," 1929.
"Casti connubii," 1930, and "Quadragesimo anno," 1931; *Pius XII*, Encycl: "Summi
pontificatus," 1939; *John XXIII*, Encycl. "Mater et Magistra," 1961, and "Pacem in
terris," 1963; particularly *Vatican Council II*, Pastoral Constitution on the Church

fulfilled by Christian doctrine. Vatican Council II declares: "The Church truly knows that only God... meets the deepest desires of the *human heart*, which is never fully satiated by earthly nourishment" (Pastoral Constitution on the Church in the Modern World, no. 41). "The Church is able to shelter the *dignity of human nature* against all wavering opinions, for example, those which either undervalue or excessively glorify the human body. By no human law can human personal dignity and liberty be so safely guarded, as by Christ's gospel, entrusted to the Church" (*ibid.*). "Only in freedom can man direct himself to righteousness, that same freedom which is so highly priced and eagerly sought by our contemporaries... Man's dignity itself requires that he act according to conscious and free choice... But man obtains such dignity when freeing himself from all slavery to passion, he seeks his goal in the free choice of righteousness and searches, with effective and sagacious diligence, for the suitable means to that end. Since man's freedom has been wounded by sin, he is unable to achieve effectively and fully such relationship with God without the help of his grace" (*ibid.*, no. 17). "The human person has a right to *religious freedom*. Such freedom consists in this, that all men must be immune from coercion on the part of individuals, of social groups, and of any human power... The right to religious freedom is rooted in the very dignity of the human person, as is made manifest by the revealed word of God and by reason itself" (Declaration on Religious Freedom, no. 2).

The universal aspirations in the intellectual and speculative order, that is, the quest for truth, which is innate to man (for, as St. Augustine puts it, there is nothing that man desires more than knowing the truth), are fulfilled by Christian revelation. Indeed, this religion offers to man definite and secure doctrines about God, the unknown Supreme Being, who is necessarily found at the end of every man's search for truth, even at the very bottom of Atheism itself, for man is naturally religious and his "soul is naturally Christian" (Tertullian, *Against Marcion* 1.10). It gives to man a suitable explanation of the origin, the course and finality of the

in the Modern World "Gaudium et spes," Dec. 7, 1965, which extensively shows the fittingness of the Christian doctrine in the present conditions of the world, regarding the individual (no. 41), society generically (no. 42), marriage and family (nos. 47–52), culture (nos. 52–62), socio-economic life (nos. 63–72), political life (nos. 73–76), and international relations (nos. 77–90).

world, by appealing to the concept of creation and to the truth of divine providence and government. It gives a suitable solution to the problem of man's own origin and destiny, which touches and troubles him intimately, particularly in some major events of life, as in suffering and failures, in catastrophe and death; such human riddle cannot be solved but through the same doctrines about God's creation and providence, and through belief in eternal life and in an ultimate settlement of things.[34]

As to the *universal aspirations in the intellectual practical order*, that is, in the order of human practical culture and civilization, which are keenly felt and promoted in the modern age, the Church has always fostered and satisfied them within the limits and exigencies of its spiritual and primary mission.[35]

In the first centuries the Church adopted the best of Graeco-Roman civilization, saved it from the general collapse of the Roman Empire, extended it to barbarian peoples together with Christian revelation, prevented it from fading away in the succeeding dark ages, and helped it to mingle with and to impregnate the rising new civilization of the Middle Ages. In the following centuries up to the present time, never did the Church cease keeping pace with the progress of culture and civilization, inasmuch as it was fitting to its primary mission which is to evangelize, not to civilize, the world. Recently Vatican Council II has directed its attention in a particular way to the values of temporal things and the ways of fostering the modern culture, also in its practical and corporal aspect.[36]

---

34 *Vatican Council II:* "Man's dignity has its foundations and its full achievement in God himself . . . Hence, when a divine foundation and the hope of an eternal life are lacking, man's dignity is most grievously injured, as is often shown by current events, and the riddles of life and death, of guilt and sorrow, remain unsolved, so that men are easily driven to despair. Meanwhile every man becomes an unsolved puzzle to himself, however obscurely he may be aware of it. For, on certain occurrences, particularly when major events of life take place, no one can simply avoid considering such a puzzle; to which God alone can supply a full and satisfactory solution, by inviting man to the knowledge of higher things and to humble search for truth" (Pastoral Constitution on the Church in the Modern World, no. 21).

35 Note the following words of Pius XI to M. D. Roland-Gosselin: "It is necessary never to lose sight of the fact that the objective of the Church is to evangelize, not to civilize. If it civilizes, it is for the sake of evangelization" (*Semaines sociales de France*, Versailles 1936, pp. 461–462).

36 The council teaches that the *human body* has its own proper value and hence no one is allowed to despise his bodily life (Pastoral Constitution on the Church, nos. 14, 41). *Temporal things in general* have their value, not only extrinsically, because

However, since material culture is only indirectly linked with the primary mission of the Church and with supernatural revelation itself, no one can reasonably expect to find necessarily in the Catholic nations a higher standard of civilization than in pagan or non-Catholic countries. On this subject of human culture or civilization, there is a general misunderstanding, due to the ambiguity of the two words themselves. Man is composed of body, intellectual faculties and moral faculties. The human culture or advancement and the human civil behavior is likewise threefold, that is, in ascending gradation of perfection, corporal, intellectual culture and moral. The moral culture and that part of the intellectual culture which is concerned with religious truth (Ethics and Theodicy) are expected to be, and are in fact, much higher in Christian nations, while the other part of the intellectual culture and the physical or corporal culture can be lower or higher or equal according to the contingent causes and circumstances. It can even happen that some of the principles of revealed ethics, as the importance of caring more about the salvation of the soul and about eternity, than about the body and temporal things, or the necessity of suffering and expiation, may lead some persons or peoples, either by false interpretation or by undue exaggeration or by the very desire for Christian perfection, to draw back or proceed at a much lower step on the path of culture and civilization. On the contrary, for opposite reasons of pagan or materialistic or atheistic trend, it may happen that other peoples or classes of people, discarding every idea of spiritual values and every hope of future life, trusting simply in their own moral liberty and devoting themselves entirely to the acquisition and development of bodily

---

they help man in the attainment of his ultimate goal, but also intrinsically, because they were made by God, who, after creating the material world "saw...it was very good" (Gen. 1:31), and because of their relationship both to the human person, for which they were made, and to Christ, to whom God ordained all things, even material (Col. 1:18) (Decree on the Apostolate of the Laity, no. 7).

Hence there should be a general concern in the Church as a whole for cultivating and promoting the construction and development of the temporal order in the right way, and directing it to God through Christ (*Ibid.*, and Pastoral Constitution on the Church, no. 39). In particular, this concern regards both the bishops, who should know that earthly things and temporal institutions are related to man's salvation and contribute to the welfare of the Church (Decree on the Bishops' pastoral office, no. 12), and to the laity, who, as in their own proper field, should cooperate in the development of human labor, technical skill, and civic culture, considering the renewal of the temporal order as their special obligation (Dogmatic Constitution of the Church. no. 36; Decree on the Apostolate of the Laity no. 7).

and material things, progress at a much speedier pace on the way
of material progress and culture, while they draw back from moral
culture.[37] Thus the Graeco-Roman culture was physically and
intellectually higher than the Hebrew, but morally much lower;
several of the modern Communistic nations, as the Soviet, seem
to proceed faster in the physical and scientific culture than some
of the Christian nations, but they descend lower and lower in the
realm of moral and religious culture.

The universal aspirations of men in the moral order, regarding both
the end of man (his final and total happiness) and the means to
that end (which are the various virtues, whose seeds were planted
by the Creator in the human conscience), are particularly fulfilled
by Christian doctrine and practice. Revelation recalls and confirms the natural truth that *man's true and final happiness* is found
only in the knowledge and love of God, who is man's beginning
and end, according to St. Augustine's maxim: "you have made
us for yourself, O Lord, and our heart is restless until it rests in
you" (*Confessions* 1.1). Moreover, it supernaturally manifests to
man the possibility and the existence of an immediate union with
God through the beatific vision, which surpasses the power and
the efficacious desire of human nature. Revelation fulfills the
aspiration of man to *virtue,* strengthening the natural motives
of the different virtues and completing them by the addition of
supernatural motives. Thus the highest virtue of *religion,* whose
seeds are naturally planted in every human conscience (for man
is naturally religious and in this sense his "soul is naturally Christian," as emphatically stated by Tertullian, *Against Marcion* 1.10),
is perfected through revelation by the removal of all kinds of false
mysticism and superstition, into which those same people often
incline who deny a personal God and check in their conscience
the true natural religious instinct. Besides, revelation adds to
natural religion a pure interior worship of the Divinity, joined to

---

37 *Vatican Council II:* "The modern world shows itself at once strong and weak,
capable of the best and of the worst deeds, while it finds wide open before itself
the road to liberty or slavery, to progress or regress, to brotherhood or hatred.
Moreover, man becomes aware that it is up to him to lead in the right direction
the forces which he has untied and which may oppress him or obey him" (Pastoral constitution on the Church in the Modern World, no. 9). "In the present time,
not a few people, excessively trusting in the progress of the natural sciences and
technical arts, have fallen into an idolatry of temporal things, thus becoming their
slaves rather than their masters" (Decree on the Apostolate of the Laity, no. 7).

a definitely determined and suitable exterior worship, consisting mainly in Christ's eucharistic sacrifice and the reception of the sanctifying sacraments. The virtue of *prudence* is freed from the admixture or adulteration of a sort of utilitarianism. The virtue of *fortitude* rises even to the palm of martyrdom. The virtue of *temperance* (which fosters the institution of temperance societies, particularly against alcoholism) is enriched and elevated by the motives of mortification and expiation. The virtue of *justice* is tempered by supernatural mercy and love, which alone are able to remove disagreement and strife in families and society, and to diffuse among men a true peace that no natural motives can promise.

The entire proof of our statement is confirmed by three signs. First, by the generally outstanding character of the life of Christian individuals, families and societies. Second, by the spontaneous testimony of individuals, converted to our faith, who acknowledged that they found in it all the benefits they had sought in vain elsewhere. Third, by the adaptability of revealed religion to all men and nations of whatever character or culture, a thing which has not happened in the case of other religions. Paganism, Buddhism, Islamism and late Judaism, continuously flourished only within the narrow limits of a single people or place.

2. APOLOGETICAL VALUE OF THE SUBJECTIVE CRITERIA

Notwithstanding its marvelous character and its subjective force of attraction, such a fulfillment of human aspirations by revealed religion is *not objectively a sufficient criterion of the fact of revelation*, that is, one which would be the basis for an evident and certain judgement that our religion has a revealed and supernatural origin, and hence is suitable for being believed and indeed one which must be believed with supernatural faith.[38] The reason is,

---

38 A rather *recent opinion* among Catholic writers holds, on the contrary, that these *subjective criteria are fully sufficient*, and even equal in strength to the objective criteria, or stronger than these, or simply the only sufficient criteria. Hence it advocates a radical change in Catholic Apologetics, to be built only, or primarily, or at least equally, on subjective criteria.

The reason for removing the traditional Apologetics (based on objective criteria, principally miracles and prophecies) and introducing a new Apologetics or a "method of Immanence" (called "Apologetics of Immanence," or "Apologetics of Adaptation," or "Apologetics of Integration") is the merely intellectual character of the old Apologetics, which is either insufficient in itself or at least inadequate to the mind of modern man.

because such a marvelous fulfillment, even taken in its entirety, *does not clearly and exteriorly bear the character of a true miracle*, that is, of a direct and extraordinary intervention of God, marking it with the seal of his testimony. Hence, absolutely speaking, it could be attributed to a natural cause or to the confluence of several natural causes, which would prove only the outstanding character of our religion, as the best among natural religions, or even as the only true natural religion; but not, however, prove it to be a supernatural religion.

Of course, some of the elements shown above, as the beatific vision of God, the eucharistic sacrifice and the sacraments, the higher motives of Christian virtues, are in themselves intrinsically supernatural, and several of the other things included in the marvelous fulfillment of human aspirations may be modally supernatural, that is produced miraculously, but the supernatural or miraculous character of both is not visible and cannot be proved with certainty, since they have only a subjective value, that is, the fulfillment of subjective aspirations. For, this subjective value of doctrines and practices is of itself indefinite and variable, according to the different psychology and customs of peoples, so that a thing which completely satisfies one, may satisfy another less or not at all. Hence we see men easily satisfied in their own religion, as a Jew, trusting only in Mosaic law and the old

---

According to *Maurice Blondel* (†1949), the founder of this new Apologetics, and his principal disciple *L. Laberthonniére* (†1932), objective criteria, particularly physical miracles, are *altogether insufficient* because the philosophical nature of a miracle, as a derogation of natural laws by God, cannot be known with certainty, as there are no fixed laws in nature, and therefore no ontological changes or exceptions of laws, but only apparent changes. Hence the only possible *Apologetics* is that of immanence.

According to others, the objective method, although valuable in itself, is *practically insufficient* for modern man, imbued as he is with rationalistic principles. Hence it must be either simply replaced by the subjective method (thus L. Ollé-Laprune, Blondel's teacher, and G. Fonsegrive, advocating simply an *Apologetics of adaptation*), or joined and strengthened with the subjective method, without which it would be insufficient (thus, among others, A. Liégé, J. Levie, A. de Bovis, N. Dunas, pleading for an *Apologetics of integration*).

Cf. Blondel, *L'action*, Paris 1893; second edition in 2 volumes, Paris 1936–37; *la philosophie et l'esprit chrétien*, 2 vols., Paris 1944–46; Laberthonniére, *Essais de philosophie religieuse*, Paris 1903; *Réalisme chrétien et idéalisme grec*, Paris 1904 (both volumes placed on the Index); Dunas, "Les problèmes et le statut de l'apologétique," *Revue de sciences philosophiques et théologiques* 43 (1959) 643–680.

For ampler knowledge of Blondel's theory and its development, see R. Aubert, *Le problème de l'acte de la foi* (éd. 2, Louvain 1950) 277–337. For a right appraisal and refutation of this doctrine, see C. Boyer, in *Gregorianum* (1935) 485–503.

revelation, a Mohammedan, trusting only the Koran, a Buddhist, resting peacefully in Brahmanic contemplation and expectation. We even see people easily shifting from one religion to another in order to find a satisfaction of some individual aspirations not found in their former religion.

Although objectively insufficient, such a criterion has nevertheless the force of a solid *probability* of the divine miraculous intervention to fulfill in the described manner all the human aspirations. By reason of its probability and especially of the force of attraction which it exercises on many people, particularly in modern times, this criterion is in practice *very useful*, at least for a start on the road to faith and as a stepping stone for the search and consideration of the objective and certain criteria, which alone are sufficient and required to elicit the judgement of evident credibility, the necessary prerequisite for the act of supernatural faith. Just as in other matters probability often leads to certitude, so such a probable criterion, with the aid of subjective inclinations and of the apologetical art of the preacher, who would fittingly and opportunely present it to the various categories of men, may lead to the willing and right consideration of the objective criteria, and through these to the certain judgement of credibility.

Moreover, it is probable that the various subjective criteria, taken all together, could be made sufficient through their change into an objective criterion, that is by considering them as *a true miracle of the moral order*, inasmuch as, in view of the natural weakness of the will and the moral inability of the intellect for a suitable acquisition of the natural truths of religion (see above, p. 75f.) it would seem impossible that the Christian religion could fully satisfy all the moral and intellectual aspirations of man without being a miraculous effect of God. But in this way we have no longer a subjective, but an objective internal criterion, to be reduced to the criterion of the sublimity and fruits of Christian doctrine. Moreover its sufficiency is not certain, as will be shown below (pp. 111–113).

10

Objective Intrinsic Criteria of the Fact of Revelation

ACCORDING TO THE SKETCH GIVEN ABOVE (P. 86), these criteria are found in and derived from the revealed truth itself, as its properties. They can be reduced to three: 1) *the sublimity of the revealed doctrine* and its marvelous fruits, shown both in 2) *the sanctity of its believers*, and in 3) *the marvelous propagation, Catholic unity, and unaltered stability of the Church.*

Like in the preceding question, we shall consider first the existence of these three properties and then their apologetical value, that is whether they are evident criteria or signs of the fact of divine revelation.

1. THE CHRISTIAN DOCTRINE IS TRULY SUBLIME IN ITS ARTICLES, AND MARVELOUS IN ITS FRUITS, THAT IS IN THE SANCTITY OF ITS BELIEVERS AND IN THE PROPAGATION, UNITY AND STABILITY OF THE CHURCH.

A. Sublimity of the revealed doctrine

The very historical *origin* of Christian doctrine bears the signs of a wondrous happening. In fact Christ did not learn it from rabbinic schools, which he did not attend, nor directly from the books of the Old Testament, for on the one hand he did not have the means and social conditions for a particular study of Scripture, as is evident from the Gospel itself, and on the other hand in his own teaching he surpassed by far the doctrines and the laws of the books of the Old Testament. Hence the wonder, that the twelve year old boy already aroused in the doctors of the temple "amazes at his understanding and his answers (Luke 2:47). And later on there was the continued admiration of the people from the beginning of his public ministry: "And all bore him witness and marvelled at the words of grace that came from his mouth. And they said: Is not this Joseph's son?" (Luke 4:22); "And when he had come to his own country, he began to teach them in their synagogues, so that they were astonished, and said: 'How did this man come by this wisdom and these miracles? Is not this the carpenter's son? Is not his mother called Mary?'" (Matt. 13:54f.) Again: "Jesus went into the temple and began to teach. And the Jews marvelled, saying: 'How does this man come by learning, since he has not studied?'" (John 7:15); "The attendants answered: 'Never has man spoken as this man" (John 7:47). Christ himself gave an answer to all such wondering, saying to the same Jews in the temple: "My teaching is not my own, but his who sent me" (John 7:16).

Likewise, the *manner of his teaching* bears an extraordinary character, as appears from the simplicity and beauty of its form (especially in the parables), from the clarity of pronouncements (cf. Matt. 5 to 7, the Sermon on the Mount), from its controversial effectiveness (Matt. 12:33ff.; Luke 11:14ff.), from the gravity and clarity of the accusations against the doctors of the law (Matt. 23:1ff.), and mainly from teaching authority shown to the people: "The crowds were astonished at his teaching; for he was teaching them as one having authority, and not as their Scribes and Pharisees" (Matt. 7:28f.).[39]

The doctrine in itself shows perfection and harmony, the two constituent parts of the concept of sublimity. This is evident as regards the *natural truths*, taught by Christ, which agree with and afford the necessary complement to whatever natural reason can find about the essence and attributes of God, and about the nature and the properties of man (Spirituality and immortality of the soul), as well as man's moral conditions (purpose of life, moral law, reward, destiny, briefly: human ethics). This perfection of doctrine is the cause of the admirable fulfillment of the intellectual and moral aspirations, of which we have spoken above (pp. 92ff.).

The same perfection and harmony appear also in the *supernatural truths* revealed by Christ. For, notwithstanding their lofty and mysterious nature, no opposition can be found either between themselves or with natural reason, but to a careful analysis they rather manifest a general fittingness and harmony.

Thus the mystery of the *Trinity* of persons in God is not opposed to the natural truth of the oneness of God, but completes it by the distinction of nature and person, and the two-fold Trinitarian processions of the Son from the Father and of the Holy Spirit from

---

39 Cf. P. Quinsat, "La maniére dont Jésus parlait." *Maison-Dieu* (1954) 59–82.

both finds an imperfect but significant illustration in the natural acts of the human intellect and will (the interior word proceeding from the intellect, and love proceeding from both). The mystery of the *Incarnation* is not opposed to divine perfection, which remains unchanged and untouched by it, and completes the notion of divine providence, particularly through the twin mystery of *redemption*, which brings this providence to its apex. The mystery of *grace*, or man's elevation to the supernatural order, completes the rational perfection of human nature. The mystery of *original sin* agrees with the inner weakness of human nature and gives a suitable explanation of its evil inclinations and of the general evil and misery in the world. The mystery of *eternal life and beatific vision* matches with the natural truth of the immortality of the soul and with a certain natural desire of seeing God in himself (cf. above, p. 72f.), and at the same time completes the mystery of grace, which is the seed of eternal life and the root of the beatific vision. The mystery of *hell* is fitting to the truths of law, justice and divine providence. *Supernatural law and ethics* are in perfect agreement with and complete the natural law and ethics (see what has been said above, on p. 96f., about the completion of natural virtues by the supernatural).

There are of course several difficult and opposed concepts, inherent to the supernatural nature of these mysteries; but, far from proving in them a real contradiction or unfittingness, they show rather their great perfection or sublimity, which consists precisely in unifying into a higher synthesis things that are opposed in a lower sphere. Thus in the mystery of Trinity, unity and plurality are joined in the same simple Being; in the Incarnation, infinite divine nature and finite human nature; in redemption, justice and mercy; in the elevation of man, nature and supernature; in the mystery of hell, and of Christ, at once redeemer and judge, the greatest mercy and the strictest justice; in Christian ethics, life with death, perfection with renunciation, contemplation with action, simplicity with prudence.

The proper perfection and originality of Christian doctrine is further shown *through its comparison with the doctrines of other religions.* For in no other religion or philosophy can we find such perfect fittingness with and completion of the truths of natural religion and ethics. In no one, *a fortiori*, are found the supernatural mysteries mentioned above nor the higher ethics based on supernatural motives. The few similarities that are found between the Christian religion and the others are only apparent or superficial, since they mingle with greater and fundamental differences regarding the proper and formal object of the various truths. Moreover they are due to some fundamental human ideas and exigencies, to which Christ himself necessarily had to adapt his religion, although it is essentially different from the others. Such are the messianic mission (as in Christ and Mohammed), the doctrinal authority (as in Christ and other religious leaders), the various cultural practices, inspired by natural religion, as prayer, sacrifice, communication with the Divinity, the rite of ablution or purification, and the sacrificial meal. Every one of these truths or practices is specifically different in the Christian religion, as is evident, for instance, in Christ, the Messiah, who is at once man and God, as well as the revealer of supernatural truths; in the Church, at once perfect visible society and Mystical Body; in Baptism, cause of interior regeneration; in the Eucharist, sacrifice of the body of Christ, really present, and immediate participation of it.

In view of such fundamental and essential differences it is also evident that the truths of Christian religion *were not derived or borrowed from any of the pagan religions or philosophies,* infected with doctrinal polytheism and fatalism, ambiguous and often shameful rites, ethical utilitarianism and personalism. All of this St. Paul includes in the following reprobation: "Do not bear the yoke with unbelievers. For what has justice in common with iniquity? Or what fellowship has light with darkness? What harmony is there between Christ and Belial?" (2 Cor. 6:14f.). Nor is Christian religion properly derived from Judaism itself, but it has only preserved, fulfilled and surpassed that indeed true and supernatural religion, thus showing its own perfection and originality.

B. *The fruits of sanctity, produced by the revealed doctrine.*

These fruits are shown both in Christ himself, at once founder of the new religion and exemplar to his followers, and in the Church, taken as a whole and considered particularly in some of its outstanding members, namely the martyrs.

The entire life of Christ, as historically related in the Gospel, is a witness to his holiness and lofty virtues. In vain did his adversaries, Scribes and Pharisees, seek anything in his actions that could be an object of calumny or accusation; hence, without fear of contradiction in the midst of one of the hottest controversies, he challenged them, saying: "Which of you can convict me of sin?" (John 8:46). And during the final showdown in the court of justice before Caiaphas "the chief priests and all the Sanhedrin were seeking false witness against Jesus, that they might put him to death, but they found none, though many false witnesses came forward" (Matt. 26:59f.), so that the judge himself had to provoke Christ to saying that he was the Son of God, to build up against him a charge of blasphemy and justify the death sentence (Matt. 26:63–66).

Christ shows a high degree of perfection in the field of every virtue. His *religion and charity toward God*, his Father, is summarized in the following declaration: "My food is to do the will of him who sent me, to accomplish his work" (John 4:34). His *charity toward his neighbor* is shown in his entire salvific mission throughout his public life, in the unceasing ministry of preaching, in the healing of sick, in the forgiveness of offenses, which made him address his traitor with the name of "friend" (Matt. 26:50) and pray for his persecutors on the cross (Luke 23:24), and finally in dying, as a criminal, in behalf of all mankind, for "greater love than this no one has, that one lay down his life for his friends" (John 15:13).

His *prudence* is manifested in the way he gradually inculcates his messianic and divine dignity, in order to avoid the false political interpretation of his mission by the common people and a reaction on the part of the Scribes and Pharisees, as well as in the indirect and efficacious manner he answers the insidious questions of the same doctors (as on the condemnation of the adulterous woman, John 8:3–9; on the tribute due to Caesar, Matt. 22:15–22; on his divine Sonship, Matt 22:46; on his teaching authority, Matt. 21:23–27). His *justice* is shown particularly in driving out the sellers and the buyers from the temple (Matt. 21:12f.) and in publicly exposing the vices of the Pharisees (Matt. 23:1–36); his *temperance*, in the simplicity and poverty of his life, such as to be able to say: "The Son of Man has nowhere to lay his head" (Matt. 8:20); his *fortitude* (combined with patience and perseverance), in bearing the continued persecution of the doctors of the law, in standing for truth against all false accusation in their court of justice. And finally in giving, through a painful and patient martyrdom, the supreme testimony of his sanctity and his divine mission.

The life of the Church shows likewise an extraordinary sanctity, and an unfailing moral fruitfulness, both in the world at large and especially in its own members.

The Church, through its doctrines and laws, has restored or improved the morals of *the world.* First in the *individuals,* for many crimes and corrupted customs, which were common and tolerated among pagans (as pederasty, sodomy, unstable concubinate, sacred prostitution), gradually fell into disuse in Christian times or were at least commonly considered as grave depravities. Secondly, in *family life,* as is clear from the restored dignity of women, the rights of children protected against the tyranny of fathers, the expulsion of polygamy and easy divorce, the prohibition of abortion and the various practices preventing human fecundation. Finally, in *civil society,* as is evident from the abolition of slavery, the care of the poor, the sick, and the weak, the abolition of political tyranny, the condemnation of racial discrimination, the protection of private property, the promotion of peace among peoples and the fostering of the so-called international law.[40]

The Church fosters and in many of its members obtains the so-called *common sanctity,* as is clear from the common observance of several difficult precepts, particularly about mortification, chastity (both in individual and in family life), sacramental confession, and of the peculiar evangelical counsels (poverty, chastity, obedience) which have given rise to many religious communities. It obtains also in several of its members a *heroic sanctity,* as is evident from the lives of Saints and particularly from the causes of canonization.

Among these, the *martyrs*[41] deserve a particular mention, for they represent of themselves a particular and outstanding witness

---

40 Among the greatest philosophers, Plato pleads to the introduction of a general form of communism, both social and domestic, by which everything should be common, including women, and *Aristotle* tries to justify absolute slavery through the principles of natural law. Both of them defend also suppression of deformed children or previous abortion (cf. Aristotle, Polit., book 7, no. 1335; however see the mild interpretation of St. Thomas, *ibid.,* lesson 12). The primitive *Roman law,* called "Law of the Ten Tables," bore such an article: "The father shall quickly kill a child conspicuously deformed" (table 4), and later Seneca, a philosopher and Nero's tutor, justified such a law and practice, by saying: "No wrath, but reason, sets apart the useless from the healthy" (*On Wrath* 1.15).

41 Martyr (from the Greek "mártus," witness) is generically understood to be one who by dying or suffering a deadly pain for the faith of Christ (hence death or pain inflicted by an enemy of the faith, as such) gives witness to Christ. For more precise

to the supernatural character of Christian religion, or a particular criterion of revelation.

As regards the *history* of martyrs,[42] in the first three centuries there were no less than twelve successive and general persecutions by decrees of the Roman emperors (the first under Nero in 64 A. D. and the last under Julian the Apostate in 363; the most violent and more general persecution was that of Diocletian from 303 to 311). In the following centuries up to the present time, persecutions have been only sporadic and local (as during the French, Russian, Mexican, and Spanish revolutions, and under the Soviet regime). It cannot be doubted that the *number of martyrs* in the Roman persecutions (which particularly come under our consideration) was very large, although it cannot be either exactly or approximately determined; this is testified by some pagan witnesses (Tacitus, *Annal.* 15.44; Pliny the Younger, *Epist.*, book 10, no. 96) and by many Christian sources (St. John, *Apoc.* 6:9–11; 17.6; Clement of Rome, *Epist. to the Corinthians* 6; Irenaeus, *Against Heresies* 4.33.9; Lactantius, *On the Death of Persecutors* 16; Eusebius of Caesarea, *Ecclesiastical History* 8.6, etc).[43]

The *condition* of martyrs, under a physical, moral, and social aspect, is manifold. Among them are found very young people (Tarcisius, Agnes), old men (Polycarp), women (Agnes, Perpetua, Cecilia, Agatha), soldiers (Sebastian), plebeians (Theodotus, Serenus), noblemen (Clemens, Apollonius), apostles (Peter and Paul), learned men (Justin, Irenaeus, Cyprian). The aforementioned pagan witness Pliny the Younger speaks of "many of all ages, of all ranks, of both sexes."

The *motive* for suffering was only one, that is, *religious faith*, which was also, directly or indirectly, the motive of persecution.

---

concept of martyrdom, see St. Thomas, *Summa Theol.* p. II-II, q. 124; E. Hocedez, "Le concept de martyre," *Nouvelle revue théologique* 45 (1928) 81–99, 198–208; R. Hedde, "*Martyre,*" *Dictionnaire de theologie catholique* 10-1 (Paris 1928) 220–233.

42   Cf. P. Allard, "Martyre," *Dictionnaire apolgétique de la foi catholique* (ed. 4, Paris 1926) 331–492; H. Grégoire, *Les persecutions dans l'empire romain*, Bruxelles 1951; E. De Moreau, *La persecution du Christianisme dans l'empire romain*, Paris 1951; *Nouvelle revue théologique* 73 (1951) 812–832.

43   The number of martyrs, up to the year 311, once greatly exaggerated by some historians (11 million according to Florés, 2 million according to Gaume), has been exceedingly reduced by some modern writers (H. Grégoire proposes much less than 10,000 in his work *Les persecutions dans l'empire romain* [Bruxelles 1951] 162, while L. Hertling, in *Gregorianum* [1944] 103–129, gives about 100,000). The Roman Martyrology counts 13,825 martyrs, which seems to be closer to the truth.

For, whatever may have been the immediate aim of the persecutors, it is certain that the Christian religion came to be considered as in radical opposition to the minimum of religious conformity, requested by the tolerant Roman law, so that Christians were considered as public enemies, under their religious standard; hence the public axiom: "Christmas are not allowed." The pagan writer Suetonius, speaking of the first persecution by Nero, says that "Christians, a class of men characterized by a new and malicious superstition, were sent to torture" (*Life of Nero* 16.2). Tertullian at the end of the second century testifies that Christians were considered as "public enemies of the gods, of the emperors, of laws, of moral customs, enemies of the whole nature" (*Apol.* 4), and because they did not sacrifice to the emperor they were "charged with sacrilege and high treason; and this was the supreme charge, nay the whole charge" (*ibid.* 10).

The *manner* of suffering, amid frightful physical and moral torments (crucifixion, burning, exposures to beasts, mockery, tears of relatives, exposure of women to houses of prostitution), shows only virtue and heroism, namely fortitude of soul, tranquility of mind, hope in God's help, meekness, charity and prayer in behalf of the persecutors themselves.

C. The marvelous propagation, Catholic unity and unaltered stability of the Church, as a fruit of the Christian doctrine.

The *propagation of the Church*[44] shows all the signs of an extraordinary event, considering its huge size (that is, its local, numerical and social expansion), its great *speed*, its scanty means, and the serious *obstacles* opposed to it.

The *size* of this propagation, as a *local or geographical expansion*, in the apostolic time itself (hence in the lapse of some seventy years, from Christ's death in the year 30 to St. John's death about the end of the first century) has no other limits than those of the Roman and civilized world. This is clear from the Acts and Epistles of the apostles and the Apocalypse. St. Paul emphatically testifies that "the gospel truth ... is in the whole world, ... has been preached to every creature under heaven" (Col. 1:6, 23; cf. Rom. 1:8). In the

---

44   Cf. J. Riviére, *La propagation du Christianisme dans les trois premiers siècles*, Paris 1907; L. Hertling, "Die Zahl der Christen zu Beginn des vierten Jahrhunderts," *Zeitschrift für katholische Theologie* 58 (1934) 243–253.

middle of the second century Justin, and at the end of the same Irenaeus and Tertullian, testify that the Christian religion had already reached beyond the very limits of the Roman Empire.[45]

The great *numerical expansion* is easily conjectured from the geographical expansion itself. The Church started with 12 apostles and 70 disciples of Christ; immediately after the Ascension 120 disciples are referred to (Acts 1:15); on the day of the first Pentecost 3000 were baptized; a little later the number of Christians grew to 5000 (Acts 4:4) and was further increased (Acts 5:14) until mention is made of many thousands (Acts 21:20). According to Tacitus, in the first persecution by Nero in the year 64 a "huge multitude" of Christians died in Rome (*Annal.* 15.44); from Pliny's epistle to Trajan toward the beginning of the second century it appears that a great part of the population in Bythinia was Christian and a century later Tertullian testifies that in Africa "almost the larger part of every city" was Christian (*To Scapula* 210). Around the beginning of the fourth century, when Constantine, the first Christian emperor, took the power, at least a fifth (some say a fourth, others a half) of the Roman Empire was Christian.

The *social expansion* is evident in the apostolic age itself. Among the apostles, besides the ten fishermen, we find a businessman (Matthew) and a learned man of the Pharisees' school (Paul). Among the other followers there is a Pharisee, doctor of the law (Nicodemus), and a nobleman (Joseph of Arimathea). Shortly after the Ascension there came to the new faith a large group of Jewish priests (Acts 6:7); Cornelius, a centurion (Acts 10:1ff.); proconsul Sergius Paulus (Acts 13:12); Dionysius the Areopagite, an influential man (Acts 17:34); a number of noble women (Acts 17:4; cf. 17:34); Crispus, the president of a synagogue (Acts 18:8); Apollo, a learned and eloquent man (Acts 8:24f.); Flavius Clement, a nobleman (Phil. 4:3); several "of the Caesar's household" (Phil. 4:22); other noble people named by St. Paul in Rom. 16:1–25. Suetonius names the aforementioned Flavius Clement and his wife Domitilla, a relative of emperor Domitian,

---

45 Justin, *Dial. cum Thryphone* 110 and 117, says generically that "there are absolutely no people of any kind" who do not adore Christ crucified. Irenaeus, *Against Heresies* 1:10, points out even Egypt and Libya. Tertullian, *Against the Jews* 7.4, mentions, among several other barbarian peoples, "the places of the Bretons, not reached by the Romans, ... and many other hidden peoples and provinces and islands, which are unknown to us and impossible to number."

both killed under the same emperor (*Life of Domitian* 10.2; 15.1). Tacitus mentions "Pomponia Graecina, a noble woman...guilty of extreme superstition" (*Annals* 13.32). Eusebius of Caesarea mentions "the mother of emperor Alexander [Alexander Severus 222–235], Mammaea by name, a particularly pious and religious woman" (*Ecclesiastical History* 6.21), in whose "household there were many Christians" (*ibid.* 6.28), and emperor "Philip [the Arab 244–249]...a Christian," as well as his wife (*ibid* 6.34, 36). Among soldiers other documents mention "the lightning legion" (cf. Tertullian, *Apol.* 5.8–12), Nereus and Achilleus, the forty martyrs of Sebaste, Sebastian and others.

In the second century the new religion finds its great Apologists among learned and outstanding men, such as Aristides, Athenagoras, Justin, Irenaeus, and Tertullian; toward the end of the same century a famous center of religious learning is founded, namely the Alexandrian school (in which was soon to flourish Origen, the greatest mind of oriental Christianity). In the year 197 Tertullian, addressing the pagans in his apologetical work, does not hesitate to assert: "We are outsiders [according to you], but we have already filled the world and everything that is yours, cities, islands, forts, city halls, assemblies, military camps themselves, regiments and companies, imperial palace, senate, law courts. We have only left the temples to you" (*Apol.* 37.4; cf. 1.7).

The *great speed* of this propagation is obvious, considering the extension of the lands reached (the whole known or civilized world) and the shortness of time, for as we have shown above, this was sufficiently done in the apostolic age itself (in 50 or 70 years), and at any rate less than three centuries after Christ's death (around 300) it was largely accomplished, when at least a fifth (probably a half) of the population of the Roman Empire was Christian.

The *means* of propagation were scanty. In human ways, the means of rapid success are principally three, namely, *pleasure*, *wealth* (which is also the basic factory of arms) and *honor*, which correspond to the three concupiscences of man, spoken of by St. John (1 Epist. 2:16). The Church did not have and did not promise such things; she was preaching mortification up to the sacrifice of one's own life, she was poor in her Founder, her apostles, most of her members, she was despised and condemned by law and science, being considered as a superstition, of Jewish origin and of sectarian character, opposed to the socially accepted standards of religion, culture and customs.

The *obstacles* to this propagation were serious. The *internal* obstacle was precisely that the new religion had nothing to offer of the naturally desirable, no pleasures, no wealth, no honors. The general *external* obstacle was that the things she had to offer were in open contradiction with the religious, cultural and moral conditions of that time, and hence met from the beginning with a stern opposition. This opposition came from the Jewish and pagan sacerdotal cast, whose temples were deserted and profits diminishing, from the people, whose customs were censured, from the philosophers, whose superior hellenic culture was despised, and finally from the public authorities, whose supreme and quasi-divine autonomy was challenged. All these obstacles came together in the one great and radical obstacle of the public and general persecutions, to which any one of the aforesaid motives could furnish the occasion and under which any ordinary religious or political movement would have been doomed to fail.

The Catholic or universal unity of the Church in its three constituent elements, government, faith and cult, is also historically evident. In the very process of this swift and universal propagation, in which other societies or institutions by reason of human passions and conditions would have met with dissentions and divisions, and would have allowed them within its limits in order to subsist, the Church constantly retained this threefold unity and carefully dropped from her membership any dissenting man or group, considering them no longer as Christ's followers.

The unaltered stability of the Church is likewise warranted by history. For, through twenty centuries the Church has constantly retained the same essential features, that is, the same essential identity of government, faith and cult, as the primitive apostolic community established by Christ, notwithstanding grave natural obstacles and reasons that seemed to call for a change. These were in sequence of time, the persecutions in the first three centuries, the great heresies of Arianism, Nestorianism and Monophysitism, the rise and expansion of Islamism, the Eastern Schism, medieval Caesaro-papism, the Great Western Schism, the Protestant Reformation, the French Revolution, and at last the combined assault of rationalism, liberalism, communism, atheism and laxism in our age.

2. APOLOGETICAL VALUE OF THESE OBJECTIVE INTRINSIC CRITERIA

Notwithstanding their marvelous and extraordinary character and their pre-eminence over the subjective criteria, these intrinsic objective criteria (that is, generically the extraordinary quality of the Christian doctrine in itself and in its fruits), *taken individually and separately as proposed above are not evident and sufficient criteria of revelation* (that is, of the fact that God has revealed), *but only very probable criteria.* On the contrary taken *all together* as one single fact having multiple facets, that is, as the Church itself, *they are not only an evident and sufficient criterion, but also the primary criterion of all*, or as Vatican Council I puts it, "an incontestable testimony" of revelation.

The reason why these criteria, taken each separately,[46] are *not evident nor sufficient*, is because each one does not clearly and visibly bear the character of a true miracle, or of the direct and extraordinary intervention of God, and hence, absolutely speaking, each could be attributed to a natural cause or to the confluence of several natural causes. This appears from a close examination of the three individual criteria, mentioned above, that is, the sublimity of the doctrine, the marvelous fruits of sanctity produced by this doctrine (in the Founder of the Church and in the members of the Church, particularly in the martyrs) and the extraordinary qualities of the Church, that is, its expansion, unity and stability.

No doubt the *doctrine in itself* bears an extraordinary character, both as to its origin in Christ and as to its articles, and hence it strongly suggests and makes highly *probable* a supernatural and miraculous intervention of God in it; for no human or natural cause can suitably explain it.

Nevertheless such a miraculous intervention of God and the exclusion of natural causes is *not absolutely certain and evident. First*, because the object itself, that is, the doctrine to be judged as a miracle, is something *indefinite*. For, if we consider the natural truths of religion (which indeed cannot be suitably known

---

46 Under the *three general headings* mentioned above (p. 100), that is, sublime doctrine, marvelous fruits of sanctity, and extraordinary qualities of the Church, we pointed out *eight more particular criteria*, namely, the origin of Christ's doctrine, this doctrine in itself, Christ's sanctity, sanctity of the members of the Church, particular sanctity of martyrs, propagation of the Church, unity of the Church, stability of the Church. Each one of these is an outstanding probable criterion.

through natural reason alone, without supernatural miraculous revelation, as we have shown above, pp. 74, 101), we cannot, *a priori* and exactly, determine what combination of such truths and in what degree of perfection and certitude they should be known by man in order to be able to reach the end of his salvation. If we consider moreover the supernatural truths, they are not clearly suitable, much less perfect and harmonious to human reason, precisely on account of their supernatural character, and need to be explained and defended as to their own suitableness, particularly against the attacks and mockery of infidels. The *second* reason is because the appreciation or proper estimate of the value of a doctrine is *variable* according to the different intellectual and moral dispositions of men. Therefore it is open to the danger of subjectivism and relativism, since what pleases one may displease another, and every single religion rests peaceably in its own philosophy judging it perfect and superior to others (see above, p. 99).

Thus one could, without falling into impossibility, explain the origin of the doctrine of Christ through the natural cause of an extraordinary intellectual capacity, and its authoritative efficacy through an extraordinary power of the will, as happened, although in much lower degree, in some of the other founders of religions, as Mohammed or Buddha; and likewise one might judge, without falling into impossibility, that the religious truths taught by those two leaders are strictly sufficient, though not perfect as Christ's doctrine, to make man able to attain the end of salvation.[47]

---

47 *Vatican Council II* discusses quite at length the various elements of religious truths found in Hinduism, Buddhism, and Islam, and their connection with the Christian religion itself. (Declaration on the Relationship of the Church to Non-Christian Religions, no. 2f.; cf. Dogmatic Constitution on the Church, no. 16).

Recently J. H. Walgrave in his work *Un salut aux dimensions du monde* (trans. from the Dutch by E. Brutsaert, Paris 1970), affirmed with a generous dose of exaggeration that divine revelation works and God speaks also through what we call pagan religions, both of the East and West, as Zoroastrianism, Hinduism, Buddhism, Islam.

On this same tendency to exaggerate the supernatural elements of non-Christian religions is partially based the claim, now spreading in Christian circles, for a *renewal of Missiology or theology of the missions*, in the sense of a work of civilization rather than evangelization, since the uncultivated peoples would have in their non-Christian religions enough means of salvation (see a description and criticism of this opinion in Civilta Cattolica 121-4 [1970] 105-110). Such a claim has certainly no foundation in the documents of Vatican II mentioned above, in which it is only stated that "the precepts and laws [of non-Christian religions] ... often reflect a ray of that Truth which enlightens all men" and that "whatever goodness and truth is found in them is considered by the Church as a preparation for the Gospel."

The extraordinary fruits of sanctity of the revealed doctrine, shown in the Founder himself and in his followers, particularly in the martyrs, suggest likewise and make *highly probable* the supernatural character of this Christian doctrine; for no natural cause can suitably explain them.

But again *they are not of themselves an evident and sufficient* criterion of revelation, for the same reason of our inability to prove with certainty the miraculous intervention of God and the exclusion of natural causes, on account of the indefinite and variable character of such criterion.

Absolutely speaking, *Christ's sanctity* could be explained (as far as it is knowable by men) in a natural way, which would establish only his natural superiority above all men and founders of other religions. The fruits of morality brought by *the Church* to the world at large concern only natural ethics; the sanctity of its members, both common and heroic, may meet with subjective and different appreciation according to the variety of people and philosophy (thus monogamy, fostered by the Church, is rejected by Mohammedans as a source of divorce and immorality). The great sanctity and heroism of *martyrs* is of course the strongest part of this criterion, for no natural cause can invincibly explain it (as pride, or passion, or fanaticism, or hope of praise, or physical coercion) considering the great number, the variety of the physical, moral and social conditions of martyrs, among them women and children, and especially their motive and manner of suffering as explained above (pp. 105–107). But again this fact could, absolutely speaking, be an effect of natural causes, as of deep conviction and enthusiasm about the Christian ideals, higher indeed than the one found in martyrs of other religions or human organizations. Moreover, finally, it is also subject to a variable appreciation of its real value.[48]

The three properties of propagation, unity and stability of the Church bear likewise a very extraordinary character, especially if taken

---

48 It should be noted that, in the course of martyrdom, real and certain *physical miracles* may occur, if for instance the sense of pain is removed or suspended (as happened in the martyrdom of Polycarp, Lawrence and Perpetua); in such cases martyrdom is an evident and sufficient criterion, not by itself, but by reason of such a certain physical miracle. Besides, martyrdom itself is for us a sure *historical testimony* of the preceding miracles and prophecies, which were the reason why the martyrs had joined and defended their faith; but in this sense martyrdom is not a criterion of revelation, but only one of the means through which we come to the knowledge of the true criteria, that is, the miracles and the prophecies.

together, and consequently they make up a very *notable criterion* of revelation or the miraculous intervention of God. For, considering all the elements involved in them, no natural cause can be advanced to suitably explain them.

Indeed the usual and principal causes of successful *propagation* in the natural order are the three objects of human concupiscence, namely, pleasure, wealth and honor, which the Church did not and could not offer, as shown above, and its necessary condition is the absence of major obstacles, especially from public authority, such as met by the Church (see p. 110).

Nor can we consider as a sufficient cause and condition of the propagation of the Church the attraction exercised by some of its doctrines, as monotheism, syncretism, and universalism, or several fortunate historical circumstances, as the diffusion of the Jewish communities in the Roman Empire, to which conational Christians could easily emigrate, or the organization of the Roman Empire, its political and cultural unity, and the religious tolerance of its laws, which paved an open and easy way to a speedy propagation. For the indubitable usefulness of these facts is not sufficient to explain such an extraordinary expansion, in view of the aforesaid scanty means and great obstacles. Moreover, those same facts could be reverted and were actually reverted into major obstacles to propagation; for the novelty and purity of the Christian doctrine and morality proved to be repugnant to the majority of the people, both ignorant and learned, and to the sacerdotal and political classes who considered the Christians as public enemies; the new religion found opposition rather than help in the Jewish communities; the unity of the Roman Empire was also the greatest obstacle to propagation, favoring the general persecutions which on account of this unity were easily planned, effectively carried out and often renewed.

The *Catholic or universal unity* of the Church as to its government, faith, and cult, cannot be suitably attributed to a natural cause in view of human passions and natural circumstances which draw every human institution into factions and parties within itself.

Likewise the unaltered *stability* of the Church, amid so many historical conditions calling for change, cannot be suitably explained through natural causes which would be no other than the three aforementioned objects of human concupiscence, namely, pleasure, wealth, and honor, not offered nor possessed by the Church. To the various exterior and interior obstacles, urging for change or dissolution, the Church opposed no other means than the affirmation of its inflexible doctrine, the defense of the divine laws, and the exhibition of its proper virtues of confidence in divine help, patience in trials, charity, and love for its own enemies.

Nor can we say that the cause of such great stability has been the wise constitution and organization of the Church, particularly the principle of supreme and unappealable authority. For the question still remains how such wise organization and supreme authority, which was also the glory and the force of the Roman Empire, was constantly kept unchanged amid so many obstacles and historical circumstances, and why the Church organization or the Church itself did not fall or decay as the Roman Empire did. The same strengthening comparison can be applied to many other important cultures and religions, some of which are entirely obsolete, as the great pagan religions of the East and of the West; others have become so aged and weakened that they survive in a state of lifeless stability or they retain only a general outline of their original features and vigor, although they have generally met no sizeable obstacles and have sprung, been protected, and kept alive by favorable causes and circumstances, as Buddhism, Islamism, and Judaism.

Notwithstanding its great force of persuasion and probability, *such a criterion is not evident nor sufficient* in itself. The reason is because these wonderful properties of the Church, absolutely speaking, could be attributed to natural causes producing an unusual and extraordinary effect, namely, the most active, unifying and stable of all natural religious societies. The marvelous expansion of the Church could perhaps be explained by a crafty and tenacious perseverance of its founders in meeting or avoiding obstacles and even converting them, as well as other favorable circumstances, into means of propagation and expansion –a policy in which the genius of St. Paul excelled. And persecution itself usually arouses among people a reaction in favor of the persecuted. The unity of the Church could perhaps be explained by an unusual and traditional ability of the hierarchy in checking human passions and the other causes of fraction and division, largely favored both by the principles of a unitarian faith and by

the totalitarian organization under one supreme and unappealable authority. The same causes could also explain the stability
of the Church. Moreover such an expansion, unity and stability is
also found to some extent in other religious cultures or societies,
as Buddhism, Islamism, and Judaism. The higher degree or excellence in which these properties are found in Christian religion
does not necessarily prove its divine origin, but only its natural
superiority, for as philosophers say, "a higher or lower degree of
perfection does not change the nature of things."

However, as stated above (p. 111), these three intrinsic criteria,
only probable in their individual force, *if they are taken together*
and combined into one single extraordinary fact having multiple
facets, *make up an evident and sufficient criterion, nay the primary
criterion of revelation, because they amount to a true and great miracle
of the moral order,* easily discernible with moral certitude and suitable to the intelligence of all people, namely, *the Church itself,* with
all that it implies.[49] This is explicitly stated by Vatican Council I
as follows: "To the Catholic Church alone belong all those many
and marvelous things which have been divinely adapted for the
evident credibility of the Christian faith. Furthermore, even the
Church itself, because of its marvelous propagation, its exceptional holiness, and inexhaustible fruitfulness in all good things,
and because of its Catholic unity and unaltered stability, is one
great and perpetual motive of credibility, and an incontestable

---

49 As we noted above, speaking of the fulfillment of human aspirations by the
Christian doctrine (p. 99), such criteria, though only probable if taken individually, are *very useful* and at times also necessary to dispose the mind to the further
examination of the extrinsic criteria (miracles and prophecies), which will give the
certitude of the fact of revelation.

Besides, some of these intrinsic criteria, even taken individually, can indirectly
acquire the strength of evident criteria, not indeed by themselves, but by being
joined with the extrinsic criteria of miracles and prophecies, as an *evident sign*
of these. For some of them are such that, unless true and extrinsic miracles had
preceded to convince men of the divine origin of Christian religion, they could not
be explained and would have no sufficient cause. Such are especially martyrdom
as death voluntarily met for that religion (see above, p. 113) and the extraordinary propagation of the same; for, as St. Augustine argues "ad hominem" against
those who deny miracles: if there were no miracles "there would be this great and
sufficient miracle, that the whole world would have believed without miracles"
(*City of God* 22.5).

Thus the Church itself, taken as a whole with all it implies and supposes, including the physical miracles and prophecies themselves, is like *a compendium of all the
criteria of revelation,* and hence the primary criterion, or the criterion by antonomasia.

testimony of its own divine mission" (Sess.3, chap.3, Denz. 3013; cf. Pius IX, Encycl. "Qui pluribus," Denz. 2279).

The reason why these probable criteria taken together make up an evident or certain criterion consisting in a true moral miracle, is not because they join together their probabilities. For an accumulation of probabilities taken materially can produce only a greater probability and not a certitude, even of an inferior degree, as "no one can give what he does not have," according to philosophers, just as many flies do not make one bird, however small. But if these probable criteria are considered formally *as convergent*, with their individual probabilities, *on the same object*, then they make up or rather they are converted into a certain criterion of truth. The reason is that such a convergence of probabilities on the same object could not be explained by any other reason than the objective truth itself; otherwise it would be an effect without a sufficient cause. Hence it is by means of an extrinsic metaphysical principle, namely, the principle of sufficient reason, that these various probable criteria are changed into one single certain criterion.

Thus the Church with all the wondrous facts and characteristics that it implies (fulfillment of human aspirations, sublime doctrine and excellent sanctity, marvelous propagation, unity and stability) becomes really an "incontestable testimony" to revelation. It is the primary criterion clearly visible to all, like a miraculous light showing the way to those who search for truth with willing and open eyes, and like "a flag set up above the nations" (Isa. 11:12; 5:26; cf. Vatican Council I, sess. 3, chap. 3).[50] The light of such a criterion is so bright that it is perceived in all its strength by the simple people, without any distinct and scientific examination of the single motives of credibility, through a sort of instinct or immediate intuition, which is the proper and principal act of our intellect.[51]

---

50 Regarding the practical manner, in which such a great motive of credibility frequently and effectively works in contemporary conversions, see D. Grasso, "Il fenomeno della Chiesa nelle conversioni contemporanee," *Problemi scelti di teologia contemporanea* (Roma 1954) 189–198.

51 About the nature and importance of the intellectual intuition in general, see J. Maritain, *The Peasant of the Garonne* (trans. from the French by M. Cuddihy and E. Hughes, New York 1968) 14–16, 110f., 137–139, 148f.

11

Objective Extrinsic Criteria of the Fact of Revelation. Physical Miracles[52]

ACCORDING TO THE DIVISION OF CRITERIA MEN-
tioned above (p. 86), physical miracles are called extrinsic criteria
because they are found outside the revealed doctrine as such. As
in the two preceding chapters, we shall consider first the existence
of physical miracles (or the historical truth of the deeds) and then
their apologetical value, that is whether they are evident criteria
or proofs of the fact of revelation.

This question is of the utmost importance to our apologetical
purpose, for two reasons. *First,* because the following chapter
on prophecies is largely dependent upon it, for prophecies are
simply one kind of miracle, although not physical but intellectual.

---

52 Brinkmann B., "Die Erkennbarkeit der Wunder Jesu," *Scholastik* 29 (1954) 345–362.

Dhanis, E., *Tractatio de miraculis,* Romae 1952; "Un chainon de la preuve du miracle," *Problemi scelti di teologia contemporanea* (Roma 1954) 63–86; "Qu'est-ce qu'un miracle?" *Gregorianum* 40 (1959) 201–241.

Evely, L., *L'evangile sans les mythes,* Paris 1970.

Garrigou-Lagrange, R., "La grâce de la foi et le miracle. Trois théories à propos de travaux récents," *Revue thomiste* (1918) 289–320.

Grant, R. M., *Miracle and Natural Law in Graeco-Roman and Early Christian Thought,* Amsterdam 1952.

Hardon, J. A., "The Concept of Miracle from St. Augustine to Modern Apologetics," *Theological Studies* 15 (1954) 229–257.

Latourelle, R., "Miracle et révélation," *Gregorianum* 43 (1962) 492–509; "Authenticité historique des miracles de Jésus: Essai de Critérologie," *Gregorianum* 54 (1973) 225–261.

Lhermitte, J., *Le problème des miracles,* Paris 1956.

Michel, A., "Miracle," *Dictionnaire de théologie catholique* 10-2 (Paris 1929) 1798–1859.

Monden, L., *Le miracle, signe du salut,* Bruges 1960.

Richardson, A., *The Miracle Stories of the Gospel,* London 1956.

Tonquedec, J. de, *Introduction à l'étude du merveilleux et du miracle,* 3rd. ed., Paris 1923; *Merveilleux métaphysique et miracle chrétien,* Paris 1955.

Van Hove, A., *La doctrine du miracle chez Saint Thomas et son accord avec les principes de la recherche scientifique,* Weteren-Bruges-Paris 1927.

Secondly, because visible miracles are the primary or certain criteria of revelation, for all the subjective and intrinsic criteria previously considered, have been found only probable, with the exception of the Church as such, which embraces all of them into a single criterion amounting to a moral miracle.

As we noticed above (p. 85), all the importance and the force of any criterion of revelation lies in its miraculous nature, that is, in the fact that it involves an extraordinary and direct intervention of God. In this sense, accordingly, there is only one criterion of revelation, miracle itself, which is found more or less probably or certainly in all the individual criteria enumerated above (p. 86). Hence the subjective and the intrinsic criteria are only probable criteria, because they are only probable miracles, and extrinsic criteria are said to be certain criteria, because they are certain miracles.

Before considering the two points just mentioned, that is, the existence and the apologetical value of the physical miracles, it is therefore fitting to give a brief explanation of miracle in general, as to its nature and possibility.

1. MIRACLE IN GENERAL

A. Nature of miracle.

The word *miracle* (in Latin "miraculum," from "mirari," to wonder)[53] etymologically means something that makes us wonder. It is properly and scientifically defined according to St. Augustine and St. Thomas: *"That which is done above the order of powers established by God in all created nature."*[54]

---

53   The word is used in the Latin Vulgate version of the Old Testament (Ex. 11:7; Num. 26:10; 1 Kgs. 14:15; Job 33:1; Isa. 21:4; 29:14; Jer. 23:32; 44:12), but not of the New Testament, in which miracles are called, according to the meaning of the original Greek words, works (John 5:20, 36), powers (Matt.13:54,58), prodigies (Matt.24:24; John 4:48), marvelous things (Matt.21:15), wonderful (or rather, unexpected) things (Luke 5:26), signs (Matt.12:38f.; 24:24; John 2:11, 18:23). Among the Fathers St. Augustine adopted and used frequently the word miracle, and hence it became classical and technical in theology and in the documents of the Magisterium since the Middle Ages.

54   St. Augustine defines it: "I call a miracle whatever appears to be difficult or unusual above the hope or the power of the one who wonders" (*On the Utility of Believing* 16.34). St. Thomas defines it more strictly: "Miracle is properly called... that which is done by God beyond the order of all created nature" (*Summa Theol.*, I, q. 110, a. 4); the context shows that by "order of nature" St. Thomas means "the acting order of nature," that is, the power of nature, the power established by God in all created nature.

What is proper and essential to miracle then, is its extraordinary character, that is, the fact that it is outside and above any law or way of acting established by God in any created nature. In this definition three elements must be carefully noticed.

First, miracle is *above the order of the powers of nature,* not necessarily above nature itself. Hence it is necessarily supernatural as to the mode in which it is done (modally or extrinsically supernatural), not necessarily as to the essence of the thing done (essentially or intrinsically supernatural; see footnote 9); hence the thing produced by a miracle can be either essentially natural (as the healing of the body) or essentially supernatural (as the healing of the soul, that is the infusion of grace), provided in both cases it is done in a supernatural way, that is, above the order of natural powers.

Second, miracle is something *above the established order* of powers. Hence things that are done by God himself but according to an established order, either natural or supernatural, are not miracles, even if they are the most important effects of God, as creation (which is the very constitution of the natural order), his providence or government of created things, his creation and infusion of a rational soul into the body, man's elevation (which is the very constitution of the supernatural order), infusion of sanctifying grace into the soul, justification, production of grace through the sacraments, the infused light of faith, the light of the beatific vision. On the contrary the proper nature of miracle is found in the following extraordinary effects: Incarnation, transubstantiation, beatific vision if temporarily granted to someone in this life (as it probably was to the Blessed Virgin), sudden justification granted outside the established laws and dispositions (as probably was St. Paul's justification on the road to Damascus).

Thirdly, miracle is above the order of *all created nature.* Hence it is an effect proper to God. Any extraordinary thing produced by an angel or devil through his own natural power and not as a mere instrument of God is not a miracle, because it is done within the established order of one created nature.

From this definition we can draw two *divisions* of miracles. The first and material division regards the nature of the thing which is done. Thus miracle is divided into *supernatural,* if the thing belongs to the essentially supernatural order (as sanctifying grace), and *natural,* if the thing belongs to the natural order, though it is done in a supernatural way. This is subdivided into *physical* miracle (as healing and resurrection), *intellectual* miracle (as prophecy and knowledge of the secrets of heart), and *moral* miracle (pertaining to the order of morals, or of the will, as change of morals). The second and formal division regards the manner in which a miracle is above the established order of the powers of all created nature, or in which it surpasses the established manner of acting of all created nature. Thus miracle is divided, in descending gradation of perfection, into *miracle as to substance* (first class miracle), if the very substance of the thing cannot be produced in any way or circumstance by a created cause (as making two bodies occupy the same place, glorification of a body similar to that which will take place in heaven, resurrection, transubstantiation, or the Incarnation), *miracle as to subject only* (second class miracle), if the substance of the thing can be produced by nature, but not in this particular subject (resurrection under another aspect,[55] restoration of sight to the blind, healing of the lame), and *miracle as to manner only* (third class miracle), if the substance of the thing can be produced by nature even in this particular subject, but not in such manner, that is, either without natural means (as cure from sickness without medicines, rain out of a clear sky), or beyond natural proportion (as the multitude of frogs produced by Moses in Egypt), or suddenly without its natural duration (as sudden cure from sickness).[56]

B. Possibility of miracle.[57]

This possibility follows from two combined reasons, that is from the fact that the natural laws (both physical and moral) are merely contingent and changeable, and that God is omnipotent,

---

55 Resurrection can be considered in two ways; specifically as a restitution of life to a *dead body*, and thus it is a first class miracle, and generically as uniting a soul to a body, and thus it would be a second class miracle, inasmuch as nature can work this union, as it does in every generation, but not in such subject, that is in a dead body.

56 This division is given and explained by St. Thomas, *Summa Theol.*, I, q. 105, a. 8; *C. Gent.* 3.101; *In 4 Sent.*, dist.17, q. 1, a. 5, qa1. In another work, *De potentia*, q. 6, a. 2, ad. 3, St. Thomas gives a somewhat different division into miracles *above nature, against nature, and beyond nature*, which is based on the difficulty of performing the work.

57 This is denied by two mutually opposed forms of positive Rationalism, which from different principles come to the same conclusion, that is, philosophical *Determinism*, which affirms the absolute stability of the natural laws and hence denies

that is able to do anything which does not involve contradiction. Indeed, all laws, either metaphysical, or physical, or moral, have their own proper and intrinsic necessity on which our certitude is based. But, unlike the metaphysical laws (which are rooted in and derived from the very essence of things and hence allow no exception whatsoever) the necessity of the physical and moral laws is only contingent or conditional, as far as the attainment of their effect is concerned, that is, it supposes that no other extrinsic cause or condition interferes to counteract and impede their effect. Thus the physical law of gravity can be opposed by a natural agent, as man preventing a stone from falling, and the moral law of parental love can be frustrated by the unusual perversion of a woman killing her child (see footnote 21).

---

any possible exception or miracle, and philosophical *Contingentism*, which denies any stability to such laws or even their very existence (conceiving every phenomenon as standing by itself without any connection with the others) and consequently denies any exception to the law since there is no law. For the first system there is no exception because there is a fixed law, for the second there is no exception because there is no law.

Determinism takes two forms. *Absolute* Determinism denies the very *physical possibility* of miracle; to this form belong all kinds of Pantheism, both materialistic and idealistic, which reduces all things, God and the world, to one being, evolving according to a constant and unchangeable law. *Relative* Determinism denies only the *moral possibility* of miracle, as something disagreeing with the attributes of God, like dignity, wisdom, and goodness; to this form belong the so-called Deists, who deny the particular providence of God (Cherbury, Voltaire, and others), and the Optimists, who claim that God created the best possible world, to whose law therefore there can be no exceptions (N. Malebranche, W. Leibniz). Absolute Determinism is also in a practical way endorsed by Positivists, who claim that the absolute fixity of natural laws is rigorously proved through scientific induction (D. Hume, J. Stuart Mill).

Contingentism is likewise expressed under two forms. *Religious* Contingentism, based on Agnosticism, considers miracle as a natural effect not yet explained by science, transformed by faith into a religious symbol and considered as a special divine intervention (Liberal Protestants, Modernists, and the Catholic defenders of the method of immanence, as Blondel and Laberthonnière, mentioned above, p. 98). *Scientific* Contingentism either denies the very existence of natural laws, considering the universe as a sort of confused aggregate and succession of phenomena without any mutual dependence or connection, so that anything can happen at any time, or, in the milder and commoner form (as that of H. Poincaré and H. Bergson), denies only the fixity of such laws, on the same basis of a lack of connection between phenomena, which makes the exception at least impossible to detect.

Against these errors *Vatican Council I* defined: "If anyone shall say that miracles are not possible, and hence that all accounts of them, even those contained in Sacred Scripture, are to be banished among fables and myths; or, that miracles can never be known with certitude, and that the divine origin of Christian religion cannot be rightly proved through them; let him be anathema" (Sess.3, can.4 on faith, Denz. 3034).

Hence, if there be an agent who would be able to counteract the action of any natural law and prevent it from reaching its natural effect, and this in a way in which no created agent can do it, there would be something done above the order of powers of all created nature, that is, a miracle. But God is such an agent, by reason of his omnipotence which extends itself to anything not involving contradiction. Therefore miracle is possible. Miracle then would consist in a direct action of God intervening into the course of natural causes or laws, either by opposing to them such an obstacle which no natural agent can oppose (as denying in such particular case the very impulse of the first and primary cause, without which no secondary cause can operate); or on the contrary by fostering their action with such favorable conditions that their effect be produced in an extraordinary manner; or by producing their effect without them; or finally by producing a special effect which they are unable to produce (cf. *Summa Theol.*, I, q. 105, a. 6).

Furthermore, miracle is not only absolutely or physically possible, on the basis of God's omnipotence (as we have shown), but also *relatively or morally* so, inasmuch as, far from being opposed to the other divine attributes, it perfectly befits them. Indeed, an obstacle or exception to the established order of natural laws does not disagree with the *dignity and loftiness of God*, as if he should not descend to such particular things in the government of the world (as Deists claim), or he should have created the most perfect world which would need no exceptions or corrections (as Optimists teach). For, on the one hand, the very particular providence of God shows on the contrary the universality of his power, of his knowledge, and of his care for creatures, and on the other hand creation of the most perfect world is not possible, otherwise God would no longer be omnipotent, being unable to do anything better. Likewise miracle does not disagree with *God's wisdom*, as if by it God would reject what he once chose or correct what he had not foreseen; nor with *God's goodness*, as if he would arbitrarily and violently intervene in the world to change the course of nature and check the natural exigencies of things. For, on the contrary, God had foreseen and wanted all the future changes and exceptions, which would follow, in due time and manner, for a wise complement and balance of the universe as well as for particular reasons proper to each miracle, not least of all the very purpose of confirming his supernatural revelation, thus paving the way to faith through the forces of nature. Hence miracle, as well as nature itself, is a bright mirror of the divine perfections.

2. CHRIST'S MIRACLES, AS TO THEIR HISTORICAL TRUTH

The supernatural origin of Christian religion can be proved by any true miracle, worked in the Church at any time, for the seal of God's testimony stamped on any miracle is a sufficient testimony. We will confine our consideration, however, to the miracles narrated in the Gospel, for they are the major testimony on whose strength and evidence the Church was first built and propagated. Moreover, among such miracles we leave out, as not necessary or less efficacious for our apologetical purpose, those performed about Christ, as the several wonders in Christ's nativity, during his public life (voice from heaven in his Baptism, during his preaching, in the Transfiguration), and in his death (the darkening of the sun, the earthquake).[58]

We consider only the physical miracles *performed by Christ himself*, either in his own body or in other persons and things, excluding of course all the many miracles mentioned only generically (as in Matt. 4:23; 8:16; Mark 1:32–34; Luke 4:40f.; 6:17–19; John 2:23; 6:2), which cannot be examined and given apologetical value.

Among such miracles there are three major ones worked by Christ in his own body, namely his Transfiguration, his Resurrection, and his entrance into the closed cenacle, and about thirty-five worked on other people or things, with a great variety of subjects and matters. These concern either spiritual beings or demons, in people possessed by them, the so-called demoniacs (at least six distinct miracles); or irrational creatures (at least nine miracles, as multiplication of loaves, change of water into wine, etc.); or men, that is, three resuscitations, more than seven cures from defect or injury of an organ (eyes, hearing, speech), many cures from various and serious infirmities (as dropsy, leprosy, paralysis for 38 years, hemorrhage for 12 years, crippled condition for 18 years).

For the sake of our apologetical purpose we can point out several groups of these miracles, and divide them according to the degree of their supernatural character into the three classes

---

58 Almost 100 particular miracles, performed by Christ or about Christ, before, in, and after resurrection, can be easily counted.

mentioned above (p. 120), namely; *Miracles as to substance:* the Transfiguration (Matt.17:1–3); entrance into the closed cenacle (John 20:19); resurrection; three resuscitations, of Jairus' daughter, of the son of the widow at Naim, and of Lazarus (Matt. 9:20–26; Luke 7:11–17; John 11:1–44). *Miracles as to subject:* several cures from organic defect or injury (eyes, hearing, speech), particularly of the man born blind (John 9:1–38); change of water into wine (John 2:1–11); two multiplications of loaves (Matt. 14:13–21; 15:32–39); the calming of the storm on the lake (Matt. 8:23–27); the walking upon the sea (Matt. 14:22–23). *Miracles as to manner;* all other miracles can be reduced to this class, especially the healing from merely functional diseases. Deliverance from diabolic possession is a more difficult type to classify, because such possession is at times coupled with a functional or organic disease, as in the epileptic demoniac, the dumb demoniac, the blind and dumb demoniac (Matt. 17:14–21; 9:32–34; 12:22–24).

The *historical truth* of such facts[59] appears from external as well as from internal criteria.

---

59   Among the aforementioned Rationalists who deny the possibility of miracles (p. 121), the older ones simply discard the historical truth of all such miracles, attributing them to a *fraud* of Christ's disciples (H. S. Reimarus) or to a mere political *fiction* of the same (H. E. G. Paulus and D. F. Strauss). The more recent ones (as Liberal Protestants and Modernists, led by A. Harnack, *Das Wesen des Christentums* [Leipzig 1902] 16ff.), generally distinguish between different miracles. They deny the historical truth of the *outstanding* miracles that are more difficult to explain, as the cure of the man born blind, the three resuscitations, and especially Christ's resurrection, to which they attribute some kind of natural error or legitimate fiction, due to the aureole with which founders of religions are usually adorned, to the general tendency among the Jews to admit miracles and the fulfillment of ancient prophecies, and to the beginning of a process of idealization of Christ's deeds immediately after his death. As regards the other *easier miracles,* they admit the historical truth but deny their supernatural character, attributing them to natural causes (see below, footnote 65).

Regarding *Christ's resurrection* in particular, which implies the two elements of true death and subsequent true life, a few of the older Rationalists reject the truth of the death of Christ, invoking a mere apparent death due to swooning or lethargy (thus H. E. G. Paulus and F. Spitta), while the others generally concede the reality of the death but deny directly the resurrection to new life, and explain the contrary affirmation of the Gospel and of the apostles in three general ways, namely:

1) Either through fraud of the disciples or of the Jews themselves, who secretly removed from the tomb and hid the corpse (the *fraud theory* held by Reimarus, Réville, Le Roy, O. Holtzmann).

2) Or through error of the disciples, deceived by some illusion or vision (of a pathological, or mystical, or objective, or spiritistic character), which made them believe they saw again Christ alive (the *error theory* held by E. Renan, A. Meyer, R. Otto, E. von Dobschütz, R. A. Hoffmann).

The external criterion is the testimony both of the evangelists, whose direct knowledge of the facts and complete veracity in relating them cannot reasonably be doubted, and of the adversaries of Christ themselves (cf. John 3:2; Mark 6:14; John 11:47; Matt. 27:42), who lacked neither the opportunity of a strict examination of Christ's miracles, nor the motive and the will to

---

3) Or through a mere but reasonable and legitimate fiction, by which a new life was attributed to Christ (the *fiction theory*). Such attribution arose in four ways. Either through the usual popular legend, adorning the life of founders (*mythical fiction*, held by F. Strauss, A. Meyer, A. Loisy). Or through the particular legend of the "savior god" rising from the dead, which was common to several hellenistic and oriental religions (*religious-syncretistic fiction*, or theory of "Religiongeschichte," held by W. Bousset and A. Loisy). Or through a popular-literary fiction, that is, a legend fashioned gradually by the addition of elements of popular literature to primitive historical elements (theory of *popular literary fiction*, "Formengeschichte" or historical forms, held by M. Albert, L. Brun, and E. Bichermann). Or through a religious symbolic process, taking originally Christ's resurrection not as a physical fact but as an ideal or symbol of spiritual resurrection and immortal life of Christ with God (theory of *symbolic fiction* held by Harnack, Loisy and the other Modernists condemned by Pius X, Denz. 3436f.; and recently by R. Bultmann, *Theologie des Neuen Testaments* [Tübingen 1958] 305; *Kerygma und Mythos* [Hamburg 1960] 1, pp. 44–48, and W. Marxsen, *Die Auferstehung Jesu als historisches und als theologisches Problem* [Gütersloh 1965] 20–35; *Die Auferstehung Jesu von Nazareth* [Gütersloh 1968]).

This last theory, as expounded by Bultmann and Marxsen, has influenced the doctrine of some *recent Catholic writers* who prefer to abstain from the word "resurrection" and replace it with the general word "life," simply declaring that by the so-called Christ's resurrection it is meant only that Christ is still alive and lives forever in a better state of glorification, and not that the individual body of Christ came back to life.

Particular commotion and criticism among Catholic circles was caused by the work of Xavier Léon-Dufour (a Scripture scholar), *Résurrection de Jésus et message pascal* (Paris, 1971; second printing with some corrections, 1972). The author keeps the word "resurrection" as the one in perfect harmony with the biblical narratives, but changes its meaning, teaching that Christ's resurrection, though a real happening, is not a historical fact in the sense commonly accepted, namely a revival of the individual body of Christ. The individual or historical body of a man is not the real component part of the human being, but only a place or a means of communication with other beings, while the real component part of the human being is the universal or cosmic body. At the moment of death the individual body, the corpse, is as it were absorbed by the universal cosmic body, never to revive. Hence when Christ died, his individual and historical body, forever dissolved, returned to the universal cosmic body, which by virtue of the resurrection was transformed and made glorious. Thus Christ's resurrection is a real fact, but not a historical fact in the sense of a revival of the dead body, historically ascertainable.

For a further explanation and criticism of this opinion see J. Galot, in *Civiltà Cattolica* (1972), vol. 2, pp. 527–540, C. M. Martini, *ibid.*, vol. 3, pp. 125–135; Ch. Journet, in *Nova et Vetera* (1972) 304–311; E. Pousset, in *Nouvelle revue théologique* (1972) 95–107; C. Spicq, in *Esprit et Vie* (1972) 76–79; M.-M. Labourdette, in *Revue Thomiste* 72 (1972) 619–633.

make it, as is particularly evident in the two miracles of the man born blind and of Lazarus. This testimony is further confirmed by that of extrinsic sources close to the facts, as the Acts of the Apostles (Acts 2:22; 3:12; 10:37f.; 2 Pet. 1:16), and the second century tradition, unanimously referring to Christ's miracles. The apologist Quadratus about the year 124 even testifies that some of those cured by Christ were still alive in his time (this is quoted by Eusebius of Caesarea, *Eccles. Hist.* 4.3). Also the Jewish historian Joseph Flavius, writing about the year 93, recalls the miracles and resurrection of Christ.[60]

The internal criterion, that is, the close examination of the narratives, shows the same historical truth. *First of all*, Christ's miracles are so numerous and so intimately connected with the other facts and words of Christ that they belong to the very substance of the entire Gospel, which without them would go crippled and unexplained; for Christ's miracles were the reason for the crowding of people around him and for the opposition of the Pharisees, as well as the occasion for him to hand on and confirm his various doctrines. In particular, if miracles were removed, the following pericopes would have to be taken out or completely changed: the reproach to Chorozain and Bethsaida (Matt. 11:20–24), Christ's power over demons (Matt. 12:23–37), the eucharistic sermon (John, chapter 6, which is almost wholly, vv. 1–70, based on the miracle of multiplication of loaves), the Pharisees' examination about Christ on the occasion of the cure of the man born blind (John, chap.9, in its entirety), the great commotion of both the people and the Pharisees on account of the resuscitation of Lazarus (John, chap. 11, in its entirety).

Secondly, the narratives of Christ's miracles are in full agreement with his character, messianic mission, and teaching.

Thirdly, the historical truth of such miracles is also confirmed by the style or manner in which they are narrated, a style which is simple, sober, life-like, spontaneous, detailed, clothed in color

---

60 *Antiquities* 18, 3:3: "At that same time Jesus lived, a wise man, if however it is right to call him a man. For he was a *performer of wonderful deeds*, a teacher of those who spontaneously accept the truth; he drew to himself many Jews as well as many Gentiles. He was the Christ. When Pilate had sentenced him, accused by the leaders of our people, to the torture of the cross, they did not cease to love him as they had done before. For *he appeared to them alive* on the third day, according to the divine prophets who had foretold these and other wondrous things about him."

and concrete circumstances, free from exaggerations, void of any pretence, deceit or contradiction, notwithstanding the variety of the fourfold source. A particular specimen of this style is found in the accounts of the Cana wedding, of the multiplication of loaves and of the cure of the man born blind (John 2:1–11; 6:1–13 and parallel texts in the synoptics; 9:1–38).[61]

As to Christ's resurrection,[62] the historical truth of the two elements implied in it, namely, a true death and a true life after death, is likewise evident from both evangelical and extra-evangelical testimony.

The evangelical witnesses of Christ's death are: the four evangelists, saying that Christ on the cross "gave up his spirit" (Matt. 27:50; Mark 15:37; Luke 23:46; John 19:30); the soldiers, who did not break his legs because they were certain of his death (John 10:32–34); the centurion, who for the same reason withdrew from guarding the cross (Mark 15:39); Pilate, inquiring from the centurion "whether he [Christ] was already dead" and hence

61 This internal coherence of the object and the style of the evangelical narratives shows also the difference, as to their historical truth, between Christ's miracles and those that are brought forth by Rationalists, under the form of a skeptical objection, from rabbinic and pagan history, as the miracles of the Pythagorean philosopher Apollonius of Tyana, of emperors Hadrian and Vespasian, of the oriental divinities Apollo, Isis, Asclepius Epidaurus, and of the religious founders Buddha and Mohammed. Cf. S. Tromp, De revelatione christiana, ed. 5, pp. 239–241 (see bibliography, ibid., p. 421).

62 Braun, F., "La résurrection de Jésus devant la critique moderne," Vie spirituelle 63 (1940) 26–52.

Daniélou, J., La résurrection, Paris 1969.

De Rosa, G. "Il cristiano di oggi di fronte alla risurrezione di Christo," Civiltà cattolica 121 (1970), vol. 3, pp. 365–377.

Fuller, R. H., The Formation of the Resurrection Narratives, New York 1971.

Haes, P. de, La résurrection de Jésus dans l'apologétique des cinquante dernières années, Rome 1953.

Kremer, J., "Ist Jesus wirklich von den Toten auferstanden?," Stimmen der Zeit 94 (1969) 310–320.

Léon-Dufour, X., "Exégèse du Nouveau Testament. Autour de la résurrection du Christ," Recherches de science religieuse 57 (1969) 583–622; "Présence de Jésus ressuscité," Etudes (1970) 593–614; Résurrection de Jésus et message pascal, Paris 1971; second printing with a few corrections, 1972.

Martini, C., Il problema storico della risurrezione negli studi recenti, Roma 1959; "La testimonianza dei primi cristiani per la risurrezione di Gesù," Civiltà Cattolica (1972), vol. 3, pp. 125–135.

Pousset, E., "La résurrection," Nouvelle revue théologique 91 (1969) 1009–1044.

Ponthot, J., "Les traditions évangéliques sur la résurrection du Christ," Lumen vitae 20 (1965) 649–673; 21 (1966) 99–118.

Résurrection (La) du Christ et l'exégèse moderne (collective work), Paris 1969.

"granting the body to Joseph [of Arimathea]" (Mark 15:44f.); Mary, his mother, and the other friends standing by the cross, whose love would have allowed no doubt about his death; the Pharisees, who not only made sure of his death, but tried to prevent even a simulated resurrection, asking Pilate to seal the tomb and have it guarded by the soldiers (Matt. 27:62–66).

Even if Christ's previous torments, as crowning with thorns, scourging, painful walking to the place of crucifixion, crucifixion itself, three hours of agony, had not been sufficient to cause death, but only a sort of syncope or lethargy, which is extremely improbable, a certain death would have violently followed from the piercing of his side with a lance and the consequent flowing of blood (John 19:34) and from suffocation due to the wrapping of the body in linen cloths and spices (mixture of myrrh and aloes, weighing about a hundred pounds; John 19:39f.) and its stay in the closed sepulchre.

Confirmation is added by extra-evangelical testimony, particularly by the preaching of the apostles, ocular witnesses, who threw the unchallenged accusation at the Jewish people, witnesses themselves and executors: "Him...you have crucified and slain by the hands of wicked men" (Acts 2:23), "The author of life you killed, whom God has raised from the dead" (Acts 3:15).

Christ's *true life after death* (and hence his resurrection) is shown by the fact that the tomb was found empty, without the body being removed by anyone, and that the body appeared again alive to the disciples.

After Christ's body was truly buried (as shown by the Gospel's description), *the tomb was found empty*, as testified both by the four evangelists (Matt. 27:57–60; Mark 15:42–46; Luke 23:50–55; John 19:38–42) and by the Pharisees themselves, who bribed the soldiers, telling them: "Say, 'His disciples came by night and stole him while we were sleeping'" (Matt. 28:13). *The body was not removed*, neither by the disciples, as is evident from this same confession of the Pharisees and from the strict vigilance of the military guard (recently enforced by an edict of Caesar Augustus or Tiberius against violators of tombs), nor by the Pharisees themselves in order to prevent any such action on the part of the disciples. This is evident from the same vigilance of the guard and from the fact that later the Pharisees would have brought forth the body in order to refute the disciples' affirmation on the resurrection.

The apparition of the living body of Christ is testified by the same four evangelists, whose veracity is warranted and fraud excluded by the general simple and spontaneous character of the Gospel, mentioned above (p. 127). Nine distinct apparitions are narrated in the Gospel: to Mary Magdalen (Mark 16:9; John 20:11–17), to the pious women (Matt. 28:9), to Peter (Luke 24:34), to two disciples on their way to Emmaus (Mark 16:12; Luke 24:13–33), to the disciples in the cenacle, twice (Mark 16:14; Luke 24:36–43; John 20:19–29), to the disciples by the Sea of Tiberias (John 21:1–14), to the apostles on a mountain of Galilee (Matt. 28:16f.; Mark 16:15), to the same immediately before the Ascension (Mark 16:19; Luke 24:44–52). Besides St. Paul testifies to three other apparitions, that is, to more than 500 disciples, to James, and to himself (1 Cor. 15:6–8; 5:5–7). Hence there were 12 distinct apparitions in all, six of which were made to the whole group of the disciples or apostles.

The truth of the testimony is warranted by the authority of the witnesses, that is, by the veracity of the disciples, for in their lives there is nothing that would suggest possibility of falsehood or fiction, and by their knowledge of the facts, which were external, visible and even collective apparitions.[63]

---

63 Hence the aforementioned *error-theory* and *fiction-theory* advanced by Rationalists and Modernists (p. 125) do not stand critical examination and the only logical course for them would be to reject or completely reshape the Gospel text itself.

Thus a *pathological error* of the disciples has no foundation, since they were not disposed to hallucination by reason of their mental balance and physical health, nor were they even thinking about the resurrection foretold by Christ, as is clear from their first movement of incredulity when they saw Christ again (Mark 16:13; Luke 24:11, 21–26, 37–41; John 20:27–29). Besides, hallucinations do not happen to many witnesses at the same time, nor to all the senses at the same time, nor to the same person many times or for a long time.

Mythical fiction (as that found in the fables about Aeneas, Romulus, and others) is something which does not endure but degenerates with time. It cannot deceive prudent men but only the popular fancy. It has some value in building up history or literature, but not interior convictions, ardent faith and a program or rule of life itself.

Likewise, *religious-syncretistic fiction* has no foundation, for it cannot be shown why and how the Christian religion would derive one of its fundamental truths from abhorred idolatrous religions, and how such adoption could have been made in so short a time.

Popular-literary fiction would also require a long time to develop and transform the original historical elements, while Christ's resurrection was commonly believed

2. APOLOGETICAL VALUE OF CHRIST'S MIRACLES

The physical miracles performed by Christ are evident and sufficient criterion of revelation, on account of their evident supernatural character.

As we noted above (p. 85), an evident and sufficient criterion of revelation is made up of three necessary elements, that is, its historical, philosophical and relative truth. Therefore, the deeds which we call physical miracles of Christ are proved to be evident and sufficient criterion of revelation, if we prove, first, their *historical truth*, or that they actually took place as they are narrated in the Gospel; second, their *philosophical truth*, or that they are true

in the Church shortly after his death, as is clear from St. Paul's first epistle to the Corinthians (15:3–11), written about the year 56.

Symbolic fiction does not agree with the historical character of the Gospel narrative, nor can it be said that such historical character is a later evolution of the primitive symbolic sense given to Christ's resurrection, for there was no sufficient time for such an evolution and the primitive Pauline teaching about the resurrection bears the same historical character. The first epistle to the Corinthians was written between the year 55 and the year 57, several years before the Gospels and the Acts; hence 1 Cor 15:3f. is the oldest Christian testimony of Christ's resurrection.

Regarding the aforementioned doubt or denial of some recent Catholic scholars about the historicity of Christ's resurrection, note the following. This resurrection, as the revival of Christ's individual body, is not directly a historical fact, historically ascertainable, inasmuch as no one witnessed or properly could witness the actual reunion of Christ's soul to his dead body. It is, however, a fact indirectly historical, of which we can acquire a moral certitude, as a conclusion from various facts which are directly historical, namely, the death and burial, the empty sepulcher, the apparitions and the conviction of the disciples about Christ's true resurrection.

The general anthropological conception, advanced by the chief dissenter, Léon-Dufour, does not agree with either philosophical or theological safe doctrine. The human soul can inform only a determined individual body, not an indefinite cosmic matter. The Church Magisterium has clearly defined that the human nature is "composed of spirit and body" (Council of Lateran IV, repeated by Vatican I, Denz. 800, 3002); hence the physical individual body is a component part of man. The Council of Lateran IV defines also that "all men shall resurrect in those same proper bodies, which they now have" (Denz. 801).

As regards Christ directly, the same Council defines that he "resurrected in his flesh" (Denz. 801), therefore, in his historical and individual body and not in a universal cosmic matter which is not flesh. The traditional doctrine teaches that the Word of God assumed a human nature composed of soul and individual body, from which he was never separated, even after the mutual separation of soul and body through death. If Christ's soul after his death would be united to the universal cosmic matter, there would result a monstrous union of the Word with the universe, a sort of "panchristism," and Christ's body would be the universe itself, assumed and transfigured by his Divinity. All our faith, piety, and liturgy are based on the individual humanity and body in which Christ was born, in which he spoke the words of divine revelation, suffered, died and offered his sacrifice on the Cross, and in which he remains with us in the eucharistic sacrament and sacrifice. All this would fall with the disappearance of the individual and historical body of Christ into the universal and cosmic matter.

miracles, that is things done by God alone (at least as principal cause) above the order of powers and laws established by him in all created nature; third, their *relative truth*, or that they were performed by Christ with the manifested intention of proving the fact of revelation, that is, that God was speaking through him. If these three things are certain, then the fact of revelation is also certain, because Christ's testimony would be approved and endorsed by God, who cannot bear witness to falsehood.[64]

The historical truth of Christ's miracles has just been proved.

Their relative truth can be easily shown, for the whole life of Christ in his words and deeds tends precisely to prove his messianic and divine mission. Christ *generically and explicitly* declares to perform his miracles in order to prove his divine mission; John 5:36: "The works which the Father has given me to accomplish, these very works that I do, bear witness to me, that the Father has sent me;" John 15.24: "If I had not done among them works such as no one else has done, they would have no sin. But now they have seen, and have hated both me and my Father" (cf. 10:25, 37, 38; 14:12). The same declaration is vividly contained in Christ's words to John's disciples asking him whether he was the Messiah to come, to whom he simply answered that his miracles

---

64   It is of course possible that God permit abuse of the gift of miracles by a man (as he permits abuse of the sacramental character by a priest), if for instance an apostate from the faith, in order to confirm his new false doctrine, would appeal to miracles performed by him when he was an apostle of the same faith. It is even possible that God work some miracles on a member or through a member of a *false religion*, as St. Thomas admits (*Summa Theol.*, II-II, q. 178, a. 2, ad. 3; *De potentia*, q. 6, a. 5, obj.5 and ad. 5). Some believe that such was the case of the Hindu ascetic, Sundar Singh (cf. *Recherches de science religieuse* 12 [1922] 1–29).

But these and similar things can be permitted by God only if no confirmation of false doctrines or religions would result from them, considering the facts and their circumstances; otherwise God would be witness to falsehood.

Thus, in the case of an apostate appealing to his past miracles for confirmation of his new false doctrine, the fallacy of his argument is clearly shown by the difference and distance between the situation in which he once performed the miracle and his present situation in which he appeals to the old miracle as a sign of his new doctrine. Miracles that are said to happen in false religions are usually false miracles because they are performed in such a way or in such circumstances that, if they were true, false religions would be approved by God. But, out of such circumstances, God can perform a miracle on a member or through a member of a false religion for different particular purposes, for instance to reward or show an outstanding virtue of an individual (as chastity, charity toward the neighbor, religious behavior), or even to show the presence of a particular element of truth found in that false religion, providing this religion as a whole does not receive any confirmation from the miracle in view of the circumstances in which it is performed.

proved who he was (Matt.11:2–5), and in his reproach to the cities of Israel, such as Capharnaum, for having seen his miracles and not believed (Matt.11:20, 23).

Christ makes the same explicit declaration in regard to some *particular* and outstanding miracles. Thus he heals the paralytic "that you may know that the Son of Man has power on earth to forgive sins" (Matt.9:6); he cures the blind because "the works of God were to be made manifest in him" (John 9:3; cf. 9:36); he brings Lazarus back to life "because of the people who stand around . . . that they may believe that you have sent me" (John 11:42). Referring to his *resurrection* he explicitly says: "An evil and adulterous generation demands a sign, and no sign shall be given it but the sign of Jonas the prophet. For even as Jonas was in the belly of the fish three days and three nights, so will the Son of Man be three days and three nights in the heart of the earth" (Matt. 12:39f.); and predicting to the apostles his return to them after death, he says: "And now I have told you before it comes to pass, that when it has come to pass you may believe" (John 14:29).

The same relative truth is *implicitly* contained in the three following circumstances. *First,* the very fact that someone works miracles while preaching a doctrine turns necessarily into a confirmation of his doctrine, and hence he implicitly intends such reference and confirmation. *Secondly,* the whole doctrine of Christ and much of his dispute with the Pharisees about his divine mission hinge upon miracles (see above, p. 126) which are, therefore, considered as the credentials of his divine mission. This is the reason why the Pharisees tried to deny the true miraculous nature of the wonders performed by Christ, attributing them to Beelzebub (Matt.12:24) and they spurned with threatening words the remark of the blind telling them: "Why, herein is the marvel, that you do not know where he is from, and yet he opened my eyes" (John 9:30). *Third,* the messianic expectation among the people was such that its fulfillment had to be shown by miracles; this is the reason why to John's disciples inquiring whether he was the Messias Christ gave no other answer than referring them to his miracles (Matt. 11:2–5). Not much later "a man among the Pharisees, Nicodemus by name, a ruler of the Jews . . . came to Jesus at night and said to him, 'Rabbi, we know that you have come a teacher from God, for no one can work these signs that you work unless God be with him'" (John 3:1f.).

The *philosophical truth* of Christ's miracles,[65] namely that they are unmistakably true miracles, due only to the direct action of God, is the most important as well as the most difficult point to be proved, considering on the one hand that we do not see God operating and on the other hand we do not know how far is to be extended or limited the power of created causes, whether physical, human, or angelic.

However, although we do not know *positively and universally* what created nature can do through its proper powers and in any circumstance, we can know *negatively* what this particular nature cannot do absolutely and taken in itself, with regard to a specific object or in a particular circumstance.

Indeed, if we consider the *specific object or effect* of some of Christ's miracles, we can have an absolute certitude that no created cause can produce it, a certitude derived from metaphysical principles as well as from common sense which is called "the perennial philosophy" and is the basis of metaphysics itself. For in those miracles which we mentioned above (p. 124) under the name of *miracles as to substance* and *miracles as to subject*, as they stand out and as they are judged by common sense itself, there takes place a *universal effect*, that is a change in the depths of "being" itself or in the very nature and essence of a thing, which, therefore, by the metaphysical principle of the necessary proportion between cause and effect, calls necessarily for a *universal cause*, that is, God himself. For God is the proper cause of being as such and of the nature and essence of things.

Thus, referring to the major miracles of the two classes, Christ's Transfiguration (or bodily glorification) implies some change in the *essence of quantity*, so that it may exhibit outwardly those extraordinary properties of brightness and color which it does not possess in its natural way (Matt. 17:2: "And his face shone

---

65 As we noted in footnote 59, Rationalists, denying the very possibility of any miracle, logically reject the philosophical truth of all Christ's miracles, and for this reason they discard even the historical truth of those outstanding miracles for which they find no explanation and they attribute the others to natural causes, that is, either to *natural powers not yet known*, or to *mental suggestion*, or to *occultism*. Thus among others E. Renan, *Vie de Jésus* (éd. 14, Paris 1873) 268–270; A Harnack, *Das Wesen des Christentums* (Leipzig 1902) 16ff., with other Liberal Protestants; A. Loisy, *L'Evangile et l'Eglise* (éd. 5, Paris 1930) 16–23, with other Modernists.

as the sun, and his garments became white as snow"). In Christ's entrance into the closed cenacle after the Resurrection there was for one moment a sort of compenetration of the body of Christ with the wall or door through which he entered, and hence the presence of two bodies in the same place, which cannot happen unless there is some change in the *essence of quantity* of either body, preventing it from occupying its natural place. Christ's Resurrection, as well as the three resuscitations he worked on others, requires necessarily a change or a direct touch in the very *essence of the body* to draw it back from corruption and dispose it again for the infusion of the rational soul.

Similar *substantial change* or touch is required in the cure of organic defects, especially in completely reshaping an organ, as in a man born blind; for organs are immediately rooted in the substance of man. The same change is required in the sudden transformation of water into wine and multiplication of the bread, for both effects naturally take place only through a slow process of various substantial changes. The two last miracles mentioned above, that is the calming of the storm on the lake and the walking upon the sea, require only a change in the essence of the quantity of the wind and of the water, by which the law of gravity is checked or regulated.

One or another modern theologian, granting that only God can produce such essential changes, denies that we can prove with certitude that such changes actually take place and they are not only apparent, due to a prodigious action of an angelic creature, who would, for instance, quickly substitute wine for water or bring loaves of bread from another place.[66]

Such an explanation certainly cannot be applied to some of the above miracles, as entrance into the closed cenacle, resuscitation, and healing of the man born blind. For, the same body of Christ which was outside is said to be inside the cenacle; the same man who was dead is said to be alive; the same man who had no sight is said to have it. Besides, if we were to explain such miracles as merely apparent facts due to the action of angelic creatures, we should say, for instance, that an angel removed the wall before the

---

66   Thus Van Hove, *op. cit.* (above, p. 119) 300, stating: "If we consider miraculous facts only under their exterior appearances, we could attribute most of them to an action of spiritual substances [angels] ... Substantial transformations themselves do not exclude an explanation of this kind."

body of Christ and then replaced it, or produced only an appearance of Christ's body before the apostles, and likewise that Lazarus actually did not rise, but an angel took his body away from the tomb and produced an appearance of Lazarus which apparently exercised all the functions of life and lasted as long as Lazarus was seen to live, and finally that the blind man did not have the sight, but an angel constantly produced in him an illusion of vision so that all the exterior objects would continually appear to him as if he had the sight. Such an explanation would not only uselessly multiply extraordinary things, but would seem also repugnant to common sense, since deception and illusion cannot last long.

Even the change of water into wine and the multiplication of bread, as well as other miracles, like instantaneous cures performed by Christ, have to be taken in their obvious sense. For, if all such things were not certain miracles just because they could absolutely be explained by a surreptitious intervention of an angelic creature, it would affect also the certitude we have of the daily events of our life, and I would not be certain, for instance, that I see, walk, eat, and that other men do these things in like manner, since possibly without my knowledge all such things are merely apparently done by an angelic creature. All of which is against common sense and out of the range of a sane mind.

As regards the miracles of the third class which we called *miracles as to manner* (most of the remaining miracles, as cures from some organic injuries of eyes, hearing and speech, and especially from functional diseases, as paralysis, dropsy, leprosy, fever), their supernatural character is known with certainty, not from the mere consideration of their object, for, absolutely speaking, this could be produced by a created cause, physical, human or angelic, but from the *circumstances, both physical and moral*, which accompany them and which prove that a particular deed cannot be produced in such a way by any created cause.

The *physical circumstances* can be reduced to three, that is, the great difficulty of the deed, the absence of natural and usual means in performing it, and its sudden, complete and permanent character. All three are found in Christ's miracles. The difficulty of the deed is clearly shown in the *various cures* from diseases, especially of the man sick with paralysis for 38 years (John 5:1ff.), of the woman crippled for 18 years (Luke 13:10–17), and of the woman with a hemorrhage for 12 years (Matt. 9:20–22). The absence of natural and usual means, as medicines and other treatment, is evident; the son of the centurion and the son of the Jewish ruler are cured from a distance, the paralytic and the leper are cured by a single word, the lepers and the woman with the hemorrhage by touch alone, the deaf mute by touch and spittle. The cure in all cases was instantaneous, complete and permanent; no sign to the contrary is shown, which would have been the occasion for doubt or incrimination on the part of the Pharisees. The same circumstances are found proportionally in miracles performed about *irrational creatures*, as the extraordinary catch of fish (Luke 5:1–11; John 21:1–11), the barren fig tree (Matt. 21:18–22), the shekel found in the mouth of the fish (Matt. 17:24–27); these were likewise difficult deeds, performed without the usual means and crowned by immediate and perfect results. The same circumstances appear in miracles regarding *spiritual creatures or demons* in the cure of demoniacs, which moreover show Christ's power over such creatures and hence a clearer sign of their supernatural character.

The moral circumstances are the morality of the performer, the goodness of the deed, its purpose, the way of acting, the means, place and time of the action; from such circumstances, which render a deed morally good or bad, one can judge whether or not it is from God or supernatural. Christ's miracles proceed from a holy man, seeking in them no gain, glory or revenge; they contain nothing immoral, harmful, dishonorable, useless, or ridiculous; they were performed for a religious purpose, in a fitting manner, with no vain, unworthy or violent means, in the right place and at the right time.[67]

---

67 Hence the three natural causes proposed by *Rationalists* (see footnote 65) did not have any influence in Christ's miracles.

Unknown natural powers could not work, at least in such physical circumstances as those which accompanied Christ's deeds.

Mental suggestion (or the medical method called psychotherapeutic) cannot explain miracles about irrational creatures, about the expulsion of demons from demoniacs, about organic diseases (as blindness, deafness, dumbness, cut off ear); to which we can associate some diseases mingled with an organic injury (as paralysis, atrophy, leprosy, dropsy, flow of blood). Hence there remain only the merely functional infirmities, or rather those that are more directly connected with nervous disorder, on which suggestion may have its psychological influence. However, suggestion is effective only in a subject psychologically apt, present, prepared by the action of the one using suggestion, who moreover works slowly and patiently

12

Objective Extrinsic Criteria of the Fact of Revelation. Prophecies[68]

IN THE ABOVE MENTIONED DIVISION OF CRITE-
rion (p. 86) we placed prophecy, along with physical miracles, as an objective extrinsic criterion of revelation. For, on the one hand it is a true miracle, although of the intellectual order, and on the other hand, it is also exteriorly recognizable with certainty by reason of the sensible manifestation of both the knowledge of a future event and its fulfillment. Thus it approaches physical miracle itself, making with it a double and primary criterion

---

and obtains his effect gradually and only imperfectly. Such characteristics are alien to Christ's miracles.

Occultism (*alias* spiritism, hypnotism, animal magnetism, animism), both as a doctrine and a practice, is based on an occult power through which extraordinary effects are obtained. Such effects are either *physical*, as telekinesis (motion of a material thing done at a distance by the will alone), levitation (by which a body is raised and kept in air without support), and materialization (formation of a new body from the fluid mass emitted by the body of the "medium"); or *psychical*, as telepathy (communication of thought to distant persons), and clairvoyance (knowledge of things distant in time or place or condition, as thoughts or secrets of heart).

Christ's miracles cannot be explained by such an occult power. The *object* is different as is clear especially for the above mentioned miracles of first and second classes (resuscitation, cure of organic diseases, change of water into wine, etc.). Particularly physical and moral *circumstances* are different; thus in spiritistic sessions things are done by a psychopathic or abnormal person (called "medium") working in an abnormal state of nervous prostration or excitement (called "trance"); total or partial fraud often takes place; the action is performed in an unbecoming manner, either frivolous or ambiguous or secret, often in the dark; the end is not religious but superstitious and a general shunning of religion.

68   Bacht, H., "Wahres und falsches Prophetentum," *Biblica* 32 (1951) 237–262. Büchel, W., "Natürliches Vorauswissen zukünftiger Ereignisse," *Scholastik* 30 (1955) 233–240.

Gils, F., *Jésus prophète d'après les évangiles synoptiques*, Louvain 1957.

Mangenot, E., "Prophétie—Prophétisme," *Dictionnaire de la Bible* 5 (Paris 1912) 728–747.

Michel, A., "Prophétie," *Dictionnaire de théologie catholique* XIII-1 (Paris 1936) 708–737.

Touzard, J., *Comment utiliser l'argument prophétique*, Paris 1911.

of revelation. Just as in the preceding chapter we will first give a brief explanation of prophecy in general, as to its nature and possibility, and then proceed to the two points of our apologetical treatment, namely, the existence of prophecies (or the historical truth of the predictions of future events and of their fulfillment) and its apologetical value, that is, whether they are evident criteria or proofs of the fact of revelation.

1. PROPHECY IN GENERAL

A. Nature of prophecy

The word prophecy (in Greek "Prophetéia," derived either from the verb "profáino," I manifest before time or for a person, or from the verb "próphemi," I speak before time or for a person) etymologically means either prediction of the future or speech for another person as a legate. Both senses are biblical; thus Isaiah and Jeremiah are called prophets because they predicted the future, while Elias and Eliseus are called prophets because they were speaking as legates of God without particularly predicting the future. Likewise both senses are patristic and theological, although the first (that is, prediction of future events) prevailed in theology, in the documents of the Magisterium and also in popular language.

In this sense prophecy is properly and strictly *defined: Certain knowledge and exterior manifestation of a contingent future event* (cf. *Summa Theol.*, p. II-II, q. 171, a. 1–3). Two elements integrate this definition, that is, knowledge of the future and manifestation of this knowledge to others. The first element which is primary and essential, as being miraculous, implies two effects in the mind of the subject, that is, the infusion of a *supernatural light,* proportioned to the object to be known (hence a light modally supernatural, as explained above, p. 69; and thus prophecy is a true miracle of the intellectual order, as noted above, p. 120), and the *presentation of such an object,* that is, of a contingent future event (or an event depending on the free will alone and therefore completely undetermined or contingent). The second element is evidently not miraculous nor essential to prophecy as such (hence if God manifests the future to a man who keeps it secret to himself, there is still a prophecy), but it is essentially required for prophecy as a sign, that is for its apologetical value, for which moreover the historical and visible fulfillment of the prediction is required. Hence two things are required in *prophecy, taken apologetically* as a criterion of revelation, namely, *prediction* (certain knowledge and exterior manifestation) of a contingent future event, and its evident historical *fulfillment.*

Prophecy, a member of the division of miracle (that is an intellectual miracle, as explained above, p. 120), cannot be divided essentially, that is, on the part of the supernatural light which is the same for the knowledge of all future events, but it is *divided accidentally,* both according to the way its object is presented to the subject, that is, whether directly in the intellect, or through the imagination, or through the exterior senses (*intellectual, imaginary,* or *sensible,* prophecy), and to the state of the subject, when receiving from God the knowledge of the future, that is, whether he is in *wakefulness,* or in *sleep,* or in *ecstasy.*

B. *The possibility of prophecy*[69] derives necessarily from two combined truths, namely, from the natural truth that God, by reason of the perfection of his knowledge and the universality of his providence, knows all future events, and from the supernatural truth

---

69   The above mentioned Rationalists, who reject the possibility of miracles in general (see, p. 121), deny consequently the possibility of this particular intellectual miracle. This denial, found likewise in other systems, springs directly from three sources.

The first is *Fatalism,* which denies liberty and contingency of things and hence removes the very object of prophecy, that is, future contingent event. Such fatalism is common to Pantheists, among whom Baruch Spinoza (*Theological Political Treatises,* chaps. 1 and 6) directly attacked the possibility of miracle in general and of prophecies in particular.

The second and opposite source is a kind of theological *Contingentism,* denying to God a definite knowledge of the future as something incompatible with human freedom and leading to fatalism. Thus Marcus Tullius Cicero (refuted by St. Augustine, *City of God* 5.9) among Stoics: Celsus, enemy of Christian doctrines (refuted by Origen, *Against Celsus* 2.20); Socinians among the first Protestants; Voltaire among Deists; Kant, founder of agnostic rationalism (*Anthropology,* § 39).

The third source is generically *Agnosticism,* common to Rationalists and Liberal Protestants (as Schleiermacher, Wegschneider, Kuenen, Lange, Sabatier), who, abstracting from the speculative possibility of prophecy, deny directly its practical possibility or its discernibility, hence inferring that prophecy has no objective value, but only a moral value and sense, as being an expression of the deep faith and morality of the men we call prophets.

Vatican Council I teaches the existence and the probative value of both miracles and prophecies: "In order that the 'obedience' of our faith should be 'consonant with reason' [cf. Rom.12:1] God has willed that to the internal aids of the Holy Spirit there should be joined external proofs of his revelation, namely: divine deeds, especially miracles and prophecies which, because they clearly show forth the omnipotence and infinite knowledge of God, are most certain signs of a divine revelation and are suited to the intelligence of all" (Sess. 3, chap. 3, Denz. 3009).

that God can reveal to man things pertaining to the supernatural order (as shown above, p. 69ff.).

2. CHRIST'S PROPHECIES, AS TO THEIR HISTORICAL TRUTH

The supernatural origin of the Christian religion can be proved by any true prophecy made in the Church at any time, because the seal of God's testimony stamped on any prophecy is a sufficient testimony. However, we shall confine our consideration to the prophecies made *by Christ himself*, as being together with his physical miracles the major testimony on whose strength and evidence the Church itself was first built and propagated.[70]

Although at first sight less noticeable than miracles, Christ's prophecies are equally scattered throughout the Gospel and are no less evident as to the definite *prediction* of future events and its exact *fulfillment*, which are the two requirements of prophecy under its historical aspect. A great harvest of such prophecies can be gathered under a threefold heading.

First in importance are the prophecies *about Christ himself*, namely, about his passion and resurrection.

Christ's passion is *predicted* not only indefinitely as to the mere fact (Matt. 9:15; 17:12; 20:22, 28; 21:33–45; 26:29; John 2:19; 3:14; 8:28; 10:17; 12:24, 32), but also with the addition of very *particular circumstances*, as Judas' betrayal, Peter's denial, Christ's deliverance into the hands of the Jewish leaders and his

---

70 Hence we leave out of our considerations:

First the *messianic prophecies* of the Old Testament about Christ, which taken all together would likewise make up an evident and sufficient criterion of Christian revelation, but only by the aid of a more careful and scientific examination, required by their less precise character (see below, pp. 149–152).

Second, the prophecies made by Christ but *not yet fulfilled* (like the prophecy about the perpetuity of the Church, as distinct from its longevity and enduring stability which is already actual, as well as the prophecy about things regarding the end of the world), because before their fulfillment they cannot be proved as true prophecies and hence they have no apologetical value, as we noted above (p. 138).

Third, that manifold and marvelous *manifestation of past and present hidden things*, often made by Christ, especially of the secrets of hearts, as the sins of the Samaritan woman (John 4:18–19, 29, 39), the interior suspicion of a Pharisee (Luke 11:38f.), the interior scorn of Simon the Pharisee about the sinful woman washing Christ's feet (Luke 7:39f.), the hostile thoughts of the Pharisees on various occasions (Matt. 9:4; 12:25; Luke 6:8), Judas' interior plan of betrayal (John 13:18). This manifestation is not about the future and hence not properly prophecy; moreover, although it is an outstanding miracle of the intellectual order and can be used as a criterion of revelation, its apologetical value is not too great, because its miraculous character is not too clear.

condemnation by them, his subsequent deliverance to the Gentiles themselves and his being mocked and spit upon by them, the scourging and the crucifixion. All these circumstances are gathered in Mark 10:32–34: "And again taking the Twelve, he began to tell them what would happen to him, saying, 'Behold we are going up to Jerusalem, and the Son of Man will be betrayed to the chief priests and the Scribes; and they will condemn him to death, and will deliver him to the Gentiles; and they will mock him, and spit upon him, and scourge him, and put him to death; and on the third day he will rise again.'" The same prophecy is found in Matthew (20:18ff.) and Luke (18:31–33) with the addition of the circumstance of crucifixion by Matthew. All four evangelists relate Judas' betrayal and Peter's denial. This prophecy in all its details was *fulfilled* to the letter, as is clear from the last chapters of the three Synoptics.

Christ's resurrection is likewise *predicted* both indefinitely (John 10:17; 11:25; 12:24; 14:19; 16:16) and with the *particular circumstance* of time, that is, "on the third day,"[71] emphasized by the double figure of the rebuilding in three days of the destroyed temple (John 2:19, 21) and of the prophet Jonas who was in the belly of the fish for three days and three nights (Matt. 12:39f., quoted above, p. 117; cf. Luke 11:29f.). This prophecy was brought up by the Pharisees themselves, both before the court of Caiaphas, as an accusation (Matt. 26:61; cf. 27:40), and before Pilate, as a precaution, for they asked him to have the sepulcher guarded for three days, because "that deceiver said: After three days I will rise again" (Matt. 27:63f.). Also the apparition after the resurrection was predicted (Matt. 26:32; Mark 14:28). This prophecy was likewise *fulfilled* to the letter, as we have shown above (pp. 128–130).

Secondly there are several general or particular prophecies *about the disciples*, all of them exactly *fulfilled*. The *general* prophecies concern the *Church*, that is, the rejection of the Jews, the conversion of the Gentiles, the expansion and stability of the Church (Matt. 8:11; 16:18 f; 24:14; 26:13; Mark 13:10; 14:9; Luke 13:29; 24:46f.; John 10:16; 12:32). Less general prophecies are about

---

71 The expression "on the third day" is found in Matt.16:21; Mark 10:34; Luke 9:22. The evangelists use also other equivalent expressions, as "until the third day," "in three days," "for three days," *"after three days"* (Matt.27:63), *"three days and three nights"* (Matt. 12:40). There is no opposition between these expressions, because even a part of the day used to be counted as a day.

the *apostles* as a group, like their flight during the passion (Matt. 26:31), the coming of the Holy Spirit upon them (John 7:39; 14:16f.; Luke 24:49; Acts 1:8; cf. 2:1ff.), the power of miracles (Mark 16:17). *Particular* or individual prophecies regard Judas' betrayal and Peter's denial (see above), Peter's primacy (Matt. 16:18f.) and martyrdom (John 21:18f.), the martyrdom of Zebedee's sons, which happened to James in a bloody manner and to John unbloodily (John 21:18–23; Acts 4:13; 5:18, 40; Apoc. 1:9).

Thirdly, two prophecies regard the *Jewish people*, namely *the spiritual downfall of Israel* or the transferring of the kingdom of God to the Gentiles, *fulfilled* in the foundation and propagation of the new Church (Matt. 8:10–12; 21:43; 24:14; Mark 13:10; Luke 21:24) and *the temporal ruin of the Jewish nation* with the destruction of Jerusalem and its temple (Matt. 24:1–35; Luke 19:41–44; 21:20–33), which was *fulfilled* in all its predicted circumstances almost within a generation. This second prophecy deserves particular attention because of its importance as an historical event and of an exegetical difficulty involved in it.

Its *importance* is evident from the detailed description of the destruction of Jerusalem and its *fulfillment* to the letter. According to the prophecy, there would be false prophets among the Jews, famines and earthquakes, a siege of the city by a Gentile army, complete destruction of Jerusalem and its temple, and captivity of the Jewish people among the nations. This all happened in the year 70, forty years after Christ's death. The general fact is attested by Roman history, according to which Jerusalem underwent a double attack of the Roman army in 66 and in 67–70, and after a long siege was captured and destroyed by Titus, afterwards emperor, who carved the event in his triumph arch, still standing in the Roman Forum. The details, given by the Jewish historian Joseph Flavius in his work *The Jewish War*, are, as predicted by Christ, the advent of false prophets before and during the siege (*ibid.* 6.5.2f.), pestilence and famine (*ibid.* 6.9.3), destruction of the temple and most of the city, with the exception of a few towers and part of the wall, left as a sign of victory and for the use of the Roman garrison (7.1.1),[72] death of the majority of the pop-

---

72 A further destruction of the towers themselves followed under emperor *Hadrian* after the year 117 on account of the rebellion of the pseudoprophet Bar Chochba. The complete destruction of what was left took place under emperor

ulation (1,100,000 persons) and captivity of the rest (97,000), destined either to be sold into slavery, or to do hard mining work in Egypt, or to the cruelties of amphitheaters, or to enhance the Roman triumph of Titus himself (*ibid.* 6.9.2f.).

The exegetical difficulty in this prophecy arises from the fact that some of the elements mingled with it do not fit the end of Jerusalem but rather the end of the world, as "the coming of the Son of Man" or the second advent of Christ, the advent of false christs who "will show great signs and wonders," the darkening of the sun and the moon, the shaking of the skies, the general resurrection (Matt. 24:23–35); all of which is said to happen within a generation: "Amen I say to you, this generation will not pass away till all these things have been accomplished" (Matt. 24:34; Mark 13:30; Luke 21:32). From this it would seem on the one hand that Christ himself, deceived by some eschatological ideas and tendencies, made a prophecy only about the end of the world within a generation, which in fact was not fulfilled, and on the other hand the first Christians, witnessing the end of Jerusalem instead of the end of the world, reshaped in an awkward manner Christ's original prophecy into a prophecy about the end of Jerusalem itself and introduced it into the Gospel. Such is the objection of Rationalists and Modernists.

However, on the one hand it is generally accepted as certain that the three Synoptic Gospels were written before the year 70, therefore before the destruction of Jerusalem,[73] and on the other hand the Gospel text is entirely genuine and not falsified by later interpolations, as serious exegetes show. This is confirmed, in our case, by the internal examination of the text itself; for, if it had been interpolated or reshaped after the destruction of Jerusalem, it would not be apparently so vague, confused and mixed up, that the exegetes are embarrassed and disagree among themselves as to

---

Julian the Apostate in 363, when the Jews, encouraged by this emperor, began to dig up the very foundations of the temple with the purpose of building a new one; in which attempt they were checked by preternatural balls of fire bursting out of the grounds, as is attested by Ammianus Marcellinus, an attendant of Julian the Apostate, *Hist.* 23.1, St. Gregory Nazianzen, *Oration about Julian* 2.4, Socrates, *Ecclesiastical History* 3.20, and Sozomen, *Ecclesiastical History* 5.22.

73 The approximate chronology of the Gospels and of the Acts of the Apostles is as follows: Matthew's Aramaic and lost gospel in the year 40–50; Matthew's Greek and present gospel in the year 62–70; Mark's gospel, 64–70; Luke's gospel, 65–70; John's gospel, 90–100; Acts of the Apostles, 62–63.

what exactly is referred to the end of Jerusalem, to the end of the world, and to both, especially with regard to that difficult assertion closing the entire pericope: "Amen I say to you, this generation will not pass away till all these things have been accomplished."

One thing is certain, namely that the Gospel text brings together a double prophecy, one about the end of Jerusalem (as is clear especially in Luke's pericope) and the other about the end of the world, and that the first has been fulfilled even within a generation.[74]

The *historical truth*[75] of such prophecies appears from external as well as from internal criteria in the same way as the historical truth of the physical miracles. Hence whatever has been said above about Christ's miracles (pp. 125 – 130) holds proportionally here as regards Christ's prophecies.

3. APOLOGETICAL VALUE OF CHRIST'S PROPHECIES

Christ's prophecies, as implying both prediction of contingent future events and its actual fulfillment, are evident and sufficient criterion of revelation, on account of their evident miraculous character.

As we stated above, speaking of miracles (p. 131f.), this apologetical value is based on three necessary elements, namely, the *historical, philosophical, and relative truth.* In other words, it has to be certain that the prophecies were made and fulfilled, that they are true miracles (although of the intellectual order), and that

---

74 Our apologetical purpose allows little importance to the question disputed among exegetes, as to the sense of "present generation." Some say that the *present generation* has to be referred to the prophecy about the end of Jerusalem; in which case it retains its proper and *historical* sense and strengthens the prophecy with the circumstance of time, matching the facts. Some on the contrary hold that it refers to the other prophecy about the end of the world; in which case the present generation is taken in an *eschatological sense*, meaning that the Jewish people, or mankind itself, will not come to an end before Christ's second advent takes place. Finally, other exegetes refer the present generation to both prophecies at once; in which case it takes a *typical or prophetic sense*, meaning that the present historical generation will not pass until both things happen, that is the end of Jerusalem in itself and the end of the world in its figure, which is shown in the end of Jerusalem.

75 Among the aforementioned *Rationalists and Agnostics*, who reject the possibility of prophecies (p. 140), some radically deny the historical truth of Christ's predictions, gratuitously attributing them to later *invention or fiction, interpolated into the Gospel* after the various events took place, to express faith in Christ or to extol his dignity. Thus H. E. G. Paulus, D. F. Strauss, R. Bultmann, A. A. Jülicher, followed by Modernists, who say that such prophecies have their origin from the later pauline doctrine of the atoning character of Christ's death, which, according to the desire of the faithful, ought to have been foreseen and predicted by Christ himself.

they were made by Christ with the manifested purpose of proving the fact of revelation, or that God was speaking through him. If these three things are certain, the fact of revelation is certain, otherwise God himself, by his miraculous intervention involved in the prophecies, would approve and endorse falsehood.

The historical truth has just been shown.

The relative truth is of itself implicit in the fact that Christ was making his prophecies in the actual exercise of his preaching as God's legate, for, this very fact turned naturally into a confirmation of his mission, and therefore he implicitly intended such reference or confirmation. Besides, this was also explicitly declared by him on several occasions; thus, after predicting Judas' betrayal, Christ added: "I tell you now before it comes to pass, that when it has come to pass you may believe that I am he" (John 13:19); predicting to the apostles his return to them after death, he declared: "And now I have told you before it comes to pass, that when it has come to pass you may believe" (John 14:29); predicting to them their future trials and persecutions, he repeated the same declaration: "But these things I have spoken to you, that when the time for them has come you may remember that I told you" (John 16:4). He predicted his resurrection as the greatest sign of his mission, thus equivalently making both, the fact of the resurrection and its prediction, the sign of his mission. (Matt. 12:39, quoted on p. 133).

The philosophical truth of Christ's prophecies,[76] namely, that they are unmistakably true miracles, due to the direct intervention of God who alone can know contingent future events, is proved by the exclusion of *natural causes, which have to be reduced to a mere*

---

76 Moderate *Rationalists*, who grant the historical truth, deny necessarily the philosophical truth of such prophecies, attributing them to a natural *power of prevision or divination*, accidentally coupled with a lucky chance.

Such power, cause of natural prophecies, would be accompanied in some extraordinary men either by *fraud and imposture*, which impels them to usurp a divine mission, or by a mere innocent *illusion*, which creates in their imagination a fictitious divine mission, or by an unusual *religious exaltation*, caused by a deeper faith and producing a kind of interior persuasion of some divine mission assigned to them.

According to this last and more common theory (developed especially by A. Kuenen and A. Sabatier) prophecy is the product of a natural and universal phenomenon of providential and normal course of history, according to which some outstanding men (as Confucius, Buddha, Zoroaster, Plato, Christ, Mohammed) connaturally rise up and express their own religious experience and aspirations, also under the form of prophecy or prediction of the future, so that it represents an object of hope rather than the knowledge of an object.

conjecture, based on a particular power of divination (either connatural or occult, that is, hypnotic or spiritistic, or even diabolic) *coupled with a lucky chance.*

Such exclusion appears from the consideration of the *subject*, or firmity of his prediction, of the *object*, which is purely contingent and very particular, and of the nature of *chance*, which is something essentially inconsistent. Indeed, it is impossible, naturally and merely conjecturing, to predict, firmly, definitely and with detailed circumstances, an event which is dependent upon the free will of God or men, remote in time, and not favored by circumstances of time and place. Besides, on the supposition that one would arbitrarily and temerariously venture such conjecture, it is impossible that such event would happen *de facto* and merely by chance, especially when it is a question of several and various predictions, for, chance is by definition something essentially inconsistent: things that happen by chance are not determined and constant.[77] But Christ's prophecies carry the aforesaid com-

---

77 From such close examination of the subject and the object it is not difficult to distinguish and detect *false prophecies*, proceeding either from a human and probable *conjecture* (due to levity, temerity, imposture, illusion, religious exaltation), or from occult natural *power of divination* (as in hypnotism and spiritism), or even from *diabolic intervention*. These are all reduced essentially to a mere conjecture, proceeding from a natural perspicacity of created intellect (human or angelic), having no firm and definite character, bearing on an indefinite object which favorable circumstances of time and place make naturally probable, and at times meeting by a lucky chance with an accidental fulfillment of their object.

Such are for instance the famous *Sibylline Oracles* of the ancient Greek religion (whose collection "Sibylline Books" was lost in the burning of the Roman Capitol in 183 B. C.; cf. H. Leclercq in *Dictionnaire d'archéologie chrétienne et de liturgie* 12-2, col. 2209–2224), partially scattered with obscurity and ambiguity, and partially interpolated after the events had taken place.

However, it is not impossible that God would permit *true prophecies also in false religions* (as we noted above about miracles, p. 132), providing they would not turn into a direct confirmation of such religions. It may even happen that a pagan or an enemy of the true religion is impelled by God to utter (consciously or unconsciously) a prophecy about or in behalf of the true religion. Such were the predictions of the pagan soothsayer Balaam, whom God compelled to make an outstanding messianic prophecy (Num. 24:15–19; cf. 2 Pet. 2:15f.; Apoc. 2:14), Caiaphas' words who, while condemning Christ, "prophesied that Jesus was to die for the nation" (John 11:41), and, according to St. Augustine (*City of God* 10.27; 18.23) and St. Thomas (*Summa Theol.*, p. II-II, q. 172, a. 6, ad 1), some of the *Sibylline Oracles*, especially the famous oracle of the Cumoean Sibyl, predicting "the great new order of times about to be born," which the poet Virgil quotes and applies to the time of emperor Augustus in his fourth eclogue. This belief in Sibylline Oracles inspired the medieval verses of our Latin liturgy: "Dies irae, dies illa, solvet saeclum in favilla, teste David cum Sibylla."

plex and definite character in their subject and object, as cursory examination of some of them will show; therefore, they are not due to a mere natural conjecture, coupled with a lucky chance.

Christ's *resurrection* could not be conjectured in any way, considering that the very object can happen only by the power and the free will of God, and is favored by no natural circumstances or dispositions. Hence it is even outside the reach of any chance.

Christ's *passion* bears unusual and unexpected circumstances which would defy any conjecture, namely: condemnation, notwithstanding his great popularity with the people up to the Sunday before his death; condemnation to death itself, rather than to exile, as was possible; death by crucifixion (not stoning), unusual among the Jews and proper to the Romans; condemnation and death by the Gentiles, not by the Jews themselves, as it would have been logical and as Pilate himself objected to the Jews (John 18:31); derision, spitting, scourging, which are very detailed and entirely contingent circumstances. Nor can one say that Christ knew from the Old Testament about the passion and death of the Messiah; for, on the one hand, all such particular circumstances are not contained in the messianic prophecies and hence they make up a prophecy themselves, and on the other hand the fact that Christ said that the passion and death prophesied about the Messiah were going to be fulfilled in his own person, constitutes a new prophecy by itself. At any rate, what kind of chance would be able to bring about such passion with such particular circumstances?

Regarding *Judas' betrayal*, although Christ through his keen sense of observation could have gradually detected Judas' disloyalty and particularly his greediness (cf. John 12:4–6), he could not naturally foresee, at least for sure and so long before it happened (cf. John 6:71f.), that he was going to betray him. For, Judas had concealed his plan so long and so well that the other apostles had no suspicion at all (cf. Matt. 26:22) and he could even to the end converse familiarly with them and with Christ (cf. John 12:4–8).

Peter's denial, rather than that of any other apostle, could not have been naturally foreseen, in view of his particular attachment to Christ, shown in several instances, as when he confessed Christ's divinity (Matt. 16:16–19: "Blessed are you, Simon Bar-Jona"), when he indignantly discarded the possibility of Christ's passion (Matt. 16:22: "Far be it from you, O Lord; this will never happen to you"), and especially when to Christ explicitly predicting his denial he vehemently protested: "Even if I should have to die with you, I will not deny you" (Matt. 26:35). Much less the particular circumstance of the cock's triple crowing could have been naturally conjectured.

The expansion and stability of the Church could not have been naturally foreseen, in view of the scanty means at her disposal and the great obstacles she would encounter (see above, p. 110).

The destruction of Jerusalem and its temple, center and base of so flourishing a people and religion, could in no way have been naturally foreseen, much less with so many and detailed circumstances. Notwithstanding the Roman yoke and its foreign character, political relations between the Jews and the Romans were not such as to suggest an imminent war, particularly because the war power of the Jewish people was so slight in comparison with that of the Romans that hardly could anyone think of a happy outcome of any war or rebellion. Furthermore, the wise Roman policy was to preserve the temples and particular monuments of the conquered peoples, even though they destroyed the cities and overturned their walls; but the temple of Jerusalem was completely destroyed by the fury of the soldiers against the explicit will of Titus himself, who entering the burning city was able to save only the upper towers. As the Jewish historian Joseph Flavius sadly remarks, no other city ever destroyed by the Romans met with such disaster. (*The Jewish War,* prologue).

We said above (p. 141) that we were not taking into consideration *the messianic prophecies about Christ in the Old Testament,* on account of their less precise character. However, as a complement of the present question on Christian prophecies, a word is to be added about these prophecies regarding their proper apologetical value.[78]

---

78   The most important and clearest messianic prophecies are found in eighteen passages, distributed as follows:

Five prophecies in the patriarchal period: Gen. 3:15 ("the seed of the woman"); Gen. 22:17f. (all nations blessed in the seed of Abraham); Gen. 49:8–12 (the King rising from the tribe of Judah); Num. 24:17–19 (the star rising from the family of Jacob; Balaam's oracle); Deut. 18:18 (the coming of the future prophet, similar to Moses).

Three prophecies in the Davidic period: Ps. 2:6–9 (the divine King); Ps. 15:9–11 (the resurrection of God's Servant); Ps. 109:1–4 (the divine King and the Priest according to the order of Melchisedech).

Ten prophecies in the period of the prophets strictly so-called: Isa. 7:14 (the virgin birth of Emmanuel); Isa. 9:1–2, 6–7 (the royal birth of the prince of peace); Isa.

Indeed, the messianic prophecies about Christ are of themselves an *evident and sufficient criterion of revelation*, because their historical, philosophical and relative truth can be known with certainty.

The historical truth appears evident from a *general and complete view of them*, as converging into a symmetrical and continuous unity of books in which they are contained, of people to which they are directed, and especially of the object which they declare.[79] The prophetic books make up an organic collection, gradually built by various authors of different character and writing in different circumstances until about the third century before Christ. The persons to whom the prophecies are addressed are one and the same Jewish people in its continuous and consistent history, with which the books themselves are intimately connected. The object of such prophecies is one and the same messianic hope of a future period of glory, peace and salvation, and such hope is made dependent on a definite person, whose character and attributes, at first outlined generically under the double aspect of savior and king (prophecies of the patriarchal period), were subsequently and progressively determined (prophecies of the Davidic period and of the time of men specifically called prophets), so that this person is distinctly said to be king, prophet and priest, Son of God, to originate in the tribe of Judah, from the line of David, by a virgin mother, in the town of Bethlehem, and one who would suffer and rise. Even discordant attributes are candidly and without hesitation predicted of him, as son of a woman and Son of God, son of David and David's Lord, humble and glorious, suffering and triumphant, dying and rising.

The *fulfillment* of such prophecies in the person and life of Christ is shown with details in the Gospel and is explicitly claimed by Christ himself. *Christ's genealogy* is traced back to David, Judah,

---

11:1–5 (the coming of the Prophet, son of David, filled with the Holy Spirit); Isa., chap. 53 entirely (the "Man of sorrows" and his passion); Jer. 23:5f. (the King, son of David); Ezech. 34:23f. (the son of David, good shepherd); Dan. 9:24–27 (the Holy of Holies, coming to restore the cult, after 70 weeks); Mich. 5:2 (Bethlehem, birthplace of the Messias); Zach. 9:9f. (the King Messias, riding a donkey); Mal. 3:1–3; appendix 5 (the King's precursor).

79   At least three of these prophecies, namely Ps. 2:1–9; Ps. 109:1–4; and Isa. 53, considered apart in themselves, show an evident character of historical truth, because they have a *literal messianic sense* which could only arbitrarily be denied, while the others could possibly be understood only in a *typical sense*, and hence they would need to be considered in the overall prophetical picture.

Jacob, Abraham, and Adam, thus showing the fulfillment of the first prophecies about the seed of the woman who was to come to save the race (Gen. 3:15), the seed of Abraham in which all nations would be blessed (Gen. 22:17f.), the star rising from the family of Jacob (Num. 24:17–19), the leader coming from the tribe of Judah (Gen. 49:8–12), the son and heir of David (Isa. 11:1–5; Jer. 23:5; Ezech. 34:23f.; 37:24f.).

Christ had his precursor in *John the Baptist*, according to the prophecy of Malachias (3:1–3; and appendix 5; both texts are referred to John by Christ himself, Matt. 11:10; 17:10–13); he was born in *Bethlehem*, the birthplace of David, according to Micheas (5:2), and of a *virgin mother* according to Isaias (7:14).

Christ explicitly claimed that he was the prophesied *Messiah* and was recognized as such by others (see above, p. 89). In his life he exercised the triple proper office of the Messiah announced by the prophets, that is, the *magisterial or prophetical office* (according to Deut. 18:18; Isa. 11:1–5); the *priestly office* (according to Ps. 109:4; Isa., chap. 53 about the "man of sorrows' dying for his people; Ezech. 34:23f. about the good shepherd; Dan. 9:24–27 about the 70 weeks), by dying on the cross, instituting the eucharistic sacrifice, substituting a new cult for the old; the *royal office* (according to Gen. 49:8–12; Num. 24:17–19; Ps. 2:6–9; 109:1–4; Isa. 9:1ff.; Jer. 23:5; Mich. 5:2; Zach. 9:9f.), entering Jerusalem triumphantly (according to Zach. 9:9f.) and declaring to Pilate that he was a king, though not of a temporal kingdom. Besides, he affirmed to be the Son of God (according to Ps. 2:6–9).

Christ ended his life through his passion as the "man of sorrows," "despised and rejected by men" (according to Isaias, chap. 53); but he did not know the corruption of the grave and arose from the dead (according to Ps. 15:9–11).

The *philosophical truth*, or miraculous character, of these prophecies is shown by the exclusion of a natural cause, that is, of conjecture coupled with lucky chance (as above, p. 148). For, it is impossible to explain through such a cause the consistency of those prophecies, notwithstanding the course of so many centuries, nor their mutual concordance, notwithstanding the great variety of prophets as to their character, time and other circumstances, in predicting long before the time (a minimum of 260 years before Christ), a fact combining many elements (the various attributes and deeds of the Messiah) and several detailed circumstances (place of birth, precursor, virgin conception, resurrection), depending on the free will of men, or even of God alone (virginal conception, resurrection), some of which were indifferent or undesirable to the people (birth in a small town, humility, ignominious passion and death, universality of the Kingdom opposed to the Jewish nationalistic ideals). Besides, even if these prophecies were one great and arbitrary conjecture, continued by many people and for so many centuries, it would still be impossible that its fulfillment should happen by a mere lucky chance, for, things do not happen fully and determinately by chance.

The *relative truth* of the same prophecies, namely, their connection with Christ's doctrine which gives to them their proper strength as a criterion of Christian revelation, is contained immediately in their very fulfillment in Christ, and thus implicitly in the intention of the prophets themselves. For, from the fact that these prophecies were fulfilled in Christ (and hence that Christ is the legate of God announced by the prophets) it follows necessarily that his teaching is from God and contains divine revelation. Besides, through his own miracles and prophecies, Christ proved that he was the legate of truth announced by the prophets and thus the Old Testament prophecies themselves received a divine confirmation.

On account of its apologetical value, the argument drawn from messianic prophecies has been constant and customary in Christian apologetics since the beginning. Christ himself insistently appealed to these prophecies as fulfilled in his person, both for his personal defense against the Jews denying his divine mission and for the instruction of the disciples and the Church. He solemnly said to the Jews: "You search the Scriptures, because in them you think that you have life everlasting. And it is they that bear witness to me, yet you are not willing to come to me that you have life" (John 5:39f.). And to his disciples after the resurrection: "These are the words which I spoke to you while I was yet with you, that all things must be fulfilled that are written in the Law of Moses and the Prophets and the Psalms concerning me ... Thus it is written; and thus the Christ should suffer, and should rise again from the dead on the third day, and repentance and remission of sins should be preached in his name to all of the nations" (Luke 24:44–47).

13
Conclusion

On the obligation of believing the revelation made by God and the genesis of the act of supernatural faith, prepared by the judgement of credibility.

As was shown above (p. 60), the formal object or the intrinsic purpose of Apologetics is to prove the evident credibility of the fact of revelation through evident criteria, or to show how a man can arrive at a sure judgment of the credibility of revelation. But there is also an extrinsic purpose to it, namely, to lead man to the act of supernatural faith itself. For this act cannot be elicited unless he has first acquired a rational evidence of the fact of revelation and elicited a certain judgment about the credibility of this fact (see above, p. 79). However, the passage from this natural judgment of credibility to the supernatural act of faith is neither necessary nor immediate, otherwise the supernatural act of faith would resolve itself into and be originated by an act of natural reason. Hence there must come, between them, an impelling act of the free will and a subsequent practical judgment by which a man affirms the obligation to believe what the speculative judgment shows as credible.

The entire process of the conversion of a man to faith includes the following steps. Since the natural law itself obliges a man to accept whatever it pleases God to reveal, even a truth of the supernatural order, as soon as he conceives a founded doubt about his natural religious belief and a solid probability about the truth of the supernatural Christian religion, he is obliged, not of course to believe as yet (since a doubtful law does not bind), but to inquire into the matter, in order to expel his doubt and to form a sure judgment about it. After this inquiry, consisting in a careful consideration the various criteria of the revealed religion, which are of themselves objectively evident and subjectively adapted to the intelligence of all, he is able to elicit the *speculative judgment of credibility* about this revealed religion ("Revelation is evidently credible"), and for this he does not need the help of grace, which however is easily granted to him (see above, p. 83).

Then, recalling the aforesaid obligation of obedience to God revealing, from this speculative judgment he proceeds under the influence of the will and the necessary help of grace to elicit the *practical judgment*, that is, the judgment about the personal obligation to believe this credible revelation ("Revelation is to be believed by me here and now"). This practical judgment is already something essentially supernatural and a proximate disposition to faith. Finally, under the influence of the will, he elicits in the intellect an *act of command to believe*, such as precedes any efficacious action of man ("Believe it"), which opens the door to faith and which, under the renewed influence of the will and of grace, is immediately followed by the *act of faith* ("I believe").

The speculative judgment of credibility does not necessarily bring in the act of faith, for the will can resist the movement of grace and interrupt the course of conversion; on the contrary the practical judgment is necessarily followed by faith, because it is the cause of the election of the will, under which the command of believing is given and the door is open to faith.

From such a process of acts and from what was said above (pp. 61, 80) it is evident that, although the natural judgment of credibility is a necessary prerequisite to the supernatural act of faith, it is in no way the *cause* of this act or the *principle* into which faith is resolved. Faith and reason live in the same intellect in a friendly symbiosis, keeping their distinct rights and objects: the judgment of credibility discharges its duties to faith, first by paving the way to it and then by remaining under that supernatural light as its rational and extrinsic foundation.

GLOSSARY OF TECHNICAL WORDS
Occurring in This Treatise

Agnosticism (from the Greek "á," a negative prefix, and "ghignósco," I know; hence, I do not know) is a philosophical system which denies the capacity of our mind to know objective truth. It is divided into *Positivistic* Agnosticism (as that of Comte and Spencer), which restricts our knowledge to experimental facts, and *Rationalistic* Agnosticism (founded by Kant), which limits our objective knowledge to an undetermined phenomenon, which makes an impression on our senses, so that all the definite concepts we have (as God, the soul, etc.) are merely subjective forms, and we cannot know whether they have a corresponding objective reality outside our mind. In this system, supernatural order, revelation, miracles, prophecies, are things whose reality cannot be ascertained. This mitigated form of Rationalism of the Kantian character was adopted among Catholics by *Modernism*, condemned in 1907 by Pius X.

Analogy means similarity of concepts and is opposed to univocity, which is identity of concepts. It is important to notice that an analogical concept is not necessarily metaphorical (as when we say: Peter is a fox), but it can be also proper; thus, if we say: Peter is son of Paul, and Christ is Son of God, the concept of sonship is proper to both Peter and Christ, although not univocal, but only analogical, inasmuch as sonship is truly found in Peter and Christ, but in different ways.

Apologetics, which etymologically means defense, is the technical name of the first part of theology which deals with the defense of revelation as a whole, against Rationalism, which denies the possibility of revelation. The defense of a particular revealed truth is more properly called apology.

Deism, etymologically from the Latin "Deus" (God), has taken historically a weakened sense in comparison to Theism, etymologically from the Greek "Theós" (God). Theism is the right philosophical system about God (called theodicy), while Deism is a rationalistic conception of the Divinity, which mutilates God in his nature and attributes in various ways, among which is found the denial of his providence (Deists were the Socinians, Cherbury, Collins, Voltaire, Rousseau). In this system revelation, miracles, prophecies, have no sense.

Essence, nature, substance of a thing are practically the same and signify the proper constituent element of something. Formally, however, this same element is called essence in relation and opposition to existence; it is called nature in relation to the acts or operations flowing from it; it is called substance in relation and opposition to the accidents placed

155

in it. Thus body and soul together are the essence of man, making him capable to exist, they are also the nature from which flow all his actions (as understanding, willing, seeing, hearing, walking, talking), and finally they are his substance, in which all his accidents are received (as intellect, will, senses, quantity, sensible qualities).

Faith subjectively is a supernatural and theological virtue dealing directly with God (as charity and hope), which makes us able to elicit the act of assenting to what God reveals (the act of faith). Objectively it is the revealed truth to which we give our supernatural assent. In this sense, which is the same as the objective revelation, we speak of truths of faith, articles of faith, symbols of faith (the Creed). In both senses Christians are called the faithful.

Fatalism is a philosophical system denying the contingency of things and consequently freedom in man. The world is conceived as a whole, enveloping and whirling in its rigid course all its parts, man included, and destiny or fate is the inescapable law of the universe. All Pantheism, whether materialistic or idealistic, is a fatalistic system, and such also is Stoicism. In this system, revelation, miracle, prophecy, have no meaning.

Immanentism is a philosophical religious system which reduces all reality to the subject (subjectivism). It began with Descartes, received a particular form with Kant, and reached its peak in the idealistic *Pantheism* of Hegel. It took a different form in *Pragmatism* (especially with William James), which is a general tendency to consider everything from the practical viewpoint, that is, in terms of action, seeking in action itself the reason of truth and certainty. It was recently adopted in Catholic Apologetics, especially by M. Blondel (†1949) and L. Laberthonnière (†1932), under the name of *"method of immanence"* or *"Apologetics of immanence,"* which gives undue importance and preference to the subjective criteria (satisfactions of human aspirations) over the objective extrinsic criteria (miracles and prophecies) in proving the divine origin of Christian religion.

Miracle, etymologically wonder, theologically is something which is above the established order of powers of every created nature and hence cannot be done but by God. Any wonder done by angels or demons or men is not a miracle, unless they work as instruments of God. Also things done by God himself according to an order established by him, are not miracles, such as creation, elevation, justification. Hence the proper and specific note of a miracle is its extraordinary character, that is, its being outside the order and laws established by God in all created things.

Modernism is a heresy which consciously or unconsciously arose among Catholics at the beginning of this century and was condemned by Pius X in 1910 in the Decree "Lamentabili" and in the Encyclical "Pascendi." It is based on three philosophical principles or systems, that is, *Kantian agnosticism*, which denies the possibility of objective knowledge, *immanentism*, which makes God and religion an effect of an inner sense or conscience, and *evolutionism*, which teaches that reality does not consist in being but in becoming. Hence religion with all its dogmas is only a fruit of a blind conscience, continually developing and expressing itself in new formulas without an objective reality that could be ascertained. In this system, supernatural order, revelation, miracles, prophecies, have no objective but only symbolic value.

Mystery etymologically and generically means something hidden, especially to knowledge, hence a secret. In theology it is taken with regard to God's revelation, and it means something which is so secret to us that it cannot be known without God's revelation. If after God's revelation such thing is perfectly clear to us (for instance if God reveals to me that in about a year or two there will be again a general war), it is a mystery in a broader sense; if on the contrary it still remains obscure as to its intimate nature, it is a mystery in the strict sense. Such are Trinity, Incarnation, revelation, grace, justification, beatific vision, etc., which we call the mysteries of our faith precisely because even after revelation they remain secret and unknown as to their intimate nature, and before the beatific vision are not seen but only believed through the obscure light of faith. All such mysteries are intrinsically supernatural.

Object of a science, or rather of any knowing faculty, is the subject matter under consideration. Material object is the concrete subject under consideration without distinction, as the concrete body which I see with my eyes. The formal object is that particular aspect or quality which is considered in the subject, as color under which my eyes see a body. The formal light is the degree of immateriality found in the formal object, which makes this object knowable, for, knowing consists in abstracting or separating an object from its material conditions.

Optimism is a theological system, held by the Protestant W. Leibniz (†1716) and the Catholic N. Malebranche (†1715), which teaches that God was morally forced by his own goodness and dignity to create the best possible world (in the case that he chose to create, as he did). Hence the natural laws, being the best, are immutable and exceptions to them, that is, miracles, are impossible. What appears to be a miracle is only an effect of angelic creatures or of natural laws still unknown.

Rationalism is a general philosophico-theological system proclaiming the absolute autonomy of the natural reason, to whose judgment all knowable object and truth is subject, including God and his world. In such system, which embraces various extreme or mitigated forms from Deism to Atheism, supernatural order and its connections, as revelation, miracles, prophecies, have no meaning at all. Rationalism takes two general forms. One extreme, or *Positive Rationalism*, especially pantheistic, either materialistic (as that of E. Haeckel) or idealistic (as that of Hegel), which denies the existence of God and of the supernatural order, identifying God with the world. The other mitigated, or *Agnostic Rationalism*, which denies the existence of God and of the supernatural order only practically, by denying that we can know such supernatural objects, even if they exist.

In the question of miracles Positive Rationalism takes two different forms, from which the denial of miracles equally follows. One is *Determinism*, which affirms the absolute fixity of the natural laws, allowing no exceptions; the other is *Contingentism*, which affirms the absolute instability of those laws, or rather their nonexistence, and therefore the impossibility of exceptions to nonextant laws.

Revelation is taken either actively, for the action of God revealing, or passively, for its effect in man. The passive revelation is taken again in two ways, namely, objectively, for the object or truth presented to the intellect of man, and subjectively, for the supernatural light infused in the intellect to enable it to understand such truth. Hence flows the difference between revelation and the other two divine lights or helps, namely, *inspiration*, given to the hagiographers who wrote the Holy Scripture, and *assistance of the Holy Spirit*, given to the infallible Magisterium of the Church. In the three cases the subject is preserved from error. But in revelation, man receives the knowledge of a truth. In inspiration he receives no knowledge but he is only moved by God in such manner as to write without error things that he already knows and also with such influence as to become only an instrument of God, principal author of the writing. In the case of the assistance of the Holy Spirit the Magisterium receives no revelation nor inspiration but merely an assistance (either supernatural or natural, but ever providential) by which it is preserved from error in its pronouncements.

Supernatural in the strict and absolute theological sense is that which is above all created nature and its powers. If it is above created nature itself, it is said to be essentially supernatural (as Trinity, Incarnation, revelation of strict mysteries, sanctifying grace); if it is only above the powers of nature, it is said to be modally supernatural (as physical miracles and prophecies). All things that we call supernatural (faith, mysteries, revelation, truths, graces of all kinds, lights, helps, virtues, etc.) belong to either of these two kinds of supernaturality.

ANALYTICAL INDEX

Analogy. Our analogical concepts have an objective value also when they are used to express revelation, 67, 71f. An analogical concept can be either purely metaphorical or proper, footnote 6

Apologetics. Meaning and use of the name, footnote 1. Its definition and object, 59f. It is an extension or a fundamental part of theology, 59. Its purpose is to prove the credibility of revelation, 59–61, 77, 153. *See Credibility, Criteria*

Augustine (St.). On the necessity of the judgment of credibility, prior to faith, footnote 24. Definition of miracle, 119, footnote 54. Words are the principal signs of the mind, 66. Man's heart is restless until it rests in God, 96

Certitude. Absolute certitude is founded on the nature of things, while conditional certitude is founded only in physical and moral laws, and hence it is divided into physical and moral certitude, footnote 21. Moral certitude of the fact of revelation is necessary for eliciting the act of supernatural faith, 79–82. This extrinsic certitude is essentially different from the intrinsic certitude of faith itself, footnote 2. Convergent probabilities may produce a true certitude, 117

Christ. The question of the historical Christ is still brought up from time to time, footnote 29. Christ's holiness and outstanding virtues as a criterion of the divine origin of his religion, 103f. The origin of his doctrine and the manner of his teaching show a wondrous character, 100f. His testimony about his divine mission, 89–91. The exercise of his magisterial function, 90f. As to Christ's miracles, prophecies, and resurrection, *see these three entries.* Besides prophecies, Christ made many miraculous manifestations of past and present hidden events, footnote 70

Church. The Church, in itself and as a whole, represents a great miracle of the moral order, and hence a certain and outstanding criterion of its divine origin, 82, 116–117. Probable criteria of its divine origin are its sublime doctrine, 100–103, 111f., its sanctity, 105–107, 112f., its expansion, unity, and stability, 107–110, 113–116. Number of the persecutions and of the martyrs of the Church, 106f. In about seventy years after Christ's death the Church reached the limits of the civilized Roman world, 107f. and at the beginning of the fourth century at least the fifth of the population of the Roman empire was Christian, 108f.

Civilization. *See Culture*

Credibility. Notion, 77f. Credibility of the fact of revelation is the proper object of Apologetics, 59–61, 77, 153. It is the rational and necessary foundation of the supernatural faith, 79–82. The proper meaning of

"Reasonable submission," stressed by St. Paul (Rom. 12:1), 75, footnote 13. *See Criteria. Faith*

Criteria. General notion and division of the criteria of revelation, 85f. They are called signs, or motives of credibility, or criteria of revelation, footnote 28. Strictly speaking there is only one criterion of revelation, namely, miracle, 85, 98, 99, 110, 118, 131. Subjective criteria (fulfillment of human aspirations) are only probable criteria, contrary to a recent opinion exaggerating their importance, 97–99, footnote 38. Objective intrinsic criteria (doctrine, sanctity and other qualities of the Church) are likewise only probable criteria, 110–117. However, such probable criteria are very useful in practice, footnote 49. The only certain criteria are physical miracles and prophecies; *see these entries*

Culture. The Church with its revealed doctrines has always fostered culture and civilization, 93–96. There is a threefold culture and civilization, namely, corporal, intellectual, and moral; Catholic peoples are expected to be superior to others only in moral civilization and in that part of the intellectual civilization which regards religion, 95f. The Church has restored and improved the morals of the world, 105f.

Desire of God, naturally felt by man, is the sign of his capacity to be elevated to a supernatural order, 72. About this natural desire much has been written in recent years, footnote 12

Faith. The rational certitude of the fact of revelation is necessary for eliciting the act of supernatural faith, 79–82. However, faith is not directly based on or reduced to such a rational credibility, 80, 154, footnotes 2 and 25. The genesis of divine faith in the intellect follows several natural and supernatural steps, footnote 66, 80, 153. Faith and reason stand in full agreement in the same human intellect, 72, 74f., 81. Demons have a natural faith, based on the evident judgment of the fact of revelation, 83. *See Intellect, Reason*

Grace is not necessary for eliciting the judgment of evident credibility of revelation, 83f.

Intellect. God's revelation involves the infusion of a supernatural light in the intellect, 67, 72–73. The human intellect has a radical capacity to reach something beyond its natural specific object, 72. The natural light and activity of the intellect is in no way disturbed by the infusion of the supernatural light of revelation, 72, 74f., 80f. *See Credibility, Faith, Reason, Revelation, Supernatural*

Martyr. Notion of martyrdom, footnote 41. Martyrs are an outstanding motive of credibility of the Christian religion, 106–107. Their history, motive, and manner of suffering, 106–107. Number of persecutions and of martyrs, 106f., footnote 43

Messias. Meaning and use of this title, footnote 31, given to Christ in the gospels, 89f. The concept of Messias in the O. T., 90f.

Miracle. Biblical use of this word, footnote 53. Nature and division of miracle, 118–121. The specific character of miracle is to be something extraordinary, that is, beyond the laws established by God in all created nature, 120f. Creation, infusion of soul in the body, elevation, justification, are not miracles, 120f. Any extraordinary thing produced by angels or demons is not a miracle, 120. Physical miracle is only modally supernatural, footnote 8. The principal division of miracles is into miracle as to substance, as to subject, and as to manner, 121f., 124, 134. The possibility of miracle is based on the contingency of the physical laws and on the omnipotence of God, 121f. Miracle is not opposed to God's wisdom and goodness, 122f. The possibility of miracle is denied by Rationalists under two opposed forms of Determinism and Contingentism, footnotes 57 and 59. They attribute miracles either to fiction or to natural causes, as unknown forces of nature, mental suggestion, or occultism, footnotes 65 and 67. False or true miracles in pagan religions, footnotes 61 and 64. Christ's miracles are historically true, 124–130. The great variety of his miracles, 124f. His greatest miracle is his own resurrection; *see this entry*. Christ's miracles are evident and certain proof of the divine origin of his religion, 131–137. In several of these miracles there takes place a universal effect, which cannot be produced but by God, the universal cause, 134–136. *See Prophecy, Supernatural*

Modernism. *See Rationalism*

Mystery, as to its notion and division, footnote 8. *See Supernatural*

Natural Laws. Physical and moral laws, unlike the metaphysical, are contingent, and hence they allow exceptions, like miracles, 121–122. Among rationalistic systems, Determinism teaches absolute fixity of the laws of nature, while Contingentism holds their complete instability; in both cases the possibility of miracle is denied, footnote 57. *See Miracle*

Necessity, either physical or moral, footnote 14

Obediential Potency, as to its notion, 72, footnote 10, and as a basis of supernatural elevation and revelation, 72f.

Pagans. The imperfect ethics of the great pagan philosophers, such as Plato and Aristotle, footnote 40. False miracles and prophecies and possibility of true miracles and prophecies among pagans, footnotes 61 and 77. Various religious truths found in Hinduism, Buddhism, and Islam, as expounded by Vatican II, footnote 47

Prophecy. Notion and division, 139f. Its proper object is a contingent future event, depending on the free will of God or man, 139. As a criterion of revelation it requires not only the prediction of a future event but also its fulfillment, 139. Its possibility is based on the universal knowledge of God and of its revelation to man, 140f. Christ's prophecies are historically true, 141–145. His principal prophecy regards his own resurrection, 142f.; among other prophecies particular importance is to be given to the one about the destruction of Jerusalem, 143–145, 149, footnotes 72–74. Christ's prophecies are certain criteria of the divine origin of his religion, for no natural cause can account for them, 145–149. The messianic prophecies of the O. T. are also certain criteria of the same truth, 149–152; they are found especially in eighteen passages of the patriarchal, Davidic, and prophetical eras, footnote 78f. Distinction between true and false prophecies, footnote 77. Rationalism denies the trueness of prophecies, on the basis of Fatalism, or Contingentism, or Agnosticism, footnote 69, and attributes them to natural divination, accompanied by fraud, illusion, or religious exaltation, footnote 76

Rationalism teaches the following: There is no supernatural order (Positive Rationalism) or at least it cannot be known by man (Agnostic Rationalism, like Modernism), footnote 7. Revelation is not necessary nor fitting, but rather harmful to human reason, 74, footnote 33. Miracle is not possible, because the laws of nature are either absolutely fixed (Determinism), or completely contingent (Contingentism), footnote 57. Christ's miracles are either historically not true, or they can be explained through natural causes, footnotes 59, 63, 65, 67. Christ's resurrection can be attributed to fraud, error, or fiction, footnotes 59, 63. Prophecies can be attributed to natural divination, coupled with fraud, illusion, or religious exaltation, footnotes 76, 77

Reason is perfected by revelation, both in the speculative and in the practical order, 74–76, 92–97. Without revelation, natural reason cannot suitably reach natural truths concerning religion and morals, 76f. See *Faith, Intellect, Revelation*

Religion. Christian religion compared to other religions and cultures, 95f., 97, 98, 102f., 111, 112, 116. It is in no way derived from other religions or philosophies, 102f.

Resurrection can be considered as a miracle either of the first or of the second class, footnote 55. Christ's resurrection is historically true, 128–130. Its miraculous character is evident from the fact that in it a universal effect takes place, which requires a universal cause, God alone, 134. Rationalists deny its historical truth, attributing it to fraud, error, or fiction, footnotes 59 and 63. Christ's prophecy about his resurrection, 142f., 147. See *Miracle*

Revelation. Biblical concept of revelation, 65f., and its definition, 66–68. Vatican II did not change the traditional definition of revelation as being essentially a speech of God, 66f., footnote 5. Distinction of revelation from inspiration and assistance of the Holy Spirit, 67. With respect to theology, revelation is its light, principle, and foundation, 59. *See Faith, Intellect, Reason, Supernatural*

Sanctity, as a fruit of Christian religion, 103–107, and a criterion of its divine origin, 112f., 116. *See Martyrs*

Supernatural. Notion and division, footnote 8. Various supernatural lights in human intellect, 67f. The existence of a supernatural order follows from the very existence of God as transcending the proper object of the human intellect, 70f. Physical miracles are supernatural not essentially but modally, 128. The supernatural truths of Christian religion are in full harmony with natural truths, 101–103. *See Faith, Reason, Revelation*

Tertullian testifies to the extraordinary expansion of the Church at his time, 109, footnote 45. His famous axiom about "the soul being naturally Christian," 93, 96

Thomas Aquinas (St.) on definition and division of miracle, 119, footnotes 54 and 56; on necessity of revelation for the suitable knowledge of natural truths, footnote 17

Vatican I. Definition of revelation, 66, its possibility, 71, fittingness and necessity, 74f., 75, footnote 17. Existence of evident criteria of revelation, especially miracles and prophecies, footnotes 2 and 69. The Church promotes human culture, footnote 33

Vatican II. Definition of revelation, 66f. On the necessity of divine help for preparation to faith, footnote 27. Revealed doctrine fulfills the human aspirations and is fitting to the present conditions of the world, 92–94. In pagan religions, as Hinduism, Buddhism, and Islam, are found several elements of truth, footnote 47

BIBLIOGRAPHY

Arcy, M. C. d', Belief and Reason, London 1944; The Nature of Belief, London 1945.

Baillie, J., The Idea of Revelation in Recent Thought, London 1956.

Balthasar, H. U. von, Word and Revelation (trans. From the German by A. V. Littledale and A. Dru), New York 1965.

Broglie, G. de, Revelation and Reason, London 1965.

Bulst, W., Revelation (tr. B. Vawter , New York 1965.

Daniélou, J., God and the Ways of Knowing (tr. W. Roberts), New York 1975.

Doronzo, E., Theologia dogmatica I (Washington 1966) 93398.

Gardiel, A., La crèdibilitè et l'apologètique, Paris 1908; 2nd ed., 1912.

Garrigou-Lagrange, R., De revelation per Ecclesiam catholicam proposita, 2 vols., 1917; 5th ed., 1950.

Latourelle, R., "La revelation comme parole, tèmoignage et rencontre," Gregorianum 43 (1962) 39–54; Theology of Revelation (trans. From the French), New York 1966; Christ and the Church; Signs of Salvation (trans. From the French by Sr. D. Parker), New York 1972.

Lèonard, A., "Vers une thèologie de la Parole de Dieu,: La Parole de Dieu en Jèsus-Christ (Tournai 1951) 11–32.

McDonald, H. D., Ideas of Revelation: An Historical Study 2 vols, London 1959–1963.

Mysterium Salutis. Dogmatique de l'histoire du salut (translation of the German collective work), I/1: Histoire du salut et revelation, Paris 1969.

Niebuhr, H. R., The Meaning of Revelation, New York 1960.

Pauwels, C. F., Apologetik, Ruremonde 1948.

Quinn, E., "Revelation: Propositions or Encounter," Downside Review 79 (1960–61) 10–21.

Rabeau, G., Apologètique, Paris 1930.

Ratzinger, J., Rahner, K., Revelation and Tradition (trans. From the German), Freiburg 1966.

Tresmontant, Cl., Le problème de la revelation, Paris 1969.

Various Authors, "La thèologie fondamentale á la recherché de son iden-titè," Gregorianum 50 (1969) 757–776.

Vatican II. La revelation divine (collective work), Paris 1968.

Waldenfels, J., Offenbarung, München 1969.

White, V., "St Thomas's Conception of Revelation," Dominican Studies 1 (1948) 3–34.

Wilckens, U., God's Revelation (trans. From the German), London 1967.

BOOK 3
The Channels of Revelation

INTRODUCTION

IN THE PRECEDING TREATISE THE FACT OF REV-
elation has been established through evident criteria. The question which now logically follows is: where do we find this revelation? What are the channels which bring it to us, so that we may
know surely and exactly what we should believe? These channels
are considered here formally as theological *"loci,"* that is, as "places"
or bases of theological investigation.

Hence this treatise is a kind of theological dialectics (theological logic, or theological methodology) and belongs to fundamental theology. But, unlike the preceding tract which is merely
apologetic, it considers the channels of revelation as the intrinsic
foundation of theology and proceeds under the light of revelation
itself. Hence it is a *dogmatic fundamental theology.*

This treatise may be defined: A scientific inquiry on the probative value of the channels of revelation, carried out under the
light of revelation itself. The channels of revelation (or "loci")
are the material object of this treatise, their probative value is
its formal object, and the light of revelation is its formal reason.[1]

The channels through which revelation comes to us, and hence
the "loci" or places where theologians find the principles and
bases for their investigation, are essentially three, namely, Scripture, Tradition, and the Magisterium,[2] with this difference how-

---

1 For the meaning of these three expressions, see our treatise on *Introduction to
Theology*, pp. 11–15, and its *Glossary*, under the entry: Object of a science, p. 49.
2 According to the list given by Melchior Cano (the founder of this treatise), and
commonly followed by later theologians the *theological "loci" would be ten*, of which
seven are taken on the part of revelation itself, namely, Scripture, Tradition, the
believing Church (the sense of the faithful), the Magisterium of the Pope, the
Magisterium of the Councils, the Fathers, the theologians; and three are derived
extrinsically from the natural reason, that is, this reason itself according to its
natural and scientific principles, the authority of philosophers, and human history.

Discarding these three extrinsic "loci," which can only lightly confirm a theological truth and help a theological investigation, all the other seven "loci" can be
reduced to three, namely Scripture, Magisterium and Tradition. In fact, the Popes
and Councils make up one general Magisterium, while the believing Church, the
Fathers and the theologians, in as much as they are witnesses of Tradition, can be
reduced to Tradition itself. The Fathers and theologians as private doctors have
only a limited and fallible authority; they will be considered under this aspect
together with the believing Church in special notes after the treatment of Tradition (pp. 188–196).

ever, that Scripture and Tradition are also deposits of revelation, that is, places in which revelation has been deposited and kept by God, while the Magisterium is only the organ (guardian, dispenser, interpreter) of revelation.[3]

This treatise is divided into two parts. The first deals with the three channels considered in themselves as to their nature and probative value, i.e., Scripture (chap. 1), Tradition (chap. 2), Magisterium (chap. 3). The second considers the theological content of these channels, particularly of the Magisterium, that is, dogma (chap. 4), theological conclusions (chap. 5), theological notes and censures (chap. 6).

---

3 With regard to terminology, until Vatican Council II Scripture and Tradition were usually called the *two sources* of revelation. Both by theologians and in the documents of the recent Magisterium thus the title of the present treatise was "On the Sources of Revelation" (together with the title "On Theological "Loci"): Pius XI speaks of the sources of revelation (Encycl. "Mortalium Animos" 1928, AAS XX 12) and Pius XII uses the same plural expression five times in his Encycl. "Humani generis" 1950 (Denz. 3886; he uses even the expression "both sources"). *Vatican II*, however, preferred a slightly different terminology, according to which the *source* of revelation is the Gospel itself (that is Christ's preaching), while Scripture and Tradition are the *deposit* (even the one *deposit*) of revelation, "entrusted" to the Magisterium.

    Following this reformed terminology, we call *source* of revelation, the gospel itself; *channels* of revelation, Scripture, Tradition, and the Magisterium; deposit (or deposits since, at least materially, they are two) of revelation, Scripture and Tradition; *organ* of revelation, the Magisterium.

PART I
The Three Channels of Revelation

1

Scripture, The Written Deposit of Revelation[4]

1. THE NATURE OF SCRIPTURE

We shall gather under this heading and briefly explain five questions which are treated extensively by biblical scholars, namely, the inspiration, canonicity, authenticity, inerrancy and interpretation of Holy Scripture. These properties are all defined or taught by the Council of Trent (Sess. 4, Denz. 1501–1508), Vatican I (Sess. 3, Denz. 3029), Leo XIII (Encycl. "Providentissimus," Denz. 3291–3293), Pius XII (Encycl. "Divino afflante Spiritu," Denz. 3825–3831), and Vatican II (Dogmatic Constitution on Divine Revelation, nos. 11–13).

Inspiration as a fact is defined by Trent and Vatican I. Its nature is described as a direct action of God into the intellect and will of the hagiographers, on account of which their writings are to be attributed to God himself as their principal author (Vatican I; Leo XIII; Vatican II). Its extension embraces all the canonical books of both Testaments, "in their entirety and in all their parts" (Trent; Vatican I; Vatican II), "in everything asserted by the inspired authors" (Vatican II) and not only in "matters of faith and morals" (Leo XIII); briefly, "everything the hagiographer asserts, enunciates, suggests" (Biblical Commission, June. 18, 1915, Denz. 3629).

Canonicity, that is, the definite canon or list of books which must be considered as inspired, is proposed as *de fide* by Trent and Vatican I.

---

4   Cf. J. Levie, "Les limites de la preuve d'Ecriture Sainte en théologie," *Nouvelle revue théologique* 71 (1949) 1009–1029; A. Bea, "Il progresso nell' interpretazione della S. Scrittura," *Gregorianum* 33 (1952) 85–105; L. Alonso-Schokel, "Argument d' Ecriture et théologie biblique dans l'enseignement théologique." *Nouvelle revue théologique* 91 (1959) 337–354; *Schrift und Tradition* (collective work), Essen 1962; *De Scriptura et Traditione* (collective work), Rome 1963; J. Dupont, "Ecriture et Tradition," *Nouvelle revue théologique* 85 (1963) 337–356, 449–468; *Mysterium salutis. Dogmatique de l'histoire du salut* (collective work translated from the German), I 2: *La révélation dans l'Ecriture et la Tradition*, Paris 1969; E. Hamel, "L'Ecriture, âme de la théologie," *Gregorianum* 52 (1971) 511–535.

The *authenticity* of the text of these books is explicitly declared by Trent and confirmed by Vatican I as regards the Latin version called the "Vulgate," by reason of its "approbation by the Church through many centuries of usage in public lectures, sermons, and explanations" (Trent, Denz. 1506; Vatican I, Denz. 3006). Two corollaries are drawn from this declaration. One is literary, namely, that the Vulgate is substantially in conformity with the original, so that it contains all and only the inspired books, as well as all the dogmatic original texts, in their sum total (although there may be a doubt or a dispute about one or another particular text, especially if it regards a modal discrepancy with the original text as critically established). The other corollary is dogmatic, namely, that the text of the Vulgate is immune from all error in matters of faith and morals, and it can be used safely and without danger of erring.

The *inerrancy* of the entire biblical text, being a mere consequence of its inspiration, can be considered implicitly defined by Trent and Vatican I, at least as regards matters of faith and morals. The absolute exclusion of all error, even in other matters, follows from the same inspiration, which makes God author of the entire text, and is considered by Leo XIII as likewise defined by the Magisterium (Denz. 3292 f).

As regards the *interpretation*, or hermeneutics, of the text, biblical scholars distinguish a *threefold sense*, namely, literal, typical, and ampler.[5]

The *literal sense* (or grammatical, historical, logical sense is that which the letter or words immediately carry and which is intended by the writer as such.[6] This is the necessary and primary sense in a biblical text, as in every speech or writing; the presence of only a typical sense would not be sufficient to justify the words of Scripture, for the typical sense must be based on the literal sense, as will be shown below. The literal sense, intended in a biblical text, is only one, at least according to the more common

---

5 The so called *accommodated sense*, based on some likeness with what is said and signified in the biblical text, is not a biblical sense. It can be used and is in fact used by preachers and spiritual writers; but this should be done with discretion and moderation. Lest such sense be mistaken for the real sense or its use involve disrespect for the sacred text. See *Verbum Domini* (1938) 272–278.

6 The literal sense can be either *proper* (as if I say: Peter is sly) or *metaphorical* (If I say: Peter is a fox). If an entire speech or pericope is metaphorical, its sense is called allegoric, and in the case of a particular form of allegory it is called parabolic (cf. *Summa Theol.*, I, q. 1, a. 10, ad. 3).

opinion. Otherwise fallacy or equivocation would be attributed to God, as was found in the oracles of pagan religions. These often carried a double contrary meaning so that the prediction would be true in either event.[7]

The *typical sense* (or real, spiritual, mystical sense) is that which is not attached to the words themselves but to the things or persons signified by the words, and therefore is not intended by the biblical writer but only by God inspiring his words. Hence, it cannot be known but through God's revelation, that is, from Scripture or Tradition or the sense of the Church, for the hagiographer himself under the inspiration and revelation, or the Church, under the assistance of the Holy Spirit, can infallibly interpret the sense of the Holy Scripture. Several typical senses are certainly proposed by the hagiographers themselves, either explicitly (Matt. 2:15, 19:36; Cor. 10:1–11; Gal. 4:23–31) or implicitly (Matt. 5:5, 26:28; Col. 2:11 f; Heb. 12:22; Apoc. 2:7).

The *ampler sense* ("sensus plenior" called also the ultra-literal or evangelical sense) would be a sense between the literal and the typical, introduced and stressed by several modern exegetes,[8] but rejected by others.[9] It would be a sense intended by God alone in the very words of the hagiographer, beyond the sense understood and intended by the latter.[10] It seems difficult to admit such a sense, for it would be at once literal (on the part of God) and not literal (on the part of the hagiographer); in such case the words would carry an extra sense which they do not have, since they are words proceeding from the mind of the hagiographer, whom God uses as an instrument. Hence, this opinion seems to proceed from a false notion of inspiration, because God inspires only and all that the hagiographer says, and the biblical text proceeds totally from

---

7 Cf. *Problemi scelti di teologia contemporanea* (Rome 1954) 251–273.

8 As A. Fernández, *Institutiones biblicae*, vol. 1, p. 390; D. P. De Ambroggi, J. Renié, D. Buzy, J. Cerfaux, J. M. Braun, M. Nicolau, J. Coppens (see *Ephemerides theologicae Lovanienses* [1958] 5–20).

9 As R. Bierberg, in *Catholic Biblical Quarterly* (1949) 182–185; J. Daniélou (see *Ephemerides theologicae Lovanienses* [1948] 119–126); G. Courtade (see *Recherches de science religieuse* [1950] 481–497).

10 This sense is used by the aforementioned exegetes, especially in explaining some of the messianic prophecies, which the prophets would not have understood in the full messianic meaning intended by God. Thus, for instance, in the Emmanuel conceived of a young woman (the Hebrew 'almâh, translated by virgin), Isaias (7:14) may have understood Ezechias, son of Achaz, while God intended Christ, the Messias.

two causes, that is, from God as principal author and from the hagiographer as God's instrument. There is no point in appealing to the case of the typical sense, intended by God and not understood by the hagiographer; for this sense is not attached to the *words* themselves, but only to the *things* signified by the words. Thus it is extrinsic to the words and is known only through the extrinsic revelation of God.[11]

2. THE PROBATIVE VALUE OF SCRIPTURE, AS A THEOLOGICAL PLACE

This value can be expressed with the following norms and rules.

First norm. Since Scripture is a true deposit of revelation, enhanced moreover by the charism of inspiration, it is a *proper, primary, privileged, and independent theological place,* from which a theologian can confidently proceed in his investigation, drawing from it certain or probable arguments, according to whether the sense of a biblical text is certain or only probable. It is true that Scripture depends on Tradition and particularly on the Magisterium with regard to the interpretation of its sense; but, once this sense has been established, theologians argue directly from Scripture, as from a proper and primary place, even before arguing either from Tradition, or from the Magisterium, which, being only the organ and guardian of the deposit of faith, is inferior to it.[12]

Second norm. Since the Vulgate version, and this alone, has been declared authentic by the Magisterium, that is, substantially in conformity with the original text, the theologian can and must take it into consideration in his labor, giving it preference to any other version or original text critically established. However, since this declaration of the Magisterium regards only the substantial conformity, in case of doubt as to the conformity of some particular text of the Vulgate with the original text as critically established, only a probable argument can be drawn from it, and, in the

---

11 With regard to the messianic prophecies, those that cannot be sufficiently explained by the literal sense, are aptly and fully explained by the typical sense, without recourse to any "ampler sense."

12 Vatican II emphasizes this inferiority, saying: "The Magisterium is not above the Word of God, but rather ministers to it, teaching only what has been handed on. Thus, by divine commission and under the assistance of the Holy Spirit, the Magisterium listens to the Word of God piously, guards it religiously and exposes it faithfully, drawing from this deposit of faith all those things which it proposes to be believed as divinely revealed" (Dogmatic Constitution on Divine revelation, no. 10).

case of *certain* discrepancy, no biblical argument can be claimed but only an argument of Tradition, inasmuch as Tradition *de facto* used the text to express its faith in a particular truth. At any rate, the critical investigation of the original text is very useful to the theologian, even for the right understanding of the Vulgate text, and hence he should be aware of the critical conclusion of the exegetes about a particular text, before introducing it into his theological elaboration.[13]

Third norm. Regarding the *interpretation of the sense of a biblical text*, we may distinguish three rules.

The first and supreme rule is the sense given by Tradition and the Magisterium, as is explicitly and repeatedly stated by the Magisterium itself. (Trent, Denz. 1507; Vatican I, Denz. 3007; Pius XII in his Encycl. "Humani Generis;" Vatican II, Dogm. Constitution on Divine Revelation, nos. 10, 12, 23, 26). In particular note the following. The morally unanimous agreement of the *Fathers* in interpreting a biblical text, if it implies a positive and firm assertion about an object considered as pertaining to faith, makes their interpretation absolutely certain, for this agreement is the voice of Tradition; on the contrary a similar agreement of mere theologians makes their interpretation only probable, because they are only fallible witnesses to Tradition. Likewise the authentic interpretation of a text, given by the *solemn Magisterium*, is absolutely certain. This is done in two ways. Either *directly* with the manifested intention of interpreting a particular text; such is the case of Rom. 5:12 on the universality of original sin, children included; John 3:5, on the necessity of true water in Baptism; Matt. 26:26ff. and parallel texts, on the Eucharist in its proper sense; John 20:22f. on the sacrament of Penance; Jas. 5:14f., on the Anointing of the Sick; Luke 22:19, on the institution of the priesthood; Matt. 16:16f. and John 21:15ff., on Peter's primacy (Denz. 1514, 1615, 1637, 1703, 1716, 1752, 3053). Or *indirectly*, by merely bringing forth a biblical text with the evident intention of confirming a particular truth; thus the Council of Trent introduces Rom. 5:12 to confirm the doctrine of original sin, and 2 Tim. 1:6f. in confirmation of the sacrament of Orders (Denz. 1512, 1766). However, such intention is not always clear, for often

---

13 Cf. Pius XII, Encyc. "Divino afflante Spiritu" 1943 (Denz. 3825).

the Magisterium quotes Scriptural texts only as a mere illustration and explanation. In this case there is no authentic interpretation, but merely a suitable use of such texts. Also the *ordinary Magisterium* enjoys per se the same authoritative interpretation, although the discernibility of its pronouncements is not so easy, by reason of the manifold elements by which this Magisterium is made up and carried out.

The second and subsidiary rule is the recourse to the so-called "analogy of faith," that is, the mutual agreement which must exist between the different truths of the same faith, so that one cannot contradict the others, but rather one can illustrate another similar to it or connected with it. For example, the Eucharist can be illustrated by the Incarnation and vice versa, the mystery of the Church by the mystery of Christ and vice versa, and the power of granting indulgences by the general power of remitting sin.[14]

The third rule (the only one left if the other two fail) is the *exegetical examination of the text*, according to the two biblical senses, the literal and the typical (since the so-called "ampler sense" seems hardly useful). Although the typical sense is truly biblical, being intended by God, and often nobler, on account of a higher object signified, the theologian should turn his attention primarily to the *literal sense*, for several reasons. *First*, because it is necessary and universal, that is, found in every word, while the typical sense is only occasionally attached to the text. *Secondly*, because it is fundamental, since the typical sense is based on it and depends on it. *Thirdly*, because it is more manifest and certain, since it is known God's revelation. *Fourthly*, because it is scientifically more efficacious, and hence more suitable to theological investigation (it is even the only one which fits an apologetical or rational purpose).[15]

---

14 This expression is found in several documents of the recent Magisterium. See Leo XIII, Encycl. "Providentissimus" (Denz. 3283); Pius X, Anti-Modernist Oath (Denz. 3546); Pius XII, Encycl. "Humani generis" (Denz. 3887); Vatican II, Dogmatic Constitution on Divine Revelation (no. 12). About the use of the "analogy of faith" in theological investigation see our treatise on *Introduction to Theology*, p. 22.

15 Cf. *Pius XII*, Encycl. "Divino afflante Spiritu" 1943 (Denz. 3829f.) *Vatican II* insists especially on the observation of the "literary forms," in which the various books were written, considered both generically, whether, for instance, their style is poetical or prophetical, or historical, and specifically, that is, with regard to the contemporary style, influenced by circumstances of time and culture (Dogmatic Constitution on Divine Revelation, no. 12).

Having clearly established the literal sense of a text the theologian should turn his attention to its *typical sense*,[16] which often is the principal sense intended by God and which has a truly demonstrative force. Thus, for example, from the fact that Melchisedech as a priest was the typical figure of Christ, as St. Paul testifies, we rightly and certainly infer that Christ, like Melchisedech, offered a sacrifice. However, the existence of the typical sense in a particular text should not be easily asserted, for it is known only by revelation which is not clear in many cases. Moreover, even when the existence of the typical sense is certain, its extension should not be unduly exaggerated; thus, from the sure fact that Melchisedech is a typical figure of Christ by reason of the superiority of his priesthood over the priesthood of Aaron, it does not necessarily follow that he is the figure of Christ also under the other characters, by which his excellence is described in genesis, and that we can necessarily infer such characters in Christ.

Hence the theologian should use only the more certain types and take them only within the more certain limits of their typicality. The apostles (particularly St. Paul) could handle the typical sense more freely and more surely on account of their charism of inspiration and revelation, and so could the Fathers, by reason of a special assistance of the Holy Spirit and of a connatural intuition, fruit of a deeper spiritual life and of an intimate familiarity with the truths of faith; but theologians do not enjoy such spiritual gifts.

---

16   Cf. *Pius XII* in the same Encyclical (Denz. 3828).

2

Tradition, The Living Deposit of Revelation[17]

1. THE NATURE OF TRADITION A) GENERAL NOTION

Tradition (in Latin "Traditio," from "trans-do," that is, I hand over; in Greek "Parádosis" from "pará-didomai," I hand over) etymologically means the action of handing over something from one to another (active Tradition), and by logical extension, it means also the thing, or object handed over (objective Tradition). In this double meaning of active and objective Tradition the word was used to signify the handing over of Christian doctrines and usages, and it became classical in Christian literature as well as in theology. Scripture speaks of doctrinal traditions of the Pharisees (Matt. 15:2, 3, 6; Mark 7:3, 5, 8, 9, 13), of heretics (Col. 2:8), and of the apostles themselves (1 Cor. 11:2; 2 Thess. 2:14; 3:6). The Fathers and the theologians up to the Council of Trent used the word Tradition only in the general and complete sense of the entire Christian revelation entrusted by Christ and the Apostles to the Church and by the Church transmitted continuously through whatever means (either written or oral). After

---

17   Cf. R. Hull, "The Council of Trent and Tradition" *American Ecclesiastical Review* 81 (1929) 469–482, 605–615; Ch. Baumgartner, "Tradition et Magistère," *Recherches de science religieuse* 41 (1953) 161–187; G. Dejaifve, "Bible, Tradition, Magistère dans le théologie catholique," *Nouvelle revue théologique* 78 (1956) 133–151. D. Van den Eynde, "Tradizione e Magistero," *Problemi e orientamenti di teologia dommatica* 1 (Milano 1957) 231–252; *Schrift und Tradition* (collective work), Essen 1962; *De Scriptura et traditione* (collective work), Roma 1963; J. Dupont, "Ecriture et Tradition," *Nouvelle revue théologique* 85 (1963) 337–356, 449–468; Y. Congar, *The Meaning of Tradition* (trans. A. N. Woodrow), New York 1964; *Tradition and Traditions*, New York, 1967; J. Ratzinger and K. Rahner, *Revelation and tradition* (trans. From the German), Freiburg 1966; *Mysterium salutis. Dogmatique de l'histoire du salut* (trans from the German), I 2: *La revelation dans l'Ecriture et la Tradition*, Paris 1969; P. Lengsfeld, "La tradition dans le temps constitutif de la revelation," *Mysterium salutis* I 2 (Paris 1969) 13–72; "Tradition et Ecriture. Leur rapport," *ibid.* 270–310; A. Kerrigan, "Doctrina Concilii Vaticani I de 'sine scripto Traditionibus'," *De doctrina Concilii Vaticani Primi* (Città del Vaticano 1969) 3–26; A. Meredith, *The Theology of Tradition*, Notre Dame, Indiana 1971; J. Pelikan, *The Christian Tradition*, 1: *The Emergence of the Catholic Tradition* (100–600), Chicago 1971.

the Council of Trent, however, by reason of the Protestant claim that the Christian doctrine is found and transmitted only in the written scripture, theologians took Tradition also in the particular and restricted sense of whatever would be found and transmitted only orally and not in the Scripture.

Hence the *objective Tradition* in theology is taken in two senses. *First* and more properly, it signifies the *integral Tradition*, that is, everything handed over in the Church from Christ and the apostles down to us, whether through inspired writings (Scripture) or orally (through other means than Scripture). *Secondly*, it signifies the *partial Tradition*, that is, only that part of doctrines and usages which is not explicitly or sufficiently found in Scripture but only in the oral Tradition.

The *active Tradition* (or the action by which Christian doctrine is transmitted) in the apostolic times consisted in preaching (Christ, the apostles, their disciples) and in inspired writings (Scripture). In the following ages it consists in common preaching, in the declarations of the Magisterium under the assistance of the Holy Spirit, in the non-inspired writings of the Fathers and of the other ecclesiastical doctors, and also, equivalently or implicitly, in various practical means by which the faith of the Church and of the people manifests itself, such as liturgical practices (liturgy), canonical laws (having dogmatic foundation), and artistic productions (archaeological, architectural, sculptural, pictorial).

b) *The proper character of Tradition as deposit of revelation*

Tradition, taken as a whole (integral Tradition) is a true and ever living deposit of revelation, whether it be written in inspired Scripture or given through other means; hence Scripture is not the only deposit of revelation or the only rule of faith.

This has been defined, as *de fide*, against older and recent adversaries[18] by the Council of Trent, declaring that "the truth and

---

18 In the second century Irenaeus and Tertullian opposed to the *Gnostics* the force of Tradition. In the fourth century *Pelagius*, founder of Pelagianism, is quoted by St. Augustine as saying: "Let us believe what we read [in Scripture], and judge as unlawful to build up what we do not read" (St. Augustine, *On Nature and Grace* 39). Not long before the rise of Protestantism, *John Wyclif* repeated: "A truth, which is not found in Scripture, does not exist" (*On Civil Power* 1.44, ed. Poole, pag, 339). The *Protestants* hold as fundamental the aphorism "Scripture is the only rule of

the discipline [first promulgated by Christ and preached by the Apostles] is contained in the written books and in the unwritten traditions, which have been received by the Apostles from the mouth of Christ himself, or under the dictation of the Holy Spirit have been transmitted by the Apostles and have come down to us as it were from hand to hand" (Sess. 4, Denz. 1501). This definition has been repeated verbatim by Vatican I (Sess. 3, chap. 2, Denz 3006) and explained more at length by Vatican II (Dogm. Constit. On Divine Revelation, nos. 7–10).

The truth of this statement of the Magisterium is also apparent from the following considerations. *First*, Christ himself wrote no books, but only preached his doctrine, and gave likewise the apostles no command to consign his doctrines to writings, but commanded them to preach them to all nations under the continued assistance of the Holy Spirit (Matt. 28:18f.; Mark 16:15; John 14:16, 26); hence Christ deposited his revelation in a living and perpetual Tradition.

Secondly, the apostles constantly claimed for themselves the office of preaching (1 Cor. 7:17; 11:23; 2 Cor. 1:18; Gal. 1:8; Col. 2:6; 2 Thess. 2:14), but never the task of writing. Hence they proposed the living Tradition as the main deposit of revelation. In particular St. Paul entrusted the same office to his disciple Timothy, saying: "Hold to the form of sound teaching which thou hast heard from me... Guard the good trust through the Holy Spirit... The things that thou hast heard from me through many witnesses, commend to trustworthy men who shall be competent in turn to teach others" (2 Tim. 1:13f.; 2:2) and he reminded the Thessalonians of his teaching given to them through his words

---

faith" (thus Luther, Melanchthon, Calvin, and all the Confessions of Protestant faith, including the Anglican).

Regarding the preaching of the apostles themselves, the Protestants teach that it was for the time being a source of revelation, but after the hagiographers consigned into inspired writing the truths preached by the apostles, this Scripture succeeded to the preached word as the only deposit of revelation and the only rule of faith. Several modern Protestants, particularly among Anglicans and French-Swiss Calvinists, grant some connatural value to Tradition in interpreting the sense of Scripture, but they hold that only Scripture has of itself the force of rule of faith. The various valuations of modern Protestants are described in the work *Scripture and Tradition*, London, 1955.

In the Catholic work *De Scriptura et Traditione* (Roma 1963) 506–512, there is a sufficient explanation of the doctrine of both the first Reformers (Luther, Melanchthon, Calvin) and the mitigated modern Protestants (I. A. Leuba, O. Cullmann, Fr. Leenhardt, M. Thurian).

and his previous letter: "Stand firm, and hold the teachings that you have learned, whether by word or by letter of ours" (2 Thess. 2:14; the letter here is pointed out not as something special and formal, but as one of the two means by which *de facto* St. Paul communicated his doctrine to the Thessalonians).

Thirdly, the New Testament Scripture does not bear the character of an official compendium of doctrines and laws, authoritatively given to the faithful, but it shows only a limited, or secondary, or occasional character. It is a collection of historical narratives on the life of Christ and on the acts of the apostles, of pastoral and instructional letters, and of future apocalyptical events, written unevenly by few of the apostles (Matthew, author of one gospel; John, author of another gospel, three short epistles and the Apocalypse; James and Jude, each author of one epistle; Peter, author of two epistles; Paul, author of most of the epistles). If the apostles had intended to leave after them the Scripture to succeed their preaching as the sole norm of faith, all of them would have cooperated, at least through a common consultation, to its drafting and they would have written it in clear and orderly manner, in the form of a code of doctrines and laws for the Church, as was done by Moses in the Old Testament for the synagogue.

Fourthly, even after the Holy Scripture, or part of it, had been written, the apostles kept appealing to the authority of their preaching; only once or twice they mentioned occasionally the authority of one or another writing of the New Testament; thus St. Peter, 2nd ep. 3:15f., mentions the authority of the epistles of St. Paul, and John in the Apoc. 1:11; 22:7, 9, 19,18f., testifies to the prophetical character of his own book; St. Paul himself in his second epistle to the Thessalonians refers to his first epistle merely as to one of the two means by which he had exposed his doctrine to them (see above).

If we compare this integral Tradition with Scripture, it is manifest that it is an older ampler and more independent deposit of revelation. It is older than Scripture, because the preaching of the revealed truth had been steadily going on for about twenty years before the oldest writings of the Holy Scripture (the two epistles of St. Paul to the Thessalonians) came out.[19] It is *ampler* than Scripture,

---

19   Christ preached his gospel for about two years before his death, which took place in the year 30 of our era, and he continued to instruct the apostles for forty

first because it includes Scripture itself, which is a written Tradition and then because it contains some truths and customs which were not consigned or sufficiently expressed in Scripture (see below). It is a *more independent* and self-sufficient deposit, because it does not depend on Scripture for its interpretation, while Scripture depends on Tradition both for its interpretation (see above, p. 175) and for its own authority since we know only from Tradition that Scripture (at least as a whole) is inspired; besides, Scripture is not absolutely necessary for the Church, but Tradition with the Magisterium as its interpreter would have been strictly sufficient.

On the other hand *Scripture enjoys a relative excellence over the unwritten Tradition*, first, because it is precisely a written document, for writings are more definite and more easily preserved from alteration (according to the aphorism "Words fly, writings remain"), and secondly and especially because it is written by God himself through the inspiration of the hagiographer. Hence we understand why God provided the Church and its Magisterium with this privileged channel, so that Christ's teaching could be handed over more surely and easily, and the Magisterium itself would be helped in its examination and finding of the revealed truth by the collation of both deposits of revelation. By reason of this intimate connection and community of purpose between Scripture and unwritten Tradition, we may say with Vatican II that they make up together one single and total deposit of revelation.[20]

We stated above (p. 179) that Tradition can be taken in two senses, that is, as integral Tradition, which includes Scripture itself, and as partial or *constitutive Tradition*, which is distinct from Scripture as to its object, because it contains some doctrines and usages not sufficiently shown in Scripture. Lately some writers have denied the very existence of *constitutive Tradition* as regards the revealed truths (not the usages), claiming that these truths

---

days after the resurrection. The apostles after the Pentecost kept on preaching for about twenty years before the first writings of the Holy Scripture, namely, the two epistles of St. Paul to the Thessalonians, were issued (about 50–51; a first gospel of St. Matthew, suppositively written in Aramaic between 40 and 50, is lost and is not part of the actual canon of Scripture). The three Synoptic Gospels and the Acts of the Apostles were written between the year 62 and the year 70; the Apocalypse about the year 95; and St. John's gospel between 90 and 100.

20   Dogmatic Constitution on Divine Revelation, no. 9f.

are contained totally in Scripture and totally in Tradition, and hence there is no constitutive but only declarative Tradition, which only explains and declares what is already sufficiently contained in Scripture.[21] This opinion was simply rejected and severely criticized by other theologians of the traditional type, as being opposed to the declarations of Trent and Vatican I (see above p. 179).[22] However, other authors have tried to follow a middle opinion, saying that all the revealed truths are in some way truly contained in Scripture, but only as to their substance, or virtually, or implicitly, or not simply, so that Tradition accidentally and truly completes Scripture.[23]

Discarding the particular features of this debate, there are four things which seem to be admitted by everyone. First, several matters concerning discipline (morals and usages) of divine origin and connected with revealed truths (for instance infant Baptism) are found in Tradition and not sufficiently in Scripture; hence there is a *constitutive Tradition* regarding these. Secondly, the canonicity and inspiration of Scripture as a whole is known only through Tradition and not through Scripture itself (see above p. 181); hence there is also a *constitutive Tradition* regarding this important truth. Thirdly, the knowledge of several truths, as derived from Scripture, is not certain unless it is completed by the data of Tradition; hence there is a *completive Tradition* in this regard. Fourthly, the knowledge of other truths derived from Scripture is

---

21   This opinion which gave rise to a sharp controversy, was proposed for the first time, at least explicitly and definitely, in 1956 by J. R. Geiselmann, "Das Missverstandnis über das Verhaltnis von Schrift und Tradition und seine Ueberwindung in der katholischen Theologie," Una Sancta 11 (1956) 131–150; *Die Heilige Schrift und die Tradition* ("Quaestiones disputatae" 18), Freiburg-Basel-Wien 1962. He was followed by several other writers, particularly by G. H. Tavard, *Holy Writ or Holy Church. The Crisis of the Protestant Reformation*, London 1959; cf. his two articles in *Theological Studies* (1962) 337–405; (1963) 278–290, and H. Holstein, "La Tradition d'après le concile de Trente," *Recherches de science religieuse* (1959) 367–390; *La Tradition dans l'Eglise*, Paris, 1960.

22   Thus H. Lennerz (who was the first to attack Geiselmann), "Scriptura sola?," *Gregorianum* 40 (1959) 39–53; "Sine scripto traditiones," *ibid.* 42 (1961) 517–522; C. Boyer, "Traditions apostoliques non écrites," *Doctor Communis* 15 (1962) 5–21; cf. *ibid.* 16 (1963) 51–57; 17 (1964) 5–19; B. Xiberta, *La Tradición y su problemática actual*, Barcelona 1964; several among the writers in the collective works *Schrift und Tradition*, Essen 1962, and *De Scriptura et Traditione*, Roma 1963, edited on the occasion of this controversy and of the opening of Vatican Council II.

23   Thus, among others, J. Beumer in the collective work *De Scriptura et Traditione* (Roma 1963) 17–40, and Y. M.-J. Congar, in *Revue des sciences philosophiques et théologiques* 48 (1964) 645–657.

further illustrated and confirmed by Tradition; and hence there is a *declarative Tradition*. These are the four ways in which Tradition truly completes and perfects Scripture.[24]

But, furthermore, it seems to us that the *constitutive Tradition* must be enlarged with regard to several other truths, which can hardly be said to be sufficiently expressed or indicated in Scripture, even implicitly, so as to be necessarily drawn from other truths, explicitly related in it. Such are, for instance, the validity of Baptism administered by a heretic or a pagan, which St. Augustine claims from Tradition alone (*On Baptism* 5.23); the necessity of Baptism for infants, or their inclusion in John 3:5, which the Council of Trent refers to the "tradition of the apostles" (Sess. 5, can. 4, Denz. 1514); the non-necessity of Communion for infants, or their non-inclusion in John 6:53, according to the same Council (Sess. 21, chap. 4, Denz. 1730); the sevenfold number of the sacraments; the cult of images, which St. John Damascene refers to Tradition (*On the Orthodox Faith* 4.16); the Immaculate Conception and the Assumption of the Blessed Virgin, truths which were developed only in later Tradition through the sense of the faithful.

However, we can say that these and all the other revealed truths are found also in Scripture in some way, inasmuch as one can always find in Scripture itself *some seed or foundation* from which they can be derived by means of the data of Tradition. Thus

---

24 These are also the conclusions briefly indicated by Vatican II (Dogm. Constit. On Divine Revelation, no. 8f.). The Council teaches: "Through Tradition the complete canon of the Sacred Books comes to be known by the Church"; "through Tradition the Sacred Writings are more fully understood and become unceasingly active"; "Tradition transmits integrally the word of God to the successors of the apostles [that is, to the Magisterium], so that through their preaching they may faithfully preserve, explain, and spread it"; "The Church draws its certitude about all the revealed things not from the Sacred Scripture alone."

The Council, therefore, attributes four things to Tradition, namely, the knowledge of the canonical books, a fuller understanding of what is contained in Scripture, the transmission of the entire revelation, and the certitude about all the revealed truths. The first two things are attributed to Tradition alone, as distinct from Scripture; of which the very first shows a constitutive Tradition, the second a completive, or at least a declarative, Tradition.

In one passage the Council says that "the apostolic preaching is expressed in a special manner in the inspired books." This refers both to the character and force of the charism of inspiration, and to the fullness of particular facts and circumstances about Christ's life and the apostolic ministry, known through the Gospels and the Acts.

we can understand better how Scripture and Tradition complete each other and make up, as it were, one single deposit of revelation having two modes of expression, interrelated and necessary for the full knowledge of a revealed truth. This seems to be the mind of the Vatican Council II, when it prefers to speak of "one deposit of revelation," as well as of Pius XII himself who, defining the Assumption of the Blessed Virgin, declares: "All these arguments and considerations of the Holy Father and theologians are based on the Sacred Writings as their ultimate foundation" (Denz. 3900).

c) Discernibility of Tradition

There are two ways, or criteria, through which we can find out for certain whether a doctrine or practice belongs to Tradition.

The *first* and primary criterion is *the declaration of the Magisterium,* especially the infallible and solemn. Hence, if the Magisterium explicitly declares that a doctrine is found in Tradition, it is certainly so; if the Magisterium merely defines or teaches a doctrine, such a doctrine is necessarily found in the deposit of revelation, and hence either in Scripture or Tradition or both.

The *second* criterion (open both to the theologian and to the Magisterium itself which, before defining a truth must inquire whether it is really contained in the deposit of revelation) is the examination of the various means through which the objective Tradition is transmitted, or in which the active Tradition consists (see above p. 179). This criterion is generically expressed in the famous statement of *Vincent of Lerins* (†before 450): "In the Catholic Church great care must be taken *that we hold what has been believed everywhere, always, and by all*" (*Commonitorium primum,* chap. 2); this is to say, that a doctrine which *de facto* is universally believed, belongs to Tradition. This universality of belief can be ascertained especially in two ways, namely through the doctrine of the Fathers and through the common sense of the faithful. Hence if the Fathers commonly teach, as a truth of faith, a doctrine not sufficiently contained in Scripture, such a doctrine has surely been transmitted or developed by Tradition; likewise, if a doctrine, whose origin cannot be ascertained through the Fathers or the Councils, is nevertheless commonly believed in the Church, it certainly comes down from Tradition.

2. THE PROBATIVE VALUE OF TRADITION, AS A THEOLOGY PLACE

This value can be expressed with the following *six norms*.

First norm. Since Tradition is a true and primary deposit of revelation, it is consequently a *proper, primary and independent theological place*, from which a theologian can confidently proceed in his investigation. It is a primary place even with respect to Scripture, in the sense explained above (p. 181). It is simply independent from Scripture, even for its interpretation, it is also independent from the Magisterium, not as to its interpretation (for the Magisterium interprets both Scripture and Tradition), but as to its probative force, as explained above with regard to Scripture (p. 174).

Second norm. In interpreting the sense of Tradition, the first and supreme rule is the *authentic declaration of the Magisterium*, as we stated also for Scripture (p. 175). However, this does not dispense a theologian from inquiring directly into the various means by which Tradition is handed over (see above p. 179), in order to clarify the truth of the magisterial declaration and to complete his own theological knowledge.

Third norm. A theological argument or investigation can be based on any of the means by which Tradition is handed over, as the Magisterium, the Fathers, liturgy, etc.; but it will be more effective, if it is *based on several at once*, in the manner of a synthesis, showing how a truth flows from the original source through the various channels and branches of the same Tradition.

Fourth norm. Among these means, the *doctrine of the Fathers* has a particular value and a greater force in any argument drawn from Tradition, because it is scientifically the surest and easiest way to find the truth; this is the reason why the argument from Tradition is often called "argument from the Fathers" and is confined mainly to their doctrine.[25] In the making of such an argument, the texts should be critically and certainly established, the doctrine should be carefully valuated, to make sure that the Fathers speak of a doctrine about faith or morals and propose it positively (not merely opiniatively) as something to be held with

---

25 We are dealing here with the Fathers only as witnesses of Tradition or as part of it. Further below (pp. 190–192) we shall consider them as private doctors having a personal and fallible authority and we will also explain the proper concept and meaning of the title "Father of the Church"

faith, and finally the morally unanimous agreement of the Fathers on such a doctrine should be established.[26]

Fifth norm. Since a particular truth can be contained in Tradition *only implicitly and later become explicit* through legitimate and logical progress in the Christian mind and conscience (see below p. 213), the argument of Tradition for such a truth consists precisely in showing how it was implicitly contained in another explicit truth since the beginning and how afterwards it progressed step by step from implicit to explicit. Thus, for the truth of the Immaculate Conception, the logical and historical steps of its progress were: the fullness of grace in Mary (the biblical "Hail, full of grace"), the comparison with the purity of Eve before the original sin (several Fathers), the greatest sanctity after that of Christ as was fitting divine maternity (Fathers and theologians, particularly S. Thomas), finally privileged immunity from original sin in conception (definition of the Magisterium).

Sixth norm. When the preceding direct ways of determining a traditional truth fail or are less efficacious (by reason of the lack of documents or the multiplicity of elements necessary to show the continuity of a doctrine with the apostolic times), the theologian may have recourse to the so-called *argument of prescription*, which, although indirect, is likewise based on Tradition.[27]

---

26 In order to have a morally unanimous agreement, it is sufficient that all the Fathers of *one age* agree; for, Tradition being one and immutable, one age cannot disagree with another. It is also sufficient that all the Fathers of *one large part of the Church*, for instance the Western or the Eastern regions, agree, while the other part does not positively disagree; for, the Church being one in faith, it is impossible that a large part of it disagrees with the other about the same faith. Likewise, it is sufficient that *several outstanding Fathers*, in various principal churches and in various places and times, agree; for, it is impossible that a large and important part of the Church be lacking in faith. It may also happen that the doctrine of *very few Fathers*, or even of *one single Father*, be sufficient, as expressing the tacit agreement of the others, if those Fathers or that Father have been recognized (particularly by the Magisterium) as doctors or defenders of the common faith in a particular circumstance or with regard to a particular dogma, as is the case of St. Athanasius in the question of Incarnation against Arianism, and of St. Augustine in the question of grace against Pelagianism.

27 This argument was sagaciously introduced and effectively used first by Tertullian in his work *On the Prescription of Heretics* (about the year 200), who transferred analogically the concept of prescription from its proper juridical object to the apologetico-theological field, Its basic principle is: "The possessor has the juridical advantage" ("Melior est conditio possidentis"); which means that no one can be disturbed in his peaceful and continued possession of something, until certain documents are brought forward to prove that he has no right on such thing. Cf. P. De Labriolle "L'argument de prescription," *Revue d'histoire et de litterature religieuse* (1906) 408–429, 497–514.

This argument can take a negative or a positive form. Its *negative form* amounts to this: The Church, in some determined age and for a long time before, has peacefully taught a doctrine as being of apostolic origin (for instance the doctrine of the seven sacraments, held explicitly from the 12th to the 16th centuries, when the Protestants attacked it). But adversaries cannot prove the non-apostolic origin of such a doctrine, or assign the author, time, place, manner, by which it would have arisen in some subsequent age. Therefore, they have no right to attack the apostolic origin of such doctrine and the Church has the title of prescription of such doctrine, that is, the right of not being disturbed in its profession.

Its *positive and stronger form*, which goes beyond the mere concept of prescription by showing the exclusion of possible causes of a post-apostolic origin of some doctrine, runs as follows: If a doctrine, which is considered apostolic, would have been introduced in some later time, this would have happened in two ways, namely, either by a common conspiracy of deception, or by a general relaxation, carelessness, and inadvertence, through which an error would have been slowly introduced. Now, both ways are excluded, in view of the diversity of places and persons, and especially of the zeal of many faithful and pastors in guarding the deposit of faith. Therefore, such a doctrine is truly of apostolic origin and pertains to Tradition.

NOTE 1. ON THE SENSE OF THE FAITHFUL AS A THEOLOGICAL PLACE[28]

We stated above (p. 185) that one of the ways of discerning Tradition, is to consult the common sense of the faithful. This common sense can be considered as one of the means by which Tradition is handed over, or rather it is an outstanding *witness to Tradition.*

The importance of this witness lies in its *infallibility,* usually called *passive infallibility* (with respect to the *active* infallibility of the Magisterium, which has a great influence on it); however it likewise has its own true active character as being also under the direct influence of the Holy Spirit. This infallibility is based on the assistance of the Holy Spirit promised by Christ to the Church as a

---

28 Cf. F. Marin-Sola, *L'évolution homogène du dogme catholique* (Fribourg, Swisse 1924) 353–392; C. Balic, "Il senso Cristiano e il progresso del dogma," *Gregorianum* 33 (1952) 106–134; W. M. Thompson, "Sensus fidelium and Infallibility," *American Ecclesiastical Review* 167 (1973) 450–486.

whole, even abstracting from the Magisterium (cf. John 14:16; 17, 20–22; 1 Tim. 3:14, where the entire Church is called "the pillar and the mainstay of the truth"). It is shown also by the following considerations. The purpose of the infallible Magisterium, which is to direct and strengthen the faith of the Christian people (cf. Matt. 16:18; 28:18–20), would be frustrated if the people would ever err in matters of faith. The Fathers in their controversies with heretics, and the Magisterium itself in its definitions, appeal to the common sense of the faithful; thus Pius IX before defining the Immaculate Conception inquired of the bishops throughout the world "what was the piety and devotion of their faithful toward the Immaculate Conception of the Mother of God;" moreover the Vatican Council II explicitly declared the infallibility of the Christian people, as a property of the prophetic office of the Church in which they share.[29]

Reason itself illustrates this truth by an analogical comparison with that kind of natural infallibility, resting on intuition, which is found in the so-called common sense. For, just as this natural sense spontaneously springs up from common natural reason, on the basis of evident general principles, and becomes an acknowledged criterion manifesting natural truth, so the common agreement of the faithful about some super natural truth can not but spring connaturally from their common faith, infused and moved in their hearts by the Holy Spirit.[30]

The principal *means of discerning* this sense of the faithful are Christian literature, the practice of prayer and devotions, popular preaching, and the monuments of Christian art itself (architectural, sculptural, pictorial).

By reason of its infallibility, this Christian sense, besides being a witness or sign of Tradition, can be taken also as a *distinct theological place*, having by itself the force of a principle of theological

---

29 "The holy People of God shares also in the prophetic office of Christ, by spreading a living testimony to Him especially by a life of faith and charity and by offering to God a sacrifice of praise, the fruit of lips praising His name (cf. Heb. 13:15). The whole body of the faithful, anointed as it is by the Holy One (cf. John 2:20 and 27), cannot be deceived in his belief. It manifests this property by means of the supernatural sense of faith of the whole people, when, 'from the Bishops down to the lowest member of the laity' [St. Augustine, *On the Predestination of Saints* 14.27] it shows a universal agreement in matters of faith and morals" (Dogmatic Constitution on the Church, no. 12).
30 Cf. Marin-Sola, *op. cit.* 382f.

argumentation. However, it must be used with careful discretion, that is, only when the universal agreement of the Christian people is certain and when it is question of principal and more common truths which alone are easily brought into explicit and general knowledge, as well as into definite and common practice, just as in the order of natural truths no one would reasonably appeal to the common sense, except in those things which are of interest to all and suitable to the intelligence and judgment of all.

NOTE 2. ON THE FATHERS OF THE CHURCH AS A THEOLOGICAL PLACE[31]

The Fathers of the Church can be considered in two ways. *First as witnesses to Tradition*, as we considered them above (pp. 175, 179, 185, 186), and thus they are a primary and sure theological place, or rather they mingle with other elements into one primary theological place which is Tradition itself. *Secondly*, they can be considered in themselves or in their capacity and value *as private doctors* in the Church, and thus they represent a particular and distinct theological place, but of secondary and mere probable value, as we shall explain below, after a brief determination of the notion of Father of the Church and of the connected notions of ecclesiastical writer and of Doctor of the Church.

Father of the Church, as a title of traditional use, was originally connected with the concept of generating others in Christian faith, and later received its full theological meaning, according to which Father of the Church is properly defined: *He who, by reason of a particular holiness, eminent and orthodox doctrine, remote antiquity, and ecclesiastical approbation, had a connatural influence in the generation of the faithful and the propagation of the faith.*

Hence four qualities are required in a man to deserve such title. *Particular holiness* is required, by reason of the intimate connection between Christian life and Christian doctrine. *Eminent and orthodox doctrine* is required by the concept of paternity in faith, lest the petty would generate the petty and the blind would guide the blind; however, the eminence of doctrine is to be understood relatively to the time and other circumstances (as is, for instance, effective refutation of heresies); orthodoxy is not affected by a particular

---

31 Cf. Y. M.-J. Congar, "Les Saints Pères, organs privilégiés de la Tradition," *Irénikon* 35 (1962) 479–498.

error, either secondary (as found in many Fathers) or material (as was St. Cyprian's error on rebaptism). *Remote antiquity*, or nearness to the beginnings of the Church, is required that one may be considered as generating and bringing to maturity the adolescent Church; this condition applies strictly to the first five centuries, (up to and including St. Gregory the Great †604), but theologians commonly extend the patristic age to the eighth century, more exactly up to St. Isidore of Seville (†636) in the West and to St. John Damascene (†about 749) in the East. *Ecclesiastical approbation* is required because only the Magisterium is qualified to judge on the orthodoxy of a writer; this approbation is given either in general, inasmuch as Councils and Roman Pontiffs in their acts refer generically to the authority of the Fathers, or in particular, and again either implicitly, if the works of a writer are publicly used in the acts of the Magisterium, or explicitly, if the works of an individual writer are commended by name (thus St. Augustine's works were directly commended by Popes Celestine and Hormisdas; Saints Cyprian, Gregory Nazianzen, Basil, Athanasius, and others, were commended by Pope Gelasius; cf. Denz. 237, 353) or even solemnly by the attribution of the special title "Doctor of the Church" (as Saints Ambrose, Augustine, Jerome, and others; see below).

Ecclesiastical writer, in the strict sense and as distinguished from "Father," is the one who enjoys antiquity but lacks one or another of the three remaining properties required in a Father, that is, holiness, orthodoxy, or approbation of the Church. Especially by reason of the lack of full orthodoxy, the title of Father of the Church is to be refused to some very outstanding ecclesiastical writers, such as Tertullian, Origen, and Eusebius of Caesarea.[32] However, in the theological argument from the Fathers or from Tradition, these and other ecclesiastical writers are included on account of the value of their remaining doctrine, in which they are at times far superior to those who are properly Fathers; such is Tertullian in apologetics, Origen in exegesis and generally in

---

32 The following are not strictly Fathers: some among the so-called Apologists of the second century, that is, Aristides, Athenagoras, and Tatian (this one on account of his heretical Encratism); likewise Tertullian (on account of his montanist heresy), Origen (who was condemned several times for some unorthodox opinions, such as the preexistence of souls and the universal eschatological rearrangement of the fate of men), Arnobius, Lactantius, Eusebius of Caesarea (who was not sufficiently exempt from Arianism), Rufinus of Aquilea (who indirectly favored Origenism), Theodoret of Cyrus and Theodore of Mopsuesta (for their connection with Nestorianism).

theology, and Eusebius of Caesarea in ecclesiastical history.[33]

Doctor of the Church is a special and specific title given by the Magisterium, since the end of the thirteenth century (starting from Boniface VIII in 1295). It was first given to some of the Fathers, and then also to theologians and other ecclesiastical writers, for both their holiness and their eminent doctrine, which in some particular matter or manner contributed to the building up of the faith. Up to the present time 32 have been declared doctors, 20 among the Fathers and 12 among theologians (of whom two are women, Catherine of Siena and Teresa of Avila). The first Fathers declared doctors by Boniface VIII in 1295 are the four great doctors of the West: Ambrose, Augustine, Jerome, and Gregory the Great; much later Pius V in 1568 gave the same title to the four great doctors of the East, Athanasius. Basil, Gregory of Nazianzus, and Chrysostom. The first theologian to receive the title was St. Thomas Aquinas (by Pius V in 1567) and the second was St. Bonaventure (by Sixtus V in 1588).[34]

The Fathers (and proportionally also the other ecclesiastical writers), not as witnesses to Tradition (see above, p. 186) but as *private doctors*, that is, when they do not propose a doctrine as to be held by faith or do not unanimously agree on such a doctrine, make up a *proper and distinct theological place, but only secondary and probable*, on which therefore a theologian can base only a probable argumentation.

However, these probable patristic arguments are not to be discarded or undervalued, for these writers greatly contributed to the increase and evolution of theological science, as is evident

---

33   Often in the same argument are included also some of the outstanding writers of the late patristic or medieval age, particularly Bede (†735), Anselm of Canterbury (†1109), and Bernard of Clairvaux (†1153).

34   The other doctors among the Fathers, besides the eight just mentioned, are: Anselm of Canterbury (declared doctor in 1720), Isidore of Seville (1722), Peter Chrysologus (1729), Leo the Great (1754), Peter Damian (1828), Bernard of Clairvaux (1830), Hilary of Poitiers (1851), Cyril of Alexandria (1882), Cyril of Jerusalem (1882), John Damascene (1890), Bede (1899), Ephraem (1920).

The other doctors among theologians, besides St. Thomas and St. Bonaventure, are: St. Alphonsus Liguori (1871), St. Francis de Sales (1877), St. Peter Canisius (1925), St. John of the Cross (1926), St. Robert Bellarmine (1931), St. Albert the Great (1932), St. Anthony of Padua (1946), St. Lawrence of Brindisi (1959), Ste. Teresa of Avila (1970), Ste. Catherine of Siena (1970). Regarding these last two Doctors, first among women to be honoured by the Church with such title, see *Civiltà Cattolica* 121 (1970), vol. 3, pp. 458–468; vol. 4, pp. 18–30; *Claretianum* 12 (1972) 257–289.

particularly of so many secondary doctrines of St. Augustine, which gave to medieval theologians the opportunity of inquiring further into various theological truths, some of which (as that on the sacramental character) reached later on the maturity of a dogma defined by the Magisterium. Naturally the force of probability in such arguments grows according to the number of Fathers who can be brought forward (short of universal agreement), to their greater nearness to the apostolic age, and to the greater authority of one or another individual Father, based on a superior intelligence, or a particular inquiry into the subject matter, or a special approbation of the Church (such is the theological authority of St. Augustine above all the other Fathers, even of the Eastern Church).

NOTE 3. ON THE THEOLOGIANS AS A THEOLOGICAL PLACE[35]

Like the fathers, theologians can be considered in two ways. *First*, as witnesses to Tradition; thus all that has been said above about the Fathers (p. 186) applies proportionally to them, although in a much lesser degree of importance and authority.

Secondly, they can be considered as *private doctors*, and in this respect they are like the Fathers, but at a lower level, a distinct theological place of secondary and mere probable value.

Theologians by definition are *Catholic men, who after the closing of the patristic age have taught or teach sacred science, either by word in the schools or (and especially) by writings, with an eminently orthodox doctrine and under the approbation of the Magisterium.*

Among the four properties required in the Fathers (see above p. 190), only two are required in a theologian, that is, no antiquity and no official holiness, but eminent orthodox doctrine and the approbation of the Magisterium.[36]

The *doctrine* must be strictly theological, although auxiliary sciences are not excluded by reason of their intimate connection with theology. It can be also a doctrine proposed only be words (as in teaching or preaching), although it is usually given

---

35   Cf. H. Lamiroy, "De auctoritate theologorum," *Collationes Brugenses* 24 (1924) 66–69; H. Van Laak, *Theses quaedam de Patrum et theologorum magisterio necnon de fidelium sensu* (Roma 1933) 33–49.

36   Hence strictly speaking all the ecclesiastical writers from the eighth century on, including St. Bede (†735), St. Anselm (†1109), and St. Bernard (†1153), are theologians, although in a stricter or more common sense, only the scientific writers from the twelfth century on are called "theologians."

or accompanied by writings. It must be eminent; for not everyone who dabbles with theology, or even teaches theology, or achieves the academic degree of doctor in theology, is properly a theologian, but only he who produces valuable theological writings, according to the common estimation, or spends a long and successful teaching career. It must be orthodox, essentially and as a whole, notwithstanding a possible secondary or material error, as we said in regard to the Fathers themselves (p. 191). The *approbation of the Church* must be at least general and implicit, that is, contained in the very fact that the words or the writings of a doctor are allowed by the vigilant Magisterium to be used in preaching, instruction of the faithful, and in the program of schools. However, also an explicit approbation has often been given to theologians by the Magisterium, either in general or in particular (as in the case of St. Thomas), and moreover some of them (twelve up to the present time, as shown above, p. 192) have been also given the official title of Doctor of the Church (first in time St. Thomas himself).[37]

Theologians, considered not as witnesses to Tradition, but as *private doctors*, that is, when they do not propose a doctrine as of faith or do not unanimously agree on such doctrine, constitute, like the Fathers themselves, although on a lower level, *a proper and distinct theological place, but only secondary and probable*, whose force is greater or lesser according to the authority and the number of the defenders of a doctrine. Such theologically probable doctrines should not be undervalued, for they often carry the seed of a future certain doctrine, which will finally gather the general agreement and pave the way to a solemn declaration of the Magisterium; at any rate, they are always useful for a deeper understanding of the revealed truths.

---

37 Among others, the following are certain and outstanding theologians: The twelve Doctors of the Church, mentioned above (among whom two women); the leaders of the better known theological schools, as St. Thomas, Scotus, Suárez; their principal predecessors and followers, as Peter Lombard, Alexander of Hales, Albert the Great, Bonaventure, Capreolus, Cajetan, Ferrariensis, Victoria, Cano, Toletus, Vásquez, Molina, Bellarmine, John of St. Thomas, St. Alphonsus Liguori, and many others up to our present time, in a special manner the authors of works used as manual or reference books in theological schools, for the instruction and formation of future apostolic preachers.

Heretical and schismatic writers, as well as those whose doctrine has been censured by the Magisterium (as Catholic Semirationalists and Semimodernists), however learned they may be in auxiliary sciences or disciplines, *are not theologians*, for lack of orthodox doctrine.

As regards the solid probability of a theological opinion, and hence its conformity with the teaching of the Magisterium, it is not sufficient that such an opinion be held by one or a few theologians, unless it is a question of a theologian especially commended by the Magisterium, particularly under the title of Doctor of the Church (such as St. Thomas), or of a few commonly recognized as weighty authorities in their field. Hence Alexander VII condemned the following laxist proposition: "An opinion, expressed in the book of a younger or modern author, should be considered as probable, as long as it is not evident that it has been rejected as improbable by the Apostolic See" (Denz. 2047).[38]

Thomas Aquinas, among and above all other theologians, may be considered as a *particular and distinct theological place*, having a stronger probable value for a sound and sure theological investigation.[39] This is based on a *very special commendation* of his works and doctrines by the Magisterium, beyond the title of Doctor of the Church, given also to several other theologians. The Magisterium, in fact, besides continuously praising and commending his doctrines through centuries since the very day of his canonization by John XXII (July 18, 1323), has recently proclaimed him *"Prince and Master of all scholastic doctors"* (Leo XIII, Encycl. "Aeterni Patris"),

---

38 This is more than a warning to that kind of theological laxism or immoderate freedom, claimed for probable opinions in the present time. Some recent writers have even gone so far as to claim for the theologians a kind of Magisterium in the Church, practically equal or at least parallel to that of the Hierarchy, based on an alleged true magisterial office which would pertain to the entire Church. Thus we read in the work *Dissent In and For the Church* (by Charles E. Curran, Robert E. Hunt, and others, New York 1969, p. 86f.): "In the face of this trend toward establishing an *exclusive* teaching prerogative in the hierarchy, recent historical studies have exercised a modifying influence by pointing out the presence of error in past papal and episcopal teaching and the correction of error by way of theological dissent. Dissent thus appears traditionally as one possible, responsible option in the theological task, and, in its own way, is an intrinsic element in the total magisterial function of the Church. The entire Church, as truly magistral, can never be contained simply and exclusively in what has become known as the *hierarchical* magisterium." See the right evaluation and criticism of this book made by J. F. Costanzo, "Academic Dissent: an Original Ecclesiology," *Thomist* 34 (1970) 636–653.

39 Cf. I. B. Raus, "L'enseignement de la doctrine de saint Thomas considérée dans ses rapports avec le Code et les écoles théologiques," *Nouvelle revue théologique* 52 (1925) 261–291, 358–380; H. Dieckmann, "De auctoritate theologica S. Thomae Aquinatis," *Scholastik* (1926) 567ff.; R. Villeneuve, "Ite ad Thomam," *Angelicum* 13 (1936) 3–23; I. M. Ramirez, *De auctoritate doctrinali S. Thomae Aquinatis*, Salmanticae 1952; "The Authority of St. Thomas," *Thomist* 15 (1952) 1–100; A. D. Lee, "Thomism and the Council," *Vatican II: the Theological Dimension* (collective work, The Thomist Press 1963) 451–492.

"Particular support and glory of the Catholic Church" (ibid.), *"Leader of Studies"* (Pius XI, Encycl. "Studiorum ducem'), *"Common or universal Doctor of the Church...whose doctrine the Church has made its own"* (ibid,), the one who occupies *"the main place"* among Catholic doctors (Paul VI, Allocution given at the Gregorian University, Sept. 10, 195).[40] Besides, the Magisterium has insistently and strongly declared that theological studies should be made according to the doctrine of St. Thomas. His *Summa Theologiae* was prescribed as a text for the Italian Seminaries by Pius X (Motu Proprio "Sacrorum antistitum") and by Benedict XV in 1920, and for Germany by this same Pope in 1921. Under the same Pontiff the Code of Canon Law proposed St. Thomas' teaching in seminaries under the form of a law: "Professors shall handle the studies and the instruction of their students according to the method, the doctrine, and the principles of the Angelic Doctor and keep these religiously" (can. 1366, §2). Pius XII in his Encycl. "Humani generis" urged the application of this canonical law. Vatican II declared that the study of speculative theology in the seminaries should be made "under the guidance of St. Thomas" (Decree on Priestly Formation, no. 16) and in Catholic schools, particularly in Universities and faculties, modern questions and investigations should be made "following in the footsteps of the Doctors of the Church, above all of St. Thomas Aquinas" (Declaration on Christian Education, no. 10).

As long as the aforementioned law remains in the Code, there is an obligation for professors of theology to follow the teaching of St. Thomas in its main principles and conclusions, or as a doctrinal body, although the weight of this obligation is judged more or less strictly or lightly by various theologians. However, no faithful or prudent son of the Church, nor any docile hearer of its Magisterium, can conscientiously overlook the fact that the Church has made the doctrine of St. Thomas its own doctrine and the Magisterium has been insistently urging the theologians to follow it, for the good of the Church and for their own good.

---

40   The three special names given to S. Thomas are: *"Angelic Doctor"* (used since the 15th century, repeated by Pius V and later commonly by the theologians and the Magisterium), *"Eucharistic Doctor"* (used in the 17th century, at least by the Salmanticenses in their treatise on the Eucharist, and repeated by Pius XI), and *"Common Doctor"* (first and pointedly introduced by Pius XI).

3

The Magisterium, Organ of Revelation[41]

1. THE NATURE OF THE MAGISTERIUM

This matter is to be examined more distinctly in the treatise on the Church, as in its proper place. Here we briefly gather a few general and essential notions, which are necessary to establish the other and principal point of this question, namely the value and use of the Magisterium as a theological place, or base of theological investigation.

Magisterium is defined as the right and the duty of teaching authoritatively the revealed truth, to which on the part of the faithful corresponds the obligation of accepting the proposed doctrine with submission of heart and mind.

It is *divided* into ordinary Magisterium and extraordinary or solemn Magisterium.

The *ordinary Magisterium* is that which is exercised in a common manner by the pastors of the Church (Pope and bishops) or under their direction, by means of ordinary papal documents or allocutions, documents of the Roman Curia, pastoral letters and allocutions of local bishops, preaching of priests, writings of Fathers and theologians, scholarly teaching and catechetical instructions. It can be either infallible or non-infallible.

The *extraordinary* Magisterium consists in a formal, explicit and solemn declaration, made only by the supreme authority in the Church, namely, the Roman Pontiff or an Ecumenical Council. Depending on the will of this authority and on the mode or

---

41 Cf. Baumgartner, Dejaifve, and Van den Eynde, cited above, on p. 10; M. Caudron, "Magistère ordinaire et infaillibilité pontificale d'après la Constitution Dei Filius [de Vatican I]," *Ephemerides theologicae Lovanienses* 36 (1960) 393–431; A. Piolanti, "Il magistero della Chiesa e la scienza teologica," *Divinitas* 5 (1961) 531–551; L. Ciappi, "Il magistero della Chiesa nel pensiero di S. S. Pio XII," *ibid.* 552–580; P. Nau, "Le magistère pontifical ordinaire au premier Concile du Vatican," *Revue thomiste* 62 (1962) 341–397; *Mysterium salutis. Dogmatique de l'histoire du salut* (trans. from the German), I/3: *L'Eglise et la transmission de la révelation,* Paris 1969.

formula of the declaration, it can be either infallible (as are the definitions of Vatican I) or non-infallible (as are the Constitutions, Decrees, and Declarations of Vatican II).

The Magisterium, both extraordinary and ordinary, is *the organ of revelation*, that is, the channel through which revelation comes to us from the deposit of Scripture and Tradition. When it proposes with infallibility a revealed truth, it becomes also *the proximate rule of faith*, that is, the norm determining for us the object to be believed, while Scripture and Tradition remain the remote rule of faith; in other words, what we believe and we have to believe is not simply the word of God contained in Scripture and Tradition, but that same word as determinately and authoritatively proposed to us by the infallible act of the Magisterium.[42] By being the organ of revelation contained in Tradition, the Magisterium becomes also part of the active Tradition, that is, one of the principal means by which the objective Tradition is transmitted, as we noted above (pp. 179, 185).

2. THE PROBATIVE VALUE OF THE MAGISTERIUM, AS A THEOLOGICAL PLACE

This value can be expressed by the following three norms.

First norm. Since the Magisterium is the organ of revelation and the proximate rule of faith, on which depend the interpretation and the presentation of Scripture and Tradition, it is a *proper, primary, independent, proximate and most efficacious theological place*, or basis of theological investigation. It is true that the Magisterium, being only an organ and a guardian and not a deposit of revelation, depends on Scripture and Tradition, as the object to be guarded and interpreted (see above, pp. 174, 182), but *subjectively on our part*, and hence for theological investigation, *it is the first theological place*, since Scripture and Tradition depend on it for the right interpretation of their sense (see above pp. 174, 175, 185).

Second norm. The ordinary Magisterium has the same theological value as the extraordinary; it is even in itself more valuable, inasmuch as it consists in the ordinary and connaturual proposition and explanation of the entire deposit of revelation, while

---

42 *Vatican I:* "By divine and Catholic faith, all those things must be believed which are contained in the written or transmitted Word of God and are proposed by the Church, either through a solemn pronouncement or through the ordinary and universal Magisterium, to be believed as revealed truths" (Sess. 3, chap. 3, Denz. 3011).

the extraordinary Magisterium has a provisional character and a particular objective, namely, that of solemnly proclaiming a particular truth or condemning a particular error.

However, on our part and for theological investigation, the extraordinary Magisterium is much more efficacious, because it has a well-determined subject (the Pope and the Council) and it manifests itself in well-defined formulas, while the ordinary Magisterium is made up of numerous and different elements, expressing themselves in various and indefinite forms. Hence it is more difficult to ascertain and to determine. This is evident as regards those truths that are only implicitly contained in the deposit of revelation and gradually are brought into explicit knowledge (such as the Immaculate Conception and the Assumption); but also those truths which, being explicit and fundamental (as the divinity of Christ, the hypostatic union, and the mystery of the Trinity), were proposed since the beginning by the ordinary Magisterium, have received a more definite and theologically more valuable formulation by the extraordinary Magisterium.

Third norm. Before using a declaration of the extraordinary Magisterium for a theological argumentation or investigation, it is necessary *to ascertain the degree of its force, its proper and direct object, and the exact sense of its words or formulas.*

Regarding the *degree of its force*, it has to be noted that not all the declarations of this Magisterium, however solemn, are definite pronouncements implying infallibility, but often they are simple authoritative explanations of a doctrine, preferred by the Magisterium and more common in the Church, or warnings, advices, persuasions, censures and prohibitions of opinions, condemnations of errors, without a definite and final judgment that the doctrine is to be held as an article of faith. Moreover, it is not always easy to ascertain whether a particular declaration carries the weight of infallibility. The surest signs of this are: a declaration made under the form of a profession of faith, as is the Creed of the Councils of Nicaea and Constantinople I; the use of the explicit formula "We define such doctrine to be a revealed truth, or to be held by faith, or under pain of incurring heresy," as in the definitions of the Immaculate Conception and the Assumption; the infliction of the note of heresy on the opposite doctrine, as is done also under the word "anathema," at least in some of the canons of Trent and Vatican I, while in other canons, especially of older Councils, this word means only excommunication, or separation from the unity of the Church.[43]

From the *proper and direct object*, which alone is infallibly defined, have to be excluded the things which are casually and incidentally asserted (usually under an indirect form), the merely explanatory propositions without which the sense of the defined truth remains unchanged, and the reasons or arguments added to prove the defined truth. For the Magisterium does not intend to define incidental or accidental determinations, nor is it infallible in arguing and proving truths but only in determining them and judging on them.

In determining the *exact* sense of the words and formulas with which this proper and direct object of the definition is expressed, careful attention should be paid to two things. *First*, to the sense which those words and formulas had at the time they were used, considering the historical circumstances and the contemporary status of the sacred science and ecclesiastical terminology (for instance, at the time of Trent and Vatican I). *Second*, to the intention and the character of the Pope or the Council defining, considering especially the circumstances which provoked the definition, the acts of the Council, as well as the character and mentality of the heretics against whom the definition was issued. From the lack of such examination, it happens at times that the words of older Councils (even of Trent itself) are unduly understood according to the developed and more definite sense which they gradually acquired in more recent theological terminology.

---

43   Hence, among recent pronouncements of the Magisterium, the surest infallible definitions are the canons of Trent and Vatican I, and the two definitions of the Immaculate Conception (by Pius IX) and the Assumption (by Pius XII).

Non-infallible documents are most of the doctrinal encyclicals of Leo XIII and subsequent Popes, and the constitutions, decrees and declarations of Vatican II.

Doubtful infallible definitions, by reason of the various judgments of theologians, are some of the most important documents of recent Popes, as the encyclical "Quanta cura" by Pius IX 1864 (against Naturalism and Socialism), the Syllabus by the same 1864 (against Rationalism), the mere chapters of Vatican I (the same holds for the chapters of Trent), the epistle "Apostolicae curae" by Leo XIII 1896 (on Anglican ordinations), the encyclical "Pascendi" by Pius X 1907 (in which Modernism is condemned as "a collection of all heresies"), the encyclical "Casti connubii" by Pius XI 1930 (on Matrimony), the encyclical "Mystici Corporis" by Pius XII 1943 (on the nature of the Church), the apostolic constitution "Sacramentum Ordinis" by the same in 1947 (on the matter and form of the Sacrament of Orders).

Moreover, it is to be noted that the definitions of the Magisterium, considered in their proper object, do not necessarily express the full positive sense of a revealed truth, since they are usually brought forth to exclude some particular error, rather than to explain directly a doctrine in itself. Hence it is necessary further to compare such definitions with the deposit of revelation (Scripture and Tradition), not so much in order to prove their conformity with it, as to grasp the fuller sense of the proposed truth.

PART II

The Theological Contents of the Channels of Revelation

THE PROPER CONTENTS OF REVELATION, AND hence of its channels, are either explicit truths, which can be called dogmas in a generic sense, or implicit truths, able to be drawn from the explicit truths themselves, which are called theological conclusions. Both are *theological contents* of those channels, because a theologian must necessarily deal with them in his scientific investigation, since there is nothing else in theology, as in any other science, than principles and conclusions. Hence, this second part of our dialectic and methodological treatise about the channels of revelation consists in a theological evaluation of both *dogma* (chap. 4) and *theological conclusion* (chap. 5). It is logical to add to this an explanation and determination of the so-called *theological notes* and censures, which imply a judgment about the agreement or disagreement of a proposition with the contents of revelation (chap. 6).

4
Dogma[44]

1. NOTION OF DOGMA

Dogma (a Greek noun, from "dokéo"=I think, I decree) etymologically signifies either *an opinion or a precept*, and in this twofold
sense it is used both in Scripture (Luke 2:1 and Acts 17:7: imperial decree; Acts 14:4: ceremonial laws of the O. T.; Col. 2:14:
God's decree) and by the Greek Fathers, who however, gradually
gave to the word the stricter sense of a *doctrinal decree or obligatory
doctrine*. With this specific sense the word was later introduced,
especially by St. Augustine and Vincent of Lerins, into the Latin

---

44 Alszeghy, Z. and Flick. M., *Lo sviluppo del dogma cattolico*, ed. 2, Brescia 1969.
Boyer, Ch., "Lo sviluppo del dogma," *Problemi e orientamenti di teologia dommatica*
1 (Milano 1957) 359–380.
  Doronzo, E., *Theologia dogmatica* 1 (Washington 1966) 491–526.
  Gardeil, A. *Le donné révélé et la théologie* (éd. 2, Paris 1912) 77–186.
  Garrigou-Lagrange, R., "Vérité et immutabilité du dogme," *Angelicum* 24 (1947)
124–139.
  Grandmaison, L. de, *Le dogme chrétien. Sa nature, ses formules, son développement*,
éd. 3, Paris 1928.
  Journet, Ch., *The Church and the Word Incarnate* 1 (tr. A. H. C. Downes, New York
1950) 338–353.
  Malevez, L., "L'invariant et le divers dans le langage de la foi," *Nouvelle revue
théologique* 95 (1973) 353–366.
  Marin-Sola, F., *La evolución homogénea del dogma católico*, Valencia-Madrid 1924.
Second edition in French (trans. B. Cambon), *L'évolution homogéne du dogme catholique*,
2 vols., Fribourg, Suisse 1924. The best and most complete work on this subject.
  Newman, J. H., *An Essay on the Development of Christian Doctrine*, new edition, New
York 1949.
  Parente, P., "La formola dommatica di fronte all cultura in evoluzione," *Doctor
Communis* 22 (1969) 89–108.
  Rahner, K., "The Development of Dogma," *Theological Investigations* (tr. C. Ernst)
1 (Baltimore 1961) 39–77.
  Rondet, H., *Les dogmes changent-ils? Théologie de l'histoire du dogme*, Paris 1960;
Histoire du dogme, Tournai-Paris, 1970.
  Schultes, R. M., "Circa dogmatum homogeneam evolutionem," *Divus Thomas*
(Piacenza) 2 (1925) 83–89, 554–564; "Eclaircissements sur l'évolution du dogme,"
Revue des sciences philosophiques et théologiques 14 (1925) 286–302.
  Various authors, *Gregorianum* 33 (1952), no. 1 (It deals entirely with the progress
of dogma).
  Vollert, C., "Doctrinal Development," *Catholic Theological Society of America* 12
(1957) 45–74.
  Walgrave, J. H., *Unfolding Revelation. Nature of Doctrinal Development*, London 1972.

Church and became classical in ecclesiastical literature. In the 17th century, however, on the occasion of the Jansenist controversy, the word received also the more strict and technical sense of a *doctrine of faith defined by the Church*. In this sense it is used occasionally in the documents of the Magisterium (Pius VI speaks of the "dogma of Transubstantiation" and Vatican I of the "dogmas proposed by the Church" and of the infallibility of the Pope as "a divinely revealed dogma," Denz. 2629, 3043, 3073). Hence "dogma" in ecclesiastical and theological use has two senses, one general, that is, any revealed truth, the other specific, that is, *a revealed truth infallibly defined by the Magisterium as to be believed of divine faith.*

In this second sense and proper definition, dogma is made up of two elements, that is, the revealed truth, which is the direct and only object of our faith, and the definition of the Magisterium, which is not the object of our faith, but only its proximate rule, that is, the necessary condition, without which we are not obliged to believe what is found in the deposit of revelation, as far as the force of the mere deposit is concerned.[45]

Whatever has been revealed by God and infallibly proposed by the Magisterium becomes a dogma to be believed with supernatural faith, whether it be a supernatural truth (as the Trinity), or a natural truth (as the existence of God, which can also be known by the natural reason, but at any rate has been also revealed), or a thing to be done (moral acts), or a particular historical fact (such as all those that make up the life of Christ). For all these objects have a close connection with the principal object of revelation (Deity) and with its proper purpose (our salvation and beatific vision).

2. THE IMMUTABILITY OF DOGMA

Dogma, once established through the revelation of God and the definition of the Magisterium, becomes *absolutely immutable*, both objectively and subjectively. It is *objectively* and essentially immutable in itself, because on the one hand God's affirmation cannot change or be proved to be false, and on the other hand the Magisterium can no longer revoke its definition, since it is a

---

45 Note, however, that the Magisterium actually proposes in a general way the whole Bible to our belief, and hence we are obliged to believe whatever is clear and explicit in Scripture. But for things and truths that are not clearly shown in it, or about which some reasonable doubt may be raised, we need an additional and particular declaration of the infallible Magisterium in order to be obliged to believe.

mere temporary condition required for eliciting the assent of faith which is irrevocable. It is also *immutable subjectively* on the part of the faithful, who cannot change or corrupt it in their knowledge, because of the infallibility of the believing and the teaching Church under the assistance of the Holy Spirit, promised by Christ.

This absolute immutability has been explicitly declared on several occasions by the Magisterium, against *Liberal Protestants and Modernists*, denying the very objective immutability of dogma, on the basis of the subjective nature of religion, and against *Orthodox Protestants and Jansenists*, denying only the subjective immutability of dogma, on the basis of their denial of the infallibility of the Church.[46] *Vatican Council I* defined: "If anyone shall say that, in view of the progress of science, the dogmas proposed by the Church could at times be understood in a sense other than that in which the Church has understood and understands them: let him be anathema "(Sess. 3, can. 3 on faith and reason, Denz. 3043; cf. chap. 4, Denz. 3020).

This immutability belongs only to dogma itself, not to its expression or *dogmatic formula*, which can vary or change as long as it does not alter or render ambiguous the concept itself, carried by the definition of the Magisterium. However, such a change depends exclusively on the Magisterium itself.[47]

---

46 *Liberal Protestants and Modernists*, based on agnostic Rationalism (see our treatise on *Revelation*, p. 5), deny the first element of dogma, that is the *objectivity of the revealed truth*. According to them religion itself and its revelation is something merely subjective and human, that is, a sense of the conscience, which changes and develops with the evolution of the consciousness of humanity, under the influence of various circumstances and cultures. Dogma is a definite formulation, in an objective form, of this subjective religious sense, and consequently it is bound to change with it, having each time only a normative and practical value, without any objective foundation. This modernistic system is explained at length and severely censured by Pius X in the Encyclical "Pascendi" (Denz. 3477–3488).

Orthodox Protestants deny the second element of dogma, that is, *the infallibility of the Magisterium* in proposing the objective revealed truth, and hence they admit the possibility of at least a partial and substantial change in things believed by the faithful, under the influence of human causes and circumstances. *Jansenists* speak of the possibility of a general obscuration or darkening of fundamental truths in the Church (cf. a proposition of the Synod of Pistoia, condemned by Pius VI, Denz. 2601). A *Günther*, a Catholic semi-rationalist, taught that the definitions of the Magisterium have only a temporary validity, and that the progress of science may demand their change (cf. his condemnation by Pius IX, Denz. 2829, and by Vatican I, Denz. 3043). A similar opinion is being spread ambiguously in recent days by the so-called "progressive theologians."

47 It is evident that, in order to express the revealed truths aptly, the Magisterium in its definitions has had to use words and expressions, current in the

3. DEVELOPMENT OR PROGRESS OF DOGMA

The absolute immutability of dogma does not necessarily exclude its development or progress, with regard to the finding and understanding of its full meaning and of its virtual implications.

The existence of the development, understood at least in a generic and indefinite manner, is evident from the fact that Christ entrusted to the Apostles and their successors the office of transmitting the deposit of revelation, which implies necessarily some kind of development in the manner of transmission, according to different times and cultures. The Church furthermore, actually has accomplished this office in many and ever more perfect ways of explaining, interpreting and defending the original revealed truths. It is also in a more definite manner declared by the *Vatican Council I* quoting the famous statement of Vincent of Lerins (see above, p. 185f.); "Therefore ... let the understanding, the knowledge, and wisdom of individuals, as well as of all, of one man as well as of the whole Church, grow and greatly progress through ages and centuries, but let such progress be only of its proper kind [i.e. homogeneous], that is within the same dogma, the same sense, and the same understanding" (Sess. 3, chap. 4 on faith and reason, Denz. 3020). *Vatican II* repeats the same declaration, pointing out

---

common language and culture (even philosophical) of each time, adapting them to fit an ecclesiastical terminology. Thus the Council of Nicaea adapted the Greek word "homoousios" ("consubstantial" — "of the same nature") to signify the numerical identity of the divine nature in Christ and in the Father, although the word can signify also a merely specific identity, as between two men; likewise the Council of Trent adopted the word "Transubstantiation," already used by the scholastic theologians, to signify the eucharistic change, declaring it to be "a very apt expression."

Only the Magisterium is competent in using or changing a dogmatic formula. In future definitions, the Magisterium will, as usual, adapt its new formulas to the culture of the time, as far as such a culture will be able to be used for the right expression of the revealed truth. As regards past definitions the Magisterium has never changed any of the principal formulas once used, both because they conform also to common sense and understanding, and because they are a safeguard against alteration of doctrines. At any rate, if, for instance, the word "Transubstantiation" should come to be changed by the Magisterium, it would necessarily be replaced by a word which would mean that the nature of bread (whatever it is that makes bread to be bread and not meat or other things) is no longer existing in the Eucharist, but has been changed into the body of Christ.

Vatican II (Constit. "Gaudium et spes," no. 62) invites theologians to adapt their teaching to the culture of the present time, but does not give them the right to discard the defined dogmatic formulas.

also the two causes of this progress, namely, the teaching of the Magisterium and the experience of the faithful.[48]

The proper nature of this development is not so easy to understand and determine, as is evident from the different explanations given by theologians. The difficulty arises from the fact that through such development we have now arrived at believing several truths which do not seem to be sufficiently contained in the deposit of revelation, but seem rather derived through an elaborate process of natural reason, based moreover on philosophical and perishable systems; such are, for instance, the sacramental character, the sevenfold number of the sacraments, transubstantiation, the sacramentality of Matrimony, the Immaculate Conception, the Assumption. To this difficulty theologians usually answer that in these and other similar cases, the development of dogma is *not objective but subjective,* that is, it consists not in an addition to a revealed object but in a further explanation and understanding of the same object; or it is also an objective progress, but only *from implicit to explicit,* that is, not again by the addition of a new object or truth, but only by rendering explicit to us an object or truth which was already implicitly contained and so believed in another object or truth which was explicitly believed in previous times. This latter and better formulation of the development of dogma is to be clarified with the following observations.

First. Throughout the Old Testament up to and including Christ and the Apostles, revelation developed *objectively by addition* of new truths, not contained, even implicitly, in the formerly revealed truths, although contained in the same reality. Hence there was a development not from reality to reality, but from one concept to another concept, really distinct from the first and not contained in it, even implicitly. Thus in the same reality of God there was a passage from the simple concept of one God to the concept of the Trinity of Persons, and in the same reality of Christ there was a

---

48 Dogmatic Constitution on Revelation, no. 8: "This Tradition, which comes down from the apostles, progresses in the Church under the assistance of the Holy Spirit. Indeed, the understanding of the things and of the words, which have been handed over, grows either by means of the contemplation and study of the faithful, who keep and compare them in their hearts (cf. Luke 2:19, 51), as well as by an intimate understanding of the spiritual things they experience, or through the pronouncements of those who have received, with the episcopal succession, the sure charism of truth. Thus the Church through succeeding centuries, moves constantly toward the fulness of divine truth, until the words of God reach their complete fulfillment in her."

passage from the concept of Messiah to the concept of God and then to the concept of Son of God. It is evident that the concept of God does not contain, even implicitly, the concept of several persons in God (otherwise we would know through natural reason the mystery of the Trinity as we know the existence of God). Likewise the concept of Messiah does not include the concept of God, nor does the concept of God include the concept of Son of God (as is clear from the person of the Holy Spirit, who is not Son of God).

Second. Such an objective development of dogma by addition of new truths is impossible in the Church, because *public revelation* has been completely given by Christ and the Apostles and has been *closed at the death of the last apostle* (that is, of St. John who died toward the end of the first century, as Catholic exegetes unanimously agree).[49] This fact, proposed equivalently by the Council of Trent (Sess. 4, Denz.1501) and more directly by Pius X in the Decree "Lamentabili" against Modernism (Denz. 3421), has been finally explicitly declared by Vatican II saying: "No further public revelation is now to be expected before the glorious manifestation of Our Lord Jesus Christ" (Dogm. Constit. on Divine Revelation, no. 4).[50]

---

49 After Christ's Ascension *public revelation continued through the apostles*, as founders of the Church, and only through them, so that whatever revelation may have been given to others of the faithful, at that time, even to the co-apostolic ministers of the Word, does not belong to public revelation or to the object of our faith. But with regard to the extent of the revelation given to the apostles themselves, we know very little from Scripture. St. Paul sometimes speaks of revelations received from the Lord, but their object is something that had already been revealed by Christ and was known by the other apostles, as the mystery of the Eucharist (1 Cor. 11:23) and the Gospel in general (Gal. 1:11–24). However, *three new revelations* seem certain from Scripture, namely, the *inspiration* of the books of the New Testament, since they were written after the Ascension, the *eschatology* consigned by St. John in the Apocalypse (cf. 1:1–3), and the so-called *Pauline privilege* (1 Cor. 7:12–15), for it can hardly be said that the apostles were instructed by Christ on such things before the Ascension. It is probable that several other things were revealed to the apostles and transmitted through oral Tradition.

50 *Private revelations*, which belong to an undying charism in the Church, have the same nature as public revelation and the same general purpose of helping the Church. Their object is either the same as the public revelation, that is, an explanation of the revealed truths, or *something new* by which public revelation may be accidentally extended. It does not, however, identify with public revelation and *does not become an object of faith* for others than the person to whom it is given and who is bound to believe it by the same supernatural faith, if he is certain of the revelation by a miraculous sign of God (either exterior, or interior in his mind). If the *Magisterium approves* such revelations (as in the case of St. Margaret Mary Alacoque about the Sacred Heart and of St. Bernadette at Lourdes), one is only

Third. Hence there remain only two ways by which dogma can develop in the Church. The first and simple way is a merely *subjective process*, consisting in a clearer explanation and understanding of a formally identical object which is contained in the deposit of revelation and was believed since the beginning. However, this is not a progress of dogma itself, but only of man in his knowledge of a dogma, and it explains only the succession of new and better formulas, expressing the same truth, such as the Divinity of Christ, not the rise and definition of new dogmas, which, as the Immaculate Conception, the Assumption, and the others mentioned above, seem entirely or formally different from the ones explicitly contained in the deposit. Hence there remains only one way of explaining a proper development of dogma, applicable to this sort of new dogmas, that is, *an objective process from implicit to explicit.* Such a process consists in this, that a truth, which is actually contained in another and hence known and believed in another, is not yet known in itself and as to its inclusion in the other, but later on, under favorable circumstances and by means of a logical and necessary process of the mind or of a forceful intuition of the Christian sense, it comes to be known as such, passing from implicit to explicit in our knowledge and in our faith, as well as in the deposit of Tradition itself. Thus, there is no change nor addition of an entirely new truth, but the same truth, explicitly believed since the beginning or at some time, is later known under a new concept implicit in it, or according to its implicit content and virtuality. For instance, from the truth or concept of Divine Maternity Tradition passed to the truth or concept of the greatest sanctity after that of Christ (included in it as a necessary consequence) and from this concept the same Tradition later passed to the concept of exemption from original sin (included in it as a necessary effect).

Fourth. This implicit inclusion of one truth in another and its subsequent extraction from the other, cannot be explained but by the existence of a necessary and infallible connection between the two, by force of which, if one is posited, the other must necessarily follow. This connection can be the connection of an *essential*

obliged to admit their fittingness as approved by the Church, but he can also, if he chooses, believe them, along with the public revelation, with the same supernatural faith. Such revelations are also useful for the *development of dogma.*

Cf. K. Rahner, "Les révélations privées," *Revue d'ascétique et de mystique* 25 (1949) 506–514; P. De Letter, "The Meaning of Lourdes," *Clergy Monthly* 20 (1958) 3–16.

property, which is absolutely inseparable from the essence of a thing, as are, for instance, intrinsic extension in regard to quantity, radical possibility of dying or of sinning which always remains in man in heaven. Or this connection can be that of an *effect to its metaphysical cause*, that is, to a cause which not only has the power of producing the effect, but also contains virtually and actually the effect itself, as the spirituality of the soul contains its immortality and God's immutability contains his eternity.[51]

Examples of development of dogmas, based on the connection of an *essential property*, are the following: The Nicene dogma of the numerical consubstantiality of Christ with the Father is a consequent property of his divine sonship, because by being Son he has necessarily the same nature as the Father and by being God he has necessarily the same individual nature as the Father. The dogma of the two wills in Christ, or the existence of a human will in him, defined by the Council of Constantinople III, is deduced from the truth that Christ is a true and perfect man, similar to us, whose essential property is the human will.

More numerous are the examples of development based on connection of *effect with its metaphysical cause*. The Ephesus dogma of Divine Maternity is drawn as a metaphysical effect from the concept of "Mother of Christ," coupled with the concepts of Christ's divinity and of a single person in Christ. From the fullness of grace, hailed in the gospel (or at any rate following from the Divine Maternity) are drawn both the Tridentine dogma of the privileged exclusion

---

51 There is of course a third way of intimate connection and inclusion, which we may call *connection of essentiality*, and which exists either between a thing defined and its definition (thus rational animal is included in man), or between the essence and its essential parts (thus the body is included in the essence of man), or between a universal thing and its particular (thus Peter is included in mankind), or between two relative things (thus the concept of son is included in the concept of father, and vice versa). However, by means of this connection, there is no real and objective development of dogma itself, but only the aforesaid subjective progress of our knowledge, about the same truth, by way of clearer and more definite formulas, or of definite equivalent concepts, which are obtained by a mere analysis of the truth, or the so-called explanatory syllogisms, as when from Christ's divine sonship we conclude that one of the other two persons of the Holy Trinity is a Father.

To this improper and subjective progress of dogma belong the various declarations of the Magisterium which express a truth, already believed, with other clearer words or formulas (as are the various symbols of faith), or with more polished and authentic words (dogmatic formulas, of which some are more definite and particular and hence they are called more strictly dogmatic formulas, as those that are found in the later councils).

of venial sin in Mary and the dogma of the privilege of Immaculate Conception. Likewise the Assumption can be drawn from the Divine Maternity or from the Immaculate Conception. Transubstantiation is implicitly contained, like an effect in its cause, in the Real Presence, considered not abstractly but as concretely expressed in the words "This is my body" (other than "Here is my body"), which are not true if the bread remains, and hence they require not only the presence of Christ but also the absence of the bread. The infallibility of the Pope, as successor of Peter, is implicitly contained, as an effect in its cause, in the amplitude of his primacy, explicitly revealed, because such ample primacy has been given to Peter and his successors with reference to all the things that are necessary to confirm the brethren in their faith and to be the rock or foundation on which the Church stands firmly, even in matters of faith.

The historical mode or way of such a development is twofold. The first is a *rational and deductive way*, by which, from a doctrine already definitely and explicitly known, another is deduced which is implicitly and necessarily contained in the former, as we have just explained. The second is an *empirical or inductive way*, consisting in this that the sense of the Christian people, by a sort of connatural intuition, perceives the necessary connection between a truth, already explicitly believed, and another, although the necessity of this connection cannot be proved in a rational and deductive way (see above, pp. 188–190).

In this second case, the common Christian sense does not create this connection between the two truths, otherwise there would be a mere pious fiction and an arbitrary invention of a dogma; but it only finds it instinctively and more easily than it would be found through a rational deductive process, which for instance, might be apparently blocked or temporarily stopped by the consideration of another dogma.

This is particularly illustrated by the case of the development of the truth of the Immaculate Conception. This truth is implicitly contained in and necessarily deduced from the fullness of grace in Mary, provided however that this fullness is understood not in any way, but in all the amplitude compatible with the dogma of the universal redemption of men through Christ. But, through a rational and deductive process, it was not clear that it should be taken in such an ample sense, which even seemed to be positively excluded by Christ's universal redemption that had to include also the Blessed Virgin; hence the majority of the great theologians in the Middle Ages (St. Thomas included) and many other afterwards were opposed to the privilege of the Immaculate Conception, until the persevering conviction of the Christian people, shown particularly in their devotion and in their interpretation of the existing feast of the Holy Conception of Mary, obliged the theologians themselves to remove the aforementioned obstacle, apparently deriving from the truth of the universal redemption, by a rational distinction between releasing redemption, common to all men, and merely preservative redemption, proper to Mary, and thus to arrive through such a forced rational process to the point where the Christian sense had easily preceded them.

The *direct causes* of such a development are included in these same two ways, that is, *theological science* and the *Christian sense;* the third and principal cause is the *Magisterium* itself, as directing the other two and closing by its solemn definition the whole development of a dogma. The *indirect causes,* or occasions, of the development are especially three. First, the necessity of refuting *errors or heresies,* which brought along the declaration of several important dogmas, as those defined by the great Councils of the first centuries and later by the Councils of Trent and Vatican I. Second, the fittingness of settling some grave doubt or controversy among Catholic doctors, such as the controversy about rebaptizing heretics at the time of St. Cyprian, which the Magisterium resolved negatively, and the medieval controversy about the rational soul as the form of the body, settled in the affirmative by the Council of Vienne. Third, the utility of strengthening the *cult and devotion* of the people, as in the case of the Immaculate Conception and the Assumption; in this regard, also private revelations may have their influence, inasmuch as they would impel the Magisterium to examine their conformity with the truths contained in the deposit of public revelation.

The *degrees or steps* of development may be described generically as follows: there is first a period of simple faith in some explicit truth, then a period of further explanation or controversy about its proper and full meaning, finally a period of precise and definite determination and formulation, or, as the case may be, of the explicit expression of a new truth, implicitly contained in the former. A more precise and important question is that of the *continuity of the dogmatic progress*, that is, whether the knowledge of revealed truth has been always progressing, or on the contrary there has been or could be a regress, notwithstanding the essential immutability of dogma, as explained above.

With regard to the *apostles*, it is certain that they had a better and deeper understanding (probably even infused) of the truths explicitly revealed; this agrees with their instruction received from Christ before the Ascension for forty days, with Christ's promise to send the Holy Spirit who would "teach them all things, all truths" (John 14:26; 16:3), and also with the manner of their doctrine (shown in the Acts and the Epistles, particularly of St. Paul). As for the implicitly revealed truths, which are now explicit to us, it is possible, but it does not seem probable that they knew them clearly and sufficiently (although some theologians think so, as Dorsch, Marín-Sola, Lercher-Schlagenhaufen); if they had thought, for instance, of the Immaculate Conception, transubstantiation, the sacramentality of Matrimony, the sacramental character, they would likely have left some signs or hints of these important, though not fundamental, truths, in their preaching consigned in the Holy Scripture.

Regarding the *post-apostolic age*, if we consider the time of elaboration of a dogma, which precedes its explicit knowledge and its definition by the Magisterium, there can surely be a kind *of general oscillation*, or even obscuration and regress, connatural to all development, as happened in the development of the truth of the Immaculate Conception, which was denied for a long time by many theologians. But in the time following the explicit knowledge and definition of a dogma, there cannot be a real general regress, such as to throw back into implicitness what has been explicit. For this would imply either a negation, or a renewed controversy, or a complete oblivion of the truth, which would be contrary to the indefectibility of the Church. However, there can be a *partial diminution or obscuration* of a dogma, in such manner that a notable part of the faithful fall into heresy, at least material, as happened to the truth of the full divinity of Christ at the time of Arianism, or that some dogma may be less clearly known or valued, as happened to the truth of the Roman Primacy at the time of Western schism and of Jansenism and Gallicanism.

5

Theological Conclusion[52]

1. NOTION OF THEOLOGICAL CONCLUSION

A theological conclusion is a proposition (or a judgment or a truth), which through a discursive process is derived from a revealed principle. It is called conclusion, because it is not revealed in itself, but only deduced from a revealed truth; it is called theological, because revealed truths are the principles of theology. Since every discursive process (usually expressed in the form of a syllogism) implies two principles or premises (major and minor) from which a conclusion is deduced, a theological conclusion may be inferred either from two revealed principles (for instance God knows the day of the last judgment, but Christ is God, therefore Christ knows the day of the last judgment) or from one principle of faith and one principle of reason (for instance, a perfect man has a human will, but Christ is a perfect man like all other men, therefore Christ has a human will).

There are two kinds of theological conclusion. One is a *theological conclusion improperly so-called, or explanatory*, which is a mere explanation of the principle and does not contain a new concept, different from what is contained in the principle, but expresses the same concept in another manner or by an equivalent concept, drawn immediately from a mere analysis of the first. This happens when one concept is included in the very essence of the other, according to the four ways explained above.[53] The second

---

52 See the bibliography, listed above (p. 205), especially Doronzo, Gardeil, Grandmaison, Marin-Sola, Schultes. Cf. also A. Gits, *La foi aux faits dogmatiques dans la théologie moderne*, Louvain 1940; J. F. Bonnefoy, in *Marianum* 12 (1950) 194–226; A. M. Elorriaga, several articles in *Estudios eclesiásticos* 1926–1929; A. M. Lubik, in *Antonianum* 36 (1961) 29–68, 173–198.

53 See footnote 51. These *four ways* of essential inclusion can be exemplified in theological conclusions improperly so-called, as follows: either the *definition* is inferred from the thing defined (as: Christ is man, therefore he is a rational animal); or an *essential part* is inferred from the whole essence (as: Christ is a man, therefore he has a soul); or a *particular* is inferred from the universal (as: Christ is man, but all men belong to the same genus or family of Adam, therefore Christ belongs to the family of Adam); or one *relative* concept is inferred from its correlative (as: Christ is a divine Son, therefore he has a divine Father).

is a *theological conclusion properly so-called*, in which three things are required; first, it must be *truly illative*, that is, bringing forth a new concept, formally distinct from the concept expressed in the principle; second, it must be also a *necessary* and scientific conclusion (for if it is only probable, it does not properly belong to the science of theology); third, it must be an *absolutely necessary* conclusion, causing an absolute certitude, because a conclusion shares in the same certitude of its principles, and the principle of a theological conclusion is a revealed truth of faith which is absolutely certain.[54]

This absolute necessity and certitude in a theological conclusion can be obtained only in two cases, namely, when the concept expressed in the conclusion is either an *essential property*, or a *metaphysical effect* of the concept expressed in the principle, as has been explained above with pertinent examples (p. 211).

2. DEFINABILITY OF A THEOLOGICAL CONCLUSION

The question is whether the Magisterium can *infallibly define, as to be held with divine faith*, not only a revealed truth, but also something logically derived from a revealed truth, that is, a *theological conclusion* properly so called.

About this question there is a variety of judgment and a real controversy among theologians, depending mainly on what is to be called a theological conclusion. Hence we shall first indicate the three things on which they all agree, and then show and try to resolve the proper point of controversy.

All the theologians agree that the Magisterium can infallibly define as to be held with divine faith the following three things. First, the theological conclusions *improperly so called*, since they are mere explanations of a revealed truth and hence they are equivalent to it. Second, those theological conclusions *which we called proper and truly illative*, as in all the examples given above (see pp. 212, 217), and which however, some other theologians consider

---

54   As we noted in the treatise on *Revelation* (p. 79), absolute certitude is founded on metaphysical (and mathematical) laws, that is, in the very essence of things, which admit no exception, while the conditional certitude is founded on physical and moral laws, which allow exceptions, and it is sufficient in physical and moral sciences.

The certitude required in a true theological conclusion is absolute and of the metaphysical order; hence, certain conclusions, which are derived from revealed principles with only a physical or moral necessity, are not truly theological conclusions, but have to be considered as mere probable theological opinions.

as improper conclusions; in either consideration, the reason of their definability is their intimate and essential connection with the revealed truth. Third, also those *proper* theological conclusions which are derived *from two principles or premises of faith*, as explained above; the reason of their definability is again their intimate and total connection with the revealed truth, since no principle of reason intervenes in the process of deduction.

The point of controversy is whether the Magisterium can infallibly define, as to be held with divine faith, also other things, no matter how we call them. Such other things would be either proper *theological conclusion* (abstracting from the above-mentioned), that is, those that everyone considers as expressing a concept truly distinct from the one expressed in the revealed principle and at the same time proceed *from one principle of faith and one principle of reason*, or the so-called *dogmatic facts*, that is, facts intimately connected with revealed truth (which, at least in our opinion, have to be reduced to theological conclusions).[55]

Because this question is somewhat ambiguous, on account of the various senses in which a proper theological conclusion is understood by theologians, we shall put it in the following general and unmistakable form: *Whether the Magisterium can infallibly define as de fide any conclusion which follows with absolute necessity and certitude from a revealed truth*. There is a twofold opinion, one denying and the other affirming.

The first and negative opinion, held by several modern theologians and particularly emphasized by R. M. Schultes, O. P.,[56] teaches that theological conclusions, expressing a truly new concept and derived from one principle of faith and one principle of reason, cannot be infallibly defined as of divine faith, because their object, being deduced partially from reason, extends beyond the revealed truth and is not homogeneous with it; the same reason holds for the so-called dogmatic facts. Of course, the Magisterium infallibly defines such things, which, though not revealed, are intimately

---

55 These *dogmatic facts* are usually divided into mere *historical facts*, on which the authority of a Pope or a Council depends (for instance, whether the Anglican Orders are valid), and *doctrinal facts or dogmatic texts*, that is, the sense of signs by which revelation is expressed (for instance, the true meaning of a word, expression, or book of an author).

56 *Art. cit.* (footnote 44). Supporters of this opinion are, among others, Billot, Hugon, Garrigou-Lagrange, Lennerz, Zapelena, De Aldama, Elorriaga.

connected with revelation, but it defines them as to be believed not with divine faith, as the revealed truths, but with an *ecclesiastical faith*. This faith is neither divine nor simply human, but is found as it were in between the two, that is, resting solely on the authority of the infallible teaching of the Magisterium; thus, while the motive of the assent of divine faith is: "I believe this because God has revealed it," the motive of the assent of ecclesiastical faith is: "I believe this because the Magisterium teaches it infallibly."[57]

The second and affirmative opinion, held by an increasing number of recent theologians and particularly emphasized by F. Marín-Sola,[58] teaches that all true and necessary theological conclusions, as well as dogmatic facts, because of their intimate and necessary connection with revealed truths, can be defined infallibly as of *divine faith* by the Magisterium.

The reasons for this *more probable opinion* are the following:

First. The Magisterium *has in fact defined*, as dogmas of *divine* faith, several true and illative theological conclusions, that is, which express a concept truly new and distinct from the one expressed in the revealed truth, and which are derived from one principle of faith and one principle of reason.

This fact is, of course, denied by the defenders of the first opinion, who say that all such conclusions, defined by the Magisterium as dogmas of divine faith, are not proper and illative conclusions, but only improper and explanatory conclusions, and they contain nothing truly new and distinct from the revealed truth. However, if this can possibly be said of some of those truths which we listed above as proper and illative conclusions (p. 212), such as the consubstantiality of Christ with the Father and the Divine Maternity, which are very close to revealed truths, it cannot be reasonably

---

57 The name of *ecclesiastical faith* was explicitly brought forward for the first time around the middle of the 17th century during the controversy with Jansenists about the definitions of dogmatic facts (see footnote 62). But the concept itself had already been inculcated by L. Molina (†1600), N. Becanus (†1624), and J. Granados (†1632), and was urged in the 18th century under the very name of ecclesiastical faith by Antoine, Tournely, and Kilber, until it became quite common in the 19th and 20th centuries.

58 *Op. cit.* (footnote 44). Supporters of this opinion are especially De Grandmaison, Gardeil, Journet, Balic, Rondet, Sauras, Bonnefoy, Roschini, Dhanis, Garcia Martinez. There are a few discrepancies among these authors (for instance, some of them extend the infallible definition of the Magisterium even to probable theological conclusions); but they all agree in the essential positive doctrine.

said of other very particular and distinct truths, defined as *de fide* by the Magisterium. Such are, for instance, among the many things defined by the Council of Trent, the permanence of concupiscence after the remission of original sin, the necessity of the intention of doing what the Church does in the minister of a sacrament, and the necessity of natural water in Baptism. Who would reasonably say, or try to explain, that all these and many other similar truths are explicitly revealed and not merely inferred from other revealed truths through a proper and illative process?[59]

Second. A conclusion which brings out a formally new concept and follows with absolute necessity and certitude from a revealed principle, even with the concourse of a principle of reason, is implicitly revealed and truly homogeneous with the explicit revealed truth. This is so because it is nothing else than the proper and intrinsic virtuality of the revealed truth itself, *actually although implicitly contained in it,* in the manner of an essential property or effect, and distinguished from it not by a real distinction, but by the so-called distinction of reason having its foundation in the reality of things (see above, p. 211). Therefore such a conclusion can be defined in the same way as the explicitly revealed truths.

Again it is not reasonable to object that such conclusions are not proper but improper conclusions; for they bring forth a new and formally distinct concept, as in the examples just mentioned. Nor can one oppose that such conclusions go beyond the revealed truth and are not homogeneous with it, since they mingle with natural reason; for, natural reason is involved only in the process of concluding, not in the object of the conclusion itself, which is directly drawn from the revealed truth, although with the help of the natural principles and of the natural reasoning. The same thing happens, essentially and proportionally, when a theological conclusion is drawn from two premises of faith (in which case all theologians admit that it can be defined as of divine faith); for in both cases a new distinct concept is drawn from a revealed truth by means of a process of natural reasoning, and the difference of the two premises of faith is accidental to this matter.

Third. Any infallible definition of the Magisterium carries with it the obligation of assenting by divine faith to the proposed doctrine. The reason is because *an infallible definition* obliges to

---

59   Cf. Gardeil, *op., cit.* (footnote 440) 171.

an infallible assent of faith (that is, an assent that cannot be deceived), and only the assent of divine faith is infallible, because only God is infallible. Hence, an assent which would be based directly on the sole authority of the Magisterium, even under God's assistance, is only an assent of fallible faith based on a fallible human authority. Hence the so-called *ecclesiastical faith* involves a contradiction, by being at once infallible and not divine, that is, infallible and not infallible. There is no middle term between divine faith and purely human faith.[60]

What has been said about the definition of theological conclusions applies likewise to the definitions of *dogmatic facts*, pronounced infallibly by the Magisterium; namely, these definitions also carry the obligation, not of the so-called ecclesiastical faith (as the aforementioned theologians claim), but of the same divine faith by which the revealed truths themselves are believed. This however, cannot be explained but by *reducing the dogmatic facts to theological conclusions*, that is, by considering them as implicitly contained in the revealed truths and brought out into explicit knowledge by the infallible declaration of the Magisterium. The inclusion of these facts in the revealed truths can be understood as that of a *particular in the universal*, not however simply and absolutely (as Peter is included in the human race), but hypothetically and conditionally, that is, on the supposition that some condition is verified.

Thus, the *dogmatic historical fact* that the Council of Trent is infallible, is implicitly contained in the general revealed truth that all ecumenical Councils are infallible, provided they are legitimate. Such a fact can be brought into explicit knowledge by merely and naturally verifying Trent's legitimacy through a reasoning process: "Every ecumenical Council is infallible in its definitions, if it is legitmate in its convocation and acts; therefore, the Council of Trent is infallible." This same process applies to other dogmatic facts, both historical and doctrinal.[61] Thus the *dogmatic doctrinal fact* of the orthodoxy or heterodoxy of a word

---

60 Marin-Sola: "The ecclesiastical faith is a useless invention" (*op.cit.* [footnote 44] I 454). Gardeil: "The so called ecclesiastical faith [is] a word and a thing entirely new, unknown to thomistic theology, a kind of fourth theological virtue, invented to designate the assent given to theological conclusions ... supported by an act of the ecclesiastical authority" (*op. cit.* [footnote 44] 183).
61 See their distinction above, footnote 55.

or proposition or text or book of an author, is contained implicitly in the revealed truth and brought out from it through the following conclusion: "All texts, which bear a sense contradictory to revealed truth, are heretical; but this particular text bears a sense contradictory to revealed truth; therefore this particular text is heretical."[62]

---

62 Such was the case of the *condemnation of Jansenius' work "Augustinus."* The Jansenists tried to weaken the strength and sense of that condemnation, distinguishing between the question of right (that is, whether a proposition taken in itself is heretical) and the question of fact (that is, whether a proposition, as contained in this particular book and as pertaining to this particular author, is heretical), and they granted the condemnation only in the first sense. But Alexander VII rejected this interpretation, declaring that "the propositions of Jansenius had been condemned in the sense intended by Jansenius himself" (Denz. 2012).

6

Theological Notes and Censures[63]

THIS QUESTION IS LOGICALLY AND METHODOLOG-
ically connected with the two preceeding questions, because the
note or critical judgment about a doctrine, as to its agreement
with revealed truth, shows its greater or lesser value as a principle of theological argumentation, according to whether it is a
doctrine of faith, or only theologically certain, or merely probable.

1. NOTION OF THEOLOGICAL NOTE AND CENSURE

"Note" or "mark" means generically a distinctive sign, while
"censure" (from the Roman office of censor) means an act of rebuke.
In ecclesiastical science, "note" is taken in two senses, namely,
apologetically, as a distinctive sign of the Church (the four notes of
the Church, called unity, sanctity, catholicity, and apostolicity), and
dogmatically, as a favorable judgment on the theological value of a
doctrine (whether it is *de fide*, or certain, or probable). Likewise
"censure" is taken both in the canonical sense of penalty (canonical censure) and in the dogmatic sense of unfavorable judgment
(theological censure). Theological note and theological censure are
often taken interchangeably, and they are also called theological
value or qualification.

They are properly *defined: a judgment about the dogmatic value of a
proposition*, or more distinctly: a judgment about the agreement or
disagreement of a proposition with a doctrine proposed by the Magisterium. If the judgment is of agreement, it is called more properly
"note;" if it is of disagreement, it is called more properly "censure."

2. HISTORY OF THEOLOGICAL NOTES AND CENSURES

Pronouncing such judgments is a part of the teaching office
of the Church, which has exercised it since the beginning in

---

63 Cf. C. Cahill, *The Development of the Theological Censures After the Council of
Trent (1563–1709)*, Fribourg, Switzerland 1955; S. Cartechini *De valore notarum
theologicarum et de criteriis ad eas dignoscendas*, Roma 1951; *Dall'opinione al dogma.
Valore delle note theologiche*, Roma 1953; E. Doronzo, *Theologia dogmatica* 1 (Washington, 1966) 526–542.

various manners. St. Paul condemns as "anathema" any one who would spread false doctrines (Gal. 1:9; cf. 1:6–8; 1 John 2:22; 4:1–3; 2 John 7 and 10). In the first centuries, the Magisterium condemned schismatics and heretics with the same censure of "anathema," which in the canons of ancient Councils meant a solemn excommunication, implying also a declaration of heresy in the case of a doctrine (see in Denzinger the various canons and decisions of the Councils of Rome, Carthage, Ephesus, Orange, Constantinople II and IV, Nicaea II). Only in the 14th century the Magisterium began to use those particular expressions and distinctions, which have become traditional and classical in theology. John XXII (†1334) condemned various errors, using for the first time four out of the five principal censures, more commonly listed by theologians, namely, *heretical, erroneous, temerarious,* and *ill-sounding* (Denz. 916, 924, 946, 979); the Council of Constance in 1418 added the fifth censure, *"offensive to pious ears"* (Denz. 1251). From then on the same censures were frequently repeated, along with other names; several of them were particularly and distinctly used by Innocent X against Jansenius (Denz. 2006), by Alexander VIII against the Jansenist Synod of Pistoia (Denz. 2601–2700). The Councils of Trent and Vatican I in their canons used consistently the word "anathema," also in the sense of heretical. Recent documents generally abstain from applying particular censures under the aforementioned names and simply condemn or proscribe errors (cf. the condemnation of Bonnetty, Günther, the Rationalists, the Ontologists, Rosmini, and the Modernists, Denz. 2811ff., 2828ff., 2841ff., 2901ff., 3241, 3466).

3. AUTHOR OF NOTES OR CENSURES, AND MANNER OF THEIR APPLICATION

The principal *author* is naturally the Magisterium, as the authentic guardian and defender of revelation. Hence this task belongs to the Roman Pontiff (acting directly or through the Roman Congregations) and to the bishops (in Councils or individually), and it is usually exercised by way of censure rather than by positive theological notes. However, also private doctors or theologians, as specialists in their field and qualified witnesses of revelation, can assign a theological censure or note; such a right was often put into practice by great universities, as those of Paris and Louvain, and is usually applied by various theologians in their writings, who try in this manner to interpret the pronouncements of the Magisterium.

The *manner* in which censures are applied by the Magisterium is various. Often an *individual* proposition is directly condemned, either with a simple censure or with several (for instance, as heretical, erroneous, and temerarious). Sometimes several propositions are condemned *together and* "*in globo,*" either equally with one or several censures or unequally and respectively, so that one or another of the assigned censures regards each proposition, without any further determination (cf. Denz. 1251, the first global censure, issued by the Council of Constance against Wyclif and Hus; Denz. 1592, against Luther; Denz. 1980, against Baius; Denz. 2332, against Jansenists, etc.).

4. DIVISION OF NOTES AND CENSURES

As there are many ways of valuating a proposition, the number and the names of notes and censures vary in the documents of the Magisterium, and in the writings of theologians. However, among the censures issued by the Magisterium, there are five which show a more definite and distinctive character, and are brought to a particular attention by theologians, namely, *heretical, erroneous, temerarious, ill-sounding,* and *offensive to pious ears.* These and many others used by the Magisterium[64] can be reduced to two general headings; some involve a doctrinal defect, either in the concept itself (heretical, erroneous, temerarious), or in its expression (ill-sounding), others involve directly only a moral defect (offensive to pious ears; under the same heading would come more serious censures, which easily involve also a grave doctrinal defect, as scandalous, blasphemous, and schismatic).

Heretical proposition (opposed to the note: *de fide*) is the gravest censure, involving a direct opposition to a proposition defined by the Magisterium as *de fide.* Such opposition can be either a direct contradiction (by saying, for instance: Christ is not a man) or a simple contrariety (Christ is an angel); in both cases there is heresy, because two contradictory, as well as two contrary propositions, cannot be true at once.[65] With this censure are connected three

---

64   See especially the Constitution "Auctorem fidei," issued in 1794 by Pius VI against the Jansenist Synod of Pistoia (Denz. 2601–2693).

65   The opposite note "de fide" is distinguished by some theologians into that "of

lower and intermediate censures, which have a peculiar and unde-termined opposition to faith, namely, *proximate to heresy* (opposite note: proximate to faith), *tasting heresy* (resembling heresy), and *suspected of heresy;* these last two imply only a probability of heresy.

Erroneous proposition (opposed to the note: *theologically certain,* or *Catholic doctrine*), which is the principal definite censure after that of heresy, implies an opposition not immediately to faith itself, but to a proposition directly and necessarily connected with faith, so that if this is denied, faith also would be denied, at least logically if not actually. Such a proposition, necessarily connected with faith, is either a strict *theological conclusion* (see above, p. 217) or the so-called *Catholic doctrine,* that is, a doctrine so intimately connected with faith that it is commonly believed to be certainly revealed, and hence proximately definable, although it has not yet been defined by the Magisterium as *de fide;* also such a point of Catholic doctrine is to be objectively reduced to a theological conclusion, although its intimate connection with faith is not known through a logical and a priori process, but through an evident sign, that is, from the fact that it is commonly thought to be a revealed truth and as such is proposed also by the Magisterium, before defining it infallibly.[66]

Temerarious proposition (opposed to the note: *highly probable,* or *morally certain*) is a less definite censure and more difficult to describe. A temerarious proposition is opposed to a proposition

---

divine faith" (which would correspond to truths as merely found in the deposit of Scripture and Tradition) and that *"of Catholic faith"* (which is attributed to truths defined by the Magisterium). But it would be better to abstain from such a dis-tinction, since there is only one faith and one object of faith, that which follows the definition of the Magisterium. Hence the expression "This is a truth of divine and Catholic faith," occurring in some documents of the Magisterium, is a mere pleonasm which brings forth the two elements necessary to constitute the object of faith, namely the revelation of God and the proposition of the Magisterium.

As shown above (p. 221), there is no such thing as an ecclesiastical faith, distinct from divine faith; consequently we discard the corresponding note and censure (truth of ecclesiastical faith, error or heresy in ecclesiastical faith), listed by the supporters of this "faith."

Hence, the triple division, divine faith, Catholic faith, and ecclesiastical faith, is to be avoided, as a cause of confusion.

66   Such are the chapters of Trent and Vatican I, the two dogmatic Constitutions of Vatican II (on the Church and on Revelation), the Encyclical "Quanta cura" and the Syllabus of Pius IX, the Encyclical "Casti Connubii" of Pius XI, the Encyclical "Humani generis" of Pius XII. However, some of these documents may be infallible definitions *de fide,* as we noted above (footnote 43).

not entirely certain but highly probable and in this sense morally certain, as being solidly founded and commonly accepted among theologians. It is called temerarious, precisely because it affirms or denies something either without sufficient foundation or against the common opinion of theologians.[67]

Ill-sounding proposition (opposed to the note: *correct-sounding*) implies a defect regarding not the truth itself but its *expression*. Such a defect consists in the inaccuracy or the ambiguity of the expression (due to the words themselves or to historical circumstances) which may lead to error about the truth; for, as St. Thomas remarks after St. Jerome, "a heresy may arise from words wrongly used" (*Summa Theol.*, I, q. 31, a. 2).[68]

Offensive to pious ears proposition (opposed to the note: *fitting for piety*) implies a defect not of doctrinal order (regarding the truth or its expression) but only *of moral order*. Such a defect consists in saying a truth, which should be kept unsaid out of reverence for holy things, or in saying it in a manner which would cause contempt for holy things; both of these things offend the sense of piety and are opposed to the virtue of religion.[69] However, such a theological offense to pious ears must not be valued and measured according to the ears of any vulgar crowd, who easily take childish offense or pharisaic scandal, but according to sound and Christian common sense.

5. INTERPRETATION AND USE OF NOTES AND CENSURES

With regard to *the interpretation* of these qualifications, careful attention should be paid to their author (whether they proceed from the Magisterium itself or from the private judgment of theologians), to their proper and historical sense, and especially

---

67 Such would be, for instance, the affirmation of an immaculate conception for St. John the Baptist; the negation of the necessity of interior intention in the minister of a sacrament, or of the objective gravity of sexual intercourse outside marriage.

68 Such would be, for instance, the following propositions: "In God there are three relative essences" (in which essence is incorrectly taken for person and may induce one to believe that in God there are simply three essences, and hence three gods); "In the Trinity the Father is the cause of the Son" (which in the strict sense of causality, as the word "cause" is understood in the Latin Church, would imply subordination and inferiority on the part of the Son).

69 Such would be, for instance, an emphasis on some moral defects or sins of the apostles or other saints (who would be highly revered), as in the following prayer: "O Magdalen prostitute, Matthew usurer, Peter perjurer, Paul persecutor, pray for us!"

to their proper force, as to the agreement or disagreement of a proposition with revealed truth. For, while the two first censures of heretical and erroneous propositions (and their opposite notes) are absolutely immutable, on account of the evident opposition of these propositions to revealed truth, the last three censures are reformable with the change of circumstances, which are the cause of the aforementioned pernicious character.

Thus, what is a temerarious proposition at one time may not be temerarious at another time, if such a proposition becomes solidly probable, after sufficient reasons for it have been advanced (for instance, the affirmation of an immaculate conception for St. Joseph is no longer temerarious, as it used to be branded). *A fortiori* an ill-sounding proposition may lose such character, when words and formulas change their meaning through historical or doctrinal evolution, as happened to those used to express the mysteries of Trinity and Incarnation. The same holds *a fortiori* for a proposition offensive to pious ears, whose offensive character has only a relative basis, so that what is offensive at one time and in some circumstances may not be such in other times or circumstances.

With regard to *the use* of notes and censures by theologians, the following observations may be suitable. These qualifications should be based on and derived from the documents of the Magisterium, when the Magisterium itself has not assigned any explicit qualification. They should be simplified as to their number and their names, as we did above; the five qualifications, just explained, seem to be sufficient, at least generally, and in particular in theological manuals for the schools; the note *"de fide"* should not be sub-divided into those of "divine faith" and "Catholic faith," much less with the addition of "ecclesiastical faith;" and the note "Catholic doctrine," if used, should be accompanied by a clear explanation, on account of its broad and somewhat ambiguous sense.

Regarding the *moral value* of these qualifications, it should be noted that only the first censure (heretical) implies a sin against faith and the loss of this virtue, while all the others imply only a sin against the virtue of religion, and the last three (temerarious, ill-sounding, and offensive to pious ears) involve also a sin against prudence.

GLOSSARY OF TECHNICAL WORDS
Occurring in This Treatise

Analogy of faith is a theological expression which adopts the philosophical term of analogy, meaning a similarity between two concepts. Hence analogy of faith means a similarity between two revealed truths, or more properly the agreement which is necessarily found between the various truths of faith, so that from one we can rightly judge about the other: thus from the perpetual virginity of Mary we understand that those who are called brothers and sisters of Christ in the Gospel are only close relatives to him.

Argument-Conclusion. Argument or demonstration is a process by which we draw a conclusion from principles. This is done in any science. Hence it is proper to theology as a science to use arguments, that is, to draw conclusions from the principles of revelation, which are the various truths revealed by God. These theological conclusions, if they follow not merely probably but necessarily from the revealed principles, can be infallibly defined by the Church Magisterium, just as the revealed principles themselves, and hence they become also the object of our faith. Thus, from the revealed truth that Christ is also a true man similar to us, it is necessarily concluded that Christ has also a human will besides his divine will, and the Magisterium explicitly defined this as an article of divine faith in the Council of Constantinople III in 681.

Faith can be taken in two ways. First in a subjective sense, that is, for the virtue of faith residing in our mind and the consequent act of faith by which we express our belief in the word of God; in this sense Christians are called "The Faithful." Secondly, faith is often taken in an *objective sense*, that is, for the objects or truths we believe, briefly the word of God. It is in this second sense that faith is taken in the following expressions commonly used in theology:

Preambles of faith are those truths about God which can be known through natural reason (such as his existence and Providence) and which therefore are presupposed to, and prepare the understanding of, the supernatural truths. *Foundations of faith* are the revealed truths themselves, briefly revelation, which is the object and hence the foundation of faith. This is the reason why the theological treatise on revelation is called fundamental theology. *Principles of faith* are the same revealed truths inasmuch as they become the principles of all theological reasoning and conclusions. *Truths of faith* are the same revealed truths considered in themselves. *Articles of faith* are more strictly the principal or fundamental truths of faith, as those contained in the Creeds or Symbols of faith.

Formula of faith is a definite expression of revealed truth, such as the various symbols of faith or the definitions of the Magisterium. *Symbols of faith* (the Creeds) are the formulas expressing the principal revealed truths. *Rule of faith* is the authoritative factor which determines for us the object to be believed; it is divided into the *remote rule* (Scripture and Tradition) and the *proximate rule* (the Church Magisterium). *Dogma of faith* (or simply dogma) is revealed truth, contained in the deposit of Scripture and Tradition, as presented to us for belief by the infallible Magisterium; dogmatic formulas are the various expressions of the same dogma in the documents of the Magisterium. *Analogy of faith* is the necessary agreement existing between various revealed truths.

Magisterium generically means teaching function or office, whether freely accepted by others or imposed upon them by social rules. It implies always a *doctrinal authority* in the sense that a master or teacher as such knows more than the disciples or listeners, and hence impresses them with his superiority and has an influence on their mind with his knowledge. But a merely human Magisterium has no practical authority, that is, it cannot force anyone's mind to accept what it says or teaches, for the human intellect is an interior faculty and hence ontologically and socially free from coercion.

God's Magisterium on the contrary has also a *practical authority*, that is, it can command to the mind of man to accept his words and his teaching, not only by virtue of his infinite and infallible knowledge (which implies a supreme doctrinal authority), but by his dominion over our intellect as well as over our whole being. Moreover, nothing prevents God from communicating this practical authority of his to a man with regard to others, to be exercised by him in God's name and as it were instrumentally, in the manner of a commissioned office. Such is precisely the *Magisterium of the Church*, which can oblige the faithful to believe its pronouncements or presentations of the word of God. For this reason it is called the authentic or authoritative Magisterium.

Reason. When we speak of natural reason, or light, or principles, in opposition to supernatural revelation, or light, or principles, we point out the proper and specific power of our intellect, working out its knowledge from its own innate principles in the light of that proper perfection that makes man a rational animal. For this proper work our intellect does not strictly and physically need any additional supernatural help from God, although in the present condition of fallen nature after the original sin, we morally need such help only to promptly and definitely understand, as we should, moral and religious truths (such as God's existence, creation, Providence, and our fundamental obligations to him and to our neighbor).

But with regard to the knowledge of truths concerning supernatural religion (such as the Trinity, Incarnation, sanctifying grace, faith, hope of beatific vision, love of friendship for God) our natural intellect is powerless and blind, and hence it needs a proportionate *supernatural help, that* is, *a higher light* (of revelation, faith, or beatific vision). This supernatural light blends, as it were, with the natural light of reason itself and makes it able to elicit a supernatural act (of knowledge, of faith, or beatific vision). Thus reason is elevated to a higher order and the rational animal becomes a partaker of the proper light of God.

Revelation is generically the manifestation of a hidden truth, either in the natural or in the supernatural order. Supernatural revelation, taken *subjectively* on the part of the act of knowledge, can signify in a broader sense any supernatural help in the line of will, or in both lines. However, strictly speaking, revelation is such a supernatural help which makes us understand directly a supernatural truth and thus it is equivalent to speech of God to man. In this strict sense *revelation* is distinguished from two other supernatural lights or helps. These are, first *inspiration*, that is, a supernatural movement of God for writing without error what God wills a man to write, given in such a manner that God becomes the principal author of the writing. This took place with the various men who wrote the Bible, called therefore the inspired books. Second, *assistance of the Holy Spirit*, by which God disposes and arranges things and human actions in such a manner as to prevent a human writer or speaker from any error in a particular work or speech (as in the case of the Pope or an ecumenical council when defining infallibly a revealed truth).

Taken *objectively*, revelation is the truth manifested to us by God through the aforementioned supernatural light, that is, the revealed truth. To this concept of revelation are referred the theological terms of source, channel, deposit and organ of revelation, of which we are about to speak in the following entry.

Source, channel, deposit, organ of revelation. All these terms carry the same general concept of means of transmission of God's revelation to man. However, there is a shade of meaning between them, by reason of which they are not used interchangeably in theology. Up until the Second Vatican Council, Scripture and Tradition were called sources of revelation; the term channel has always kept an indefinite meaning and attribution. Vatican II suggested a change in theological terminology by using the term source of revelation only to signify the Gospel itself, and the term deposit to signify Scripture and Tradition. Hence the terminology, as it stands now, is the following. The *source* of revelation is the Gospel preached by Christ; Scripture and Tradition are the *deposits* (or rather one total deposit) of revelation (or the channels containing revelation); the Magisterium is the *organ* of revelation (or the channel immediately transmitting revelation to us). To use a common image, the living water of revelation comes down from the Gospel as its original source; it is gathered into the water tower of Scripture and Tradition; from this it is finally channelled to us, for our immediate needs and obligations, through the pipeline of the Magisterium. Of course it is up to our good will and savoir-faire to turn the faucet the right way in order to get from the indefectible pipeline of the Magisterium the limpid water, gathered into the unbroken reservoir of Scripture and Tradition from the inexhaustible source of the Gospel.

Theological "Loci" are called the places in which theologians find the proper principles of their investigation and demonstrations. The ten theological "loci" usually listed after Melchior Cano (†1560), their first illustrator (namely, Scripture, Tradition, Believing Church, the Magisterium of the Pope, the Magisterium of the Ecumenical Councils, the Fathers, the theologians, natural reason, the authority of philosophers, and history), can be reduced to three (omitting the last three which are merely extrinsic and confirming "loci"), namely, *Scripture, Tradition, and the Magisterium,* which are also channels of revelation and rules of faith.

ANALYTICAL INDEX

Analogy of faith, an expression used by theologians and insisted upon by the Magisterium, is the mutual agreement which necessarily exists between the various truths of faith, 176.

Apostles. After Christ's Ascension the apostles received several public revelations, footnote 49, but with the death of the last apostle (St. John who died about 100) public revelation was closed forever, 210. The apostles had a deeper understanding of the revealed truths, at least of those which are explicitly revealed, 215.

Believing Church. The sense of all the faithful about a doctrine of faith, or a doctrine connected with it, is witness to Tradition, 185, 188–190. It carries also infallibility in matters of faith, 188. It can be compared to the natural common sense with regard to the first principles of reason, 189, 213. It is an influential cause of the development of dogma, 213f.

Censures (theological). *See Notes (theological)*

Channels (of revelation) are divided into deposits of revelation (Scripture and Tradition, which can be considered as one total deposit) and organ of revelation (the Magisterium), footnote 3, 182. *See Source (of revelation)*

Conclusions (theological). In the strict sense a theological conclusion is a proposition necessarily derived from a revealed truth by means of a discursive process of our natural reason, 216f. It is distinguished from a mere explanation of the revealed truth and also from a proposition which follows only probably from a revealed truth, 216f. Various examples of theological conclusions 212, 219. To theological conclusions are to be reduced the so-called dogmatic facts, that is, those historical or doctrinal facts that are necessarily connected with the revealed truth, 217; *see Dogmatic facts.* The Magisterium can infallibly define theological conclusions, but it is disputed whether in that way they become the object of divine faith (as is more probable) or of an inferior kind of ecclesiastical faith, 217–222; *see Faith (ecclesiastical)*

Deposit (of revelation). *See Channels (of revelation)*

Doctors (of the Church). *See Fathers (of the Church)*

Dogma. In the strict sense dogma is a revealed truth infallibly defined by the Magisterium as to be believed of divine faith, 206f. It is objectively immutable with regard to the defined truth itself, 206f., but it undergoes development and progress with regard to the formulation and the logical implications of the revealed truth, 208–215. This progress is both subjective, as to a clearer understanding of the truth, and also objective, consisting in the passage of a truth from implicit to explicit, 209–214. Nature of this passage and various examples, 211–213. Historical ways and causes of the development of dogma, 213–215. There can be in the history of the Church an obscuration or regress about a revealed truth, totally so before its solemn definition by the Magisterium, and only partially afterwards, 215. See Conclusion (theological). Faith (divine), Revelation

Dogmatic facts are those historical or doctrinal facts that are necessarily connected with a revealed truth, such as the orthodoxy or heterodoxy of a doctrine or writing of an author, and the legitimacy of a Pope or Council, 218, 221f. They are to be reduced to theological conclusions; see this entry. They can be infallibly defined by the Magisterium, but it is disputed whether they become the object of divine faith (as is more probable) or of an inferior kind of ecclesiastical faith, 218–222; see Faith (ecclesiastical)

Faith (divine). Scripture and Tradition are only the remote rule of faith, while the Magisterium is its proximate rule, infallibly determining for us the object to be believed, which thus becomes dogma of faith; see Dogma Magisterium Scriptures Tradition. A "de fide" proposition is the first theological note, to which a heretical proposition is directly opposed, 225; see Notes (theological)

Faith (ecclesiastical). as to its origin, its supporters, and its weakness, 218, 221, 228, footnote 65. See Conclusions (theological). Dogmatic facts

Faithful. See Believing Church

Fathers (of the Church). They can be considered in two ways, that is, as witnesses to Tradition, 175, 179, 185, 186, 190, and as private doctors, 190, 192. Considered as witnesses to Tradition, their doctrine is the principal part of what is called argument of Tradition, 186; in this argument the doctrine of the Fathers should be carefully valuated, 186; see Tradition. Considered as private doctors, their doctrine is the basis of a secondary and mere probable argument in theology, 192. The four qualifications required to be a Father of the Church, 190f. Distinction between Fathers and both ecclesiastical writers and Doctors of the Church, 191f. List of the Doctors of the Church, 192

Inspiration. Its notion and extension, 171f. It gives to Scripture its importance and its relative excellence over Tradition, 182, footnote 24. However, we know only from Tradition itself that Scripture, as a whole, is inspired, 181, 182

Magisterium (of the Church). Notion and division into ordinary and extraordinary 197f. The ordinary Magisterium has the same value as the extraordinary, 175, 198. The Magisterium is the channel and the organ of revelation as well as the proximate rule of faith, and under this consideration it is for us more important than Scripture and Tradition, footnote 3, 198f. The Magisterium declares the sense of Scripture, 175, 198, and of Tradition, 185, 198. It is, however, inferior to Scripture and

Tradition inasmuch as these are the deposit of revelation from which the Magisterium derives its doctrine, 174. The Magisterium is also part of Tradition, taken integrally, 179, 185. It is the basis of the strongest argument in theology, 198; for this purpose the various pronouncements of the Magisterium should be carefully valuated, 198–201. The Magisterium is one of the causes of the development of dogma in various ways, 208, 214. Once infallibly defined by the Magisterium, a truth becomes formally a dogma of faith, 206f., objectively immutable, 206, and subjectively free from a general obscuration or regress in the Church, 214f.

Modernists deny the objective value and immutability of dogma, footnote 46

Notes (theological). Their notion and distinction from theological censures, 223f., their history, 223, author, 224f., division, 225–227, interpretation and use, 227f. The principal notes are three, namely, a proposition of faith, a proposition theologically certain, and a proposition greatly probable, to which three censures are opposed, that is, heretical, erroneous, and temerarious propositions, 225f.

Prescription (theological), as to its value and the manner in which it should make up a theological argument, 187f.

Protestants discard Tradition as a rule of faith, holding firmly to their aphorism "Scripture alone," footnote 18; they deny also the infallibility of the Magisterium and the immutability of dogmas defined by it, footnote 46

Revelation. Its object; *see Conclusions (theological). Dogma.* The means of its transmission or channels (which come down to us from the Gospel, its source) are Scripture and Tradition, as deposits of revelation, and the Magisterium, as its organ; *see these three entries.* Public revelation, given by Christ and partially continued through the apostles after his Ascension, has been definitely closed at the death of the last apostle (St. John who died about 100), 210f. Private revelations are not an object of faith, even after their approbation by the Magisterium which only declares them to be in harmony with faith and Christian life, footnote 50

Scripture. Regarding the senses of biblical texts, *See Sense (biblical).* Chronology of the various biblical writings, footnote 19. Scripture is not properly the source of revelation, but its channel and deposit, footnote 3, 174. Comparison between Scripture and Tradition as to their value under the aspect of deposit of revelation, 179–185. The interpretation of biblical texts depends on Tradition and on the Magisterium, 174f. *See Inspiration. Magisterium. Tradition. Vulgate*

Sense (biblical) is usually divided into literal, typical, and ampler, 172–174. The third sense, introduced by some modern scholars under the name of "sensus plenior," seems difficult to admit, 173. The literal sense is practically the most important, 176f. The typical sense should not be easily asserted because it is known only through God's revelation, 177

Source (of revelation), according to the new terminology introduced by Vatican II, is the Gospel itself and not Scripture and Tradition, which are only the deposit of revelation, footnote 3. *See Channels (of revelation)*

Theologians, as distinct from the Fathers of the Church, 192f. Not everyone who teaches theology or even holds a doctorate in theology is properly a theologian in the theological sense, but to be qualified as such two things are required, namely, eminent doctrine and approbation (at least implicit) of the Magisterium, 194f. Theologians, considered as private doctors, are the basis of a probable argument in theology, especially in the case of general agreement, 194f. Theologians have no Magisterium of their own but they are only commissioned to teach by the authentic Magisterium, footnote 38. Theological reasoning is an influential cause of the development of dogma, 211–213

Thomas Aquinas. His doctrine can be considered as the basis of a strong probable argument in theology by reason of its very special approbation by the Magisterium, which considers St. Thomas as the "Doctor Communis," 195–196. Vatican II points him out as the guide to be followed in Catholic schools and theological faculties, 196. He was the first among theologians to be declared Doctor of the Church, 192

Tertullian, who introduced and effectively used the so-called argument of prescription, footnote 27, is not properly speaking a Father of the Church because of some important errors in matters of faith, 191

Tradition is a channel and a deposit of revelation, footnote 3, 178–179, 185. Taken integrally, it implies all the means through which the revealed truth is transmitted, including Scripture and the Magisterium, 179, 185, 189. The restrictive sense, which opposes and distinguishes Tradition from Scripture, has been introduced by the theologians only after the Council of Trent, 179. Comparison between Tradition and Scripture in their value as deposit of revelation, 179–182. Ambiguous controversy among recent authors about the very existence of the so-called constitutive Tradition which would contain some truths not sufficiently contained in Scripture, 182–185. Tradition depends on the Magisterium as to its interpretation, 185, 198. The argument of Tradition should be carefully valuated, 185–187. *See Fathers (of the Church)*

Vatican Council II introduced a new terminology, calling the Gospel alone source of revelation, and Scripture with Tradition only deposit of revelation, footnote 3. It considers also Scripture and Tradition as one total deposit rather than two deposits of revelation, 182, 185. The Magisterium is not above the word of God but merely its channel and organ, footnote 12. The mind of the Council about the so-called constitutive Tradition, footnote 24. The sense of all the faithful in matters of faith is infallible, 189. On the development of dogma, 208f. Public revelation has been closed forever at the death of the last apostle, 211. This Council issued no definitions of faith, even in the two dogmatic constitutions on revelation and the Church, footnote 66

Vulgate, or the Latin version of the Bible, as to its authority and theological use, 172, 174

BIBLIOGRAPHY

Cano, M., *De locis theologicis* (posthumous work, first edited at Salamanca in 1563; the last edition is found in *Melchioris Cani Opera Theologica*, 3 vols., Rome 1900).

Casado, F., "En torno a la génesis del 'De locis thologicis.'" *Revista española de teologia* 32 (1972) 55–82.

Doronzo, E., *Theologia dogmatica* 1 (Washington, D.C. 1966) 399–544.

Gardeil, A., "La notion du lieu théologique," *Revue des sciences philosophiques et théologiques* 2 (1908) 51–73, 246–276, 484–505; "Lieux théologiques," *Dictionnaire de théologie catholique* 9-1 (Paris 1926) 712–747.

Lang, A., *Die Loci Theologici des Melchior Cano und die Methode des dogmatischen Beweises*, München 1925.

Lubac, H. de, *Sources of Revelation* (trans. From the French), New York 1968.

Marcotte, E., *La nature de la théologie d'après Melchoir Cano* (Ottawa 1949) 110–162.

Mysterium salutis. Dogmatique de l'histoire du salut (translation of the German collective work), I/2: *La révélation dans l'Ecriture et la Tradition*; I/3: *L'Eglise et la transmission de la revelation*, Paris 1969.

BOOK 4
The Church

INTRODUCTION

1. PARTICULAR CHARACTER OF THE TREATISE

This treatise is comparatively new in theology and is still in the making, painfully acquiring its specific features. Its difficult character arises from the complex nature of the Church, which extends its connections and ramifications into other treatises of theology, as those on the Incarnate Word, Trinity, sacraments, faith, revelation, the last things. Indeed, the Church is the continuation of the Incarnation, the Mystical Body of Christ animated by the Holy Spirit, the sacrament of salvation, the rule of faith, the organ of revelation, the pilgrim people searching out its way to the new Jerusalem.

In the Middle Ages there was no distinct treatise on the Church, but its various elements were loosely placed, according to their formal aspect, in different parts of theology. Thus the doctrine of the Mystical Body was expounded within the question of the capital grace of Christ and the doctrine of the authority of the Church in the question on the rule of faith, as appears from the *Summa Theologiae* of St. Thomas. After the Council of Trent, the first distinct treatises on the Church began to take shape, with the purpose of defending the authority of the Hierarchy against the attacks of the Protestants. Later they developed into more ample works, frequently including also the matter of revelation, with the same apologetical purpose against the new attacks of Rationalism. Even when positive dogmatic elements were amplified and stressed in this treatise, it kept the ambiguous apologetical-dogmatic features of an ecclesiological symposium, aiming principally at showing and defending the external and *social aspect* of the Church, without any particular consideration of its intimate nature as the Mystical Body of Christ.

This *spiritual aspect* of the nature of the Church has been emphasized by modern theologians and endorsed by Pius XII in his Encyclical "Mystici Corporis" in 1943, resulting in a general effort to reshape the principal lines of this treatise. More recent theologians have also emphasized *the ecumenical and eschatological aspects* of the Church, as the pilgrim People of God leading all nations and searching out the way ahead until it will meet the coming Lord. This view has been endorsed by the Vatican Council II.[1]

2. THE OBJECT OF THIS TREATISE

The general notion of the Church is contained and manifested in the three expressions that have become its proper names, that is, *Church, Catholic Church* and *Mystical Body.* All other expressions, such as People of God, Kingdom of God, Temple of God, House of God, Spouse of Christ (see below, pp. 260–263), are not proper names in theological terminology, but only short paraphrases of the nature of the Church

Church (from the Greek "Ecclesía, i.e., convocation) etymologically means assembly, convention, meeting of people, either as the act of assembling or as the people assembled. In this twofold sense the word was used by Greek classic writers to signify *political conventions.* In the Septuagint Greek version of the *Old Testament* the same word occurs 95 times, usually as the translation of the Hebrew gâhâl, which is also translated by the word "synagogue"; it means a *political-religious convention*, proper to the Jewish theocratic people.[2] In the N.T the word occurs about 114 times to signify (except in Act. 7:58; 19:23–40) the Christian communities and often the *Universal Church* itself.[3] In the Gospel it occurs three times and in Matthew alone, used by Christ Himself (Matt. 16:18: "Ecclesiam meam," in the universal sense; 18:17 twice, in a particular sense). Christ usually uses the expression "Kingdom of God" or "Kingdom of Heaven."[4] The word in early Tradition became the proper name of the universal Christian congregation.

---

1 On these developments of the treatise, see: *L'ecclésiologie au XIX siècle* (collective work), Strasbourg 1959; Stanislaus Jáki, *Les tendances nouvelles de l'ecclésiologie,* Rome 1957; R. X. Redmond, in *Proceedings of the Catholic Theological Society of America 1962,* pp. 139–160; R. Ortuño, in *Angelicum* (1966) 458–510 (see also other writers in the same fasc. 3–4 of this periodical); Y. M-J. Congar, in *Revue des sciences philosophiques et théologiques* (1967) 250–258.

2 The first book, in which the Greek translation uses the word "Ecclesia" (Church) is Deuteronomy, 4:10; 9:10; 18:16 ("The day of the assembly"); 23:1–8 ("The community of the Lord"); 31:30 ("The assembly of Israel").

3 This universal sense is found in Matt. 16:18; Eph. 1:22; 3:10, 21; 5:23, 24, 25, 27, 29, 30, 32; 1 Cor. 10:32; 12:28; 15:9; Gal. 1:13; Phil. 3:6; Col. 1:18, 24.

4 We do not know what Aramaic word Christ used in those three places. According to some scholars (as Zapelena and Cullmann), he probably used the word "gehala" which corresponds to the aforementioned Hebrew word "qâhâl" (Church or Synagogue).

Catholic Church (in Greek "Katholiké Ekklesía"; "katholicós," total, from "katá," according to, and "hólos," whole, entire), means total or universal Church.

The word "*Catholic,*" in the sense of total or universal, is used by classic writers, both Greek and Latin; thus Aristotle (*Rethor,* 1.2.15; *Analyt. Poster.* 24) speaks of catholic, that is, universal, as opposed to individual, of catholic expression, and of catholic demonstration. It is used also in the Septuagint version of the O. T. (Ex. 20:11; Ezech. 13:3, 22; 17:14; Amos 3:3, 4; Dan. 3) and once in the N. T. (Acts 4:18: "Not to speak ... at all [kathólou = in no way]").

The combined expression "*Catholic Church*" is not biblical, although it has some foundation in Matt. 26:13 and Mark 14:9, who speak of the "Gospel preached in the whole world." It is formally patristic. It was used for the first time at the beginning of the 2nd century by St. Ignatius of Antioch († about 107), disciple of St. John the Evangelist (*Epistle to the Christians of Smyrna* 8.2: "Where Christ Jesus is, there is the Catholic church"). It occurs four times about the middle of the same century in the epistle of the church of Smyrna on the martyrdom of St. Polycarp, addressed "to all communities of the world, belonging to the Catholic Church" (inscription; cf. 8.1; 16.2; 19.2).

In the third century it became already a common and technical proper name for the true Church as distinct from heretical sects; it is used by the most important writers, such as Clement of Alexandria (*Miscellanies* 7.18), Origen (*On Canticles* 2.14; *On Matt.,* no. 50), Tertullian (*Against Marcion* 4.4; *Prescriptions* 30), St. Hippolytus of Rome (*Philosophumena* 9.12), the author of *Didascalia* (chaps. 1, 8, 9, 10, 11, 13, 24, 25), and St. Cyprian who gave the title *On the Unity of the Catholic Church* to one of his principal writings. In the fourth century the name was introduced into various Symbols of the Faith and finally into the universal Creed of the Council of Constantinople I in 381 (Denz. 150: "One, holy, Catholic, and apostolic Church").[5]

---

5 It may be that the original meaning of "Catholic Church" referred directly to the *intrinsic totality* (the Church, which has all the means and doctrines of salvation), rather than to the *extrinsic or extensive totality* (the Church, which is everywhere, the greater and universal Church). At any rate this second meaning was soon added, as appears from the explanations of the word given in the 4th and 5th centuries by Cyril of Jerusalem (*Catech.* 18.23), Optatus of Milevis (*On the Schism of the Donatists* 1.26), Augustine (*Epist.* 52.1; *Epist.* 92.23), and Vincent of Lerins (*Commonitorium I,*

Mystical Body (of Christ)[6] is not strictly a proper name of the Church, but rather a technical expression of the proper nature of the Church, which is now used so commonly and emphatically that it has become the equivalent of a proper name. It has its origin in the Bible, at least essentially in so far as St. Paul calls the Church the *"Body of Christ"* (Rom. 12:4f.; 1 Cor. 12:27; Col. 1:18; Eph. 1:22f.) The Fathers completed the expression by adding the adjective "spiritual" and calling the Church *"Spiritual Body"* which is perfectly equivalent to "Mystical Body (Clement of Alexandria, *Miscellanies* 7.14; Tertullian, *Against Marcion* 5.19; Gregory the Great, *Morals* 34.4.8).

The expression "Mystical Body" as such, was coined in the Middle Ages. It appeared, probably for the first time, in the *Summa Aurea* of William of Auxerre (†1231) and became common among the theologians of the 13th century. It was soon adopted also by the Magisterium, first by Boniface VIII in his famous Encyclical "Unam sanctam" of 1302 (Denz. 870) and then frequently by other Roman Pontiffs up to the present time. Vatican I brings it forth in the prologue of the Constitution on Catholic Faith ("The entire Mystical Body of Christ") and Vatican II uses it three times in its Dogmatic Constitution on the Church (nos. 7, 50, 54). Pius XII in particular took it as the title of his important encyclical on the nature of the Church, ("Mystical Body" 1943) and proposed it as the proper definition of the Church, explaining at length the reason why "the Body of Christ, which is the Church, must be called mystical" (Denz. 3809).

From these three names we gather *the general notion of the Church* as being an assembly of people and hence some kind of society (Church), universal in character (Catholic Church) and spiritual in nature (Mystical Body). But, when it is question of defining it scientifically, that is, of striking the essential note under which every other element must be leveled and measured, theologians feel doubt and uneasiness. The reason is the aforementioned double aspect of the Church (p. 242), as being at once a social external reality and a spiritual invisible entity. These two notes,

---

chap. 2: "We must hold what has been believed everywhere, always, and by all. For this is truly and properly Catholic"). Hence the complete sense of the expression "Catholic Church" is: the Church that has all and is in all.

6   As to the origin of this expression, see H. De Lubac, *Corpus Mysticum* (éd. 2, Paris 1949) 13–19, 116–135.

mutually opposed in character, seem to exclude each other, at least from the essence or nature of the Church. For, if the Church is essentially a society, as older theologians customarily defined it, it is essentially exterior and hence not essentially spiritual or mystical; if, on the contrary, the Church is essentially a Mystical Body, as recent theologians choose to define it, it is essentially interior and hence not a visible society.

It seems, however, that both notes and aspects can be brought into unity under the concept of Mystical Body or supernatural society, *defining the Church properly and essentially as follows: The Church is a Mystical Body of Christ, that is, a supernatural union of men in Christ, based on the vital influence of the Holy Spirit and the exterior bonds of faith, worship, and government.* The suitableness of this definition will be shown below in the proper place (pp. 256–270).

3. DIVISION OF THE TREATISE

For the sake of simplicity we distribute the entire matter into seventeen consecutive chapters. These, however, are placed in a logical order, according to four lines of thought, as follows;

1. Institution and purpose of the Church	Chap. 1
2. Nature of the Church	
Intimate nature (the Mystical Body)	Chap. 2
Exterior structure	
The true and perfect society	Chap. 3
Its threefold power	Chap. 4
The two degrees of the power of jurisdiction	
Primacy	
Primacy of Peter	Chap. 5
Primacy of the Roman Pontiff	
Existence	Chap. 6
Nature	Chap. 7
Property of infallibility	Chap. 8
Episcopacy	
Divine origin	Chap. 9
Collegial nature	Chap. 10
Monarchical form	Chap. 11
The three degrees of the power of Orders, episcopate, presbyterate, and diaconate	Chap. 12

3. The members of the Church
  In general   Chap. 13
  The laity in particular   Chap. 14
4. Resulting elements
  Properties of the Church
    Intrinsic properties   Chap. 15
    Extrinsic marks   Chap. 16
  Activity of the Church in the world   Chap. 17

1

Institution and Purpose of the Church

THIS GENERAL AND INTRODUCTORY CHAPTER gathers into a brief synthesis the two extrinsic causes, which brought the Church into existence, namely, its efficient cause, or founder, and its final cause, or the purpose which moved the founder to such an institution. It is, therefore, a general inquiry into that striking phenomenon which sprang out of the life of Christ into the world, and appeared to all men like "a flag set up above the nations."[7]

Statement. *In order to complete and continue the history of salvation, Christ instituted the Church, that is, a spiritual and visible union of men having for its purpose the salvation of souls.*

Theological note. This statement is an *article of faith,*[8] repeatedly proposed by the ordinary infallible Magisterium and again

---

7 Isa.11:12; 5:26. Cf. Vatican Council I, sess. 3, chap. 3.
8 It is denied by a twofold heresy. *Modernists* (especially A. Loisy, *L'Evangile et l'Eglise* [éd. 5, Paris 1930] 33–70) deny that Christ had the intention of founding a *union* of men, that is, a kingdom of God present in this life. According to them, Christ, deceived by eschatological ideas, that is, convinced that the end of the world was approaching, intended to announce a mere eschatological kingdom of God, namely, a heavenly and glorious kingdom, which would start with the imminent end of the world and in which the world would be transformed and the Messiah glorified. Such was the historical preaching of Christ himself, as appears from a few scattered passages reflecting the original gospel (as Matt. 10:23; 16:28; 24:34; 26:64). After Christ's death, when this eschatological expectation appeared frustrated, the first Christians changed the character of the kingdom of God, proposed by Christ, and introduced into their gospels a kingdom of this present life, at once spiritual and external, having only an ultimate and remote eschatological term. This heresy is exposed and condemned by Pius X in the Decree "Lamentabili" (Denz. 3433) and in the Encyclical "Pascendi" (Denz. 3492).

Renewed interest in Modernism and favorable judgement on it is shown in the following recent publication: E. Poulat, *Histoire, dogme et critique dans la crise moderniste*, Paris 1962; J. J. Heaney, *The Modernist Crisis*, London 1969; O. Rousseau, *Le mouvement théologique dans le monde contemporain. Liturgie, dogme, philosophie, exégèse*, Paris 1969; J. A. Hartley, *Thomistic Revival and the Modern Era*, Toronto 1971.

Liberal Protestants (especially A. Sabatier, *Esquisse d'une philosophie de la religion*, Paris 1897, and A, Harnack, *Das Wesen des Christentums*, Leipzig 1900) deny that

solemnly declared by *Vatican I*, in the following opening words of its Constitution on the Church: "[Christ] the eternal shepherd and the bishop of our souls, in order to render perpetual his beneficial work of redemption, decided to build the holy Church, in which all the faithful would be gathered as in the house of the living God, with the bond of the same faith and charity" (Denz. 3050).

The proof of our statement is made manifest by the simple consideration of the history of salvation, from the fall of Adam to the redemptive work of Christ, which was to be the beginning of a new eschatological era. This history is briefly and aptly outlined by *Vatican II*, stating: "The eternal Father...[from all eternity] had decided to gather in the holy Church all those who would believe in Christ. The Church, already foreshadowed since the beginning of the world, then suitably prepared through the history of the people of Israel and by the Old Covenant, and finally established in the new era, has been made manifest through the outpouring of the Spirit and will reach its glorious fulfillment at the end of the world."[9]

The history of salvation began immediately after the fall of Adam with the promise of the future Redeemer made by God: "I will put enmity between you and the woman, between your seed and her seed; he shall crush your head, and you shall lie in wait for his heel" (Gen. 3:15). In this promise the Church is also implicitly foreshadowed, as the mystical body of the future Redeemer.

In the *patriarchal period*[10] up to the establishment of the synagogue through Moses, the divine plan of salvation was carried out in a rather individual manner, through private helps, inspirations, and revelations, having, however a bond of intentional cohesion and continuity on the part of God. This appears especially from the four successive messianic prophecies uttered in this period: Gen. 3:15, just quoted, about the saving seed of the woman; Gen. 22:17f., about all nations to be blessed in the seed of Abraham;

Christ had the intention of founding an *external union* of men, with a determined faith or doctrine and a definite form of worship, to be followed by all. He only gave a general religious impulse, or founded a purely spiritual and internal union, consisting in an intimate religious sense of the filial relationship between man and God, which Christ particularly experienced and by word and example communicated to other men. The external and definite aspect and organization of Christian religion is due to a later evolution made by the primitive Church, under the influence of Judaism, Hellenism, and Roman political organization.

9   Dogmatic Constitution on the Church, no. 2.
10   Cf. Ch. Journet, *L'Eglise du Verbe Incarné* 3 (Bruges-Paris 1969) 349–412.

Gen. 49:8–12, about the future leader rising from the tribe of Judah; Num. 24:17–19, about the star rising from the family of Jacob. This status of supernatural economy contains the *first embryo of the future Church*. In it the messianic hope was carried on, the figure of the future founder of the Church was gradually shaped up as the saving seed of the woman, the blessed seed of Abraham, the rising star from Jacob, the coming leader from Judah. Also the first draft of a covenant was outlined between God and Noe (Gen. 6:18: "I will establish My covenant with you") and later between God and Abraham (Gen. 22:18: "In your descendants all the nations of the earth shall be blessed").

The blessing given by God to Abraham was the origin of the *second embryo of the future Church*, namely, the synagogue founded by God through Moses, a prophetical figure of Christ.[11] The general features of the Church began clearly to appear through the three elements which successively made up the synagogue. There was first the direct election of Israel as *"the People of God"* (Ex. 6:7; Deut. 7:6) or "the Kingdom of God" (Ex. 19:6; Num. 23:21; Deut. 33:5). There followed an *explicit covenant*, drafted in the form of a law on mount Sinai (Ex. 24:12). Finally a *definite form of cult* or public religion was established, with temple, ark of the covenant, altar, rites and priests (Exodus, chaps. 25–30). In this second period the messianic hope increased and the prophetical picture of Christ was fully outlined, as to his divine sonship (Ps. 2:6–9), kingship (*ibid.*), priesthood (Ps. 109:1–4), teaching function (Deut. 18:18), virginal birth (Isa. 7:14), passion (Isa. 52), and resurrection (Ps. 15:9–11).[12]

In these same prophecies the Church is also outlined as the future universal and spiritual kingdom to be founded by the Messiah. Particularly Jeremiah prophesies the Church as the New Covenant, saying: "Behold the days shall come, saith the Lord, and I will make a new covenant with the house of Israel and with the house of Juda. Not according to the covenant which I made with their fathers, in the day that I took them by the hand to bring them out of the land of Egypt: the covenant which they made void,

---

11   Cf. Journet, *ibid.* 412–518; P. Touilleux, *L'Eglise dans les Ecritures. Préparation et naissance*, Paris 1968.
12   About these and other messianic prophecies sees our treatise on *Revelation*, pp. 149–152.

and I had dominion over them, saith the Lord. But this shall be the covenant that I will make with the house of Israel after those days, saith the Lord: I will give My law in their bowels and I will write it in their heart: and I will be their God, and they shall be My people" (31:31–33).

Thus these two successive periods in the history of salvation, namely, the patriarchal and the Mosaic, were essentially *a symbolic figure and a historic preparation of the Church*, the New People of God and the New Covenant. St. Paul, speaking of the laws and happenings of the Old Testament, states: "All these things happened to them as a type, and they were written for our correction, upon whom the final age of the world has come" (1 Cor. 10:11).

Hence, "when the fullness of time came, God sent his Son, born of a woman, born under the law" (Gal. 4:4), that same ruler who was to come for all the nations (Gen. 49:10), to bring to them the *New Covenant*, to gather among them the *New People of God*, the *New Kingdom of God*, the *New Assembly or Synagogue*, the *Church.*[13]

After the short ministry of John the Baptist, the forerunner prophesied by Malachy (3:1–3; appendix 5), who announced to the people that "the kingdom of heaven was at hand" (Matt. 3:2), Jesus of Nazareth "began to preach and to say, Repent for the kingdom of heaven is at hand" (Matt. 4:17), for "until John came, there were the Law and the Prophets; since then the kingdom of God is being preached" (Luke 16:16).

As far as we know from the Gospel, Christ practically always calls His ministry *"the kingdom"* (of God or of heaven); only three times He calls it *"the Church,"* the name which became current in the apostolic preaching (see above, p. 243).[14]

This Kingdom or Church is manifestly presented by Christ as a *spiritual and visible union of men*. The very names of Kingdom and Church imply the concept of union and suggest also a visible or external union; the reference of this Kingdom to God and to heaven expresses also its spiritual character.

---

13 Cf. Journet, *op. cit.* 574–602; Touilleux, *loc. cit.*
14 The various expressions occurring in the Gospel are: *Church;* Matt. 16:18; 18:17. *Kingdom of God* (in the three Synoptics, especially in Luke): Matt. 12:28; 21:43; Mark 1:14, 15; 4:20; Luke 4:43; 6:20; 10:9, 11; 13:18; 16:16; 17:20, 21; 18:16; 19:11; 21:31; 22:18. *Kingdom of heaven* (only in Matthew): Matt. 3:2; 5:3, 10; 10:7; 11:12; 13:11, 24, 31, 33, 44, 45, 47; 16:19; 18:23; 19:14; 20:1; 22:2; 25:1 *Kingdom:* Matt. 8:12; 14:19, 38. *His Kingdom:* Luke 1:33. *My Kingdom:* John 18:36. *The Gospel of the Kingdom:* Matt. 4:23; 9:35; 24:14; Mark 1:14.

The concept of *union* is emphasized in the hierarchical character of the Church, which makes it also a proper social union, that is, a true society. This will be shown directly below in chapter 3. It suffices at present to refer to the main passages in which Christ gives the apostles and their successors the threefold power of teaching (Matt. 28:18–20), ruling (Matt. 18:18; 16:18f.), and sanctifying (Matt. 28:18–20; John 20:21f.). At any rate, the very communication in the same purpose and same means of salvation (faith and cult, as Baptism and the Eucharist) involves some kind of union. Christ speaks of His followers as "one fold... under one shepherd" (John 10:16) and prays His Father "that all may be one" (John 17:21).

The *spiritual* character of this union follows likewise from the spirituality for its purpose (see below) and its means (faith, cult, laws expounded by Christ particularly in his sermon on the mountain in Matt. chaps. 5–6).

Its *visible* or external character is manifest in many ways. The messianic kingdom, foretold by the prophets, which Christ affirms to be fulfilled in His own kingdom, was described as visible and external (cf. Isa. 2:2–4; Dan. 2:44; 7:13f. 27; Mal. 1:11). The members of Christ's Kingdom are visible and external, as appears from the parables about this kingdom, in which the good and the bad live together, like wheat and tares in the same field, like good and useless fish in the same net, like men clothed with the nuptial garment at the banquet and those lacking it (Matt. 13:1–50; 22:1–14). The duties to be performed in this kingdom are likewise external, as public preaching (Matt. 10:32f.). *A fortiori* the aforementioned threefold power given by Christ to His apostles show the external character of His Kingdom.[15]

The purpose assigned by Christ to His Church is *the salvation of souls*, that is, their sanctification required for eternal life. Generally speaking, the reason why the Church was instituted is the continuation of the history of salvation, but this history

---

15 The two heresies of *Modernists* and *Liberals*, related in footnote 8, cannot be directly disproved here from the testimony of the Gospels, since they deny the historical truth of the texts concerning the institution and the proper character of the Church. Hence their refutation is to be found in the works of the Catholic exegetes, who prove the genuineness and historicity of the Gospels.

Regarding Christ's prophecy about the end of the world, on which Modernists particularly base their opinion of the eschatological idea and error of Christ, see our treatise on *Revelation*, pp. 143–145.

took up a new mode in this last period and Christ assigned a new and specific purpose to the Church. The proper purpose of the old economy and covenant was not directly to sanctify the people, but rather to convey and transmit the messianic faith, through which men were sanctified as it were by anticipation, that is, in virtue of a foregoing application of the merits of the future Redeemer; in this sense the saints of the Old Testament can be said to belong to the New Testament and to be members of Christ's Body.[16]

On the contrary, after the messianic hope has been fulfilled, the Church founded by Christ shares in the same sanctifying purpose and is destined to continue and perpetuate the redemptive work of Christ. Such is the purpose explicitly assigned to it by the Saviour, saying: "As Thou hast sent Me into the World, so also I have sent them into the world" (John 17:18; cf. 17:19–26); "As the Father has sent Me, I also send you" (John 20:21); "All power in heaven and on earth has been given to Me. Go, therefore, and make disciples of all nations, baptizing them..., teaching them to observe all that I have commanded you" (Matt. 28:18–20).

To this purpose are directed all the operative means with which Christ endowed his Church, as the office of teaching the faith necessary for salvation and administering the sacramental instruments of sanctification. To the same purpose was directed the whole doctrine and ministry of the apostles, as shown in their Acts and Epistles and insistently emphasized by St. Paul, stating: "On behalf of Christ, therefore, we are acting as ambassadors" (2 Cor. 5:20); "Through whom we have received the grace of apostleship to bring about obedience to faith among all the nations" (Rom. 1:5); "I have written to you rather boldly... brethren... because of the grace that has been given to me by God, that I should be a minister of Christ Jesus to the Gentiles: sanctifying the gospel of God, that the offering up of the Gentiles may become acceptable, being sanctified by the Holy Spirit" (Rom. 15:15f.).

The foundation of the Church sealed *ipso facto* and implicitly the *abrogation of the Synagogue and of the Old Covenant*, which remained only in the books, as a shining figure of the future and a dead skeleton of the past.

---

16 Cf. St. Thomas, *Summa Theol.*, III, q. 8, a. 3, ad. 3.

This is equivalently contained in the old prophecies, particularly of Jeremias about the new and better covenant (see above p. 249) and of Malachias about the new sacrifice replacing the levitic sacrifice in the future (1:10f.). It is also directly signified in the New Testament. Christ says that the Old Law and the prophets had their force only until the coming of John the Baptist (Luke 16:16), the divine cult is no longer confined to the temple of Jerusalem (John 4:21), the Kingdom of God is taken away from the Jewish nation and given to other worthy people (Matt. 21:43; cf. 8:11), the new covenant is sealed in His own blood (Luke 22:20; cf. 1 Cor. 11:25, and compare with Ex. 24:8). St. Paul teaches that the Old Law was only a tutor preparing the people for the coming of the new faith and therefore it has ended its function (Gal. 3:24f.) and the Old Testament has been made void in Christ (2 Cor. 2:14), who sponsored a better testament (Heb. 7:22; 8:6), rendering obsolete the former (Heb. 8:13).

This abrogation follows necessarily from the very nature and laws of the new Church, which are directly opposed to the essential elements of the synagogue, namely, from the new faith, which is no longer about the future Messias; from the new cult, which replaced circumcision with Baptism and is no longer confined to the temple of Jerusalem; from the universality of the new institution, which removes the old Jewish boundary. However, if we consider the old institution as a period of the same progressing history of salvation and a stepping stone for the coming of the new one, it can be said to be still alive in the Church, as in the "New People of God" and the "New Israel" whose foreshadowing was the purpose and the soul of the past. Such abrogation and fulfillment of the synagogue took place, by right and fundamentally, at the very moment of the death of Christ on the cross, but *de facto* and actually was in force only since the day of Pentecost, when through the effusion of the Holy Spirit the New Law was officially proclaimed and the new Church publicly presented to the world.

The Church itself, although a perfect fulfillment of the old covenant and the last covenant of God with man, has not acquired all its perfection as yet, but carries in its breast the *eschatological tension* toward the invisible and eternal realities it announces, and bears in its heart all the anxieties of a pilgrim people, foreign to the land and searching out its way ahead toward the second coming of the Lord and its own dissolution into the city of the new Jerusalem.[17]

---

17 About this eschatological character of the Church see below, pp. 453–455.

2

The Intimate Nature of the Church[18]

AS SHOWN IN THE PRECEDING CHAPTER, THE
Church, in its general features, is external and internal, physical
and mystical. However, since these two characters are at first
glance mutually opposed, they cannot equally constitute the intimate nature of the Church, which is one simple entity. Hence the
Church must essentially consist either in an external society, to
which are extrinsically attached a supernatural purpose and some
internal spiritual elements, or an internal and spiritual community,

---

18   St. Thomas, *Summa Theol.*, III, q. 8 (on the capital grace of Christ).

Antón, A., "Hacia una sintesis de las nociones 'Cuerpo de Cristo' y 'Pueblo de Dios'
en la ecclesiologia," *Estudios eclesiásticos* 44 (1969) 161–203.

Bouyer, L., *L'Eglise, Corps du Christ et Temple de l'Esprit*, Paris 1970.

Cerfaux, L., *The Church in the Theology of St. Paul* (trans. from the French), St.
Louis, Mo. 1959.

Congar, Y., *L'Eglise sacrement universel du salut*, Tournai, 1967; "La personne
'Eglise.'" *Revue thomiste* 71 (1971) 613–640.

De Wal, V., *What Is the Church?*, Valley Forge, Pa. 1970.

Dupuy, B. D., "Le mystère de l'Eglise. Bibliographie organisée," *Vie Spirituelle*
104 (1961) 70–85.

Gherardini, B., "Per una ecclesiologia di comunione," *Divinitas* 16 (1973) 389–414.

Glorieux, P., *Nature et mission de l'Eglise*, Paris 1963.

Gruden, J. C., *The Mystical Christ*, St. Louis, Mo. 1938.

Hammer, J., *The Church is a Communion*, New York 1964.

Journet, Ch., *L'Eglise du Verbe Incarné*, 2: *Sa structure interne et son unité catholique*
(Paris 1951) 50–96, 510–705.

Küng, H., *The Church* (tr. R. and R. Ockenden) New York 1968.

Lubac, H. de, *The Church: Paradox and Mystery* (trans. J. R. Dunne), Staten Island,
New York 1970.

Martelet, G., "De la sacramentalité propre à l'Eglise," *Nouvelle revue théologique*
95 (1973) 25–42.

Mersch, E., *Theology of the Mystical Body* (trans. C. Vollert), St. Louis, Mo. 1951.

Mühlen, H., *Una mystica persona. Eine Person in vielen Personen*, Paderborn 1964,
2nd ed, 1967. French translation: *L'Esprit Saint dans l'Eglise*, 2 vols. Paris, 1969.

O'Rourke, J., "The Church as People of God in the New Testament," *Divinitas*
13 (1969) 655–670.

Rahner, K., *The Church and the Sacraments* (tr. W. J. O'Hara), New York 1963.

Ramirez, E., "Relaciones entre el cuerpo fisico y el cuerpo mistico de Cristo,
"*Mysterium* 27 (1968) 37–48.

Semmelroth, D., *Die Kirche als Ursakrament*, Frankfurt 1953.

Tromp, S., *Corpus Christi quod est Ecclesia*, 3 vols., Roma 1937–1960 (Important
work, with abundant bibliography at the end of each volume).

which extends into an external and social structure, so that it be in all its elements, both internal and external, something simply mystical, that is, a supernatural mystery. The first consideration seems to have chiefly inspired older theologians, by reason of their primary apologetical purpose, the second has been leading recent theologians toward a deeper understanding of the proper nature of the Church in its purely dogmatic aspect.

Agreeing with this theological development, which is manifestly favored by the recent Magisterium since the specific Encyclical "Mystical Body" of Pius XII in 1943, but shunning at once undue exaggerations, we move on to the following doctrine.

Statement. *The Church, considered in its intimate nature, is essentially the Mystical Body of Christ, that is, a supernatural union of men in Christ, based on the vital influence of the Holy Spirit and the external bonds of faith, worship and government.*

No *theological note* can be assigned to this assertion, as such, that is, as an interpretation of the intimate nature of the Church. However, the three elements *de facto* implied in it, namely, that the Church is a Mystical Body or a supernatural union, that it is animated by the Holy Spirit, and that its members are gathered by the threefold bond, are all theologically certain and belong to the Catholic doctrine proximately definable.

The proof for our statement is derived from the channels of revelation, that is, the Magisterium, Scripture, and Tradition, as well as from theological reasoning.

The doctrine of the Magisterium has been aptly gathered, explicitly expounded, and further determined by *Pius XII in his Encyclical "Mystical Body"* of 1943 (AAS, vol. 35, pp. 193–248; cf. Denz. 3800–3822).[19] Here is the doctrinal summary of this Encyclical:

---

19 The major elements, contained in the Encyclical, are found sufficiently expressed, but not logically assembled, in the *preceding documents of the Magisterium* explicitly emphasizing that the Church is a Mystical Body, of which Christ is the head and to which men are incorporated as members through Baptism, and remain such as long as they do not visibly break the bond of their union.

Boniface VIII, who, as noted above (p. 244), was the first to adopt the theologians' expression "Mystical Body" in his Encyclical "Unam Sanctam" of 1302, declares that Christ in the *head* of this body and that Christians are united in it by *one faith and one Baptism* (Denz. 870). The *Councils of Florence and Trent* teach the same thing, that is, that Christ is the head, we are the members through Baptism and through the union of faith and charity; Trent determines the concept of head, saying that *Christ exercises his supernatural influence* in us (Denz. 1314, 1546, 1638, 1671).

1. Regarding *the nature of the Mystical Body*, which is the best possible definition of the Church (no. 13), it must be noted that the attribution "Mystical" does not mean that the Church is a mere *spiritual body* (no.14), that is, united only by the internal bonds of faith, hope, and charity (nos. 70–76). On the contrary, this body is also something *"concrete and visible"* (no. 14), that is, endowed both with external means of sanctification, or sacraments (no. 18), and *"with the external bonds* of one profession of faith, worship, and government" (nos. 68f.). There is no opposition or distinction between the visible body and the mystical body of the Church, but it is one and the same body having two aspects mutually complementary (nos. 62–66). Hence appears the distinction of the Mystical Body from both physical and moral bodies (nos. 62–66).

2. *Members of the Mystical Body* are only those who keep the aforementioned external bonds of faith, worship, and government (no. 21). Sinners themselves are members as long as they keep those three bonds (no. 22); souls in purgatory and catechumens may be considered as members (no. 99). Pagans, heretics, schismatics, and persons excommunicated, are not members (nos. 21, 100–102), "even if they may be inclined toward the Mystical Body of the Redeemer by a kind of unconscious desire and hope" (no. 101).

3. *The influential principles of the Mystical Body* are two, namely, Christ, as the head, and the Holy Spirit, as the soul. *Christ is the head*, by reason of His excellence and perfection (nos. 35, 47), by reason of His government, both invisible and visible through the Pope and the bishops (nos. 36–42), and especially by reason of His *interior influence* of illumination and sanctification (nos. 48–50), on account of which Christ lives so intimately in the Church that He can be called not only the head of the body but also the body itself, and vice versa the Church can be called the "alter ego" (the other self) of Christ (nos. 50–53, 77f., 92). *The*

Pius IX emphasizes the bond of faith, stating that "religious communities, which are separated from the Catholic Church, can in no way be called member or part of this Church" (Apostolic letter "Iam vos omnes" 1868, Denz. 2997f.) *Vatican I* emphasizes in the Mystical Body the "communion of its members with its *visible head* [i.e., the Roman Pontiff]" (Sess. 3, prologue). *Leo XIII* adds a new element, declaring that "while Christ is the head of the Church, *the Holy Spirit is its soul*" (Encycl. "Divinum illud" 1896, AAS 29, p. 650).

Holy Spirit is "the soul of the Church," because through his influence he works and dwells both in the Head and in the other members, and joins them together (nos. 54–56, 60, 79f.). *The Blessed Virgin* may be considered both as the most excellent member, by being filled with the Holy Spirit more than any other creature, and as an influential element, because "she is the mother of all the members of Christ" (nos. 108f.).

In this Encyclical there are two outstanding notes by which the Catholic doctrine of the Mystical Body has been further determined, namely, that the Mystical Body and the Catholic Church as an external society are *perfectly equivalent* in extension (so that no man belongs to the Mystical Body unless he belongs to the Catholic Church) and that *the soul* of the Mystical Body or of the Church is no other than *the Holy Spirit.*

Vatican Council II has briefly repeated the same doctrine in its Dogmatic Constitution on the Church (cf. especially nos. 7, 8, 13–16).[20] In some of the expressions it seems at first glance to extend the concept of member of the Church by a distinction between a full incorporation and an inferior manner of pertaining to the Church; but it is only question of a less precise theological formulation, or rather of a more solicitous pastoral outlook, as will be shown below (pp. 412f.).

---

20 The most pertinent and apt passage about the function of Christ and the Holy Spirit in the Mystical body, is the following: "The Head of this body is Christ... From Him 'the whole body, supplied and built up by joints and ligaments attains a growth that is in God' (Col. 2:19). He continually diffuses into his body, that is, the Church, the gifts of functions, through which by his power we mutually render the services necessary for salvation, so that, following the truth with love, we may through all things grow up into Him, who is our head (cf. Eph. 4:11–16 according to the Greek text).

"In order that we may continuously acquire new strength in Him (cf. Eph. 4:23). He made us share in his Spirit, who, being one and the same in the Head and in the members, vivifies, unifies, and moves the whole body, in such a way that His function could be compared by the holy Fathers to the function which the soul, principle of life, discharges in the human body" (no. 7).

By reason of her relationship with Christ, as his Mystical Body, and of her saving mission and purpose, Vatican II applies to the Church also the general concept of *sacrament* (Efficacious sign of grace), calling the Church "the universal sacrament of salvation" (Dogmatic Constitution on the Church, nos. 9 and 48; Pastoral Constitution on the Church, nos. 42 and 45). Cf. Y. Congar, *L'Eglise sacrement universel du salut*, Tournai, 1967; G. Martelet, "De la sacramentalité propre à l"Eglise," *Nouvelle revue théologique* 95 (1973) 25–42; Ch. Journet, "Le mystère de la sacramentalité. Le Christ, l'eglise, les sept sacrements," *Nova et Vetera* 49 (1974) 161–214; B. Gherardini, "Veluti sacramentum...," *Doctor Communis* 23 (1975) 74–122.

The doctrine of Scripture on the Mystical Body is eminently Pauline.[21] It is expounded by the Apostle in four epistles, Rom. 12:4–8; 1 Cor. 12:12–27; Eph. 1:22 f; 4:11–16; 5:21–32; Col. 1:18; 2:13, 19. It can be summarized as follows:

1. *The Church is called the body of Christ:* Rom. 12:5; 1 Cor. 12:27; Eph. 1:23; 4:12; 5:23, 30; Col. 1:18; 2:19 (as we noted above, p. 244, the complete expression "Mystical Body" does not occur). This body is considered as the "pleroma" of Christ, that is, His extension, completion, fullness: Eph. 1:23; 4:13. The reason why the Church is called the body of Christ is the diversity of members and functions: Rom. 12:4–8; 1 Cor. 12:12–27; Eph. 4:11–16; Col. 2:19, as well as their communication in the same vital principle, which is the Holy Spirit: 1 Cor. 12:13; Eph. 4:4.

2. *Christ is the head of this body:* Eph. 1:22; 4:15; 5:23; Col. 1:18; 2:19. He is the head, not only by reason of priority and perfection: Eph. 1:22f. Col. 1:17–20; but also on account of His influence, both exterior, through the constitution of the hierarchy: Eph. 4:11f., and interior, by causing salvation and grace: Eph. 4:15f.; 5:23; Col. 1:20.

3. *The Holy Spirit is an influential principle in this body:* 1 Cor. 12:13; "For in one Spirit we were all baptized into one body... and we were all given to drink of one Spirit;" Eph. 4:4f.: "Preserve the unity of the Spirit in the bond of peace: one body and one Spirit..., one Lord, one faith, one Baptism"; Phil. 2:1: "Fellowship [of Christians] in the Spirit," Although St. Paul never calls the Spirit the soul of the Church and very seldom speaks of Him in direct connection with the body of Christ (for his conception of this body is prevalently Christological), nevertheless the concept of soul of the Church, later proposed by the Fathers, is implicitly contained in the prevalent influence which the apostle attributes to the Spirit in several passages; this Spirit unites and feeds the faithful into one body (1 Cor. 12:13; Eph. 4:4f., Phil. 2:1 just quoted); He makes them the temple of God (1 Cor. 6:19; Eph. 2:22), He is given to them (1 Thess. 4:8; 1 Cor. 2:12), he lives in them (Rom. 8:9f.; 1 Cor. 3:16), sanctifies them (1 Cor. 6:11), makes them sons of God (Rom. 8:15; 1 Cor. 2:10–14).

The Fathers repeat and amplify this Pauline doctrine, particularly in their explanation of the various texts of the apostle. Among them

---

21 Among the authors cited in footnote 18 see especially Cerfaux, Mersch, and Tromp.

two doctors stand out as to abundance and clearness of concepts, namely, in the East St. Cyril of Alexandria (cf. *Comment on John* 1.11, MG 74.558f.) and in the West St. Augustine, who shows how our predestination and grace derive from Christ's predestination and grace, as from the head into its members, through the influence of the same Spirit (*On the Predestination of Saints* 15.31, ML 44.982f.; cf. *On the Gift of Perseverance* 24; *Comment. on John*, tr. 108.5).

Moreover, several Fathers bring forth into explicit formulation the concept of *soul of the Church* attributed to the Holy Spirit. St. John Chrysostom: "Just as in a body there is one spirit [i.e., one soul], which holds and unifies what is made up of various members, so also here [i.e., in the Church]" (*Comment. on Eph.*, hom. 9.3, MG 62.72).[22] St. Augustine: "The Holy Spirit is for the body of Christ, what the soul is for the body of man. The Holy Spirit does in the whole Church, what the soul does in all the members of one body" (*Sermon* 267.4, ML 38. 1231; cf. *Sermon* 268.2; *On John*, tr. 26.13; tr. 27.6). Pseudo-Gregory the Great: "Just as one soul vivifies the various members of a body, so the Holy Spirit vitalizes and enlightens the whole Church. Just as Christ, who is the head of the Church, was conceived of the Holy Spirit, so the holy Church, which is His body, is filled with the same Spirit, that it may live" (*Comment. on the Penitential Psalms* 5.1, MG 79. 602).[23]

Besides the Pauline metaphor of the body, there are *several other expressions and metaphors*, manifesting the Church as a supernatural union of men in Christ, which from their biblical source passed likewise into the other two channels of revelation. Here is a brief explanation of each.

---

22 Several texts of other Greek Fathers are collected by S. Tromp, *De Spiritu Sancto Anima Corporis Mystici*, 1: *Testimonia selecta e Patribus Graecius*, Romae 1932.

23 Likewise *the theologians of the Middle Ages* reaffirmed the concept of the Holy Spirit soul of the Church, although they rather insisted on the Christological aspect of the Mystical Body. Cf. Peter Lombard, *On 1 Cor.* 12.11–17; *On Eph.* 4.1–6, and Albert the Great, *On the Sacrifice of the Mass* 2.9.

St. Thomas, *In 3 Sent.*, dist. 13, q. 2, a. 1, qa. 3.: "The Holy Spirit is the ultimate and principal perfection of the mystical body, like the soul in the natural body;" Opusc. *On the Symbol of the Apostles*: "The soul, which vivifies this body, is the Holy Spirit;" *Summa Theol.*, II-II, q. 183, a. 2, ad. 3: "Like in the natural body the various members are kept together by the power of a vivifying spirit and they separate at its departure, so likewise in the body of the Church peace among the different members is kept by the power of the Holy Spirit, who vivifies the body of the Church;" III, q. 8, a. 1, ad. 3: "The Holy Spirit is compared to the heart, because he vivifies it and unites the Church in an invisible manner" (here St. Thomas shifts to the equivalent and more subtle concept of heart).

Kingdom of God, or Kingdom of heaven.[24] This expression, already used in the Old Testament for the Jewish people (see p. 249), is name that Christ gave to his works, as we noted above (pp. 242, 250).[25] The biblical concept of divine Kingdom does not exactly coincide with the Church, for there was a past kingdom of God before the Church in the Old Testament and there will be an eternal kingdom after the Church in heaven; hence the kingdom of God is at once past, present and future. However, since the Church is the full realization of the old and the preparation of the future, she carries in herself all the archaeological baggage of the past and all the eschatological hopes of the future. This is the reason why Christ taught the Church to pray: "Our Father..., thy kingdom come." In whatever ampler or stricter meaning it is taken, this expression means that the Church is a union of men subject to God and sharing in divine goods, all of it in the supernatural order, as is evident from the circumstances and from the comparison of the texts.

People of God is equivalent to the preceding expression, but adds to it the more intimate character of a special election. It is frequently used in the Old Testament (for the first time in Ex. 6:7 at the moment of the election: "I will take you as my own people").[26] In the New Testament it is used very rarely, perhaps on account of its nationalistic flavor, to signify the Church as the new People of God; 1 Pet. 2:10: "You are now the people of God"[27] (cf. Osee 2:24); 2 Cor. 6:16: "They shall be my people;" the same is said in Heb. 8:10 and Apoc. 21:3 (these words are a quotation, in prophetical sense, of Ex. 6:7; Lev. 26:12; Jer. 31:33; Ezech. 37:27). Recently Vatican Council II has frequently used this name for the Church to signify both the messianic fulfillment

---

24   Cf. L. Cerfaux, *The Church in the Theology of St. Paul* (tr. G. Webb and A. Walker), New York 1959; *Ephemerides theologicae Lovanienses* 2 (1925) 181–198; *Recueil Lucien Cerfaux* 2 (Gembloux 1954) 365–387.

25   In footnote 14 we gave the different passages, in which this expression occurs in the Gospels, especially through the mouth of Christ. Also St. Paul uses it quite frequently (Acts 19:8; 20:25; 28:23, 31; Rom. 14:17f.; 1 Cor. 6:9; 15:24f.; Eph. 5:5; Col. 1:12; 4:11), although much more frequently he uses the new name "Church" (63 times in the epistles; see above, footnote 3).

26   Rather than under the impersonal form "People of God" the expression occurs usually with a possessive pronoun "My, thy, his People": Ex. 6:7; Lev. 26:12; Num. 27:17; Deut. 7:6, 26; 14:21; 26:19; 32:9; 3 Kgs. 8:51; Ps. 78:13; Isa. 1–3; 40:1; Jer. 31:33; 51:7; Ezech. 37:27; Osee 2:24, and frequently in the Psalms and the Prophets.

27   However equivalent expressions are used in Acts 15:14; 18:10; Rom. 9:25; Tit. 2:14; 1 Pet. 2:9.

and the eschatological tension of the "pilgrim Church," as a people coming from the wilderness of the older condition and searching ahead for the promised land where it will meet the Lord.[28]

Building of God—Temple of God.[29] Christ himself compared the Church to a building, Matt. 16:18: "Upon this rock I will build my Church." St. Paul quite frequently calls the Church "Building of God" and "Temple of God" (1 Cor. 3:9, 16:17; 6:19; 2 Cor. 6:16; Eph. 2:21 f; 4:12, 16). He also explains this image, saying that the Christians are built on the foundation of the apostles and prophets with Christ as the chief corner stone, on which the whole structure grows up into a temple of God, with the cooperation of each member of the body of Christ, working according to his measure through every joint of the structure (Eph. 2:19–21; 4–12, 16). St. Peter extends the equivalent image of the spiritual temple through the concept of spiritual priesthood and sacrifice (1 Pet. 2:5).

The Church as the temple of God is the figure of the heavenly *"New Jerusalem,"* which, like a "Holy City," is built on the "foundation of the twelve apostles," and in which there is "no temple, for the Lord God almighty and the Lamb are the temple thereof" (Apoc. 21:1f., 14, 22); "Jerusalem which is above ... is our mother" (Gal. 4:26). On account of this intimate relationship between the type and the antitype, the Church itself can be called "The New Jerusalem" as it is called "The New Israel," with reference to the old; in fact, both are likely involved in the passages of St. John and St. Paul. On the biblical image of the Church as a building is based the beautiful description of the construction of the spiritual tower in the book of Hermas, written toward the middle of the second century (*The Shepherd,* Vis. 3.3–7; Sim. 9.1–10).

House of God. Family of God. Our Mother. These are three biblical Pauline expressions carrying the same general concept of a family tie with God. Only the first is found as such in St. Paul, 1 Tim. 3:15: "The house of God, which is the Church of the living God;" Heb. 3:6: "Christ is faithful as the Son over His own house. We are

---

28 See above, p. 253. In its Dogmatic Constitution on the Church, the Council uses such expressions as: "The Church, that is, the people of God" (no. 13), "The New People of God" (nos. 9, 13), "The New Israel" (no. 9, from Gal. 6:16: "The Israel of God"), "The members of the People of God" (no. 13). The same expression "People of God" occurs in nos. 16, 17, 18, 26, 30, 31, 32, 33, 41, 44, 45, 50.
29 Cf. J. Daniélou, *Le signe du Temple ou de la présence de Dieu,* Paris 1942; Y. Congar, *Le mystère du Temple,* Paris 1958.

that house." The second expression is equivalently contained in Eph. 2:19: "You are ... members of God's household." The third is involved in Gal. 4:26: "Jerusalem which is above ... is our Mother," as we noted above.

Both Tradition and the Magisterium frequently have used these expressions.[30] "House of God" is used by Vatican I (Constitution on the Church, prologue). "Family of God" is used by Trent (Sess. 14, chap. 2: "Household of faith"), Pius XI (Encycl. "Divini illius Magistri"), John XXIII (Allocution "Laetamur admodum" 1960), Vatican II (Dog. Constit. on the Church, no. 27). "Mother" is used by Pius XI ("Pia Mater Ecclesia," Encycl. "Casti connubii" 1930), John XXIII (Encycl. "Mater et Magistra" 1961), Vatican II (Dogm. Constit. on the Church, nos. 6, 15).

God's tillage. Christ's branches. The first figure belongs to Paul, the second to John. 1 Cor. 3:9: "You are God's tillage;" John 15:5: "I am the vine, you are the branches" (cf. 15. 1–6). The same concept is carried out by the image of the "olive tree" (Rom. 11:16–24) and by the parable of the "vineyard" (Matt. 21:33–44). The image of the vine and the branches is particularly exploited by St. Augustine (*On John*, tr. 80.1), the Council of Orange in 529 (can. 27, Denz. 394), and the Council of Trent (Sess. 6, chap. 16, Denz. 1546).

Sheepfold, Sheep. Both images are proper to John, 10:1–16 (where Christ is shown as the "good Shepherd," the Christians as the sheep, the Church as the sheepfold). The Church is the sheepfold, which Christ, "the Prince of the shepherds," (1 Pet. 5:4), "the shepherd of our souls" (*ibid.* 8:25), entrusted to Peter, saying: "Feed My lambs ... Feed My sheep ... " (John 21:15–17). Vatican Council I opens its Constitution on the Church with the words: "The eternal Shepherd and Bishop of our souls [1 Pet. 2:25]" (Denz. 3050).

Spouse of Christ. The spousal character of the relation between Christ and the Church was figured in the Old Testament through the same general image of the spousal union of God with Israel, and is often inculcated by Christ Himself in the Gospel (Matt. 9:15; 22:2–4; 25:1–13; Mark 2:19; Luke 5:34; 12:35–38; 14:16–24). But the explicit and direct image of the Church as the spouse of Christ is proper to Paul and John.

---

30   As regards Tradition, cf. J. Plumpe, "Ecclesia Mater," *Transactions of the American Philological Association* 70 (1939) 535–555; *Mater Ecclesia. An Inquiry into the Concept of the Church as Mother in Early Christianity*, Washington 1943; K. Delahaye, *Ecclesia Mater chez les Pères des trois premiers siècles*, Paris 1964.

Paul brings forth this image twice; once with regard to the particular church of Corinth, which has been, as it were, given by him to Christ as a virgin spouse (2 Cor. 11:2f.: "I betrothed you to one spouse, that I might present you a chaste virgin to Christ"), and again with regard to the universal Church, declaring that *Christ loved the Church as a spouse*, the way a husband must love his wife, and he gives as the reason the fact of the mystical body itself, that is, because we are members of Christ's body (Eph. 5:23–32).[31]

John in the Apocalypse introduces the Church as the *"Spouse of the Lamb"* (21:9), both in her terrestrial exile, in which she is longing for the Lord (22:17: "And the Spirit and the bride say: Come"[32]) and in her eternal dwelling, where "the holy city, the New Jerusalem, comes down out of heaven from God, made ready as a bride, adorned for her husband" (21:2).

Theological reasoning[33] demands that the intimate nature of the Church be evaluated according to its proper purpose, as happens in every other thing, for, the purpose of some thing is the sign and

---

31   On this text is based the typicality of the sacrament of Matrimony, Eph. 5:32: "This is a great mystery, I mean in reference to Christ and to the Church." Concerning the use and sense of the title "Spouse" or "Bride of Christ," see C. Chavasse, *The Bride of Christ, Enquiry into the Nuptial Element in Early Christianity*, London 1940.
32   Here John translates into Greek the Aramaic expression *"Marana-tha"* (Lord, come), commonly used by the first Christians in their meetings. Paul at the end of his first epistle to the Corinthians keeps the Aramaic form of this exclamation.
33   Cf. *Summa Theol*, III, q. 8 (on the capital grace of Christ). Some recent authors, as T. Zapelena, *De Ecclesia Christi 2* (ed. 2, Roma 1954) 372–378, say that the doctrine of St. Thomas on the Mystical Body does not agree with that of St. Paul and of Pius XII in the Encyclical "Mystical Body," because it considers the Mystical Body only in its spiritual aspect, overlooking its external and social aspect, so that the Mystical Body would include also those who do not actually belong to the Church, as the angels, the saints of the Old Testament, the souls in Purgatory and in heaven, and any non-Catholic or non-Christian who is justified or receives a supernatural grace outside of the Church. Such criticism is refuted by Ch. Journet in *Bulletin thomiste* 8-2 (1952) 363–373, and J. Hamer, *L'Eglise est une communion* (Paris 1962) 71–86.
There is something true in both opinions. If we consider only the capital grace of Christ from which flows every effect of grace into any creature and at any time, we can with St. Thomas speak of the Mystical Body also in an *ampler sense*, and thus include all the aforementioned subjects (who moreover are in some way connected with the present Catholic Church), namely, the Church of the Old Testament, all men who are justified or receive a supernatural movement outside the Catholic Church and belong to it *de iure* if not simply *de facto*, the Church of the other life, both purgatorial and triumphant. But in the strict sense, which is proposed by Pius XII, the Mystical Body is properly and directly confined to the present and visible Catholic Church. Also Vatican Council II tends to take the Mystical Body in an ampler sense, as we noted above (p. 258).

the sign and the measure of its nature or intrinsic form. But the proper purpose of the Church is essentially spiritual or mystical, that is, the salvation or sanctification of souls, as shown above (p. 252). Therefore, the intimate nature of the Church is essentially spiritual or mystical, that is, it is all involved in the mystery of grace and the principles of grace.

Furthermore, the Church is union of men, who, on account of that spiritual purpose, communicate exteriorly in the same profession of faith, the same form of worship, the same laws under one authority, and share interiorly in the same life of grace, imparted to them by the same principles, that is, by Christ, whose human nature is the instrumental cause of every grace or supernatural effect, and by the Holy Spirit, who is the principal cause of the same effect. Therefore, *the Church is essentially the Mystical Body of Christ.* It is a body, because it is a union of men having the same purpose and sharing in the same kind of life; and thus it is not different from the natural civil society. It is a mystical body, because its purpose and life are supernatural, that is, belong to the mystery of grace.[34] Finally, this mystical body is the body of Christ, because its purpose and life derive proximately from the influence of Christ himself, under the principal movement of the Holy Spirit.

Hence this Mystical Body, which is the Church, can be aptly defined: *A supernatural union of men in Christ, based on the vital influence of the Holy Spirit and the exterior bonds of faith, worship, and government.* In this definition, the supernatural union is the *form,* in which the Church is at once similar to, and different from, other societies; similar, because it is a union; different, because it is a supernatural union. Christ and the Holy Spirit are the *vital and interior principles* of this union; Christ is the principle in the manner of a *head,* keeping together and moving supernaturally the other members; the Holy Spirit is the principle in the manner of a *soul,* infusing supernatural life in both, head and members, and moving

---

34 Carefully distinguish the *three kinds of body, the physical, the moral or social, and the mystical.* The first is properly a body, the second and third are called body only analogically and metaphorically, deriving precisely such metaphor from the physical body. In the mystical body the unity of the members and the influence of the head and of the soul are less strict than in the physical body, as is clear; but they are more strict, and in this sense more proper, than in the moral or social body. The reason is because the life, which vivifies the mystical body, is primarily interior; its soul, namely, the Holy Spirit, dwells inside it, and both, the soul and the head (Christ), act into the members not only exteriorly but also and principally interiorly.

the other members through the head itself. The three exterior bonds are the *external instruments* of this mystical union and, as it were, the visible face of this supernatural but human organism. The vital influence of both, head and soul, considered concretely in its effect of sanctifying grace and other supernatural gifts (sanctifying grace, virtues, gifts of the Holy Spirit, actual graces, miraculous gifts), can be called the *life* of this body, or its supernatural joints and organs, through which the soul and head operate.

A further explanation about the various principles and members of the Mystical Body:

Christ is the head, that is the principal member, in the three ways in which the corporal head excels above the other members.

First, He is principal member in the order of intention, because His grace precedes the grace of all the others in God's predestination, and it is the exemplary cause to which all the other graces are made similar. Second, He is principal member in the order of perfection, because His grace is the greatest and has even a plenitude of relative infinity. Third, He is principal member especially in the order of *influence*, inasmuch as, by reason of this plenitude of grace, He produces grace in the other members. And He produces it in two ways, namely, through an *exterior* influence of government, inasmuch as He instituted, maintains, and supports the organs of authority in the Church (Roman Pontiff and bishops), and especially through an *interior* influence, at least of the *moral* order (that is, through merit and satisfaction, principal cause of our grace) and probably also of the physical order (inasmuch as His humanity would be the proper and physical instrument of His Divinity).[35]

Only Christ can be properly called head of the Mystical Body and hence of the Church. This title and concept cannot be attributed to the Holy Spirit, because He is above the order of

---

35   A further explanation of the nature and influence of the so-called *capital grace* of Christ belongs to the treatise on the Incarnate Word. Pius XII in his Encyclical explains at length the various manners in which Christ is head of the Church and exercises his influence on it (see above, p. 257).

As regards the *physical causality* of the humanity of Christ (as well as of his sacraments), it is a subject of dispute among theologians. St. Thomas, the thomists and many other theologians admit it, as being in closer harmony with the expressions of Tradition. Others deny it, and are satisfied with a moral or intentional causality. This question is also directly considered in the treatises on the Incarnate Word and on the sacraments.

grace and He is not similar to the members, as the head must be. Nor to the angels, the saints, and the Blessed Virgin, because they have no exterior influence in the Church and their interior influence through merit and satisfaction is limited and dependent on Christ's influence. Nor to the Roman Pontiff himself, because he has only an exterior influence and moreover limited and vicarious, on account of which he can be called head of the Church only in the limited sense of exterior society, not in the full and proper meaning of the Church, which is essentially a Mystical Body.

The Holy Spirit is the soul of the Church or of the Mystical Body.[36]

In view of the Traditional and Magisterial doctrine exposed above (pp. 256–260), no one can deny that the concept and name of soul of the Church is aptly attributed to the Holy Spirit, as to the primary influential principle of the life of the Mystical Body. But it can be questioned whether the concept of soul is not more properly applicable to *sanctifying grace*, which is, like the soul in a body, a form informing and residing in the subject, rather than to the Holy Spirit, who does not inform the subject but is only an exterior principle, efficiently influencing in it.

In fact, before the Encyclical "Mystical Body" of Pius XII, theologians commonly taught[37] that the soul of the Church is properly

36   Antón, A., "El Espiritu Santo y la Iglesia. En busca de una fórmula para el misterio de la Iglesia," *Gregorianum* 47 (1966) 101–113.

Charue, A. M., "Le Saint-Esprit dans 'Lumen Gentium,'" *Ephemerides theologicae Lovanienses* 45 (1969) 359–379.

Congar, Y., "Le Saint-Esprit et le Corps apostolique réalisateurs de l'oeuvre du Christ," *Revue des sciences philosophiques et théologiques* 36 (1952) 613–625; 37 (1953) 24–48; "Pneumatologie ou 'Christomonisme' dans la tradition latine," *Ephemerides theologicae Lovanienses* 45 (1969) 394–416.

Dagens, Cl., "L'Esprit Saint et l'Eglise dans la conjoncture actuelle," *Nouvelle revue théologique* 96 (1974) 225–245.

De Letter, P., "The Soul of the Mystical Body," *Sciences ecclésiastiques* 14 (1962) 213–234.

Delhaye, Ph., "L'Esprit-Saint et la vie morale du chrétien," *Ephemerides theologicae Lovanienses* 45 (1969) 432–443.

Dockx, S., "L'Esprit-Saint, âme de l'Eglise," *Ecclesia a Spiritu Sancto edocta. Hommage à Mgr Gerard Philips* (Gembloux 1970) 65–80.

Esprit Saint (L') et l'Eglise, (collective work), Paris 1969.

Mühlen, H., *Una Mystica Persona. Eine Person in Vielen Personen*, Paderborn 1964; 2nd ed. 1967. French translation: *L'Esprit dans l'Eglise*, 2 vols., Paris 1969.

Tromp. S., *Corpus Christi quod est Ecclesia*, 3: *De Spiritu Christi Anima*, Roma 1960 (Important and exhaustive disputation on this subject.)

37   Among others, Wilmers, De Groot, Billot, Van Noort-Verhaar, Schultes, in their well-known treatises on the Church.

sanctifying grace (or rather the supernatural organism common to all the just) and its body is the social external society. In this view the Mystical Body itself would coincide with sanctifying grace, so that the Church would be made up of two bodies, the mystical body or sanctifying grace, and the social body or its exterior elements. The Holy Spirit then would be only an outer efficient cause of the Church, influencing from outside in both interior and exterior elements, without being part of either body, and in this extensive sense he was at times called also soul of the Church.

But the Encyclical reshaped the concept of Mystical Body by joining in it both the interior and the exterior elements of the Church, so that Church and Mystical Body are perfectly equivalent. Hence sanctifying grace lost its importance as the animating principle of the Mystical Body, and the Holy Spirit took its place in the common evaluation of modern theologians, manifestly favored by Pius XII in his Encyclical and more recently by the Vatican Council II (see above, p. 258).

The reason for this more probable and now common opinion[38] is the following. Since the Mystical Body is not a physical body, we cannot apply to it the concept of soul as an informing principle, so that a single reality would inform all the subjects of the Mystical Body and reside in them. Such a concept does not fit either the Holy Spirit, because He does not inform a man, or sanctifying grace, because, though informing each man individually, it is not one single reality in all the individuals, but divides into many various forms in different subjects. Hence the only concept, under which the soul can be applied to the Mystical Body, is that of an efficient principle, which would be the cause of all vitality and activity in the Church and would be found one and the same in all the members, including the head itself.

But such a concept applies only to the Holy Spirit. In fact sanctifying grace is not found in all the members, not in sinners, it is not the same in all the others, it is not the cause of all the exterior

---

38 A few recent theologians try to follow a middle course, distinguishing a *double soul*, one *uncreated*, merely efficient and only indwelling, namely the Holy Spirit, and the other *created*, properly inhering and informing, that is, sanctifying grace. Thus Journet, *op.cit.* (in footnote 18) 565–579, 601–675, and E, Sauras, *El Cuerpo Místico de Cristo* (Madrid 1952) 736–744. But such multiplication would change the very concept of soul and destroy the analogy of the Mystical Body with the physical body; for only one soul is conceivable in a body, since the soul is the principle of specification and unity of the whole being.

activities of the Mystical Body (as the exercise of the triple power of Order, jurisdiction and Magisterium, which is valid without the state of grace); the capital grace of Christ itself resides only in Christ, nor is it the cause of the exterior activities of the members.

On the contrary, the Holy Spirit is numerically one and the same in all the members, as indwelling in all the just and at least influencing all the members, even sinners whom He keeps in their faith and moves to conversion. He is also the cause of all the activities of the Mystical Body. As regards the interior activities, He keeps faith and hope in the sinners and moves them to conversion, He infuses sanctifying grace, augments it, moves man to the acts of virtues, adds actual graces. Regarding the exterior activities, He exercises a direct influence into the acts of the aforementioned triple power, at least with His assistance, and grants also extraordinary graces or particular charisms, which are never lacking in the Church. Hence the Holy Spirit is truly the soul of the Mystical Body in two ways: first, because of his *indwelling* in the Church, properly in the souls of its better and numerous members, on account of whom the whole Church with its own sinners is dear to the Spirit, and secondly, because He is the first and universal principle of all the activities in the Church, both in its interior and exterior life.

All the other members of the Mystical Body, besides Christ the Head, are to be considered and distributed in different degrees and dignities, according to the way they partake of the influence of the Soul, that is, of the Holy Spirit, either in the interior and higher order of sanctification or on the exterior and lower level of the charismatic activity of the Church (cf. Eph. 4:11–16).

Hence, after *Christ the Head*, the first member of the Mystical Body and of the Church is the *Blessed Virgin*, on account of the highest dignity and sanctity of her Divine Maternity, which makes her also Mediatrix, Co-Redemptrix, "Principle of generation for all the members of Christ" (Encyclical "Mystical Body," no. 109; see above p. 257), "Mother of the Church" (Paul VI). Extending to this first member the analogy of the physical body, theologians call Mary either the secondary head of the Church, or the heart of the Church, or the neck of the Church (this last image, introduced by St. Bernard, seems to be the best, because it expresses the first member connecting the rest of the body with the head). Next comes *St. Joseph*, for there is no higher dignity than that of being foster-father of Christ, as truly as one can be, short of physical generation, and simply husband of the Mother of God. The third place is due to the twelve *apostles*, who, notwithstanding their physical death, are still morally alive, as the foundation of the permanent Church (cf. Eph. 2:20; Apoc. 21:14). These are the three principal members, or the main "joints of the system," as St. Paul puts it (Eph. 4:16).

The remaining faithful are secondary members according to the "measure of each single part" (Eph. 4:16). This measure is various, both in the interior order of sanctification, whose degrees are known only to the indwelling Spirit, and in the lower order of exterior charisms, which are either stable and constitutional, as those of the *Roman Pontiff and the bishops*, or transitory and individual, as those that are distributed by the Holy Spirit when and how he chooses.[39]

From the fact that the Mystical Body is connected with the external bonds of faith, worship and government, it follows that the Mystical Body and the Roman Catholic Church are perfectly equivalent. Hence all and only those are members of the Mystical Body who are actually members of the Roman Catholic Church. But about this question more will be said below, in the chapter on the members of the Church (pp. 411ff.).

---

39 Hence Pope and bishops, as such, that is, as invested with the constitutional charism of their dignity and abstracting from their interior dignity or indignity, are really mystical members and hence sacred and mystical persons. They are even, according to Pius XII, "primary and principal members, because through them, by command of the Divine Redeemer, the functions of Christ, as doctor, king, and priest, are perpetuated" (Encycl. "Mystical Body," no. 17).

3

The Exterior Structure of the Church[40]

AS NOTED ABOVE (P. 255), THE CHURCH, AS A Mystical Body, is made up of two elements, both of them spiritual and supernatural, that is, the interior vital influence of the Holy Spirit, and the exterior bonds of faith, worship and government.

The first element has been sufficiently explained in the preceding chapter, nor is it fitting to delay on it any longer, unless we wish to bring into this treatise several other important questions, as those concerning the capital grace of Christ and the indwelling of the Holy Spirit, and hence cripple the treatises on the Incarnate Word and the Trinity in order to extend beyond proportion the treatise on the Church.

The three bonds of faith, worship, and government, that is, exterior profession of faith, participation in the sacrifice and the sacraments, and obedience to the established authority, which show the visible face of the Church and its social structure, can be considered in two ways. First, as mere ligaments connecting the members into one body, and in this manner they will be considered below in the chapter on the members of the Church (pp. 410ff.). Second, as instruments of the inner life of the Mystical Body, inasmuch as they depend on the triple power of the Church, namely, the Magisterium, or the power of teaching (which is the

---

40 Alberigo, G., *Lo sviluppo della dottrina sui poteri della Chiesa universale. Momenti essenziali tra il XVI e il XIX secolo*, Roma 1964.

Grelot, P., *Le ministère de la nouvelle alliance*, Paris 1967.

Journet, Ch., *L'Eglise du Verbe Incarné* 1 (éd. 2, Paris 1955) 101–114, 124–148.

López Ortiz, J., "Doctrina católica sobre la naturaleza jurídica y soberana de la Iglesia," *XIV Semana Española de Teologia* (Madrid 1955) 119–135.

Müller, J., "Il concetto della Chiesa come 'società perfetta' in S. Tommaso d'Aquino e l'idea moderna della sovranità.'" *Rivista internazionale di scienze sociali* 97 (1923) 193–204, 301–308.

Sorge, B., "E superato il concetto tradizionale di dottrina sociale della Chiesa?" *Civiltà Cattolica* 119 (1968), vol. 1, pp. 425–436.

Stickler, A. M., "Lo sviluppo della dottrina sui poteri della Chiesa universale," *Seminarium* 16 (1964) 652–673.

source of the bond of faith), Orders, or the power of ministering (which establishes the bond of worship), and Jurisdiction, or the power of binding (which is the origin of the juridical bond). This triple power in the ecclesiastical society is nothing else but the extension of the triple function of Christ, as prophet, priest, and king, and consequently, the extension of the influence of the Head of the Mystical Body from the inner joints to the outer structure.

This second consideration is the subject of the present and following chapters (chaps. 3 – 12) and will necessarily claim for itself the principal and lengthier part of this treatise under its proper dogmatic aspect. This integral treatment concerns *the social structure of the Mystical Body*, as to its general character of a true exterior society, its aforementioned triple power, and the various subjects who share in this power.

In this chapter we consider only the general character of *a true and perfect society*.

A *true society*, properly so called, is a moral and stable union of men for the purpose of achieving a common good. This purpose cannot be effectively reached without an authority, due to the variety of members having different ideas and inclinations and to the multiplicity of means to be evaluated and brought into practice. Hence authority is an immediate and essential property of true society, as the effective principle of union and operation; there can be no true society without some kind of true authority. A *perfect society* is that which has for its purpose some good, perfect and complete in a definite order, and possesses of itself all the means necessary to attain that purpose; by reason of this self-sufficiency, it is also independent of any other society. Such is, in the natural order, only the civil society, while family is a true but imperfect society depending on the civil society itself, because it cannot reach its proper purpose in the order of natural good without the help of the civil society.[41]

Statement. *The Church is a true and perfect society.*[42]

Theological note. It is *de fide* that the Church is a *true society*; this is currently taught by the ordinary Magisterium and is implicitly

---

41 Cf. St. Thomas, *Summa Theol.*, I-II, q. 90, a. 3, ad. 3.
42 *The true social character of the Church* is rejected first of all by a twofold radical

error, that is, by *Modernism*, denying that the Church, as founded by Christ, is a *stable union* and replacing it with a mere eschatological movement, and by *Liberal Protestantism*, denying that the Church is an *external union* and replacing it with a purely internal movement. Both errors were expounded above (footnote 8), as rejecting the very existence or foundation of the Church as a union of men.

Directly against our present assertion on the true social character of the Church are two less radical errors among both orthodox and liberal Protestants, which, granting an external aspect of the ecclesiastical community, deny its *authoritative element*, and hence its true social character.

Orthodox Protestants (since Luther, *Captiv. Babyl*, §On Orders; Calvin, *Instit*. 14.20; 19.22; Melanchthon, *Theological Loci*, §On ecclesiastical power) distinguish a two-fold Church, one invisible (the congregation of the just, or of the predestined) and the other visible. In this there is no established authority and no distinction between laity and clergy. Since, however, not every Christian is fit to preach Christ's message, there must be some kind of public ministry, implicitly wanted or in principle established by Christ, but without social or public authority properly so-called.

Among recent *Liberal Protestants* there is a marked tendency to soften the radical doctrine of the older Liberals, mentioned above, by giving importance also to the external element of the Church, deprived, however, of any true authoritative character. Thus, the so-called "Dialectic Theology" of Karl Barth (*Kirchliche Dogmatik*, vols. 1 and 2, München 1932 and 1938; *Dogmatik im Grundriss*, Zürich 1947) teaches that the Church is really visible and communitarian, attached to some particular men and place, based only on divine trust, subject to no human authority but only to the ruling of Scripture. Another tendency is the so-called "*Neue Consensus*" (i.e., New Agreement), which conceives the Church as the "People of God" or the "New Israel," having both interior and exterior elements, as a "society of hearts and rites"; thus, M. Goguel, F. J. Leenhardt, Ph.-H. Menoud, J. L. Leuba, (*L'institution et l'événement*, Neuchâtel 1950), and O. Cullman, (*Christology of the New Testament* [trans. from the French, rev. ed.], Westminster, Md., 1964; *Christ and Time* [trans. from the French, rev. ed.], Westminster, Md. 1964).

The perfect social character of the Church is denied by all those who, in doctrine or practice, consider the Church as subject to the State or civil society; for, the denial of the independence of the Church supposes necessarily the denial of its social perfection.

This error, historically called *Caesaropapism or Regalism* (meaning usurpation and exercise of the supreme authority in ecclesiastical matters by emperors and kings) began among ecclesiastical circles in the Middle Ages. As a doctrine it was first brought forth by *Marsilius of Padua* († about 1327) in his famous work *Defender of peace*, condemned as heretical by John XXII (cf. Denz. 941–946), then again by *John Wyclif* and *John Hus*, both condemned by the Council of Constance in 1415 (cf. Denz. 1166, 1209), finally and with greater emphasis by *Gallicanism* in the 17th century.

Gallicanism is a general politico-religious movement, started in France in defense of the rights of the French Church against the alleged usurpations of the Roman Pontiff and publicly endorsed by the "Articles of the Gallican Clergy" in 1682. Notwithstanding the condemnation of these articles by Alexander VIII (Denz. 2281–2285), the movement spread out also in Germany, under the name of *Febronianism* (from the writer Justin Febronius whose real name was John Nicholas Hontheim †1790), in Austria, under the name of *Josephism* (from emperor Joseph II, †1790), and even in Italy, where the *Synod of Pistoia* in 1786 denied the authority of the Church in exterior matters (condemned by Pius VI in 1794; cf. Denz. 2604f.).

The more recent Liberalism, prevailing in many modern States, which inspires its policy in the principle of complete separation between Church and State, is also based on an implicit denial of the independence and perfect social character of the Church.

or equivalently contained in some of the infallible definitions of the extraordinary Magisterium, particularly in the definition of Vatican I according to which the Pope has the full and supreme power of jurisdiction in the Church. It is a *Catholic doctrine, at least theologically certain* and proximately definable, that the Church is a *perfect society*; this is explicitly taught by the extraordinary Magisterium since the Syllabus.

The proof for our statement is taken directly from the channels of revelation as well as from theological reasoning.

The Magisterium stood for its rights in this matter and manifested its doctrine since the Middle Ages, when the pretenses and usurpations of civil rulers in ecclesiastical matters began to take a menacing shape. The first doctrinal declaration was brought forth by Boniface VIII in his famous Bull "Unam sanctam" of 1302, in which, against the Regalism of Philip IV, "The Fair," king of France, he affirmed the principle: "The temporal power must be subordinate to the spiritual ... The spiritual power is above any earthly power, in dignity and nobility" (Denz. 873). Shortly after this document in 1327 *John XXII* condemned as heretical the doctrine of Marsilius of Padua on the subjection of the Pope to the emperor (Denz. 941–946) and in the following century the *Council of Constance* in 1418 condemned similar regalistic propositions of John Wyclif and John Hus (Denz. 1166, 1209). Finally in the 17th century *Alexander VIII* rejected the mitigated regalism advanced by the French Gallicans in 1682 (Denz. 2281–2285) which was followed one century later by the Jansenist Synod of Pistoia, condemned by Pius VI in 1794 (Denz. 2604f.).[43]

In the more recent time of the 19th–20th centuries, when Liberalism and Laicism subtly distinguished between perfect and imperfect society and advocated a complete separation between the Church and the civil society in order to inculcate the denial of the independence of the Church, the Magisterium took up the duty of explicitly and repeatedly declaring that the Church is *a true and perfect society, possessing all the means necessary to achieve its supernatural purpose, completely independent from the State and supreme*

---

43 Against Protestantism, denying the existence of a true hierarchy in the Church, the *Council of Trent* directly defined this truth as *de fide* (Sess. 23, can.6, Denz. 1776). However, the Council defines directly only the hierarchy of *Orders*, which is not of itself (purely as a right to minister) sufficient to constitute a true society but only a ministerial association, unless it is combined with the power of jurisdiction.

in its own order. This is a summary of the doctrine repeated by the Roman Pontiff for a century since the *Syllabus of Pius IX* in 1864.[44]

In Scripture all the elements of a true and perfect society are sufficiently indicated with regard to the Church. This appears from the simple examination of the elements with which Christ endowed the Church and of the manner in which the apostles interpreted and applied Christ's institution.

Christ speaks of founding a building (Matt. 16:18), of inaugurating a kingdom (above, p. 260), of gathering a flock in a sheepfold (see above, p. 263). These images are vague of themselves and absolutely speaking could be applied to a merely spiritual union or movement, but in the biblical context they receive a concrete sense and inculcate the concept of a true society, since the same images are applied by the prophets to the synagogue

---

44 The *Syllabus* condemned the following proposition: "The Church is not a true and *perfect society*, completely free, nor is it endowed with its proper rights given to it by its divine founder, but it is up to the civil power to determine which are the rights of the Church and the limits within which it may exercise such rights" (prop. 19, Denz. 2919). Likewise it rejected the misleading proposition: "The Church must be set apart from the State, and the State from the Church" (prop. 55, Denz. 2955).

Vatican Council I defined as de fide that "the Roman Pontiff has the full and supreme power of jurisdiction over the universal Church" (Sess. 4, can. 3, Denz. 3064).

Leo XIII in his Encyclical "Immortale Dei" 1885 expounds and determines more at length the doctrine of the Syllabus, stating: "The Church ... is a *society perfect in its order and in its right*, because by the will and gift of its founder, it possesses in itself and by itself all the necessary means for its safety and its action ... God has divided the care of the human race between two powers, namely, the ecclesiastical and the civil, one entrusted with the divine and the other with human matters. *Both of them are supreme, each in its own proper order*" (Denz. 3167f.).

Pius XI: "The Church is a supernatural society..., *perfect in itself,* because it is endowed with all the means needed to achieve its purpose, that is, the eternal salvation of men. Hence it is also a society *supreme in its order*" (Encycl. "Divini illius Magistri," Denz. 3685).

Pius XII: "Christ willed that the union of men which he founded should be a *society perfect in its kind* and endowed with all the juridical and social elements" (Encycl. "Mystical Body," no. 63, AAS 35, p. 224).

Vatican II: "The political community and the Church are *mutually independent and self-governing* in their proper field. Both, however, under a different title serve to the personal and social vocation of the same men. They shall discharge such service more effectively for the benefit of all, if both strive to increase wholesome mutual cooperation, having due regard also to the circumstances of place and time" (Constitution on the Church in the Modern World, no. 76). However, the Council claims complete freedom of the Church from civil authority, declaring that "the Church ... does not lodge her hope in privileges conferred by civil authority. Indeed, she stands ready to renounce the exercise of certain legitimately acquired rights if it becomes clear that their use raises doubt about the sincerity of her witness or that new conditions of life demand some other arrangement" (*Ibid.*) (see also the Decree on the Bishop's Pastoral Office, no. 20).

which was a true society and which Christ intends to replace with the new building, the new kingdom, and the new flock. Furthermore, Christ explicitly points out the four elements which constitute a true society, namely, the people, the purpose, the means, the authority. The people are "all nations" (Matt. 28:19) or "every creature" (Mark 16:15), for he wills a universal union; the purpose is a specific supernatural good, the salvation of souls (John 20:11: "As the Father has sent me, I also send you"); the means are faith and sacraments (Matt. 28:18–20; Mark 16:15f.); the authority regards baptizing, teaching, binding and loosing (Matt. 16:18f.; 18:18; John 20:21f.).

The truth and force of this authority is exemplified by Christ in the pericope on fraternal correction: "But if thy brother sin against thee, go and show him his fault, between thee and him alone ... If he do not listen to thee, take with thee one or two more so that on the word of two or three witnesses every word may be confirmed. And if he refuse to hear them, appeal to the Church, but if he refuse to hear even the Church, let him be to thee as the heathen and the publican. Amen, I say to you, whatever you bind on earth shall be bound also in heaven; and whatever you loose on earth shall be loosed in heaven" (Matt. 18:15–18).

The apostles, interpreting and applying what Christ had instituted, organized the faithful into several well-defined communities and exercised over them a true authority, which is the typical sign of a true society. This authority is shown particularly in the Council of Jerusalem, in which the apostles decided how the faithful should act in regard to certain prescriptions of the Jewish law. After the discussions they issued the following decree: "*The Holy Spirit and we have decided to lay no further burden upon you but this indispensable one,* that you abstain from things sacrificed to idols and from blood and from what is strangled and from immorality; keep yourselves from these things, and you will get on well. Farewell" (Acts 15:28f.). Soon after this Council, Paul "travelled through Syria and Cilicia, and strengthened the churches and commanded them *to keep the precepts* of the apostles and presbyters" (Acts 15:41).

The social character of the Church is particularly evident from *the words and the acts of St. Paul,* the great organizer of Christian communities. He tells the presbyters of Ephesus: "Take heed to yourselves and to the whole flock in which the Holy Spirit *has placed you as bishops, to rule the Church of God"* (Acts 20:28). As soon as he had spread the Gospel and made new converts in various regions, he "appointed presbyters for them in each church" (Acts 14:22). He also felt the need of special legates who, as Timothy and Titus, would themselves "appoint presbyters in every city" (Tit. 1:5) and would in full govern a particular church, exercise judgement and ordain new *"presbyters who rule"* (1 Tim. 5:17–22).

The role of a bishop is thus outlined to Timothy: "Preach the word, be urgent in season, out of season; reprove, entreat, rebuke, with all patience and teaching" (2 Tim. 4:2). The *legislative and coercive power* is clearly shown by St. Paul particularly in the epistles to the Thessalonians and the Corinthians. He tells the Thessalonians "to do the things that *we enjoin*" and "if anyone does not *obey our word*... do not associate with him" (2 Thess. 3:4, 14). He praises the Corinthians because they "hold fast *my precepts* as I gave them" (1 Cor. 11:2) and distinguishes between *his own precepts* and the precepts of the Lord (1 Cor. 7:10–12); he speaks with authority when he explains to them how to behave about the use of things that have been sacrificed to idols (1 Cor. 10:23–32), the headdress of women in church (1 Cor. 11:1–17), the celebration of the Eucharist (1 Cor. 11:17–34), and the use of particular charisms (1 Cor. 14:26–40). He exercises his power of *coercion*, particularly in the case of the incestuous man at Corinth, menacing to "come to you with a rod" and meanwhile "passing judgement" on him and excommunicating him "with the power of our Lord Jesus" (1 Cor. 4:21; 5:1–5); again in his second epistle to the Corinthians he warns them, menacing to "act severely, according to *the power that the Lord has given me*" (2 Cor. 13:2, 10).

With regard to *Tradition*, it is evident that at least toward the end of the second century the Church was everywhere organized, according to the same pattern, into a true and perfect society and was recognized to be such as of divine right. In particular the Fathers of the 4th century explicitly defend the *superiority and independence of the Church* against the first usurpations in ecclesiastical matters made by the Christian emperors, who inaugurated the so-called Byzantine Caesaropapism (see footnote 42).[45]

---

45 Athanasius flatly tells the arian emperors to mind their own business (*History of the Arians* 52, MG 25.755). Hosius of Cordova in his letter to emperor Constantius tells him: *"God gave the empire to you and entrusted the ecclesiastical matters to*

It will suffice, therefore, to give a summary of the doctrine of the Apostolic Fathers (from the end of the first century through the second century), particularly Clement of Rome († about 95), the author of the *Didache* (about the beginning of the 2nd century), Ignatius of Antioch († about 107), Polycarp († about 155), Hermas (about the middle of the same century), Justin († about 156) and Irenaeus († about 202).

The existence of a true hierarchy is expressed in several ways. The ecclesiastical ministers are said to be "constituted" in their place (Clement of Rome, *Epist. to the Corinthians* 44.1f.) or to obtain "the place of the presbytery" (Polycarp, *Epist. to the Philippians* 11.1); these expressions show that the presbytery is not a mere title of honor, but a public office to which one is taken up and in which he is placed. The first verbal distinction between ministers and "laity" appears at this time (Clement of Rome, *ibid.* 40.5). The ministers are given various names which imply authority, as assessors (those who hold the first seats), prefects, presidents (Hermas, *Shepherd*, Vis 2.2.6; Justin, *Apol. I* 65: "The one who presides over the brethren"). The bishop governs the community of the faithful and presides in the place of God (Ignatius of Antioch, *Epist. to the Magnesians* 6.1); to the other presbyters obedience is due on the part of the faithful (Clement of Rome, *Epist. to the Corinthians* 57.1); the ecclesiastical presidents possess particularly the magisterial power (Irenaeus, *Against Heresies* 3.3.1: "The apostles handed over their own magisterial place to their successors").

The divine origin of this hierarchy is expressed in three ways. First, implicitly in the apostolic succession, affirmed by Clement of Rome and Irenaeus. Second, equivalently, by saying that the apostles, having received Christ's command to preach the Gospel, started such a work and chose bishops and deacons for the same function (Clement of Rome, *ibid.*, chaps. 42 and 44), solemnly asserting that "where the bishop is, there is the Church" (Ignatius of Antioch, *Epistle to the Christians of Smyrna* 8.2). Third, explicitly. According to Ignatius, "bishops, presbyters, and deacons are

---

us" (ML 8.1329). Hilary of Poitiers in a writing addressed to the same emperor protests against civil courts judging ecclesiastical persons (ML 10.557). Gregory of Nazianzus in a speech to his citizens tells secular princes and prefects: "By the law of Christ you also are subject to my empire and to my throne" (MG 35.975). Ambrose in his epistle to emperor Valentinian tells him: "In matters of faith the bishops usually judge the emperors, not the emperors the bishops (*Epist.* 21.4, ML 16.1046).

named to their office in conformity with Christ's will, who makes them firm through His holy spirit" (*Epistle to the Philadelphians, address*); the bishop of Philadelphia "obtained the ministry of governing the people by the benign will of the Father and of the Lord Jesus Christ" (*ibid.* 1.1). Onesimus and Ignatius are bishops "by the grace of God" (ibid. 1.3) or "by the will of God" (*Epistle to the Christians of Smyrna* 11.1). According to Clement of Rome and Irenaeus, the ecclesiastical ministers are so clearly instituted by God that they were even foretold by Isaias 60.7. (Such is the sense given by these Fathers to the words of Isaias: "I will make thy visitation peace, and thy overseers justice").

Theological reason cannot prove from other principles the institution of the Church as a *true society*; it is a fact shown only through Scripture and Tradition. Absolutely speaking, Christ could have given to his followers faith and sacraments without any particular social bond or authoritative guidance, leaving to men themselves the rational choice of getting together into some form of true society and authoritative supervision, humanly and democratically established. However, the utmost *fitness* of a social divine organization of the spiritual and visible union brought by Christ among men is evident, considering on the one hand the nature of religion in general, which is essentially external and social, according to the nature of man, and on the other hand the good of the faith itself and of the sacraments instituted by Christ, which could not be easily kept free from alteration and integrally transmitted in the course of the ages unless through a definite and hierarchical society.

Moreover, once the social character of the Church is established from the channels of revelation, its perfect social character can be theologically proved; in other words, if the Church is a true society, it is necessarily a *perfect and independent society*, according to the definition of perfect society given above (p. 272). In fact, *the purpose* of salvation of souls is a complete and perfect good in its proper supernatural order, because it covers and unifies the entire life of a man, enveloping in itself all other particular purposes we can think of, in the same supernatural order, as prayer, worship, evangelization, education, science; in the same manner, the good of temporal happiness envelops and unifies all the particular purposes and activities of man in the natural order, as science, arts, voyages, commerce, industry. Furthermore, the Church received from its divine founder all *the means* necessary and sufficient for achieving such a purpose, namely, faith, which perfects the intellect, worship, which as a cause of sanctification reaches the will, and government, which reaches both intellect and will through the regulation of exterior acts.

From the fact that the Church is a perfect society, it follows necessarily that it is also completely *independent* from the civil society which is likewise perfect in its own natural and inferior order. Moreover, given on the one hand the superiority of its order and purpose and on the other hand the inseparability of the two orders which cover the life and the actions of the same man, it follows logically that the Church is a society superior to the civil society and *reaches it indirectly*, so that, in the case of conflict in mixed matters and obligations, the right of the Church prevails, as the right of God prevails over the rights of man, according to the word of Peter: "We must obey God rather than men" (Acts 5:29; cf. 4:19–31; 5:18–28; 23:1–5).

This is the basic principle regulating all the *relations between Church and State*, between the supernatural and the natural societies.[46] Hence in things merely temporal, which do not interfere with the supernatural good and the salvation of souls, the Church as such has nothing to say and no rights to claim, following Christ's warning: "My kingdom is not of this world" (John 18:38); "Render therefore, to Caesar the things that are Caesar's and to

---

46   Cf. H. De Lubac, "Le pouvoir de l'Eglise en matière temporelle," *Revue des sciences religieuses* 6 (1932) 329–354; J. C. Murray, "Contemporary Orientations of Catholic Thought on Church and State in the Light of History," *Theological Studies* (1949) 177–235; "Leo XIII on Church and State: The General Structure of the Controversy," *ibid.* (1953) 1–31; G. Saraceni, *La potestà della Chiesa in materia temporale e il pensiero degli ultimi cinque Pontefici,* Milano 1951; A. Abate, *La potestà indiretta della Chiesa,* Roma 1957; J. N. Moody (ed.) *Church and Society,* New York 1953; B. Monsegu, "La tesis del Estado laico a la luz de la teologia y de la historia," *XIV Semana Española de Teologia* (Madrid 1955) 219–270; Ch. Journet, *L'Eglise du Verbe Incarné* 1 (éd. 2, Paris 1955) 328–331; A. De Bovis, *"L'Eglise du Verbe Incarné* 1 (éd. 2, Paris 1955) 328–331; A. De Bovis, "L'Eglise dans la société temporelle," *Nouvelle revue théologique* 79 (1957) 225–247; R. Moya, "Naturaleza de la potestad de la Iglesia en materia temporal," *Angelicum* 36 (1959) 383–410; 37 (1960) 53–69; G. Martelet, "L'Eglise et le temporel. Vers une nouvelle conception," *L'Eglise de Vatican II* (éd. G. Barauna, trad. Y. M.-J. Congar, Paris 1966), vol. 2, pp. 517–539; Various authors, "Church and State," *New Catholic Encyclopedia* (New York, 1967), vol. 3, pp. 726–758; L. Spinelli, *Problematica attuale nei rapporti tra Chiesa e Stato,* Modena 1970; R. Guénon, *Autorità spirituale e potere temporale,* Milano 1972.

God the things that are God's" (Matt. 22:21). But in things that are either purely spiritual or closely connected with the spiritual good of man, in such a way that they are notably favorable or harmful to it, the Church can and must, in the measure in which circumstances prudently suggest it, vindicate its rights, appealing to the words of its Founder: "All power in heaven and on earth has been given to Me. Go, therefore, and make disciples of all nations" (Matt. 28:19).[47]

It goes without saying that in such mixed or connected matters the best practical way is the mutual cooperation between the two powers, as is wisely suggested by Leo XIII in his Encyclical "Immortale Dei" (Denz. 3172) and by Vatican II quoted above in footnote 44. On the other hand a systematic withdrawal or mutual disregard is generally harmful to both, and if in some circumstances a practical seclusion on the part of the State may be useful to the Church, a theoretical and doctrinal separation of both powers is a heresy, involving the negation of the Church as a perfect and independent society. For this reason it has been explicitly condemned in the Syllabus (see above, footnote 44).

---

47 The Church has the right to *possess temporal goods* of different kinds in order to propagate the faith, to provide decent life for its ministers, to build churches or places of worship, to celebrate the sacrifice, the sacraments, and other acts of divine cult, to build and support seminaries and schools. It has the right of *urging the faithful*, even in the way of taxation, to supply temporal goods necessary for the acts of cult and the support of its ministers. It has also the right to acquire and exercise a *temporal power*, in the fashion of a civil society, in the measure in which it would be necessary to protect its action and independence; such was the past Roman State up to 1929 and such remains the actual Vatican City, as a reduced dimension of that State.

4

The Threefold Power of the Church[48]

THE CHURCH, BEING A PERFECT SOCIETY, IS NEC-
essarily endowed with the *power of jurisdiction*, which is essential
to every perfect society[49] and which involves three functions,
namely, the legislative (law making power), the judicial (power
of judging whether individual actions conform to the law), and
the coercive (power of punishing unlawful actions, which is an
extension of the judicial).

But, unlike the civil society, the Church has also two peculiar
means for the attainment of its supernatural purpose of salvation
of souls, namely, faith and the sacraments. Hence the question
arises, whether these two means are the basis of two additional
powers in the Church, which are not found in the civil society,
namely, the *power of Orders*, that is, the exclusive right of performing and administering the sacraments, and the *power of Magisterium*, that is, of teaching authoritatively the doctrines connected
with the salvation of souls.[50]

---

48 Cf. Fuchs, *Magisterium, Ministerium, Regimen. Vom Ursprung einer ekklesiolo-
gischen Trilogie*, Bonn 1940; T. Zapelena, *De Ecclesia Christi* 1 (ed 4, Romae 1946)
170–197; 2 (1954) 119–171; I. Salaverri, "La triple potestad de la Iglesia," *Mis-
celenae Comillas* 14 (1950) 5–84; Ch. Journet, *L'Eglise du Verbe Incarné* 1 (éd. 2,
Paris 1955) 69–241; 307–425; *Problems of Authority*, London 1961; E. Doronzo,
De Ordine 1 (Milwaukee 1957) 197–489; 3 (1962) 23–88.

49 As St. Thomas notes (*Summa Theol.*, II-I, q. 90, a. 3, ad. 3), a true but imperfect
society, like the family (see above, p. 272), has no jurisdiction properly so-called
and the authority of such society can issue only statutes, precepts, orders, but no
proper laws. The same applies to judgment and coercion.

50 All the above mentioned *adversaries* (footnote 42) who deny that the Church
is a true or a perfect society, consequently reject all three powers. However, some
of them attack particularly one or another power. Thus the power of Orders was
rejected by *Wyclif, Hus*, with their followers, and by the *Protestants*, as a consequence of their negation of a true priesthood in the Church. The power of Magisterium was first attacked by the Cathari in the 12th century, then by the followers
of Wyclif and Hus, and finally it was radically eliminated by the Protestants, for
whom the only rule of faith is Scripture. Likewise the power of jurisdiction is
rejected by the Protestants on the assumption that Christ gave to Christians, and to
all of them, the mere commission of spreading the Gospel and ministering Baptism

The analogical concept, common to these three powers, is the public right of exercising an action about the members of the Church. But the power of Orders merely implies the right of *acting*, that is, of performing and administering the sacraments, without imposing an obligation, while the two other powers imply the right of imposing an obligation ("potestas ius dicendi," that is, the power of saying what is right and what is wrong). The further distinction between these two is that the power of jurisdiction regards things to be done, that is, obliges to do exterior things and actions (like in the civil society), while the power of the Magisterium regards truths to be believed and obliges to assent with the intellect itself and the will (unlike the civil power or any other human power).

Statement 1. *The Church is endowed with the power of Orders, that is, with a proper and exclusive right to dispense the means of salvation through ministers divinely ordained for this purpose.*[51]

Theological note. The existence of a proper and sacerdotal hierarchy, and hence of the power of Orders, divinely instituted, is *de fide*, often defined by the Magisterium and more solemnly by the Council of Trent.

The doctrine of the Magisterium has been handed on in three steps, following the three historical moments in which the existence of the sacerdotal hierarchy has been denied with the same general purpose of extending to all the faithful the administration of the two means of salvation, faith and sacrament. First, the Lateran Council IV in 1215 defined against the Albigenses that only an ordained priest can perform the Eucharist (Denz. 802). Then the *Council of Constance* in 1418 compelled the followers of Wyclif and Hus to admit that only a priest, to the exclusion of any layman, can hear sacramental confession (Denz. 1260; cf. 1277). Finally the *Council of Trent* defined as *de fide* against the Protestants the existence of the power of Orders divinely instituted (Sess. 23, can. 6, Denz 1776; see below pp. 184f.).

This same doctrine was repeated by the Councils Vatican I (Constit. on the Church, Denz. 3050) and Vatican II (Dogmatic Constit. on the Church, nos. 18, 32).

---

and the Eucharist. The Jansenist *Synod of Pistoia* attacked particularly the coercive power of the hierarchy.

51 This assertion will be completed below (pp. 387ff.) by the doctrine of the threefold degree of the hierarchy of Orders.

With regard to Holy Scripture, the very existence of the power of Orders or sacred hierarchy in the *synagogue* which was the figure and the preparation of the Church, suggests the existence of a similar power in the Church. If the adversaries object that there is no sacrifice to be offered in the New Testament and hence no power of Orders, we answer that on the contrary there is a eucharistic sacrifice instituted by Christ, as is shown in the treatise on this sacrament; besides, even if there were no sacrifice, the power of Orders would have its sufficient reason for the purpose of administering the sacraments, as Baptism, and in general for performing the acts of worship and dispensing the means of salvation.

As a matter of fact, *Christ* chose the apostles and handed on only to them His divine mission of salvation. *In a general way* He "made them fishers of men" (Matt. 4:19), He sent them into the world for the same work for which He was sent by the Father (John 17:18; 20:21), so that they would bring forth lasting fruits of sanctification (John 15:16). In particular He entrusted to them alone definite means of sanctification, namely, Baptism (Matt. 28:19; Mark 16:16), Penance (John 20:21–23: "Whose sins you shall forgive, they are forgiven them"), Eucharist, and Orders (Luke 22:19: "Do this in remembrance of me").

The Acts and Epistles show that the apostles, applying Christ's institution and interpreting his will reserved this ministry to themselves and to other chosen and ordained persons. Thus particularly the ministry of Baptism (1 Cor. 1:12–17; Acts 2:41; 8:11, 12, 16, 28; 10:48, etc.), Confirmation (Acts 8:14–20; 19:5), Eucharist (Acts 2:42; 20:7; 27:35), Anointing the Sick (Jas. 5:14f.), Orders (Acts 6:1–6; 13:3; 14:22; 1 Tim. 4:14; 2 Tim. 1:6).

This power given to the chosen apostles was constitutional, that is, *was to last with the Church* and to be transmitted unceasingly to definite successors of the apostles. This follows from the very purpose of this power, which is the sanctification of all men. For Christ told the apostles to take faith and Baptism to "all nations" (Matt. 28:19), to "the whole world, to every creature" (Mark 16:15f.), "to the very ends of the earth" (Acts 1:8), which could not be done by the apostles alone in their physical life and person, but only through their successors. This is confirmed by the fact that Christ promised the apostles that He would assist them in their work and "be with them all days, even unto to consummation of the world"

(Matt. 28:20), and for the same purpose He would send to them the Holy Spirit who would "dwell with them forever" (John 14:16). A further confirmation comes from the fact that the apostles since the beginning entrusted their own power to other ministers, considering them as divine heralds of the same mission. Thus St. Paul tells the presbyters of Ephesus that "the Holy Spirit has placed them as bishops, to rule the Church of God" (Acts. 20:28) and St. Peter compares the presbyters to himself and to Christ, describing them as "shepherds" under the Prince of shepherds (1 Pet. 5:4) and calling himself a "fellow-presbyter" (*Ibid.* 5:1).

Tradition in the second century shows the sacred ministry so intimately connected with the hierarchy that it is difficult to distinguish in the texts cited in the preceding chapter (p. 278) what refers to Orders and what to jurisdiction or Magisterium.

The entire function of the hierarchy is frequently called *"Liturgy,"* which suggests the concept of cult, although the specific cultic meaning of this word was determined later and in this period the word is used to signify any ecclesiastical ministry, though not cultic, just as the word "diaconia" (service, ministry).[52]

---

52   The Greek word *"leiturgia"* derives from "léitos," i.e., concerning people ("laós," people) and "érgon," i.e., work, deed. Originally in profane language it meant public function, and "leiturgós" meant a public officer.

The word in its various forms ("leiturgia, leiturgéo [I perform the function], leiturgós, leiturgicós") is frequently used in the Bible (version of the O. T. and original of the N. T.). In the N. T. it occurs 15 times (only in Luke and Paul), six times in the specific sense of sacred cult (Luke 1:23; Acts 13:2; Heb. 8:2, 6; 9:21; 10:11), nine times in the more general sense of ministry connected with religion, as the ministry of the word and charity (Rom. 13:6; 15:16, 27; 2 Cor. 9:12; Phil 2:17, 25, 30; Heb. 1:7, 14). Only once the word signifies probably the cult of the N. T. (Acts 13:2).

The Fathers of the second century adopted the word in the general sense of ecclesiastical ministry; cf. Clement of Rome, *Epist. to the Corinthians* 40f.; *Didache* 15; Hermas, *The Shepherd*, Sim. 9.27. 2f.; Irenaeus, *Against Heresies* 1.1. Later on it received the specific sense of cultic ministry.

The Greek word *"diaconia"* (of uncertain etymological origin) derives proximately from the verb "dióco" (I follow) and is used by pagan writers in the sense of acting service (not servitude or slavery), as that of house servants and especially of waiters at tables. In the New Testament the word is used also for the sacred ministry of the apostles (Acts 1:17, 25; 20:24; 21:19; Rom. 11:13; 2 Cor. 4:1, 63; 1 Tim. 1:12) and of the bishop (only once, 2 Tim. 4:5). The kindred name "diáconos' (deacon) is attributed to Christ himself, called "deacon [minister] of the circumcision" (Rom. 5:8), to simple faithful working for the cause of Christ and called "God's or Christ's deacons" (2 Cor. 6:4; 11:23), to an individual woman, Phoebe by name, particularly helping the church at Cenchrae (Rom. 16:1: "the deacon," i.e., the deaconess), and to particular ministers, inferior to presbyters and bishops (three times, Phil. 1:1; 1 Tim. 3:8, 12). This last sense prevailed since the second century.

At any rate, the cultic character of the ecclesiastical hierarchy is shown by its intimate connection with the principal acts of cult, as public prayer, administration of Baptism, Penance, Anointing of the Sick, and particularly the Eucharist (see especially Ignatius of Antioch, *Epistles to Eph.* 5.2; *Smyrn.* 8.2; *Philad.* 8.1; *Polyc.* 5.2; and Justin, *Apol. I* 65, 67).

In the following period, *up to the beginning of the 5th century*, the sacerdotal character of the hierarchy is brought into full light.

In the 3rd century, the very expressions "sacerdos-sacerdotium-sacerdotale" (priest, priesthood, priestly), not used in the preceding century (probably for fear of confusion with the ministers of the Jewish law), are frequently used, especially by Tertullian and Cyprian. The bishop is called priest, high priest, pontiff; the power or office is called sacerdotal; the class (order, college, body) of ministers is likewise called sacerdotal. The book *Apostolic Tradition* (probably of Hippolytus of Rome, †235) describes distinctly the ordination of the sacred ministers.

In the 4th century the same sacerdotal character is greatly emphasized. Particular monographs are edited on the priesthood, eminent among others that of St. John Chrysostom. The title "sacerdos" is given also to the presbyter, generally with the qualification of "sacerdos" of second order, to distinguish him from the bishop, priest of first order or high priest (Jerome, *Epist.* 79; *On Jer.* 3.13; Optatus of Milevis, *On the Schism of Donatists* 1.3; pseudo-Ambrose, *On 1 Tim.* 3.8–10; Innocent I, *Epist.* 25.6). St. Augustine testifies: "Bishops and presbyters are now properly called priests" (*City of God* 20.10). *The Apostolic Constitutions* (compiled about the year 400) describe at length the various sacerdotal functions (Book 3, chap. 10; book 8, chaps. 5,28).

Theological reasoning draws the existence of the power of Orders from the very nature of the Church as a perfect society. For one of the means necessary to the Church for achieving its purpose of sanctification of souls is the cult (particularly the sacraments), besides faith, to which corresponds the power of Magisterium. But all the means through which a perfect society achieves its purpose must be in the hands of its authority. Therefore, the cult must belong to the authority, that is, must be administered authoritatively by ministers having the power *ad hoc*, to the exclusion of others. Of course God could have instituted the Church with only the power of jurisdiction, leaving to private persons indiscriminately the care of administering the sacraments; but in that case the Church would be only an imperfect society, while the civil society is perfect and complete with the sole power of jurisdiction.

Statement 2. *The Church is endowed also with the power of Magisterium, that is, with a proper and exclusive right of teaching authentically the revealed truth.*

Theological note. De fide, equivalently defined by both the ordinary and the extraordinary Magisterium (Vatican I).[53]

The Magisterium in the first centuries brought its own existence to knowledge in a practical manner, through conciliar or extraconciliar decrees by which it proposed various doctrines and condemned contrary errors. In the Middle Ages, when several pseudo-spiritualistic sects, namely, the Cathari and the Waldensians (12th century), the Fraticelli (Little Friars; 14th century), the Wycliffites and Hussites (15th century), claimed for all the faithful the right of publicly preaching the Gospel, thus implicitly denying the existence of a Magisterium, they were directly and solemnly condemned, respectively by the Council of Lateran IV in 1215, John XXII in 1318, and the Council of Constance in 1418. When Protestantism began to attack explicitly the Magisterium as a whole, Leo X condemned several pertinent propositions of Luther (props. 27–30), among which we read the following most radical assertion: "It is certain that it is not in the power of the Church or the Pope to determine articles of faith or even laws regarding morals or good acts" (Denz. 1477; cf. 1478–1480).

Recent documents from Vatican I to Vatican II explicitly insist on the existence and weight of the Magisterium. Particularly important are the following declarations of *Vatican I* on which the other documents depend: "God ... instituted *the*

---

53   There is no vicious circle in the fact that the Magisterium infallibly defines its own existence. For the Magisterium is not the source nor the deposit of revelation but only its interpreter, and it receives this truth about its existence and infallibility from revelation, consigned by God in Scripture and Tradition. In other words, God revealed that there is in the Church an infallible Magisterium and at the same time made such Magisterium able to infallibly find out its own existence in the deposit of revelation, like any other truth.

Church as a guardian and teacher of the revealed truth"; "The Church received the apostolic function of teaching, and with it the order of guarding the deposit of faith." and hence the Magisterium becomes also the *proximate rule of faith*, inasmuch as "by divine and Catholic faith all those things must be believed which are contained in the written or transmitted word of God and are proposed by the Church, either through an extraordinary pronouncement or through the ordinary and universal magisterium, as truths divinely revealed and to be believed" (Sess. 3, chap. 3, Denz. 3011, 3012, 3018).

The same doctrine has been confirmed by Leo XIII (Encycl. "Satis cognitum," Denz. 3305), Pius XI (Encycl. "Divini illius Magistri," Denz. 3686), Pius XII (Encycl. "Humani generis," Denz. 3884; and "Mystici Corporis," AAS 35, pp. 214, 238), and Vatican II which aptly presents together the threefold power of Orders, Magisterium and jurisdiction (Dogmatic Constit. on the Church, no. 20f.).

Scripture shows Christ giving the apostles the power of teaching, to last forever in the Church (see above, p. 284). He generally entrusts to them His own mission (John 17:18; 20:21). He explicitly gives them the command "to teach all nations" (Matt. 28:19f.) and "preach the gospel to every creature" (Mark 16:16); He prays the Father for the apostles and "for those also who through their word are to believe in Me" (John 17:20); He considers contempt to their teaching as contempt to Himself, saying: "He who hears you, hears Me; and he who rejects you, rejects Me" (Luke 10:16).

The exercise of this Magisterium by the apostles is shown in the Acts and Epistles, particularly through St. Paul's ministry. The Apostle explains why such power has been given, namely, to preserve the faithful from error and false doctrines (Eph. 4:14). He emphasizes the weight of the Magisterium as being able to bring the mind of men into submission (see 2 Cor. 10:5: "Bringing every mind into captivity to the obedience of Christ").

Tradition in the second century speaks through the mouth of Irenaeus. He teaches that "the apostolic tradition is kept in the various churches, through the succeeding presbyters," that is, through the bishops, "to whom, as to their successors, the [apostles] transmitted their own magisterial function" and who "with the succession in the episcopacy received *the charism of truth*" (*Against Heresies* 3.2.2; 3.3.1; 4.26. 2; MG 7.847, 848, 1053). Hermas in his visions received a book of revelation with the order of "consigning it to the presbyters, "more precisely to the bishop, Clement by name, who should "send it to the other cities" (*The Shepherd*, Vis. 2.4.2f.). The common belief of the subsequent patristic age is aptly expressed in the following short sentences of Origen and Augustine. Origen, speaking of the variety of opinions occuring among doctors, states: "Only that truth is to be believed, which is in no way at variance with the ecclesiastical and apostolic tradition" (*On Principles* 1.2, MG 11.116). Augustine utters his famous paradox: "I would not believe the Gospel, if I were not compelled by the authority of the Catholic Church" (*Against the Epistle of Manichaeus* 5.6; ML 42.176).

Theological reasoning proceeds exactly in the same manner as above with regard to the power of Orders. Since the doctrine of faith is one of the two means necessary to the Church to achieve its purpose of salvation, it must be in the hands of the authority, otherwise the Church would not be a perfect society (see above, p. 286). Therefore, besides the power of Orders, there is also the power of ecclesiastical Magisterium.

Statement 3. *The Church is endowed with the power of true jurisdiction, which implies three functions, namely, the legislative, the judicial, and the coercive.*

Theological note. The entire assertion is a Catholic doctrine, *at least theologically certain* and proximately definable, as being currently and firmly taught by both the ordinary and the extraordinary Magisterium, and constantly brought into practice by the Church. As regards the legislative function, the assertion seems *de fide*, equivalently contained in the definition of Trent (see below).

The Magisterium equivalently taught this doctrine as many times as it taught that the Church is a perfect society, for jurisdiction is the basic and necessary power of any perfect society. Hence all the documents cited above (p. 274) for the social character of the Church are pertinent here. It suffices to add a few explicit expressions.

The Council of Trent defines as *de fide* that a man is "obliged to observe *the laws* of God and of the Church" (Sess. 6, can. 20, Denz. 1570). In these words the legislative function seems equivalently defined, taking the word "law" in its proper meaning with regard to the Church, as it is taken with regard to God. *Pius VI* against the Jansenist Synod of Pistoia quotes explicitly the three functions of the jurisdiction, declaring that is leading to heresy to deny that the Church "has a God-given power, not only to direct by means of advice and persuasion, but also to command with *laws*, and to coerce and compel by external *judgment* and healthful *punishment*, guilty and contumacious persons" (Denz. 2605). *Pius IX* in his *Syllabus* condemns a proposition teaching that "the Church has no coercive power" (Denz. 2924). *Leo XIII* from the fact that the Church "is a perfect society" infers the three functions, that is, "a true and proper power of passing laws and the consequent power of judging and punishing" (Encycl. "Immortale Dei"). *The Code of Canon Law* declares the same three functions (Cans. 196, 1553, 2214). *Vatican Council II* uses a milder and pastoral expression for the power of jurisdiction, calling the bishops "ministers of government" (Dogmatic Constit. on the Church, no. 20).[54]

With regard to *Holy Scripture*, the three jurisdictional functions appear sufficiently in the texts given above (pp. 275–277) to show that the Church is a perfect society.

Likewise the sense of *Tradition* is manifest from the texts brought forth in the same place (pp. 277f.), although the documents of the second century speak of the three powers of Orders, Magisterium and jurisdiction as one integral power without distinction. Since the beginning of the 3rd century the distinction of jurisdiction is marked by the disciplinary canons of the Councils. In the 4th century the jurisdictional character of the ecclesiastical power is particularly emphasized by the Fathers in their defense

---

54 The original has: "Gubernationis ministri." It seems that the translation: "Officers of good order," made in some publications, is too mild and does not render the exact authoritative meaning of the original.

The Latin word "gubernatio" means originally the piloting of a ship (Cicero) and was soon used by the classics to mean the government of the republic. The same authoritative meaning is kept in all modern languages. At any rate the Council by using the expression "ministers of government" did not intend to undervalue the jurisdictional power of the Church, but only to emphasize its truly ministerial character, as being for the service of Mystical Body (see below, pp. 292–293).

of the independence of the Church against the Byzantine Casearopapism (see above, footnote 45).

The judicial power of the bishop is vigorously described in the following passage of the *Didascalia Apostolorum* (Teaching of the Apostles), one of the oldest juridico-liturgical works, written in the course of the 3rd century: "Let the bishop instruct and admonish all his people about all these things . . . Let him love all men, for he is the upright judge. All the decorous things that are in men, should be found in the bishop. For if the pastor is clear of all wickedness, he can also compel his subjects . . . Judgement is the sword, the Gospel is the bugle, the bishop is the explorer, placed above the Church" (Book 2, chap. 11, p. 6).

Theological reasoning infers the power of jurisdiction from the nature of the Church as a perfect society. Even considered generically as a society, or if it were only an imperfect society in the manner of a family, the Church would still need some kind of true authority, some shadow of jurisdiction, regulating the exterior actions of its members (see above p. 272), and hence an authority distinct from the powers of Orders and Magisterium which would also regulate the external actions regarding cult and faith. But, as a perfect society, it needs a true and proper jurisdiction, without which there can be no real and efficacious laws to compel the members to do things necessary for the good order of the community, nor would the society itself be completely free and independent from any other society.

This jurisdiction in every society implies necessarily *three functions*, namely, the *legislative*, the *judicial*, and the *coercive*. Indeed, jurisdiction is the power of directing the community to the achievement of its purpose and hence of deciding about all the means that are necessary for that purpose. But for such direction it is necessary, first to propose under obligation the means to be taken, and in this the legislative and principal function consists; then to provide that these means are actually taken or that these laws are observed, and from this there derive two mutually complementary functions, that is, the judicial, which passes sentences on the actual application of the laws as well as on the corresponding penalties to be given for violations, and the coercive, which constrains by force these violations and applies these punitive sentences.

Note 1. *On the properly ministerial character of the power of the Church*[55]

Because men are equal in natural dignity, no man has a natural authority on the others, but every true authority is from God, and in this sense it is essentially a ministry, that is, a power entrusted by God as a service to others in the society.[56] But for the ecclesiastical authority there are two additional reasons why it is essentially a ministry or service, a *"liturgia"* (function for the people) or a *"diaconia"* (service), as it was called in the 2nd century (see above, pp. 284f.).

The first reason is because the rectors of the Church in their triple exterior power are actually and properly acting *as ministers of Christ,* who is still present with His authority, although visibly absent until the Second Coming; as St. Paul acknowledges: "On behalf of Christ, therefore, we are acting as ambassadors" (2 Cor. 5:20). This is true not only with regard to the power of Orders which is usually called ministry and in which priests are moreover mere instruments of Christ, actually (and probably also physically) influencing through them, but also with regard to the power of Magisterium and jurisdiction; hence the Pope is Christ's Vicar rather than simply head of the Church, even as to its exterior and social structure.

The second reason is because this social structure itself is not the whole Church, but only the exterior part of the *Mystical Body,* in which, according to the nature of a body, all the members cooperate to the good of the whole and thus help each other and work each to the service of the others (see Eph. 4:11–13). Undoubtedly the service contributed by those who exercise exterior authority is different and even mystically nobler than the

---

55   Cf. M. Lohrer, "La hiérarchie au service du peuple chrétien," *L'Eglise de Vatican II* (ed. by Barauna, trans. into French by V. M.-J. Congar, Paris 1966), vol. 3, pp. 723–740 (with bibliography at the end); Y. M.-J. Congar, "La hiérarchie comme service selon le Nouveau Testament et les documents de la Tradition," *L'Episcopat et l'Eglise universelle* (Paris 1962) 67–132; J. L. McKenzie, *L'evangile et le pouvoir dans l'Eglise,* Paris 1970; T. Flamand, *Saint Pierre interroge le Pape,* Paris 1970; D. Comporta, "Libertà ecclesiale. Appunti per una antropologia giuridico-teologica," *Divinitas* 17 (1973) 313–354.

56   St. Paul calls the secular authority "deacon or minister of God." Rom. 13:1–4: "Let everyone be subject to the higher authorities, for there exists no authority except from God, and those who exist have been appointed by God...[The authority] is God's minister [diáconos] to thee for good."

service afforded by the other members (see footnote 39), but it is still a service, to be rendered to others with ardent zeal, profound humility, and cooperative condescendence, following the warning of the Apostle: "Tend to the flock of God..., governing ... willingly... eagerly, not ... as lording it over your charges, but becoming from the heart a pattern to the flock" (1 Pet. 5:2f.). Christ Himself set the example, saying: "The Son of man also has not come to be served but to serve" (Mark 10:45; cf. Matt. 20:28).

This cooperative condescendence on the part of the Pope and bishops is based on the fact that the external mission of salvation is not confined to the hierarchy, but extends also to the whole community, as being under the influence of the Holy Spirit, soul of the Mystical Body. Hence the authority must prudently acknowledge, approve, and foster the cooperation of the faithful in ecclesiastical provisions and decisions, and particularly detect and support the influence which the Holy Spirit exercises both in the manner of ordinary inspirations and also through extraordinary charismas which are never lacking in the Church, following the warning of the Apostle: "Do not extinguish the Spirit. Do not despise prophecies. But test all things; hold fast that which is good" (1 Thess. 5:19f.).

This ministerial aspect of the ecclesiastical hierarchy is particularly emphasized by the *Council of Vatican II* (Dogm. Constit. on the Church, nos. 12, 20, 24, 30, 32).

Note 2. *On the proper distinction of the three powers*

The power of Orders is specifically and adequately distinct from the other two, because it implies only the right of doing something without imposing an obligation. As to the other two, they both give rise to an obligation, regarding either things to be done (jurisdiction) or truths to be believed (Magisterium). The jurisdiction is certainly the direct source of such obligation, so that the Pope or the bishop himself (not God) is the one who directly obliges the faithful, with a power previously given him by God. The Magisterium also gives rise to the obligation of believing a truth or holding a doctrine. But it is disputed among theologians whether the Magisterium is the direct cause of the obligation or only the condition or occasion of an obligation coming directly from God after the Magisterium has proposed a doctrine (in the way, for instance, in which the Pope receives directly from God the primacy over the Church, after his election by the Cardinals, which is only a condition required for him getting the primacy).[57]

In the first case, which seems more probable, we have to draw the following conclusions. First, the Magisterium is *properly authoritative*, that is, direct cause of obligation, like jurisdiction. Second, such authority comes directly from God as a special charism, for only God can compel the intellect of man to believe a truth. Third, the Magisterium is not opposed to jurisdiction, taken as a source of obligation, but only regards a different object, that is a truth to be believed instead of a thing to be done; in this way we can say that there are *only two powers*, namely, Orders and jurisdiction. In the second case, the Magisterium is not properly authoritative, but only *authentically declarative* (that is, it does not command to believe, but it declares a truth, which God then commands to believe); hence it is directly opposed, like the power of Orders, to jurisdiction, and we have *three directly distinguished powers*, namely, Orders, Magisterium, and jurisdiction.

Note 3. *On the power of Orders*

This power shows several *characteristics*, in opposition to the other two powers, with regard to its name, existence, nature, and object.

Regarding the *name*, up to the 12th century the three powers were called jurisdiction or key of the Church. In the 13th century a distinction was made between the key of Orders and the key of jurisdiction (cf. St. Thomas, *Summa Theol.*, II-II, q. 39, a. 3; *Suppl.*, q. 19, a. 3). Since then this power of Orders acquired and retained its proper name, while the other two remained together under the name of jurisdiction until the 19th century, when they were separately considered under the two names of Magisterium and jurisdiction. Hence the threefold division.

The power of Orders comes into *existence* or is given to a man "*ex opere operato*," that is, through a sacrament, and remains in him indelibly and unchangeably (it cannot be removed, or bound, or

---

57   This controversy has been raised especially by Zapelena and Salaverri (cited in footnote 48), the former holding the first view, the latter the second.

given twice, or increased, or diminished). The other two powers on the contrary, are acquired not necessarily and simply through a sacrament, but in the case of papal primacy it is acquired through a human and irrevocable election, based on divine right, and in the case of episcopacy it is acquired through the sacramental ordination only to a certain extent and it is bound by the primacy itself with regard to its exercise (see below, pp. 373f.).

The *nature* of the power of Orders, considered physically, is a *sacramental character*, that is, something physical, impressed in the soul and essentially supernatural, while the other two powers consist only in something moral, that is, in a right, which is only extrinsically supernatural. Considered morally, the same power of Orders consists also in a right, but, unlike the others, this right is only the right of doing things, that is, of performing the acts of cult, not of imposing to men things to do or truth to believe. Hence there is no jurisdiction formally involved in it, although the episcopal character carries with it the radical exigence of the power of jurisdiction and the sacerdotal character requires the combined action of the exterior jurisdiction in order to operate in the sacrament of Penance.

The *object* or act of this power is essentially the offering of the sacrifice and the performance and administration of the sacraments. There are, however, some extra-sacramental actions of a cultic character, affecting the validity and existence of the sacraments themselves, which can hardly be reduced to the mere power of jurisdiction, as is usually done by the theologians, but seem rather to claim their allegiance to the power of Orders. Such are particularly the determination of the matter and form of some sacraments, the faculty given to a simple priest for administering Confirmation or even Ordination, the placing of impediments to the validity of the sacrament of Matrimony, the solution of all sacramental Matrimony which has not been consummated.

Hence it seems more logical to extend the power of Orders, or rather to distinguish two kinds of power of Orders. One is the *sacramental power*, received in the three ordinations of diaconate, presbyterate, and episcopate, which concerns only the performance of sacrifice and sacraments. The other is the *non-sacramental* or merely liturgical power of Orders, concerning the aforementioned acts about the valid conditions of the sacraments, which, together with jurisdiction and Magisterium, stretches beyond the episcopate, reaching the Supreme Pontificate. Thus in this supreme degree of the ecclesiastical hierarchy the three powers of Order, Magisterium, and jurisdiction reach their apex, unifying without confusion all power of binding and loosing in one and same person who, as Vicar of Christ, is at once the Pontiff, the King, and the Doctor of the Church.

Note 4. *On the power of Magisterium*

From what has been said above (pp. 282, 293), it appears that the nature of this power is the right of teaching authentically doctrines regarding the salvation of souls, that is, revelation and things connected with revelation. The two words *"Authentic Magisterium"* describe it essentially and distinguish it from the other two powers of Orders and jurisdiction.

Under the aspect of *Magisterium*, such power has three properties and three functions. Its three *properties* are: to be constantly *alive*, that is, extant and exercised at all times (while a dead master teaches only through past works or words); to be *external* (while God teaches through internal inspirations); to be merely *transferring* the revelation, once made and forever closed. Its three *functions* are: *teaching*, that is, presenting the revealed truths through simple preaching and doctrinal expository documents; *interpreting* ambiguous or less clear expressions; *judging* about things or doctrines, disputed or erroneous.

Under the aspect of *Authentic*, this Magisterium is *authoritative*, in the sense that it gives rise to an obligation on the part of those to whom it addresses its pronouncements (whether it is the proper cause or a mere condition of such an obligation, it is disputed, as explained above, p. 293). Hence it is a divine *charism*, for no human power can oblige man's intellect and will to assent to a truth, nor any human authority has ever attempted to impose such an obligation. As a particular property, it carries with it the weight of *infallibility*, although not in all its pronouncements, as will be explained below, together with the division of the Magisterium in extraordinary and ordinary (see pp. 351–353).

Note 5. *On the power of jurisdiction*

Jurisdiction is the most fundamental power, considering the Church as an external perfect society. Hence it is intimately connected with the other two powers and reaches the entire external behaviour of a member of the Church, even in matters connected with the other two powers. Such matters are: practice of external cult (for instance, assistance to Sunday Mass, annual confession, paschal communion), external obligatory profession of faith, external obedience to the pronouncements of the Magisterium (with this are connected the excommunication of heretics, while simple declaration of heresy in a man is an act of the Magisterium, and the prohibition of discussing certain matters or continuing a doctrinal controversy).

As to the extension of the three particular functions, namely, legislative, judicial, and coercive, note the following.

The legislative function reaches, at least indirectly, also *internal acts*, that is, those acts that are necessarily connected with the exterior acts which are directly prescribed; for instance, if the Church prescribes the reception of the sacrament of Penance, or the application of a Mass, or the recitation of the divine office, it prescribes also indirectly the act of attrition, or the intention of applying the Mass, or the intention of praying. Whether it can reach such acts also directly in themselves, it is disputed among the theologians, but the negative opinion is more probable.[58]

The same power reaches directly the *internal "forum,"* both sacramental and *non-sacramental.* In the first "forum" it gives to a priest the jurisdiction required for the *penitential absolution*, which is a judicial act, and in the second it grants indulgences and dissolves the obligation of a vow or an oath. In both cases there is no

---

58   The question is whether the Church can prescribe to elicit purely internal acts, for instance, that on Sundays or on other particular circumstances Catholics should make an internal act of faith or charity. A few recent theologians, as Straub, Cappello, and Zapelena, have thought so, on the basis that such acts are a means to achieve the proper purpose of the Church, that is, sanctification of souls. But the more common opinion, held by St. Thomas (*Summa Theol.*, I-II, q. 1, a. 4). Suárez, St. Alphonsus, Billot, Ottaviani, and others, reasonably deny it, because jurisdiction, as a source of obligation, concerns not the Mystical Body as such, but only its social and external structure, just like the jurisdiction of the civil society. Nor does it matter that Orders and Magisterium reach directly internal acts, for these are special and charismatic powers not flowing from the nature of the Church formally as a society.

act imposing an obligation, but only the granting of something; the first case implies only the concourse of the power of jurisdiction with the power of Orders in the same act of absolution, the second case implies an extension of the legislative power intro granting favors, privileges and freedom from some obligations, as happens also in civil society.[59]

The judicial function has naturally the same extension as the legislative, and therefore it reaches all matters of faith and morals, as well as all disciplinary matters and temporal things, inseparably connected with both. In this is founded the common distinction of a threefold forum, that is, the ecclesiastical or canonical forum (understood as external forum, in opposition to the internal, both sacramental and non-sacramental), the civil or secular forum, and the mixed forum.

The coercive function implies the infliction of spiritual punishment or privation of spiritual goods (as excommunication or suspension from sacred ministry), as well as of temporal punishment, or privation of temporal goods (whether purely temporal, as pecuniary fine, infamy, prison, exile, or of mixed character, as privation of ecclesiastical benefice). Such temporal punishment, applicable in the measure and manner allowed by circumstances of place and time, far from being opposed to the spiritual purpose of the Church, is fitting to its social structure and is usually more efficacious, considering human reactions and inclinations.[60]

---

59 Hence the Church reaches directly internal acts *in four ways*, namely, through the power of *Orders*, through the power of *Magisterium*, through the power of jurisdiction in the sacrament of *Penance*, and through this same power, in the manner of dispensation, when granting *indulgences* and dissolving the obligations of *vows and oaths*. No one of these cases involves the imposition of an obligation.

60 The Church has the natural right to use physical coercion, or call on the secular power for its defense or for the application of its coercive decisions. Whether it has also the right of inferring *capital punishment* in its own forum or raising an *armed* force for its defense, it is disputed (cf. St. Thomas, *Summa Theol.*, II-II, q. 11, a. 3; 1.64, aa.3–4; Journet, *op. cit.* [above in footnote 48] 307–425). It seems, however, that capital punishment, as well as mutilation or corporal torture, is not, of itself and abstracting from present social conditions, suitable for achieving the spiritual purpose of the Church nor does it agree with the nature of the Mystical Body and the example of the Founder, who took no revenge but died on the cross.

Note 6. *Schematic division of the power of the Church, as of divine right*

Powers of Orders (liturgical, sanctifying power).

> *Sacramental* (strictly called power of Orders): received in the three sacramental ordinations and aiming at the performance of the sacrifice and the sacraments.
>
> *Non-sacramental* (merely liturgical, only mediately sanctifying): residing only in the R. Pontiff and the bishops and regulating the valid conditions of the sacraments.

Power of Magisterium: binding to accept doctrines.

Power of Jurisdiction (disciplinary, canonical power): binding to perform external actions or loosing an obligation.

> *Properly binding*: directly inferring an obligation.
>
> > *Legislative*: law making function.
> >
> > *Judicial*: judging function.
> >
> > > In the external forum.
> > >
> > > In the internal sacramental forum (power of loosing or binding).
> >
> > *Coercive*: punishing function.
>
> *Dispensing* favors and freedom from obligations.
>
> > In the external forum.
> >
> > In the internal non-sacramental forum (power of loosing).
> >
> > > Loosing the obligation of temporal punishment through indulgences.
> > >
> > > Loosing the obligation of a vow or oath.

5

Peter's Primacy[61]

IN THIS AND THE FOLLOWING SEVEN CHAPTERS
we consider the ecclesiastical hierarchy, that is, the persons in
whom resides the aforementioned threefold power, or rather the
various degrees of these powers, namely, the *primacy and episco-pacy*, as the two degrees of jurisdiction and Magisterium, and the
episcopate, presbyterate, and diaconate, as the three degrees of the
power of Orders.

Starting from the primacy, we consider it in this chapter as it
was found in St. Peter, not however as a personal charism but as
a constitutional endowment of the Church, to be transmitted to
Peter's successors, who are in fact the Roman Pontiffs, as will be
shown in the following chapter.

In Peter's dignity we must *distinguish formally between apostleship
and primacy*, that is, between Peter as apostle and Peter as Pope
or juridical head of the universal Church; the same distinction
applies proportionally to the other apostles who can be considered
as apostles and as bishops. It is theologically certain that Christ
instituted the apostleship, that is, a college of twelve members,

---

61 Afanasieff, N. (and other separated Orientals), *La primauté de Pierre dans l'Eglise
orthodoxe*, Neuchâtel, 1960

Benoit, P., *Exégèse et théologie* 2 (Paris 1961) 250–284: "La primauté de S. Pierre."

Brown, R. E. et al., *Peter in the New Testament*, Minneapolis New York 1973.

Cerfaux, L., "Saint Pierre et sa succession." *Recherches de science religieuse* 41
(1953) 188–202.

Cullmann, O. (protestant), *Peter, Disciple, Apostle, Martyr* (trans. from the French
by V. F. Filson), rev. ed., Westminster, Md. 1962; "Petra, Petros, Kephas," *Theologische Woerterbuch zum Neuen Testament* 6 (1959) 94–112.

Journet, Ch., *The primacy of Peter from the Protestant and from the Catholic Point
of View* (trans. from the French), Westminster, Md. 1954.

Karrer, O., *Um die Einheit der Christen, Die Petrusfrage*, Frankfurt 1953.

Obrist, F., *Echtheitsfragen und Deutung der Primatstelle Mt. 16.18 in der Deutschen
protestantischen Theologie der letzten dreissig Jahre*, Münster 1961.

Panikkar, R., "'Super hanc petram.' Due principi ecclesiologici: la roccia e le
chiavi," *Legge e Vangelo* (Brescia 1972) 135–146.

Rigaux, B., "Saint Pierre et l'exégèse contemporaine," *Coucilium*, no. 27 (1967)
129–152.

Rimoldi, A., *L'apostolo S. Pietro. Fondamento della Chiesa, principe degli apostoli e
ostiario celeste, nella Chiesa primitiva dalle origini al Concilio di Calcedonia*, Roma 1958.

to whom He entrusted an authoritative mission (jurisdiction and Magisterium) to be transmitted to their successors. This is clearly taught by the Council of Trent (Sess. 23, chaps. 1 and 4, Denz. 1764, 1768) and Vatican I (Sess. 4, chap. 3, Denz. 3061), stating that the bishops are the successors of the apostles, and more emphatically by Vatican II, which adds that Christ "established the apostles after the manner of a permanent group, over which He placed Peter, chosen from among them" (Dogm. Constit. on the Church, no. 19; cf. nos. 18–20).

However the apostles as such, besides the constitutional pontifical power to be transmitted to their successors, had a proper personal dignity to which several extraordinary and not transmissible gifts were attached and which constitute properly the so-called *Apostleship*,[62] as distinguished from the simple pontificate of both the bishops and the Pope. As regards the power of Orders, the apostles had a clearer knowledge of its revelation,[63] as appears, for instance, from the words of St. James on the Anointing of the Sick (Epist. 5:14f.) and from St. Paul's statement on Matrimony (Eph. 5:32). As to the Magisterium, they had three special charisms, namely, inspiration in writing, infallibility in teaching, and public revelation (which was closed at the death of the last apostle). As to jurisdiction, each apostle had the right to preach the Gospel to all nations, and to found and rule particular churches, notwithstanding Peter's true primacy, which did not restrict the free ministry of the other apostles in the same manner in which the episcopal jurisdiction is now depending on

---

62 The name Apostle (from the Greek "apóstolos," that is, one who is sent for some business or some mission) is found 80 times in the N. T., especially in the epistles of St. Paul and in the Acts. Referring to Christ's chosen disciples, Matthew calls them "*the twelve apostles*" (10:2; cf. 10:5; Luke 9:1; Mark 6:30; John 13:16) and Luke says that Christ himself "*named* [them] *apostles*" (6:13). The word "twelve" by itself is often used as a name to designate the apostolic group ("The Twelve;" Mark 4:10; 6:7; 9:34; Luke 8:1; 22:3; John 6:71f.; 20:24).

Besides the twelve, the same name is given to *Christ* himself (Heb. 3:1), to *Matthias* who took Judas' place (Acts 1:25f.), to *Paul* who calls himself apostle at the beginning of several of his epistles (Rom., 1 and 2 Cor., Gal., Eph., Col., 1 and 2 Tim., Tit.), to *Barnabas* (Acts 14:4, 14).

Paul himself is not an apostle in the original sense, for he is not counted among the twelve. But the dignity of apostleship applies to him equally as to the others, and he himself emphasizes this (1 Cor. 9:1; 15:9–11; Gal. 1–12), although calling himself "the least of the apostles, and not worthy to be called an apostle, because I persecuted the Church of God" (1 Cor. 15:9).

63 See our treatise on *The Channels of Revelation*, p. 215.

the Roman Pontiff; hence St. John, who was still living under the pontificate of Clement of Rome, the third successor of St. Peter, was inferior to him in the line Pontificate and superior in the line of Apostolate.

Here we consider in Peter not his apostleship, in which he was equal to the other apostles, but only his *primacy*, that is, the supreme degree of jurisdiction (and Magisterium[64]), given directly and immediately to him, formally as the head of the Church, and hence to be transmitted to others after him.

Statement. *Christ gave directly and immediately to Peter a true primacy of jurisdiction, to be lasting forever in the Church.*

Theological note. Both the existence and the perpetuity of Peter's primacy are *de fide*, defined by Vatican I.

The Magisterium has declared and defined this doctrine in three steps, following the three steps taken successively by its adversaries, who explained the social constitution of the Church either as oligarchic (rule of a group), or as democratic (rule of the people), or as simply non-hierarchic (absence of true authority).[65]

---

64   What we say about jurisdiction applies also to Magisterium, because these two powers, unlike the power of Orders, are intimately linked together (see above, pp. 293, 294).

65   The denial of Peter's primacy is based on three errors about the social constitution of the Church, which is considered as a society either oligarchic, or democratic, non-hierarchic.

The first error teaches that the Church, as founded by Christ, has an *oligarchic* constitution, namely, that Christ gave the supreme authority of the Church to the *apostolic college* as a whole, granting at the same time to Peter only a certain primacy of honor or direction. Thus the *separated Oriental* theologians, since the 11th century (the time of their separation) and specially since the 16th century. Some of them admit, however, the primacy only as a personal non-transmissible privilege of St. Peter. The same general opinion is held by the *Anglicans* and by the so-called *Old Catholics* who withdrew from the Catholic Church when the Vatican Council I defined the Petrine and Roman primacy. Cf. M. Jugie, in *Dictionnaire de théologie catholique* 13-1 (Paris 1936) 344–391; Afanasieff, *loc. cit.* (above, footnote 61).

The second error teaches that the Church has a *democratic* constitution, namely, that Christ gave the supreme authority not directly and immediately to Peter, but to the *Christian people*, from whom it is transmitted to Peter and his successors. This error is held by all the *Caesaropapistic and Regalistic theories*, mentioned above (footnote 42), which deny the Petrine primacy of jurisdiction in order to deny or lower the supreme authority of the Pope. The condemnation of this error, as expressed by Marsilius of Padua, Hus and his followers, the Synod of Pistoia, and other Gallicans, is found in Denzinger, nos. 942, 1207, 1263f., 1999, 2594–2596, 2602f.

The third error teaches that the Church has a *non-hierarchic* constitution, that is, it is not a true external society, but either a merely internal and spiritual movement

When the separate *Orientals* first denied Peter's primacy by attributing it to the entire apostolic college, his primacy was explicitly declared by *Leo IX* in the year 1053 in his Epistle to Michael Caerularius, founder of the oriental schism ("Peter and his successors have the unlimited judgment over the entire Church," Mansi 19.638), by the *council of Lyons II* 1274 (Denz. 861), by *Clement VI* in his Epistle to the Armenians 1351 (Denz. 1053), and by the *Council of Florence* in its Decree for the Greeks 1439 (Denz. 1307).[66] The same declaration is repeated in all these documents, namely, that Peter had a true primacy of jurisdiction and that the Roman Pontiff is his successor in it.

When *Caesaropapism and Regalism*, since the Middle Ages up to the end of the 18th century, denied the same primacy with the intention of lowering the papal authority, the Magisterium constantly repeated the same doctrine, condemning each affirmation in particular.[67] The founder of this doctrinal Caesaropapism, Marsilius of Padua († about 1327), flatly affirmed: "Blessed Peter the Apostle had no greater authority than the other Apostles ... Christ left no head in the Church nor made anyone his vicar" (Denz. 942). This proposition was condemned as heretical by *John XXII* in 1327. The last descendant of Caesaropapism, the Gallican Synod of Pistoia 1786, declared that "the power of ecclesiastical ministry and jurisdiction derives in the pastors from the community of the faithful ... [and hence] the Roman Pontiff did not receive his ministerial power from Christ in the person of Blessed Peter but from the Church;" this affirmation was condemned as heretical by *Pius VI* in 1794 (Denz. 2602f.).

When finally recent *Modernism and Liberalism* denied even the hierarchical constitution of the Church, depriving it of all true authority,[68] *Vatican Council I* (1870) solemnly defined the primacy of both Peter and his successor the Roman Pontiff as a dogma of divine faith, stating: "If anyone shall say that blessed Peter

---

(thus *Modernists and Liberal Protestants*), or an external community lacking true authority as far as Christ's institution is concerned (thus *Orthodox Protestants* and some of the *recent Liberal Protestants*). About this error, in which the primacy is radically eliminated, a fuller explanation has been given above (footnote 42; see in Denz. 1475f., 3455, the direct denial of Peter's primacy by Luther and the Modernists).

66 See the definition of the Councils of Lyons and Florence, quoted below, p. 88.
67 See footnote 65.
68 *Ibid.*

the Apostle was not made by Christ the Lord the prince of all the Apostles and the visible head of the entire militant Church, or that he directly and immediately received by the same Jesus Christ our Lord only a primacy of honor and not a primacy of true and proper jurisdiction: let him be anathema;" "If anyone shall say that it is not by reason of an institution of Christ the Lord himself or of a divine right that blessed Peter should have never-ceasing successors in the primacy over the entire Church; or that the Roman Pontiff is not Peter's successor in that same primacy: let him be anathema" (Sess. 4, can. 1f., Denz. 3055, 3058; the two corresponding chapters explain the doctrine more at length).[69]

The same teaching has been confirmed by the more recent Magisterium, as the documents of *Leo XIII* (Encycl. "Satis cognitum" 1896, AAS 28. 726–728), *Pius XII* (Encycl. "Mystical Body" 1943, AAS 35.210f.), and *Vatican II*, which simply refers to and integrally confirms the definition of Vatican I (Dogm. Constit. on the Church, no. 18).

In *Scripture*[70] two texts exhibit directly Peter's primacy, namely, Matt. 16:18f., under the form of a promise, and John 21:15–17, under the form of its actual bestowal.

Matt. 16:18f.: "And I say to thee, thou art Peter, and *upon this rock I will build My Church*, and the gates of hell shall not prevail against it. And I will give thee *the keys of the kingdom* of heaven; and whatever thou shalt *bind on earth* shall be bound in heaven, and whatever thou shalt *loose on earth* shall be loosed in heaven."[71]

---

69   Cf. U. Betti, *La Constituzione dommatica "Pastor aeternus" del Concilio Vaticano I* (Roma 1961) 585–647; the same is reprinted in the collective work *De doctrina Concilii Vaticani Primi* (In Civitate Vaticana 1969) 309–360.

70   Cf. Benoit, Cerfaux, Cullmann, Journet, Rigaux, listed above, footnote 61.

71   The aforementioned adversaries (footnote 65) explain the first and principal part of this text in three ways. Some (as A. Harnack and more recently M. Goguel) deny its *authenticity*, saying that it does not belong to Matthew's gospel but was interpolated later in order to support Peter's authority. Others (as W. G. Kümmel and R. Bultmann in *Theologische Blaetter* [1941] 265–310) deny its *historical truth*, saying that the words belong to Matthew but not to Christ, and Matthew attributed them to Christ for the same purpose of establishing Peter's authority.

Others more numerous, granting both authenticity and historical truth of the words, change their obvious meaning, saying that they do not refer to Peter, but either *to faith*, which had been professed by Peter in the preceding verse 16: "Thou art the Christ," or *to Christ* himself, so that faith or Christ are said to be the rock upon which the Church is built; thus the meaning of the words would be: "You are blessed, Peter, for having confessed your faith in me, for faith is, or I am, the

The text in its entirety is *authentic*, that is, it belongs to Matthew and was not interpolated later into Matthew's gospel. For it is found in all codices and versions critically established. It is also mentioned through allusions or short quotations in several documents of the 2nd and 3rd century; Tertullian, Origen, and Cyprian quote it in its entirety, No objections can be raised from the fact that Mark and Luke do not contain these words; nor from the presence of the word "Church," unusual in the Gospel, for it occurs again twice in Matthew 18:17, even in connection with the same power of the keys.

Likewise the text is *historically true*, that is, it refers to the words spoken by Christ himself and not invented by Matthew to support Peter's authority before the community. For it matches perfectly with the evangelical context (as the peculiar attachment of Peter to Christ and his confession of faith) and with the exercise of Peter's authority in the primitive Church, as shown in the Acts. It would also be highly improbable that Peter's authority would have sprung and grown so fast without the utterance of these words by Christ.

As to their *meaning*, first of all, these words *refer to Peter, not to faith in general or to Christ* (as the adversaries of the primacy interpret[72]). The whole pericope (Matt. 16:16–19) is addressed manifestly to Peter, therefore also the words "Upon this rock I will build My Church." The second part of the text about the keys which is clearly addressed to Peter, implies the same concept of supreme authority in the Church. Peter's name, given him by Christ since the beginning (John 1:42), means rock; as a matter of fact Christ used the Aramaic word "Kepha," which means rock, but the evangelists in their Greek narration through out the gospels used the masculine form "Pétros" instead of "Pétra," which is

---

rock upon which I will build my Church." This explanation, already given by the first Protestants (Luther, Calvin, Melanchthon, and Zwingli) and commonly by the Oriental theologians, has been again brought forth by several recent Liberals (as F. Kattenbusch, K. L. Schmidt, O. Linton, and A. Oepke).

Finally a few recent authors, particularly O. Cullmann (*loc. cit.*, above, footnote 61), grant that by such words a primacy has been given to Peter, but only as a *personal privilege*, not as something to be transmitted and perpetuated.

Such various interpretations of the text are exposed by Cullmann himself and by F. M. Braun, *Aspects nouveaux du problème de l'Eglise*, Freiburg (Schweiz) 1944. See also Rigaux, cited above, footnote 61.

72   See preceding footnote.

in Greek the equivalent of rock[73]; hence it perfectly matches with the following words, "And upon this rock I will build my Church."

If these words referred to faith or to Christ, there would be no logical process in Christ's discourse; it would run as follows: "You are Peter ("Rock"), and upon this rock, which is the faith or myself, I will build My Church;" on the contrary the whole pericope logically runs as follows: "You are blessed, Simon, son of Jona, for having expressed your faith in my Divinity. Hence I tell you that, while Simon by name, you are in reality a rock, for upon you, as a rock, I will build my Church, and consequently I will give you the keys of the kingdom and the power of binding and loosing whatsoever on earth."

Secondly, the same words express *a true primacy of jurisdiction*. This is *equivalently* contained in the three metaphors used by Christ, namely, the rock upon which the ecclesiastical society is founded, the *keys* of the kingdom of heaven, and the power of *binding and loosing*. The fundamental rock is for a building the principle of its stability and firmness (cf. Matt. 7:24f.), as authority is for society. The keys are the sign of property-right over a house; in ancient times, especially by oriental customs, giving the keys of a city to the enemy was the sign of its surrender; the keys were also given to a new governor as the sign of his power; the Bible uses also elsewhere the metaphor of the keys in the sense of power (cf. Isa. 22:21f.; Apoc. 1:8; 3:7; 9:1; 20:1–3; Luke 11:52). Likewise the metaphor of binding and loosing is often used in the New Testament in the sense of authoritative action (cf. Matt. 5:17–19; 18:18; 23:4; John 5:18; 7–23; 20:21f.).[74]

Thirdly, the *perpetuity* of the primacy is not explicitly signified in the text, but it is implicitly contained in and logically inferred

---

73 Christ said: "Thou art kepha ["petra," rock], and upon this kepha I will build my Church." John once recalls the name Cephas, as first given to Peter by Christ: "Thou art Simon, the son of John: thou shalt be called Cephas (which interpreted is Peter)" (1:42). Paul, referring to Peter, often calls him with the Aramaic name Kepha (1 Cor. 1:12; 3:22; 9:5; 15:5; Gal. 2:11, 14).

74 A Catholic exegete is not allowed to doubt the value of the scriptural argument from Matt. 16:18f. as well as from John 21:15–17 in favor of Peter's primacy, at least under the light of the interpretation of Tradition, which is one of the rules of Catholic exegesis. In fact Vatican I, after quoting the two texts, declares that Peter's primacy is "a manifest doctrine of the sacred Scriptures, as always understood by the Catholic Church" (Sess. 4, chap. 1, Denz. 3054). However, R. E. Brown (*loc. cit.*, above in footnote 61) declares that there is no biblical evidence of St. Peter's primacy.

from the same metaphor of the fundamental rock of the Church; for the foundation must last as long as the building lasts, and hence the primacy must be perpetual like the Church.[75] The same conclusion can be inferred, though with less evidence, from the other two metaphors, for the keys of the kingdom and the power of binding and loosing are given to Peter without restriction of time.

John 21:15–17: "When, therefore, they had breakfasted, Jesus said to Simon Peter, 'Simon, son of John, doest thou love me more than these do?' He said to him, 'Yes, Lord thou knowest that I love Thee.' He said to him, *'Feed my lambs.'* He said to him a second time, 'Simon, son of John, dost thou love Me?' He said to him, 'Yes, Lord, thou knowest that I love Thee.' He said to him, *'Feed my lambs.'* A third time He said to him, 'Simon, son of John, dost thou love Me?' Peter was grieved because He said to him for the third time, 'Dost thou love Me? And he said to Him, 'Lord, Thou knowest all things, Thou knowest that I love Thee.' He said to him, *'Feed my sheep.'*"

The text is *authentic*, for on the one hand it is found in all codices and versions and on the other hand it matches in style and words with the rest of the fourth gospel. Non-Catholic exegetes point out the double epilogue of the gospel, found in 20:30f. and 21:24f., which would show that John ended his gospel with 20:30f. and hence that the whole of chapter 21 is a later addition; but nothing proves that this addition was not made by John himself, in order to dispel the false opinion of some of the faithful about his immortality (see 21:23) or to endorse the primacy of Peter which had already passed to his Roman successors and not to himself.[76] It is not certain, however, that John himself wrote the second epilogue (21:24f.), which could have been added by a disciple.

---

75 Cullmann, *loc. cit.*, denies the legitimacy of such conclusion, saying that the only thing which can be inferred is that Peter, as head of the first community of Jerusalem, was the first rock on which the Church began to be built. However, Christ did not say that Peter would be the rock of the Church of Jerusalem, or only of the beginning of the Church, but simply of the Church. Hence Cullmann's interpretation falsifies the text.

76 Peter died in 64. He had three successors in Rome till the end of the first century, namely, Linus, Anacletus, and Clement (†97, more probably 101) under whom John died (in 95, more probably a few years later). According to Irenaeus (*Against Heresies* 3.1.1), who in his youth had known Polycarp, John's disciple, the apostle wrote his gospel on his return to Ephesus from exile after the death of emperor Domitian in 96. If this is exact, John died toward the very end of the first century.

Peter's *primacy* is made manifest by the metaphor of the shepherd, which by itself indicates care, guidance, and ownership, and in the biblical use means particularly authority. In fact under such figure the O. T. signifies the royal dignity of David (2 Kgs. 5:2), of Cyrus (Isa. 44:28), of God (Isa. 40:11; Jer. 22:3; Ezech. 34:10), of the Messiah (Jer. 23:1–8; Ezech. 34:23; 37:24); particularly in the N. T. Christ applies to Himself the ancient prophecies about the Messiah as a shepherd (Matt. 9:36; 18:11–14; Mark 6:34; Luke 15:2–6; especially John 10:16, the entire parable of the good shepherd). Both the supreme power and its *perpetuity* are shown in the fact that all the sheep of Christ without distinction are entrusted to Peter's care.

The two texts of Matthew and John are mutually illustrative. A further confirmation for both is supplied by the Acts of the Apostles which show the actual exercise of Peter's primacy in the first Christian community. Peter gathers the brethren for the election of Matthias (1:15–26); on the day of Pentecost he receives the new recruits into the Church (2:14–42); he punishes Ananias (5:1–11); he goes with John to Samaria to confirm the new Christians (8:14–24); he admits into the Church the first pagans (10:1–48 and 11:1–8); he presides over the first council at Jerusalem (15:1–21). Paul himself manifestly acknowledges Peter's authority; after his conversion he goes to Jerusalem to see Peter (Gal. 1:18) and he repeats the voyage at the beginning of his ministry (Gal. 2:1–10); in the Council of Jerusalem he submits to Peter's decision the controversy about the observation of the mosaic prescriptions by the converted gentiles (Acts 15:1–35); the very fact of his later remonstrance to Peter's practice in Antioch over that same question of the mosaic prescriptions, shows his recognition of Peter's authority, which was the reason why many Jewish Christians were following his example and withdrawing from the converted Gentiles (Gal. 2:13f.).

Tradition offers many testimonies of Peter's primacy, which can be gathered and briefly indicated under the following three headings.

Peter received a true power. He is "*Christ's vicar*" (Ambrose, *On Luke* 10.175, ML 15.1942). He is "the pastor of the Church" (Augustine, *Against Faustus* 22.70, ML 42.445). To him Christ gave "the helm of the Church" (Leo I, *Serm.* 3.2f., ML 54.145f.).

Peter received a supreme power. He is "the only one chosen among the twelve, as chief" (Jerome, *Against Jovinianus* 1.26, ML 23.258). "Only on him Christ built the Church" (Cyprian, *On the Unity of the Catholic Church* 4, ML 4.514). "To him the primacy has been given" (Cyprian, *ibid.*). "The primacy among the disciples" (Augustine, *On Ps.* 108.1, ML 37.1431f.). He is *"the prince of the apostles"* (Eusebius of Caesarea, *Eccl. Hist.* 2.14, MG 20.171), "The head of the apostles" (Chrysostom, *On John*, hom. 88.1, MG 59.478–480). He is "the doctor of the whole world" (Chrysostom, *ibid*). He received "all power in heaven" (Chrysostom, *On Matt.*, hom. 54.2, MG 58.534f.). "Peter rules over all priests and pastors" (Leo I, *Serm.* 4.2, ML 54.149f.). "Through Peter Christ gives to the bishops the key of heavenly things" (Gregory of Nyssa, *On Mortification*, MG 46.311). Christ "never gives anything to others but through him" (Leo I, *ibid.*)

Peter received a never-ceasing power. He "personifies the Church" (Augustine, *Epist.* 53.2, ML 33.196); hence "Where Peter is, there is the Church" (Ambrose, *On Ps.* 40.30, ML 14.1134). "As the thing that Peter confessed in Christ is everlasting, so the thing that Christ established in Peter never ceases" (Leo I, *Serm.* 3.2f., ML 54.145f.). Peter "is always living in his successors" (Philip, apostolic legate in the Council of Ephesus, Denz. 3056), who occupy *"Peter's Chair"* (Jerome *Epist.* 15.1, ML 22.355; Augustine, *Against the Epistle of Manichaeus* 4.5 ML 42.175; Leo I, *Serm.* 3.2 f, ML 54.145f.), in whom "Peter's power is alive" (Leo I, *ibid.*), so that "through Leo and Agatho [Roman Pontiffs] Peter himself spoke" (Acclamation of the Fathers in the Councils of Chalcedon and Constantinople III).

The sense of Tradition is summarized in the following common slogans: *"Christ's Vicar"* (Ambrose), *"Prince of the Apostles"* (Eusebius of Caesarea), *"Peter's Chair"* (Jerome, Augustine[77], *"Where Peter is, there is the Church"* (Ambrose).[78]

---

77 Cf. A. Trapé, "La'Sedes Petri' in S. Agostino," *Miscallanea Antonio Piolanti* 2 (Roma 1946) 57–76.

78 Some ambiguous expressions are to be noted. *Tertullian* in his attack against the "Edict of Callistus" (very probably the Roman Pontiff) seems to deny the perpetuity of the primacy (or at least of the full primacy), stating that "the clear intention of Christ was to confer it personally to Peter" (*On Chastity* 21.9f., CCL 2.1327). But he was at that time a Montanist heretic.

Cyprian says that "the other apostles were what Peter was, being invested with a common and equal honor and power" (*On the Unity of the Catholic Church* 4). But

The traditional sense is also confirmed by *archaeological monuments* in which Peter is represented under the image of Moses, or as holding the Keys, or as a shepherd carrying a sheep, or sitting on a rock or chair, or as receiving from Christ the volume of divine law.[79]

Theological reason can prove with certainty the institution of a *true and perpetual primacy* of jurisdiction in the Church, from the fact that the Church is a true and perfect society, as shown above (pp. 272ff.). For there is no perfect society without a first principle of authority and order, and a society cannot be perpetual if its authority is not perpetual.

But the institution of *Peter's primacy* as such, both as monarchic (rather than oligarchic or democratic) and as Petrine, that is, that Christ should have given the supreme power of the Church only and directly to one man and moreover to that individual man, cannot be proved, because also the oligarchic or democratic form of government is rational and sufficient and any apostle or other person could have been chosen as head of the Church.

However, the fittingness of a *monarchic* primacy for the Church is shown by a twofold reason. First, because such a primacy is the best means for easily achieving and firmly maintaining ecclesiastical unity.[80] Second, because it reflects and actualizes, in the manner of a human participation, the unity and sovereign character of the kingship of Christ which is ever present and influential in the

---

he also adds that Christ gave a primacy to Peter to keep the unity in the Church (*ibid.*). See below, p. 319.

Augustine in some passages attributes to Christ and not to Peter the words "Upon this rock I will build my Church," because, he says, "it has not been said to him: Thou art a rock but thou art Peter ['non petra, sed Petrus]" (see *Retractations* 1.21.1, ML 32.618). But this is due only to his ignorance of the Aramaic language, that is, of the proper value of the Aramaic name "Kepha." At any rate, he also judges as probable the attribution of those words to Peter.

79 Cf. H. Lecelercq, "Pierre (Saint)," *Dictionnaire d'archéologie chrétienne et de liturgie*, 14-1 (Paris 1939) 935–973; A. Giuliani, "Il primato di S. Pietro nell'' iconografia paleocristiana (secoli II–VI)," *Miscellanea franciscanna* 65 (1965) 235–284.

80 This reason is given by several Fathers, as Jerome (*Against Jovinianus* 1.26) and Cyprian (see footnote 78). It was particularly emphasized by *Vatican Council I*, saying that Peter's primacy was instituted "so that the episcopacy itself be one and undivided, and through the mutual cohesion of the pastors the entire society of the faithful be kept in the unity of faith and communion" (Sess. 4, prologue, Denz. 3050). This statement has been repeated by *Vatican II* (Dogm. Constit. on the Church, no. 18). The same reason is expounded by St. *Thomas*, C. Gent. 4.76; cf. *Summa Theol.*, I, q. 103, a. 3.

Church, so that the one single Pastor, actually ruling the Church, be represented by one single vicar as another Christ on earth.

The election of *Peter*, as this individual person, is founded on a particular predilection of Christ for him, shown on several circumstances, as well as on Peter's attachment to Christ and enthusiasm for His cause; no doubt that Peter's natural temperament and qualities made him also fit for such an office. The election of *an apostle*, as the first holder of the primacy, has an evident fittingness, because, through that, the ecclesiastical primacy has been dignified by the apostolic seal and its existence has been, as it were, permanently rooted in the apostolic foundation.

For this reason the Church is really and permanently founded on Peter, as on its rock, and Peter is, as it were, the permanent vicar of Christ, so that the subsequent Pontiffs hold the ecclesiastical primacy and the vicarious office for Christ inasmuch as they morally carry in their physical person and temporal succession the very person of peter. And this is the meaning of the traditional expressions: "Where Peter is, there is the Church," "Peter lives, rules and speaks in his successors," "Every Pontiff sits in Peter's chair," "Papal documents are signed by the seal ring of the Fisherman." All such expressions are but an echo of Christ's promise: "Thou art Peter, and upon this rock I will build My Church," which is perpetually true of every Pontiff inasmuch as he morally carries in himself the person of Peter.

6

The Primacy of the Roman Pontiff[81]

SINCE PETER'S PRIMACY IS TO LAST INDEFINITELY through his successors, as shown in the preceding chapter, the question arises: who is *de facto* Peter's successor? And since the only one who claims for centuries to be Peter's successor is the bishop of Rome, the precise question is whether he really is what he claims to be.

The inquiry is confined to the *mere fact*, although it is a truly dogmatic one, that is, intimately connected with revelation and as such capable of being infallibly defined.[82]

Hence we abstract from further questions, both dogmatic and historical, namely, whether the Petrine primacy has been bound to the Roman See by divine and unchangeable right or by a merely human and reformable decision; whether Peter was ever actually present in Rome and died there; whether he was also bishop of Rome; whether the city of Rome and the Roman See will be eternal on account of the perpetuity of the primacy. Such secondary questions, though historically interesting in themselves, have no

---

81   See bibliography given for the preceding chapter, footnote 61.

Conte, P., *Chiesa e primato nelle lettere dei papi del secolo VIII*, Milano 1971.

Cullmann, O. (protestant), *Peter, Disciple, Apostle, Martyr* (trans. from the French by V. F. Filson), rev. ed., Westminster, Md. 1962.

D'Ercole, G., *Communio, Collegialità. Primato e "Sollicitudo omnium ecclesiarum" dai Vangeli a Constantino*, Roma 1964.

Journet, Ch., *L'Eglise du Verbe Incarné* 1 (éd. 2, Paris 1955) 541–567; *Primauté de Pierre* (Paris 1953) 115–140.

Lattazi, U., *Il primato romano*, Roma 1961.

Lemeer, B. M., "Autour du primat de Rome," *Angelicum* 31 (1954) 161–179.

Maccarone, M., *Vicarius Christi. Storia del titolo papale*, Roma 1952; "'Cathedra Petri' e lo sviluppo dell'idea del primato papale dal II al IV secolo," *Miscellanea Antonio Piolanti* 2 (Roma 1967) 37–56.

Sánchez, J. H., *De initio potestatis primatialis Romani Pontificis*, Romae 1968.

Thiis, G., *La primauté pontificale. La doctrine de Vatican I. Les voies d'une révision*, Gembloux 1972.

82   On the nature and definability the so-called *"dogmatic facts,"* see our treatise on *The Channels of Revelation*, pp. 218–222, and here below, pp. 353–355.

essential bearing on the fact under consideration, which must be determined independently of them. Hence they will be briefly examined only at the end of this chapter in additional notes.

Statement. *The Roman Pontiff is by divine right Peter's successor in the primacy.*

Theological note. This statement is *de fide*, more than once defined by the extraordinary Magisterium, more solemnly and distinctly by the Vatican Council I.[83]

---

83 The same three errors, mentioned above (footnote 65), which deny the Petrine primacy, deny consequently the Roman primacy. In the first and second errors, about the oligarchic and democratic constitution of the Church, the principal reason why Peter's primacy, at least perpetual, is denied, is because it logically infers the Roman primacy, which is the main sign of contradiction.

The undeniable material fact of the primacy, firmly claimed and constantly exercised for centuries by the bishop of Rome, is attributed to several natural causes and is given various historical beginnings.

The *natural causes* would be the following. First, the political preeminence of the city of Rome, which naturally gave origin to the prestige of the Roman Church (this is the more common opinion, held by Modernists, according to prop. 56 condemned in the decree "Lamentabili," Denz. 3456, and by A. Harnack, M. Goguel, O. Cullmann, several Oriental theologians, particularly A. Lebedev in his Russian work on the primacy of the Pope). Second, the particular zeal and charitable behaviour of the Roman community toward other churches, which made Ignatius of Antioch say in his letter to the Roman Church that "it presided over the universal community of charity" (thus Cullmann). Third, the influence of the false papal Decretals, written by pseudo-Isidore in the 9th century, which exaggerated the power of the Roman Pontiffs (thus several Orientals, particularly Chrysostom Papadopoulos). Fourth, the ambition and usurpations of the Roman clergy in the first centuries and of the Roman Pontiffs in the Middle Ages (thus several Orientals).

The *time (and author)* of the rising primacy would be, either the 2nd century under Pope Victor (Harnack, Goguel); or the 3rd century under the influence of Pope Callistus or Cyprian (R. Sohm); or the 4th century, under the influence of emperor Gratian who gave the Roman Pontiff the right of judging bishops (J. Turmel); or the 5th century when Leo the Great changed the primacy of mere direction into that of jurisdiction (B. I. Kidd); or the 7th century under the influence of the Germans and Anglo-Saxons (I. Haller); or the 9th century at the time of Pope Nicholas I under the influence of the aforementioned false Decretals (several Orientals); or finally the 11–13th centuries under the influence of authoritarian Popes (several Orientals).

Among these errors the attitude of the *Oriental theologians* is to be noted, for being particularly opposed to the Roman primacy and for having made the first historical attempt to overthrow it. The papal primacy was first equivalently rejected in the 9th century by *Photius*, patriarch of Constantinople and initiator of the schism, who, however, admitted Peter's primacy (see *Quest. to Amphil.* 97, MG 101.607). Photius' schism was consummated in the 11th century by *Michael Caerularius*, patriarch of Constantinople, who was excommunicated by Leo IX (see above, p. 74). The oriental theologians commonly followed in the same denial and since the 17th century, supported by the Protestants, they consigned it also in their Symbolic Books, such as the *Confessions of faith of Critopoulos* (1625), of *Peter Moghila* (1640),

Doctrine of the Magisterium. The Roman Pontiffs themselves constantly through centuries (since Clement of Rome toward the end of the first century) affirmed and exercised their primacy, particularly in the first ecumenical Councils, as will be shown below in the argument from Tradition. In a doctrinal and definite manner the Magisterium proposed this truth as *de fide* in the following three ecumenical Councils.

The Council of Lyons, which dealt with the question of the reunion of the Orientals with Rome, in the profession of faith presented to and accepted by the Greek emperor Michael Palaeologus in 1274, defines: "The same holy Roman Church holds the supreme and full primacy and power over the universal Catholic Church. She truly and humbly acknowledges to have received this primacy with the fullness of power from the Lord Himself in the blessed Peter, prince and summit of the Apostles, *whose successor is the Roman Pontiff*" (Denz. 861).

The Council of Florence, dealing again and more directly with the same oriental question, defines in the Decree for the Greeks in 1439: "We define that the holy Apostolic See and the Roman Pontiff hold the primacy over the entire world, and that the same Roman Pontiff is the *successor of the blessed Peter*, prince of the Apostles and true vicar of Christ" (Denz. 1307).

The Vatican Council I in 1870 defined the same truth more solemnly and distinctly in the two canons quoted above (p. 304). The doctrine is explained more at length in the two corresponding chapters.[84]

---

and of *Dositheus* (1672). Finally in the 19th-20th centuries there followed three anti-Roman declarations of patriarch *Anthimus VI* in 1848 (in reply to Pius IX), of patriarch *Anthimus VII* in 1895 (in reply to Leo XIII), and of the *Congress of Oriental Churches held at Moscow* in 1948.

The Oriental church was broken up into various *autocephalous* (self-governing) *churches*, whose common juridical bond is not clearly defined.

The *reasons* of their opposition to the Roman primacy are: the dignity of Constantinople, as the new Rome; the equal dignity of the oldest patriarchates of Jerusalem and Antioch; Peter had no definite see, and even if he was the bishop of Rome, the Pope succeeds him only as bishop of Rome; the Church is a Mystical Body and hence it has only a mystical chief, Christ himself; the Roman primacy introduces two heads into the Church and is detrimental to Christ's primacy; it lowers the authority of the bishops, making them mere vicars of the Pope, and makes the universal Councils useless.

84   The same doctrine is proposed, although not solemnly defined, in all the other documents listed above (pp. 302–304), together with the doctrine of the Petrine primacy.

Tradition[85] supplies us with three arguments, namely, dogmatic, apologetical, and historical.

The dogmatic argument amounts to this. The Church for several centuries, before the oriental schism (9th–11th centuries) questioned the Roman primacy, acknowledged it universally by words and deeds. Such a universal agreement in a fact, on which largely depend the discipline of morals and the doctrine of faith, cannot involve an error in view of the assistance promised by Christ to the Church in the person of the apostles. The truth of the universal agreement will be shown in the historical argument.

The apologetical argument is drawn from the perpetuity of Peter's primacy. Since this is perpetual, it has to be easily found somewhere in the Church. But no one, except the Roman Pontiff, claimed to be Peter's successor and actually exercised the primacy. Therefore, Peter's succession and primacy is in the Roman Pontiff or it is nowhere.

The historical argument needs a preliminary general clarification. In view of the natural evolution of all human institutions, even of divine right, and of the revealed truths themselves as to their full knowledge on our part, no one could reasonably expect to find, especially in the documents of the first period, a clear and definite expression of the Roman primacy. However, since the very beginning of the postapostolic age and throughout the whole second century, there appear several suggestive signs, whose constancy and convergence direct an unprejudiced mind to the persuasion or at least to a strong conjecture that in the Roman See Christ's promise and prophecy of the perpetuity of Peter's primacy was gradually taking shape. Under this general and comprehensive light the first documents of Tradition, which, taken separately

---

85 In the holy *Scripture* nothing is said about the connection of Peter's primacy with the Roman see, except a probable allusion to Peter's coming to Rome (see below, footnote 100), which at any rate would not be a decisive fact in this question. Since Peter died in the year 64, Paul in 67, and John at the end of the century, the only allusion to a Roman successor of Peter, already extant, could be found, either in the last pastoral epistles of Paul (1 and 2 Tim. and Tit., written between 63 and 67 when Paul was in prison in Rome for the second time, awaiting his death sentence) or in the works of John; but the character of these writings does not demand such an allusion.

At any rate the silence of the holy Scripture is immaterial to the present question, which does not regard a doctrine (as the primacy), but only a fact, that is, the connection of the Roman See with Peter's primacy. Besides, the holy Scripture is not the only channel of truth, but it is completed by Tradition, especially as regards facts connected with revelation.

and examined critically, are unable to give us the certitude of the fact, acquire their theological and truly historical value, as so many clear manifestations of a general persuasion, founded on some apostolic fact or word, which gradually through centuries acquired a more definite and clear expression, particularly with regard to the amplitude of the Roman primacy.

In the 2nd century we find several suggestive signs of this primacy, involved in the clear testimony of a certain pre-eminence of the Roman Church, shown particularly by Pope Clement of Rome, Ignatius of Antioch, Irenaeus, and Pope Victor.

Clement of Rome, third bishop of Rome (after Linus and Anacletus), in a letter to the Corinthians about the year 96, steps into the religious affairs of that distant and important church of Pauline foundation, to check a revolt of the faithful against their presbyters. In this letter he excuses himself for *"intervening so late"* into that disturbance and asks the rebels, *"to obey the orders given them by God through him"* and send back to Rome his legates with the good news of a restored peace (chap. 63, no. 2). The only thing missing here to show the primacy is the title of such an intervention and whether his right regards the universal Church or only the church of Corinth. This, however, is shown by the great authority which the other oriental churches attached to that letter, using it in their public readings (see Eusebius of Caesarea, *Eccles. Hist.* 3.16; 4.23) and by the words of Irenaeus, stating toward the end of the second century that Clement had in that letter "announced to the Corinthians the tradition he had recently received from the apostles" (*Against Heresies* 3.3.3).

Ignatius, bishop of Antioch († about 107) in his letter to the Romans speaks of the church "which presides in the Roman region . . . which *presides to charity,"* that is, to *the community of the faithful* (address), which *"teaches and commands"* (3.1), and which will *"govern,"* together with Christ, his own church during his absence (9.1). The force of these expressions, very different from those used by Ignatius in his various epistles written to other churches, gives to the text the following connatural sense: "The church, which is located in the Roman region, is the president Church, presiding, teaching and commanding over the entire union of charity, that is, the entire body of the faithful; hence, it will govern the church of Antioch during the absence of its bishop." Nothing in the text shows that Ignatius is speaking of the Roman Church only as a particular self-governing church.

Irenaeus, bishop of Lyons († about 202), in his work *Against Heresies* has several expressions pointing to the pre-eminence of the Roman See. "This Church of Rome is very great, very old, universally known, *founded and constituted by the two apostles Peter and Paul*," "The blessed apostles, founding this church, gave to Linus the episcopal function of its administration. Anacletus succeeded to Linus, and then Clement, who saw the apostles and conversed with them, was the third to receive the episcopacy after the apostles;" "*By reason of the more powerful superiority of this Church, it is necessary that the entire Church, that is, the faithful of every place, agree with it; in this church the faithful of all places have always kept the apostolic Tradition*" (Book 3, written before the year 190, chap. 3, nos. 1–3; MG 7.848–851). The pre-eminence of the Roman church is manifest in the whole text, from its powerful superiority (an expression which brings forth the concept of authority), and from the necessity for all faithful to agree with it.[86]

Victor, Roman Pontiff (189–199), showed his primacy by solving authoritatively the so-called paschal controversy about the day on which Easter should be celebrated. Because the churches of Asia Minor, based on an old local custom, celebrated it on the same day on which the Jews celebrated their Paschal festivity, the Pope ordered them to adopt the contrary and common custom of

---

86 In this most famous and discussed text of Irenaeus some of the words may be twisted or lessened in their meaning. The common opinion of Catholic scholars understand the word "superiority" (Latin "principalitas") in the sense of authority, the word "necessary" in the sense of moral necessity or obligation, and the words, "in this Church" as referred to the Roman Church. Thus the sense of the pericope would be: "The Roman Church has a more powerful *authority*, and hence all the faithful of every place *are obliged* to agree with it, and in fact they agree with it, for through it all the faithful keep the apostolic Tradition."

On the contrary, non-Catholic scholars and a few among Catholics understand "superiority" as apostolic origin, "necessity" as a mere logical necessity, and the words "in this Church" as referring to the universal Church. Thus the sense would be: "The Roman Church has a more powerful apostolic origin (since it is founded by Peter and Paul), and hence it is logical that there be a doctrinal agreement between the Roman Church and the universal Church, in which the apostolic Tradition is kept." If this violent contortion of the text is legitimate, there would be no Roman Primacy expressed in it.

Cf. D. J. Unger, "St. Irenaeus and the Roman Primacy," *Theological Studies* 13 (1952) 389–405; B. Botte, "A propos de l'Adversus haereses III, 3, 2 de saint Irenée," *Irénikon* 30 (1957) 156–163; *Bulletin de théologie ancienne et médiévale* 6 (1950) 99–101.

the Roman church and of the other churches. For this purpose he ordered that local synods in various churches decide on the matter, and having obtained the agreement of all the churches, except those of Asia Minor, he threatened to excommunicate these (thus Eusebius of Caesarea, *Eccl. Hist.* 5.23–25, MG 20.490–510).[87]

In the 3rd century we find in the same African church two major doctors, Tertullian and Cyprian, who, while exhibiting a substantial testimony of the Roman primacy, were led into bitter ecclesiological controversies, which made them undervalue the full implication of their previous statement.

Tertullian († after 222) in the Catholic period of his activity writes: "If you turn toward Italy, you find *Rome whence the authority comes to us* [in Africa]. *How happy that church is, to which the apostles gave copiously the entire doctrine together with their blood"* (*On the Prescription of Heretics* 36.2, CCL 1.216). The first words however, do not necessarily mean that the Roman church has authority over the African, but that the African church, having been founded by the Roman, had received from this its authoritative apostolic character. In his semi-montanistic period Tertullian writes: "The Lord left the keys to Peter and through him to the Church" (*Remedy Against the Sting of Scorpions* 10.8, CCL 2.1088); here he does not say to whom Peter's keys are now entrusted in the Church. In his montanistic and clearly heretical period he attacks the Edict of Callistus (the Roman Pontiff) about the remission of sins, stating that in Matt. 16:18f. on the primacy "Christ's clear intention was to confer it personally to Peter alone" (*On Chastity* 21.9f., CCL 2.1327). While clearly denying the primacy, he also clearly *testifies that Callistus claimed the primacy.*

---

87 The sense of these and other documents of minor importance such as those of *Hermas* (*The Shepherd*, *Vis.* 2.4.3), *Dionysius of Corinth* (cf. Eusebius of Caesarea, *Eccles. Hist.* 4.23), and Abercius, bishop of Hierapolis (see Rouet de Journel, *Enchiridion Patristicum*. no. 187), is confirmed by the custom of going to Rome for religious purposes. The purpose was either to get a surer knowledge of the common faith, as is evident from the journeys of Polycarp (cf. Irenaeus, *Against Heresies* 5.24), Abercius, and Hegesippus (cf. Eusebius, *ibid.* 4.11.21f.), or to get some protection for ambiguous doctrines or heresies through a simulated Roman approbation, as was the case of Cerdo (cf. Irenaeus, *ibid.* 5.3f.), and the two leaders of Gnosticism, Marcion and Valentinus, who opened their schools in Rome.

The aforementioned *Abercius* in the famous *Epitaph*, which he wrote for his own sepulcher, gives the following account of his journey to Rome: "He [Christ the Shepherd] sent me to Rome to contemplate majesty, and to see a queen golden-robed and golden-sandalled; there I saw a people bearing a shining mark [i.e., of Baptism]."

Cyprian (†258) in his principal work *On the Unity of the Catholic Church* and in several passages of his letters written to Pope Cornelius and to the Roman clergy, clearly manifests his belief in the Roman primacy. But later in his baptismal controversy with Pope Stephen he shows not only a practical disagreement with the authority of the Roman See or a simple incoherence between his theory and his practice, but a real doctrinal disagreement and a deficient valuation of the Roman primacy. In other words, *he constantly admitted a true primacy but he did not grasp its full implications*, holding that it is limited by the rights of the bishops, at least in disciplinary matters. This error is not surprising in such an ecclesiologist as Cyprian if we consider the complex character of the baptismal controversy, the antiquity of that period, and the fullness and extension of the primatial power, knowledge of which requires necessarily a certain process of maturation.

In his work *On the Unity of the Catholic Church* Cyprian teaches that the reason why Christ gave to Peter the primacy, actually represented by the Roman Pontiff, is because it safeguards the unity of the Church: *"In order to manifest the unity of the Church, Christ (established one chair), through his authority he disposed that such unity would be originated from one...* (The primacy is given to Peter, to show one Church of Christ and one chair)... How can anyone who opposes and resists the Church, (*who abandons Peter's chair, on which the Church is founded*), believe to be in the Church?" (ML 4.514)[88]

In his *Epistle to Pope Cornelius*, written in 252, Cyprian complains that African schismatics "dare to sail [for Rome] and take letters to the *chair of Peter and to the principal Church* which is the origin of the sacerdotal unity" (*Epist.* 59.14, CV 3-2, p. 683). The expression "principal Church" does not mean the older church,

---

88 There are two recensions of this work. The words, which we placed between parentheses and which lay a further stress on Peter's primacy, belong to the shorter recension, of disputed authorship. Some scholars, as Hartel (in his critical edition in the Vienna Patrology) and J. Le Moyne (*Revue Bénédictine* [1937] 70–115) attribute it to an unknown African writer of the 4th century, while the majority of scholars (J. Chapman, Batiffol, D'Alès, Ernst, Van den Eynde, Bevenot) attribute both recensions to Cyprian, who would have recast the work (either the longer or the shorter recension) for controversial purposes.

Cf. M. Bevenot, *St. Cyprian's "De Unitate" Chap. 4 in the Light of the Manuscripts* (Rome 1938) 1–13; L. Campeau, "Le texte de la primauté dans le 'De catholicae Ecclesiae unitate' de S. Cyprien," *Sciences ecclésiastiques* 19 (1967) 81–110, 255–276.

nor the more excellent church, but the fontal church, that is, the active and permanent principle of the unity of the Church.[89]

The aforementioned baptismal controversy of Cyprian with Pope Stephen, while containing a partial error or insufficiency in Cyprian's doctrine, is a striking testimony of the Roman primacy, as generally recognized in the Church. Indeed, Stephen did not fear or delay to intervene authoritatively into the ecclesiastical affairs of another so powerful a church as Carthage, confiding in the fact that "he held Peter's succession, on whom the foundations of the Church are placed," as Firmillian complains in his letter to his friend Cyprian with regard to the same controversy (*Epist.* 75.14, among Cyprian's epistles, CV 3-2, p. 821).

From the 4th century to the end of the patristic age, as the persecutions expired and freedom of action was given to the Church, the Roman primacy received a fuller expression and manifested its influence more effectively. This is shown in the *patristic literature, in the declarations of the Roman Pontiffs, and in the acts of the Ecumenical Councils.*

The Fathers' doctrine can be summarized under the following headings.

The series of Roman Pontiffs starts with Peter. Optatus of Milevis: "In the city of Rome the episcopal chair was given to Peter...In this unique chair, which is the first of the [divine] endowments, first sat Peter, to whom Linus succeeded...[The list of the Roman Pontiffs continues]" (*On the Schism of the Donatists* 2.2, MC 11.947–949). Likewise Augustine draws the list of the Roman Pontiffs, starting "from Peter's See," "from Peter himself" (*Against the Epistle of Manichaeus* 4.5, ML 42. 175. *Epist.* 53.2, ML 33.196).

The Roman See is "Peter's See" or "Peter's Chair." See Augustine, just quoted. Peter Chrysologus: "Pay heed obediently to the things that have been written by the most blessed Pope of the Roman city, for the blessed Peter, who lives and presides in his own see, bestows faith to those who seek the truth" (*Epistle to Eutyches,* founder of Monophysitism, MG 54.743).[90] Jerome: "I keep the unity in communion with your Beatitude, that is, with Peter's chair. I know that the Church has been built

---

89 Both of these texts have inspired the prologue of the Constitution on the Church by *Vatican I* (Denz. 3050).
90 The phrase "Who lives and presides" has been used by *Vatican I* (Denz. 3057).

upon that rock" (*Epist.* 15.1, to Pope Damasus, ML 22.355).

The Roman See is the *"Apostolic Chair"* or the *"Apostolic See."* Augustine: "The sovereignty of the Apostolic Chair was always in the Roman Church" (*Epist.* 43, ML 33.163); "Apostolic See" (*Serm.* 131.10, ML 38.734).

The Roman Church presides as a sovereign over all the other churches. Gregory of Nazianzus: "It presides over all" (*Poems*, 2.1.12, MG 37.1068); Theodoret of Cyrus: "That most holy see holds in many ways the sovereignty over the churches of the entire world, especially because it kept immune of heretical corruption, and never a dissenter sat in it, but everyone kept the integrity of the apostolic gift" (*Epist.* 116, MG 83.132).

The Roman See is the source of all rights in the Church. Ambrose: "From that See derive into all, the rights of the venerable communion" (*Epist.* 11.4, ML 16.986).[91]

"Rome has spoken, the case is closed" ("Roma locuta est, causa finita est"). This famous axiom derives from Augustine, saying about the debate on Pelagian heresy: "Concerning this question two conciliar decisions have been sent to the Apostolic See: also rescripts came from there, hence the trial is over" (*Serm.* 131.10, ML 38.734).

The Roman Pontiffs themselves constantly asserted their primacy, as is shown in the following summary of their doctrine.

They apply to themselves *Christ's words to Peter,* Matt. 16:18f.: "Thou art Peter..." and John 21:15–17: "Feed My lambs..." Thus Siricius, Boniface I, the "Decree of Gelasius," Hormisdas, Pelagius I, Nicholas I (Denz. 184, 234, 350, 363, 446, 640).

The Roman Pontiff received the primacy from Christ Himself. The "Decree of Gelasius" (by a private author about the beginning of the 6th century): "The Roman Church received the primacy through the evangelical voice of the Lord and Savior" (Denz. 350); Nicholas I: "The privileges of the Roman Church are established in the blessed Peter by the mouth of Christ" (Denz. 640).

The Roman Pontiff is Peter's moral person. Siricius: "[The Roman Pontiff is] the apostolic rock" (Denz. 184). Innocent I: "Whenever a question of faith is dealt with, all must refer only to Peter, that is, to the one who bears his name and his honor" (Denz. 218). Leo I: "The blessed Peter did not leave the government which he

---

91 *Vatican I* has adopted this beautiful expression in its definition (Denz. 3057).

received ... In his See [that is, the Roman] his power is alive and his authority is visible" (*Serm.* 3.2f., ML 54.145f.).[92]

Peter remains in his successors. See Leo I, just quoted. Philip, apostolic legate to the Council of Ephesus: Peter "is always living in his successors" (Denz. 3056).

The Roman Pontiff is "Peter's heir" (Siricius, Denz. 181) and has *"Peter's See"* (Leo I, quoted above; Gelasius, quoted below).

The Roman Pontiff has "the care of all the churches" (Innocent I, Denz. 218; Leo I, *Serm.* 5.2 ML 54.153). He is "the head of all the churches" (Boniface I, Denz. 233; "Decree of Gelasius," Denz. 350; Hadrian I, Mansi 12.1081).

The Roman Pontiff decides and judges on all ecclesiastical matters and is judged by no one. Boniface I: "It is certain that the last settlement of things depends on his decision, which is irreformable" (Denz. 234f.) Gelasius I: "The See of the blessed Peter has the right of judging over all churches and no one can judge its decision; the canons allow to appeal to it from all parts of the world, but no one can appeal from it to any other authority."[93] Nicholas I: *"The first see is judged by no one"* (Denz. 638, against Photius).[94]

The eight ecumenical Councils[95] (from the Nicene I in 325 to the Constantinopolitan VI in 870), which were all celebrated in the East before the schism took place, offer an outstanding practical testimony to the Roman primacy, inasmuch as they were assembled and held with the explicit compliance of the Roman See and in the presence of its legates (with the exception of Constantinople I and II), and submitted their acts and final decisions to the approbation of the Roman See. Moreover, in some of them explicit declarations of the Roman primacy were uttered.

The Council of Constantinople I in 381 voted a canon giving the bishop of that city "a primacy of honor *after the Roman bishop,* because the City itself is a younger Rome" (Can. 3). This shows

---

92 *Vatican I* uses part of this text (Denz. 3057).

93 Quoted by A. Thiel, *Epistulae Romanorum Pontificum,* epist. 26 (Brunsbergae 1868) 399.

94 This juridical maxim is quoted verbatim by Nicholas from the acts of a pseudo-Synod of Sinuassa (work of an unknown forger, about the year 500). However it is essentially contained in the words of Gelasius I (†496) and Boniface I (†422) just quoted. The Code of Canon Law adopted it; can. 1556: *"The First See is judged by no one"* ("Prima Sedes a nemine iudicatur").

95 Cf. J. Chapman, *The First Eight General Councils and Papal Infallibility,* London 1908; T. Dolan, *The Papacy and the First Councils of the Church,* St. Louis, Mo. 1910.

at least a general acknowledgement of the Roman primacy. At any rate, such a canon was never approved by Rome, as being detrimental to the bishops of Alexandria and Antioch, who were already given a similar honor by the preceding Council of Nicaea I in 325.

In the Council of Ephesus in 431 the authoritative influence of Pope Celestine I is manifest. The Council was presided over by Cyril of Alexandria through the Pope's explicit commission. The pontifical legates read to the Council Celestine's epistle, which was received with acclamation, and after the deliberations they subscribed and confirmed the acts. One of the legates, Philip by name, in his allocution made an explicit and remarkable declaration of the Roman primacy, which is quoted by Vatican I in its Constitution on the Church (Denz. 3056; see above, p. 322).

Likewise *the Council of Chalcedon* in 451 clearly testified to the Roman primacy. Before the Council, both parties, namely, Eutyches, founder of Monophysitism, and the patriarch Flavian, who had condemned his doctrine, appealed to Pope Leo I. In the course of the Council the papal legates declared that they brought to the Council "the orders of the Pope of the city of Rome." After the public reading of Leo's dogmatic epistle of Flavian, the Fathers uttered the acclamation: *"Peter has spoken through Leo."* In their synodical epistle sent to the Pope the Fathers again acknowledged that Leo had spoken "as interpreter of the voice of blessed Peter." Having ended their dogmatic decisions, the Fathers in the absence of the papal legates voted the famous can. 28, confirming the third canon of Constantinople I about the primacy of honor for the patriarch of this city; but the legates and the Pope refused to approve it.

The Council of Constantinople II, held in 553 against the will of Vigilius, became legitimate only when this Pope, brought by force to Constantinople, ill-treated, and excommunicated by the Council, finally gave his approval to its decisions.

The Council of Constantinople III in 680–681 condemned Monothelitism in the presence of the papal legates. The epistle, previously sent to the emperor by Pope Agatho, was acclaimed by the Fathers with the words: *"Through Agatho Peter has spoken."* It is true that the Council solemnly condemned Pope Honorius, Agatho's predecessor, but the object of the condemnation was the religious policy of Honorius rather than his doctrine, and only in this sense does this condemnation seem to have been approved by Pope Leo II.

The Council of Nicaea II in 787 was likewise held in the presence of the papal legates and its decisions were confirmed by Pope Hadrian I.

The Council of Constantinople IV, held in 870 in the presence of the legates of Pope Hadrian II, accepted the so-called "Formula of faith of Hormisdas" against christological errors, in which the Roman primacy is explicitly asserted (cf. Denz. 363, 365).

Note 1. *On the right by which the primacy is bound to the Roman See*

From what we have seen it follows that the primacy is *de facto* attached to the Roman See, namely, that in the present circumstances whoever is legitimately made bishop of Rome, is ipso facto the primate of the universal Church, Peter's successor, and Christ's Vicar.[96] The necessary bond between the primacy and the Roman see was made by St. Peter himself and not by any of his successors, for on the one hand it regards the foundations of the Church, which belong to the apostles, and on the other hand the documents of Tradition draw up the list of the Roman Pontiffs, starting from Peter himself.

The further and *disputed question* is, by what right did St. Peter attach his primacy to the Roman see? Several theologians (as Billot, Schultes, D'Herbigny, Journet, Lattanzi) hold that it was done by *divine and irreformable right*, that is, by the will of Christ, telling Peter or later revealing to Peter to do so, or explicitly approving a previous choice personally made by Peter. Others (as Franzelin, Zapelena, Salaverri) soften this opinion, saying that it was done by a *strictly apostolic and irreformable right*, that is, by Peter himself, but as an apostle, laying the Church's foundation

---

96 It should be noted, however, that this bond between the primacy and the Roman episcopacy does not consist in a mere juxtaposition or addition of the two titles in the same person, but in the *absorption of the Roman episcopacy into the universal episcopacy or primacy*. In other words, the Pope is not bishop of Rome and Pope, but is simply Pope and by that is the bishop of Rome, or he is bishop of Rome and on account of that he is Pope. There remains only a virtual distinction in the same person between the two titles, inasmuch as they could have been separated.

The reason for such absorption of the Roman title into the universal title is because the first adds nothing to the second (that is, no more power nor different power) and it is like a particular power with regard to a universal power. The same would happen if the Pope would reserve to himself also some other diocese besides Rome and be for instance also bishop of New York; but in that case he would be Pope not because he would bishop of New York but always because he is bishop of Rome.

under the general impulse of God. Finally few others (John of St. Thomas, *On Summa Theol.*, II-II, disp. 1, q. 1, nos. 14, 15, 20; Ballerini, Mendive) hold that it was done by a *simple ecclesiastical or primatial right*, that is, by Peter simply as Pope, hence by a right *reformable* by any of his successors.

Each of the three opinions has some probability. The first is at least extrinsically more probable, as held by most of the theologians and apparently favored by the Magisterium.[97] The second is rather ambiguous and should be logically reduced to the first or the third. The third opinion has some degree of probability which might grow in the future, but which now is extrinsically very slim.

If this right is irreformable (according to the first and second opinions), it follows that *Rome and the Roman diocese are in some way eternal*, like the primacy attached to them. Some theologians (as Billot and Schultes) explain this eternity in a material and geographical sense, saying that Rome and its diocese will never be destroyed; others (as Journet and Salaverri) explain it only in a formal and juridical sense, saying that if Rome be destroyed, the one who succeeds the last bishop of that city would still be juridically the Roman bishop and his new diocese would be juridically Rome itself under a new material and geographical condition.

Note 2. *On the historical manner in which the primacy was bound to the Roman see, or whether St. Peter was in Rome and was bishop of Rome*[98]

---

97 This opinion seems to be favored by several expressions of the Magisterium, saying that the fact was done "by divine preordination" (Leo I), "by Christ himself" (Gelasius), "by God as author" (Gregory I), "by divine command" (Hadrian I), "by divine revelation" (Innocent III), "by Christ's choice" (Leo XIII: "Jesus Christ chose and reserved to himself only the Roman City. He ordered that the See of his Vicar should be here forever" (AAS 31 [1899] 645).

However some of such expression can be referred only to the law of succession and not to the condition of succession (that is, its connection with the Roman See); others (as that of Leo XIII) can be understood in the sense of an indirect influence of God, that is, through Peter's personal choice.

98 Besides Cullmann, Jornet, and Rimoldi, listed above (footnote 61), see H. Lietzmann, "The Tomb of the apostles ad Catacumbas," *Harvard Theological Review* (1923) 147ff.; *Petrus und Paulus in Rom*, Bonn 1915; 2nd ed. 1927; *Petrus Romischer Martyrer*, Berlin 1936; O. Marucchi, *Pietro e Paolo a Roma*, Roma 1934; B. Altaner, "War Petrus in Rom?," *Theologische Revue* 36 (1937) 177–188; "Neues zur Petrusfrage," *ibid.* 38 (1939) 365ff.; J. Ruysschaert, "Les documents littéraires de la double tradition romaine des tombes apostoliques," *Revue d'histoire ecclésiastique* 52 (1957) 791–831; D. W. O'Connor, *Peter in Rome. The Literary, Liturgical, and Archaeological Evidence*, New York 1969.

The preceding question about the juridical manner in which the primacy was attached to the Roman see does not depend on the question about the particular manner in which it was bound to it, for instance, by Peter being present in Rome and being also bishop of Rome. In fact Peter could have named his Roman successor from far away or in Rome itself without being bishop of Rome, saying, for instance, that, at the moment of his death, a certain person would be bishop of Rome and succeed him as Pope, or that the one who would be bishop of Rome at that time would succeed him. However, the natural historical way of making that connection would have been through the physical presence of Peter in Rome and even through his own Roman episcopate; moreover, these two historical facts would confirm and make more intelligible the principal and dogmatic fact of the extant connection between Peter's primacy and the Roman see.

The great probability, or moral certitude, of both facts (especially of Peter's Roman sojourn and martyrdom), is admitted commonly by Catholic scholars and granted by several Protestants. It has also been confirmed by the Vatican Council I.[99] It is based on many convergent literary testimonies and a few liturgical and archaeological documents.[100]

---

99 All *Catholics* admit Peter's Roman sojourn and martyrdom; only one or another doubts about his Roman episcopate as not agreeing with the fact that the apostles were continually traveling and founding various churches (thus P. Benoit in *Revue biblique* 60 [1953] 574.) Vatican I affirms both facts, stating: "[Peter] lives and presides and exercises his judgement up to this time and always in his successors, the bishops of the holy Roman See, founded by him and consecrated with his blood" (Sess. 4, chap. 2, Denz. 3056). All *Protestants* deny Peter's Roman episcopate. Most of them deny also his Roman sojourn, which is admitted by others, as A. Harnack, H. Lietzmann, H. von Campenhausen, and O. Cullmann.

100 In *Scripture* there are four allusions to Peter's sojourn in Rome. The first and surer is 1 Pet. 5:13: "The Church which is at Babylon greets you"; there was no sizable city of Babylon at that time, and on the other hand under that name Rome is probably indicated in Apoc. 4:8; 17:5; 18:2; hence Peter wrote his epistle from Rome. The second is Acts 12:17: "And he departed and went to another place"; coming out of prison about the year 42–43, Peter disappears from the scene of the Acts until the Council of Jerusalem in 49–50; he could have gone to Rome during that time. The third is Rom. 15:20–22, where Paul tells the Romans that he had not come to see them as yet, "lest I might build on another man's foundation"; this important man may be Peter. The fourth is Apoc. 11.3–13 about the "two witnesses...[whose] bodies will lie in the streets of the great city"; several modern scholars see in these Peter and Paul killed in Rome.

Supposing the truth of such allusions, Peter got out of prison in 42–43 and went to Rome; he came back to Jerusalem in 49–50; he was in Rome again much

Clement of Rome in his epistle to the Corinthians (see above, p. 316), speaking of Peter and Paul, seems to associate them to the other Roman martyrs (5.3–7; 6.1). *Ignatius of Antioch* in his epistle to the Romans says that he is not speaking to them with authority "like Peter and Paul" (4.3); the context suggests that he means "like Peter and Paul had spoken among them." Papias, bishop of Hierapolis about the year 130 and auditor of John the evangelist, testifies that Peter wrote his first epistle from Rome, which he calls Babylon (thus Eusebius of Caesarea, *Eccles. Hist.* 2.15, MG 20.171–174); this would be the first clear testimony of Peter's Roman sojourn. *Dionysius*, bishop of Corinth about 170, testifies that "both [Peter and Paul] went together to Italy, and having instructed the Romans, suffered martyrdom at the same time" (Thus Eusebius, *ibid.* 1.25, MG 20.210). *Irenaeus*, writing about the year 180, testifies that "the Roman church was founded and established by the two most glorious apostles Peter and Paul," who "gave to Linus the episcopal function of its administration" (see above, p. 317).

At the end of the same century we find a document of particular importance, due to the fact that its author is a Roman and that he testifies that the sepulchers of the two apostles are visible to everyone: *Gaius* or (Caius), a Roman priest under Pope Zephyrinus (199–217), in his book *Against Proclus*, the Montanist, to this heretic who was boasting that in his church the "sepulcher of Philip" was kept, answers: "But I can show the sepulchers of the apostles. For, whether you go to the Vatican place or to the Ostian, there will come up to your sight the sepulchers of those who founded that church" (cited by Eusebius, *ibid.* 2.25, MG 20.210; cf. 3.26).

In the 3rd century, *Clement of Alexandria* testifies that Peter wrote his first epistle from Rome (cf. Eusebius, *ibid.* 2.15). *Tertullian* says that the two apostles gave to the Roman church "their doctrine with their blood," and that Peter was crucified like Christ and Paul beheaded like John the Baptist (*On the Prescriptions of Heretics* 36.2f.). *Origen* testifies that Peter in Rome "was crucified with his head downwards" (cited by Eusebius, *ibid.* 3.1, MG 20.215).

In the 4th and 5th centuries several complete lists of the Roman Pontiffs, starting from Peter, are brought forth, following the pattern of those exhibited in the 2nd century by Hegesippus and

---

later and from there he sent his two epistles to the churches of Asia; he died there during the persecution of Nero.

Irenaeus (cf. Eusebius, *ibid.* 4.22; 5.6; see above, p. 317). Eusebius of Caesarea starts his list by saying that Peter was "bishop of Rome for 25 years" (which seems to be a personal amplification) and he adds that "Peter and Paul died in Rome" during Nero's persecution (*Chronical,* book 2, in St. Jerome's translation, ML 22.449f., 454). The anonymous author of the *Chronographer* of the year 354, a valuable compilation of historical documents, in his seventh document, called Liberian Catalogue, gives the list from Peter to Liberius (†366). A list is given also by Optatus of Milevis, St. Augustine (both quoted above, p. 320), and Epiphanius who states that "Peter and Paul were the first apostles as well as the first bishops of Rome" and they were both "killed on the 12th year of Nero" (*Against Heresies,* her. 27, MG 41.371).

Among *liturgical documents* are found two feasts of St. Peter, thus related by the aforementioned *Chronographer:* "On the month of February. VIII Calends of March [that is, on the 22nd of February] birth of Peter of the chair" (which can mean either Peter's martyrdom or his taking over the Roman See). "On the month of June, III Calends of July [that is, the 29th of June] about Peter at the Catacombs and Paul at the Ostian road, during the consulate of Tuscus and Bassus (258)."[101]

Regarding the *archaeological monuments,* the results of the excavations made in 1915 under the basilica of St. Sebastian near the Catacombs (where, according to the *Liber Pontificalis* of the 6th century, the bodies of Peter and Paul had been kept for some time), were very slight, for only several inscriptions in honor of the two apostles were found. The results of *Vatican excavations,* started in 1939 under the basilica of St. Peter, were much more important, but not conclusive with regard to a sufficient evidence of St. Peter's tomb in that place.[102]

---

101 Scholars dispute about the exact meaning of these two feasts. Cf. H. Leclercq, "Pierre (Saint)," *Dictionnaire d'archéologie chrétienne et de liturgie* 14-1 (Paris 1939) 855–876; Cullmann, *loc. cit.* (above, footnote 61).

102 Cf. *Esplorazioni sotto la Confessione di S. Pietro in Vaticano* (collective work and official publication), 2 vols., Rome 1951 (see especially pp. 119–144); Cullman, *loc cit.* (above, footnote 61); J. Ruysschaert, "Recherches et études autor de la Confession de la Basilique Vaticane (1940–1958). Etat de la question et bibliographie," *Triplice omaggio a Sua Santità Pio XII* 2 (Città del Vaticano 1958) 33–47; E. Kirschbaum, *The Tombs of St. Peter and St. Paul* (tr. J. Murray), New York, 1959; M. Guarducci, *The Tomb of St. Peter. The New Discoveries in the Sacred Grottoes of the Vatican* (tr. J. McLellan), New York 1960; D. W. O'Connor, *Peter in Rome. The*

Undoubtedly the very fact that the emperor Constantine built the basilica in that exact place, notwithstanding extraordinary topographical difficulties, is a sign of a traditional conviction that it was the place of the tomb or at least of the martyrdom of the apostle, testified by the aforementioned Roman priest Gaius. Furthermore, the excavations have brought to light the remainders of a small tomb, which seems to have commanded the orientation of the basilica in its difficult construction and which could be the sepulcher Gaius was speaking about; but no bones or ashes have been found in it, nor any mention of the apostle in the inscriptions immediately surrounding it.

Note 3. *On the various requirements for obtaining or losing the primacy*

In order to *obtain* the primacy five things are required. First, the *masculine sex*, which is the only one fitted for the threefold power of Orders, Magisterium, and jurisdiction.[103] Second, the *age of discernment*, that is, the use of reason, without which a man is unable to govern; this condition is not required for Ordination. Third, the quality of *member of the Church*, for no one can be head if he is not a member; hence a man not yet baptized, or heretic, or schismatic, or solemnly excommunicated, cannot be made Pope. Fourthly, *lawful election*, whose manner has been various in different ages, according to rules established by the Pope alone. In the first centuries the election was made by the Roman clergy, and since the late Middle Ages by the cardinals. It is disputed whether the Pope could choose his own successor.[104] Fifthly, acceptation by the one elected, for

---

Literary, Liturgical, and Archeological Evidence. New York-London 1969.

103 The case of the medieval *Pope Joan*, who would have been surreptitiously elected and would have governed the Church for about two years, between Leo IV (†855) and Benedict III (†858), is a pure fable, invented in the 13th century and widely circulated up until the 16th century, when it was scientifically refuted by Catholic scholars and later also by Protestants. Cf. H. Thurston, "Pope Joan," *The Month* (1914) 450–463; F. Vernet, "Jeanne (La Papesse)," *Dictionnaire apologétique de la foi catholique* 2 (éd. 4, Paris 1924) 1253–1270.

104 It is denied by older theologians as Cajetan and Bellarmine, but admitted by several modern authors, as Wernz, Cappello, Granderath, Grisar, Straub (*De Ecclesia*, vol. 1, p. 596).

The reason given for this affirmative opinion is that the Pope in such case would not really elect his successor, but would only put a condition which would have its effect in the future, just as when he establishes the mode of election by others. However, this seems a fallacious reason, because in the second case the Pope does

the electors are not givers of the power, but only a condition for the action of God, who is not supposed to force such heavy burden on the one who does not feel ready to bear it. Besides, the Pope can freely resign the primacy, hence he can *a fortiori* refuse it.

If the newly elected is only a priest, or a deacon, or a layman, he must receive the episcopal consecration, in order to be fully head, pastor, and pontiff of the Church. However, it is very probable that before this consecration he can fully exercise jurisdiction and Magisterium (like making a universal law, defining a truth, assembling a Council)[105]; on the contrary it is uncertain whether he would still remain a Pope if he would simply refuse to be consecrated.

The primacy *can be lost* in four ways. First, by *physical death;* hence the deceased person is no more Pope either in the other life or if he should miraculously revive; he remains however a bishop by reason of the indelible sacramental character. Second, by *moral death,* that is, by manifest and perpetual insanity; just as the lack of the use of reason is an impediment for obtaining the primacy, so also it is a cause for losing it. Third, by *spiritual death,* that is, through formal and public heresy (if it could happen in a Pope as a private doctor),[106] by reason of which he ceases to be member of the Church and hence he is no longer its head. Fourth, by a voluntary *abdication;* as he voluntarily accepted the primacy, so can the Pope freely withdraw from it.[107]

---

not have a direct influence on the election made by others, while in the first case he exercises an elective action which will have its effect at the moment of his death. The two facts brought forth from ancient history, namely, that of Felix IV who in 530 chose Boniface II as his successor and of this same Boniface choosing Vigilius, can be suitably explained as mere commendations to the future electors.

105   This is denied by some theologians, as Sánchez, *loc. cit.* (above, footnote 81). However the Code of Canon Law (can. 219) seems to suggest it and Pius XII simply asserted it in his Allocution to the Second World Congress of the Lay Apostolate, Oct. 5, 1957 (see *Documentation Catholique* 54 [1957] 1415).

106   Some theologians (as Palmieri and Straub) simply admit the possibility of a Pope falling into formal and public heresy, as apparently shown by some historical cases (see below, p. 130f.). Others (as Dorsch, D'Herbigny, Salaverri), granting the speculative possibility, deny the practical possibility of such case, considering the assistance promised by Christ to the Church and the grave disturbance which the Church would suffer through the downfall of its head.

107   This case happened at least twice in history. St. Celestine V (canonized in 1313) resigned in 1294, feeling unable to govern the Church by reason of political and ecclesiastical disturbances. Gregory XII was asked to resign in 1415 by the Council of Constance for the good of the Church, in order to make less difficult the end of the Western Schism.

7

The Nature of the Primacy of the Roman Pontiff[108]

THE PRIMACY OF THE ROMAN PONTIFF, AS ESTAB-
lished in the preceding chapter, implies some kind of true and
supreme power of jurisdiction, as distinguished from a mere
pre-eminence of honor or a simple power of general direction
over the entire Church. We shall now determine the nature of
this power, that is, its vigor and extension

We may distinguish three concepts with which the Vatican
Council I describes the Roman primacy, namely *episcopal, supreme,*
and *universal power.*

Episcopal power itself implies three notes, that is *full, ordinary*
and *immediate* power. *Full power* is taken both intrinsically, as to
all the functions of the power and not only as to some superior
rights, and extrinsically, as to all the objects or causes concerned,
whether doctrinal or disciplinary. *Ordinary power* (as distinguished
from delegated or vicarious or extraordinary power) is that which
is attached to the office itself and is exercised in one's own name
and right, and in all circumstances. *Immediate power* is that which
reaches the subjects directly, without passing through or using
the influence of another inferior power. Such is also the power of
a bishop, although in his limited church or diocese. *Supreme power*
is that which has no equal or superior power. *Universal power* is
taken here only with reference to the subjects, that is, the power
which reaches the universal Church in all its particular churches
and all its individual members.

Statement. *The primacy of the Roman Pontiff is a universal, episcopal, and supreme power in the Church.*

Theological note. The entire assertion is *de fide,* defined in the
three Councils of Lyons, Florence and Vatican I, in the first two

---

108   See the bibliography given above for the existence of the primacy (footnote
81) and below for the episcopacy and its collegiate nature (footnotes 156 and 167).

Councils only under the general expression of a plenitude of power, in the third under the explicit concept of episcopal, supreme, and universal power, in the sense just explained. However, the word "episcopal" does not occur in the definition itself, but only in its explanation, and hence the episcopal power, under the name and indefinite concept, is not defined and is only proximate to faith; but its specific concept of a "full, ordinary and immediate" power is directly and *verbatim* defined as *de fide* in the canon.[109]

The Magisterium since the Middle Ages has declared the nature of the primacy under the general concept of a plenitude and superiority of power, which embraces all the other qualities, distinctly expressed by the Vatican Council I. Its declarations generally

---

109   The first two errors mentioned above (footnotes 65 and 83), which deny both the Petrine and the Roman primacy, on the basis of an oligarchic or democratic constitution of the Church, come back here, under different forms and in connection with other trends of heretical movement, to attack especially the episcopal and supreme power of the Pope. All such errors can be gathered under three names, that is, episcopalism, conciliarism, and caesaropapism.

Episcopalism stresses beyond measure the rights of the bishops, limiting the Pope's episcopal authority over the universal Church, that is, his full, ordinary, and immediate power. Such was the effort of *Cyprian* and his friend *Firmilian* in the 3rd century (see above, pp. 318–320), of *Gallicanism* in the 17–18th centuries (see footnotes 42 and 65), which moreover denied the supreme authority of the Pope, and of *Anglicanism*, which denied also the primacy itself (see above, footnotes 65 and 83).

Conciliarism denies the supreme authority of the Pope in favor of the Ecumenical Council (or of the Christian people represented by the Council). Its essential doctrine is that the Church itself is superior to the Pope and that in the case of an unworthy Pope (especially if heretical), or of a doubtful Pope by reason of a general schism in the Church, there is no other remedy but to appeal to the authority of the Church itself through an Ecumenical Council.

This doctrine began to take shape among the medieval *canonists* (cf. B. Tierny, *Foundations of the Conciliar Theory* [Cambridge 1955] 55–67), increased with the birth of Caesaropapism in the 13th century, when the first appeal to a general Council against the Pope was uttered under Philip IV, king of France, and reached its climax at the time of the Western Schism (1378–1417), when many canonists and theologians, especially of the Parisian school, explicitly proclaimed the superiority of the Council over the Pope during the celebration of the three Councils of Pisa (1409), Constance (1415), and Basel (1434) (cf. P. De Vooght, in *Irénikon* [1963] 61–75, and in *Istina* [1963] 57–86). It revived again in the 17–18th centuries under the form of *Gallicanism* (see above, footnote 42), combined with trends of episcopalism and caesaropapism (see the various Gallican propositions, condemned by the Magisterium, in Denz. 2281–2285, 2594–2597, 2602f.).

Caesaropapism denies the supreme authority of the Pope in favor of the King or any civil authority, based on the principle that Christ gave the supreme authority immediately to the Christian people, from whom it is communicated to the Pope, through the King or the civil authority. Of the history of this heresy and its ramifications into Gallicanism we have spoken above (footnote 42).

followed step by step the various errors which tried to lessen the full meaning of the keys given by Christ to Peter and his successors.

Boniface VIII in 1302 against the rising Caesaropapism vindicated to the Roman Pontiff "the *supreme power*, which only by God and by no man can be judged," "a power which is above any earthly power" (see above, p. 274). *Clement VI* in his Epistle to the Armenians in 1351 insists at length on the "plenitude of power," declaring that the Roman Pontiff "received immediately from Christ all the power of jurisdiction, which Christ Himself in His human life had as the head, over the entire and universal body of the militant Church" (Denz. 1054; cf. 1052–1065 where the various rights of the Pope are expounded).

The *Councils of Lyons II* (1274) and *of Florence* (1439) proposed to the Orientals as an article of faith that "the Roman Church obtained the *supreme and full* primacy and principality over the entire Catholic Church" (Lyons, Denz. 861) and that to the Roman Pontiff "was given by our Lord Jesus Christ the *full power* of guiding, ruling and governing the universal Church" (Florence, Denz. 1307). After the rise of Conciliarism, claiming the superiority of the Council over the Pope, *Martin V* and *Eugene IV* rejected those parts of the declarations of the Councils of Constance and Basel in which this theory was inculcated.[110] *Alexander VIII* and *Pius VI* condemned similar Gallican theories (Denz. 2281–2285, 2594–2597, 2602f.).

The definition of the Vatican Council I in 1870 was not, therefore, something new, but only a further explanation and determination of the doctrine already defined as *de fide* by the Councils of Lyons and Florence; the Vatican Council itself declares the intention of "renewing the definition of the Ecumenical Council of Florence" (Denz. 3059).

The Vatican definition[111] reads as follows: "If any one, therefore, shall say that the Roman Pontiff has only a function of

---

110　These two Popes finally approved the decisions of both Councils, except whatever was "prejudicial to the right, the dignity, and preeminence of the holy Apostolic See, and to the power given to it by Christ" (Denz., before nos. 1151–1195). Cf. P. De Vooght, *Les pouvoirs du Concile et l'autorité du Pape au Concile de Constance*, Paris 1965; G. Hofmann, "Papato, Conciliarismo, Patriarcato (1438–1439)," *Miscellanea historiae pontificiae* 2 (Roma 1940) 3–82; J. Lecler, *Le Pape ou le Concile? Une interrogation de l'Eglise médiévale*, Paris 1973.

111　Cf. Betti, *loc. cit.* (above, footnote 69); W. F. Dewan, "Preparation of the Vatican Council's Schema on the Power and Nature of the Primacy," *Ephemerides theologicae*

inspection or direction, and not *the full and supreme power of juris-diction over the entire Church*, not only in things regarding faith and morals, but also in things concerning the discipline and government of the Church spread all over the world, or if he shall say that the Roman Pontiff has only the principal parts, and not the whole fulness of this supreme power, or that this power of his is not *ordinary and immediate on all and single churches as well as on all and single pastors and faithful*: let him be anathema" (Sess. 4, chap. 3, at the end, Denz. 3064).

In this definition the three notes of our statement are contained, namely, *universal* (the word is not expressed in direct form, but the concept is emphatically brought forth), *episcopal* (the word is expressed only in the body of the chapter: "Which is truly episcopal,"[112] but the concept is given in the definition with its three parts: full, ordinary, and immediate), and *supreme*. In the chapter which precedes the definition, the doctrine is fully expounded.

The same doctrine is repeated in the subsequent documents of the Magisterium, as in the encyclical "Satis cognitum" of *Leo XIII*, who says that "the power of the Roman Pontiff is supreme, universal, and of full right" (Denz. 3308f.) and in the Dogmatic Constitution on the Church of *Vatican II* which simply confirms the definition of Vatican I and calls the Roman Pontiff "Pastor of the entire Church [having] full, supreme and universal power" (nos. 18, 22).

Lovanienses 36 (1960) 23–56; "'Potestas vere episcopalis' au premier Concile du Vatican," *L'Episcopat et l'Eglise universelle* (collective work; Paris 1962) 661–687, reproduced in the collective work *De doctrina Concilii Vaticani Primi* (In Civitate Vaticana 1969) 361–382.

112   Dewan, in the article cited in the preceding footnote examines the manner in which the expression "Truly episcopal power" was introduced into the final schema of the definition, and its sense. Episcopal power is equivalent to ordinary and immediate power; it has been added to signify that the Pope has the same kind of power on each faithful of any diocese as the bishop has on the faithful of his particular diocese, and hence he can reach each faithful in any case and directly without passing through the bishop.

Some Fathers in the Council were opposed to the expression "universal bishop" or "episcopal power" given to the Pope, fearing a lesion to the rights of the bishops. But it is only a question of name, for the same concept is found in the two words "ordinary and immediate." Besides, the title itself is traditional. The Roman Pontiff has been called "Bishop of bishops," "Ecumenical bishop," "Bishop of the Catholic Church" (Council of Chalcedon), "Bishop of the Roman and universal Church" (Leo I, thus calling himself; see Mansi 52.698). Gregory the Great, disliking the title "Ecumenical bishop," preferred the expression "Servant of the servants of God" (see *Epistles* 18, 20, 21, 43), which has been used by recent Popes.

The meaning of Scripture and Tradition is in full harmony with the Vatican definition, as appears from the simple and unrestricted manner in which the primacy is attributed to the Roman Pontiff.

A cursory analysis of the two biblical texts on the primacy (quoted above, pp. 304–308) shows its unlimited amplitude through the three metaphors under which it is proposed. The entire Church is built on one *rock*; hence the Roman Pontiff is the principle of unity and firmity, that is, the authority with regard to anything that is part of the Church. The *keys* of the kingdom of God are given to Peter and his successors simply and without conditions; hence he decides on all causes and persons. Christ's *sheep* are simply and without restriction entrusted to Peter, for whatever care is necessary and whatever food is needed.

The *Fathers* (quoted above, pp. 316–324) never say or signify that the power of the Roman Pontiff is restricted. Even *Cyprian*, who represents the only discordant voice, did not dare to say it explicitly, although by his words and deeds he seemed equivalently to deny the fulness of this power and advocate some kind of ambiguous episcopalism. *Irenaeus* simply affirms that all the faithful must agree with the Roman Church "by reason of its more powerful superiority." *Ambrose* does not fear to say that the Roman See is the source of all rights in the Church. According to *Innocent I*, in questions of faith all must refer to Peter, who has the care of all the churches. According to *Boniface I, Gelasius I,* and *Nicholas I,* the Roman Pontiff decides and judges on all ecclesiastical things and cannot be judged by anyone; hence the traditional juridical axiom, "The First See is judged by no one," The plenitude of the primatial power is also shown in the practice of the Roman Pontiffs during the patristic age, as in the intervention of *Clement of Rome* in the revolt of the Corinthian church, of *Victor* into the Asian paschal controversy, of *Stephen* into the baptismal practice of the African church, and of the Popes who followed into the celebration and decisions of the eastern ecumenical Councils.

The principal objections, which can be raised and in fact were raised by the adversaries of the fulness of papal power, may be reduced to the following. *First,* an *episcopal power* of the Pope over the entire Church would establish two authorities of the same kind over the same subject, which is impossible; besides, it would reduce extremely the power of the bishops, making them like vicars of the Pope. *Second, a supreme power* of the Pope would be unable to safeguard the good of the Church in the case of an heretical or doubtful Pope; hence there must be an extraordinary higher power, as that of the universal Council, at least for such cases of extreme necessity.

Answer to the first objection. The two powers of the Pope and of a bishop are of the same kind (that is, episcopal), but not of the same order; one is superior and the other is subordinate, and hence they can exercise their influence on the same subject, according to the mode and the limits of subordination. Even in the natural order God and man are both causes of the same kind, that is, principal causes, but not of the same order, for God is the first cause and man is the secondary cause of his own action, while neither obstructs the influence of the other.[113] Hence the power of the bishop is in no way diminished nor reduced to that of a vicar, but it is simply a subordinate power, although principal and truly episcopal in its own line.

Answer to the second objection. A similar case of grave disturbance for the Church could occur with a general council whose orthodoxy or legitimacy would be doubtful, especially in time of general schism in the Church, in which moreover it may happen that several opposed councils are assembled and several Popes are elected by them. The case of an heretical Pope (the practical possibility of which may even be doubted)[114] can be solved by the action of a Council, not authoritatively deposing the Pope, but merely declaring that he is no longer the head as he is no longer a member of the Church. The case of a doubtful Pope can be solved by a conclave of cardinals or a general Council, with the help of divine Providence which never abandons the Church; thus the Council of Constance solved the case of the three Popes John XXIII, Benedict XIII, and Gregory XII, by deposing the first two as clear intruders and asking the third (the legitimate one) to resign voluntarily for the good of the Church, so that all doubt would be removed in the mind of the many faithful who had followed in good faith the two antipopes.

---

113   Cf. St. Thomas, *In 4 Sent.*, dist. 17, q. 3, a. 3, qa. 3, ad. 3.
114   See footnote 106.

8

Infallibility of the Roman Pontiff[115]

WHAT HAS BEEN SAID IN THE TWO PRECEDING
chapters about the existence and the nature of the papal primacy, applies equally to both powers of jurisdiction and Magisterium, which are intimately linked together under the general
expressions "power, authority, jurisdiction."[116] In chapter 4 we
have treated sufficiently of the nature of the two powers and
their distinction (see pp. 287ff.). Hence the only question now
to be considered, in order to complete our treatment, is that of
infallibility, which is a quality proper to the Magisterium. We
discuss it directly with reference to the Pope, who is its principal

---

115   Castelli, E. (ed.), *L'infaillibilité. Son aspect philosophique et théologique*, Paris 1970.
Cauldron, M., "Magistère ordinaire et infaillibilité pontificale d'après la Constitution 'Dei Filius'," *Ephemerides theolgicae Lovanienses* 36 (1960) 393–431.
    Chavasse, A., "La véritable conception de l'infaillibilité papale d'après le Concile
du Vatican," *Eglise et unité* (Lille 1948) 57–91.
    Ciappi, L., "Crisis of the Magisterium, Crisis of Faith?," *Thomist* 32 (1968)
147–170.
    Eglise infaillible ou intemporelle? (collective work), Paris 1973.
    Fenton, J. Cl., "The Doctrinal Authority of Papal Encyclicals, "*American ecclesi-
astical Revue* 121 (1949) 136–150, 210–220; 125 (1951) 53–62; 128 (1953)
177–198.
    Fichtner, J., "Papal Infallibility: A Century Later," *American Ecclesiastical Review*
163 (1970) 217–243.
    Flick, M., "Chiesa permissiva e Chiesa repressiva," *Civiltà Cattolica* 124 (1973).
vol. 3, pp. 455–466.
    Journet, Ch., *L'Eglise du Verbe Incarné* 1 (éd. 2, Paris 1955) 567–578.
    Kenny, J. P., "The Positiveness of the Infallibility of the Church," *American Eccle-
siastical Review* 156 (1967) 242–256.
    Nau, P., "Le magistère pontificial ordinaire, lieu théologique," *Revue thomiste*
56 (1956) 389–412; "Le magistère pontifical ordinaire au premier Concile du
Vatican," *ibid.* 62 (1962) 341–397.
    Nicolosi, S., "L'infallibilità Attualità e indefettibilità di una definizione." *Aquinas*
15 (1972) 635–657.
    Ruffino, G., *Gli organi dell'infallibilità della Chiesa*, Torino 1954.
    Thils, G., "L'infaillibilité de l'Eglise 'in credendo' et 'in docendo,'" *Salesianum* 24
(1962) 298–335; *L'infaillibilité pontificale. Sources–conditions–limites*, Gembloux 1969.
    Tierney, B., *Origins of Papal Infallibility 1150–1350. A Study on the Concepts of
Infallibility, Sovereignty, and Tradition in the Middle Ages*, Leiden 1972.
116   As noted above (p. 294), the two powers remained under the same name of
jurisdiction until the 19th century, when the nominal distinction into jurisdiction
and Magisterium was made.

and original subject, leaving to an additional note at the end of this chapter the explanation of the infallibility which belongs to the other two subjects, namely, the ecumenical Council and the believing Church. The question on the infallibility of the Pope is usually thus phrased: *Whether the Roman Pontiff is infallible when speaking "ex cathedra."* To suitably resolve this question, a previous explanation of the two expressions "infallibility" and "speech *ex cathedra*" is in order.

Infallibility is generically understood as immunity from error. This immunity can refer either to the act (as if I say: This assertion is true, that is, free from error) and thus it is properly called *inerrancy*, that is, the actual fact of not making errors (for instance, of a man who always states the truth, we can say that he is inerrant), or to the potency, and this is properly called *infallibility*, that is, the impossibility of making an error. This is either absolute, essential, and unparticipated, as is found in God's knowledge alone, or hypothetical, accidental, and participated, as can take place in a man if God gives him a supernatural help always to state the truth. This help can be either an interior light of revelation (as in the prophets), or an interior movement of inspiration (as in the writers of Holy Scripture), or a simple divine assistance, which disposes human persons and events in such a manner that a man cannot be led into error and when he speaks he cannot propose an error.[117] The infallibility attributed to the Pope is only of this third kind. Undoubtedly this infallibility does not dispense the Pope from a previous inquiry as to whether a doctrine is actually contained in the deposit of revelation; however his infallibility does not depend on such an inquiry, but only on the divine assistance, so that if the Pope speaks *"ex cathedra,"* what he says is infallibly true.

Speech "ex cathedra" is an expression used by Vatican I in its definition of the infallibility of the Pope and it has become classical in theology.[118] According to the explanation given by the Council itself, it involves four conditions for the papal discourse to be infallible. First, *on the part of the subject,* or the Pope, he must

117 About the distinction of these three supernatural helps, see our treatise on *Revelation*, p. 67.
118 It is based on Christ's words: "The Scribes and the Pharisees have sat on the chair [cathedra] of Moses" (Matt. 23:2f.) and on the patristic title "Cathedra Petri" (Peter's Chair) for the Roman See (see on p. 320). It has been used by theologians off and on before the Council, but not as a technical expression.

speak formally *as head of the entire Church;*[119] however, for this it is not necessary that he speak materially and directly to the whole Church, for, even in a document directed to a particular church or person, if it implies a doctrine regarding the entire Church, he is understood to speak to or for the whole Church (such is, for instance, the epistle of Clement VI to the Armenians, Denz. 1050ff.). Second, *on the part of the object,* this must be a doctrine pertaining to *faith and morals* and proposed as to be held by the Church. Third, *on the part of the form,* or the mode of teaching, the doctrine must be presented *authoritatively,* namely, with the supreme power of the primacy. Fourth, it must be presented also *definitively,* that is, as something no longer subject to doubt or controversy.

Statement. *The Roman Pontiff is infallible when speaking ex cathedra.*

Theological note. The statement is *de fide,* defined implicitly by the Councils of Lyons II and Florence, explicitly and distinctly by Vatican I.[120]

---

119   Thus the Pope is considered not as a private doctor (as when he writes a book or individually joins a dispute among theologians), but as a *public person.* However, he is not considered only as a symbol of the papal See, as if the expression "The Pope is infallible" would only mean that the See as a whole is infallible but not each single man sitting in that See, is infallible (this was the famous ambiguous distinction of the Gallicans between the See and the Sitting); but he is taken as an *individual person.* Moreover he is taken as *distinct and independent from the Church,* inasmuch as his decisions have their value of themselves and not from the agreement of the Christian people. However, he is *not considered as opposed or separate from the Church,* for he is precisely the immediate and principal subject of the infallibility of the Church itself. Hence the Pope is considered as a person, who is public, individual, distinct but not separate from the Church.

120   The Pope's infallibility is logically denied by all those who deny either his primacy, as Protestants and the separated Orientals (footnotes 65 and 83), or the fulness of his primacy, as Conciliarists and Gallicans (footnote 109). On the occasion of the Vatican definition, also several Catholics, even inside the Council, joined their voice of dissent, and some other withdrew from the Church, forming a separate church under the name of Old Catholics.

Among *Protestants,* the *Anglicans* in the 39 articles of their faith stated that the general Councils can err and sometimes erred, even in things regarding God, and hence whatever is decided by them does not have any authority, unless it can be shown that it has been derived from the Scripture (art. 21; this article has been removed by the American Episcopalians). Recent Protestants generally deny infallibility as a lesion to religious freedom; but this reason has been rejected by Karl Barth, who says that neither the extrinsic authority taught by Catholics nor the individual religious freedom advanced by new Protestantism is the rule of faith, but Christ alone in his evangelical teaching.

The *Orientals* attacked particularly the Vatican definition, declaring it to be the principal obstacle to the union with Rome; thus patriarch Anthimus VII in

The Magisterium implicitly proposed this truth as many times as it taught the primacy and its fulness, especially in the two *Councils of Lyons and Florence*, which uttered definitions of faith (see above, pp. 314, 333f.); the Vatican Council itself in the explanation of its definition quotes these two Councils, as proposing the infallibility

---

his reply to Leo XIII in 1895, A. Maltsev (supporter of the union), S. Bulgakov, Chr. Papadopoulos, and the Congress of Oriental Churches held at Moscow in 1948 (see footnote 83).

The *Conciliarists* of the 15th century logically rejected papal infallibility in their negation of the primacy. The Council of Constance, under the influence of the French theologians John Gerson and Peter d'Ailly, in its first sessions declared that "everyone, in whatever state or dignity, even papal, is found, is obliged to obey the general council in things regarding faith" (Mansi 27.585, 590).

The *Gallicans* clothed their negation with two insidious distinctions, saying that a papal decision "is not an irreformable judgement unless the consent of the Church is obtained" (Denz. 2284) and that although the Papal *"See"* is infallible, its individual "occupant" is not infallible. This distinction, already suggested by John Gerson in the Council of Constance, was first *verbatim* coined by J. B. Bossuet (†1704) and emphasized by other Gallicans. Cf. A. G. Martimort, *Le gallicanisme de Bossuet*, Paris 1953. Alexander VIII in 1690 condemned the following explicit statement of the Jansenists; "The assertion about the infallibility of the Roman Pontiff in defining questions of faith is futile and often disproved" (Denz. 2329).

Remnants of Gallicanism and Episcopalism showed up in the first *Vatican Council* itself. Out of 601 Fathers, about 83 were opposed to the definition as inopportune; among these, 47 were opposed to the truth itself. Most of these dissenters left Rome before the last ballot, declaring in a letter to the Pope that they were leaving because they did not want to say *"Non placet* publicly in the face of the Father."* The principal dissenters were Darboy, archbishop of Paris, Dupanloup, archbishop of Orleans, Maret, dean of the faculty of La Sorbonne in Paris, the two Cardinals of Praga and Vienna, the well known historiographer Hefele, bishop of Rotterdam, and Strossmayer, bishop of Diakovàr in Croatia, who made himself a name for his stubborn and active opposition. However, all these bishops within one or two years declared their submission to the definition.

A more serious opposition came from several professors of the various universities in Austria and Germany, who after the definition withdrew from the Church in 1871 and founded their own schismatic church, under the name of *Old Catholics*. Their first bishop was a lay professor, J. H. Reinkens, consecrated in 1873 at Rotterdam by the Jansenist bishop Heykamp of Deventer. Cf. C. B. Moss, *The Old Catholic Movement: Its Origin and History*, London 1948.

Recently, after the second Vatican Council confirmed again the doctrine of papal infallibility, its direct denial has once more crept into *Catholic circles*, arousing a sharp controversy.

The principal challenger of the defined truth is the Swiss theologians *Hans Küng* in his work *Unfehlbar? Eine Anfrage*, Einsiedeln 1970; English translation by E. Quinn: *Infallible? An Inquiry*, New York 1971; see also the following articles written by Küng in self-defense: "Im Interesse der Sache. Antwort an Karl Rahner," *Stimmen der Zeit* 187-1 (1971) 43–64; 187-2 (1971) 105–122; "Why I Am Staying in the Church," *America* 124-11 (1971) 281–283; *Fehlbar? Eine Bilanz*, Zürich—Einsiedeln—Koeln 1973.

According to Küng, papal infallibility lacks philosophical, biblical, historical, and theological foundation.

of the Roman Pontiff. Moreover, a direct reference to infallibility is made by the Council of Lyons stating: *"If any questions about faith arise, they must be settled by his judgment"* (Denz. 861) and by the Council of Florence, calling the Pope "head of the entire Church and father and *doctor of all Christians* (Denz. 1307). There

Under the viewpoint of *philosophy*, only God is infallible. Any human proposition is subject to possible error, it is essentially problematic, it can be true or false, as well as true and false at the same time.

The only text brought forth from *the Bible*, Luke 22:32, does not speak of infallibility nor of Magisterium, and at any rate we cannot prove that it concerns others than Peter, such as his successors. The apostles never claimed infallibility for themselves and consequently Pope and bishops cannot claim it, as successors of the apostles; besides, it cannot even be proved that they succeed to the apostles directly and exclusively, nor that the bishops are of divine institution and hold an authentic Magisterium. Only the Church as a whole succeeds to the apostles, and likewise the Magisterium is a general charisma pertaining to theologians, whose doctrines are judged only by the whole Church, as the community of the faithful.

As regards *history*, the testimony of Tradition proves nothing, because the doctrine of papal infallibility may have been built against or beyond the Gospel. Moreover, the very existence of such testimony is doubtful; that doctrine was first shaped in the 11th century under the influence of false Decretals, as an expression of papal totalitarian power. The three conciliar testimonies of Constantinople I, Lyons II, and Florence, brought forth by Vatican I in its definition, belong to Councils not universally acknowledged as ecumenical.

Papal infallibility cannot be inferred *theologically* from other truths. First it does not follow from the internal exigence of faith, for faith is not bound to infallible propositions; doctrinal propositions may have a binding force and a defensive character, by reason of historical circumstances, but not a definitive character of perpetual value. Indeed, it is possible that the Christian message demand the infallibility of one or another particular proposition; however, this cannot be presumed, but must be strictly proved, which is not the case for papal infallibility, as explained above. Second, papal infallibility does not follow from the assistance promised by Christ to the Church, for this promise concerns not the infallibility of the Church but its *indefectibility*, or the unceasing continuity of the truth in the Church, namely, that notwithstanding all possible errors the Church is kept in the truth, or Christ's message remains unceasingly in her, with his presence and the presence of the Holy Spirit.

This truth of the indefectibility of the Church, or of its infallibility understood as indefectibility, is precisely the fundamental problem which was overlooked by Vatican I in its definition; hence this Council did not define a problem which it did not see or it defined only the indefectibility of the Church in papal pronouncements. Consequently, denying papal infallibility is not necessarily opposed to the Vatican definition.

For an ampler explanation and criticism of this doctrine, embodying many errors and several contradictions, see K. Rahner, "Kritik an Hans Küng, *"Stimmen der Zeit* (1970) 361–377; (1971) 145–160; (Rahner ed.), *Zum Problem Unfehlbarkeit, Antworten auf die Anfrage von Hans Küng*, Freiburg – Basel – Wien 1972; Y. Congar, in *Revue des sciences philosophiques et théologiques* (1970) 613–618; M. Loehrer, in *Schweizerische Kirchenzeitung* (1970) 544–548 and in *Der Seelsorger* (1971) 60–65 (see English version in *Worship* [1971] 273–289; G. De Rosa, in *Civiltà Cattolica* (1971),

is also a direct statement about papal infallibility in the epistle of *Clement VI* to the Armenians, which is considered as an infallible document by several theologians. Clement among other doctrinal questions asks the Armenian patriarch: *"Whether you believed and still believe,* that only the Roman Pontiff can definitely settle doubts arising about the Catholic faith, by an *authentic definition, to which one must irrevocably adhere;* and that everything he defines to be true, using the power of the keys given him by Christ, is in fact true and Catholic, and what he defines as false and heretical must be believed to be so" (Denz. 1064).

Hence the definition of *Vatican I* appears to be only an explicit and more definite declaration of what the Magisterium had already at least implicitly proposed. This important definition reads as follows: "With the approval of the Council we teach and define to be a revealed dogma of faith: that the Roman Pontiff, *when he speaks ex cathedra,* that is, when in the exercise of his function *as pastor and doctor of all Christians* he defines *with his supreme Apostolic authority a doctrine on faith and morals to be held by the whole Church,* has, through the divine assistance promised to him in blessed Peter, that same infallibility with which the divine Redeemer wanted His Church to be endowed in defining a doctrine of faith and morals. Hence such definitions of the Roman Pontiff are irreformable of themselves and not by the consent of the Church. If, however, anyone shall dare — God forbid — to contradict this definition of ours: let him be anathema" (Denz. 3073–3075). We have already pointed out all the essential elements of this definition.[121]

---

vol. 1, pp. 126–139, 228–240; J. T. Ford, in *Thomist* (171) 501–512; various in *Theology Digest* (1971) 104–132.

The same denial of papal infallibility has been explicitly held or endorsed by several other writers, such as Fr. Simons, *Infallibility and the Evidence,* Springfield, Ill. 1968; L. Dewart, *The Foundations of Belief,* New York 1969; R. Schwager, "Vorgegeben und trotzdem frei," *Orienterung* (1970) 227–229, 241–243; B. Tierney, *Origins of Papal Infallibility 1150–1350,* Leiden 1972.

This erroneous doctrine has been explicitly rejected by the *Sacred Congregation for the Doctrine of the Faith* in its *Declaration In Defense of the Catholic Doctrine on the Church Against Certain Errors of the Present Day,* June 24, 1973 (AAS 65 [1973] 400–404). See its commentary in *Civiltà Cattolica* 124 (1973), vol. 3 pp. 139–150, and *Clergy Review* 58 (1973) 944–962.

Moreover, on February 15, 1975 the same Sacred Congregation issued an explicit and direct warning against Küng's opinion (see the text in *Civiltà Cattolica* [1975], vol. 1, pp. 582f.).

121 Cf. Betti, *op. cit.* (above, footnote 69) 627–657; Cauldron, Chavasse, and Thils (cited in footnote 115).

Vatican II simply refers to and integrally confirms this definition (Dogm. Constit. on the Church, no. 18), adding also a short résumé of it, in which it is worth noting a twofold peculiarity, that is, the direct reference to Luke. 22:32 about Peter confirming the brethren in their faith, and the expression "When he proclaims [the doctrine] with a definite act," instead of "When he speaks *'ex cathedra.'*" (No. 25).

The Sacred Congregation for the Doctrine of the Faith has again declared and explained this doctrine, rejecting its erroneous interpretation brought forth by some recent theologians (Declaration in defense of the Catholic Doctrine on the Church against certain errors of the present day, June 24, 1973, *AAS* 65 [1973] 400–404).

Scripture contains the infallibility of the Roman Pontiff (as Peter's successor) implicitly in the two texts (Matt. 16:18f., John 21:15–17; see pp. 304–308), in which the existence of the primacy is explicitly exhibited and from which its fulness is immediately drawn. These three truths, namely, the primacy, its fulness, and its infallibility, are consequent to each other, as implicit to explicit. For, the primacy over the Church would not be purely and simply a primacy, as described in Scripture, if it would not imply the fulness of power, both of jurisdiction and Magisterium, and this power would not be truly and simply full if it were not infallible, because it would lack that indefectibility in faith which has been promised by Christ to the Church (Matt. 28:19f.; John 16:13).

The very analysis of *the four metaphors*, under which the primacy is described, leads to the same conclusion. The Roman Pontiff would not be the *rock* on which the Church is founded if he were not infallible, for faith is one of the essential elements of the Church and, therefore, if the rock fails in faith, the Church fails with it. The *keys* of the kingdom of heaven would be inefficacious, if the doorkeeper could not use them securely by reason of his fallibility in faith, which is one of the gates of this kingdom. The ruler of the Church could not effectively *bind and loose* in matters of faith, if he were fallible in these matters; he would be like the blind man leading the blind. A fallible *shepherd* would be unable to feed the sheep with a safe and certain doctrinal food, nor could a fallible doctor teach the Church, which on the one hand is infallible on account of the assistance promised by Christ

(Matt. 28:19f.; John 16:13) and on the other hand is obliged by the same Christ to listen to this doctor (Luke 10:16).

A direct confirmation of the same conclusion is drawn from the following text of *Luke* 22:31f.: "Simon, Simon, behold, Satan has desired to have thee, that he may sift thee as wheat. But I have prayed for thee, that *thy faith may not fail;* and do thou, when once thou has turned again, *strengthen thy brethren.*"[122] Here Peter's faith is manifestly shown as indefectible and as means of strengthening the faith of others. The only question which could be raised is whether the words refer to Peter as a private person, strengthening the faithful during his life, or as the head of the Church exercising a function to be perpetuated in his successors. This second sense is strongly inculcated by the consideration of two other similar texts. First, by the evident difference between this text and John 17:4, 20, in which Christ prays the Father for all the apostles and the faithful, while here he prays only and directly for Peter. Second, by the striking parallelism between this text and Matt. 16:18f., on the primacy; there it is a question of the "gates of hell [which] shall not prevail" against the Church solidly founded on Peter, the rock, and here it is a question of Satan sifting Peter's faith which will not fail. In both texts Christ makes a special promise to Peter under the form of an affirmation or a prayer: "And I say to thee — But I have prayed for thee."[123]

Tradition does not bring forth the infallibility of the Roman Pontiff with a formal and definite expression, as Vatican I does. This truth is virtually contained in and necessarily derived from two other truths explicitly and currently taught by Tradition, namely,

---

122 In the words "When once thou hast turned again" there is a minor textual difficulty, which, however, has no bearing on our question. Some exegetes (as Lagrange) refer them to Peter's conversion from his future denial during the passion, which is predicted by Christ further below (v. 34f.); some others (as Maldonatus) take the word "turned" (in the Latin version "conversus") in the adverbial sense of "conversely" or vice versa ("And you vice versa, or on your turn, strengthen your brethren in that faith which you once denied").

123 Such a primatial sense is commonly given to this text by the Fathers and the Magisterium. See Ambrose, *On Faith* 4.5; Chrysostom, *On Acts* 3:1–3; Cyril of Alexandria, *On Luke* 22:31f.; Leo I, *Serm.* 4; Gelasius I, *Epist.* 14; Gelasius II, *Epist.* 3; Gregory the Great, *Epist.* 5.20; Agatho, in his epistle to the emperor on the occasion of the Council of Constantinople III; Leo IX in his epistle to Caerularius: Innocent III in his epistle to the patriarch of Constantinople (Denz. 775); Leo XIII, Encycl. "Satis cognitum;" *Vatican Council I* (using the text as a confirmation, without however authentically and directly declaring its primatial sense; Denz. 3070); *Vatican II* (Dogm. Constit. on the Church, no. 25).

that the Church is infallible or indefectible in faith, according to Christ's promise (Matt. 28:19f.; John 16:13), and that this same Church is obliged to agree with the judgment and the doctrine of the Roman Pontiff in matters of faith. From these two premises necessarily follows the conclusion that the Roman Pontiff is infallible, otherwise the Church would be obliged to agree also with a false doctrine taught by the Pope and err with him, which is against the premise of the indefectibility of the Church.

Under the light of these two principles the following clear facts and explicit affirmations acquire their probative and conclusive value, although each one taken separately would not necessarily infer the infallibility of the Roman Pontiff.

1. *The major questions or causes of debate* in matters of faith were often brought to the Roman Pontiff or authoritatively reserved by himself for their final settlement. Such are, among many others, the cases of Pope Victor in the oriental controversy (see p. 317), of Pope Cornelius in the African schism of Felicissimus (p. 319), of the Popes who intervened into the Montanist movement (cf. Tertullian, *Against Praxeas* 1.5), of Pope Dionysius deciding on the orthodoxy of Dionysius archbishop of Alexandria (cf. Athanasius, *On the Doctrine of Dionysius* 13 and 18; Eusebius of Caesarea, *Eccles. Hist.* 7.26), of Pope Julius I rejecting the condemnation of Athanasius by the Council of Antioch (*Epistle to the Antiocheans*, ML 8. 905–908; cf. Denz. 132). All these facts manifest a general persuasion that the final decision in matters of faith or connected with faith belongs to the Roman pontiff, and suggest his infallibility.

2. *All the ecumenical Councils* held in the East, up to the beginning of the oriental schism (9th century), in which matters of faith were principally decided, were celebrated under the influence of the Roman Pontiffs, especially with regard to their final doctrinal decisions (see pp. 323f.). This shows also the doctrinal independence of the Roman Pontiff from the general Councils, and hence from the Church.

3. The Roman Pontiff is called *"The Doctor of truth."* Ignatius of Antioch:" [The Roman Church] teaches and commands" (p. 316); the pseudo-Clementines (3rd century) call the Roman Pontiff "the doctor of truth...[to whom Christ] entrusted the chair of truth" (nos. 2, 17, interpreted by Rufinus, MG 2.35f., 53f.); Peter

Chrysologus: "The Pope of the Roman city...bestows faith to those who seek the truth" (see p. 368).[124]

He is *the rule of faith*. Irenaeus: "It is necessary that with it [i.e., the Roman Church] agree the faithful of every place" (see p. 316); Philip, legate of the Pope at the Council of Ephesus (see p. 323): "Pillar of faith" (which is a direct allusion to 1 Tim. 3:15: "The Church of the living God, pillar and mainstay of the truth").

He is the *arbiter of faith*, whose judgment is final and unappealable. Augustine: "Rome has spoken, the case is closed" (p. 321); Peter Chrysologus: "We, the bishops, cannot judge on questions of faith without the agreement of the bishop of the Roman city" (*Epistle* to Eutyches, founder of Monophysitism, ML 54.743); Innocent I: "Whenever a question of faith is dealt with, all must refer to Peter" (Denz. 218); Boniface I, Gelasius I, and Nicholas I: "The first see is judged by no one" (p. 322).

4. The Fathers testify to the fact that *the Roman See never admitted a single error in faith* and they give as the reason for this Christ's promise included in Peter's primacy (Matt. 16.18). Jerome: "I thought I should consult Peter's chair and the faith enhanced by the apostolic tongue. Only in you the heritage of the Fathers is kept unaltered" (*Epistle* 15, to Damasus Pope, ML 22.355); Pope Hormisdas: "Such words spoken by Christ [Matt. 16.18] are confirmed by the facts, for the Catholic religion has always been kept unspotted in the Apostolic See..., in which the entire and true firmness of the Christian religion is found" (Denz. 363, 365).[125]

Hence one understands the logical self-reliance with which the medieval Popes began to express their infallibility with more explicit formulas, starting from Leo IX who in his epistle of 1053 to Michael Caerularius, founder of the oriental schism, states that the faith of Peter and his successors "has never failed and shall never fail" (Mansi 19.638f.).

---

124 The title *"Doctor of Christians"* was later used by the Councils of Lateran IV, Lyons II, Florence, and Trent. A similar title *"Mother and Teacher"* is given to the Roman Church by the same Councils (Denz. 807, 811, 850, 1699, 1749, 1868) and was used as the title of one of his encyclicals by John XXIII ("Mater et Magistra" 1961).
125 The so-called "Formula of faith of Hormisdas," sent to Constantinople by Hormisdas in 515 to be signed by priests returning to the Church from the schism of Acacius, patriarch of Constantinople, is a very important historical document, as it was commonly accepted in that same century by the Orientals and was later promulgated by the Council of Constantinople IV in 870, shortly before the oriental schism began with Photius. Vatican I quotes the words of this council (Denz. 3066).

In order to solve the objections, which were raised and uniformly repeated through centuries by the various opponents of the papal infallibility, and are now again being circulated by daring dissenters among Catholic scholars, notice the following.

1. The infallibility of the Roman Pontiff is in no way *opposed or detrimental to the infallibility of the Church or of the ecumenical Councils.* As will be explained below (pp. 349f.), the Church's general infallibility has three different subjects, namely, the believing Church, the teaching Church through the Councils, and the teaching Church through the Pope. Each of these is infallible in its own manner and in its own order, without confusion or opposition.

2. *The old and repeated dissent* against papal infallibility in the Catholic Church does not prove that it is not a part of the revealed truth or is not contained in a perpetually consistent Tradition. It only shows that this is a truth not formally and explicitly, but only equivalently or implicitly revealed, and hence it was naturally subject to intermittent denial or doubt for various doctrinal and political reasons. Furthermore, this dissent is not very old, nor general, nor decisive. It started in the 14th century with the secular Caesaropapism, attacking the primacy itself rather than its infallibility; it developed rapidly in the 15th century, favored by the confused condition of the Western Schism, striking likewise at the primacy itself; it quickly expired with the expiration of the schism in the Council of Constance (1414–1418). It revived again, supported by the political power and clothed in ambiguous formulas, within the general nationalistic reclamations of Gallicanism and likewise disappeared quickly with the political power itself. Its last revival appeared within and without the Vatican Council I at the time of the definition, lasted hardly a year or two, and had only the sad result that a small group of dissenters withdrew from the Church and formed the congregation of the so-called Old Catholics. After the explicit definition of papal infallibility by the Vatican Council and the peaceful possession of the truth by the universal Church for a full century, there is no room or dogmatic excuse for the daring dissenters of the present progressive age, who wander about like a sterile group of New Catholics.

3. *The historical cases of errors made by some of the Roman Pontiffs,* particularly by Liberius, Vigilius, and Honorius, involve a historical and canonical question rather than a dogmatic difficulty. For

in all of them it is a question either of an uncertain historical fact, or of a matter prevalently disciplinary, or of a doctrine proposed not definitively and *ex cathedra*.

Liberius (†366), after firmly defending the faith against Arianism, through pressure and exile was compelled to endorse the Arian formula of faith. However, scholars do not agree on whether he really endorsed any Arian formula at all, and if so, whether this was the truly heretical formula of the Anomoeans, that is, the pure Arians who simply denied the divine nature of the Word, or the ambiguous formula of the Semi-Arians, followers of Basil of Ancyra, who taught only that the Word is similar to the Father, a doctrine which could be understood in a Catholic sense. Even if he endorsed the first formula, nothing proves that the required condition for a definition *ex cathedra* are found in his action; his renewed opposition to Arianism after his exile shows rather the opposite.

Vigilius (†555), after opposing the Council of Constantinople II for condemning the so-called Three Chapters (that is, the writings of Theodore of Mopsuesta, Theodoret of Cyrus, and Ibas, bishop of Edessa), was brought to Constantinople, ill-treated, and excommunicated by that Council, and finally approved its decisions. However, his previous opposition concerned a disciplinary matter, that is, the opportuneness of condemning the authors of those Nestorian writings, already dead, while his subsequent approbation concerned the renewed condemnation of the Nestorian heresy.

The case of *Honorius* (†638) is apparently more difficult, inasmuch as in his letter to Sergius, patriarch of Constantinople, he seemed to encourage this heretic to spread Monothelitism, that is, a doctrine denying the human will of Christ; this doctrine was afterwards solemnly condemned by the Council of Constantinople III (680–681; see above, p. 324). However, from the simple analysis of the letters sent by Honorius to Sergius it clearly appears that he did not intend to define anything, but only suggested to Sergius not to speak either of one or of two wills in Christ and to leave out such questions as irrelevant. In this he failed in two ways; first through lack of natural shrewdness, which prevented him from seeing that he was ill-informed by Sergius about the controversy on the human will of Christ, and secondly through lack of prudence for not inquiring any further into the matter. It is true that the Council of Constantinople III condemned the already-deceased

Honorius as heretical, but Leo II in his confirmation of this Council explained that this condemnation was to be understood not in the sense of a formal heresy on the part of Honorius, but of a grave pollution of the immaculate Church, inasmuch as through his action Honorius helped to spread the heresy.[126] Other minor cases of alleged papal errors are not worth mentioning.[127]

Note 1. *On the threefold subject of infallibility*

We have spoken only of the infallibility of the Pope, as being the principal infallibility of the Church. However, the ecumenical Council is also infallible in teaching, and likewise the universal Church, as the congregation of faithful, is infallible or indefectible in believing. Hence there are *two kinds of infallibility*, that is, one *in teaching* (which is called active) and the other *in believing* (which is called passive, only in opposition to the other), and there are *three subjects* endowed with infallibility, i.e., *the Pope, the ecumenical Council*, and *the Church* as a whole (to which also the Pope and the Council belong, considered merely as faithful).[128]

Since the active and passive infallibility are formally distinct, also their subjects are formally and adequately distinct, although

---

126 Cf. E. Amann, "Honorius Ier," *Dictionnaire de théologie catholique* 7-1 (Paris 1927) 93–132.

127 This applies also to the case of the condemnation of the astronomer *Galileo Galilei*, which has been so much publicized by reason of its modern appeal and its fitness for anti-Catholic propaganda. Galileo, holding the new theory of the rotation of the earth around the sun, was condemned as "suspected with heresy" by a decree of the Holy Office under Urban VIII in 1633. This condemnation *was not a direct act of the Pope*, much less a definition *ex Cathedra*, but a declaration of the fallible Holy Office, although acting under the general approbation of the Pope. Furthermore, the reason and the object of the condemnation was not the theory itself, but its presumed implications in the explanation of the texts of the Holy Scripture; hence the *question was disciplinary rather than doctrinal*.

The Holy Office may have failed for lack of natural perspicacity in judging that theory as necessarily implying an opposition to the sense of the biblical texts, and also for lack of prudence in mingling prematurely with questions directly scientific in themselves. But it is not fair to harshly and hastily condemn a decision issued by the Sacred Congregation for the sole purpose of protecting the Holy Scripture from profane intrusions, at a time when the heliocentric theory was still a mere hypothesis, rejected by many. On the part of the Holy Office there was merely a mistake, maybe also an act of excusable imprudence; nothing else.

Cf. E. Vacandard, "Galilée," *Dictionnaire de théologie catholique* 6-1 (Paris 1947) 1058–1094; Journet, *op. cit.* (above, footnote 115) 457–462.

128 About the nature of the passive infallibility see our treatise on *The Channels of Revelation*, pp. 188f. See also Vatican II, Dogm. Constit. on the Church, no. 12, and the Sacred Congregation for the Doctrine of the Faith, Declaration about the doctrine on the Church, June 24, 1973.

Pope and Council, materially and individually considered, are part of the subject of passive infallibility. On the contrary the two subjects of the active infallibility are not adequately distinct, since the Pope is the head of the defining Council and a body cannot be without the head.

There is, however, a further *question disputed* among the theologians, as to whether the Pope and the Council are *two distinct and immediate subjects of infallibility*, or only one, namely, the Pope, who defines either along or together with the bishops.[129] The first opinion holds that there are two subjects, on the ground that Christ promised infallibility not only to Peter but also to the apostolic college as a whole (Matt. 18:18; 28:20) and that it is difficult to understand how infallibility could derive from the Pope into the bishops, and how each bishop would really be a judge in a conciliar definition (thus Franzelin, Pesch, De Guilbert, Ruffino, Betti, Gagnebet[130]). The second opinion teaches that the Pope is the only immediate subject of active infallibility, because he is the only head of the Church, the rock on which the entire Church rests, the pastor guiding all the faithful, even the bishops as assembled and defining in Council (thus Palmieri, Billot, Straub, Zapelena, Lattanzi[131]).

This second opinion seems more logical and probable, otherwise there would be two distinct supreme powers in the same society. Hence the Pope, even in the Council and acting in a collegiate manner with the other bishops, defines as a Pope, that is, as the supreme head of the Church, and not as one of the bishops, merely presiding over the Council. However, such a conciliar definition is not equivalent to the papal definition *ex cathedra*, because the Pope can define either alone, that is, *ex cathedra*, or together with the bishops and with their juridical cooperation, that is, through a real conciliar action. Hence, instead of saying that the Council is infallible because the Pope in the Council is infallible, we should

---

129   This question regards not only the subject of infallibility, but generically the subject of the supreme power in the Church, of which infallibility is a particular and outstanding property.

130   R. Gagnebet, "De duplici subiecto unicae potestatis supremae," *Acta Congressus Internationalis de theologica Concilii Vaticani II, Romae 1966 celebrati* (Typis Polyglottis Vaticanis 1968) 118–128.

131   U. E. Lattanzi, "Episcopalis Collegii ad Papam relatio," *Acta Congressus Internationalis de theologia Concilii Vaticani II, Romae 1966 celebrati* (Typis Polyglottis Vaticanis 1968) 136–145.

properly say: The Council is infallible, because, on account of its union with the Pope, it shares in the very papal infallibility.[132]

Note 2. *On the twofold manner in which the active infallibility is exercised, that is, through the extraordinary and the ordinary Magisterium*[133]

We have briefly explained above (p. 296f.) the nature and the immediate properties of the power of Magisterium. Here we complete its treatment, considering its division into extraordinary and ordinary Magisterium[134] and its peculiar property of infallibility.[135]

The Magisterium is called *extraordinary or solemn* by reason of the extraordinary manner in which it teaches a doctrine, with regard both to the material (or verbal) expression and especially to the formal expression of the authoritative judgment, inasmuch as this proceeds in an absolute and decisive manner. Otherwise it is called *ordinary*. Hence the difference between the two is only accidental, although it has a great practical importance as to our knowledge of the obligatory doctrine, which is much easier to distinguish when proposed by the extraordinary Magisterium.

The extraordinary Magisterium is found both in the Pope and in the bishops. The Pope exercises it through the more solemn documents called Encyclicals, Bulls, and Constitutions. The bishops exercise it through a collegiate action in union with the Pope, either within an ecumenical Council (as it has been usually done up to the present time), or without a formal Council, by an equivalent

---

132   There is still a *third opinion*, already proposed by some of the Fathers in Vatican I and again revived by a few theologians after Vatican II by reason of the collegiality taught by this Council. According to this opinion, the immediate subject of infallibility and of the supreme power in the Church is only one; however, it is not the Pope, but the episcopal college, in which the Pope acts as head and the others as members, so that even when the Pope defines *ex cathedra*, he defines as the head of the college. In other words, the supreme power in the Church is essentially collegial or composed, in which Pope and bishops have their respective part.

On this opinion, as it was proposed in Vatican I, see J. Hamer, in *Revue des sciences philosophiques et théologiques* (1961) 21–31. On the same, as proposed by recent writers (as Rahner, Dejaifve, Schillebeeckx, and Congar), see Y. Congar, in *Estudios eclesiásticos* (1970) 408–415.

133   Cf. Caudron, Fenton, and Nau, cited above, footnote 115.

134   The distinction of these two kinds of Magisterium is clearly brought forth by Vatican I (Sess. 3, chap. 3, Denz. 3011) and Pius XII (Encycl. "Humani generis," Denz. 3885). Vatican I teaches also the infallibility of the ordinary Magisterium (*ibid.*).

135   In the treatise on *The Channels of Revelation* (pp. 197–206.) we have shown that the Magisterium is the channel or organ of revelation and, when it defines infallibly, it becomes also the proximate rule of faith.

action, that is, a direct and concordant consultation with the Pope (which mode, very rare in past times, might become more frequent and may prove more effective in the future, by reason of practical difficulties inherent to the celebration of general Councils).

The ordinary Magisterium is also found both in the Pope and in the bishops.[136] The Pope exercises it through allocutions, radiophonic pronouncements, particular epistles to individual cardinals, or bishops, or societies, and also indirectly through the decisions of the Roman Congregations. The bishops exercise it by their individual action in each diocese, instructing the faithful, either directly through pastoral letters, allocutions, declarations, or through others, as pastors, theologians, catechists, writers.

This division of the Magisterium into extraordinary and ordinary does not correspond to the other division into *infallible and noninfallible* Magisterium, for both the extraordinary and the ordinary Magisterium can be either infallible or noninfallible, both in the Pope and in the bishops.[137] In all cases the Magisterium is infallible if it teaches authoritatively and definitively a doctrine as a revealed truth to be held with divine faith. As regards the bishops assembled in a Council with the Pope, their extraordinary Magisterium is not necessarily infallible; thus Vatican I defined several doctrines infallibly, while Vatican II, as far as it can be ascertained, defined nothing infallibly. As regards the Pope, only those documents are infallible which contain the four notes of a definition *ex cathedra*; these, however, can be found not only in those more solemn encyclicals that are usually called definitions *ex cathedra*, like the definitions of the Immaculate Conception and the Assumption, but also in some other outstanding encyclicals, as long as it can be ascertained that the Pope is authoritatively teaching a doctrine as revealed and as to be held with divine faith. This is not always easy to ascertain (see pp. 355–357).

---

136   One or another recent theologian (particularly Caudron, *loc. cit.*, in footnote 115) denies that the Pope exercises also an ordinary Magisterium and attributes this only to the bishops. But Pius XII himself makes an explicit distinction between extraordinary and ordinary Magisterium in papal documents (Encycl. "Humani generis," Denz. 3885).

137   Cf. F. A. Sullivan, "On the Infallibility of the Episcopal College in the Ordinary Exercise of Its Teaching Office," *Acta Congressus Internationalis de theologia Concilii Vaticani II, Romae 1966 celebrati* (Typis Polyglottis Vaticanis 1968) 189–195; A. B. Vaughan, "The Role of the Ordinary Magisterium of the Universal Episcopate," *Proceedings of the Catholic Theological Society of America* 22 (1967) 1–19.

Note 3. *On the twofold object of infallibility*[138]

The object of the Magisterium, whether infallible or not infallible, is generically speaking revelation (called technically deposit of faith, doctrine of faith, doctrine of faith and morals). Since the main function of the Magisterium about revelation is twofold, that is, to propose it and to guard it, its object also is twofold. The principal and direct object is the revealed truth itself, which for this reason is called *formally revealed* (either explicitly or implicitly). The secondary, indirect, and extensive object whatever may be intrinsically connected with revelation, which for this reason is called *virtually revealed;*[139] this connection with revelation, or virtual inclusion in it, is either an internal connection of logical inference, and then the virtually revealed is a *theological conclusion,* or merely an external and practical connection, and then the virtually revealed is called a *dogmatic fact.*[140]

The object of *infallibility* extends as far as the object of the Magisterium itself; it is, therefore, both the formally revealed and the virtually revealed.

As regards the *formally revealed,* the infallibility of the Magisterium is *de fide,* at least implicitly defined by Vatican I in the definition of the infallibility of the Pope which is said to be about "the doctrine of faith or morals;" it is also explicitly confirmed by Pius XII in his encyclical "Humani generis" (Denz. 3884–3886) and

---

138   See what has been said about dogma and theological conclusions in the treatise on *The Channels of Revelation,* pp. 203–222.

139   The extension of the Magisterium to this object is shown both from its connection with revelation and from the fact that the Church condemned several philosophical doctrines not agreeing with revelation, as those of Rationalism, Semirationalism, and Modernism (Denz. 2858–2861, 3018, 3042, 3405, 3407, 3425). It is also explicitly declared by Pius XII (Denz. 3886).

140   The nature of theological conclusions and of dogmatic facts as well as their connection with revelation has been expounded in the treatise on *The Channels of Revelation,* pp. 216–222.

A *dogmatic fact* in itself is not a doctrine, but a fact which is inferred from a revealed truth by reason of an extrinsic connection with it, inasmuch as the revealed truth cannot be suitably explained and kept without it. In this sense it has to be reduced to a theological conclusion, as we explained in that same treatise (p. 221).

It is divided into *historical fact,* on which the very transmission of the revealed truth depends, such as the legitimacy of a Pope or a Council, and *doctrinal fact,* which involves an implicit judgment about the revealed truth, that is, about the connection of something with revelation: such are *the dogmatic text* (i.e., the judgment about the orthodoxy or heterodoxy of a particular writing according to the mind of its author), *disciplinary decrees, canonization of saints,* and *approbation of religious orders.*

by Vatican II (Dogm. Constit. on the Church, no. 25); it follows, furthermore, from the simple reason that, if the Magisterium is infallible about anything, this is at least and primarily about its principal object, namely, revelation.

As regards the *virtually revealed*, the infallibility of the Magisterium has not been infallibly defined as yet; hence it is not *de fide*. It is, however, *theologically certain*, and even proximate to faith, as is evident from its intrinsic connection with the revealed truth, for the Magisterium cannot infallibly declare and keep the revealed truth, unless it be infallible also about those things which are intimately connected with it and whose denial would logically infer the denial of the revealed truth itself.

This connection is evident in *theological conclusions*, which are linked with revelation by a necessary logical bond.

It is also evident in the various *dogmatic facts*.[141] Indeed, if the Church were not infallible in declaring a *historical fact*, such as the legitimacy of a Pope or of a Council, it could accept their definitions as truths of faith and thus err about the revealed truth.[142] Likewise, if the Church were not infallible about *doctrinal facts*, that is, dogmatic texts, disciplinary decrees, canonization of saints, and approbation of religious orders, it could propose to the faithful something to be done or held which is opposed to the revealed truth. In the judgment about a *dogmatic text*, that is, about the orthodoxy or heterodoxy of an author, the knowledge of the revealed truth is involved.[143] The *disciplinary decrees* (especially the universal ones, as canon law and liturgy) have doctrinal foundation and they are made according to the principles of faith and morality. In *canonization*[144] the Church definitely declares that a man has led a holy life in harmony with the evangelical principles of perfection, that he is now in heaven, and that he

---

141   See preceding footnote.
142   As noted above (p. 312), the succession of the bishop of Rome in Peter's primacy is also a dogmatic historical fact.
143   About the famous case of the condemnation of the doctrines contained in the work *Augustinus* by *Cornelius Jansenius* (cf. Denz. 2012), which gave birth to the expression "dogmatic fact," see our treatise on *The Channels of Revelation*, p. 222; J. Carreyre, "Jansénisme," *Dictionnaire de théologie catholique* 8-1 (Paris 1923) 500–522; A. Gits, *La foi ecclésiastique aux faits dogmatiques dan la théologie moderne*, Louvain 1940.
144   Cf. F.-J. Rieda, "Infallibility of the Pope in his Decree of Canonization," *Jurist* 6 (1946) 401–415; E.-W. Kemp, *Canonization and Authority in the Western Church*, London 1948.

can be an object of cult, of prayers, and imitation.[145] By the *final approbation of religious orders* the Church judges on the conformity of their rules with the doctrine of faith and morals, as well as their aptitude to lead their members to Christian perfection.

It is disputed among theologians, whether the virtually revealed, once infallibly defined by the Church, is believed with divine faith (like the formally revealed itself) or only with a so-called *ecclesiastical faith*. We examined this question in the treatise on *The Channels of Revelation* (pp. 217–222), showing that also the virtually revealed becomes necessarily an object of divine faith.

Note 4. *On the means of knowing whether a particular declaration of the Magisterium is an infallible definition*[146]

The Magisterium in its declarations does not use, and is not bound to use, any particular and explicit formula.[147] Hence the infallible character of a definition must be gathered either from the type of its formulation or from its circumstances.[148]

The surest *formulas* are those in which the Magisterium explicitly or equivalently declares that a doctrine is a revealed truth, or must be believed,[149] or that the contrary doctrine is a heresy, or deserves the anathema.[150] Such expressions are found together or

---

145 *Beatification*, on the contrary, is not a final judgment, but a preparation and a step toward the final judgment of canonization. Hence it is not an object of infallibility. This is the reason why the Pope, after examining the miracles attributed to the one who has been beatified, declares in his decree "de tuto" that the final step of canonization can be safely taken.

146 Cf. C. M. Berti, S. M. Meo, H. M. Toniolo *De ratione ponderandi documenta Magisterii ecclesiastici*, Romae 1961. A criticism of the current valuation of the documents of the Magisterium by theologians is brought forth by B. Sesboüé, "Autorité du Magistère et vie de foi ecclésiale," *Nouvelle revue théologique* 93 (1971) 337–362.

147 Undoubtedly the constant use of a technical or unequivocal formula would be in full harmony with modern mentality and very useful to theologians, who often wonder and dispute whether a solemn documents bears the seal of infallibility. Cf. Fr. M. Bauducco, in *Antonianum* 37 (1962) 395.

148 Vatican II, speaking of the declarations of the Roman Pontiff, states that they must be interpreted "according to the mind and will manifested by him, which is known principally from the character of the documents, or from the frequent presentation of the same doctrine, or from the manner of its verbal expression" (Dogm. Constit. on the Church, no. 25).

149 This is equivalently signified also in the fact that the Church proposes a doctrine under the form of a *profession of faith*. Such are, for instance, the Symbols of faith brought forth by the Councils of Nicaea I and Constantinople I, and by Pius IV (Denz. 125, 150, 1862–1870).

150 The term "anathema" per se means generically separation from the Church; hence in disciplinary canons it means solemn excommunication, and in doctrinal

separately in the canons of Trent and Vatican I and in the encyclicals on the Immaculate Conception and Assumption, which are undoubtedly infallible definitions.

When such formulas are wanting, there remain only two ways of discerning, with lesser or greater probability, the infallible character of a definition. The first is the valuation of the various circumstances accompanying the definition; these make evident, for instance, the infallible character of the definitions of the Councils of Ephesus, Chalcedon, Constantinople II and III. The second is the *judgment of the theologians*, which, however, is quite various and hesitant, as is to be expected; hence the infallibility of one and same document is admitted or denied or questioned by different authors. In view of the uncertainty, resulting from both the valuation of the circumstances and the judgment of the theologians, we may classify among doubtful infallible definitions: the decisions of the Council of Constance against Wyclif and Hus, the Decree for the Armenians by the Council of Florence, the Bull of Leo X against Luther, the Bull of Pius VI against the Council of Pistoia, the encyclical "Quanta cura" and the Syllabus[151] of Pius IX, the encyclical "Pascendi" against Modernism by Pius X, the encyclical "Casti connubii" of Pius XI, the encyclicals "Mystici Corporis" and "Humani generis," and the constitution "Sacramentum Ordinis" of Pius XII.[152]

---

canons, as those of Trent and Vatican I, it means also implicitly the note of heresy. This is the common judgment of the theologians about the canons of these two councils; it has been questioned without sufficient foundation by a few recent authors, as R. Favre, in *Bulletin de littérature ecclésiastique* 47 (1946) 226–241; 48 (1947) 31–48; A Lang, in *Münchener Theologische Zeitschrift* 4 (1953) 133–146; P. Fransen, in *Scholastik* 25 (1950) 492–517; 26 (1951) 191–221; 27 (1952) 526–556; in *Ephemerides theologicae Lovanienses* 29 (1953) 657–672; in *Bijdragen* 14 (1953) 363–387; Z. Alszeghy, M. Flick, in *Magistero e morale* (Bologna 1970) 128–133; in *Gregorianum* 52 (1971) 599, 627. This new opinion is examined and refuted by F. Garcia Martinez, in *Revista española de teologia* 15 (1955) 637–653.

151 Regarding the widely discussed infallible character of this very important document, on which several of the definitions of Vatican I are based, see L. Brigué, "Syllabus," *Dictionnaire de théologie catholique* 14-2 (Paris 1941) 2877–2923.

152 *Vatican II* seems to have issued no infallible definition whatsoever. To the principal dogmatic Constitution on the Church the following declaration of the Theological Commission was officially appended: "In view of conciliar procedures and of the pastoral purpose of the present Council, this Holy Synod defines, as things of faith and morals to be held by the Church, only those which it openly declares to be such." As a matter of fact no declaration of this kind is found, even in the principal section of chapter 3, that is, nos. 18–22, in which the important doctrine on episcopacy is expounded. Cf. U. Betti and J. Ratzinger, in *L'Eglise de*

Moreover, once the infallible character of a definition has been established, three things remain to be determined, namely, its extension, or the parts which are infallibly defined, its proper and direct object, and its formulation or the exact meaning of the words, as we explained in the treatise on *The Channels of Revelation* (pp. 198–201).

Note 5. *On the quality of the assent due to the definitions of the Magisterium, both infallible and non-infallible*[153]

Since the Magisterium can define, either infallibly or non-infallibly, both the formally revealed and the virtually revealed, three cases must be distinguished.

The infallible definition of a truth *formally revealed* obliges to the assent of *divine faith*, under pain of losing this same theological virtue. As we explained in the treatise on *The Channels of Revelation* (pp. 198, 206f.), such a definition becomes a proximate rule of faith and a condition of the object of faith, which is then properly called dogma, that is, a truth revealed by God and proposed by the Magisterium.

The infallible definition of a truth or fact only *virtually revealed* (see above, p. 354) obliges likewise to the assent of *divine faith*, at least according to the more probable opinion which we chose in the treatise on *The Channels of Revelation* (pp. 287f.); however other theologians are satisfied with the so-called ecclesiastical faith, in which supposition there is no reason why a dissenter would be heretical and lose the theological virtue of faith.

Every other *non-infallible definition* of the Magisterium[154] obliges seriously to a *religious assent*, both *external*, and *per se internal*, shown at least by a *prudential and opinative manner of*

Vatican II (dir. G. Barauna, French edition by M-J. Congar, Paris 1966), vol. 2, pp. 211–218; vol. 3, pp. 787–790.

153   Cf. Journet, *op. cit.* (above, footnote 115) 451–462; Fr. M. Bauducco, "Quale assenso si debba ad alcuni documenti del magistero ecclesiastico," *Antonianum* 37 (1962) 393–399.

154   The Magisterium here is taken integrally, for the episcopal as well as the papal teaching authority. The papal Magisterium itself is understood both for the one exercised immediately by the Pope and for the one exercised through the Roman Congregations, whose decrees are approved by the Pope either in a generic manner ("in forma communi"), when they are issued under the proper name of the Congregation, or in a specific manner ("in forma specifica"), when they are issued in the name and authority of the Pope himself.

judgment.[155] This religious assent is distinct from the assent of divine faith, both as to its principle, which is not the virtue of faith but the virtue of religion, and as to its object, which is not God's word but the word of the Church having its teaching authority from God. It implies abstention from any external manifestation of dissent. It implies also an internal act of compliance, both of the will and of the mind, adhering to the doctrine of the Magisterium as true and certain if one sees no founded reason for the opposite doctrine, or adhering to it as more probable and practically safer if one sees a founded reason for the opposite. This is the prudential and opinative way of judging, required *per se.* But, since it is a question of non-infallible Magisterium in which an error is possible, in the rare case in which a man is truly and objectively certain of such an error, then *per accidens* he morally can, and psychologically must, withdraw his judgment and interiorly dissent, because presumption or doubt must necessarily yield to truth.

---

155   This assertion is *certain*, being explicitly endorsed by the Magisterium. Besides proposing *generically* the obligation of accepting the decrees of the Magisterium (Vatican I, Denz. 3045; repeated by Pius XII, Denz. 3884), the *external assent* is emphasized by Pius XII (Denz. 3885) and the *internal assent* itself by Pius X (Denz. 4307, 3503) and Vatican II, stating: "Bishops, teaching in communion with the Roman Pontiff must be revered by all as witnesses to divine and Catholic truth; the faithful must agree with the teaching of their Bishop in matters of faith and morals and adhere to it with a *religious submission of the soul. This religious obedience of the will and of the mind* must be paid particularly to the authentic Magisterium of the Roman Pontiff, also when he does not speak *ex cathedra*" (Dogm. Constit. on the Church, no. 25).

9

Divine Origin of the Episcopacy[156]

WE NOTED ABOVE (P. 301) THAT CHRIST INSTI-
tuted the apostleship, that is, a group of twelve to whom He
entrusted the office of founding the Church. We also distinguished
in the same apostles two functions, that is, the apostleship properly so-called, having for its purpose the founding of the Church,
and the pontificate, having the power of ruling the Church once
founded. Then in chapter 5 we proved that in the line of pontificate Christ chose among the twelve apostles Peter, to whom

---

156   The recent and particular bibliography about the collegial nature of the epis-
copacy will be given in the following chapter (footnote 167).
  Anciaux, P., L'episcopat dans l'Eglise, Bruges 1963.
  Barlêa, O., Die Weihe der Bischoefe, Presbyter und Diakone in vornicaenischer Zeit,
München 1969.
  Benoit, P., "Les origines de l'episcopat dans le Nouveau Testament," Exégese
et théologie 2 (Paris 1961) 232–246; "Les origines apostoliques de l'épiscopat,"
L'évêque dans l'Eglise du Christ (Paris 1963) 13–57.
  Betti, U., La dottrina sull'Episcopato nel capitolo III della constituzione dommatica
Lumen Gentium, Roma 1968.
  Colson, J., L'evêque dans les communautés primitives, Paris 1951; Les fonctions ecclé-
siales aux deux premiers siècles, Paris 1954.
  Doronzo, E., De Ordine 1 (Milwaukee 1957) 82–489, 612–962.
  Dupuy, B-D., "La théologie de l'épiscopat," Revue des sciences philosophiques et
théologiques 49 (1965) 288–342.
  Eglises chrétiennes et épiscopat (collective work), Tours 1966.
  Episcopat (L') et l'Eglise universelle (collective work, ed. Y. Congar, B.-D. Dupuy),
Paris 1962.
  Evêque (L') dans l'Eglise du Christ (collective work), Paris 1963.
  Lécuyer, J., "Episcopat," Dictionnaire de spiritualité 4 (Paris 1960) 879–907;
"Orientations présentes de la théologie de l'épiscopat," L'Episcopat et l'Eglise univer-
selle (Paris 1962) 781–812; "La triple charge de l'évêque," L'Eglise de Vatican II (dir.
G. Barauna, French edition by Y. M.-J. Congar, Paris 1966), vol. 3, pp. 893–914;
"La succession des évêques d'Alexandrie aux premiers siècles," Bulletin de littérature
ecclésiastique, n. 2 (1969) 81–99.
  Michiels, A., L'origine de l'épiscopat, Louvain 1900.
  Rahner, K., "Ueber den Episkopat," Zeichen der Zeit (1963–64) 161–195;
(Ratzinger, J.), Episkopat und Primat, Freiburg i. Br. 1961.
  XVI Semana Española de teologia: Problemas de actualidad sobre la sucesión apostólica,
Madrid 1957. XXII Semana Española de teologia: Teologia del episcopado, Madrid 1963.
  Torrell, J.-P., La théologie de l'épiscopat au premier Concile du Vatican, Paris 1961;
"Les grandes lignes de la théologie de l'épiscopat au Concile du Vatican. Le point
de vue officiel," Salesianum 24 (1962) 266–282.

He gave the primacy over the other apostles and over the entire Church, a primacy to be lasting forever through Peter's successors; and in chapter 6 we showed that Peter's successors are the Roman Pontiffs. Now the question arises whether also the subordinate pontificate of the other apostles was to be perpetuated, by divine right or by the will of Christ. More exactly and concretely we ask: whether by the will of Christ there are in the Church, *besides and under the Roman Pontiff, other hierarchs*, having their proper and ordinary power of ruling and teaching, those who since the origins have been given the technical name of bishops.[157]

The ecclesiological doctrine on episcopacy, recently completed by the Vatican Council II, involves two other questions besides the divine origin of the episcopacy, namely, about its collegial nature and its monarchic form, which will be expounded in the two following chapters. In these three chapters we consider episcopacy only under the aspect of the double ruling power of jurisdiction and Magisterium; the third ministerial power of Orders will be considered in chapter 12, in the general question of the three degrees of the hierarchy of Orders.

---

157 We express the question with these terms because the divine origin of the bishops is not necessarily bound to their succession to the apostles, for they could have been instituted by Christ just as pastors of the Church, without being successors of the apostles, who would have had a personal general power in the Church, not to be transmitted to others. Such is precisely the opinion held by a few older theologians, as Bellarmine (*On the Roman Pontiff*, book 1, chaps. 9 and 11; book 4, chap. 23) and Suárez (*On Faith*, disp. 10, sect. 1, nos. 4 and 12). However, the common teaching of the theologians, supported by the documents of the Magisterium, holds that the bishops are instituted by Christ, also formally as successors of the apostles. On this question see Journet, *op. cit.* (above, footnote 115) 492–499.

As regards *the name "bishop,"* derived from the Latin "episcopus," note the following. The original Greek word "episcopos" (from "epi," above, and "scopéin," to inspect, to observe) etymologically means inspector or observer. It was soon given an authoritative meaning and it commonly signified superintendent, prefect, president, judge, in the profane as well as in the biblical patristic literature.

In the O.T. (Greek version or Greek original text) the word occurs at least fourteen times, and in two places God himself is called bishop (Job 20:29, where the Greek version has "episcopos" as a translation of the Hebrew "El," which is the name of God; Wisd. [Greek original] 1:6: "God is the witness [episcopos] of his inmost self"). In the N.T. it occurs five times, namely, Acts 20:28; Phil. 1:1; 1 Tim. 3:2; Tit. 1:7; 1 Pet. 2:25; in the first four places it designates the head of a particular Christian church and in the last Christ himself, called "bishop of your souls" (the English version has: Guardian of your souls"). In the patristic literature since the second century (as is clear from the epistles of Ignatius of Antioch) it became the technical name of the head of a particular Christian church, even in the sense of monarchic bishop.

Statement. *Episcopacy, generically considered, is of divine origin, that is, Christ Himself established that, besides and under the Roman Pontiff, there be in the Church other hierarchs, who, as successors of the apostles, hold their proper and ordinary power of ruling and teaching.*

Theological note. This statement has not yet been defined as *de fide* by the extraordinary Magisterium, but it has been so constantly and decisively taught by it, especially after Vatican I, that it is a Catholic doctrine, at least *theologically certain* and proximately definable.[158]

---

158   The divine origin of episcopacy is radically denied by all those who deny the very social nature of the Church, as *Modernists* and *Liberal Protestants*, or its hierarchical constitution, as *Orthodox Protestants* (see above, footnote 42).

Among Orthodox Protestants, episcopacy is more directly rejected by the *Presbyterians*, who teach absolute equality among Christian ministers. The Anglicans, the American Episcopalians, and the Scandinavian Lutherans, admit episcopacy to be of divine institution only in the general sense of an undetermined "essential ministry," distinct from a secondary and undetermined "dependent ministry," both however deprived of true authority and provided only with a kind of managing and directive function. See our Latin work *De Ordine* 1 (Milwaukee 1957) 131–170, 623–625; I. Asheim and V. R. Gold (eds), *Episcopacy in the Lutheran Church? Studies in the Development and Definition of the Office of Church, Leadership*, Philadelphia 1970.

Midway between orthodox and liberals are found several moderate recent Protestants, such as E. Brunner, R. Bultmann, K. Barth, and O. Cullmann, whose general teaching about the social structure of the Church has been indicated above (footnote 42). In particular Barth teaches that the external element of the Church should be reduced to a minimum and true authority expelled, for all episcopal or presbyteral system is rather harmful to Christ's Church (see *Désordre de l'homme et dessein de Dieu* 1 [1949] 95–107), Cullmann teaches that the pontifical authority, of both Peter and the other apostles, was a mere historical fact, or a temporary power, not to be transmitted to any successors (see above, footnotes 71 and 75).

The historical rise of the episcopacy in the Church is generically explained through a natural evolution of the primitive charismatic Church into a hierarchic Church, which gave birth to the monarchic episcopate itself. There are three more specific theories.

The first teaches a *monarchic evolution*. That is, since the beginning the various churches chose or accepted, as their rector, one influential man, who later grew in authority until he became a true monarchic bishop (thus F.-C. Baur and J.-B. Lightfoot).

The second opinion holds an *oligarchic evolution*. That is, at the beginning Christian communities were ruled in common by a college of presbyters, until one of these prevailed, marking the distinction of one bishop and a college of presbyters (thus K. Weizsaecher and A. Ritschl), or the communities were ruled by two colleges of bishops and presbyters until these mingled into one from which later rose the bishop (thus E. Hatch and A. Harnack).

The third opinion teaches a *democratic evolution*. That is, the primitive church was merely charismatic, ruled only by the Holy Spirit through charisms, and hence a charismatic anarchic democracy. Afterwards the spiritual rights of the community were given up into the hands of a few or a college of presbyters, which constituted an oligarchy. Finally the rights of the college passed into the hands of one

The Magisterium has solemnly declared this doctrine especially in the three Councils of Trent, Vatican I, and Vatican II. Other minor documents will be named below.

The Council of Trent teaches that, among other degrees, the bishops principally belong to the ecclesiastical hierarchy and are superior to the priests, having *"succeeded in the place of apostles"* and *"having been placed by the Holy Spirit to govern the Church of God"* (Sess. 23, chap. 4, Denz. 1768). It also defines as *de fide:* "If anyone shall say, that in the Catholic Church there is no hierarchy, *instituted by divine ordinance,* which is made up of bishops, presbyters and ministers: let him be anathema" (Can. 6, Denz. 1776).

The Council's doctrine and definition concern directly the episcopacy only as a power of Orders, as is evident from the mention of other degrees, that is, presbyters and ministers (inferior orders); but indirectly it reaches also the power of jurisdiction, as follows from the general character of the words expressing the apostolic succession in the government of the Church. It is true, however, that from this Tridentine doctrine and definition, as it stands, the divine origin of the episcopacy, as a power of jurisdiction, cannot be inferred directly and with certainty. The full implication of the definition (can. 6) will be given below (pp. 391f.).

Vatican I directly teaches, although in passing and without defining, that *"Christ willed* that there be shepherds and doctors in the Church unto the consummation of the world, just as He sent the apostles, whom He had chosen" (Sess. 4, prologue, Denz. 3050). It also determines, again cursorily but clearly and specifically, the apostolic origin and the proper nature of the episcopal power of

---

monarchic bishop; hence the evolution consisted in a double resignation of rights and a double step from democracy to oligarchy and from oligarchy to monarchy (thus E. Renan. A. Sabatier, R. Sohm).

The principal authors of this general theory of evolution are E. Hatch, *The Organization of the Early Christian Churches,* London 1881; A. Harnack, *Die Gesellschaftsverfassung der kristlichen Kirchen im Altertum,* Giessen 1883; R. Sohm, *Kirchenrecht,* 1: *Die geschichtlichen Grundlagen,* Leipzig 1892; *Wesen und Ursprung der Katholizismus,* Leipzig 1909.

The various theories are expounded at length in our Latin work *De Ordine* 1 (Milwaukee 1957) 625–645. See also N. F. Josaitis, *Edwin Hatch and Early Church Order,* Gembloux 1972.

There is also among *Catholic scholars* a milder theory, holding only a *mediate divine institution of episcopacy.* But it regards especially, if not exclusively, episcopacy as a power of Orders, and hence it will be considered below in the proper chapter (in footnote 199).

jurisdiction, stating: "The supreme power of the Sovereign Pontiff does not in any way constitute an obstacle to that *ordinary and immediate episcopal jurisdiction*, by which the bishops, called *by the Holy Spirit* [cf. Acts 20:28] to succeed *in the place of the Apostles*, feed and govern individually, as true pastors, the flocks assigned to them. On the contrary, their power is strengthened and protected by the supreme and universal pastor" (Chap. 3, Denz. 3061).[159]

Vatican II in its Dogmatic Constitution on the Church (called "Lumen gentium," i.e., "Light of Nations," from its opening words, based on Luke 2:32; John 1:9; 8:12) repeated and further determined the doctrine of the two preceding Councils about the divine and apostolic origin of the episcopacy, abstracting from the particular addition on the collegial nature of the same power, which will be examined below (p. 371). This further determination consists in three things.

First, there is an explicit affirmation of the *"divine institution"* of the episcopacy: "This sacred Synod teaches that by divine institution bishops have succeeded in the place of the Apostles, as shepherds of the Church" (no. 20); this affirmation is not found in the text of Trent, which uses the more vague expression "instituted by divine ordinance," and moreover applies it directly not to the power of jurisdiction but to the power of Orders; however, the same explicit affirmation is found in several documents which preceded Vatican II, as in those of Leo XIII, the Code of Canon-Law, and Pius XII, quoted below.

Second, there is a particular stress on the two parallel binomials *"Peter and apostles"* and *"Roman Pontiff and bishops:"* "Just as, by the Lord's will, saint Peter and the other Apostles make up one apostolic college, so in an equal manner the Roman Pontiff,

---

159 The first Constitution on the Church, issued by Vatican I, which deals only with the primacy of the Roman Pontiff, was to be followed by a second Constitution on the Church, which would have dealt especially with the episcopacy in its relation to the primacy. The interruption of the Council, on account of the occupation of Rome by the Italian King, is the reason of the incomplete doctrine of the Council on episcopacy.

Regarding this doctrine and the acts of the Council, see the collective work *De doctrina Concilii Vaticani Primi* (In Civitate Vaticana 1969) 383–487; Torrell, *loc. cit.* (above, footnote 156); J. Cl. Fenton, "The Vatican Council's Unfinished Business," *American Ecclesiastical Review* 142 (1960) 217–224; J. Arrieta, "La colegialidad episcopal: Un tema en vista al proximo Concilio," *Estudios eclesiásticas* 38 (1963) 5–56.

Peter's successor, and the bishops, successors of the Apostles, are joined together" (No. 22).

Third, there is an explicit declaration, never made before by the Magisterium, on the *sacramentality of episcopacy*, as the ontological foundation of the powers of jurisdiction and Magisterium themselves, from which the very divine origin of the episcopacy is further strengthened, since all the sacraments are of immediate divine institution; this is the real new acquisition brought forth by the Council, although it concerns directly only the power of Orders. The Council declares: "The sacred Synod teaches that through the episcopal consecration the fulness of the sacrament of Orders is conferred ... Moreover the episcopal consecration, together with the office of sanctifying, confers also the offices of teaching and governing, which, however, according to their nature cannot be exercised but in hierarchical communion with the Head and the members of the College" (No. 21).

There are three minor documents, issued between the two Vatican Councils, which paved the way to Vatican II. *Leo XIII* states that "the bishops succeed to the Apostles" and he includes episcopacy among the things that "are in the Church *divinely established*" (Encycl. "Satis cognitum," Denz. 3307, 3310). *The Code of Canon Law* takes a step further than Trent, stating: "*By divine institution* the sacred hierarchy, under the aspect of Orders, is made up of bishops, priests, and ministers, and under the aspect of jurisdiction, is composed of the supreme pontificate and the subordinate episcopacy; other degrees were also added through the institution of the Church" (Can. 108, § 3; can. 329, § 1). *Pius XII*, while teaching the divine institution of the episcopacy, stresses very strongly its subordination to the Roman Pontiff, through whom the divine power is communicated to the bishops: "[The bishops] enjoy ordinary power of jurisdiction, immediately given to them by the Roman Pontiff. Hence they must be venerated by the people as successors of the Apostles by *divine institution*" (Encycl. "Mystical Body," Denz. 3804); "The power of jurisdiction which is given to the Supreme Pontiff directly by divine right, comes down to the bishop *from the same right*, but only through Peter's successor," (*Epistle* to the people of China in 1955, AAS 47.9).

Scripture does not show any explicit reference to the divine origin of the episcopacy; no evangelical text signifies that Christ told the apostles that they should have successors, nor any passage of the Acts or the Epistles shows an explicit declaration of the apostles themselves about the necessity of such a succession. However, this is *implicitly contained in the perpetuity of the apostolic ministry*, which is equivalently signified in Scripture, in three ways.

First, the very fact that Christ chose and carefully prepared an apostolic college for the office of preaching the evangelical message and establishing an ecclesial community in which that message should be kept and transmitted, suggests that He had also the intention of perpetuating such an apostolic office, so that it would belong to the very constitution of the Church. This suggestion is strengthened by the fact that Christ instituted Peter's primacy as something to be perpetuated; for Peter is shown not only as the head of the Church but also as the head of the apostolic college; hence, as the head had to be perpetuated, so also his college would naturally follow in the same path of unending duration.

Second, Christ equivalently signified that the apostolic office would be perpetual, for He ordered the apostles themselves (not the faithful generically) to take the gospel and the sacrament of Baptism *to all nations*, promising them His perpetual assistance *onto the consummation of the world* (Matt. 28:19; Mark 16:15; Acts 1:8). He also promised the apostle to send to them the Holy Spirit, who would "dwell with them *forever*" (John 14:16) and prayed the Father "not for these only, but for those also *who through their word are to believe*" (John 17:20). All such orders and promises, made to the apostles for an unlimited future when they would be no longer on earth, have no sense if there are no successors in whom the apostles' office and person is morally perpetuated.

Third, Christ's intention about the perpetuity of the apostolic ministry is manifested in a practical manner by the promptness and the care with which the apostles since the beginning appointed various ministers, not only to help them in their work but also to take direct charge and complete management of the various communities, considering them as "fellow-presbyters" and shepherds," "who tend the flock of God" (1 Pet. 5:1–4), whom "the Holy Spirit has placed as bishops to rule the Church of God" (Acts 20:28) and who "take care of the Church of God" (1 Tim. 3:5).

Some among these ministers were certainly bishops properly so called, namely, *Timothy, Titus* (see the three corresponding epistles

of St. Paul), and *the rectors of the seven Asian cities* of whom John
speaks in the Apocalypse (Chap. 2f.). As to the many other persons, indifferently called bishops or presbyters (in the Acts and
the Epistles),[160] it is disputed among scholars, whether, independently of these names, they were all simple priests, as many
modern authors believe (Prat, Steinmann, Holtzmeister, Puzo,
Médebielle, Bardy, Spicq, Renié, etc.), or all true bishops, as very
few hold (Petau and Perrone), or some priests and some bishops, as the more common opinion holds (many Fathers, most of
the older exegetes and theologians, a few modern exegetes, as
Simon-Prado and Bover).[161] At any rate, there is no doubt that
the apostles themselves before their death established many true
bishops throughout the universal Church; at the death of St. John
(about the year 100) all the Asian churches were organized, even
in the strict form of a monarchic episcopacy, as is evident from
the epistles of Ignatius of Antioch who died shortly after the
apostle (about 107).

Tradition[162] in its *first period* (2nd–3rd centuries) testifies to
the divine origin of the episcopacy in three ways.

First, implicitly, by comparing the ecclesiastical hierarchy to
that of the Old Testament, which was manifestly instituted by
God through Moses, and by declaring the apostolic succession
of bishops. Clement of Rome, who was a disciple of the apostles
(cf. St. Paul, Phil. 6:3) and the third successor of St. Peter, comparing the hierarchies of the two Testaments, sees in Isa. 60:17
a prophecy about bishops and deacons (*Epistle to the Corinthians,*
chaps 40, 44);[163] the same comparison is made by Origen (*On Lev.*

160   They are named presbyters in Acts 11:30; 14:23; 15:2, 4, 6, 22, 23, 41;
16:4; 20:17; 21:18; 1 Tim. 4:14; 5:17, 19; Tit. 1:5; Jas. 5:14; 1 Pet. 5:1f.; 1 John
1; 3 John 1. They are named *bishops* in Acts 20:28; Phil. 1:1; 1 Tim. 3:1 f; Tit.
1:7 (always by St. Paul).

161   The Magisterium seems to favor this third opinion by frequently using the
aforementioned text Acts 20:28 with reference to the bishops. Thus Trent (above,
p. 362), Vatican I (p. 363), Pius XI (Encyl. "Ubi arcano"), Pius XII (Encycl. "Mediator Dei" and "Munificentissimus Deus"), John XXIII (Encycl. "Ad Petri cathedram"
and Epistle "Princeps pastorum"). We expounded this question in our Latin work
De Ordine 1 (Milwaukee 1957) 745–792.

162   We expounded this argument quite at length in the same work *De Ordine,* pp.
227–489, examining the individual testimonies of Tradition. Here below (p. 395)
we will also complete this argument speaking of the episcopacy as a power of
Orders.

163   Isa. 60:17 in the Vulgate reads: "And I will make thy visitation peace, and
thy overseers justice." The Greek version has: "I will make thy magistrates peace,

6.3) and Cyprian (*On the unity of the Catholic Church* 18f.). Irenaeus particularly insists on the apostolic succession of the bishops, showing the unity of the bishops with the apostles in the same doctrine and in the same ministry (*Against Heresies*, books 3 and 4) and Tertullian calls the bishops "the transmitters of the apostolic seed" (*On the Prescription of Heretics* 32).

Second, the Fathers declare the divine origin of the episcopacy *equivalently* under various expressions. The bishops were established by the apostles (Clement of Rome, *loc. cit.*); but the apostles would have no right of handing over their divine power to others, unless Christ willed it. The bishops are compared to the apostles in their establishment, their authority, and their relation to the Church (Origen, *On Matt.* 61; *On Prayer* 28; Cyprian, *Epist.* 33). The bishops belong to the Constitution of the Church, and are morally identified with the Church; this is particularly stressed by Ignatius of Antioch through his axiom: "Without these [i.e., bishop and priests] there is no Church" (*Epistle to the Trallians* 3.1); "Where the bishop is, there the people should be, just as where Christ is, there is the Catholic Church" (*Epistle to Smyrna* 8.2),[164] and by Cyprian, whose entire ecclesiological doctrine can be summarized in these words: "The Church is established on the bishops" (*Epistle* 33).[165]

Third, the same truth is set forth *explicitly* in the following expressions: The bishops are "appointed according to the will of Christ" (Ignatius of Antioch, *Epistle to the Philadelphians*, address). They are sent by God to govern His household, the Church (Ignatius of Antioch, *Epistle to the Ephesians* 6.1; Origen, *On Matt.* 61). They are established and ordained by God (Origen, *ibid.*; Cyprian,

---

and thy bishops justice," that is, "I will give you peaceful and just rulers." Such interpretation, or accommodation of the text to the ecclesiastical hierarchy, is made also by Irenaeus, *Against Heresies* 4.26.2, Chrysostom, *Sermon Against the Jews and the Gentiles* 7, and Jerome, *On Isa.* 17.61.

164   The testimony of Ignatius is extremely important, for he is the first apostolic Father (immediately after Clement of Rome) and a disciple of the apostles. He was probably ordained by the apostles (likely by St. John, residing in the same Asian region). He held the Antiochean episcopate since the year 70 (in which he succeeded to St. Peter after Evodius). He died in 107 or 110, only a few years after St. John. Besides, his epistles bear an outstanding testimony not only to the apostolic succession of the episcopacy, but also to the establishment of the monarchic episcopate itself.

165   The divine origin of the episcopacy is the characteristic note of Cyprian's ecclesiology, just as the apostolic tradition and succession of the episcopacy is the proper character of the ecclesiology of Irenaeus.

Epistles 48 and 55). The bishop is elected "by God's will" and "by God's grace" (Ignatius of Antioch, *Epistles to Philad.* 1.1, *to Smyrna* 11.1, *to Ephes.* 1.3). The institution of bishops and deacons has been foretold by God in Isa. 60:17 (Clement of Rome, cited above; Irenaeus, *Against Heresies* 4.26.2).[166]

The subsequent Tradition (4th and 5th centuries) testifies to this truth in the same three ways, and with particular force.

The divine origin of episcopacy is *implicitly* propounded and stressed by Eusebius of Caesarea, giving the list of the bishops who succeeded in the principal sees, from the apostles to the beginning of the fourth century, and by Epiphanius, bringing the complete series of the thirty-seven bishops who succeeded the apostle James in the see of Jerusalem.

The *equivalent* affirmation of the same truth is stressed especially by referring the apostolic succession of the bishops to Peter himself. Ephraem: "The bishop has received his power from Peter" (*Hymns on Epiphany* 7). Athanasius, speaking of the legitimate form of ordination, states: "I am declaring to you what we received from the blessed Peter" (*Apology Against the Arians* 36). Ambrosiaster: "The Order, started by the apostle Peter, is kept up to the present time through the line of the succeeding bishops" (*Questions on the Old and New Testaments*, q. 110). Innocent I: "The apostleship and the episcopacy had their beginning in Christ through the holy apostle Peter" (*Epistle* 2).

The *explicit* affirmation is contained in the following expressions: "In the bishop the plenitude of the Divinity dwells corporally" (Pseudo — Jerome, *On the Seven Orders of the Church* 5 and 7). "[Christ] made us shepherds" (Caesarius of Arles, *Serm.* 232). "The bishops of the churches of God are established by God" (Basil, *Epist.* 42.4). "God entrusted to you the government of the Church" (Basil, *Epist.* 4.195). "God himself brought you to the chair of the apostles" (Basil, *Epist.* 197 to Ambrose bishop of Milan). "The Savior established such things [i.e., the things which regard episcopacy]" (Athanasius, *Epistle to Dracontius*). "[God] willed that individual bishops should govern individual churches" (Ambrosiaster, *On 1 Cor.* 12:28).

---

166   See footnote 163.

10

Collegial Nature of the Episcopacy[167]

WE HAVE ESTABLISHED IN THE PRECEDING CHAP-
ter that by divine right the bishops succeed to the apostles in their
hierarchical pastoral office. We now inquire about the collegial
nature of this succession, namely, whether the bishops succeed to
the apostles not only individually, each as pastor of a particular
church, but *also and primarily in a collegial manner*, each as part of
a college of pastors, which immediately succeeds to the apostolic
college and through which every single consecrated bishop, even
non-residential, shares in the apostolic office of teaching and
ruling the Church.

The expression *"episcopal college"* is taken here in a juridical
sense, not however strict and profane, that is, for a group of equals,
but in a broader and ecclesiastical sense, such as implied by the
second Vatican Council itself, that is, for a group of pastors having

---

167   Part of the bibliography given in footnote 156 is also pertinent here.

Bertrams, W., *De relatione inter episcopatum et primatum*, Romae 1963; *Il potere
pastorale del Papa e del Collegio dei Vescovi*, Roma 1966; various articles, in *Civiltà Cattolica* (1964) 436–455; *Gregorianum* (1965) 343–354; *Euntes Docete* (1967) 59–70.

Collégialité (La) épiscopale (dir. Y. M.-J. Congar), Paris 1965.

Colson, J., *L'épiscopat catholique. Collégialité et primauté dans les trois premiers siècles
de l'Eglise*, Paris 1963.

Congar, Y., "La collégialité de l'episcopat et la primauté de l'évêque de Roma
dans l'histoire," *Angelicum* 47 (1970) 403–427.

Dejaifve, G., "Le premier des évêques," *Nouvelle revue théologique* 82 (1960)
561–579; Les Douze Apôtres et leur unité dans la tradition catholique," *Ephemerides theologicae Lovanienses* 39 (1963) 760–778.

D'Ercole, G., *Communio – Collegialità – Primato e "Sollicitudo omnium ecclesiarum"
dai Vanyeli a Constantino*, Roma 1964.

Eglise (L') de Vatican II (dir. G. Barauna, French edition by Y. M.-J. Congar, Paris
1966), vol. 3, pp. 763–889 (various articles on collegiality under biblical, theological, and historical aspects).

Huerga, A., "Sacramentalidad y colegialidad del episcopado," *Angelicum* 45
(1968) 328–344; "Primato e collegialità. La struttura monarchico-gerarchica
della Chiesa nei due Concilii Vaticani," *Sacra Doctrina* 15 (1970) 233–265.

Lécuyer, J., *Etudes sur la collégialité épiscopale*, Lyons-Le Puy 1964.

Moeller, Ch., "Origine et développment du thème de la collégialité à Vatican II,"
Euntes Docete 20 (1967) 445–458.

Warnholtz, C., *The Nature of the Episcopal Office According to the Second Vatican
Council*, Washington 1968.

equal and universal rights in the government of the Church, to the extension permitted and limited by the primacy of the head of the college, the Roman Pontiff.[168]

A certain collegial nature has always been attributed to the episcopacy by the theologians, in the sense that all the bishops together make up both the ordinary Magisterium, spread all over the entire Church, and the extraordinary Magisterium exercised in the assembly of the ecumenical Council. But a further question, hardly touched in the past by one or another theologian of minor importance,[169] has been explicitly raised and affirmatively resolved by several recent theologians, that is, whether collegiality, or membership in the episcopal body, is not a mere consequence of the episcopal charge in a particular diocese, received from the

---

168 *The word "college"* (and a fortiori "collegiality"), as applied to the bishops, is new in theology as well as in Tradition; hence it needs a definite sense and a continued theological and ecclesiastical usage to be fully incardinated into classical theology.

The Latin word "collegium" (from "cum" with, and "lego," I choose) etymologically means a union of chosen persons. In profane language it means either a moral bond between men having a common quality or purpose (class, category, guild, corporation, company, school, of doctors, lawyers, workers, students, etc.), or a juridical bond between men juridically equal (such probably was the sense of the word as applied to the senate in Roman right and such is the sense of ecclesiastical colleges and "college of the Cardinals" in the Code of Canon Law, canons 99, 100, 231, 237, 1053, §3).

The word, as applied to the bishops, is not biblical; the apostles themselves are not called a college, although they are signified as a special group under the name "The Twelve" (see above, footnote 62). Likewise, the word is hardly patristic or magisterial; it occurs only in some papal letters of the 4th – 5th centuries and occasionally in later documents (see below, footnote 176). It has been foreign to the use and the mentality of theologians up to the present time, when finally, through the efforts of some recent authors it has been accepted by the Vatican Council II under the expression "Episcopal College" to signify the proper juridical bond which unites the bishops as successors of the apostolic group.

The Council, however, in order to avoid the ambiguity of the word and to remove from it the profane juridical sense of a group of men juridically equal, uses also interchangeably the words "order" and "body" of the bishops. Moreover, in a "Prefatory Note," read by the Secretary General of the Council by order of "a higher authority" (presumably the Pope) before the final vote on the Constitution of the Church, the meaning given by the Council to the expression "episcopal college" is explained as follows: "College is not understood in a strictly juridical sense, that is, in the sense of a group of equals, who would consign their power to their president, but in the sense of a stable group, whose structure and authority are to be deduced from Revelation."

169 Particularly I. V. Bolgeni, who clearly set forth the modern opinion in his works *Fatti dogmatici*, 1788 and *L'episcopato ossia la podestà di governare la Chiesa*, 1789. Cf. M. R. Gagnebet, "L'origine de la juridiction collégiale du corps épiscopal au Concile selon Bolgeni," *Divinitas* (1961) 431–493.

Roman Pontiff, as has been commonly held by theologians, but the primary and fundamental reason and origin of all episcopal power and of its relation to the primacy of the Roman Pontiff. The second Vatican Council has adopted this view within moderate limits, bringing the two opinions to a harmonious equilibrium, as will be explained in the following statement.

Statement. *Episcopacy is in its nature essentially collegial, in this sense that a bishop, by virtue of his sacramental consecration and on condition of his hierarchical communion with the Roman Pontiff, becomes ipso facto a member of the apostolic college. From this collegial incorporation he automatically acquires an ontological participation of the sacred functions, by which he is actually appointed to exercise with the entire college the care concerning the universal Church, according to the mode determined by the Roman Pontiff for such a collegial action. From the same incorporation he also acquires a radical aptitude to exercise a particular office or to govern with proper and ordinary right a particular church, which aptitude is made effective only through a concession of the Roman Pontiff.*

Theological note. This statement is a brief paraphrase of the doctrine, solemnly declared, though not defined as *de fide*, by Vatican II.[170] Hence it cannot be rejected or questioned without *considerable temerity*. It can also be called a Catholic doctrine, in the space of a few years passing from implicit to explicit with impelling speed which the greater part of the theologians between the two Vatican Councils could hardly foresee.

The debates about the nature and origin of the episcopal power, held in the preceding Councils of Trent and Vatican I, did not afford any positive contribution to this question. On the contrary a similar theory on episcopal collegiality, proposed in some exaggerated terms by a few Fathers in Vatican I, was promptly discarded by the Deputation on faith.[171]

Vatican II in its Dogmatic Constitution on the Church (chap. 3, particularly nos. 21–23) considered directly the question of the collegial nature of episcopacy and essentially determined it,

---

170 See footnote 152 about the dogmatic value of the Constitution on the Church.
171 See above, footnote 132. About the discussion at Trent, see our work *De Ordine* 2 (Milwauke 1959) 103–108; G. Alberigo, "Le potestà episcopali nei dibattiti tridentini," *Il Concilio di Trento e la riforma tridentina* (Trento 1963) 1–53; Bertrams, *locis cit.* (above, footnote 167).

leaving further details to the dispute of theologians.[172] Since it is a doctrine proper to the Council and matured in the Council, we shall propound it, following step by step the conciliar teaching.

The biblical foundation of this doctrine[173] is briefly indicated by the Council in the words of Matt. 18:18, by which all the apostles received from Christ a general power of binding and loosing, similar to the one given to Peter, and of Matt. 28:16–20 about the collective mission of preaching and baptizing, given likewise by Christ to all of them. There are, however, several other hints of the same doctrine, namely, the collective election of the apostles (Mark 3:14); their collective name "The Twelve" (Mark 4:10)[174]; the collegial manner in which the apostles exercised their power, as shown in the Acts, particularly in the case of the election of Matthias (1:15–26), of recruiting new Christians on the day of Pentecost (2:14, 37f.), of electing the first deacons (6:1–6), of confirming already baptized faithful (8:14), of receiving in the Church the first gentiles (11:1–18), of settling the question of Mosaic observances in the first council of Jerusalem (15:1–31; cf. Gal. 2:11–14).

The patristic foundation,[175] proposed by the Council, bears only a *practical character.* It consists in the universal solicitude toward the common good of the Church, shown by the bishops in the patristic age, by their epistles spontaneously sent to the Roman Pontiff and to other bishops, concerning general questions of faith and discipline, by the convocation of particular and general councils, and by the particular practice of calling neighboring bishops for the consecration of a new bishop (No. 22). As a matter of fact the *doctrinal* patristic foundation is very slim; the only thing that can be gathered from the patristic literature is a particular, and somewhat exaggerated, collegial mentality in Cyprian (manifested especially in his work *On the Unity of the Catholic Church;* see above, p. 319); and some explicit expressions of episcopal solidarity in

---

172   The same doctrine is also briefly summarized by the Council in the Decree on the Bishop's Pastoral Office in the Church, nos. 1–7.

173   Cf. St. Lyonnet, "La collégialité épiscopale et ses fondements scripturaires," *L'Eglise de Vatican II* (direct. G. Barauna, French edition by Y.M-J. Congar, Paris 1966), vol. 3, pp. 829–846.

174   See footnote 132.

175   Cf. J. Hajjar and G. Dejaifve in the collective work on Vatican II just referred to, pp. 847–890.

the papal letters of Celestine I, Sixtus I, Leo I, Felix I, and Gelasius I, in which also the word "college" occurs.[176]

The doctrine itself, taught by the Council, can be summarized in the following seven points.

1. By divine institution the episcopal college is *proportionally equivalent to the apostolic college*, according to the twofold binomial "Peter-apostles" and "Pope-bishops." The word college is not taken in the strict juridical sense of a group of equals, for the head of the episcopal college, the Pope, is such by his own right, and enjoys the primacy over the Church. This is the reason why the episcopal group is indifferently called college, order, or body (No. 22).

2. By reason of this proportional equivalence between the two colleges, the episcopal college succeeds to the apostolic in the *supreme and full* power over the universal Church, which, however, cannot be exercised without the agreement of the Head (No. 22). Since the Pope, even in the College, keeps always his primatial power over the entire Church and can act also outside the College, this College is not only the only supreme power in the Church, but, in the line of power, distinction must be made between the Pope alone and the Pope with the College.[177]

3. Each bishop becomes member of the College "*by virtue of the sacramental consecration and by the hierarchical communion with the Head and the members of the College*" (No. 22). This assertion is very new and very important, because it proposes the incardination

---

176 Celestine I, *Epistle* 18.1, to the Council of Ephesus: "For it is a sacred college to which veneration is due." Leo I, *Epistle* 5.2: "With those who are united to us by the charity of the college." Cf. J. Lécuyer, "Le collège des évêques selon le pape Célestin Ier," *Nouvelle revue théologique* 86 (1964) 250–259; G. Medico, "La collégialité épiscopale dans les lettres des pontifes romains du Ve siècle," *Revue des sciences philosophiques et théologiques* 49 (1965) 369–402.

177 The text reads: "The order of bishops is also the subject of supreme and full power." The "Prefatory note of explanation" adds to these words the following declaration: "This must necessarily be admitted, lest the fulness of the power of the Roman Pontiff be injured ... In other words the distinction is made not between the Roman Pontiff and the bishops taken together, but between the Roman Pontiff taken alone and the Roman Pontiff together with the bishops."

This confirms the thesis of the existence of *two, inadequately distinct, subjects* of the supreme power and infallibility, mentioned above (p. 350). But it leaves open the disputed question whether the immediate subject is double, or only one, and in this second case, whether it is the Pope, from whom the authority derives into the college, or the college itself, in the sense that the Pope gets his power because he is the head of the college (see above, pp. 350f.). It is evident that this last supposition, held by a few recent authors, does not fully agree with the words of the "Prefatory note," just quoted.

to the episcopal college as an effect of the sacramental consecration, thus putting a necessary bond between the two powers
of Orders and jurisdiction and making the first the foundation
of the other. This also resolves negatively the preceding debate
among theologians, as to whether the episcopal jurisdiction is
given to the bishop by the Roman Pontiff, at least as regards the
general jurisdiction on the universal Church as a member of the
College. From the fact that this general jurisdiction is given by
virtue of the sacramental consecration, it does not follow that it
is properly a sacramental effect, as is the physical sacramental
character, otherwise it would be indelible like this character and
could not be conditioned by the communion with the College,
which is extinguished through heresy, schism, or excommunication; it is, therefore, a moral effect conditioned by the sacramental
consecration.

4. Besides the membership in the College, "*the episcopal consecration, together with the office of sanctifying* [the power of Orders],
confers also the offices of teaching and of governing [the two powers
of Magisterium and jurisdiction], which, however, according to
their proper nature, cannot be exercised but in hierarchical communion with the Head and the members of the College" (No. 21).
This teaching is a mere explanation of the preceding, naming and
binding together the three powers of Orders, Magisterium, and
jurisdiction.

The "Prefatory note of explanation" adds three declarations to
this text. First, in the consecration the bishop receives only "an
ontological participation of the sacred offices" of teaching and
governing, that is, *only the office* (Latin "munus"), and not the
exercise of the office, or *the power*, understood as power actually able to act; this is later given to the bishop by a canonical
or juridical determination, consisting either in the granting of a
particular office or in the assignment of subjects.[178] Second, the

---

178 This declaration is rather *ambiguous or misleading*. Hence some theologians
understand this ontological power, as a true power, actually existing but unable
to act; others understand it not as an actual power but as a radical capacity to
receive the power through the subsequent canonical mission. It seems, however,
that two kinds of powers should be distinguished, namely, the one related to the
universal Church, which the bishop actually and fully receives in his consecration
by his incardination to the college, and the other related to a particular office or
church, which the bishop receives only radically in his consecration and actually
by the subsequent canonical determination.

recent documents of the Magisterium which speak of the power given to the bishops immediately by the Pope (see Pius XII, above, p. 364) must be understood as referring not to the office but to its determination. Third, the ontological office received in the consecration cannot be exercised without hierarchical communion with the college: whether this regards only the lawfulness or also the validity of the acts, is a matter of free discussion, especially with regard to the actual practice of the separated Orientals.[179]

5. The supreme power of the College, to which each bishop is associated by virtue of his consecration, is exercised through a *collegiate action* in two ways, namely, either in a solemn manner, such as an *Ecumenical Council,* or through some other ordinary action of the bishops living in different parts of the world, provided the Pope calls for such an action or approves it (No. 22). From this it follows that the Ecumenical Council is not necessary, since there are two other ways of providing for the good and the necessities of the Church, namely, the personal supreme power of the Pope and some other kind of collegial action.[180]

6. Besides the membership in the episcopal college and the universal collegial power deriving from it, a bishop by virtue of his consecration acquires also *a radical aptitude for governing, with proper and ordinary right, a particular church,* which is brought into actual power by the aforementioned canonical determination.[181] Although this power does not extend to other particular churches

---

According to the Council, every consecrated bishop, by being a member of the college, has the right to be present at an ecumenical Council (Decree on the Bishop's pastoral office, no. 4); hence, before receiving any canonical mission, he exercises with the other bishop the supreme power of teaching and governing.

179 Cf. I Zuzek, "La giurisdizione dei vescovi ortodossi dopo il Concilio Vaticano II," *Civiltà Cattolica* (1971), vol. 2, pp. 550–562.

180 The Council in its Decree on the Bishop's Pastoral Office in the Church (no. 5) advised the introduction of a particular mode of collegial action, by the institution of the so-called "*Synod of bishops,*" which was in fact established by Paul VI through the Motu Proprio "Apostolica sollicitudo" in 1965 and has been functioning thereafter. Cf. R. Laurentin, *Le Synode permanent. Naissance et avenir,* Paris 1970; H. Fesquet *Le Synode et l'avenir de l'Eglise,* Paris 1972.

181 Hence the past controversy, whether the bishop receives his power immediately from God or from the Roman Pontiff, comes to a final solution. Namely, the bishop receives by virtue of his consecration, and consequently immediately from God, the office of teaching and governing the universal Church, whose exercise, however, depends on the ruling of the Pope, and the radical aptitude for governing a particular diocese. He receives, therefore, immediately from the Pope the free exercise of the first office, and the actual power for the second.

nor *a fortiori* to the universal Church, each bishop, as a member of the episcopal college, must have a particular solicitude also for other churches (No. 23)[182]

7. *The relationship between primacy and episcopacy* is manifest from all the preceding doctrine. First, the Pope can act alone without the College, in any manner and at any time, while the College can never act without the Pope, since without the head there is no collegial body nor collegial action. Second, the exercise of collegial action of any kind depends, as to its time and manner, on the Pope. Third, the general office of teaching and governing the Church, which a bishop acquires in his consecration, cannot be exercised except in communion with the Pope and according to the mode determined by the Pope for the collegial action. Fourth, the radical aptitude for governing a particular diocese, which a bishop likewise acquires in his consecration, is brought to actuality only by the Pope, through different modes established or permitted by him.

Note 1. *On the infallibility of the episcopal college*

The infallibility of the episcopal college in its Magisterium, both extraordinary (Ecumenical Councils) and ordinary (any other collegial action, formal or equivalent), is a mere consequence of its supreme power in the Church. It is also explicitly declared by Vatican I, whose words make it proximate to faith, and by Vatican II with a particular stress.[183] The biblical

---

182   The Council points out the various ways in which this universal solicitude of a bishop should go into practice (no. 23). For the same purpose, in its Decree on the Bishops' Pastoral Office (no. 36–38) it strongly recommends both the ancient practice of provincial and plenary councils and the modern practice of the so-called episcopal conference, for which it sets forth some definite rules.

183   *Vatican I*; "By divine and Catholic faith all those things must be believed which are contained in the written or transmitted word of God and are proposed by the Church, either through a solemn pronouncement or through the ordinary and universal Magisterium, as revealed truths to be believed" (Sess. 3, chap. 3, Denz. 3011). As the Deputation of faith declared, this definition does not concern the infallibility of the Roman Pontiff (which is defined in sess. 4, chap. 4), but of the bishops.

Vatican II: "The bishops do not enjoy individually the prerogative of infallibility. However, they pronounce Christ's doctrine infallibly, when, while teaching authentically matters of faith and morals, they concur in the same sentence as to be definitely held. This is so, even if they are dispersed in different parts of the world, provided they keep the bond of unity among themselves and with Peter's successor. The same is more evident, when, assembled in an Ecumenical Council, they are teachers and judges for the universal Church in matters of faith and morals; hence their definitions must be accepted with the submission of faith" (Dogmatic Constitution on the Church, no. 25).

foundation is placed in the same texts, Matt. 18:18; 28:16–20, brought forth to prove the collegial nature of the episcopacy. Indeed, the power of binding and loosing in matters of faith cannot be effectively exercised if the holder of this power can himself fail in those matters, and Christ has promised to the apostles and their successors his assistance, without restriction, in their teaching of the faith. The Fathers manifestly consider the episcopal succession to the apostles as carrying with it the charism of truth and consider the decision of the Ecumenical Council as irrevocable (cf. Athanasius, *Epistle to the Africans*; Ambrose, *Epist.* 21.14; Leo I, *Epist.* 114 to the Council of Chalcedon; Gregory I, *Epist.* 25). The Ecumenical Councils themselves in their decisions proceed authoritatively and definitively, thus bearing testimony to their own infallibility.

Whatever has been said above (pp. 349–358), speaking of the infallibility of the Pope (as to its division, its object, the means of discerning an infallible document, and the assent due it), applies proportionally to the infallibility of the episcopal college.

Note 2. *On the Ecumenical Council*[184]

As shown above (p. 374), the Ecumenical Council is only one solemn manner in which the action of the episcopal college and its supreme authority and infallibility are exercised. Hence it is not absolutely necessary for the government of the Church, since there are two other ways for it, namely, the exercise of the primatial power of the Pope and the collegial action of the bishops exercised in another ordinary manner. This explains the fact that there were so few Ecumenical Councils in the long history of the Church: 21 councils in 20 centuries. (The first, Nicaea I, was celebrated as late as 325; three full centuries elapsed between Trent and Vatican I).[185] This also might be the cause of a still

---

184   Cf, C, Raab, *The Twenty Ecumenical Councils of the Catholic Church*, Westminster, Md. 1959; J. L. Murphy, *The General Councils of the Church*, Milwaukee, Wis. 1960; H. Jedin, *Ecumenical Councils in the Catholic Church*, New York 1960; *Le Concile et les Conciles. Contributions à l'histoire de la vie conciliaire de l'Eglise* (collective work), Paris 1960; Fransen, P. "The Authority of the Councils," *Problems of Authority* (ed. J. M. Todd, Baltimore 1962) 43–78; De la Brosse, *Le Pape et le Concile*, Paris 1965.
185   The 21 Councils, with their name, date, ruling Pope, and principal matters defined, are the following:
1. *Nicaea* I, 325, under Sylvester I, about the divinity of the Word, against Arianism.

smaller number of such Councils in the future, due on the one hand to the difficulties inherent to their celebration and on the other hand to an easier way of collegial action by reason of the modern means of quick and sure communication.

However, the general utility of such Councils, considered both in themselves and especially with regard to the past era, is evident. For, in the face to face collegial action of the bishops, the union among the members and with the head of the episcopal college is tangibly shown and greatly fostered, the common decisions and

2. *Constantinople* I, 381, under Damasus, about the divinity of the Holy Spirit, against Macedonianism.

3. *Ephesus*, 431, under Celestine I, about the unity of Person in Christ, against Nestorianism.

4. *Chalcedon*, 451, under Leo I, about the distinction of two natures in Christ, against Monophysitism.

5. *Constantinople* II, 553, under Vigilius, against some remnants of Nestorianism, called the "Three Chapters."

6. *Constantinople* III, 680, under Agatho, about the presence of a human will in Christ, against Monothelitism.

7. *Nicaea* II, 787, under Hadrian I, about the legitimacy of the cult of images, against Iconoclasm.

8. *Constantinople* IV, 869–870, under Hadrian II, about the removal of Photius from his see.

9. *Lateran* I (Rome, Lateran palace), 1123, under Callistus II, about ending the investiture conflict between Pope and emperor.

10. *Lateran* II, 1139, under Innocent II, against papal schism and ecclesiastical disorders.

11. *Lateran* III, 1179, under Alexander III, about reformation of the clergy and condemnation of the Cathari.

12. *Lateran* IV, 1215, under Innocent III, about papal primacy, secrecy of confession, and condemnation of the Cathari.

13. *Lyons* I, 1245, under Innocent IV, against emperor Frederick II.

14. *Lyons* II, 1274, under Gregory X, about the reunion of the Greek Church with the Latin.

15. *Vienne*, 1311–1312, under Clement V, about the soul as form of the body, against Peter Olivi.

16. *Constance*, 1414–1418, under Martin V, about ending the Western Schism and condemnation of Wyclif and Hus.

17. *Florence*, 1439–1445, under Eugene IV, about the reunion of the Greek Church and the doctrine on the Procession of the Holy Spirit from the Father and the Son and on the sacraments.

18. *Lateran* V, 1512–1517, under Julius II and Leo X, about Church reforms and relation between Pope and Council.

19. *Trent*, 1545–1563, under Paul III, Julius III, and Pius IV, about Scripture and Tradition, original sin, justification, sacraments, Church discipline.

20. *Vatican I* (Rome, in the Vatican palace), 1869–1870, under Pius IX, about revelation (against rationalism), primacy and infallibility of the Pope.

21. *Vatican II*, 1962–1965, under John XXIII and Paul VI, about pastoral and general renewal, world-wide outlook, revelation, nature of episcopacy.

definitions are more diligently prepared and clearly proposed, the final documents are more promptly promulgated and applied by the bishops in their particular dioceses, the definition of a truth takes up the character of a profession of faith, made simultaneously and as it were by a lively unanimous voice uttered by the entire universal Magisterium.[186]

As regards the *nature and conditions* of an Ecumenical Council, as distinct from any other collegial actions of the bishops, note the following.

First, the Council is a *physical and local convention* of the entire episcopate under the direction of the Roman Pontiff, to decide about doctrines and discipline concerning the universal Church. Therefore, there is no Council if there is no physical and local convention (as in any other kind of collegial action, provoked or approved by the Pope), or if the entire episcopate is not represented, speaking however of moral entirety; this would be realized even if a smaller number of bishops, representing various and principal particular churches, would assemble, or decide, with the Pope.

Second, the Council's *procedure* is made up of three steps, namely, its *convocation*, its *celebration*, and its final *decision*, each under the approbation of the Roman Pontiff.[187] Any of these steps, if not approved, is not conciliar; however, if the final step, namely, the final decision is approved, the Council is simply a true Ecumenical Council; thus the Councils of Constantinople I and II, celebrated without the Pope's approval, became Ecumenical Councils later when they received the approval of their decisions, and likewise the Council of Constance became ecumenical only in its last five sessions.

Third, *Council's members* by right (right of convening, celebrating, and deciding) are all and only those who are actually members of the episcopal college, since the moment of their

---

186 These reasons are briefly expounded by the Vatican Council I itself, in the prologue of its third session.

187 This has been solemnly declared by the Council of Lateran V in 1516 (Denz. 1445) and again recently by Vatican II stating (after the Code of Canon Law, cans. 222, 227): "A council is never ecumenical if it is not confirmed or at least accepted as such by the successor of Peter. It is a prerogative of the Roman Pontiff to convoke these councils, to preside over them, and to confirm them" (Dogmatic Constitution on the Church, no. 22).

consecration. Hence all consecrated bishops, both residential and titular, have the right to attend a Council,[188] to the sole exclusion of those who withdrew from the communion with the college and its head.[189]

---

188   This is explicitly stated by Vatican II (Decree on the Bishop's Pastoral Office, no. 4). In the past there was a doubt about the titular bishops.
189   Since the exercise of any collegial action depends on the Roman Pontiff (see above, pp. 162, 163, 166), probably the Pope can restrict such right in the individual bishops, so as to convoke to the Council only a limited number, required and sufficient to represent morally the entire episcopal college.

11

Monarchical Form of the Episcopacy[190]

AS SHOWN IN CHAPTER 9, THE EPISCOPACY IS OF divine origin, at least in the sense that by the will of Christ there must be in the Church, besides and under the Pope, some other hierarchs, ruling the various parts of the Church with their own full and ordinary power. From this also follows that these hierarchs cannot be reduced to mere vicars of the Pope or have only a partial power over the faithful, so that, for instance, one would take care of matters of faith and another of matters of discipline about the same people. Each must have the complete care of the same people, whatever may be its designation, whether by the common place, or race, or language, or rite, or any other possible condition suitable to modern civilization.

However, the form of this full right episcopacy could be twofold, that is either collegial and oligarchic, in the sense that several bishops would have in common and equally the complete hierarchical care of the same particular Christian church, or unitary and monarchic, in the sense that only one man would have such a complete charge, whether with the subordinate help of other bishops or not. The question here is precisely whether this second *monarchical form of episcopacy, which is in fact constantly and universally practiced in the Church at least since the second century,* is also of divine and unchangeable institution, or is due to merely human and contingent causes, rooted in the apostolic usage itself.

Statement. *The monarchical form of the episcopacy is probably of divine origin.*

This assertion, denied not only by Liberal Protestants but likewise by several Catholic scholars,[191] seems sufficiently based on

---

190 Cf. Ch. Journet, *L'Eglise du Verbe Incarné* 1 (éd. 2, Paris 1955) 502–512, 527–529, and our work *De Ordine* 1 (Milwaukee 1957) 831–836, 955–962.

191 It is logically denied by all the *Liberal Protestants*, who reject the divine origin of episcopacy itself, explaining the historical rise of the monarchic episcopate

a twofold reason. *First, on the historical* fact that the monarchical form of episcopacy ascends without interruption to the apostolic age; such a venerable start and firm constancy connaturally suggest an underlying intention of Christ Himself, made manifest through the apostles and their practice. *The second and dogmatic reason* is the testimony of Tradition and of the Magisterium, which seems to point to a divine institution.

The historical facts are the following. Within the second century, at least in its second half, all the churches are monarchically constituted, as everyone acknowledges. At the very beginning of the same century the monarchic bishop is found in six churches of Syria and Asia Minor, namely at Antioch, Ephesus, Magnesia, Tralles, Philadelphia, and Smyrna, as testified by *Ignatius of Antioch* (†107 or 110) in his epistles. A few years earlier, toward the end of the first century *St. John* in his Apocalypse speaks of the "angels" of seven churches in the same region, that is, of Ephesus, Smyrna, Pergamum, Thyatira, Sardis, Philadelphia, and Laodicea; these angels are the bishops of those churches (not their guardian angels, as a few exegetes wish to interpret), shown by the context and by the fact that just a few years later Ignatius of Antioch testifies to the presence of a monarchic bishop in three of these churches, Ephesus, Smyrna, and Philadelphia.

About the same time (in 96) the church of Rome sent its epistle to the Corinthians (see above, p. 316), which, according to three writers of the second century namely, Dionysius of Corinth, Hegesippus, and Irenaeus (whose testimony cannot seriously be doubted), was written by Clement, bishop of Rome; the fact that he did not send the letter under his name does not prove that he was only the president of a college ruling the Roman church.[192]

---

through an evolution of a monarchic, or oligarchic, or democratic type, as indicated above (footnote 158). According to them, the true monarchic episcopate started at the beginning of the second century in some Asian churches and within the same century progressively prevailed everywhere, even in the Roman Church, in which there was no true monarchic bishop until Anicetus or Soter (*ca.* 155–170). Their principal argument is the silence of documents about a monarchic bishop, both in the apostolic age and in several churches, till the middle of the second century.

Among *Catholic scholars*, J. Colson (*L'évêque dans les communautés primitives* [Paris 1951] 14,111f., 123f.) and P.-T. Camelot (*Ignace d'Antioche. Polycarpe de Smyrne* ["Sources chrétiennes," no. 10, Paris 1951] 45–48) hold likewise that in the first part of the second century in several churches prevailed the collegial system of government, until the Asian monarchic system was extended to all churches.

192 This could be attributed either to a sense of a personal humility, or to the

In the preceding *apostolic age*, the apostles themselves were equivalently monarchic bishops in the particular churches founded by each one, since they kept them under their absolute control, governing them directly or through special legates or through the local presbyterium, as is manifested particularly by the epistles of St. Paul. Furthermore, the church of Jerusalem, mother of all the others, appears since the beginning monarchically constituted, first under Peter (Acts 6:1–6; 12:17) and later under James (Acts 15:13–22; 21:18; Gal. 1:19; 2:12). Among the closest co-operators and legates of St. Paul, Timothy and Titus appear to be in full charge respectively at Ephesus and Crete, and, if they were only simple legates of St. Paul for the time being, they likely succeeded the apostle in those churches after his death, as a later tradition also testifies. Other rectors, called presbyters or bishops in the Acts 20:28, 1 Tim. 3:5, 1 Pet. 5:14 (see above p. 152), seem to have had full charge of their communities.

Clement of Rome, disciple of the apostles, in his epistle to the Corinthians (about 96) testifies that the apostles "constituted the aforementioned [bishops and deacons] and then they ordered that after their death, other worthy men should take over their ministry" (44.2).

There is no particular reason why we should not accept the historical truth of the episcopal catalogues, made by Eusebius of Caesarea toward the end of the third century and based on the older testimonies of Julius the African, Irenaeus, and Hegesippus. According to them, the monarchic episcopate ascends without interruption to the apostles themselves in four of the principal churches, that is, of Jerusalem (James), Rome (Peter), Antioch (Peter), and Alexandria (Mark).

All these facts show with sufficient evidence that the monarchic episcopate has its origin from the apostles, inasmuch as they constituted several monarchic bishops, or at least signified their

---

reverence for Peter's memory, who was still ruling the Roman church in the person of his successor, or to the Roman collegial mentality and usage, which made official acts and decrees go under the famous heading "The Senate and the People of Rome." This could also explain the fact that Ignatius of Antioch addressed one of his epistles to the Romans without mentioning their bishop, as he does on the contrary in the other epistles to the Asian churches, unless the reason for this silence is because Ignatius did not sufficiently know the name or the person of the Roman bishop.

will that such bishops should take their succession after their death. From this truth we can deduce a solidly probable argument for the divine origin of the monarchic episcopate. Indeed, it would be difficult to explain why the apostles founded and organized the various churches in such a concordant manner that the monarchic episcopate was soon and everywhere to arise and propagate, unless they were moved at least by a faithful interpretation of Christ's intention, if not by an actual impulse of the Holy Spirit.

The dogmatic reason for the same conclusion is supplied by the testimony of the Fathers and of the Magisterium. The strength of this argument lies in *a continuous affirmation or persuasion that in every church there should be only one bishop*; its weakness, however, or uncertain value, comes from the possibility of attributing such expressions to the mere fact, that is, to the actual monarchic constitution, which being as old as the apostolic age, is commonly understood as unchangeable.

Ignatius of Antioch, speaking of the bishop, whom in fact he shows only as monarchic, considers him as something pertaining to the very constitution of the Church (see above p. 367). To Novatian, who claimed the papacy, *Cyprian* objects that he cannot be the legitimate bishop of Rome because Cornelius was elected before him and there can be no more than one bishop in the church (*Epistle* to Iubainanus), and the same *Cornelius* complains about Novatian, saying: "Did therefore this defender of the gospel ignore that there must be only one bishop in the Catholic church?" (*Epistle* to Fabius, Denz. 109). Cornelius in his epistle to Cyprian quotes also the following confession made by those who returned to him from the schism of Novatian: "We do not ignore that there is only one God and one Lord Christ in whom we have believed, one Holy Spirit, and that there must be only one bishop in the Catholic [church]" (*Epist.* 49.2, among Cyprian's epistles). *Ambrosiaster* states: "Because all things come from one God the Father, he established that individual churches should be governed by individual bishops" (*On 1 Cor.* 12.29, ML 14.256). Likewise *Jerome*: "Undoubtedly there could not be several bishops in the same city" (*On Tit.* 1.5, ML 26.597).

Vatican I teaches that the bishops, who are established by the Holy Spirit to succeed the apostles, govern the various churches individually (above, p. 357). *The Code of Canon Law* affirms that "the bishops are the successors of the apostles and they are placed at the head of the individual churches *by divine institution*" (Can. 329, § 1). Vatican II, speaking of "bishops governing the particular churches entrusted to them," teaches that "the Holy Spirit unfailingly preserves the *form of government established by Christ the Lord in His Church*" (Dogm. Constit. on the Church, no. 27). All such expressions seem to direct our mind to the idea of the divine origin of the monarchic episcopate, although they could be referred only to the divine institution of the episcopacy as such, abstracting from its monarchic form.

A *theological reason* of fittingness may be deduced from the parallelism between primacy and episcopacy. Just as the Pope's primacy in ruling the universal Church is undoubtedly monarchic, so it is fitting that the subordinate episcopacy be likewise monarchic in the government of the particular churches. As Christ, one single and principal Pastor, is aptly represented in the universal Church by one single vicar, so it is fitting that He be represented by one single vicar in each particular church.

Note. *On the origin, nature, and division of the power of the monarchic bishop*[193]

The bishop's power with regard to a particular church is proportionally the same as the Pope's power over the universal Church, with the evident exception of the supreme character and fulness of the Pope's primacy, which reaches all the particular churches themselves and their individual members. Hence, according to Vatican II (Dogm. Constit. on the Church, no. 27), the bishop is a true pastor, "to whom the habitual and daily care of his sheep is entrusted completely," "a vicar and legate of Christ," "sent by the Father to govern his family," not only "through his counsel, exhortations, and example," which is proper to domestic regulation, but also "by his authority and sacred power," "by the virtue of which, he has the sacred right and the duty before the Lord to make laws on his subjects, to pass judgment on them, and to moderate all the things which regard the regulation of worship and of the apostolate."

---

193   Cf. Ch. Journet, *L'Eglise du Verbe Incarné* 1 (éd. 2, Bruges 1955) 502–512; J. Lécuyer, "La triple charge de l'évêque," *L'Eglise de Vatican II* (dir. G. Barauna, French edition by M.-J. Congar, Paris 1966), vol. 3, pp. 891–914.

As regards its *origin*, the episcopal power is founded upon and derives from the sacramental consecration, but not simply in all ways. Only the power of Orders is actually and simply given in the consecration; the power of jurisdiction and Magisterium is given only radically and it derives actually and formally from the appointment of the Roman Pontiff, as has been explained above (pp. 375f.).

As regards its *division*, the bishop's power is threefold, that is of *Orders, jurisdiction, and Magisterium*, while the Pope as such, lacks the power of Orders which would be above that of the bishop, at least speaking of sacramental power of Orders (see above, pp. 295, 299). By reason of the power of Orders, a bishop regulates the worship of his Church and sanctifies the faithful through the sacrifice and the sacraments, particularly through Confirmation, which is practically reserved to him in the Latin Church, and Holy Orders, of which he is the proper and sole minister.[194] By reason of the power of jurisdiction, a bishop can issue true laws, obliging even "*sub gravi*," he can establish a true judicial court and trials, and apply canonical sanctions; however, this power is restricted by the general laws issued by the Roman Pontiff for the universal Church. By reason of the power of Magisterium, a bishop is the authentic doctor in his church, although not infallible, who has the right and duty of teaching, interpreting, and defending the revealed truth, and to whose pronouncements religious assent is due (see above, pp. 357–358).[195]

---

194 The episcopal power of Orders will be directly considered in the next chapter, in the general question of the three degrees of the hierarchy of Orders.

195 *Vatican II* in its Decree on the Bishop's Pastoral Office in the Church (nos. 8, 11–18) expounds more definitely the manner of exercising this threefold episcopal power.

12

The Threefold Degree of the Power of Orders, Episcopate, Presbyterate, and Diaconate[196]

IN CHAPTER 4 WE HAVE ESTABLISHED THE EXIS-
tence and the nature of the power of Orders. We now complete
its treatment with the question of the hierarchy of Orders, that is,
the persons in whom this power resides, or the various degrees in
which it is divided, namely, the episcopate, the presbyterate, and

---

196 The bibliography about the episcopate, as including also the power of Orders,
has been given above (footnotes 156 and 167). A particular bibliography on the
diaconate will be given below (footnote 211). The following list concerns the three
degrees together, *as a whole ministry*, and *particularly the presbyterate*, which has
been lately the object of much discussion, regarding its nature, its standing in the
modern world, and its contemporary crisis.

Bouyer, L., "The Ecclesiastical Ministry and the Apostolic Succession." *Downside
Review* 90 (1972) 133–144.

Bovis, A. de, "Le presbytérat, sa nature et sa mission d'après le concile du Vatican
II," *Nouvelle revue théologique* 89 (1967) 1009–1042.

Bunnik, R. J., *Priest for Tomorrow* (trans. F. Wilms), New York 1970.

Caprile, G., "Il Sinodo dei Vescovi. Seconda assemblea generale. Discussione sul
sacerdozio ministeriale: principii dottrinali, parte pratica," *Civiltà Cattolica* 122
(1971), vol. 4, pp. 262–271, 366–386.

Colson, J., *Les fonctions ecclésiales aux deux premiers siècles*, Paris 1954; *Ministre
de Jésus-Christ ou le sacerdoce de l'Eglise*, Paris 1966.

Congar, Y., *Ministères et communion ecclésiale*, Paris 1971; "Quelques problémes
touchant les ministères,"" *Nouvelle revue théologique* 93 (1971) 785–800.

Coppens, J., "Le sacerdoce chrétien," *Nouvelle revue théologique* 92 (1971) 225–
245, 337–364; see *Ephemerides theologicae Lovanienses* (1972) 138–149.

Danneels, G. et al., *Le Prêtre. Foi et contestation*, Paris 1970.

Delorme, J. (ed.), *Le ministère et les ministères selon le Nouveau Testament. Dossier
exégétique et réflexion théologique*, Paris 1974.

Denis, H., "La théologie du presbytérat, de Trente à Vatican II," *Vatican II. Les
Prêtres* (Paris 1967) 193–232.

De Rosa, G., "Preti nuovi per un mondo nuovo," *Civiltà Cattolica* 122 (1971), vol.
2, pp. 321–355, vol. 3, pp. 455–467.

Doronzo, E., *De Ordine* 1 (Milwaukee 1957) 612–692.

Galot, J., "Le sacerdoce dans la doctrine du Concile [Vatican II]." *Nouvelle revue
théologique* 88 (1966) 1044–1061; *Visage nouveau du prêtre*, Gembloux 1970.

Giblet, J., "Les prêtres," *L'Eglise de Vatican II* (dir. G. Barauna, French edition by
M.-J. Congar, Paris 1966), vol. 3, pp. 915–941.

the diaconate. Once this is established, we will have completed the treatment of the ecclesiastical hierarchy as a whole, according to its two branches of jurisdiction, which resides in the primacy and episcopacy, and of Orders, which includes the three degrees of episcopate, presbyterate, and diaconate. However, the power of Orders is considered here simply as a moral power of ministering the means of sanctification, abstracting from the further question of its sacramentality (that is, whether it is conferred through a

Greely, A., *New Horizon for the Priesthood*, New York 1970.

Guittard, A., Bulteau, M. G., *International Bibliography on the Priesthood and the Ministry*, Montreal 1971.

Henrich, Fr. (ed.), *Existenz probleme des Priesters*, München 1969.

James, E. O., *The Nature and Function of Priesthood*. London 1955.

Klostermann, A., *Priester für Morgen*, Innsbruck, Tyrolia, 1970.

Kollar, N., "Old and New in the Theology of the Priesthood," *American Ecclesiastical Review* 164 (1971) 145–153.

Küng, H., *Why Priests? A Proposal for a New Church Ministry* (tr. R. C. Collins), Garden City, N. Y. 1972.

Lash, N., Rhymer, J. (eds.), *The Christian Priesthood. The Ninth Downside Symposium*, London and Danville, N. J. 1970.

Lécuyer, J., *Le sacerdoce dans le mystère du Christ*, Paris 1957.

Lemaire, A., *Les ministères aux origines de l'Eglise. Naissance de la triple hiérarchie: évêques, presbytres, diacres*, Paris 1971.

Masi. R., "Per una teologia del presbiterato," *Euntes Docete* 20 (1967) 99–132.

Meagher, G. (ed.), *Priest: Person and Ministry*. Dublin 1971.

Mierzwinski, T. T. (ed.), *What Do You Think of the Priest? A Bibliography on the Catholic Priesthood*, New York 1972.

Mohler, J. A., *The Origin and Evolution of the Priesthood: A Return to the Sources*, Staten Island, N. Y. 1970.

Moingt, J., "Caractère et ministère sacerdotal," *Recherches de science religieuse* 56 (1968) 563–589.

Mosshamer, O. *The Priest and Womanhood* (tr. R. J. Voight), Baltimore, Md. 1964.

Nicolau, M., *Ministros de Cristo. Sacerdocio y sacramento del Orden*, Madrid 1971.

Prêtre (Le) hier, aujourd'hui, demain ("Travaux du Congrès d'Ottawa 1969"), Paris 1970.

Prêtres (Les) dans la pensée de Vatican II, Paris 1966.

Priesterliche (Der) Dienst ("Quaestiones Disputatae," nos. 46–47) (collective works), 2 vols., Freiburg i. Br. 1970.

Rambaldi, G., "La figura del sacerdote secondo il Sinodo del 1971," *Doctor Communis* 27 (1971) 41–65.

Richards, M., "Priesthood and Ministry: A Bibliographical Survey," *Clergy Review* 59 (1974) 320–326.

Spicq, C. *The Mystery of Godliness* (tr. J. Martin), Chicago 1954.

Stockums, W., *The Priesthood*, St. Louis, Mo. 1942.

Theology (The) of Priesthood (collective work), London 1969.

Various Authors, "Esquisse d'une théologie des ministères," *Revue des sciences religieuses* 47 (1973) 3–138.

Wuerl, D. W., "The Third Synod: Bishops on the Ministerial Priesthood," *Homiletic and Pastoral Review* (1972) 48–56.

sacrament and consists in a physical sacramental character), a question which belongs to the treatise on the sacraments and cannot be discussed here.

Since the noun Order and the two kindred terms Hierarchy and Sacerdotal Office have a close connection and they are often used interchangeably, a preliminary explanation of the three terms, as to their sense and usage, will be helpful.[197]

Order, considered both in the sense of a state or condition and in the sense of persons who are in a state or condition, is taken in four ways in ecclesiastical terminology. First, for the various conditions of the *members of the Church,* inasmuch as some are constituted in authority and others are not; thus we speak of the hierarchical order and of the lay order. Second, exclusively for the *hierarchical order,* as including the three powers of Orders, Magisterium and jurisdiction. Third, only for the power or *hierarchy of Orders* (episcopate, presbyterate, diaconate), and this is the more common sense in Tradition. Fourth, in the very strict sense of *sacramental Order* that is, the power of Orders as given through a sacrament, and this is the technical sense in theology since the Middle Ages.

---

197 The meaning and the use of the word "bishop" has been expounded above (footnote 157). The word *"presbyter"* (which in the vernacular language has been changed into that of priest), according to its original Greek noun "presbuteros" or "presbutes" means senior or prior in age, and by extension it acquired also the twofold sense of predecessor (historically prior) and prior in dignity or authority (because in ancient customs old age was regarded as a title for particular influence in public affairs). In such triple sense the word is used in profane literature and in the bible of both Testaments.

In the N. T. the word, taken in the third hierarchical sense, designates both the Jewish dignitaries (constantly in the Gospel, Matt. 16:21; 21:23; Mark 8:31; 11:27; Luke 9:22; 20:1) and the rectors of the Christian communities (in the Acts and the Epistles; Acts 11:30; 14:22; 15:2, 4, 6, 22, 23, 41; 16:4; 20:17; 21:18; 1 Tim. 4:14; 5:17, 19; Tit. 1:5; Jas. 5:14; 1 Pet. 5:1, 2, 5; 2 John 1; 3 John 1). As noted above (p. 152), it is disputed whether these Biblical presbyters were bishops or simple priests. At any rate, since the beginning of the second century, the name presbyter began to be reserved to simple priests, and the name bishop to true bishops, as is evident from the epistles of Ignatius of Antioch.

The word *"deacon"* (in Greek "diáconos," from "dióco," I follow), means minister, that is, servant, and in this original sense it is used also by profane writers. In the N. T. the Greek word occurs thirty times, eight times in the Gospel, twenty-two times in the epistles of St. Paul, usually with a religious sense, and in three texts (Phil. 1:1; 1 Tim. 3:8, 12) in that specific hierarchical sense, which became common in Tradition since the beginning of the second century. About the various senses of both words "diáconos" and "diaconia" (deaconry) in the Scripture, see above (footnotes 52 and 56).

Hierarchy (a noun made up from the two Greek words "hierá," sacred things, and "arké," power) means sacred power, or those who hold the sacred power. Hence it implies the three powers of Orders, Magisterium and jurisdiction, which are all sacred, and it corresponds to Orders in the second sense just mentioned. However, in the common as well as in the theological usage, the power of jurisdiction tends to usurp this name.

Sacerdotal Office (in Latin "Sacerdotium," probably from "sacra," sacred things, and "do," I give) signifies the proper function of a priest, which, according to the common concept in all religions, consists in mediating between God and man, handing over as it were the sacred things, that is, the gifts of God to men and the worship of men to God, which consists mainly in the sacrifice.[198]

In ecclesiastical usage sacerdotal office is taken in three senses. First, broadly for the entire *hierarchy of Orders*, episcopate, presbyterate, and also diaconate. Second, only for the sacrificial Order, namely *episcopate and presbyterate* (Trent, Vatican I and Vatican II call the bishops priests). Third, in a very strict sense, only for the *presbyterate* as distinguished from the episcopate; hence the presbyter is called either priest without qualification, or simple priest, or priest of the second order (Trent and Vatican II speak simply of bishops and priests).

Statement. *Orders, or sacerdotal power and hierarchy, by immediate divine institution is combined of three degrees, namely, episcopate, presbyterate, and diaconate.*

Theological note. The immediate divine institution of the hierarchy of Orders, generically considered and abstracting from the three degrees, is *de fide* defined by Trent, sess. 23, can. 6. At least the mediate divine institution of the three degrees is *theologically certain*, as following from that same definition of Trent. The immediate divine institution of the three degrees is certain in

---

198   The Greek word "ieréus" (Hebrew "Kôhên" or "Kômer;" Latin "Sacerdos," priest) in Scripture designates either *the ministers of the old law* (Matt. 8:4; Mark 1:44; Luke 1:5; 5:14; Heb. 5:1; 7:1, 3, 14, 20, 23), or *Christ* himself (only in Heb. 5:5f.; 7:11, 15, 17, 21, 26; 8 1, 3, 4; 10:21), or *all the Christians* in the metaphorical sense of their spiritual and internal priesthood (1 Pet. 2:5, 9; Apoc. 1:6; 5:10; 20:6). The ministers of the new law are never called priests ("ieréus," "sacerdos"), probably in order to avoid confusion with Jewish or pagan ministers who were technically called priests. However, later in Tradition this name was commonly given to the ministers of the Church, as we shall see now.

the sense that its negation would now be *temerarious*, according to the doctrine of the Code of Canon Law and of Vatican II.[199]

The *Magisterium* since the Middle Ages has taught and defined the immediate, divine institution of the power of Orders generically considered, as we have shown above (p. 283). The same

---

199   As noted above (footnotes 42 and 50), *Protestants* deny the divine institution of all kinds of ecclesiastical authority properly so called, whether of Orders, or Magisterium, or jurisdiction. Such an authority is foreign to the three forms of ministry practiced in their churches, namely, the episcopalian, the presbyterian, and the independent organization. The Anglicans (and the American Episcopalians) admit the divine institution of a kind of undetermined "essential ministry" which was later determined in the form of episcopacy, but, as far as the divine institution is concerned, this ministry is void of proper authority and a fortiori of sacerdotal character (see footnote 158).

Particularly and unanimously they reject the power of Orders as to its properly *sacerdotal and sacrificial character*. This is a logical consequence of their fundamental dogma of justification only through faith in Christ, based on the ampler doctrine of the absolute sufficiency of Christ's priesthood and sacrifice, which excludes the necessity and fitness of any other means of salvation, such as the Church, the sacrifice, the sacraments, and particularly the power of Orders which is like the compendium and the origin of all the others.

Regarding the episcopate, as distinct from the presbyterate (and hence the distinction between the two orders), its divine institution was simply denied in the fourth century by Aërius, an ascetic of Pontus (cf. Epiphanius, *Against Heresies* 75.4; Augustine, *On Heresies* 53); in the 14th century by Marsilius of Padua, teaching the equality of all ministers by Christ's institution (Denz. 944), and John Wyclif, saying that at the beginning there were only presbyters and deacons and that the other degrees of the hierarchy were introduced through ambition of power (Denz. 1178, 1265); in the 16th century by the Protestants, among whom the *Presbyterians* developed against the Anglicans their particular thesis of the absolute parity of all ministers.

Several Catholic theologians denied the immediate institution of the three degrees of Orders by Christ and admitted only some kind of *mediate institution*, which can be described in the following manner. Christ immediately instituted only the priesthood generically and without determination of degrees; later the apostles or the Church determined or divided the fulness of this power into various degrees, which appeared clearly and firmly established, according to the threefold branches, in several churches at the beginning of the second century and were gradually extended to all churches in the course of the same century. This opinion takes two forms. Some theologians, as P. Pourrat and P. Batiffol, say that Christ instituted only *an essential sacerdotal principle*, which the Church determined into three particular branches. Others, more numerous, as C. Baisi, Y. Congar, M. J. Gerlaud, H. Lennerz, L. Marchal, H. Bouëssé, and A. Michel, say that Christ instituted some kind of *global power*, which the Church divided into three parts. Since the superior degree includes the inferior, this opinion can be expressed also by saying that Christ instituted only the episcopate, as implying a total sacerdotal power, from which the Church separated the other two degrees.

Cf. Pourrat, *La théologie sacramentaire* (éd. 2, Paris 1907) 283–286; Batiffol, *Etudes d'histoire et de théologie positive* (première série, éd. 8, Paris 1926) 257–266; Congar, "Faits, problèmes et réflexions à propos du pouvoir d'Orde et des rapports entre le presbytérat et l'épiscopat," *Maison-Dieu* 19 (1948) 125–128.

divine institution for the three degrees in particular is declared sufficiently by the Council of Trent and explicitly by the Code of Canon Law and Vatican II.

The Council of Trent[200] defines: "If anyone shall say that in the Catholic Church there is no hierarchy, instituted by divine command, which is combined of bishops, presbyters, and ministers: let him be anathema" (Sess. 23, can. 6, Denz. 1776). In this canon the immediate divine institution of the power of Orders, generically considered, is directly and explicitly defined. Regarding the three hierarchical degrees, at least their mediate divine institution is implicitly proposed, in this sense that the Church could not divide such a power into degrees unless through an authority given her by God. But their immediate divine institution cannot be necessarily deduced from this canon, as it stands, because the canon does not say that the hierarchy is divinely instituted "as combined of bishops, presbyters, and deacons," but "*which is combined of . . .* " This uncertainty has been removed by the two following documents.

The Code of Canon Law, can. 108, §3, states: "*By divine institution the sacred hierarchy, as regards Orders, is combined of bishop, presbyters, and deacons;* as regards jurisdiction, it is combined of the supreme pontificate and the subordinate episcopate; other degrees were also added by Church's institution"; can, 329, §1: "Bishops are successors of the Apostles and by divine institution they are placed over individual churches, which they govern with ordinary power under the authority of the Roman Pontiff." The Code has doctrinal authority and moreover it reflects the current doctrine of the Church. Divine institution, in current ecclesiastical terminology and teaching, is understood as immediate divine institution, as opposed to the institution by the Church through a power divinely given to it; this opposition is also explicitly marked here by the Code.

Vatican II[201]: "Just as the office given by Christ individually to Peter, first among the Apostles, is permanent and is to be transmitted to his successors, so also the office of shepherds of the

---

200   Cf. our work *De Ordine* 2 (Milwaukee 1959) 100–110; E. Boularand, "Le sacerdoce de la loi nouvelle d'après le décret du Concile de Trente sur le sacrament de l'Orde," *Bulletin de littérature ecclésiastique* 56 (1955) 193–228; Ch. Journet, "Vues récentes sur le sacrement de l'Ordre," *Revue thomiste* 53 (1953) 83–86.
201   Cf. Bovis, Denis, Galot, Giblet, Lécuyer, *Prêtres,* cited above, (footnote 196).

church given to the Apostles is permanent and is to be exercised by the sacred order of Bishops. Hence the Sacred Synod teaches that *by divine institution Bishops have succeeded in the place of the Apostles*, as shepherds of the Church" (Dogm. Constit. on the Church, no. 20). "Christ, whom the Father sanctified and sent into the world (John 10:36), through His Apostles made their successors, namely the Bishops, partakers of His consecration and His mission. These legitimately handed on to various ecclesiastical individuals and in various degrees their ministerial office. Thus the *divinely instituted ecclesiastical ministry* is exercised in different degrees by those who from ancient times have been called Bishops, Presbyters, and Deacons" (no. 28). The Council teaches directly only the immediate divine institution of the episcopate; as to the other two degrees, it teaches at least that they exercise, as well as the bishop himself, the ministry divinely instituted.

Scripture, in the Acts and Epistles, exhibits at least two classes of ministers besides the apostles themselves, namely, those who are called *deacons* and those who are indifferently called *presbyters or bishops*. Moreover, two ministers, Timothy and Titus, are shown as special legates of St. Paul with particular authority (similar legates may also be Tychicus, Artemas, Silas, Epaphras, Archippus, and Epaphroditus).[202]

Deacons, as a class of ministers distinct from the presbyters-bishops, are mentioned three times, twice certainly and under that very name (Phil. 1:1; 1 Tim. 3:8–13), once very probably but with no special name (Acts 6:1–6: the election of the seven men). In the first two places the deacons are shown as true hierarchical ministers, distinct from the laity, inferior to the bishops, and united to them in honor and obligations. As to the third passage, it is disputed whether the seven men, especially elected by the apostles, were only ministers destined to temporal and economic office (according to A. Steinmann and H. Lennerz), or special and temporary hierarchical ministers, inferior to the apostles and of the kind of the presbyters-bishops instituted a little later (thus J.-X. Funk, S. Gaechter, and J. Kahmann), or finally real deacons, of the same

---

202 Mention is also made of some charismatic men, called by St. Paul apostles, prophets, evangelists, and doctors (1 Cor. 12:4–11, 28–30; Rom. 12:6–8; Eph. 4.11f.). But it is uncertain and disputed whether these are distinct from the ordinary hierarchs and whether they constitute a true *charismatic hierarchy*. See our work *De Ordine* 1 (Milwaukee 1957) 627f., 713–741, 797–805, 821–823.

kind as those shown in the other two passages. (This is the common opinion of Catholic authors, following the traditional interpretation, since Irenaeus, *Against Heresies* 1.26.3; 3.12.10; 4.15.1).

Presbyters-bishops. As we noted above (p. 152), it is disputed whether the same or different persons are designated under these two names and, abstracting from this question, whether they were all bishops, or all simple priests, or some of them bishops and others priests.

The *presbyters* are shown first in the church of Jerusalem, as rulers with St. James (Acts 11:30; 15:2, 4, 6, 22, 23, 41; 16:4; 21:18), then in the churches founded by St. Paul (Acts 14:23), and finally in the various churches of Asia (Acts 20:17, 28; 1 Tim. 4:14; 5:22; Tit. 1:5; Jas. 5:14; 1 Pet. 5:1). The *bishops* are shown in the churches typically Pauline (Act. 20:28; Phil. 1:1, 1 Tim. 3:2; Tit. 1:7). Both presbyters and bishops are certainly endowed with authority; they are placed "by the Holy Spirit to govern the Church of God" (Acts 20:28) and to "govern God's flock" (1 Pet. 5:2), they administer the Anointing of the Sick (Jas. 5:14f.), they are placed in their charge through the laying on of hands, that same rite through which the sacred ministers were later ordained (Acts 14:23; 1 Tim. 5:22; Tit. 1–5); they are also distinct from the deacons (Phil. 1:1; 1 Tim. 3:8–13).

Paul's legates, particularly Timothy and Titus, show manifestly a hierarchical and episcopal character in both lines of jurisdiction and Orders. *Timothy* is sent by the Apostle to the Thessalonian, Corinthian, and Philippian churches, to exhort, confirm, and admonish them (1 Thess. 3:2; 1 Cor. 4:17; 16:10f.; Phil. 2:19); he governs with full right the church of Ephesus (1 Tim. 3:14f.; 4:11f.); he judges the presbyters (1 Tim. 5:19); he examines the qualities of bishops and deacons to be ordained (1 Tim. 4:14; 2 Tim. 1:6f.); he ordains the ministers (1 Tim. 5:22); his sacerdotal and episcopal character is shown by this last action, by the fact of the full charge of the church, and by his own ordination, received through the imposition of the hands of St. Paul and of the presbyters. The same applies to *Titus*, who governs with full right the church of Crete, admonishing authoritatively (Tit. 2:1, 15), checking on false doctors (1:10–13; 3:10), examining the dignity of bishops to be elected (1:7–9), ordaining presbyters and placing them in charge of various cities (1:5).

All this manifests clearly the existence of *at least two degrees* of the hierarchy of Orders in the apostolic age, besides the apostles themselves who were certainly bishops. *Deacons* are found in the two churches of Philippi and Ephesus, and very probably also in the primitive church of Jerusalem. *Bishops* are at least Timothy and Titus; to whom very probably the "angels of the churches" of Asia, referred to in the Apocalypse, are to be added (see above pp. 365, 382). The existence of the third degree, that is, *the presbyterate*, cannot be proved with certainty; it depends on the hierarchical quality of the aforementioned presbyters-bishops, whether they were all bishops or not; since the negative opinion is much more probable, it follows that such a third degree was already extant and numerous in the apostolic age.

The *divine origin* of this hierarchy is reasonably inferred from the promptness and uniformity with which the apostles established other ministers, their future successors, with similar hierarchical and sacerdotal power. By this they showed that such an institution belongs to the very essential and perpetual constitution of the Church, according to the will of Christ himself. It is not necessary to say that Christ directly signified to the apostles the precise form, in which their hierarchical power should be transmitted to others, such as is found in the three degrees of episcopate, presbyterate, and diaconate. The apostles, as founders of the Church, were acting under the assistance of Christ, the direct impulse of the Holy Spirit, and the gift of revelation, which was publicly closed only at their death. Hence, the institution of the three hierarchical degrees, as pertaining to the constitution of the Church, is still immediately divine, or *divine-apostolic*, and immutable like the Church itself.[203]

Tradition shows the three degrees of the hierarchy established since the beginning of the *second century* in several Asian churches, as is evident from the epistles of Ignatius of Antioch (see above, p. 382). In the other documents of the same period, as the writings of Clement of Rome (see p. 383), *Didache* (chap. 14f.), Hermas (*Shepherd*, Vis. 3.5.1; Vis. 2.4.2f.; 3.9.7), Justin (*Apol. I* 65, 67), only the bishops and the deacons are explicitly mentioned. But this silence about the presbyters does not prove their non-existence, because, in view of the still fluctuating terminology and of the

203 See the same work 508–518, 665–689.

community of the presbyters with their bishop, these may be fittingly indicated under the plural name of "bishops." Even Ignatius of Antioch fails to mention his own presbyters, while explicitly mentioning the presbyters of all the other Asian churches to which he writes, and on the contrary Polycarp in his epistle to the Philippians mentions the presbyters but not the deacons of his own church, who are mentioned by Ignatius of Antioch in his epistles to the church of Smyrna and to Polycarp.

The *sacerdotal* character of the hierarchy is shown especially by Ignatius of Antioch, stating that the presbyter can celebrate the Eucharist and baptize with the permission of the bishop (*Epistle to Smyrna* 8.1f.) and that the deacons "are the ministers of the mysteries of Jesus Christ" and "they are not ministers of food and drink but of the Church of God" (*Epistle to the Trallians* 2.3).

In the *3rd century* the threefold hierarchy is explicitly, constantly, and universally exhibited. The ambiguity and synonymity of the two names "bishop" and "presbyter" are removed, by reserving the first name to the first degree. The *sacerdotal character* is more definitely expressed in many ways. The word "priest" (Latin "sacerdos," Greek "ieréus;" see footnote 198) is introduced and attributed simply to the bishop, or also to the presbyter under the double distinction between the priests and the deacons, or between the high priest and the other priests; even deacons are sometimes said to belong to the sacerdotal or priestly class.[204]

The presbyter's functions are: oblation of the sacrifice and reconciliation of sinners in the absence of the bishop (Cyprian, *Epistles* 9, 10, 11, and 12); assistance to the bishop in the Mass and in the ordination of new presbyters, to whom the assistant presbyters impose the hands without ordaining (*Apostolic Tradition*); anointing and baptism of catechumens with the bishop's permission (*Apostolic Tradition*). *The deacon's functions* are: reconciliation of public sinners in urgent cases and in the absence of the bishop and presbyters (Cyprian, *Epist.* 12); cooperation in the Mass, by

---

204 Origen: "The priests or the prince of priests" (*On Lev.* 7.1). Cyprian: "The priests and the ministers" (*Epist.* 66 and 72); "The presbyters are united with the bishop in the sacerdotal honor" (*Epist.* 54). The Council of Antioch in 269 calls bishops, presbyters, and deacons "the sacerdotal class" (MG 20.710–719). Tertullian simply distinguishes in the Church between priest and laity (*On Prescr.* 41; *On Monogamy* 12). Origen says that also deacons have the right to "the sacerdotal honorarium" (*On Josue* 17.3).

bringing to the bishop the matter to be consecrated (*Apostolic Tradition*) and by distributing communion (*Apostolic Tradition*), especially the chalice (Cyprian); assistance to the presbyter in Baptism (*Apostolic Tradition*) and even administration of Baptism with the permission of the bishop (*Didascalia of the Apostles*).

In the *4th century and at the beginning of the 5th century* there is a greater precision of terms and an ampler evolution of the sacerdotal functions of the presbyter and of the deacon. The synonymity of the terms "bishop" and "presbyter" is practically eliminated. The term "priest" (Latin "sacerdos") becomes the proper name of the two first degrees (Augustine, *City of God* 20.10: "Bishops and presbyters are now properly called priests in the Church"); (bishop) and simply "the priest," or "the second priest," or "the priest of the second order" (Optatus of Milevis, *On the Schism of the Donatists* 1.13).

As regards the proper *functions*, the *presbyter* emerges singularly, both in the hierarchical and in the sacerdotal line, by reason of the expansion of the churches and the necessity of the pastoral care. To him are commonly attributed celebration of the sacrifice, preaching (once strictly reserved to the bishop), ordinary administration of Baptism, reconciliation of sinners, Confirmation (only in the East), Anointing of the Sick, benediction of the people. In his emphatic exaltation of the presbyterate St. Jerome does not hesitate to say: "What does the bishop do, that the presbyter does not do, with the exception of ordination?" (*Epist.* 146.1).

Also the *deacons* grew in authority and importance, to the point of being at times guilty of hierarchical usurpations to the detriment of the presbyters, for which they were often rebuked by Councils and Fathers.[205] The deacons belong to the "sacerdotal

---

205   Cf. Council of Arles of 314, can. 18; the Council of Nicaea I of 325, can. 18; Ambrosiaster, *Questions on the Old and New Testaments*, q.101; Jerome, *Epist.* 146.1; *On Tit.* 1.5; *Dialogue between a Luciferian and an Orthodox* 9.

St. Jerome in his attack against the pretentious behavior of the Roman deacons uttered several exaggerated expressions about the dignity of presbyters, giving the impression that *he denied the distinction between bishops and presbyters*, as far as divine right is concerned. He says that such degrees are based on a mere accidental distinction of honor (*Epist.* 146) and were introduced later in the Church for the sake of order and unity to prevent schism, and hence "by an ecclesiastical custom . . . rather than by a true institution of the Lord" (*On Tit.* 1.5).

However, such expressions (uttered also by two other contemporary writers, namely, Ambrosiaster, *On 1 Tim.* 3:8–10; *Questions on the Old and New Testaments*, q.101, and pseudo-Jerome, *On the Seven Orders of the Church*) can very probably be

catalogue" (*Constitutions of the Apostles*, book 8, chap. 47, no. 8),
as "established in the third priesthood," "not as priests, but as
ministering to the priests" (Optatus of Milevis, *On the Schism of
the Donatists* 1.13). Their cultic function is about the same as in
the preceding century and concerns principally the celebration
of the Eucharist; among other things deacons attend to the good
order among people at the door of the Church and inside the
Church during the eucharistic celebration; they call the people's
attention to some of the parts of the Mass; they invite people to
exchange the kiss of peace; they dismiss the people at the end
of the celebration.

From the 5th to the 12th century there is a further determination, along the same general lines, of both the doctrine and the
practice of the presbyteral and diaconal ministerial dignity. This
is due especially to the multiplication of the liturgical books (as
The Testament of Our Lord Jesus Christ, *The Canons of Hippolytus*, *The
Old Statutes of the Church*, the various *Sacramentaries* and *Church
Orders*), and of particular works dealing directly with the ecclesiastical orders and offices (as those of Isidore of Seville, Rabanus
Maurus, Amalarius of Metz, and pseudo-Alcuin).

The *presbyter* is commonly called priest, while the bishop is
called pontiff; pseudo-Dionysius the Areopagite distinguishes the
"order of bishop," the "order of priests," and the "liturgic order"
(deacons). The deacon is no longer the exclusive minister of the
bishop, but also of the priest. The sacraments of the Eucharist
and Penance, as well as preaching the divine word, are regular
functions of the priest. The oblation of the sacrifice is considered

---

understood in the right sense, if we consider the common doctrine of the other
Fathers, from which Jerome could not so easily withdraw, the intimate connection
and proximity of the two orders of episcopate and presbyterate, on account of
which they often come under the same name, the polemic purpose and context,
which here, as in other cases, led Jerome to rhetorical exaggerations, and finally
other passages, in which he makes a clear distinction between bishops and presbyters, as when he says that only the bishops are the successors of the apostles,
while the presbyters are the successors of the other seventy disciples of Christ
(*Epist.* 14.9; 41.3; 58.5; 75.6; *On Mich* 2.9; *On Jer.* 13.12f.).

At any rate, such ambiguous expressions, uttered by Jerome, Ambrosiaster, and
pseudo-Jerome, were the seed which gave rise in the Middle Ages to the double
opinion, according to which the episcopate is not distinct from the presbyterate as
an Order, but only in the line of jurisdiction, or at least is not a sacramental order.

On the whole question and difficulty rising from Jerome's doctrine, see our work
De Ordine 2 (Milwaukee 1959) 49–93.

as the specific function of a priest (pseudo-Alcuin, *Book of the Divine Offices*, chap. 36; Yves de Chartres, *Serm.* 2; Peter Lombard, *Sent.* 1. 4, dist. 24).

The *deacon* becomes intimately associated to the priest, as his minister. Caesarius of Arles counts him among the priests, speaking of "all the priests of the Lord, not only the bishops, but also the presbyters and the ministers of the Church" (*Serm.* 183.1) and Isidore of Seville emphatically states: "Without the deacons the priest has a name, but he has no office" (*On Ecclesiastical Offices*, book 2, chap. 6, no. 1). The principal functions of a deacon are two, namely, the reading of the Gospel and the distribution of the chalice in communion; the writers of the 12th century already mention the handing over of the book of the Gospels in the ordination of a deacon.

So far we have shown the existence of the three degrees of Orders, since the apostolic age through the various periods of Tradition. There remains to show that Tradition testifies also to their *immediate divine origin.* Regarding the first and principal degree, the episcopate, this has already been done above (pp. 153–156), for the testimonies brought forth to prove the divine institution of the episcopacy as a power of jurisdiction, refer to the bishop integrally and concretely, as vested with the twofold power of jurisdiction and Orders. Considering now the three degrees together, the positive testimony of Tradition is manifested in the three following manners.

First, the Fathers explicitly and constantly *attribute to God himself* the existence of the three degrees of the power of Orders and not only of this power in its generality. Such affirmation would be an improper and deceptive exaggeration, if these orders were instituted by the Church.

Clement of Rome, speaking of the ecclesiastical offices, states that God "Himself by His most excellent will determined where and by whom they must be celebrated" and that the apostles "having received [Christ'] command ... went out to announce the coming of the kingdom of God. Hence preaching the word through lands and cities ... they established bishops and deacons for those who were to believe" (*Epistle to the Corinthians* 40–44). Ignatius of Antioch speaks of "the bishop, his presbyters and deacons, appointed according to the will of Christ" (*Epist. to Philad.*, address) and signifies that these degrees belong to the very constitution of the Church, saying: "Without these there is no Church" (*Epist. to Trall.* 3.1). Cyprian states: "By God and through God His priests are established in the Church" (*Epist.* 69); "Divine law determines the persons and the qualities required in the persons who are to serve at the altar and celebrate the divine sacrifices" (*Epist.* 68). Pseudo-Jerome says that the function of deacon "was given by God to this order" (*On the Seven Orders of the Church* 5). Chrysostom, addressing deacons, states: "God adorned you with this honor" (*On Matt.*, hom. 82.6). Pseudo-Dionysius the Areopagite, comparing the episcopate with the other two degrees, writes: "The divine law lavishly granted to this order more sacred functions in His service than to the other orders" (*On Eccl. Hier.* 5).

Second, the Fathers compare and assimilate, as to their divine origin, the degrees of the ecclesiastical hierarchy *with the degrees of the Mosaic hierarchy*, which was manifestly of immediate divine origin. This comparison first made by Clement of Rome (who also interprets Isa. 60.17 as a prophecy of this ecclesiastical hierarchy; see above, p. 153), was frequently repeated by the Fathers (Origen, *On Josue* 17.3; Cyprian, *Epist.* 68; Ambrose, *Epist.* 63.48; Jerome, *Epist.* 146) and in liturgical documents (*Apostolic Tradition, Didascalia, Constitution of the Apostles*).

Third, the Fathers frequently *refer to the apostles* the institution of the three degrees, thus implicitly signifying the divine institution itself, as explained above (p. 395). Clement of Rome has been quoted above. Epiphanius states: "The successions of the bishops and of the presbyters have been established by the apostles in the house of God" (*Against Heresies* 79.3). *The Constitutions of the Apostles* put the following words in the mouth of the apostles: "After his [i.e., Christ's] ascension we elected bishops, presbyter, and deacons, according to His command" (book 8, chap. 46).

Theological reasoning shows the fittingness of the institution of several degrees in the hierarchy of Orders. On the one hand this is useful to both the ministers and the faithful, for it makes the administration of the sacraments and in general the performance of the divine cult much easier. On the other hand, it manifests the perfection and amplitude of the sacred power itself, aptly distributed into various offices, such as the total care of the Mystical Body, belonging to the bishop, the consecration of the Eucharistic

Body of Christ, pertaining specifically to the simple priest, and the service or assistance to both on the part of the deacon. To this a double confirmation may be added from the distribution of the *civil power* itself into several degrees and especially from the divine institution of three degrees in the *Mosaic hierarchy*, namely, the high priest, the simple priests, and the levites or ministers.

Furthermore, if the three degrees of the sacred hierarchy were not immediately *instituted by God* but by the Church, according to the opinion of some theologians (see footnote 199), the Church would have power on the very essence of the priesthood, one of the constitutive elements of the Christian society, which however is said to be founded only by Christ and the apostles, and likewise it would have the power on the very substance of the sacrament of Orders, by dividing it into three sacramental degrees, which does not agree with the teaching of the Council of Trent, stating that the Church has no power whatsoever on the substance of a sacrament (Sess. 21, chap. 2, Denz. 1728).

Note 1. *On the proper functions of the three degrees of Orders*

The bishop,[206] as successor of the apostles who are Christ's vicars, inherits from them the complete charge of his church with Christ's triple office of *teacher, ruler, and priest.* Above (p. 385) we have briefly outlined this threefold office of the episcopal charge, following the doctrine of Vatican II.[207] The two first offices, although not directly and formally sacerdotal, are intimately connected with the sacerdotal office, like in Christ Himself, by reason of the same subject and of the same purpose, which is the sanctification of the People of God and the building of the Mystical Body. On account of this connection, those two powers are founded on the sacerdotal power and are given with it in the same sacramental consecration, in the manner explained above (p. 373).[208]

---

206   Cf. Vatican II, Dogmatic Constitution on the Church, nos. 19–27; Decree on the Bishop's Pastoral Office in the Church; Colsen, Lécuyer, and Renard, cited above (footnote 196).

207   The Council in the same Constitution on the Church recalls this threefold office several times (nos. 20, 21) and explains each in particular (no. 25, on the office of teacher; no. 26, on the office of priest; no. 27, on the office of ruler).

208   To avoid confusion, it must be noted that the power of teaching and ruling can be understood in two ways. First, in a *broader sense,* that is, as the right to hand the word of God in the exercise of the sacred ministry itself or in connection with it (as in the Mass, in the sacrament of Penance, on various occasions when preaching

As is evident from the historical outline given above (pp. 395–398), in the primitive Church (2nd century), the bishop reserved to himself practically the entire exercise of the power of Orders, so that priests and deacons gave him a mere assistance or an accidental and subsidiary cooperation. In later periods, by reason of the expansion of the churches and the consequent necessity of the common good of the faithful, the exercise of that power was increasingly extended to priests and deacons, especially with regard to the more common and necessary sacraments of Baptism, Penance, and the Eucharist, as well as the preaching of the divine word. Hence the bishop retained only the administration of the two typically episcopal sacraments of Confirmation and Orders, besides the general regulation and supervision of the entire worship and ministry. This practice and discipline has been confirmed also by Vatican II (Dogmatic Constitution on the Church, no. 26).

The priest,[209] by virtue of his sacramental ordination, shares also, in a different manner and at lower degree than the bishop, in Christ's threefold function, *magisterial, royal,* and *sacerdotal.*[210]

In the primitive Church (2nd century) the priestly exercise of the power of Orders was very limited and rather occasional. In the 3rd century it was extended, particularly with regard to the two typically priestly sacraments of the Eucharist and Penance. By the end of the 4th century, all the sacraments, with the exception of Ordination, (and of Confirmation in the West), were currently

---

is suitable) and to regulate worship. Thus, these two powers are inherent to the power of Orders itself, or are connected with it, and we can say that the power of Orders is not restricted to the function of sanctifying the faithful, but implies also the function of instructing them and regulating the administration and reception of the acts of worship, or that it brings along some power of instruction and regulation. Secondly those two powers under the particular name of Magisterium and jurisdiction, are taken in the strict sense of authoritative teaching and of law-making authority. In this sense the power of Orders does not involve any power of teaching or ruling, and it is specifically distinct from Magisterium and jurisdiction; it is not even necessarily accompanied by them (see above, pp. 293, 294f.).

209   *Vatican II* explains the offices of the priest in the Decree on the Ministry and the Life of Priests and in the Decree on Priestly Formation. A good commentary on these decrees is found in *Les Prêtres. Décrets "Presbyterorum ordinis" et "Optatam totius"* (dir. J. Frisque and Y. Congar), Paris 1968. Cf. the bibliography given above (footnote 196).

210   Only, however, in the broader sense, explained above (footnote 208). A priest has no divine Magisterium or jurisdiction in the proper sense, which belongs only to the Primacy and the episcopacy. Whatever true Magisterium or jurisdiction may be given to priests, either by Canon Law or by a direct concession of the bishop or the Pope, is only an ecclesiastical Magisterium and jurisdiction.

administered by simple priests; even the typically episcopal function of preaching began to be entrusted to them. Between the 7th and 11th centuries the administration of the Eucharist and Penance and the preaching of God's word were considered as the *threefold proper function of a priest*.

The deacon,[211] by virtue of his sacramental ordination, shares likewise, in a different ministerial manner and on the lowest level, in Christ's threefold function of *prophet, king, and priest*. His power is a pure service, according to the proper sense of his name ("diáconos," follower, servant; "diaconia," service); it is however, a service to the sacerdotal minister and in the sacerdotal line, and for this reason the Fathers say that the deacon belongs to the sacerdotal class and he is established in the third sacerdotal degree.

His teaching functions, or ministry of the word, is reduced to the *reading of the Gospel* and in general of the Holy Scripture (to the exclusion of preaching as such, which belongs to the priest); for this reason the book of the Gospels was introduced into the ordination of a deacon since the Middle Ages. His sacerdotal function is the administration of the *eucharistic communion* (in times past, especially under the species of wine). His royal function is reduced to some kind of *surveillance* over the people, especially

---

211 Vatican II did not issue any special decree about deacons. *Paul VI* supplied the matter in his Motu Proprio "Sacrum Diaconatus ordinem," June 18, 1967 (AAS 59 [1967] 697–704), in which he gives also the norms for the restoration of the ancient *stable diaconate* and the admission of *married men* to this order.

Brassell, P. V., "A Married Diaconate?," *Heythrop Journal* 3 (1962) 377–388.

Colson, J., *La fonction diaconale aux origines de l'Eglise*, Paris 1960; "Les diacres," *Vie spirituelle* 116 (1967) 442–467.

Diacre (Le) dans l'Eglise et dans le monde d'aujourd'hui (dir. P. Winninger and Y. Congar), Paris 1966.

Diakon (Der) heute (collective), Würzburg 1970.

Diakonia in Christo. Ueber die Erneuerung des Diakonates (ed. K. Rahner and H. Vorgrimler), Freiburg 1962.

Echlin, E. P., *The Deacon in the Church: Past and Future*, Staten Island, N. Y. 1971.

Hornef, J., "Diakonat und Zoelibat," *Seelsorger* 27 (1956–57) 545–549; *Kommt der Diakon der frühen Kirche wieder?*, Wien 1959.

Kerkvoorde, A., "Eléments pour une théologie du diaconat," *L'Eglise de Vatican II* (dir. G. Barauna, French ed. Y. M.-J. Congar, Paris 1966), vol. 3, pp. 943–991.

Nolan, R. T., *The Diaconate Now*, Washington, D. C. 1968.

Schamoni, W., *Familienvaeter als geweite Diakone*, Paderborn 1953.

Tihon, P., "Quelques études sur le diaconat," *Nouvelle revue théologique* 87 (1965) 602–605.

Winninger, P., *Vers un renouveau du diaconat*, Paris 1958; "Les ministères des diacres dans l'Eglise d'aujourd'hui," *L'Eglise de Vatican II* (dir. G. Barauna, French ed. Y.M-J. Congar, Paris 1966), vol. 3 pp. 993–1009.

in the practice of worship. In the first centuries, also the *administration of the temporal goods* of the Church was entrusted to deacons, perhaps in memory of the "service at tables" which was the occasion of the first ordination of deacons (Acts 6:1–6); this function was the cause of the great importance of the ancient deacons, as well as of the practical downfall of the diaconate in the Middle Ages. Vatican II has inculcated the restoration of this temporal function, speaking of the deacon's "offices of charity and administration."

The same Council has extended the deacon's functions beyond those four offices, that is, to the solemn administration of *Baptism*, assistance to and blessing of *Matrimony*, application of the sacramentals, performance of the funeral and burial rites.[212]

In ancient times the diaconate was considered as *a stable office*, that is, as a permanent degree of the hierarchy, at least *per se* and without necessarily precluding the access to a higher degree (as a matter of fact many Popes of the Middle Ages ascended directly from the diaconate to the papacy). Later, by reason of the great number of both priests and clerics in the minor order, who were able to perform the diaconal functions, the diaconate gradually lost its importance and was finally reduced to the condition of a transitory degree or stepping stone to the presbyterate, as happened also to the subdiaconate and the minor orders.

In recent years, by reason of the diminishing number of priests (especially in missionary lands) and the increased necessity of diaconal functions (especially with regard to catechetical instruction and the administration of the necessary sacraments of Baptism and eucharistic Viaticum), there has been an impelling movement among writers and hierarchs[213] for the *restoration of the ancient stable diaconate*, which would be conferred also to *married persons. The Vatican Council II* has accepted both requests, leaving the application of this reformed diaconate to the decision of the individual bishops, to be approved by the Pope, and keeping the law of celibacy still generally attached to the diaconate,

---

212 Hence the deacon becomes also *ordinary minister* of rites of which he was before only extraordinary minister, such as the solemn administration of Baptism and the distribution of eucharistic communion.

213 The movement was first started in Germany by J. Hornef in 1949 and strengthened with solid arguments by W. Schamoni in 1953 (both cited above, footnote 211).

especially for the levites who aspire to the priesthood (Dogm. Constit. on the Church, no. 29).[214]

Note 2. *On the origin and nature of the subdiaconate and the minor orders*[215]

Besides the three degrees of episcopate, presbyterate, and diaconate, which are certainly of divine institution (and also sacramental, as will be shown in the treatise on the sacrament of Orders), the ecclesiastical hierarchy of Orders numbered five inferior degrees, that is, the subdiaconate and the so-called minor orders, namely, the acolyte, the exorcist, the lector, and the ostiary (however, in the oriental rite there are only two orders below the diaconate, namely, the subdiaconate and the lector).[216] As will be shown below, these orders have been suppressed or completely reformed for the Latin Church. There remains, however, a two-fold historical question regarding their origin and their nature, namely, whether they were in the Latin Church (and still are in the Oriental Church) divinely instituted and sacramental. We shall first give a historical sketch of the appearance of these orders in the various churches, and then indicate the two opinions of theologians with regard to that combined question.

As regards *history*, the first mention of a minor order, namely of the *lector*, is made about the end of the 2nd century by Tertullian

---

214   As mentioned above (footnote 211), *Paul VI* issued a special document to regulate this matter. In a subsequent Motu Proprio "Ad Pascendum," Aug. 15, 1972 (AAS 64 [1972] 534–540) a few rules have been added concerning the rite of admission to the Diaconate. Among other things it is required that the candidate receive the institution to the newly reformed ministries of Lector and Acolyte (see below) and subsequently be admitted as a candidate to the Diaconate through a special ceremony determined by the Ordinary. It is also established that married deacons cannot marry again in the case of death of their wives.

215   Cf. M. Quera, "El Concilio de Trento y los Ordenes inferiores al Diaconado," *Estudios eclesiásticos* 4 (1925) 337–358; J. Périnelle, P. Boisselot, "Six ordres de 'ministres' préparent au sacerdoce," *Vie Spirituelle* 31 (1932) 225–240; M. Coppenrath, "Les ordres inférieurs: degrés du sacerdoce ou étapes vers la prêtrise," *Nouvelle revue théologique* 85 (1959) 489–501; E. Doronzo, *De Ordine* 2 (Milwaukee 1959) 313–445.

216   *Tonsure*, that is, the ceremony which formerly preceded the conferring of the minor orders, was not properly and theologically an Order. However, in the Code of Canon Law (can. 950) it was juridically assimilated to the Orders under the same name, because it was the first rite through which a man entered the clerical order and became canonically a cleric. This ceremony, of pagan and Jewish ancestry, was introduced into the Church at the latest in the 8th century, very probably in the 6th century, as appears from the writings of Gregory the Great (†604; *Epist.* 2.38; 9.21).

(*On Prescription* 41.6–8); from which mention a more ancient origin of this order is reasonably inferred. The second mention is found about the middle of the 3rd century in the *Apostolic Tradition* (commonly attributed to Hippolytus of Rome), which speaks of both lector and subdiaconate. The third mention, that of the subdiaconate, occurs about the same time in the oriental liturgical book *Didascalia of the Apostle* (some scholars, however, believe that the text is a later interpolation). The fourth and more important mention is found about the same time in the epistle of Pope Cornelius (251–253) to Fabius, bishop of Antioch, in which he testifies to the existence of *all five orders* in the Roman church; from his words it can be inferred that these orders had been practiced in Rome for some time before him, at least under his predecessor Fabian (236–250).[217] The existence of similar orders in the African church in the same period is testified by Cyprian (†258) in his epistles.

In the 4th and 5th centuries the testimonies are more frequent. In the oriental church the binomial "subdeacon-lector," indicated by Athanasius (*Epistle to Dracontius*, MG 25.766), became more stable in following centuries and has been kept unchanged up to the present time. In the Western church the fivefold list is brought forth again at the beginning of the sixth century in the *Old Statutes of the Church* and in the so-called *Apocrypha of Symmachus*, from which they passed into the writings of Isidore of Seville, Rabanus Maurus, Amalarius, pseudo-Alcuin, and later into the various Sacramentaries, Orders, and Pontificals. These ritual books stabilized the use of the five orders in the Latin Church up to the present time.

As regards their *origin and nature*, the common opinion of the theologians up to the Council of Trent held their *divine origin and sacramentality*. After the Council this opinion was gradually abandoned by many, on account of the new positive and historical

---

217 Complaining about the schismatic Novatian, who had claimed the papacy (see above, p. 384), he writes to Fabius, bishop of Antioch: "Did, therefore, this defender of the gospel ignore that there must be only one bishop in the Catholic Church? He did not, however, ignore — how could he? — that in the [Roman Church] there are forty-six priests, seven deacons, seven sub-deacons, forty-two acolytes, fifty-two between exorcists, lectors, and ostiaries, more than fifteen hundred widows and needy people to whom God's grace and goodness supplies nourishment" (cited by Eusebius of Caesarea, *Eccles. Hist.* 6.43.11; see Denz. 109).

studies which showed the late origin and the fluctuating existence of these orders; but it was again defended by several theologians in the present century.[218]

The reasons which lend *some probability* to this opinion are the following. The Councils of Florence and Trent, while declaring the doctrine on the sacrament of Orders, bring forth these orders together with the major ones, marking no distinction (Florence, Denz. 1326; Trent, sess. 23, chap. 2f., Denz. 1765f.). Trent declares that these orders exist "since the beginning of the Church" (*ibid.*). Trent (can.6, Denz. 1776) and the Code of Canon Law (can. 108, §3) teach that the hierarchy of Orders, which is divinely instituted, "is combined of bishops, presbyters, and ministers" (see p. 286); the word "ministers" here refers not only to deacons but to all the inferior orders. These orders appear since the beginning of the third century without any sign of novelty; hence their origin should be attributed to the apostolic age. In them is found everything needed for a sacrament, that is, matter, form, and spiritual effect.

The second and *negative opinion*, first proposed by Durandus of St. Pourçain (†1334) and followed only by a few great theologians before the Council of Trent, such as Cajetan, Francis of Vitoria, and Dominic Soto,[219] grew stronger after the Council until it became absolutely prevalent in recent times.

The reasons for this *much more probable* opinion are the following. Recent documents of the Magisterium give no importance to these orders. The Code of Canon Law states that "by divine institutions there are in the Church clerics distinct from the laity, although not all the clerics are of divine institution" (can.107). Pius XII in his Constitution "The Sacrament of Orders" makes no mention of these orders. Likewise Vatican II in its Constitution on the Church constantly speaks of the three superior orders and only once in passing mentions the others, apparently eliminating

---

218   It is held by St. Thomas (*Summa Theol., Suppl.*, q. 35, a. 2; q. 37, a. 2) and the other great doctors of the 13th century; later by such theologians as Capreolus, Cano, most of the Tridentine doctors, Suárez, Bellarmine, John of S. Thomas, Billuart; in the present century by Lépicier, Pègues, Gerlaud, Audet, Thomas, Henry, Campo, and Journet. This last theologian strangely states that these orders were sacraments only up to 1947, when Pius XII by his Constitution on the Sacrament of Orders reduced them to the condition of mere ecclesiastical sacramentals (cf. in *Revue thomiste* [1953] 107f.).

219   These four theologians doubted also the sacramentality of the diaconate.

them from the sacramental line.[220] As regards the Councils of Florence and Trent, the former did not issue an infallible document on the sacraments in its Decree for the Armenians, the latter teaches that Order is a sacrament, but does not say that all the orders are that sacrament.

Especially from the *historical Tradition* it is sufficiently evident that these orders are not sacramental nor of divine origin. For, unlike the episcopate, the presbyterate, and the diaconate, they do not exist since the beginning, they are not the same in all the churches, and above all they were mutable through the ages. Thus in the Latin church itself some of these orders, as the exorcist and the ostiary, were discontinued for quite a while and became practically inexistent; the proper function of the acolyte in the primitive Roman rite was totally different from the function later attributed to it under the influence of the Gallican rite; the function of the subdiaconate itself is different in the Latin Church and in the Oriental Church; at present in the Latin Church they are only two, the Lector and the Acolyte, and these two are no longer minor orders but mere ministries of no clerical character.

As regards *theological reasoning*, the proper matter, used since the apostolic age for conferring the sacred power, namely, the laying on of hands, is lacking in these orders. Their proper functions do not require a special supernatural power or character and can be as well performed by lay persons, such as carrying candles, reading the Scriptures, opening or closing the doors of the church.

Paul VI by his Motu Proprio "Ministeria quaedam," Aug. 15, 1972 (AAS 64 [1972] 529–534) has completely reformed, or rather suppressed, these inferior orders in the Latin Church, reducing them from five to two, namely, *the Lector and the Acolyte*, and depriving these two of their nature and dignity of orders, that is, of degrees pertaining to the hierarchy of Orders. They are only simple *ministries*, no longer reserved to those who are destined to receive the sacrament of Orders, but communicable also to the laity.

---

220 We say "apparently," because there is some ambiguity in the following passage, in which the inferior orders are mentioned: "Also the ministers of the inferior order [below priesthood], first of all the deacons, share in a particular manner in the mission and grace of the Supreme Priest... The clerics..., called by the Lord and set aside as his portion..., prepare themselves for the office of ministers" (no. 41).

The particular norms set in this document are the following.

1. Tonsure, which marked the entrance into the hierarchy of Orders, is simply abolished; the diaconate itself is at once the entrance into the clerical hierarchy and its first order.

2. Whatever cultic office may be found below the Diaconate is no longer an order but merely a ministry.

3. Any such ministry is not reserved to those that are destined to receive the sacrament of Orders, but is communicable also to lay persons.

4. Actually there are only two ministries, commonly established for the entire Latin Church, namely, the Lector and the Acolyte. Hence the ostiary, the exorcist, and the subdeacon himself, are commonly abolished. However, the Acolyte in some places may be called Subdeacon, depending on the judgment of the regional Episcopal Conferences; moreover, these Conferences may obtain from the Holy See the establishment of other ministries for their respective regions, such as ostiary, exorcist, or catechist.

5. The principal office of the Lector is the reading of the Word of God (to the exclusion of the Gospel) in the liturgical assembly, that is, in the Mass and other sacred ceremonies. The general and ordinary office of the Acolyte is his service to the altar, that is, to help the Deacon and the Priest in their liturgical actions, especially in the celebration of the Mass, thus replacing the abolished subdeacon; as an extraordinary minister he can also distribute Holy Communion and expose the Blessed Sacrament for the adoration of the faithful.

6. The institution (no longer ordination) of these two ministries, from which women are still excluded, is performed by the Ordinary (respectively the Bishop or the Major Religious Superior), according to a ceremony established by the competent Congregation of the Roman Curia.

7. The candidate to Diaconate and Priesthood must first receive the two ministries of Lector and Acolyte, as a suitable preparation for those two Orders.

13

The Members of the Church[221]

THE MEMBERS OF A SOCIETY ARE THE FIRST OF its constituent elements, that is, the material of which society is made up, and for this reason they are called its *material cause* in philosophical terminology; the other element is the union of these members, which makes them formally a society, distinct from a loose gathering of people, and for this reason it is technically called the *formal cause* of society. In chapters 2 and 3 we have considered the formal cause of the Church, both as Mystical Body and as external society. Hence we complete here the treatment of the constitution of the Church by the consideration of its members without which there is no union, so no society, no Mystical Body.

A double question logically occurs on this subject, one about the *requirements for membership*, or the necessary conditions for being a member of the Church (both as Mystical Body and as external society), the other about the *different states or classes* in which the members of the Church are divided, as of divine institution, that is, the hierarchical order and the laical order. In the present chapter we consider only the first question, reserving the second for the next chapter.

---

221 Bandera, A., "The Composition of the People of God," *Thomist* 33 (1969) 405–455.

Boisvert, L., *Doctrina de membris Ecclesiae iuxta documenta Magisterii recentiora,* Montréal 1961.

Brunet, R., "Les dissidents de bonne foi sont-ils membres de l'Eglise?," *Problemi scelti di teologia contemporanea* (Roma 1954) 199–218.

Dacquino, P., "De membris Ecclesiae, quae est Corpus Christi," *Verbum Domini* 41 (1963) 117–139.

Fenton, J. C. "Contemporary Questions About Membership In the Church," *American Ecclesiastical Review* 145 (1961) 39–57.

Journet, Ch., *L'Eglise du Verbe Incarné* 1 (éd. 2, Bruges 1955) 43–62; 2 (1951) 1056–1080.

Strotmann, D. Th., "Les members de l'Eglise," *Irénikon* 25 (1952) 249–262.

Valeske, U., *Votum Ecclesiae*, 2 vols. München 1962.

Vatican II: The Theological Dimension (collective work, ed. A. D. Lee, The Thomist Press 1963) 59–140.

Vodopivec, G., "Membri 'in re' ed appartenenza 'in voto' alla Chiesa," *Euntes Docete* 10 (1957) 65–104.

The answer to this question would seem very easy at first glance, for, since the Church is a union of men in Christ based on the vital influence of the Holy Spirit and the external bonds of faith, worship, and government, as we defined it above (p. 256), it logically follows that all and only those are its members, who are found under the influence of the Holy Spirit and under the three external bonds. However, the question becomes less clear if we consider the fact that also people who lack those external bonds are under the influence of the Holy Spirit and many of them are in one way or another still connected with the Church.

Hence, to avoid confusion, we divide the question into *three points:* First, whether the external ecclesiastical society is *perfectly equivalent* to the Mystical Body, so that only the members of the external society are members of the Mystical Body. Second, *who are de facto the members* of the Church.[222] Third, what is the relationship between those *who are saved or moved by the Holy Spirit outside the Church* and the Church itself.

Statement 1. *The external ecclesiastical society is perfectly equivalent to the Mystical Body, so that the Mystical Body is no more nor less than the Catholic Church itself and the members of the Mystical Body are only those who are members of the Catholic Church.*[223]

The *biblical foundation* for this assertion can be seen in Eph. 4:4–15, where St. Paul, pointing out the Mystical Body, speaks of "one body, one spirit . . . one faith, one Baptism," one Magisterium

---

222   The concept of *member*, in this moral and mystical body which is the Church, is to be understood properly, although analogically with regard to the physical body (see above, footnote 34). Hence it implies both an actual organic *cohesion* with the head and the other members, and some *participation* in the life of the whole organism under the actual influence of its soul.

The concept of *subject* of the Church is different from that of member, because it implies only subjection to the laws of the Church and its obligations, which are founded on the mere Baptism. Hence the quality of subject, just like the indelible Baptism, is found in every baptized person, whether he is a member or not. Cf. the Code of Canon Law, can. 87; S. Thomas, *Summa Theol.*, Suppl., q. 22, a. 6, ad. 1.

223   This assertion has become quite common among recent theologians, especially after the encyclical "Mystical Body" issued by Pius XII in 1943. However, it has been denied by several theologians, who directly inquired into the nature of the Mystical Body (as Fr. Jügensmeier, E. Mura, E. Mersch, Y. Congar, L. Cerfaux, V. Morel) and who teach that the Mystical Body extends beyond the social body of the Church, embracing all those who are saved or supernaturally influenced by God outside the Catholic Church. Cf. Y. Congar, *Chrétiens désunis. Principes d'un "oecuménisme" catholique*, Paris 1973; L. Cerfaux, *La théologie de l'Eglise suivant saint Paul* (Paris 1948) 283–292.

and one ministry. All such things are applicable only to the visible Church, out of which and beyond which, therefore, no Mystical Body can be found. In the same text the triple bond of Baptism, faith, and union with the authority is indicated.

The explicit doctrine is set forth by the *Magisterium*, especially in recent documents. Already *Boniface VIII* in his bull "Unam sanctam" of 1302 speaks of *"the Catholic Church..., which represents one mystical body*, whose head is Christ..., in which there is only 'one Lord, one faith and one baptism' [Eph. 4:5]" (Denz. 870). *Pius IX*, in his Apostolic Letter "Iam vos omnes" 1868, issued on the occasion of the Convocation of the Vatican Council I, in which he invites all non-Catholics to join the Church, explicitly declares: "No on can deny or doubt that Jesus Christ Himself . . . built His only Church upon Peter . . . so that through baptism all men could be gathered into His mystical body . . . *Religious societies, which are separated from the Catholic Church...cannot be called member or part of that same Church* [which Christ has built]" (Denz. 2997f.).

Pius XII in his encyclical "Mystical Body" 1943 directly sets forth the identity between the Catholic Church and the Mystical Body. This Body of Christ is not merely spiritual but also "concrete and visible" (no.14); its members are only those who keep the three external bonds of faith, worship, and government (no.21), hence *pagans, heretics, schismatics, and persons excommunicated, are not members of the Mystical Body* (nos.21, 100–102), *"even if they may be inclined toward the Mystical Body of the Redeemer by a kind of unconscious desire and hope"* (no. 101; see above, p. 257). The Mystical Body is the *very definition of the Catholic Church*: "In order to define and describe this true Church, which is the holy, Catholic, apostolic, Roman Church, nothing can be found more noble, more excellent, more divine, than that pronouncement, by which it is called 'the Mystical Body of Christ'" (no.13). In his encyclical "Humani generis" 1950 Pius XII insists on the same doctrine, admonishing: "Some believe that they are not bound by the doctrine, set forth a few years ago in our Encyclical Epistles and based on the sources of revelation, which teaches that the Mystical Body of Christ and the Catholic Church are one and same thing" (AAS 42 [1950] 571).

Vatican II repeats the same doctrine: "The society equipped with hierarchical offices and the Mystical Body of Christ . . . are not to be considered as two things, but they form one complex reality, which combines the human and the divine elements . . . This is the only Church of Christ, which in the Creed we profess as one, holy, Catholic, and apostolic . . . This Church, constituted and organized in this world as a society, *subsists in the Catholic Church"* (Dogm. Constit. on the Church, no. 8). With the softer and ecumenical expression "This Church *subsists* in the Catholic Church" instead of "This Church *is* the Catholic Church," the Council does not deny the absolute identity between the Mystical Body and the Catholic Church, but intends only to suggest that outside the Catholic Church there are some ecclesiastical and mystic elements, which belong to the Catholic Church itself (see below, pp. 416–420).

Statement 2. *In order to be truly and strictly a member of the Church and of the Mystical Body, one must receive Baptism and keep the resulting union of faith, government, and worship, which is broken by heresy, schism, or excommunication.*

It is at least *theologically certain* and proximately definable that Baptism is the first and fundamental requirement for acquiring the Church's membership. This has been constantly and explicitly taught by the extraordinary Magisterium, particularly by the Council of Florence (Denz. 1314), the Council of Trent (Denz. 1626, 1671), Pius IX (Denz. 2997), Pius XII (Encycl. "Mystical Body"; see below), Vatican II (Dogm. Constitution on the Church no. 14); according to these documents, Baptism is the door of the Church and the means through which a man becomes a member of the Church or of the Mystical Body.

The requirement for not losing the Church membership is the *unbroken threefold union of faith, government, and worship,* which is a necessary consequence of Baptism. This statement, in its generality and abstracting from further determination explained below, is certain in the sense that the opposite opinion would be *at least temerarious.* This is based on the explicit doctrine of the recent Magisterium. *Pius IX* explicitly states that non-Catholic religious societies are not members of the Church founded by Christ (quoted above, p. 412). *Pius XII* distinctly declares: "Only those must be considered as members of the Church, who have received the bath of regeneration, who profess the true faith, and have not miserably withdrawn from the union of the Body nor have been separated from it by the legitimate authority on account of very serious offenses" (Encycl. "Mystical Body," no.21, Denz. 3802). *Vatican II* states: "Those are *fully incorporated* into the society of the Church, who ... are joined to Christ in the Church's visible structure, that is, through the bonds of the profession of faith, of the sacraments, and of the ecclesiastical government and communion" (Dogm. Constit. on the Church, no.14). Here again the Council uses the softer and ecumenical expression "fully incorporated," to suggest the idea of some kind of incomplete and improper incorporation to the Church, applicable to those who are not actually in the Catholic Church (see below, pp. 416ff.).

Hence the following persons are *certainly not members* of the Church in the true and strict sense: *non-baptized persons* (except the catechumens), *formal and public heretics, formal and public schismatics*, and those who are *solemnly excommunicated* as persons to be avoided (insofar as it appears from the form of the excommunication that the Church intends to separate them from its social body).

On the contrary, all other sinners, no matter how wicked they may be, remain certainly members of the Church.[224] The reason for this is because these sinners do not break any of the three bonds, which make up the ecclesiastical unity, and on the other hand, by keeping their faith, they share in a low degree in the influence of the Holy Spirit, who is the soul of the Church (see above, pp. 267–269, where we have also spoken of the other true members of the Mystical Body). However, all these sinners, guilty of grave transgressions, are likened to *dead or maimed members*, as being deprived of the full life of grace and of the prevailing influence of the Holy Spirit.

As regards all the other persons, whose membership is questioned among theologians and who for this reason may be called *doubtful members*, we hold the following.

Souls in purgatory are not truly and strictly members of the Church, because they are no longer in the visible and hierarchical Church nor under the threefold bond of faith, government, and worship. The reason why Pius XII lists them among the members ("Mystical Body," no. 99), is because these souls (at least many of them) were

---

224 This is explicitly stated by Pius XII in the encyclical "Mystical Body" (no. 22) and by Vatican II in the Dogmatic Constitution on the Church (no. 14).

in this life members of the Church, and hence they are considered as departed members, still in the care of the Church through its prayers and suffrages, just as in the natural order dead persons are still considered as members of their family through the love and the memory of the survivors.

Catechumens are not truly and strictly members of the Church, since they are not yet baptized and hence they are still outside the door of the Church. Pius XII and Vatican II seem to assimilate them to the members of the Church because they are united to the Church by their desire of Baptism and incorporation, and by the love and care which the Church has for them.

Persons invalidly baptized are not members of the Church, although they are apparently members and they are treated as members, as long as the invalidity of their Baptism remains unknown. The fact of being reputed as members does not make them members, for reputation is not reality. Some theologians (as Straub and Pesch) consider these as true members, objecting that otherwise we would not know where the visible Church is, since the validity of Baptism is not something visible. To this we answer that the validity of Baptism in ordinary circumstances is morally certain, as is morally certain the correct application of the matter and form and the intention of the minister; moreover, supposing the indefectibility of the Church, it is absolutely certain that at least the greater number of the faithful are validly baptized.

Formal but purely internal heretics, that is, those who do not exteriorly manifest their heretical mind and the loss of their faith, more probably *are not members* of the Church, because the internal faith is the lowest degree of the vital influence of the Holy Spirit and of supernatural life, which vivify the Mystical Body. Pius XII states that members of the Body are "those who profess the true faith" and that the reason why sinners are still members is because they "keep their faith;" but an internal heretic can hardly be said to profess the true faith or keep his faith. However, several theologians (as Straub, Billot, Pesch, Schultes, D'Herbigny, Rahner, Morel) consider these heretics as true members.

Formal but only internal schismatics are true members of the Church, because they keep their interior faith, while the internal dissent from the authority does not break the bond with the Church which is essentially an external society. On this all the theologians agree,

Purely material heretics or schismatics, that is, "bona fide" such, more probably *are not members* of the Church, because sincerity and good faith does not furnish reality and these persons *de facto* do not share in the Catholic faith and government. If the contrary opinion, held by some theologians (as Franzelin, Caperan, Malvy, D'Herbigny, Morel), were true, most of the faithful of the dissident churches would be members of the Catholic Church, which does not agree with the above general statement of Pius IX (p. 412).

Persons solemnly excommunicated (by the excommunication called anathema or a declaration of persons to be avoided), *are not members* of the Church, because the Church by this action intends not only to punish them canonically, but also to separate them from its body. This is shown by the formulas of this sort of excommunication, in which the separation from the Church is explicitly expressed,[225] and from the traditional doctrine in theology about the three ways of losing *de facto* the Church membership, that is, through heresy, schism, or excommunication, which doctrine has been endorsed by Pius XII (quoted above p. 413). However, some recent theologians (as Dieckmann, D'Herbigny, Sauras, Journet, Guarnieri) think that the Church does not in fact intend to separate such excommunicated persons from its body. It is only question of interpreting the mind of the Church.

Statement 3. *Abstracting from the dignity of a true and proper member of the Church, "all men … belong to the Catholic unity or are related to it in various manners, the Catholic faithful as well as all other believers in Christ, and also universally all men, who are called to a salvation by the grace of God.*[226]

The reason for this doctrine, particularly inculcated by Vatican II, is because "outside the visible structure of the Catholic Church *several elements of sanctification and truth are found*, which, as gifts proper to Christ's Church, impel men to Catholic unity" (Dogm. Constit. on the Church, no. 8).[227] Hence this general and imperfect

---

225 See the general form of solemn excommunication referred in the *Roman Pontifical*, and the individual excommunication issued against some priests by Pius X (AAS 3 [1911] 54) and by the Holy Office (AAS [1922] 593).
226 Vatican II, Dogm. Constit. on the Church, no. 13; cf. nos. 14–17. The same doctrine is expounded by the Council in the Decree on Ecumenism and in the Declaration on the Relationship of the Church to Non-Christian Religions.
227 Cf. the Decree on Ecumenism, no. 3.

communion of all non-Catholics with the Catholic Church, beyond true and proper membership, is based on two things, namely, on the influence of God's grace or of the Holy Spirit, which extends outside the Church, and particularly on the various elements of sanctification and truth, which are found in other religions and in all men, and which, as proper goods of the Catholic Church, impel or dispose men to the unity with this Church.

The first degree, which may be called a true communion, or imperfect and improper incorporation, is found in various manners and fulness in *all Christians*, especially those who are baptized, whether schismatics or heretics. All of them have the name and faith of Christ, admit the Holy Scripture as a source of revelation and as a norm of faith and morality, believe in the Trinity and in Christ's divinity, administer the sacrament of Baptism and in some way also the Eucharist (the Orientals even keep in full all the sacraments, especially Orders, which is one of the essential elements of the Catholic Church as a society).[228] "Besides," as Vatican II remarks, "they share with us in prayers and other spiritual benefits; they are also in some way joined with us in the Holy Spirit, who through his gifts and graces exercises among them his sanctifying influence, and strengthened some of them to the extent of the shedding of their blood" (Dogm. Constit. on the Church, no. 15).[229]

The second degree, which must be called a mere *connection of destination* rather than communion, is found in various ways and fulness in all *non-Christians*. First in the *Jews*, to whom the messianic Christian promise was made, from whom came to us Christ and his apostles according to the flesh and who faithfully keep the Old

---

228 Vatican II in the Decree on Ecumenism uses stronger expressions than in the Constitution on the Church in favor of the separated Christians. See also E. Lamirande, in *Istina* 10 (1964) 25–58, and Chr. Butler, in *L'Eglise de Vatican II* (dir. Barauna, French ed. Y. M.-J. Congar, Paris 1966), vol. 2, pp. 651–668. In order to remove false interpretations of the Vatican doctrine brought forth or suggested by some theologians, the *Sacred Congregation for the Doctrine of the Faith* declared: "The followers of Christ are not permitted to imagine that Christ's Church is nothing more than a collection (divided, but still possessing a certain unity) of churches and ecclesial communities. Nor are they free to hold that Christ's Church nowhere really exists today and it is to be considered only as an end which all churches and ecclesial communities must strive to reach" (Declaration in Defense of the Catholic Doctrine on the Church Against Certain Errors of the Present Day, June 24, 1973).

229 See below, pp. 442, 443.

Testament, source of revelation and of infallible divine promises.[230]
Second, it is found in the other *monotheistic* peoples, particularly
the *Mohammedans*, who adhere to Abraham's faith and adore one
God, who is merciful and will in the future judge all men.[231] Third,
it is also found in all *other pagan peoples*, who in different manners
through shadows and figures search for that "Unknown God," who
"is not far from any one of us," "since it is he who gives to all men
life and breath and all things" (Acts 17:23–28).[232]

Regarding the pagans, Vatican II remarks: "Eternal salvation
can be attained also by those who without fault of their own do
not know Christ's gospel, and yet with sincere heart seek God
and under the impulse of grace strive to do his will, known to
them through the judgment of their conscience. Nor does divine
Providence refuse the necessary help for salvation to those who
without personal fault have not arrived to the explicit knowledge
of God, and strive, with the help of divine grace, to find the right
path. For, whatever element of goodness and truth is found in
them, is regarded by the Church as an evangelical preparation
and as a gift of the One who enlightens all men that they may
obtain life" (Dogm. Constit. on the Church, no. 16).[233]

Note. *On the traditional maxim "Outside the Church there is no
salvation."*[234]

As regards its history, this maxim was born in the 3rd century.
Apparently the first Father who uttered it, was Origen, writing:

---

230 Cf. G. Baum, "Note sur les relations d'Israel et de l'Eglise," *L'Eglise de Vatican
II* (dir. G. Barauna, French ed. Y. M.-J. Congar, Paris 1966), vol. 2, pp. 639–650;
A. Bea, *La Chiesa e il popolo ebraico*, Brescia 1966.

231 Cf. G. Thils, in the same work *L'Eglise de Vatican II* cited in the preceding
footnote, pp. 669–680.

232 Regarding the elements of spirituality, found in different religions, as in
primitive peoples and in the civilized religious philosophy of Hinduism, Brah-
manism, and Buddhism, see A. Ravier, *La Mystique et les mystiques*, Paris 1965;
R. Panikkar, *Le mystère du culte dans l'hindouisme et le christianisme*, Paris 1970; J.
Moffit, "Inter-religious Relations" A Key Confrontation" *American Ecclesiastical
Review* 168 (1974) 341–351.

233 See the letter of the Holy Office to the archbishop of Boston, Aug. 8, 1949
(Denz. 3866–3873), on the false interpretation of the maxim "Outside the Church
there is no salvation." given by the rigorist priest Leonard Feeney, who for his
obstinacy was nominally excommunicated in 1953. Cf. the *American Ecclesiastical
Review* 127 (1952) 308ff.

234 Capéran, L., *L'appel des non-chrétiens au salut*, Paris 1962.
    Congar, Y. M.-J. "Au sujet du salut des non-catholiques," *Revue des sciences reli-
gieuses* 32 (1958) 53–65.

"Outside this house, that is, outside the Church, no one is saved" (*On Josue*, hom. 3.5, MG 12.841). About the same time Cyprian repeated it: "Outside the Church there is no salvation" (*Epist.* 73.21, CV 3-2, p. 795). Since the Middle Ages the Magisterium itself made use of this axiom quite often, declaring also that it expresses a dogma of faith; thus Innocent III (Denz. 792), the Council of Lateran IV (Denz. 802), Boniface VIII (Denz. 870), the Council of Florence (Denz. 1351), Pius IX (Denz. 2867), the Holy Office in 1949 (Denz. 3866, in the case of Leonard Feeney).

Since this maxim seems at first glace to contradict another truth of faith about God wanting the salvation of all men, the recent Magisterium, has softened the rigor of the expression by declaring that a man can be saved outside the Church by reason of his subjective disposition and good faith, and also of his unconscious desire and connection with the saving Church itself. Thus Pius IX (Allocution "Singulari quadam"), Pius XII (implicitly in the words quoted above, p. 412), the Holy Office (Denz. 3870–3872, in that same case of Leonard Feeney), Vatican II (quoted above, pp. 416f.).

Hastings, A., "The Universality of Salvation," *Clergy Review* 51 (1966) 190–213.

Heislbetz, J., *Theologische Gründe der nichtchristliche Religionen*, 1967.

Journet, Ch., *L'Eglise du Verbe Incarné* 2 (Bruges 1951) 1081–1114; 3 (1969) 403–408.

King, J. J., *The Necessity of the Church for Salvation in Selected Theological Writings of the Past Century*, Washington 1960.

Kunnumpuram, K., *Ways of Salvation: The Salvific Meaning of Non-Christian Religions According to the Teaching of Vatican II*, Poona (India) 1971.

McBrien, R., *Do We Need the Church?*, New York 1969; *Church: the Continuing Quest*, Newman Press 1970.

Neuner, J. (ed.), *Christian Revelation and World Religions*, London 1967.

Nyss, H., *Le salut sans l'Evangile. Etude historique et critique du problème du "salut des infidèles" dans la littérature théologique récente (1912-1964)*, Paris 1966.

Rahner, K., *Theological Investigations* (trans. from the German) 5 (Baltimore, Md. 1965) 115–134.

Ratzinger, J., *Das neue Volk Gottes*, Patmos 1969; "Hors de l'Eglise point de salut," *Pour une nouvelle image de l'Eglise* (Gembloux 1970) 49–62.

Roeper, A., *The Anonymous Christian*, New York 1966.

Santos Hernández, A., *Salvación y paganismo. El problema teológico de la salvación de los infieles*. Santander 1960.

Schlette, H. R., *Toward a Theology of Religions*, New York 1966.

Thils, G., *Propos et problèmes de la théologie des religions non-chrétiennes*, Paris 1966; "'Ceux qui n'ont pas reçu l'Evangile," *L'Eglise de Vatican II* (dir. G. Barauna, French ed. Y. M.-J. Congar, Paris 1966), vol. 2, pp. 669–680.

Walgrave, J.-H., *Un salut aux dimensions du monde* (trans. from the Dutch by E. Brutsaert), Paris 1970.

Combining together the two truths of faith, namely, that the Church is a means absolutely necessary for salvation and nevertheless a man can be saved without actually belonging to the Church, the complete sense of the maxim "Outside the Church there is no salvation" implies three things. First, since the Church is the Mystical Body of Christ, *only in the Church are found all the means of salvation*, and therefore, only in the Church men are regularly and commonly saved (Vatican II, Decree on Ecumenism, no. 3). Second, *all means of salvation belong to the Catholic Church*, even those that are found accidentally outside the social structure of this Church (Vatican II, Dogm. Constit. on the Church, no. 8, quoted above, p. 214; Decree on Ecumenism, no. 3). Third, consequently all those who are saved or supernaturally helped by God outside the Catholic Church *belong in one way or another to her* and they are connected with her at least by an implicit desire (Vatican II, Dogm. Constit. on the Church, no. 15, quoted on p. 215; Holy Office, Denz. 3870).[235]

---

235 Some recent writers, as Rahner, Ratzinger, Schlette, Roepers, Heislbetz, and Walgrave (see bibliography in the preceding footnote) unduly emphasize the saving efficacy of the means of salvation that are found in non-Christian religions, to the point of suggesting the idea that these religions are de facto an *ordinary means of salvation* and hence the Church membership is only a mere privileged status or condition.

According to *Rahner*, those religions contain an anonymous or implicit Christianity, through which God works salvation, while the Catholic Church represents, as it were, the sacrament of salvation, that is, the *external sign* of what God is anonymously offering to all men. According to *Ratzinger*, the Church is only *a communal servant of mankind*, chosen by God as a messianic people to perform a mediatorial service of proclamation, worship, and action in behalf of humanity, similar to that of Christ, her founder: hence the Church is not called to make all men her members, but to stand for all men in the universal work of redemption done by Christ, to which she is associated.

With such and similar interpretations the axiom "Outside the Church there is no salvation" is deprived of all its theological vigor and is gently evaporated into an elastic ecumenical formula.

14

The Laity[236]

BY DIVINE INSTITUTION THE MEMBERS OF THE
Church are divided into two classes, the hierarchical and the laical.
The first class, more important in the Church under the aspect
of external society, has been considered in chapters 5–12; the
second class, no less important in the life and the growth of the
Mystical Body, deserves also a special treatment, which has been
developed in recent years under the name of "laical theology" or
"theology of the laity."

Theologians in the past, focusing their apologetical efforts and
their dogmatic consideration on the hierarchy of the Church, paid
no special attention to the lower social class which makes up the
greater part of the Mystical Body and of the People of God. Both
in theology and in Canon Law itself the laity was overlooked or

---

236   Congar, Y. M.-J., *Lay People in the Church*, (tr. D. Attwater, Westminster, Md.
1957; rev. ed. 1965), translation of the important French work, *Jalons pour une
théologie du laïcat*, éd. 3, Paris 1964; *Sacerdoce et laïcat*, Paris 1962; *Christians Active
in the World* (trans. from the French), New York 1968.

Eglise (L') de Vatican II (dir. G. Barauna, French ed. Y. M.-J. Congar, Paris 1966),
vol. 3, pp. 1011–1101: "Les laïcas dans l'Eglise (chapitre IV de la Constitution)."
Four important articles are found here, written by Schillebeeckx, Chenu, Koser,
and Gozzini.

Gerken, J. D., *Toward a Theology of the Layman*, New York 1963.

Giordano, G. M., *La teologia spirituale del laicato nel Vaticano II*, Roma 1970.

Kraemer, H. (Protestant), *A Theology of the Laity*, London 1958.

*Laici in Ecclesia. An Ecumenical Bibliography on the Role of the Laity in the Life and
the Mission of the Church*, Genève 1961 (a Protestant publication).

Laïcs d'aujourd'hui (collective work), Rome 1971.

Newman, J. H., *On Consulting the Laity in Matters of Doctrine* (ed. J. Coulson), New
York 1962.

Philips, G., *The Role of the Laity in the Church* (tr. J. A. Gilbert and J. Moudry),
Chicago 1955.

Schillebeeckx, E., "The Layman in the Church," *Doctrine and Life* 11 (1961)
336–375, 397–408; *The Layman in the Church* (trans. M. H. Gill), New York 1963.

Schmaus, M. *et al.*, *Theologie im Laienstand*, München 1966.

Scott, J. R. W., *One People: Layman and Clergy in God's Church*, Downers Grove,
Ill. 1970

Tucci, R., "Recenti publicazioni sui laici nella Chiesa," *Civiltà Cattolica* 109 (1958),
vol. 2, pp. 178–190.

Vatican II: The Theological Dimension (collective work, ed. A. D. Lee, The Thomist
Press 1963) 262–316.

only offhandedly mentioned,[237] until under the Pontificate of Pius XI there has been both a practical and a doctrinal movement for an equitable promotion of the laity.

Several reasons occasioned and favored this movement. First, the general and ever-increasing *secularization* of civil society and civilization with its breaking off from the religious and ethical order, which showed the importance and necessity of the lay apostolate in the world and was the reason for the institution of the so-called "Catholic Action" by Pius XI.[238] Second, the *liturgical movement*, started under Pius X and doctrinally confirmed by Pius XII in his Encyclical "Mediator Dei" in 1947, which fosters the community spirit. Third, *the doctrine of the Mystical Body* emphasized by several modern theologians and authoritatively endorsed by Pius XII in his Encyclical "Mystical Body" in 1943, which shows the nature and importance of the collaboration of all members for the common good of the body. Fourth, the doctrine of the *universal priesthood of the faithful*, founded on the basic sacraments of Baptism and Confirmation, which shows that also the laity shares in a particular manner in Christ's priesthood. Fifth, the *ecumenical movement* started privately by some theologians, tacitly approved by the Holy See and finally officially proposed by Vatican II, which, on the basis of the twofold doctrine of the Mystical Body and the universal priesthood, promotes some suitable approach and union with the separate Christians whose faith and religion is also essentially founded on the same Baptism.

The general *notion* of the laity is brought forth by its very name, which according to the original Greek noun " laós" (people; "laicós," popular) and in profane, biblical, and ecclesiastical usage, means people, as distinct from the ruling class.[239] Hence

---

237 The *Code of Canon Law* does not carry a comprehensive section on the laity, but treats of it scatteredly and separately, pointing out obligations rather than rights. It has only about 40 canons on the laity out of 2414 canons. The third part of the second book under the title "On the Laity" treats only of the associations of the faithful.

238 Cf. Pius XI, Encyclical, "Ubi arcano" 1928 and "Non abbiamo bisogno" 1931; Epistle "Quae nobis" to Cardinal Bertram 1928; T. M. Hesburgh, *The Theology of Catholic Action*, Notre-Dame, Ind. 1946.

239 All scholars agree that this was the distinct and specific sense of the word in the profane as well as in the sacred usage. It has been convincingly proved by I. De la Potterie, "L'origine et le sens primitif du mot 'Laïc,'" *Nouvelle revue théologique* 80 (1958) 840–853.

the laity is the people of the Church and in the New Testament it is called the People of God (1 Pet. 2:10: "You are now the People of God;" see other texts above, p. 261). As regard its specific *definition*, the Code of Canon Law (can. 948) points out only the negative concept of distinction from clerics (lay=non cleric), while recent theologians have added to it the two positive concepts of active members of the Church and of men having a direct relationship and ordination to the profane and secular world. *Vatican II* has gathered these three concepts into the following definition: "The laity are all the faithful, *except the members of the sacred Orders and of the religious societies*, who, having been incorporated to Christ through Baptism and become the People of God, share in their own manner in the sacerdotal, prophetical, and royal functions of Christ and *carry out their part in the mission of the entire Christian people with regard to the Church and the world*" (Dogm. Constit. on the Church, no. 31).[240]

Statement. *The laity, that is, the members of the Church who do not belong to the hierarchical Orders or to religious societies, by virtue of the sacraments of Baptism and Confirmation share, in their own non-hierarchical manner, in the priestly, prophetical, and kingly functions of Christ, and consequently in the apostolic mission of the Church derived from these functions, both within the Church itself and particularly in the secular world at large.*

---

240 Hence there are *two notions of laity*. One *broader*, which implies only distinction from the clergy and includes also the members of religious societies, and the other *strict* which implies distinction also from religious societies (which represent a special class or state of perfection among the members of the Church.

This *religious state* does not belong to the constitution of the Church established by Christ, and, although based on evangelical counsels, is in itself and formally an ecclesiastical and canonical institution, promoting moral perfection in some members of the Church. For this reason it does not necessarily belong to this dogmatic treatise on the Church, but rather to moral and canonical treatises, regarding Christian morality and ecclesiastical laws.

Vatican II, in its pastoral outlook, aptly joins a brief and substantial treatment of this state to its Dogmatic Constitution on the Church (nos. 43–47), to which it adds also a special Decree on the Appropriate Renewal of the Religious Life.

Further explanations on these Vatican documents about religious are found in the collective work *L'Eglise de Vatican II* (dir. G. Barauna, French ed. Y. M.-J. Congar, Paris 1966), vol. 3, pp. 1139–1190. See also J.-M.-R. Tillard, *Les religieux au coeur de l'Eglise*, Paris 1969; J. Beyer, "Premier bilan des chapitres de renouveau," *Nouvelle revue théologique* 95 (1973) 60–86; M.-M. Labourdette, "La vie religieuse aujourd'hui," *Revue thomiste* 73 (1973) 257–272.

Explanation of the two parts of this statement, namely, of the sharing of all faithful both in Christ's functions and in the Church mission.[241]

A. *Sharing of all the faithful in the threefold, priestly, prophetical, and kingly function of Christ.*

1. The *priestly function* of the faithful, or the so-called, *universal priesthood*,[242] coalesces of two elements, or is exercised in two ways.

The first element is merely *spiritual* (the spiritual sacrifice, or worship, or host). It consists in the sanctity of life, that is, in the

---

241 As noted in the Statement, the sharing of the faithful in the mission of the Church is founded on their sharing in the function of Christ, and this in its turn is founded on Baptism and Confirmation, because these two sacraments make of man a full Christian and give him a double character, which is a participation of the priesthood of Christ, carrying along also the other two functions of prophet and king. This effect of the two sacraments is proved and explained in the proper treatise on the sacraments.

242 Vatican II, Dogmatic Constitution on the Church, no.34.

Arrieta, J. S., "Pueblo de Dios sacerdotal: El sacerdocio comun de los fieles," *Estudios eclesiásticos* 46 (1971) 303–338.

Carré, A.-M., *Le sacerdoce des laïcs*, Paris 1960.

Cerfaux, L., "Regale sacerdotium," *Revue des sciences philosophiques et théologiques* 28 (1939) 5–39.

Coppens, J., "Le sacerdoce royal des fidèles: un commentaire de 1 Pet. 2:4–10," *Mélanges Charue* (Gembloux 1969) 61–75; see another article more general cited above, footnote 196.

Dabin, P., *Le sacerdoce royal des fidèles*, 2 vols., Paris 1941, 1950.

De Rosa, G., "Il sacerdozio 'comune' dei fedeli nella Tradizione della Chiesa," *Civiltà Cattolica* 123 (1972), vol. 4, pp. 350–357, 538–549; "Teologia del sacerdozio 'comune' dei fedeli, *ibid.* 124 (1973), vol. 1, pp. 131–143, 231–239.

Doronzo, E., *De Ordine* 2 (Milwaukee 1959) 445–609.

Espeja, J. "El sacerdocio regio del pueblo cristiano," *Ciencia tomista* 91 (1964) 77–130.

Feuillet, A., "Les 'sacrifices spirituels' du sacerdoce royal des baptisés (1 P 2, 5)" *Nouvelle revue théologique* 96 (1974) 704–728; "Les chrétiens prêtres et rois d'après l'Apocalypse," *Revue thomiste* 75 (1975) ho-66.

Hesburgh, T. M., *The Theology of Catholic Action*, Notre Dame, Ind. 1946.

Lécuyer, J., "Essai sur le sacerdoce des fidèles chez les Pères," *Maison-Dieu* 27 (1951) 7–50.

Palmer, F., "The Lay Priesthood: Real or Metaphorical?," *Theological Studies* 8 (1947) 574–613; cf., 10 (1949) 235–250.

Philips, G., "Un peuple sacerdotal, prophétique et royal," *Divinitas* 5 (1961) 644–705.

Rea, J. E., *The Common Priesthood of the Members of the Mystical Body*, Westminster, Md. 1947.

Teologia del sacerdocio. Sacerdocio ministerial y laical, Burgos 1970.

Torrance, T. F., *Royal Priesthood*, London 1955.

Verhaegen, G., "The Priesthood of the Laity," *The Way* 5 (1965) 23–33.

Vorgrimler, H., "Das Allgemeine Priestertum," *Lebend Zeugnis* (1964) 92–113.

acts of the various virtues, especially of charity and religion, exercised in the various states of Matrimony, virginity, religious life. It is founded not formally on the sacramental character but on sanctifying grace. We can say with Vatican II (Dogm. Constit. on the Church, no. 34) that, through this spiritual priesthood and sacrifice, "the world is consecrated to God," especially by the laity.[243]

The second element is *ritual or sacramental*, because it is founded properly on the sacramental character. It consists in receiving the other sacraments, in the apostolate of faith (connected more directly with the sacrament of Confirmation, which makes a man soldier and witness to Christ), in conferring Baptism in the case of necessity, in being a quasi-minister of Matrimony, in a kind of active participation in the offering of the sacrifice of the Mass, in administering communion in the case of necessity, in dispensing also some of the sacramentals of the Church,[244] in being also called to the newly established ministries of Lector and Acolyte (see above, pp. 408f.).

Both elements are called priestly in an improper and metaphorical sense, for the proper priesthood is essentially hierarchical (see above, pp. 294f.). The Sacred Congregation for the Doctrine of the Faith in its Declaration of June 24, 1973 states explicitly: "These [i.e., the common priesthood and the hierarchical priesthood] differ from each other not only in degree but also in essence."

2. *The prophetical or doctrinal function of the laity consists in some activity* with regard to the knowledge and diffusion of the faith and the sacred doctrine, which however, is deprived of the authentic and authoritative character, proper to the hierarchical Magisterium. This function embraces the following.

First, the *sense of the Christian people* in doctrines of faith, of which we spoke in the treatise on the Channels of Revelation (pp. 188–190, 213f.) and which enjoys a kind of passive infallibility, sometimes preceding the infallible definition of the Magisterium (see above, p. 349).

---

243 The expression "Consecration of the world," as attributed to the lay apostolate, was first used by Pius XII (Allocution to the second congress on the lay apostolate in 1957, AAS 49, p. 927). Cf. M.-D. Chenu, "Les laïcs et la 'consecratio mundi,'" *L'Eglise de Vatican II* (dir. G. Barauna, French ed. Y. M.-J. Congar, Paris 1966), vol. 3, pp. 1035–1053; *Nouvelle revue théologique* (1964) 608–618.
244 This last function is permitted and commended by Vatican II (Constitution on the Sacred Liturgy, no. 79).

Second, the *private charisms* (as miracle, prophecy, revelation, visions, knowledge of the secrets of hearts, gift of languages), which were frequent in the primitive Church (cf. 1 Cor. 12:1–11; 14:6, 26) but were never lacking in the history of the Church, as is evident from the lives of saints.[245]

Third, the *apostolate of the word*; for, at least in a general manner, "on all Christians is laid the splendid burden of working to make the message of salvation known and accepted by all men throughout the world;"[246] just as simple faithful, besides the apostles and the other hierarchs, worked to spread the Gospel in the primitive Church, so modern faithful should also strive, according to their means and circumstances, to spread the evangelical message in their environment, subject to the rights and the direction of the hierarchy.

Fourth, the *apostolate of life*, that is, the living preaching of the example in Christian practice; Vatican II refers this apostolate to "the prophetic office fulfilled by Christ through the laity,"

---

245 Vatican II speaks of such "special gifts given to the faithful" by the Holy Spirit, distinguishing them into *"outstanding charisms"* and *"more simple and widely spread charisms,"* whose existence and exercise must be controlled by the authority (Decree on the Apostolate of the Laity, no. 3; Dogm. Constit. on the Church, no. 12; cf. no. 30).

As regards the charisms that are said to happen in the so-called *Pentecostal Movement*, spreading among Catholics, see E. D. O'Connor, "The New Theology of Charisms in the Church," *American Ecclesiastical Review* 101 (1969) 145–169; idem, *The Pentecostal Movement in the Catholic Church*, Notre Dame, Ind. 1971; "Charism and Institution," *American Ecclesiastical Review* 168 (1974) 507–525; W. J. Hollenweger, *The Pentecostals: The Charismatic Movement in the Churches* (trans. from the German by R. A. Wilson), Minneapolis 1972; Fr. A. Sullivan, "The Pentecostal Movement;" *Gregorianum* 53 (1972) 237–266; D. W. Faupel, *The American Pentecostal Movement: A Bibliographical Essay*, Wilmore, Ky. 1972; J. V. McHale, "The Charismatic Renewal Movement," *The Furrow* (May 1973) 259–271; J. Giblet, "Le movement pentecotiste dans l'Eglise Catholique aux U. S. A.," *Revue théologique de Louvain* 4 (1973) 469–490; D. L. Gelpi, *Pentecostalism: A Theological Viewpoint*, New York 1973; H. Thwaites, "Pentecostalism," *Faith* 5 (1973), no. 3, pp. 12–15 (this writer is utterly opposed to Pentecostalism); P. Hocken, "Catholic Pentecostalism: Some Key Questions," *Heythrop Journal* 15 (1974) 131–143, 271–284; A. Barruffo. "Il 'Rinnovamento Carismatico' nella Chiesa Cattolica" *Civiltà Cattolica* 125 (1974), vol. 2, pp. 22–36, 332–346; R. Laurentin, *Pentecôtisme chez les catholiques. Risques et avenir*, Paris 1974.

246 Vatican II, Decree on the Apostolate of the Laity, no. 3. Cf. M Sauvage, *Catéchèse et laïcat. Participation des laïcs au ministère de la Parole et mission du frère enseignant dans l'Eglise*, Paris 1962; *L'apostolat des laïcs. Décret "Apostolicam Actuositatem,"* Paris 1970; J. H. Nicolas, "Les laïcs et l'annonce de la parole de Dieu," *Nouvelle revue théologique* 93 (1971) 821–848 (he states that laymen could be given permission to preach during liturgical offices).

inasmuch as "the power of the Gospel shines forth in their daily, family, and social life."[247]

Fifth, *the apostolate of science*, that is, of the theological and apologetical science, which is not an exclusive privilege of the clerics, as is evident from the history of the Church, which brings forth so many outstanding doctors and defenders of the faith, who were laymen or wrote their works while they were still laymen.[248]

Sixth, *the apostolate of free opinion*, for, as Vatican II states, "laymen, by reason of the knowledge, competence, and importance which they may enjoy, have the right and sometimes the obligation to declare their views on things concerning the good of the Church;"[249] these words in their generality refer not only to the discipline but also to the doctrines of the Church.

3. *The kingly function*, as regards the government of the Church, may be exercised by laymen in two ways, namely, through an indirect influence into the laws and decisions of the hierarchy, by way of suffrage, or advice, or petition, and also through a limited participation in some of the public offices which are not of divine but of merely ecclesiastical institution. We may exemplify this with four instances.

First, it is suitable in itself and, according to the present circumstances of time and customs, it would be desirable, that the Christian people have some kind of *consultative suffrage*, in the election of their pastors, in the assignment of some ecclesiastical offices, and in the decisions of the Councils themselves. This has been done to a certain extent in the apostolic period (cf. Acts 6:3–7; 15:4, 22; 1 Tim. 3:7), in the patristic age (when bishops were appointed with the compliance of the people[250]), and also in more

---

247 Dogmatic Constitution on the Church, no. 35.
248 Thus in the patristic age, Justin, Tertullian, Clement of Alexandria, Lactantius, Prosper of Aquitania, Socrates, Sozomen. In more recent period, Pius II (Piccolomino), Cardinal Contarini, Cardinal R. Pole, Marcellus II (Cervini), who all wrote in their lay period. In the modern age, Chateaubriand, De Maistre, Goerres, Donoso Cortés, A. Nicholas, Veuillot, Maritain, Gilson, who remained simple laymen. The Church has recently given the title of "Doctor of the Church" to two women, St. Theresa of Avila and St. Catherine of Siena. Cf. Fr. Coudreau, "Lay Responsibility in the Church's Theological Mission," *Lumen Vitae* 28 (1973) 609–630.
249 Dogmatic Constitution on the Church, no. 37.
250 Cf. Clement of Rome, *Epistle to the Corinthians* 44; Cyprian, *Epist.* 14; 16.4; 17.1; 55.8; 59.5; 67.5. The author of the *Life of St. Augustine*, Possidius, his disciple and friend, testifies: "In ordaining priests and clerics he thought that the consent of the greater number of the faithful and the custom of the Church should be

recent times insofar as laymen were admitted as observers in the Ecumenical Councils from Lateran IV to Trent.[251]

Second, it would be very suitable to modern time and mentality to allow *an indirect influence of laymen in the making of ecclesiastical laws*, by way of given and accepted advice and desire, or freely manifested opinion, or adherence to some previous lay initiative. This holds both in things purely ecclesiastical and in mixed matters, in which the very knowledge, competence, and authority of laymen would afford a great help to the ecclesiastical legislator in the preparation of his laws for the good of the entire Church. This is also acknowledged by Vatican II (Dogm. Constit. on the Church, no. 37).

Third, it would also be useful that some upright and distinguished laymen be called *to share in some ecclesiastical dignities and offices*, which are of mere ecclesiastical institution and have no immediate connection with the sacred ministry. Such are the members of the Roman Curia, the members of the Vatican diplomatic corps, the apostolic delegates and nuncios themselves in their relation not to the bishops of a country but to its civil government.[252] The reason for this is the same as for the preceding provision.

Fourth, it would be suitable to modern age and circumstances to entrust to laymen *the administration of the temporal goods of the Church*, under the general supervision and examen of the hierarchy. This would be fitting to the evangelic spirit of poverty, to the spiritual freedom and efficacy of clerics in their sacred ministry. and also to the prosperity of the temporal goods of the Church, which

---

followed" (21, ML 32.51). Cf. R. G. Howes, "Consultative Process in the Church," *American Ecclesiastical Review* 168 (194) 422–430.

251 Vatican I simply excluded them, while Vatican II admitted them (even women), as mere auditors (listeners). In France, Spain and England, the particular councils of the 6th–7th centuries were celebrated in the presence of laymen, who sometimes signed the acts, and in the 7th–9th centuries several mixed councils (combined of clerics and laymen) took place. However this was done by reason of the great influence of the secular power at that time and it was the occasion of several abuses. To prevent similar abuses Vatican II expressed "the wish that in the future no righs or privileges regarding the election, nomination, presentation, or designation to the episcopal office, be any longer granted to civil authorities" (Decree on the Bishop's Pastoral Office in the Church, no. 20).

252 Cf. A. Doglio, *De capacitate laicorum ad potestatem ecclesiasticam, praesertim iudicialem*, Roma 1962; D. Dehler, "On the Ascension of the Layman to Ecclesiastical Offices," *Revue de l'Université d'Ottawa* 40 (1970) 127–139.

would be entrusted to men usually more capable and competent than clerics in temporal affairs. The Code of Canon Law (can. 1521, §2; cf. cann. 1495–1551) partially provides for this, but it does not make such lay administration universal (in the Church as a whole, in the diocese, in the parish) nor full and ordinary.

B. *Sharing of the laity in the apostolic mission of the Church.*

Such a participation in the saving mission of the Church, usually called the *lay apostolate*, consists in the various activities deriving from the participation in the threefold functions of Christ, which we have just described. Two things remain to be explained, namely, its mode and its peculiar and specific character.

The mode in which this apostolate is exercised is threefold. The *ordinary* apostolate consists in the aforementioned works of the spiritual priestly function, by which the laity consecrate the world to God (p. 425), and in the various works of the prophetical function, which makes up the testimony of the word and of life (p. 425). The *extraordinary* apostolate is exercised by the laymen in two ways, either by making the Church present and operative in those places and circumstances in which the Church cannot work through other means or persons, or by providing some sacred services (as Baptism, preaching, sacramentals) when the ordained ministers are lacking or are hindered by persecution.[253] The *special* form of apostolate consists in an immediate cooperation with the apostolate of the hierarchy, which is exercised either by all those who in many ways directly help the clerics in the sacred ministry, or by some individuals who are called by the authority to share in the ecclesiastical offices (see above, p. 428). Furthermore, these three modes of apostolate can take either an individual form, to which all faithful are obliged to a certain extent, or a social and organized form, such as the so-called Catholic Action.[254]

---

253 Cf. Vatican II, Dogm. Constit. on the Church, nos. 33, 35.

254 The Catholic Action, first founded by Pius XI (see above, p. 422), was later organized under various forms in different countries. There are now many approved associations in the field of apostolate, under the name of Catholic Action or similar names, which are highly commended by Vatican II in its Decree on the Apostolate of the Laity, nos. 18ff. Paul VI by his Motu Proprio "The Catholic Church of Christ" 1967 instituted a "Council of Laymen" for the purpose of fostering the exercise and the practice of the lay Apostolate.

The peculiar and specific character of this lay apostolate[255] lies in its *direct connection with temporal things and the secular world*, which are immediately and vitally reached, sanctified, and consecrated to God by the laymen. This direct connection with temporal things, proper to the layman, is not to be understood on the part of the object reached by him, for his apostolate extends also to actions and things within the Church, but on the part of the subject or the person itself, in the sense that a layman, while he lives and in the way he lives in the secular life and in the midst of a secular world, exercises according to his conditions a sacred apostolate, both within the Church, by helping and partially completing the ministry of the clerics, and without the Church in the secular world, in which he leads his daily life and from which he is not separated by a clerical or religious state.

Hence the layman, in his quality of layman, exercises his apostolate in the three circumstances of his life, namely, in his *individual life* (as also clerics and religious do in their own conditions), in his *family life*, as a married man or woman (which is common but not exclusive to laymen, since there are also married clerics), and in his *social life*, according to the manifold aspects of professional, cultural, civic, national, and international activities (which life, as a state, is per se proper to a layman, since clerics and religious are normally excluded from it).

Such an apostolate is properly lay, but it is not profane; on the contrary it is a sacred and truly ecclesiastical activity, which the Church or the Mystical Body itself exercises through some of its members, exteriorly and hierarchically inferior but mystically equal to clerics, according to that essential and higher equality which is the bond of all the members of the Mystical Body in Christ the Head.[256]

---

255   Cf. Vatican II, Dogmatic Constitution on the Church, nos. 31, 32, 34, 36; Decree on the Apostolate of the Laity, nos. 2, 7, 16; *L'Apostolat des laïcs Décret "Apostolicam actuositatem"* (collective work under the direction of Y. Congar), Paris 1970.
256   See the same Vatican Constitution on the Church, no. 32.

15

The Properties of the Church[257]

WITH THE PRECEDING CHAPTER WE HAVE COM-
pleted the consideration of the four causes, which bring the
Church into existence (the two extrinsic causes, i.e., the efficient
and final, pointed out in chap. 1) or constitute its essence (the
two intrinsic causes, i.e. formal and material, expounded directly
in chaps. 2, 3, 13, 14). We now logically proceed to the consideration of the properties of the Church, which necessarily derive
from its essence and are intimately connected with its four causes.

All such properties can be reduced to the four qualities solemnly indicated by the Council of Constantinople I in its symbol
(Denz. 150), namely, *unity, sanctity, Catholicity,* and *apostolicity.*
These four qualities can be considered in two ways. First, dogmatically and in themselves, or formally as *properties* flowing from the
essence of the Church, and this is the direct subject of the present

---

257   Congar, Y. M.-J., "L'Eglise est sainte," *Angelicum* 42 (1965) 273–298; *L'Eglise,
une, sainte, catholique et apostolique,* Paris 1970.

Dulles, A., "The Church, the Churches, and the Catholic Church," *Theological
Studies* 33 (1972) 199–234.

Harle, P. A., "La notion biblique d'apostolicité," *Etudes théologiques et religieuses*
40 (1965) 133–148.

Jourent, Ch., *L'Eglise du Verbe Incarné* 1 (éd. 2, Paris 1955) 673–724 (apostolicity); 2 (Paris 1951) 903–934, 1115–1128 (sanctity), 1191–1297 (unity and
Catholicity); "La sainteté de l'Eglise: Le livre de Jacques Maritain," *Nova et Vetera*
46 (1971) 1–33.

Jugie, M., *Où se trouve le Christianisme intégral? Essai de démonstration catholique,*
Paris 1947.

Mysterium salutis. Dogmatique de l'histoire du salut (trans. from the German), IV:
L'Eglise, sainte, une, catholique, apostolique, Paris 1970.

Renwart, L., Fisch, J. M., "La sainteté du Peuple de Dieu," *Nouvelle revue
théologique* 87 (1965) 1023–1046; 88 (1966) 14–40.

Reveillaud, M., "L'apostolicité de l'Eglise chez les Pères," *Etudes théologiques et
religieuses* 40 (1965) 149–164.

Santoro, G., "La natura delle Note della vera Chiesa," *Sapienza* 6 (1953) 257–271,
394–402.

Thils, G., "La notion de catholicité de l'Eglise dans la théologie moderne," *Ephemerides theologicae Lovanienses* 13 (1936) 5–73; *Les notes de l'Eglise dans l'apologétique
catholique depuis la Réforme,* Gembloux 1973; "La 'via notarum' et l'apologétique
contemporaine," *Angelicum* 16 (1939) 24–49.

Witte, J. L., "Die Katholizitaet der Kirche," *Gregorianum* 44 (1961) 193–241.

chapter. Second, apologetically and with regard to use, or formally as *marks* or signs, by which it can be ascertained which is the true Church founded by Christ, whether it is only the Roman Catholic Church; this will be the subject of the next chapter.

Property here is understood in the strict sense of a quality which derives directly from the specific essence of a thing and hence is found only in it.

Unity is taken integrally, that is, both extrinsically and intrinsically. Hence the unity of the Church means that the Church is numerically one, not two or three (extrinsic unity), and that is formally one, in all its constitutive elements, as having one faith, one worship, and one government (intrinsic unity).

Sanctity is taken both passively (sanctity itself, as existing in a person) and actively (the means of sanctification). Hence the sanctity of the Church means that the Church is holy in its members (passive sanctity) and that it has all the means to sanctify men (active sanctity).

Catholicity, which etymologically signifies totality or universality, is taken both extrinsically and intrinsically (see above, footnote 5). The extrinsic catholicity of the Church means that the Church extends to all men, with regard to their condition (to all races), time (to all ages as long as mankind lasts), and place (to all nations everywhere); its intrinsic catholicity means that the Church has all that it must have according to Christ's institution, that is, all the doctrines and all the means of salvation.[258]

Apostolicity means identity of the Church at all times with the primitive Church of the apostolic age, with regard to all its essential elements, that is, faith, worship, and government.

Statement. *Unity, sanctity, Catholicity, and apostolicity, are true properties of the Church flowing from its specific nature and hence necessarily found in it.*

258 Regarding this extrinsic Catholicity in its third element of place (the so-called *geographic Catholicity*), note that it is to be taken not absolutely, but morally and relatively. In other words the Church is Catholic or universal, if it has an *expansive force* tending to reach all places and all peoples and in fact it is *found everywhere in a conspicuous manner and with a considerable number of members*, taking into account time, place and people. Hence it is not against the Catholicity of the Church if in the first days of its expansion it was not yet actually everywhere, or if some numerous people, as that of China, is now not sufficiently reached by the Church, or if the greater number of mankind is not Catholic.

Theological note. It is *de fide*, defined by the Magisterium, both ordinary and extraordinary, that the Church is one, holy, Catholic, and apostolic, taking these four qualities generically and indistinctly. The Church professes this faith in the Constantinopolitan Creed, constantly and universally used. If we take those qualities distinctly in the essential sense explained above, the statement is *theologically certain* and proximately definable. This theological note is based on the documents of the Magisterium here below.[259]

---

259 The *Protestants* in logical conformity with their denial of the social nature of the Church (see footnote 42), admit the four properties of the Church only partially and in a limited sense, especially with regard to unity and apostolicity. As regards *unity*, they logically deny the extrinsic unity, namely, that the Church must be only one society, and admit the intrinsic unity only as to some fundamental articles of faith and the two baptismal and eucharistic rites of worship. *Sanctity* is likewise reduced to extrinsic justification through faith in Christ and the two means of Baptism and the Eucharist. *Catholicity* extrinsically is understood only as a force of expansion, not as a fact, and intrinsically it is restricted to the aforementioned articles of faith and two sacraments. *Apostolicity* is denied, as regards government, and it is restricted to the same articles of faith and sacraments, as regards faith and worship.

Such denial or restriction of the four properties was the cause of the so-called *ecumenical movement*, born in the Protestant church in the last century with the purpose of building up some sort of pan-Christendom on the denial of the extrinsic unity of the Church. This movement was first started by Anglicans, through the foundation of the "Association for the promotion of the reunion of Christendom" at London in 1857. It took a new practical and successful shape much later, when in 1910 a general congress was held in Edinburgh under the name of "World Missionary Conference." Several other general congresses have been held, up to the present time, under the name of "World Conferences on Faith and Order" and since 1948 under the third name of "The World Council of Churches." The doctrinal result of this movement has been the reduction of faith to a minimum agreeable to all, that is, the doctrine about Christ, God and Savior. The practical and fruitful result has been to show and agree on the fact that separation is harmful to Christianity and that at least the union in faith is an essential property of the Church as founded by Christ.

About the history of this movement, see S. R. Rouse and St. Ch. Neill (eds.), *A History of the Ecumenical Movement 1517–1948*, London 1954, 2nd ed. 1967. About its doctrine see G. Thils, *Histoire doctrinale du mouvement oecuménique*, éd. 2, Louvain 1963; B. Lambert, *Ecumenism: Theology and History*, London 1967.

The separated *Orientals* commonly speak of the four properties of the Church which they profess in the Constantinopolitan Creed. However, by reason of the schism, some ambiguity or restriction can be observed in the concept of unity and catholicity. The *unity of government* does not agree with the lack of the Supreme Pontificate. *Extrinsic Catholicity* is understood only as an expansive force, not as the fact of being conspicuously everywhere, since the Orientals are behind the Protestants in this kind of expansion. The lay theologian A. S. *Khomiakov* (†1860) introduced among the Russian theologians a new concept of Catholicity, called "Sobornost" or collegiality (from the Russian "sobor," convention); the Church would be Catholic in the sense that it is synodal, that is, in conformity with the agreement of all, or to the free unanimous opinion.

The Magisterium constantly proposed the four properties together, since the fourth century; in recent documents one or another property is distinctly and separately considered.

The fourfold formula has been proposed, very probably for the first time, in the Creed defined by the *Council of Constantinople I* in 381: "I believe in one God ... and one, holy, Catholic, and apostolic Catholic" (Denz. 150).[260] From the Middle Ages to the present time the Magisterium has repeated this formula in the major documents of faith; thus Leo IX in 1053 (Denz. 684), Innocent III in 1208 (Denz. 792), the Council of Lyons II in 1274 (Denz. 854), Boniface VIII in 1302 (Denz. 870), Vatican I in 1870 (Denz. 3001 with 3013), Vatican II (Dogm. Constit. on the Church, no. 8).

Pius IX, through the Holy Office in the epistle to the bishops of England in 1864, directly explains the doctrine of the four properties or marks of the Church applying them to the Roman Catholic Church. "By divine authority the true Church of Jesus Christ," he declares, "is constituted by and discerned from the fourfold mark, which we profess in the Creed, and each of these marks is so bound with the others that it cannot be set apart from them. Hence that same Church which is called Catholic and is truly such, must also shine with the prerogatives of unity, sanctity, and apostolic succession" (Denz. 2888).

Unity is particularly stressed by Leo XIII (Encycl. "Satis cognitum," Denz. 3304), Pius XI (Encycl. "Mortalium animos"), the Holy Office ("On the ecumenical movement" 1949), John XXIII (Encycl. "Ad Petri Cathedram" 1959 and "Aeterna Dei" 1961), Vatican II (Dogm. Constit. on the Church, no. 8). *Sanctity* by Vatican I (Denz. 3012) and Vatican II (*ibid.*, no. 39). *Catholicity* particularly by Vatican II, which extends it in some degree to all men, even those who actually are outside the Catholic Church (*ibid.*, no. 13; see above, pp. 213f.). *Apostolicity*, with regard to government, by Vatican I and II, in their doctrine about the succession of the Roman Pontiff to Peter and of the bishops to the other apostles (Denz. 3050f., 3056–3058; Dogm. Constit. on the Church, no. 18).

These four properties of the Church are solidly founded on *Scripture* and *Tradition*, and suitably confirmed also by *theological reasoning*.

---

260 However, some scholars think that this Creed is derived from an older Symbol of faith, reported in 374 by Epiphanius in his *Ancoratus* (a synopsis of Christian doctrine). In this Symbol exactly the same words occur (see Denz. 42).

1. UNITY OF THE CHURCH[261]

Scripture implies the extrinsic unity of the Church, or the existence of one Church, in the various images of *one flock* and *one fold* (John 10:14–16; 21:15–17), *one house* built on one rock (Matt. 16:18f.), *one moral body* (1 Cor. 12:12–30; Eph. 4:4f.). The same follows from the unity of government, because several societies cannot be established formally under the same government. The intrinsic unity of *faith and worship* follows from Christ's command to preach the same Gospel to all nations and baptize them (Matt. 28:18–20; Mark 16:15–17), and from St. Paul's affirmation: "One faith, one baptism" (Eph. 4:5). The unity of *government* is founded on Christ's words giving the apostles the authority of preaching to all men and baptizing them all, and in St. Paul's words about "the pastors and teachers [established by Christ] in order to perfect the saints for a work of ministry, for building up the body of Christ" (Eph. 4:11f.).

The Fathers often stress both the extrinsic and the intrinsic unity of the Church. Two among older testimonies will suffice. *Irenaeus:* "The Church, spread all over the world, diligently keeps, as living in one house, the preaching and the faith once received; and in like manner it believes that doctrine with one soul and one heart, and harmoniously preaches, teaches, and hands it over, as it were with one mouth. For, notwithstanding the difference of tongues in the world, the force of tradition is one and the same" (*Against Heresies* 1.10.2, MG 7.551). *Cyprian* in his entire work *On the Unity of the Catholic Church* stresses very emphatically this truth against the dangers of schism: "There is one God, one Christ, one Church, one faith, one people solidly united into a body by the bond of agreement. Unity cannot be broken, nor can the unity of this body break asunder" (Chap. 23).

Theological reasoning draws the unity of the Church from the unbreakable unity of its various elements. The purpose of the Church is one and indivisible, the salvation of souls; its founder is one, God through Christ; its soul is one, the Holy Spirit; its head is one, Christ in his humanity; its inner life is one, sanctifying grace; its faith is one, in one divine revelation; its basic means is one, Baptism onto one regeneration. If all the other elements are one, also the people and the government must be one, by force

---

261 See Journet, cited in footnote 257.

of the principle of sufficient reason; for there is no reason why plurality of churches and authorities should be built on the unity of purpose and nature.

2. SANCTITY OF THE CHURCH[262]

Scripture shows the active sanctification in the means instituted by Christ, namely, faith and the sacraments. The passive sanctification of the members of the Church is stressed by the apostles; St. Paul speaks of "a glorious church, having no spot or wrinkle or similar blemish...[which is] holy and undefiled" (Eph. 5:27) and of "the acceptable people, pursuing good works" (Tit. 2:14); St. Peter calls the Christians "a chosen race, a royal priesthood, a holy nation" (1 Pet. 2:9).

The Fathers likewise stress frequently the holiness of the Church. Irenaeus: "Where the Church is, there is the Spirit of God; and where the Spirit of God is, there is the Church and all grace" (*Against Heresies* 3.24). Cyril of Jerusalem: "The Catholic [Church]...cures and heals all kinds of sinners; but she in herself is endowed with all kinds of virtues, with regard to facts, to words, and to all spiritual gifts" (*Catech.* 18.23).

Theological reasoning draws the same conclusion. For, all the elements of the Church are holy and tend to sanctify the souls. Its purpose is precisely the salvation of souls; its author is the Redeemer; its soul is the Holy Spirit; its head is Christ by reason of his capital grace; its life is sanctifying grace; its means are supernatural faith, spiritual worship, and spiritual government. All these things would be to no purpose, if they would not *de facto* produce abundant fruits of sanctification in the members of the Church.

The presence of many sinners in the Church does not affect the essential and total sanctity of the Church. There is always a great number of good members. Several of these possess also a high degree of holiness which makes up abundantly for the blemish of others in the same Mystical Body, for the degree of perfection is not measured by quantity but by quality (thus one holy man may please God more than a hundred wicked men displease him). Sinners themselves are under the influence of the Holy Spirit, who keeps in them faith and impels them to conversion, and under this aspect they are really part of the Holy Church and the Mystical

---

262   See Congar, Journet, Renwart, listed in footnote 257.

Body, which suffers for them and expiates for them, trying to pour again into its mortified members the undying stream of its life.

3. CATHOLICITY OF THE CHURCH[263]

Scripture implies the intrinsic catholicity of the Church in its indefectibility, based on the assistance of Christ and of the Holy Spirit (Matt. 28:19f.; John 16:13). The extrinsic or extensive catholicity is contained in the prophecies of the Old Testament about the universality of the messianic kingdom (Gen. 22:17f.; 49:8–12; Ps. 2:6–9), and in Christ's evangelical words. Christ compares "the kingdom of heaven to a grain of mustard seed, which, when it grows up, is larger than any herb and becomes a tree, so that the birds of the air come and dwell in its branches" (Matt. 13:31f.); he affirms that "this gospel of the kingdom shall be preached in the whole world, for a witness to all nations" (Matt. 24:14); he orders the apostles "to go and make disciples of all nations" (Matt. 28:19; cf. Acts 1:8). The fact of the quick and universal expansion of the Church in the apostolic age itself is shown in the Acts and Epistles.[264]

The Fathers stress particularly the extrinsic catholicity, taking in this sense the very name "Catholic Church" which became the proper name of the Church in Tradition (see above, p. 243). Cyril of Jerusalem: "When you travel across cities, but do not just inquire where things belonging to the Lord are, for also wicked sects and heresies strive to prove the legitimacy of their dens under this name; do not even inquire where the Church is, but where the Catholic Church is; for this is the proper name of this holy mother of ours" (*Catech.* 19.7). Pacianus: "Christian is my name, Catholic my surname; the former designates and signifies me, the latter shows and proves what I am . . . Hence our people are distinguished from heretics when they are called Catholics" (*Epist.* 1.4). Augustine: "[The Church] is Catholic, and it is called Catholic not only by its members but also by all its enemies" (*On the True Religion* 7.12; cf. *Against the Epistle of Manichaeus* 4.5). By considering the name "Catholic" as the proper name of the Church, the Fathers implicitly signify that the Church is essentially universal, tending by its inner necessity to be everywhere and to embrace all men.

---

263 See Journet, Thils, Witte, listed in footnote 257.
264 See our treatise on *Revelation*, pp. 107–109.

Theological reasoning can deduce from the nature of the Church its extrinsic catholicity, considered only as an inner *exigency* of the Church, namely, that the Church tends dynamically to universal expansion. This follows from its purpose, which is the salvation of all souls, and from Christ's explicit command to evangelize all nations. *The fact* of the universal expansion in the apostolic age is probably to be attributed to a true miracle, worked by God to show the divine origin of the Church and the truth of revelation. In the following ages the Church proceeded in its expansion through natural causes and without any general miracle; but such miracle would certainly be repeated by God, if, due to extraordinary circumstances of physical and moral order, it should happen that the Church would be reduced again to a handful of men.

4. THE APOSTOLICITY OF THE CHURCH[265]

The Apostolicity of the Church, taken as the integral identity of the Church at all times with the primitive apostolic Church with regard to its three essential elements of faith, worship, and government, follows from the indefectibility of the Church, promised by Christ (Matt. 28:19f.; John 16:13). If we take it particularly with reference to the government, as the unbroken and formal succession of hierarchs in the governing office of the apostles, it follows also from the words of Christ, conferring to the apostles (especially to Peter) a perpetual power over the Church (Matt. 16:18; 18:18; 28:20), which cannot be true unless through a formal succession of others to the apostles. This property of the Church is frequently stressed by the Fathers, particularly by Irenaeus (*Against Heresies* 3.3 1–7, quoted above, p. 316) with regard to the apostolicity of the faith, and by Irenaeus, Tertullian, and Cyprian (cited above, pp. 366f.) with regard to the apostolicity of government.

From the fact that the four qualities are attributed to the Church as true properties, that is, as things deriving from its nature, it follows that they are *exclusive to the Church* and that they are so intimately bound together, that one cannot be without the others and if one is missing the others also are missing.

---

265   See Harle, Journet, Reveillaud, listed in footnote 257.

16

The Marks of the Church, Showing the Trueness of the Catholic Church[266]

THE FOUR PROPERTIES OF THE CHURCH, INDI-
cated in the preceding chapter, namely, unity, sanctity, Catholicity, and apostolicity, by reason of their visibility and their inseparability from the Church, become also marks or signs of the true Church of Christ, that is, the means of surely discerning which is the true Church of Christ among those which claim this title. Hence the present apologetical question is whether those four properties are found only in the Catholic Church, which thereby is shown to be the only true Church founded by Christ.[267]

Statement. *The four properties or marks of the true Church, namely, unity, sanctity, catholicity, and apostolicity, are found only in the Catholic Church, which is, therefore, the only true Church instituted by Christ.*

---

266   See bibliography given above (footnote 257).
267   The efficacy of this traditional argument, called the *"way of the marks,"* for proving that the Catholic Church is the true Church, has been questioned by a few recent theologians, particularly by Thils, *loc. cit.* (above, footnote 257), whose reasons were efficaciously refuted by T. Zapelena, "De via notarum in recenti quodam opere," *Gregorianum* 19 (1938) 88–109, 445–468.

The reason for this opinion is that on the one hand the traditional argument supposes several things that are denied by non-Catholics and which are included in the four properties as described above, and on the other hand these properties can be found, at least in a lower degree, also in other churches. Hence, they say, the quicker and more efficacious way of proving the trueness of our Church is the *"empirical way,"* that is, the consideration of the Catholic Church as a whole under the aspect of a true miracle.

However, the first way is traditional and cannot be simply discarded. Moreover, it is based on the four qualities which are true properties of the Church and can be found only in the one Church of Christ. The so-called empirical way is directed only to Christians, followers of other churches, who already admit the fact of revelation and the divine institution of the Church, not to unbelievers to whom the fact of revelation must be proved through miracles. Furthermore, proving the miraculous nature of the Catholic Church, after the oriental schism and the Protestant reformation took place, would be at least as difficult as proving that it possesses the aforementioned four properties.

439

1. *Unity is found in the Catholic Church.* This Church is *numerically one.* It never allowed within its boundary the formation or existence of several churches with distinct government, but promptly expelled from its body all groups of dissidents, even when such action seemed to be detrimental to the salvation of some souls, as is the case of the two schisms of Orientals and Protestants.[268] The Catholic Church is also *formally one* in its three constitutive elements of faith, worship, and government.

2. *Sanctity shines in the Catholic Church.* The *active sanctity,* that is, the means of sanctification (faith and sacraments), are kept without change or adulteration; the various dogmas defined by the Magisterium since Trent (as sacramental character, transubstantiation, Immaculate Conception, pontifical primacy and infallibility, Assumption) do not represent a change in the faith but a legitimate and necessary progress in the knowledge of revelation. The *passive sanctity,* that is, the fruits of sanctity in the members of the Church, is manifested in the general observance of the *common laws* of God and of the Church (some of which are quite difficult to human frailty, as mortification, chastity, sacramental confession) and in the morality of life which is quite common among Catholics in comparison with the members of other churches. Moreover the *religious orders,* which flourish abundantly in the Catholic Church, are efficacious means of higher holiness through the evangelical counsels of poverty, chastity, and obedience. Also *heroic holiness,* duly and strictly examined by the Church in the process of canonization, has constantly given to this Church its saints and its martyrs.[269]

---

268 The case of the *Western Schism,* although general and continued (1378–1417), does not make an objection against the unity of the Church, because it was not a true and formal schism, at least generally among the people. For, all believed in the necessity of one supreme ecclesiastical authority, and they only disputed and dissented about the actual subject of this authority, that is, who was the real Pope among the several pretenders.

269 From the 12th century, when Alexander III (†1181), for the first time reserved to the Holy See the canonization of saints, up to the 16th century, 53 saints were canonized. After the reform of the process of canonization, introduced by Leo X, Sixtus V, and especially Urban VIII (1625), up to the Code of Canon Law (1917), 113 more saints were added (80 of them from the 19th century). After the stricter form of Canonization, introduced by the Code, many other canonizations took place (34 of them under Pius XI).

Also, *martyrs* were never lacking for the defense of the Catholic faith on the occasion of particular persecutions, as in Spain after the invasion of the Mohammedans, in the northern countries of Europe during the Protestant reformation, in

3. *Catholicity is also evident in the Catholic Church.* As to the *intrinsic Catholicity*, that is, the totality of the articles of faith and of the sacramental means of sanctification, it is evident that the Church never abolished or corrupted any of them; the Orientals and Protestants themselves complain only about addition of things which, however, can be proved to be only a legitimate development of the principles of revelation. Of course under this aspect our argument does not have much apologetical value, since it supposes a long and laborious determination of the articles of faith and of the sacraments instituted by Christ.

The *extrinsic Catholicity*, or local and numerical extension, of the Catholic Church is particularly shown by the dynamic and missionary spirit with which this Church tends to reach all countries and peoples in the world, constantly retaining that universal extension it had before the Oriental schism and the Protestant secession. What the Church lost in extension through the Oriental schism was counterbalanced by its extension into Poland, Ruthenia, Hungary, Scandinavia and the Baltic regions in the 11th-12th centuries, and in Asia and Africa in the 14th-15th centuries; what it lost through the Protestant secession was again brought to balance by the evangelization of both Americas. Also the number of the members of the Catholic Church is great, both absolutely and relatively to the members of the other Christian communities, whose combined number is inferior to that of the Catholics.

4. *The apostolicity of the Catholic Church*, that is, its identity with the apostolic Church in faith, worship, and government, requires a long and laborious demonstration in order to become evident. For, Orientals and Protestants claim that this Church added some non-apostolic doctrines or sacraments to the apostolic deposit of revelation and deny that the Roman Pontiff is Peter's successor in the primacy. Besides, the Orientals have a true apostolic succession in their bishops. Hence, the argument drawn from this particular note seems apologetically ineffi-cacious. However, the apostolicity can be established through inference from the other properties, for, as we noted above (p. 438), all properties, flowing from the essence of the Church, are

---

various countries during the more recent political revolutions, as the French, the Russian, the Mexican, and the Spanish.

necessarily bound together and if one of them is missing, all the others are also missing.

5. In the *Protestant church* the four properties are not found, although several elements of each remain. Evidently there is no *unity* of government, and hence not one church but several congregations mutually independent; there is not even unity of faith, since they all agree only in a few fundamental articles, as the ecumenical movement has made it sufficiently clear (see above, footnote 259).

As regards *active sanctity*, the only two means of salvation admitted by Protestantism, namely, Baptism and faith in Christ, do not seem sufficiently efficacious to produce, keep, and foster holiness and morality in a man. As regards *passive sanctity*, neither the examples of some of the founders (as Luther and Henry VIII), nor the abolition of clerical celibacy and religious state, are means or signs of holiness. Undoubtedly there are among the Protestants several elements of morality and sanctity, sincerely acknowledged also by Vatican II (see above, p. 417), as the moral and interior life of many people in good faith who seek God in their heart, the heroic sanctity of some exceptional soul,[270] a restoration of some religious life among Anglicans and Calvinists,[271] but the sum total of all this does not seem sufficient to make up that general sanctity which is the proper character of the Church of Christ, as is evident from a comparison with the elements of sanctity found in the Catholic Church.

Catholicity lacks its foundation which is unity. The unity in some fundamental articles of faith is not sufficient to deserve the name of Catholicity even in that line, for faith refers indivisibly to all the truths which one believes. As regards extension, the Protestant

---

270 Such is the case of the famous Hindu ascetic *Sadhu Sundar Singh*, a convert to the Anglican church, who seemed also to perform miracles. Cf. L. de Grandmaison, "Le Sadhu Sundar Singh et le problème de la sainteté hors de l'Eglise catholique," *Recherches de science religieuse* 12 (1922) 1–29.

In 1925 the House of Clergy of the Anglican church canonized several saints, or rather proposed the addition of several saints to the liturgical calendar, namely, Tertullian, Catherine of Siena (the only saint of the Catholic calendar), John Wyclif, King Henry VI (†1471), archbishop Cranmer (†1556), archbishop Parker (†1575), archbishop Land (†1645), King Charles I (†1648), John Wesley (†1791, founder of the Methodists), John Keble (†1866), Florence Nightingale (†1910). Cf. V. Maulucci, *Vi sono santi tra i cristiani non cattolici? Apporti per l'ecumenismo*, Assisi 1970.
271 Cf. A. Urrutia, "Familiae religiosae apud Anglicanos," *Commentarium pro religiosis* 27 (1948) 90–103, 206–223; 28 (1949) 67–83.

churches are found practically everywhere in the world; but each individual church lacks universal extension, for each one still carries the genetic birth mark of the particular people or nation in which it was founded, as is the case of the German Lutherans, the English Anglicans, and other Congregations (Presbyterians, Baptists, Methodists, etc.) which had their origin among the nordic peoples of Europe and spread in foreign countries among populations derived from them. Nor has subsequent proselytism and missionary work notably changed this individualistic character, as to warrant the name of Catholicity.

Apostolicity does not agree with the break with Tradition, proper to Protestantism, for apostolicity is guaranteed by succession and continuity. Hence all the elements of doctrine and rites, identical to the apostolic age, which are kept in Protestantism (baptism, the Eucharist, faith in Christ, episcopacy in its principle), are not formally apostolic, because they are not derived from the apostles through legitimate handing over, but they were borrowed from the Catholic Church when the reformers withdrew from it.

6. *The separated Orientals* lack the *unity* of government, by reason of their rejection of the primacy, and they are consequently divided into several churches. As regards *sanctity* they retain all the elements of the active sanctity (faith and the seven sacraments); but their influence into the passive sanctity of the members does not seem sufficient to make it the mark and property of the Church wanted by Christ, notwithstanding the many fruits of sanctity, even heroic, flourishing among the people in good faith.[272] There is no intrinsic *Catholicity* for lack of unity in government, nor extrinsic catholicity, as shown by the lack of missionary spirit and of worldwide expansion; the oriental churches are truly orientals, that is, bound to eastern regions or

---

272 The Greeks have canonized only a few saints, among others Gregory Palamas (author of strange doctrines) and Mark of Ephesus (famous for his opposition to the Latins in the Council of Florence). Much more important is the canonization in the Russian church, started in 1721, when emperor Peter the Great instituted the Sacred Synod. At least 140 saints have been canonized, chosen among those who lived in Russia since the beginning of Christianity in that country. Cf. Pl. De Meester, "La canonizzazione dei santi nella chiesa russa ortodossa," *Gregorianum* 30 (1949) 393–407; G. P. Fedotov (ed.), *A Treasury of Russian Spirituality*, London 1952; I. Kologrivof, *Essai sur la sainteté en Russie*, Bruges 1953; Maulucci, *loc. cit.* in footnote 270.

peoples. The *apostolicity* is missing insofar as the oriental bishops, although truly and materially succeeding to the apostles, lack the formal or juridical succession, as they are separated from the communion with the successor of Peter or (abstracting from the Pope's primacy) from the other bishops.

17

Activity of the Church in the World[273]

THE CHURCH, MYSTICAL BODY, THROUGH ITS VIS-
ible and social structure, lives and acts in a wider world; hence its
activity must extend beyond its proper religious sphere of internal
government and ministry and reach also the external environment of the world at large. This exterior activity, as regards its
object, is twofold, one *human and temporal*, the other religious and
supernatural; this second activity is threefold, namely, *missionary*,
with regard to the pagan world, *ecumenical*, with regard to the
Christian world outside the Catholic boundary, and *eschatological*,
with regard to the ultra-temporal world, populated by all those
who, from different earthly conditions and societies, have died
in the peace of Christ.

These four kinds of ecclesiastical activity are indirectly connected with the four properties of the Church and with its four
causes. The human and temporal activity may be connected
with the apostolicity and with the efficient cause of the Church,
inasmuch as Christ's command of "preaching the gospel to every
creature" (Mark 16:15) reaches indirectly also all the material
"creation [which] groans and travails in pain until now" (Rom.
8:22), and both the Church and the material creature were made
by the same "Creator Spirit" and by the same Christ "King of
the universe" and were ordained to the same purpose of the
supernatural renovation of the world. The missionary activity

---

273   Vatican II, Pastoral Constitution on the Church in the Modern World; J.
Daniélou, *L'Eglise face au monde*, Paris 1966; *L'Eglise dans le monde de ce temps. Etudes
et commentaires autour de la Constitution "Gaudium et spes" de Vatican II avec une étude
sure l'encyclique "Populorum progressio,"* 2 vols., Paris 1967–1968; E. Schillebeeckx,
Le monde et l'Eglise, Bruxelles 1967; J. B. Metz, *Pour une théologie du monde* (trad.
de l'allemand par H. Savon), Paris 1970; J. A. Wiseman, "Schillebeeckx and the
Ecclesial Function of Critical Negativity," *Thomist* 35 (1971) 207–246; J. Wright,
The Church Hope of the World (ed. D. Wuerl), Kenosha, Wis. 1972.

   See special bibliography on each of the four activities of the Church below, footnotes 274, 278, 281, 284.

is connected with the Catholicity of the Church and with its material cause which is the universality of men to be gathered into one People of God. The ecumenical activity is referred to the unity of members. The eschatological activity is connected with the sanctity of the Church and hence with its final cause which is the sanctification and salvation of souls and which is fully accomplished for each man only in the other life, where images and shadows vanish, and for all mankind at the end of times, when with the coming of the Eternal Shepherd the pilgrim Church will rest.

1. THE HUMAN AND TEMPORAL ACTIVITY OF THE CHURCH[274]

This activity, which may be called Christian and Catholic humanism, is twofold; one concerns temporal goods, the other social affairs.

The first activity is based on and revolves about the following four native rights which the Church has with regard to *temporal goods*. First, "the right of acquiring, keeping, and administering temporal goods, freely and independently from the civil authority, for the attainment of its proper purposes" (Code of Canon Law, can. 1495, §1: cf. §2). Second, "the right ... of obliging the faithful to furnish the goods which are necessary for the divine worship, for an honorable life of the clerics and other ministers, as well as for other ecclesiastical purposes" (*Ibid.*, can. 1496).[275] Third, the right of acquiring, retaining, and exercising a *civil principality or state*, arising from favorable historical circumstances and necessary or fitting for the protection of the personal independence of the Roman Pontiff and his freedom of action in the government

---

274 Cf. Vatican II, Pastoral Constitution on the Church in the Modern World (see also the various allusions to temporal things in the Dogmatic Constitution on the Church, nos. 13, 31, 35, 37); G. Martelet, "L'Eglise et le temporel. Vers une nouvelle conception," *L'Eglise de Vatican II* (dir. G. Barauna, French ed. Y. M.-J. Congar, Paris, 1960) vol. 2, pp. 517–539; P. Kurtz and H. Dondeyne, *A Catholic Humanist Dialogue: Humanists and Roman Catholics in a Common World*, Buffalo, N.Y. 1973.

275 Also Vatican II stresses such obligation of the faithful, with regard to priestly remuneration. Recalling the biblical statements Luke 10:7 and 1 Cor. 9:14, the Council declares: "Therefore, if an equitable remuneration for priests is not otherwise provided for, the faithful themselves in whose behalf priests labor, are bound by a true obligation, to see that the necessary aid is given them to lead a decent and respectable life" (Decree on the Ministry and Life of Priests, no. 20).

of the Church.[276] Fourth, the prevailing right of deciding in mixed matters which interest both the ecclesiastical and the civil power (see above, pp. 280f.).

The second temporal activity of the Church, regarding *social affairs*, is based on the right and the duty of the Church to intervene and spread its doctrine and its light on all the temporal manifestations and problems of human life and of human consortium, which particularly in the modern age are suddenly brought up and rapidly developed. In all this the Church exercises its proper spiritual influence in two ways. First in a negative way, by correcting and healing, through its moral and supernatural principles, the various errors or defects occurring in philosophical, moral, economic, political, and cultural doctrines; secondly, also in a positive way, by completing these doctrines in their own proper field through its principles and contributions of a superior order, so that there be a philosophy, or ethics, or economics, or culture and arts, authentically Christian.[277]

2. THE MISSIONARY ACTIVITY OF THE CHURCH WITH REGARD TO THE PAGAN WORLD[278]

Missionary activity is taken here not in the general sense of evangelization of all non-believers (including those who, living in

276 Such is the Roman State, which had its origin in the 8th century, was violently suppressed in 1870 through the occupation of Rome by the King of Italy, and was restored in 1929 under the reduced dimensions of Vatican City through the Lateran Treaty. Cf. M. Vaussard, *La fin du pouvoir temporel des Papes*, Paris 1964; Ch. Journet, *L'Eglise du Verbe Incarné* 1 (éd. 2, Bruges 1955) 578–609.

277 See Journet, *op. cit.* 255–269. Vatican II explains this activity of the Church quite at length in its Pastoral Constitution on the Church in the Modern World. After a general introduction on the conditions of modern times (nos. 1–10), in the first part of this Constitution (nos. 11–45) the Council expounds the Catholic doctrine on man, on the world, and on the relationship of the Church to it. In the second part (nos. 46–93), the Council points out the principal and most urgent problems of the present time and their efficacious solutions and remedies, such as the dignity of matrimony and family (nos. 47–52), the right promotion of culture (nos. 53–62), the economic and social life (nos. 63–72), the life of a political community (nos. 73–76), universal peace to be fostered and the society of nations to be promoted (nos. 77–90).

The doctrine of this Constitution has been completed by the Council in the Declaration on Religious Freedom and in the Decree on the Instruments of Social Communication (press, cinema, radio, television, etc.)

On religious freedom cf. R. Coste, *Théologie de la liberté religieuse. Liberté de conscience, liberté de religion*, Gembloux 1969.

278 Vatican II, Declaration on the Relationship of the Church to non-Christian Religions; Decree on the Church's Missionary Activity; Dogmatic Constitution on the Church, no. 17.

Christian countries, never had faith or lost it), but *in the strict sense* of the sending of ministers of the Gospel to foreign pagan countries, so that through their action Christ's faith and his Church be extended to new peoples and particular churches be founded among them.[279]

As mentioned above (p. 446), this activity is connected with the Catholicity of the Church and with its material cause, which is the universality of men to be gathered into one flock of Christ; hence, through the property of Catholicity, this activity belongs to the very nature of the Church, which is essentially missionary.[280]

Its *origin* lies remotely in the double trinitarian mission of the Son by the Father to save all men and of the Holy Spirit by the Son to impel the Church founded by Him to continue this divine mission. Proximately it is founded on Christ's direct command to the apostles to evangelize all nations: "As the Father has sent Me, I also send you" (John 20:21); "Go, therefore, and make disciples of all nations" (Matt. 28:19). Its *reason and purpose* are rooted in the mystery of the will of God about the salvation of all men, as actualized not only imperfectly through a direct divine action in the souls, but also perfectly through the work of the Incarnate Word, which is now carried on by the Church, His Mystical Body. Its *mode* is explained at length by Vatican II in its Decree on the Church's Missionary Activity (nos. 10–42), which treats of the preaching of the Gospel, of the foundation and organization of new churches, of the missionaries themselves, and of the cooperation of the entire Church to the work of the missionaries.

Cuming, G. J., *The Mission of the Church and the Propagation of the Faith*, Cambridge, Mass. 1970.

Heney, A.-M., *Esquisse d'une théologie de la mission*, Paris 1959.

Journet, Ch., *L'Eglise du Verbe Incarné* 2 (Bruges 1951) 1205–1251.

Le Guillou, M.-J., "La vocation missionnaire de l'Eglise," *L'Eglise de Vatican II* (dir. G. Barauna, French ed. Y. M.-J. Congar, Paris 1966), vol. 2, pp. 681–698.

Power, J., *Mission Theology Today*, Maryknoll, N. Y. 1971.

Thils, G., "L'idée missionnaire dans l'enseignement de la théologie dogmatique," *Ephemerides theologicae Lovanienses* 36 (1960) 478–481.

279 This definition of the missionary activity, commonly called of the foreign missions, is given by the Council itself in the aforementioned Decree on the Church's Missionary Activity (no. 6).

280 Cf. Vatican II, the same Decree, nos. 2 and 6.

3. THE ECUMENICAL ACTIVITY OF THE CHURCH WITH REGARD TO THE NON-CATHOLIC CHRISTIAN WORLD[281]

The ecumenical activity, understood generically as a direct and urgent invitation to the separate Christians to join mother Church again, has been a constant practice of the Roman Pontiffs.

---

281 Vatican II, Decree on Ecumenism (followed by the establishment of a Commission for the application of this Decree). Cf. Decree on Eastern Catholic Churches, nos. 24–29

Acta Congressus Internationalis de theologia Concilii Vaticani II Romae a. 1966 celebrati (Typis Polyglottis Vaticanis 1968) 648–766.

Adams, M. (ed.), *Vatican II on Ecumenism*, Dublin-Chicago 1966.

Avenir (L') de l'Eglise et de l'Oecuménisme, Paris 1969.

Congar, Y. M.-J., *Chrétiens désunis. Principes d'un "Oecuménisme" catholique*, éd. 2, Paris 1965; *Ecumenism and the Future of the Church*, Chicago 1967.

Daniélou, J., "Le Protestantisme dans des voies nouvelles," *Etudes* 277 (1953) 145–156.

D'Ercole, G. and Stickler, H. M. (eds), *Comunione interecclesiale, Collegialità, Primato, Ecumenismo. Acta conventus internationalis de historia sollicitudinis omnium ecclesiarum, Romae 1967*, Romae 1972.

Goodall, N., *Ecumenical Progress. A Decade of Change in the Ecumenical Movement 1961–1971*, London 1972.

Hamer, C., "Dialogue and Unity in the Teaching of the Second Vatican Council," *Clergy Review* 54 (1969) 13–26.

Homrighausen, E. G., "The Church in the World," *Theology Today* 26 (1970) 446–455.

Hurley, M., *Theology of Ecumenism*, Cork 1969.

Iung, N., *Bilan de l'oecuménisme contemporain*, Paris 1971.

Karrer, O., *Ouverture oecuménique de Vatican II*, Paris 1969.

La Brosse, O. de, "L'intercommunion, chemin vers l'unité?" *Angelicum* 47 (1970) 214–229.

Lanne, E., "L'avenir de l'oecuménisme." *Irénikon* 44 (1971) 306–330.

Lambert, B., "La Constitution [de Vatican II] du point de vue catholique de l'oecuménisme," *L'Eglise de Vatican II* (dir. G. Barauna, French ed. Y. M.-J. Congar, Paris 1966), vol. 3, pp. 1263–1277.

Lebeau, P., "Vatican II et l'espérance d'une Eucharistie oecuménique," *Nouvelle revue théologique* 91 (1969) 21–46.

Marranzini, A., "Prospettive per l'intercommunione," *Civiltà Cattolica* (1971), vol. 3, pp. 143–150.

Nouvel (Un) âge oecuménique (collective work), Paris 1966.

Nouvelle (Pour une) image de l'Eglise (Gembloux 1970) 175–266.

Renwart, L., "L'intercommunion," *Nouvelle revue théologique* 92 (1970) 26–55.

Rondet, H., *De Vatican I à Vatican II. Ouverture à l'oecuménisme*, Paris 1969; *De Vatican I a Vatican II. Ouverture au monde*, Paris 1969.

Situation (La) oecuménique dans le monde (collective work), Paris 1967.

Thils G., *Histoire doctrinale du mouvement oecuménique*, éd. 2, Louvain 1963; *Le décret sur l'oecuménisme du deuxième Concile du Vatican*, Paris 1966, *Syncrétisme ou catholicité?*, Paris 1967; *"L'Eglise et les églises. Perspectives nouvelles en oecuménisme*, Bruges 1967.

Willebrands, J., *Oecuménisme et problèmes actuels*, Paris 1969.

Witte, J., "The Basis of Intercommunion," *Gregorianum* 51 (1970) 87–111; cf. *ibid.* 50 (1969) 63–92, 291–342.

This is evident from the various approaches and dealings made in the Middle Ages, which brought the Orientals to the union with Rome in the Councils of Lyons and Florence, and from the various invitations more recently sent to the separated brethren since the pontificate of Pius IX up to the Council of Vatican II, that same period in which the so-called "ecumenical movement" was born and laboriously progressed among Protestants. On the contrary, if the ecumenical activity is understood specifically as a practical and public movement of convention or mutual action of Christians for the purpose of fostering the union of all Christians, we must acknowledge that it is a Protestant initiative, which has been quite prosperous for about sixty years (see above, footnote 259). The Holy See has been constantly opposed to it on the presumption of danger of perversion or confusion on the part of the faithful,[282] until *Vatican II*, "recognizing the signs of the times," which have removed this danger and rather increased the hope of attracting the separated brethren to the Catholic unity, spontaneously agreed with the ecumenical movement and in its solemn *"Decree on Ecumenism"* proposed it under a moderate and typically Catholic form.

The principles and cautions for this Catholic ecumenism, as set forth by the Council itself, are the following.

a) *"God's Church is only one,"* that same Church which has been established by Christ under the apostolic college and Peter's primacy (nos. 2f.). Only in this Church "the fullness of unity, wanted by Christ" can be found (nos. 3f.).

b) *"Division [among] Christians is opposed to Christ's will,* scandalous to the world, and detrimental to the most sacred work of preaching the gospel to every creature" (no. 1).

---

282   The principal doctrinal documents are the two Encyclicals "Satis cognitum" of *Leo XIII* in 1896 and "Mortalium animos" of *Pius XI* in 1928, which directly declare the principle of the oneness of the Church, identified with the Roman Catholic Church. The principal disciplinary documents, forbidding Catholics to publicly join the ecumenical movement, are three declarations of the *Holy Office*, the first 1864 in the form of a letter to the bishops of England (Denz. 2885–2888; see above, p. 235), the second ("Cum compertum") in 1948 under the form of admonition, the third ("Ecclesia Catholica") in 1949 under the form of a practical instruction.

Also the *Code of Canon Law* set forth an explicit prohibition, saying: "Catholics must abstain from engaging in disputations or conferences, especially of public character, with Non-Catholics, without permission from the Holy See or, in urgent cases, from the Ordinary" (can. 1325, §3).

c) The damnable divisions and rifts, which have occurred in the Church and for which "at times both sides were to be blamed" *can no longer be imputed* "to those who are now born in such [separated] Communities and are imbued with the faith in Christ; hence the Catholic Church embraces them with fraternal reverence and affection" (no. 3).

d) The separated Communities lack that "fullness of unity which Jesus Christ willed" and that "fullness of grace and truth with which the Catholic Church has been entrusted." However, *they possess several elements of salvation*, both in the line of doctrine and worship, "which come from Christ and lead to him [and which] belong by right to the Church of Christ" (no. 3; see above, p. 214).

e) Today, under the impulse of the Holy Spirit, "*the ecumenical movement*" has been steadily growing, through "various activities and initiatives... which aim at fostering the unity of Christians." Hence "all the Catholic faithful are exhorted to *recognize the signs of the times* and to take active part in the ecumenical work" (no. 4).

f) This work is carried out in *two general ways*. First, in a *negative way* by removing certain impediments, particularly by psychological character, as "words, judgments, and actions, which do not respond with fairness and truth to the condition of our separated brethren and hence make mutual relations with them more difficult." Second, also in a *positive way*, that is, by means of "a dialogue between competent experts, in which each one explains deeply the doctrine of his Communion and clearly brings out its distinctive character; through such dialogue everyone acquires a truer knowledge and a more just appreciation of the doctrine and life of both Communions" (no. 4).

g) *Two supreme norms* must preside over this work, namely, *charity and truthfulness*. Full charity will foster concern, help, and prayer for the separated brethren, while sincerity and humble charity will suggest a careful appraisal of whatever should be renewed and achieved in our own Catholic family (no. 4). *Truthfulness* demands that "the entire [Catholic] doctrine be clearly explained; nothing is more foreign to ecumenism than a false irenicism, which harms the purity of Catholic doctrine and obscures its genuine and true meaning" (no. 11); such a whitewashed irenicism is soon to cause suspicion and displeasure in the sincere dissidents themselves, for there is nothing that man loves more than truth, or trusts more than truthfulness.

From this it follows that it is fitting to the charitable spirit of ecumenism to overlook some *moral or doctrinal defects* in the teaching of our separated brethren and rather direct our attention to the "common heritage [of goods and truths]...recognizing the riches of Christ and virtuous works in the lives of others who are bearing witness to Christ, sometimes even to the shedding of their blood" (no. 4). But on the other hand it is not conformed to true and truthful ecumenism to positively disregard all original blemish and much less to canonize, as it were, the schismatic or heretical movement of the founders, interpreting it as an authentic Christian and Catholic movement for renovation, which suffered some illogical deformity.[283]

h) Since the doctrinal dissent between Catholics and non-Catholics, objectively considered, seems incurable as long as the separated brethren rigidly adhere to the original lines of their systems, the purpose of Christian unity sought through the ecumenical movement is to be expected *from the good moral dispositions of both parties*, from the renovation of Christian life, and particularly from the common prayer for unity, for which Christ Himself once prayed to the Father. These good dispositions can be brought about and developed only by the Holy Spirit Himself, who not without reason stirred up this universal ecumenical movement among the followers of Christ. Vatican II points

---

283 Some Catholic ecumenists easily accuse traditional ecclesiology for its apologetical method and purpose, turned against non-Catholic systems. Some also advocate a historical revision of the origins of the Oriental schism and of the Protestant reformation. Some introduce Luther as a man essentially religious, who originally expressed true Catholic perceptions, although he later fashioned them into a unilateral system, which was the cause of his dissent with the hierarchy

Such ecumenistic views are stressed particularly by Congar in the work cited above (footnote 281), *Chrétiens désunis*, and in the article "Luther vu par les catholiques, ou de l'utilité de faire l'histoire de l'histoire," *Revue des sciences philosophiques et théologiques* 34 (1950) 507–518. They are refuted by Journet, *L'Eglise du Verbe Incarné* 2 (Bruges 1951) 56f., and Llamera, "Legitimidad del ecumenismo católico," *XXII Semana Española de teologia* (Madrid 1953) 310–318.

With regard to the true doctrine of Luther and Calvin, see Ch. Boyer, *Luther. La doctrine*, Rome 1970; *Calvin et Luther. Accords et différences*, Rome 1973.

The recent ecumenical statements or agreements on the Eucharist and the Ministry, issued respectively at *Windsor* and *Canterbury* (1973) by Catholic and Anglican theologians, seem to be in direct disagreement with the ecumenical principles or norms indicated by Vatican II. Cf. C. J. Dumont, in *Istina* (1973) 155–207; E. Holloway, D. Knowles, and Chr. Derrick in *Faith* (1974), no. 2, pp. 2–18.

out: "This conversion of the heart and sanctity of life, along with private and public prayers for the unity of Christians, should be considered as the soul of the entire ecumenical movement, and can rightly be called 'spiritual ecumenism'" (No. 8; cf. nos. 5–8).

4. THE ESCHATOLOGICAL ACTIVITY OF THE CHURCH WITH REGARD TO THE ULTRA-TEMPORAL WORLD[284]

Eschatology (from the Greek "éschata," last things, and "lógos," speech) means speech about the last things; it is one of the names given to the last treatise of theology about the end of man and of the world (death, judgment, hell, purgatory, heaven). In the same general meaning the eschatological activity of the Church is understood here as an essential and universal tension of the Church toward the future life and condition, that is, the manner in which the Church acts with regard to the end of the present earthly life and of this visible world, and consequently also with regard to those who live in the other ultra-temporal world, who are usually called the Suffering Church and the Triumphant Church.

This eschatological character or tension permeates the Church, in its entirety and in each of its specific elements, that is, in its soul (the Holy Spirit), its head (Christ), its vital energy (grace), its external bonds (faith, government and worship).

Considering the Church *integrally*, its eschatological character is manifested by the various names and images which describe it (see above, pp. 241–244, 259, 260–263). The four names "Church, Mystical Body, Kingdom of God, People of God" have an eschatological meaning. The very proper name "*Church*," which etymologically means convocation, shows the Church as a herald ever calling through the desert of this world and preparing the path to the Lord (cf. John 1:23, from Isa. 40:3) and as "a standard

---

284   Vatican II, Dogmatic Constitution on the Church, chap. 7.

Dahl, N. A., "The Parables of the Growth," *Studia theologica* 5 (1951) 132–166.

Haughey, J. C., "Church and Kingdom: Ecclesiology in the Light of Eschatology," *Theological Studies* 29 (1968) 72–86.

Molinari, P., "Caractère eschatologique de l'Eglise pérégrinante et ses rapports avec l'Eglise Céleste," *L'Eglise de Vatican II* (dir. G. Barauna, French ed. Y. M.-J. Congar, Paris 1966), vol. 3, pp. 1193–1216.

Schmaus, M., "Il problema escatologico nel Cristianesimo," *Problemi e orientamenti di teologia dommatica* 2 (Milano 1957) 925–959.

Schnackenburg, R., *God's Rule and Kingdom* (transl. from the German), New York 1963.

set up unto the nations [Isa. 11:12]...inviting to itself those who have not yet believed."[285] Thus the Church is of its nature pilgrim and missionary[286] and consequently lives and works eschatologically.

The other proper name *"Mystical Body"* carries also the eschatological concept of a vital organism which grows continually, acquiring new members and unceasingly perfecting them "until we all attain to the unity of the faith and of the deep knowledge of the Son of God, to perfect manhood, to the mature measure of the fullness of Christ" (Eph. 4:13). The Church is called also *"Kingdom of God"* as a kingdom in the making, which continually expands in this world to attain its completion at the end of time when its king will appear again. It is called likewise *"People of God,"* with reference to the prophetical name of the people of Israel, travelling through the desert toward the promised land; thus the new People of God is essentially a group of "wayfarers" and "a pilgrim Church," tending through the lands and times of this world to the place of eternal rest.[287]

The six *images*, with which the nature of the Church is illustrated, carry the same eschatological concept. The Church is the *"Temple of God,"* which is unceasingly being built and will have its completion only in heaven. She is the prophetical *"New Jerusalem,"* whose fulfillment will be an eternal Jerusalem (Apoc. 21:1f., 14, 22; Gal. 4:26). She is the *"House of God,"* the *"Family of God,"* *"Our Mother,"* who continually begets new children and grows into a numerous people. She is *"God's tillage and vineyard,"* which must be unceasingly labored; *"Christ's branches,"* which must extend; the *"Olive tree,"* on which extraneous wild branches have continually to be grafted. She is *"Christ's sheepfold and flock,"* to which "other sheep [must be added] that are not of this fold...[until] there shall be one fold and one shepherd" (John 10:16). She is the *"Spouse of Christ,"* who is kept waiting for the nuptials of the Lamb and who from this earthly exile cries to her bridegroom with the voice of the Spirit she has inside: "Come!" (Apoc. 22:17: "And the Spirit and the bride say, 'Come!' and let him who hears say, 'Come!'").

---

285 Vatican I, sess. 3, chap. 3, Denz. 3014.
286 Vatican II, Decree on Ecumenism, no. 2.
287 Vatican II, Decree on Ecumenism, no. 2; Dogmatic Constitution on the Church, nos. 6, 9, 46, 49, 50. In these and other passages the Council uses or inculcates the concept of *"Pilgrim Church."*

Likewise the *specific elements of the Church* have an eschatological character. The *Holy Spirit*, who is the soul of the Church, works only invisibly, waiting for His future revelation in heaven. *Christ*, who is its head, works also invisibly, waiting for his future second coming. *Grace*, the vital energy through which the influence of the Spirit and of Christ is exercised, is a mere seed which is to develop into an eternal tree. *Faith*, the first external bond of the members, is only "the substance of things to be hoped for, the proof of things that are not seen" (Heb. 11:1), that is, a provisional light to be replaced by the light of glory (1 Cor. 13:12).

The *government* is likewise something provisional, exercised in a vicarious fashion under the invisible ruling of Christ, while the flock is waiting for the coming of "the Prince of shepherds" (1 Pet. 5:4). The *worship* itself has an eschatological signification. All the sacraments signify three things, the present conferring of grace, the past passion of Christ, and the future glory in heaven; particularly the Eucharist, center of all worship, is essentially a memorial in which "the death of the Lord is proclaimed, until He comes" (1 Cor. 11:26), and Baptism, basis of all worship, is an image making us similar to Christ in the mysteries of his death and resurrection, and giving us the right to our future resurrection (Rom. 6:3–11).

This eschatological tension and activity of the Church is also the cause of that peculiar communication of the Pilgrim Church with the Suffering and Triumphant Churches of the ultra-temporal world, which is called the *Communion of Saints*. This mystery, which is directly considered in the treatise on the Last Things as in its proper place, is a "vital fellowship,"[288] or mutual communication and exchange of the supernatural goods, made in a manner proportionately fitting to the triple state, in which all those who lived or died in Christ are found, namely on earth, in purgatory, and in heaven. This exchange from us on earth is made in the way of worship for the blessed in heaven and of suffrage for the souls in purgatory, while from both of these groups it comes down to us by way of example and petitions to God.

---

288 Vatican II in the Dogmatic Constitution on the Church (nos. 49–51) deals quite at length with this subject.

GLOSSARY OF TECHNICAL WORDS
Occurring in This Treatise

Apostolic is called anything which is in agreement or connection with the Apostles; thus we speak of apostolic age, college doctrine, creed, Church.

Apostolicity is the identity of the true Church at all times with the primitive Church of the apostolic age, with regard to all its essential elements, namely, faith, worship, and government. Together with unity, sanctity, and Catholicity, it makes up the four properties or marks by which the true Church founded by Christ can be distinguished.

Bishop (from the Greek "episcopos," made up of "epi" = above, and "scopéin" = to observe, to inspect) etymologically means observer or inspector, and by usage it received an additional authoritative meaning of president, prefect, judge. The Greek text of the Old Testament calls God bishop (Job 20:29; Wisd. 1:6) and in the New Testament Christ is called by St. Peter "bishop of your souls" (1 Pet. 2:25). In the Acts and Epistles this name appears only four other times to designate without further determination the head of a particular Christian church (Acts 20:28; Phil. 1:1; 1 Tim. 3:2; Tit. 1:7). Since the beginning of the second century, as is evident from the epistles of Ignatius of Antioch, the name has the technical meaning which has been kept up to the present time, that of the monarchical head of a particular part of the Church, or diocese. *See Clergy. Collegiality.*

Canonization is a solemn and definitive pronouncement of the Magisterium, declaring that a man led a holy life in harmony with the principles of evangelical perfection, he is now in heaven among the blessed and he is the object of public worship in the whole Church. Such pronouncement is infallible, because it bears on an object necessarily connected with revelation, called dogmatic fact; it is therefore, the source of an obligation of faith for us. But theologians dispute whether this is divine faith itself, as the one due to the infallible definition of a revealed truth, or an inferior kind of ecclesiastical faith.

The so-called *Beatification* bears on the same object, but it is not yet a definitive pronouncement and hence it is not infallible. It is only a first step to canonization itself, by which the Magisterium recognizes the holiness of a man (then called only blessed, not yet saint) and permits his public cult to a certain extent and under certain conditions.

Canonization was first reserved to the Holy See in the 12th century by Alexander III and the process of canonization was thoroughly reshaped by Urban VIII in 1625 and codified under a strict form in the Code of Canon Law in 1917. From the 12th to the 16th century, 53 new saints, and from that time up to the Code of Canon Law 113 saints were canonized; many more were added in the following period (34 of them under Pius XI alone).

Among Protestants, the Anglican church canonized several saints, namely, Tertullian, Catherine of Siena (the only Catholic), John Wycliff, King Henry VI, Cranmer, Parker, Land, King Charles I, John Wesley, John Keble, Florence Nightingale (†1910). Among separated Orientals, the Greek church has canonized very few saints, such as Gregory Palamas and Mark Ephesus; on the contrary the Russian church, since the institution of the Sacred Synod by emperor Peter the Great in 1721, has canonized at least 140 saints, only among men who lived since the beginning of Christianity in Russia.

Catholic (from the Greek "katá" = according to, and "hólos" = whole, entire) means whole or universal. The combined expression "Catholic Church," for the true Church that has all the means of salvation, came into use as early as the 2nd century, starting from St. Ignatius of Antioch († about 107). After the Reformation this title was commonly used to designate the traditional Church from which the reformers had withdrawn (hence Catholic faith, Catholic nation, Catholics), but rather recently, by reason of a protest both from some Protestants and from orthodox Orientals, this Church is given the name of Roman Catholic Church.

Catholicity is one of the four properties or marks of the true Church of Christ, expressing the universality which must be found in it, both with regard to men, who have to be reached in their moral entirety, in all times, place, conditions (extrinsic catholicity), and with regard to the means of salvation, as doctrines of faith and practical means, which have to be possessed by the Church integrally (intrinsic catholicity). This is expressed by St. Pacianus, bishop of Barcelona (at the end of the 4th century) in his famous slogan: "Christian is my name, Catholic my surname."

Charism (from the Greek "chárisma" = gift, an extension of "cháris" = grace, favour) is taken in theology especially for the supernatural transitory graces, called also "graces freely given," in opposition to permanent and habitual graces (called "graces making a man acceptable" to God, such as sanctifying graces, virtues, and gifts of the Holy Spirit). These graces, given to individuals for the good of the community, are powers or knowledge of a miraculous nature (as physical miracles, revelations, prophecies, visions, knowledge of the secrets of heart).

They were very frequent in the primitive Church (see several lists of them in 1 Cor. 12:8–10, 28–30; Rom. 12:6–8; Eph. 4:11f.) in view of the growth and propagation of the faith: St. Paul even seems to speak of a charismatic group or hierarchy, made up of apostles, prophets, evangelists and doctors (*ibid.*), not however distinct from the ordinary hierarchy. The same graces are never lacking in the Church, as is evident from the lives of saints; they are also widely spread by the Holy Spirit among the faithful in lower degrees and less manifest manners, so that often they are not clearly noticed by the subject receiving them and by others.

At any rate, the existence and exercise of these graces in their exterior and public manifestation must be controlled by the authorities in order to avoid confusion, abuse, and falsehood, for many good people easily imagine many things and take for granted that they are impelled by Holy Spirit rather than by their own more or less pious imagination.

Church (from the Greek "ekklesía" = convocation, meeting, assembly) is the name given by Greek writers to political conventions, by the hagiographers of the Old Testament to the political-religious conventions of the Jewish people, called also *synagogue* (cf. Deut. 18:16; 31:30, etc.), and finally by Christ himself to his religious institution (only three times in the Gospel, Matt. 16:18; 18:17). The use of this name is very frequent in the Acts, Epistles, and Apocalypse (more than 100 times) to signify either *particular Christian communities* or the *universal congregation* itself (for this latter sense see Eph. 1:22; 3:10, 21; 1 Cor. 10:32; Gal. 1:13, etc.).

Every group of Christians, whether legitimate, or heretical or schismatic, claimed through the ages this evangelical name (Matt. 16:18: "Upon this rock I will build by Church"). Only Christ himself at the end of all ages will point out his Church among the assembled nations; meantime for the purpose of salvation he marked her with the four notes of unity, sanctity, Catholicity, and apostolicity, that she may be recognized by men of good will, for according to the prophecy of Isaias, God "lifted her up as a sign to the nations afar off" (5:2).

Clergy (from the Greek "cléros" = lot, part) indicates the body of all the persons reserved for the divine cult and the care of the Christian people, as if they were the lot of the Lord. In this sense clergy is opposed to laity (see *this entry*) and the Christian congregation is divided into clerics and laymen. Clerics themselves with regard to the hierarchy of Orders were formerly divided into major clerics (bishops, priests, deacons and subdeacons) and minor clerics (acolytes, exorcists, lectors, and ostiaries). The major order of subdiaconate and the four minor orders have now been removed from the hierarchy of Orders which has in the Latin church only the three degrees of episcopate, presbyterate, and diaconate, divinely instituted and sacramental. Each one of these is received through a ceremony, called ordination, which is the sixth sacrament of the Church.

Besides this hierarchy of Orders, there is also a hierarchy of *jurisdiction* and *Magisterium* (*see these entries*) which comprises only two degrees by divine institution, namely, papacy and episcopacy (see *Roman Pontiff. Bishop*), and many others of purely ecclesiastical institution (as patriarch, archbishop, pastor, vicar). Thus a bishop has two dignities, namely, order and jurisdiction; the Pope by sheer election gets only the supreme jurisdiction, but by the previous or subsequent episcopal consecration he receives also the dignity of the episcopal order and becomes even the immediate bishop of the universal Church; a priest by virtue of his divine ordination receives only the power of Order, but by ecclesiastical law or grant he can get also various degrees of jurisdiction.

Collegiality is a new technical term, introduced by the second Vatican Council together with the corresponding doctrine about the episcopal dignity. It means the necessary membership of every bishop in the episcopal college which succeeds to the apostolic college itself in the Church. In other words, every bishop by virtue of his consecration becomes ipso facto a member of a college of hierarchs, which succeeds to the college of the twelve apostles in the government of the Church.

Communion of Saints is a vital fellowship, or mutual communication and exchange of supernatural goods (prayers, suffrages, merits), between the faithful living on earth (the militant Church) and those who died in peace with God and are either in purgatory (the suffering Church) or in heaven (the triumphant Church). This truth is based on the reality of the one Mystical Body of Christ and we confess it as an article of faith in the Creed of the Apostles, according to the formula contained in the Roman Order at least since the 9th century.

Council or synod is an assembly of bishops for the purpose of defining doctrines concerning faith and morals or determining regulations of ecclesiastical discipline. It is called *particular Council* if it represents only one part of the Church, whether one single province made up of several dioceses (provincial council), or several provinces (plenary council). No particular council is infallible. It is called universal or *ecumenical council* if it represents, at least morally, the entire Church, and hence it is one solemn and extraordinary manner in which the episcopacy exercises its collegiality; it has no value nor does it even exist, unless presided or approved by the Pope, at least in its last period of final decisions, if not in the preceding phases of convocation and celebration. It enjoys infallibility in its definitive pronouncements in matters of faith and morals.

The Church in its 20 centuries of existence celebrated only 21 ecumenical councils, the first in Nicaea in 325 after three centuries from its birth, the latest at the Vatican in 1962–1965, which issued several important Constitutions and Declarations but no infallible definitions.

Creed (from the Latin "Credo" = I believe), or Symbol of faith (from the Greek "sumbállo" = I put together), is an extended formula containing the fundamental truths of faith (especially about God, Trinity, Incarnation, to which other truths were added later, concerning the Church, Baptism, Communion of Saints, life everlasting). It is an extension of a primitive apostolic "rule of faith" expressing the mystery of the Holy Trinity.

Among the many Creeds, used in old ages in various churches, two are important for us and commonly used in the Western Church, namely, the *Creed of the Apostles*, used especially in private practice and in Catechisms, according to the formulation found in the Roman Order of the 9th century, and the *Nicene-Constantinopolitan Creed* (defined by these two Councils respectively in 325 and 381), which we use in the liturgy of the Mass. In this Creed is found that solemn profession of the four properties and marks of the Church: "I believe ... one, holy, Catholic, and apostolic Church."

Deacon (from the Greek "diáconos," deriviation of "dióco" = I follow) means minister, that is, servant. In the New Testament it occurs thirty times, usually in a religious sense, and three times (Phil. 1:1; 1 Tim. 3:8, 12) in that specific hierarchical sense which became common since the beginning of the second century. The kindred word "diaconía" was often used in the general meaning of service to signify any ecclesiastical ministry. Deacon is the third and lowest degree in the hierarchy of Order and usually a stepping stone to the priesthood. His functions and attributions have varied through the ages, according to his proper character of servant to the bishop and the priest. The second Vatican Council has amplified his functions and has also restored the diaconate to the ancient type of a stable office, granting moreover, the promotion of married men to this order.

Definition, as a *philosophical term*, means properly a proposition which expresses clearly and briefly the nature of a thing, by indicating the genus, to which it belongs, and the specific difference, which distinguishes it from another thing belonging to same genus (thus rational animal defines and distinguishes man from the irrational animal or brute). As a *theological term*, definition or dogmatic definition is a solemn pronouncement of the Magisterium on matters of faith and morals, and more strictly an infallible pronouncement. Thus we speak of a defined dogma, such as the definitions of the Immaculate Conception and Assumption.

Encyclical – Bull – Constitution are solemn papal documents on matters of faith and morals, or connected truths. An *encyclical* (from the Greek "encúclios" = circular, periodical) is a letter sent by the Pope to all the bishops in order to speak his mind through them to all the faithful about a particular point of doctrine, morals, or discipline. It is not necessarily infallible. Famous among others are in recent times the various Encyclicals of Leo XIII on thomism, marriage, State, government ("Immortale Dei"), liberty, biblical studies, social problems ("Rerum novarum"), as well as the encyclicals against Modernism ("Pascendi") by Pius X, about Christian marriage ("Casti connubii") and social problems ("Quadregismo anno") by Pius XI, about the Mystical Body ("Mystici Corporis") by Pius XII.

A *Bull* (from the Latin "Bulla," which was the imprint of a seal to authenticate public documents), is one of the most solemn documents, either dogmatic or disciplinary; it has a lead seal (the "bulla") attached to it and bearing on one side the name of the Pope and on the other side the names of Saints Peter and Paul; it bears also the introductory formula: "X[the Pope's name as Paul or Pius] Episcopus Servus Servorum Dei"; famous among others are the Bull "Unam Sanctam" of Boniface VIII in 1302 about the authority of the Church and the Bull "Ineffabilis Deus" of Pius IX in 1854 defining the Immaculate Conception.

Likewise an *Apostolic Constitution* is a very solemn definition of the same kind and force as a Bull; very important Constitutions are the "Auctorem fidei" 1794 of Pius VI against the Jansenist Synod of Pistoia, the "Sacramentum Ordinis" 1947 of Pius XII on the matter and form of the sacrament of Orders, and the "Munificentissimus Deus" 1950 of Pius XII defining the Assumption of the Blessed Virgin.

Ex Cathedra is the proper qualification of an infallible definition of the Pope. The expression, recalling the "Cathedra Petri" (the Chair of Peter) in which the Roman Pontiff sits, was coined by the first Vatican Council in its definition of the papal infallibility. The same Council explains its sense as follows. The Pope is infallible when he speaks *"ex cathedra,"* namely, when as *pastor* of the universal Church he proposes a *doctrine* of faith and morals *authoritatively* and *definitively*. Hence four conditions are required — one on the part of the Pope, one on the part of the object proposed, and two on the part of the pronouncement itself. The infallible definitions of the ecumenical Councils are not called *ex cathedra* because the Councils do not sit "in cathedra" and because of the peculiar solemnity involved in the pronouncement of the Head of the Church, through whom St. Peter speaks and on whom the Church is built as on its unshakeable rock.

Forum (Latin word meaning an outdoor place, especially where commercial or political business was transacted) is a juridical and canonical term which signifies the competent authority, especially with regard to its judicial function. Hence three fora are distinguished, namely, the ecclesiastical or *canonical forum* (divided into external forum and internal forum, which is sacramental with regard to Penance and nonsacramental with regard to granting indulgences or dispensing from vows and oaths), the civil or *secular forum*, and the *mixed forum*.

Hierarchy (from the Greek "hierá" = sacred, and "arké = authority) etymologically means sacred power, but by usage it signifies the persons endowed with power, rather than the power itself. Hence it is the body of persons partaking in ecclesiastical power. Since this power is two-fold, namely, power of Orders (or ministration) and power of jurisdiction (or commandment), there is a twofold hierarchy, the *hierarchy of Orders* with the three degrees of episcopate, presbyterate, and diaconate, and the *hierarchy of jurisdiction* with the two degrees of papacy and episcopacy, as far as divine institution is concerned. By ecclesiastical institution the first hierarchy was formerly completed with five orders, inferior to the diaconate, which are now suppressed, and the hierarchy of jurisdiction is amplified with various additional degrees, both above and below the episcopacy. *See Clergy.*

Infallibility is to be distinguished from *indefectibility* (absence of any defect, such as decay, sin, error), from *impeccability* (absence of sin), and from *inerrancy* (the fact of not making error); it means the impossibility of making errors. This can be obtained by means of three kinds of

461

supernatural help, namely, through an interior light of revelation (like in the prophets), or through inspiration properly so-called (as in the writers of Holy Scriptures), or through any other kind of assistance of the Holy Spirit. When we speak of the infallibility of the Church we refer to the third help of God. The subject of this infallibility is threefold, namely, *the believing Church*, or the faithful as a whole body, and the teaching Church divided into *the Pope* alone and *the ecumenical Council* (or rather the Pope with the rest of the apostolic college).

Jurisdiction. There are three kinds of power in the Church, namely, the *power of Orders*, that is, the exclusive right of performing and administering the acts of worship (particularly the sacraments), the power of teaching, or *Magisterium*, involving on the part of the faithful the obligation of assenting to its pronouncements, and the *power of jurisdiction*, that is, of obliging the faithful to perform exterior acts regarding ecclesiastical policy.

This third power, which is common to civil authority in its natural order, involves, also in the Church, three functions, that is, the legislative function, which regards the making of laws, the judicial function or the right of judging on the application of ecclesiastical laws (canonical forum), and the coercive function, that is, the right of punishing any violation of these laws, through the privation of spiritual goods (as excommunication or suspension from sacred ministry) or of temporal goods (as privation of ecclesiastical benefice, pecuniary fine, infamy, prison, exile, not however capital punishment or corporal torture which do not seem to agree with the nature of the Mystical Body).

Laity (from the Greek "laós" = people) are all the Christian people as distinct from the clerics (broader definition) and from the members of religious communities (stricter definition). By virtue of their sacramental character received in Baptism and Confirmation, laymen truly share in a nonhierarchical manner in the priestly, prophetical, and kingly functions of Christ himself, and consequently also in the manifold apostolic mission of the Church.

This lay apostolate, or spreading of Christ's doctrine and laws in the world, is an apostolate of good life, of spoken word, of acquired science, of free opinion humbly manifested to the authority, of closer cooperation to the work of the hierarchy itself (Catholic Action), and in general an apostolate through which temporal things themselves and the secular world at large are sanctified and consecrated to God. Thus the life of a layman is not profane but sacred and truly ecclesiastical, for it cooperates, no less than the life of clerics and religious although in a different manner, to the construction of the Mystical Body of Christ in which all members are proportionally equal.

Liturgy (from the Greek "léiton" = concerning people, adjective of "laós" = people, and "érgon" = work, deed) originally meant any public function, and liturgist ("leiturgós") meant public officer. The word, in its various forms of noun, adjective, and verb, occurs 15 times in the New Testament, six times in the sense of sacred cult (Luke 1:23; Acts 13:2; Heb. 8:26; 9:21; 10:11). The Fathers at the beginning adopted it in the general sense of any ecclesiastical ministry; only much later it received the specific meaning of *cultic ministry.*

According to this traditional meaning, liturgy is essentially the celebration of the Eucharist and of the other sacraments, to which the administration of the sacramentals and the recitation of the divine office are attached. The liturgical books are the Missal, the Pontifical, the Ritual, and the Breviary. The liturgical science can be reduced partially to Canon Law (or law of the Church in cultic matters) and partially to Tradition (for liturgy is an outstanding witness to the traditional belief and sense of the Christian people, according to the aphorism: "The law of prayer is the law of faith.").

Magisterium. See Glossary of the preceding volume on *The Channels of Revelation.*

Marks of the Church, or characteristic properties by which we can distinguish which is the true Church instituted by Christ, are unity, sanctity, Catholicity, and apostolicity, expressed in the Nicene-Constantinopolitan Symbol, or the Creed we use in the Mass.

Mystical Body is a technical expression, first coined in the Middle Ages but based on St. Paul's formula "Body of Christ," which points out the essential nature of the Church and hence its best definition. It means that all the faithful make up one total body of a spiritual character and of vital influence, in which the Holy Spirit is the soul, Christ is the head, and all the others are the members, distributed in different degrees and dignities, according to the manner in which they partake the supernatural influence of the soul, that is, of the Holy Spirit.

Old Catholics are a small schismatic Church, originated a century ago by a group of dissenters (mostly professors of various universities of Austria and Germany), as a protest against the definition of the papal primacy and infallibility by the first Vatican Council (1870). Refusing submission, they withdrew from the Catholic Church in 1871 and founded their own schismatic church under the name of Old Catholics; their first bishop was a lay professor, J. H. Reinkens, who was consecrated in 1873 by the Jansenist bishop Heykamp of Deventer in the diocese of Utrecht in Holland. Even in their most flourishing period (about 1878) they did not reach a very conspicuous number of members (about 100,000 in all) and they are now in a state of no public importance.

Order (from the Latin "ordo" = order, rank) in general is the correct and proportionate disposition of several things with regard to an end or common purpose. In ecclesiastical terminology Order has a double sense, one strictly canonical, that is, *religious order* (the major religious communities with solemn vows, as Dominicans and Franciscans), and one theological, that is, the *power of Orders* as distinct from the power of jurisdiction and Magisterium. This power has three degrees, namely, episcopate, presbyterate, and diaconate, given through a ceremony which is called ordination and constitutes the sacrament of Orders. *See Clergy Jurisdiction.*

Orientals, separated from the Roman Catholic Church since the 11th century through the influence of Michael Caerularius, patriarch of Constantinople, form a distinct Church, commonly called Eastern Orthodox Church, or rather an agglomeration of several autocephalous (self-governing) churches, usually national, having a common faith but not common supreme authority, under a primacy of sheer honor recognized to the patriarch of Constantinople. After the constitution of the Sacred Synod in Russia by emperor Peter the Great in 1721, the two major groups of the Orthodox Church are the *Greek* and the *Russian* churches with their respective patriarchs in Constantinople and Moscow.

The chief object of dissent from the Roman Catholic Church, which gave rise to schism in the Middle Ages, is the papal primacy, reinforced by the first Vatican Council with its explicit definition of both the primacy and the infallibility of the Pope. Several attempts of reunion were made since the Middle Ages, particularly in the Councils of Lyons in 1274 and Florence in 1439, but they did not produce lasting fruits. After the second Vatican Council new attempts are being made under renewed dispositions of good will and Christian fraternity on both sides.

Papacy-Pope. *See Roman Pontiff.*

Priest (from the Latin "presbyter" and originally from the Greek "presbúteros" or "presbútes" = elder) in profane literature and in the Bible has a threefold sense, namely, prior in age (senior), prior in time (predecessor, historically prior), and prior in dignity or authority. In the third hierarchical sense the rectors of the Christian communities are called presbyters in the New Testament (Acts 11:30; 14:22; 15:2, 4, 6, 22, 23, 41; 16:4; 20:17; 21:18; 1 Tim. 4:14; 5:17, 19; Tit. 1:5; Jas. 5:14; 1 Pet. 5:1, 2, 5; 2 John 1; 3 John 1). It is disputed among scholars whether these biblical presbyters were simple priests or bishops. At any rate, since the beginning of the second century the name "presbyter" began to be reserved to simple priests, just as the name "bishop" was reserved to true bishops, as is evident from the epistles of St. Ignatius of Antioch († about 107).

In traditional terminology the bishop is also called priest, being the highest degree of the priesthood (the high priest) and the common expressions of the priestly dignity are likewise attributed to him, such as sacerdotal office, power, character, class, ordination.

The simple priest is the second degree of the hierarchy of Order (*see Clergy. Jurisdiction. Order*). His principal offices are the celebration of the Eucharist and the administration of the other sacraments, except Ordination which is reserved to the bishop; with regard to jurisdiction, it may be given to him by ecclesiastical right, in different degrees and manners proportioned to the necessary care of the souls, as is evident from the institution of pastors and vicars. The actual participation of priests in the exercise of both the power of Orders and the power of jurisdiction has been various in different ages.

In the first two centuries most of the sacred ministry was ordinarily reserved to the bishop; from the third century on, the participation of the priest became increasingly more extended, so that toward the end of the 4th century all the sacraments, with the exception of Ordination (and of Confirmation in the West), were currently administered by simple priests, and between the 7th and 11th centuries the administration of the Eucharist and Penance and the preaching of God's word were considered as the threefold proper function of a priest.

Religious societies. The word "religion" (from the Latin "religio" of uncertain etymology, either from "relegere" = to read over, or "reelig-ere" = to choose again, or "religare" = to bind) means *a moral bond between man and God*, and hence the knowledge of God and the performance of duties toward him. There is a twofold religion, one natural, based on our natural knowledge of God (his existence and providence), and the other supernatural, based on additional direct revelation of God about his intimate mysteries (as the Trinity and Incarnation).

Besides this philosophical and theological meaning, religion has acquired since the Middle Ages the canonical sense of *a society of men or women* particularly bound to God by the three vows of poverty, chastity, and obedience, and living together under a common rule approved by the ecclesiastical authority. Before the 13th century, such societies sprung up in the Church as it were spontaneously, under the impulse of a saint, and kept on flourishing without any particular and official approbation of the authority (thus for instance the great orders of Benedictines and Augus-tinians). Toward the end of the 12th century Innocent III reserved to the Holy See the approbation of religious orders, and he himself approved the Trinitarians (1198), the Dominicans (1206), and the Franciscans (1209). All religious communities founded before the Council of Trent have solemn vows (which involve more radical effects) and they are called specifically religious orders, while those that followed this Council have only simple vows and are called properly religious congregations. The approbation to religious societies can be given either by the local bishop or the Holy See; hence the distinction between societies of diocesan or pontifical right.

This religious state is not directly of divine but of ecclesiastical or canonical institution, although it is based on and inspired by the three evangelical counsels, corresponding to the three vows. Religious do not belong to the laity in the strict sense, unless we understand laity only as opposed to clergy. The fact of belonging to a religious society does not make a man holy but only provides him with easier means of sanctifi-cation, while outside of any religious society a man can get to the same or to a higher degree of holiness through rougher means.

Roman Pontiff [The] is the Vicar of Christ (not his successor), the successor of St. Peter in the primacy over the universal Church, the immediate pastor of all the faithful (notwithstanding the immediate but secondary pastorship of the local bishop), the bishop of Rome (probably eternally so), the patriarch of the Western Church, the primate of Italy, the metropolitan archbishop of the Roman Province, the pastor of the Church of St. John Lateran. He enjoys the primacy, that is, the fullness of the threefold power of Orders, Magisterium, and jurisdiction over the entire Church. He is infallible in his definitions, which by reason of their intrinsic solemnity are called *ex cathedra*, that is, proceeding from St. Peter's chair and as it were from St. Peter's mouth, as was expressed by solemn acclamation in the Councils of Chalcedon and Constantinople III: "Through Leo and Agatho Peter has spoken."

On the level of sacramental Order the Pope is no more bishop than any other bishop, since the episcopacy is the plenitude of priesthood, but on the level of nonsacramental Order the Pope excels all the bishops together, because he is the bishop of the whole world and possesses a higher liturgical power on the regulation of sacramental and nonsacramental worship, as well as on the very validity of some sacraments.

Hence we understand the reasons of the following statements of ecclesiastical writers: "Rome has spoken, the case is closed" (St. Augustine), "The first see is judged by no one" (Nicholas I), "Fidelity to the Roman Pontiff is the characteristic mark of a Catholic" (St. Robert Bellarmine), "He who bites the Pope dies from it" (Joseph De Maistre).

Rome, capital of the civilized world and cradle of the unending western civilization at the time Christ founded the Church, was soon to become capital of the Christian world with the fall of the Roman empire. By reason of the sojourn of St. Peter in Rome and his Roman episcopacy, which cannot be reasonably doubted, the Petrine and papal primacy was attached to the see of Rome, either under divine inspiration or by St. Peter's own choice. In either case this primatial bond is very probably irreformable by any successor of St. Peter.

From this it follows that Rome and the Roman diocese are in some way eternal, as is eternal the primacy attached to them, in the sense that Rome will never cease to exist, or at least in the sense that, if Rome and the Roman diocese were materially destroyed, the one who would succeed the last bishop of that city would still be juridically the Roman bishop, and his new diocese, wherever it may be, would still be juridically Rome itself under a new geographical outfit. Thus the hazardous prophecy or wish of the Roman poet Horace, according to which never will anything greater than Rome appear under the sun, has been fulfilled through the eternal papacy, by which "Christ himself has become a Roman" (Dante Alighieri in his *Divine Comedy*) and his followers are called Romans.

Tertullian, while still a Catholic, wrote: "If you turn toward Italy, you find Rome whence the authority comes to us. How happy that Church is, to which the apostles gave copiously the entire doctrine together with their blood" (*On the Prescription of Heretics* 36.2). The same acclamation is repeated in the liturgical office of the feast of Saints Peter and Paul: "O happy Rome! for thou hast been consecrated with the glorious blood of the two princes, and, clad in purple with their martyrdom, thou alone outshine all the beauties of this world."

Society is twofold, one natural, based on the natural law, and the other supernatural, based on a supernatural revealed law; both of them are either perfect or imperfect. The *natural perfect society* is the civil society, now organized in the manner of nations or states under a monarchical or democratic regime, necessarily endowed with the power of jurisdiction, comprising the triple legislative, judicial, and coercive function. The natural imperfect society is *the family*, which does not have in itself all the means necessary for its purpose and lacks true jurisdiction, so as to become necessarily part of the civil perfect society. The *supernatural perfect society* is the one single Church founded by Christ, which is a Mystical Body endowed not only with the power of jurisdiction but also with the higher powers of Orders and Magisterium. An imperfect society in this supernatural order is *the religious society*, which imitates the natural family but is only of canonical approbation, not of divine institution.

Salvation means the attainment of the supernatural end of man, which is the direct possession of God through beatific vision, called heaven or glory. Hence in this life we reach no salvation as yet, but we can reach sanctification which is the way to salvation and consists in sanctifying grace, the seed of glory. Salvation of souls is the proper purpose of the Church as it was the proper purpose of its Founder, who "for us men and for our salvation came down from heaven ... and became man "(Creed). The Church could not work for the salvation of souls if it were not essentially holy in itself, that is, holy in its members and sanctifying in all its social means; hence one of the essential properties of the Church is sanctity, as we profess in the Creed, and "outside the Church there is no salvation," according to the traditional axiom.

ANALYTICAL INDEX

Anglicans deny Peter's primacy or its transmission to the Roman Pontiff, footnote 65, as well as the infallibility of the Pope and of the ecumenical Council, footnote 120; however, the American Episcopalians removed art. 21 of the Anglican faith which denies the infallibility of the ecumenical Council, footnote 120. Anglicans admit the divine origin of the episcopacy in a general sense, footnote 199. In 1925 the Anglican church canonized several saints, among whom Catherine of Siena, footnote 270. *See Protestants (Orthodox)*

Apostle. Sense and use of this word, footnote 62. St. Paul is not an apostle in the strict original sense proper to the Twelve, but he received the same dignity and authority as the others, footnote 62. The apostleship of St. Peter and of the others is distinct from St. Peter's primacy and the episcopacy of the other apostles, 300f. As founders of the Church, the apostles are the noblest members of the Mystical Body after the Blessed Virgin and St. Joseph, 269

Apostolicity (of the Church), as to its general notion, 431f., as a property of the Church, 438f., and as a distinctive mark of the Church, 441

Augustine (St.) unusually refers to Christ himself rather than to St. Peter the words: "Upon this rock I will build by Church," footnote 78. His paradox: "I would not believe the Gospel if I were not compelled by the authority of the Catholic Church," 289. His famous statement which has been condensed into the following axiom: "Rome has spoken, the case is closed," 321, 346

Barth (K.) denies any true authoritative element in the Church, footnotes 42 and 158. *See Protestants (Liberal)*

Bishop. Meaning and origin of the name bishop, footnote 157. Divine origin of the episcopacy, 361–368. Various non-Catholic theories explain the rising of episcopacy through natural causes, footnote 158. Episcopacy is the first degree of the hierarchy of Order divinely instituted; *see Orders (Power of)*. Collegial nature of the episcopacy, stressed recently by the theologians and the Magisterium, 369–376; *see Collegiality*. The episcopal consecration is sacramental, 373. By virtue of this consecration each bishop *ipso facto* belongs to the apostolic college ruling the Church, and consequently gets the three powers of Orders, Magisterium, and jurisdiction, 373–376. The episcopal college is infallible in defining matters of faith and morals, 376f. Also the monarchical form of the episcopacy is probably of divine origin, 381–385; its historical beginning and development, 382–384, 395–400; its nature and attributions, 385f., 401f. *See Deacon. Priest. Roman Pontiff*

Boniface VIII in his famous Bull "Unam sanctam" on the freedom of the Church, 274, 333, was the first Pope to use the expression "Mystical Body" to designate the Church, 244, 411, footnote 19

Caerularius (Michael), patriarch of Constantinople in the 11th century, openly denied the primacy of the Roman Pontiff and inaugurated the oriental schism, 303, 346, footnote 83. *See Photius*

Caesaropapism is a doctrine which denies the supreme authority of the Pope in favor of Caesar, that is, of the civil power, 303, footnotes 42, 65, 83 and 109. *See Gallicanism. Marsilius of Padua. Regalism*

Canonization is an object of the infallibility of the Church, as a dogmatic fact connected with revelation, 354f. History of canonization and number of canonized saints, footnote 269. Canonization among Anglicans, footnote 270, and orthodox Orientals, footnote 272

Cathari reject the Magisterium, 287, footnote 50

Catholicity (of the Church), as to its general notion, 431f., as a characteristic property of the Church, 437f., and as a distinguishing mark of the Church, 440f. Catholicity is taken both extrinsically and intrinsically, that is, the true Church must extend to all men and possess all the elements required by Christ's institution, 431f. The famous slogan of St. Pacianus: "Christian is my name, Catholic my surname," 438. The Catholicity of the Roman Church is shown by its dynamic and missionary spirit, 440f.

Charisms, that is, private and temporary gifts given by God to individuals for the good of the community (such as miracles and prophecies), are never lacking in the Church, 426, footnote 245. In the early Church there was even a charismatic hierarchy, footnote 202

Christ is the founder of the Church, 250–254, and the head of the Mystical Body, according to St. Paul, 259, Pius XII, 257, and theological reasoning, 265f. Through his capital grace Christ moves the Church both interiorly and exteriorly, 266

Church. Difficulty of shaping a proper treatise on the Church, due to its double aspect of exterior society and Mystical Body, 241f. Attempt at a proper definition of the Church, 244f., 255f., 263–265, 411. The three proper names Church, Catholic Church, and Mystical Body, 242–244; other names showing the mystical nature of the Church, 260–263, particularly Kingdom of God, 261f., People of God, 249, 253, 261, Mother Church, 262f. The preparation of the Church in the history of salvation, 247–250, 253f. The Church is essentially a Mystical Body, 256–270. Notion of physical, moral, and mystical bodies, footnotes 34 and 222. The Catholic Church and the Mystical Body are perfectly equivalent, 257, 258, 270, 411–413. The three bonds uniting the members of the Church, that is, faith, worship, and government, correspond to the three powers of the Church, namely, Magisterium, Orders, and jurisdiction, 271; *see* *these three entries* and *Members (of the Church)*. On the ministerial character of the powers of the Church, 292–293. The Church has the right of possessing temporal goods and, if necessary, also a temporal power, as is the case of Vatican City, 446, footnote 47. As to the temporal, missionary, ecumenical, and eschatological activities of the Church, *see these four entries. See Society. State*

Collegiality. Meaning and use of this word, especially according to Vatican II, 369–371. Recent increment of the doctrine of episcopal collegiality, 371. Episcopacy is essentially collegial in the sense that every bishop by virtue of his consecration becomes *ipso facto* a member of a college of hierarchs, which succeeds to the college of the apostles in the government of the Church, 371–376. *See Bishop*

Communion of Saints is a vital fellowship, or mutual communication and exchange of supernatural goods, between the faithful living on earth and those who died in peace with God, 455

Conciliarism is a theory holding the superiority of the ecumenical Council over the Pope. It began among medieval canonists, increased under the form of Caesaropapism in the 13th century and received its formal shape in the 15th century in the three councils of Pisa, Constance, and Basel, footnote 109. It denies also the infallibility of the Pope, footnote 120. *See Caesaropapism. Gallicanism. Regalism*

Council (Ecumenical), as to its definition, nature, conditions, and usefulness, 377–380. It is one solemn manner of exercising episcopal collegiality, 374f.; *see this entry*. List of the 21 ecumenical councils, footnote 185. They were relatively few in the long history of the Church, in fact about one every century as an average; the first took place at Nicaea almost three centuries after the birth of the Church, and three full centuries elapsed between Trent and Vatican I, 377

Cullmann (O.), a modern moderate Protestant, understands St. Peter's primacy as a mere personal privilege not to be transmitted, hence he denies the primacy of the Roman Pontiff, footnotes 71, 75, 83 and 158. However, he admits as certain St. Peter's Roman sojourn, footnote 99. *See Protestants (Liberal)*

Cyprian (St.) stressed emphatically the unity of the Church, 435f., and chose it as the title of one of his works, 243. He was one of the first writers to use the traditional axiom, "Outside the Church there is no salvation," 419. He brought forth an important testimony on the divine origin of the episcopacy, 367, and on the apostolic origin of the monarchical episcopate, 384. On the contrary he seems not to have grasped the full implication of the papal primacy, 318–320, footnote 109

Deacon, as to the origin and use of the name, 285, 292. It is the third degree of the hierarchy of Orders, divinely instituted; *see Orders (Power of)*.

Its historical development and its proper functions, 393–399, 401–405. Restoration of the ancient type of stable diaconate and admission of married men to this order, endorsed by Vatican II, 405

Ecumenism, or ecumenical movement, was started among Protestants by reason of their broad doctrine concerning the unity of the true Church of Christ, which they limit to a few fundamental articles of faith, 449, footnote 259. Catholic ecumenism, recently promoted by Vatican II, has its own proper principles, cautions, manners, and general norms, 242, 449–453

Episcopalism, to be distinguished from the Protestant Episcopalian Church, is a doctrine urging beyond measure the rights of the bishops as against the rights of the papal primacy; it has been adopted by Catholic Gallicans and Protestant Anglicans, footnotes 109 and 120. See *Anglicans. Gallicans*

Episcopacy. See *Bishop*

Eschatology, or rather the eschatological aspect and activity of the Church, has been recently emphasized by theologians and endorsed by Vatican II, 241, 254, 445, 446, 453–455. The Church, as the Pilgrim People of God on earth, is essentially eschatological, tending to the future goal of the other life and expecting the second coming of the Lord, 453–455

Fathers (of the Church), as to their use of the names "Catholic Church," 242f., and "Spiritual Body" which gave origin to the expression "Mystical Body" in the Middle Ages, 244. They also call the Holy Spirit soul of the Church, 260. See *Tradition*

Forum is threefold, namely, ecclesiastical (divided into the external and internal), civil (or secular), and mixed, 297. See *Jurisdiction*

Gallicanism is the French Regalism, claiming the rights of the French Church against the alleged usurpations of the Roman Pontiff, footnote 42. It blends in its system various remnants of older Caesaropapsim, Conciliarism, Episcopalism, and Regalism, footnote 109; see *these four entries*. It denies Peter's primacy, footnote 65; it limits the primacy and infallibility of the Pope, distinguishing between the infallibility of the "See" and the fallibility of "the occupant," footnotes 109, 119 and 120

Holy Spirit (The) is the influential principle in the Church, according to St. Paul, 259, and the soul of the Church, according to Pius XII, 257, the Fathers, 260, and the theologians, footnote 23. The reason why the soul of the Church is the Holy Spirit rather than sanctifying grace, 267–268

Hus (John) denies the primacy of both the Pope, 274, footnote 42, and St. Peter, footnote 65, as well as the very existence of the three powers of Order, Magisterium, and jurisdiction in the Church 283, 287, footnote 50

Ignatius of Antioch (St.) was the first to use the name "Catholic Church," 243. By reason of his antiquity († ca. 107), he is an important witness of the primacy of the Roman Pontiff, 316f., of the divine origin of episcopacy, 367, of the apostolic origin of its monarchical form, 382f., 384f., 395, and of the existence of the three degrees of the hierarchy of Orders, 395f.

Indulgences are granted by the Church by virtue of its jurisdictional power, 298, footnote 59

Infallibility, or impossibility of erring under certain conditions, is a property of the Magisterium, based on divine assistance, not, however, on revelation or inspiration, 338f. With regard to the twofold manner, ordinary and extraordinary, in which infallibility is exercised by the Magisterium, *see this entry.*

The subject of infallibility is threefold, that is, the Pope, the ecumenical Council (or rather the episcopal college), and the believing Church as a whole, 349–351. The episcopal college is infallible, whether acting in an ecumenical Council or in other ways, 376f. It is disputed whether the Pope and the episcopal college are one or two distinct subjects of infallibility and of supreme jurisdiction, 350f.

The object of infallibility is twofold, that is, the formally revealed, and the virtually revealed, such as the theological conclusions and dogmatic facts (orthodoxy of a book, legitimacy of a Council, canonization, approbation of religious societies), 353–355. On the means of knowing whether a particular document of the Magisterium is infallible, 355–357. Assent of faith is due to the infallible definitions of the Magisterium, and religious assent is due to any other of its pronouncements, 357–359. On the infallibility of the Roman Pontiff, *see this entry*

Irenaeus (St.) testifies that the Roman See was founded by Peter and Paul, 327. His famous text about the Roman primacy is the object of different interpretations, escpecially on the part of non-Catholic scholars, footnote 86

Jansenism in political matters blends with Gallicanism, footnote 42. The Jansenistic Synod of Pistoia denied the primacy of St. Peter and of the Pope, 303, footnotes 65 and 83, and the coercive power of the Church, 290, footnote 50. Jansenius was repeatedly condemned by the Holy See, footnote 143. See *Gallicanism*

Jerome (St.) in his fight against the Roman deacons uttered a strong and ambiguous affirmation about the identity of priests and bishops as to their power, footnote 205

Jurisdiction is the essential power of any perfect society, 282, 297, and hence it is necessarily found in the Church, 289–292, according to its three functions, the legislative, the judicial, and the coercive, 291f. The Church's legislative function reaches also internal acts, at least indirectly,

297. Its judicial function reaches directly internal acts in the sacrament of Penance, 297. By virtue of its coercive power the Church can inflict spiritual as well as temporal punishment, except probably capital punishment and corporal torture, 298. *See Forum. Powers (of the Church). Society*

Laity. The theology of the laity, recently emphasized by theologians and Vatican II, has been prepared by several recent doctrines and movements in the Church, 421–423. Notion of laity, 423, footnote 240. The distinction between clergy and laity has been explicitly pointed out for the first time by Clement of Rome toward the end of the first century, 278.

The laity, by virtue of its incorporation to Christ through Baptism and Confirmation, shares in the priestly, prophetical, and kingly functions of Christ and in the consequent apostolic mission of the Church, 423–430. Among other things, the laity enjoys active participation in the offering of the Eucharistic sacrifice, occasional private charisms of God, manifestation of free opinion and humble advice to the authority, Christian sense in matters of faith, participation in the proper apostolate of the Church (for instance under the form of the so-called Catholic Action), and particularly active sanctification of temporal things and consecration of the secular world to God, 425–430. *See Members (of the Church)*

Leo XIII on the Church as a perfect external society, 290, footnote 44

Liberalism, prevailing in modern nations since the last century, inspires its policy in the principle of complete separation between Church and State, 281, footnote 42. *See State (or civil society)*

Liturgy, as to the sense and use of the word, 284f., 292

Magisterium. Notion, 271, 282, existence in the Church, 287–289, properties and functions, 293f. Division into ordinary and extraordinary Magisterium, value and infallibility of both, 351–353. Also the Pope exercises the ordinary besides the extraordinary Magisterium, 352. The Magisterium in its pronouncements is the source of an obligation of assent, coming directly either from the Magisterium itself or from God, 293, 296.

The principal pronouncements made by the Magisterium regarding the Church are: on the Mystical Body, 256–259; on the Roman Pontiff's primacy and infallibility, 297f., 333–335, 339–343; on the divine origin of episcopacy, 362–364, and its collegiality, *see this entry*; on the title "Mother Church," 262f.; on the axiom "Outside the Church there is no salvation," 419; on the four properties of the Church, 433–435. *See Infallibility. Jurisdiction. Powers (of the Church)*

Marsilius of Padua is the founder of the caesaropapistic or regalistic doctrine on the subjection of the Pope to the civil power, 274, 303, footnotes 42 and 65. *See Caesaropapism. Regalism*

Mary, Blessed Virgin, is the Mother of the Church and the first member of the Mystical Body, 257, 269

Members (of the Church). Notion of member of a society and distinction from subject of the same, footnote 222. Strictly speaking, only the members of the Catholic Church are members of the Mystical Body, 411–413. Strictly speaking, only those are members of the Church and of the Mystical Body who are baptized and afterwards keep the three bonds of faith, worship, and obedience to Church authority, 413–418; some ambiguous or disputed cases in this matter, 414–416.

The various members of the Mystical Body according to Pius XII, 257, and to theological reasoning, 269–270. The Pope and the bishops are special members of the Mystical Body, 269. Vatican II extends the concept of member of the Church by a broader distinction between complete and incomplete incorporation or bond of men to the Catholic Church, 258f., 412, 416. Thus all men belong in some way to the Catholic Church by reason of various elements of salvation, scattered also among non-Catholics, non-Christians, and mere pagans, meaning of the traditional axiom: "Outside the Church there is no salvation," 418–420. With regard to the clergy and the laity, as members of the Church, *see these two entries. See also Church*

Missionary Activity of the Church and its relation with the pagan or secular world at large, emphasized by Vatican II, 447f.

Modernists deny the foundation of the Church by Christ, footnotes 8 and 15, its nature as a true society, footnotes 42 and 65, and the divine origin of episcopacy, footnote 158

Mystical Body is a technical expression for the Church, first coined in the Middle Ages, but based on St. Paul's "Body of Christ" and the patristic "Spiritual Body," 244. The Mystical Body is the very essence of the Church; *see this entry*

Old Catholics, a small schismatic church started in Germany, Austria, and Switzerland in 1871, as a protest against the Vatican definition of the infallibility of the Pope, which has no longer any public importance, deny Peter's primacy or its transmission to the Roman Pontiff, and particularly papal infallibility 347, footnote 120

Orders (Power of). Name and notion of the power of Orders, 282, 293, 294f., 389, and its existence in the Church, 283–287. This power is given "ex opere operato" through a sacrament and consists in a permanent physical character, 294, 299. We may, however, distinguish a twofold power of Orders, one sacramental, and the other merely liturgical, 295, 299. The expressions "sacerdos" (pries), "sacerdotium" (priestly office), "sacerdotale" (priestly, sacerdotal), for the ministers of the New Testament began to be used only in the 3rd century, 289.

The power, or hierarchy of Orders, by immediate divine institution is combined of three degrees, namely, episcopate, presbyterate, and diaconate, 390–401. Meaning and use of the names bishop, priest, and deacon, 393–398, footnotes 157 and 197. Taking Magisterium and jurisdiction in a broad sense, they are in some way included in the power of Orders but strictly and properly they are totally distinct from it, footnote 208. *See Bishop. Deacon. Jurisdiction. Powers (of the Church). Priest. Subdiaconate-Minor Orders*

Orientals (Orthodox). Orthodox theologians either deny St. Peter's primacy or admit it only as a personal privilege not to be transmitted, 303, footnotes 65 and 71. Hence they mainly and directly deny the primacy of the Roman Pontiff, footnote 83, and his infallibility, footnote 120. They profess the four properties of the Church mentioned in the Constantinopolitan Creed itself, but they attribute to them a restrictive sense, especially with regard to unity and Catholicity, footnote 259.

In the Orthodox church there is no unity of government, no extrinsic catholicity or universal expansion, and no formal apostolicity as long as its bishops are not in communion with the Apostolic See or the successor of St. Peter, 443f. The Greek church has officially canonized very few saints, while the Russian church since 1721 has canonized at least 140 Russian saints, footnote 272

Pagans. Non-Christian monotheists (Jews and Mohammedans) or polytheists (simply called pagans), belong in some way to the unity of the Catholic Church, by reason of the various elements of truth which they have and through which the Holy Spirit, soul of the Catholic Church, may work their salvation, 417f.

Penance, as a sacrament, involves an act of true jurisdiction, 297, 299

People of God is an emphatic expression, used both in the O.T. for Israel the chosen people and in the N.T. for the Church, 249, 253, 261, and recently inculcated by Vatican II, 261

Peter (St.) The name Peter (from the Greek "Pétros," with which the Gospel translates in the masculine form the original Aramaic word "Kepha" = Greek "Petra" = rock) was given directly by Christ to Simon, footnote 73. Peter died in the year 64, while St. John, who survived all the other apostles, died at the end of the first century under Pope Clement of Rome, Peter's third successor, footnote 76. St. Peter's primacy must be distinguished from his apostleship, common to the other apostles, 301f. St. Peter received from Christ a true primacy or a full power of Magisterium and jurisdiction over the entire Church, 302–311. The exercise of this primacy by Peter is shown in the Bible, 308. Its fittingness, 310f. Why was this primacy given to St. Peter personally rather than to another apostle, 309f. Expressions of St. Peter's primacy in Scripture and Tradition: "Rock" of the Church (Matthew), "Shepherd" of all the faithful (John), "Christ's Vicar" (Ambrose), "Pastor of the Church" (Augustine), "Prince of the Apostles" (Eusebius Caes.), "Peter's Chair" (Jerome, Augustine), "Where Peter is there is the Church" (Ambrose), 304, 307, 308, 310. With regard to Peter's Roman sojourn, *see Rome*. *See Roman Pontiff*

Photius, patriarch of Constantinople in the 9th century, was the first among Orientals to deny the primacy of the Roman Pontiff, thus paving the way to schism, which took place in the 11th century through the work of patriarch Michael Caerularius, footnote 83. *See Caerularius (Michael)*

Pius XII in his Encyclical "Mystical Body" proposed this same expression as the proper definition of the Church, 244, 256, 412. Doctrinal summary of this Encyclical, 256–258. Pius particularly emphasizes the doctrine of the Holy Spirit as the soul of the Church, which has since become common among the theologians, 257f., 267f. The Catholic Church and the Mystical Body are perfectly equivalent, 258. Members of the Church and of the Mystical Body are only those who are united to it by the triple bond of Baptism, faith, and government, 257, 413

Pope. *See Roman Pontiff*

Powers (of the Church). The three powers of Order, Magisterium, and jurisdiction are a participation of the triple function of Christ, as prophet, priest, and king, 272. Hence they are also an extension of the influence of Christ as the head of the Mystical Body, 272. The Pope and the bishops, as holders of this threefold power, are special members of the Mystical Body, footnote 39. Notion and distinction of those three powers, 282f., 293f. Each of them reaches also internal acts, footnote 59. Schematic division of all the powers in the Church, 299. Theologians debate the question whether there are two subjects or only one subject of the supreme power and infallibility in the Church, 350f., footnote 177. *See Bishop. Church. Jurisdiction. Magisterium. Orders. Peter (St.). Roman Pontiff*

Priest is the second degree of the power or hierarchy of Orders, divinely instituted; *see Orders (Power of)*. Historical development of this degree, 393–398. Its proper sacerdotal character is explicitly brought forth since the 3rd century, 396. St. Jerome's ambiguous assertion about the identity of priest and bishop, footnote 205. Functions of the priest, 393–398, 402f. *See Bishop. Deacon*

Primacy. *See Peter (St.). Roman Pontiff*

Properties or Marks (of the Church). The four characteristics of the Church, namely, unity, sanctity, Catholicity, and apostolicity, can be considered as properties deriving from its essence, 431–438, and as marks distinguishing the true Church founded by Christ from others, 439–444. They were formulated for the first time by the Council of Constantinople I in its Creed, 433. For the apologetical purpose their consideration is still valuable in the present time, footnote 267. *See the corresponding four entries just named*

Protestants (Liberal) teach that the Church is not an external society but a purely internal union or movement; some recent authors, however, softened this doctrine, giving a relative importance also to the exterior elements of the Church, with the exclusion of any true authority, foot-notes 8, 15, 42 and 65. In particular they all deny the divine origin of episcopacy, footnotes 158 and 191. *See Barth. Cullmann. Protestants (Orthodox)*

Protestants (Orthodox) distinguish a twofold church, one purely interior, the other exterior, built on preaching and sacraments (at least Baptism) but deprived of true authority and admitting no distinction between laity and clergy, footnotes 42 and 65. Consequently they reject the pow-ers of jurisdiction, Order, and Magisterium, 283, 287, footnotes 50 and 199, St. Peter's primacy, footnote 71, and his Roman sojourn, footnote 99, the primacy and infallibility of the Roman Pontiff, footnote 120, the divine origin of episcopacy, footnote 158. However, Anglicans, Epis-copalians, and Scandinavian Lutherans admit the divine institution of episcopacy understood generically as an undetermined essential ministry, footnote 158.

Protestants admit the four properties of the Church only in a limited manner; this gave rise among them to the so-called ecumenical movement, footnote 259; *see Ecumenism*. Protestants cannot claim for their churches the four marks of the true Church; they have no unity of government and strictly no unity of faith, since they agree only in some fundamental truths; they have no active sanctity, that is, all the means of salvation, for Baptism and mere faith in Christ are insufficient to foster holiness; nor internal catholicity, that is, all the doctrines of faith and all the means of sanctification; nor apostolicity, by reason of their break from Tradition, which is the only guarantee of connection with the apostolic Church, 441–443. In 1925 the Anglican Church canonized several saints, footnote 270. *See Anglicans. Protestants (Liberal)*

Regalism is a general politico-religious doctrine or movement, started in the 14th century by Marsilius of Padua, which fosters the subjection of the ecclesiastical power to the civil authority, footnote 42. Consequently it denies also St. Peter's and the Roman Pontiff's primacy, 303, footnote 65. *See Caesaropapism. Gallicanism. Marsilius of Padua*

Religious societies are not strictly and directly of divine institutions but of ecclesiastical or canonical origin, footnote 240. Members of these societies do not belong to the laity in the proper sense of this word, but only in the narrower sense of persons distinct from clerics, footnote 240. The approbation of religious societies is one of the objects of the infalli-bility of the Magisterium, by reason of its connection with the revealed truth, 354f.

Roman Pontiff. The adversaries of papal primacy point out several natural causes of its historical rising, footnote 83. The historical argu-ment for papal primacy, 315–324. Some traditional expressions: "Peter's See—Peter's Chair—Apostolic Rock—Living Peter—Peter's Heir—Peter speaks through the Pope's mouth—Rome has spoken, the case is closed—The First See is judged by no one," 320f. The existence of the papal primacy does not depend on the question whether St. Peter came to Rome, although this fact is very probable, 312; *see Rome.* Papal primacy implies episcopal, supreme, and universal authority over the entire Church 332–336.

The Roman Pontiff is infallible when speaking *ex cathedra*, 339–348. This expression implies four conditions, namely, that the Pope speak as head of the whole Church, that he propose it authoritatively and definitively, 338f. The Fathers call the Roman Pontiff: Doctor of truth (Ignatius of Antioch), Rule of faith (Irenaeus), Arbiter of faith (Augustine: "Rome has spoken, the case is closed"), 346. The alleged cases of grave errors, attributed especially to Popes Liberius, Vigilius, and Honorius, 348f.

The Roman Pontiff has the right of acquiring and retaining a civil power or state (as is the case of the Vatican City), footnote 47 and 276. The fullness of the papal power is not opposed to the true power of the bishops, 336, nor does the supreme authority of the episcopal college diminish the papal primacy, 373, 375, 379. On the requirements for obtaining or losing the primacy, 329–330. The Pope can freely resign, as was certainly done twice in history, by Celestine V and Gregory XII, footnote 107. Disputable questions are the following: whether a Pope elected but not yet consecrated bishop can immediately exercise his supreme jurisdiction, 330; whether the Pope can choose his successor, 329; whether a Pope privately falling into heresy is no longer Pope, 330. *See Peter (St.). Rome*

Rome. The dogmatic question of the papal primacy is independent of the historical question whether St. Peter came to Rome and moreover was bishop of Rome, 313. However, even these two facts are very probable, or rather morally certain from historical testimonies, 325–329. Various lists of the Roman Pontiffs ascending to St. Peter in ancient testimonies, 328. Uncertain results of Roman excavations connected with this matter, 329f. The Church primacy was *de facto* bound by St. Peter to the Roman See, 324, either by divine right and instigation or by the Apostle's personal choice, and, at least in the first case, the fact is irreformable and the see of Rome is eternal, 324f. *See Peter (St.). Roman Pontiff*

Sacrament. The episcopal consecration is sacramental or rather the fullness of the sacrament of Orders, 373

Salvation. History of salvation from the fall of Adam to the foundation of the Church by Christ, 246–254. Salvation of souls is the proper purpose of the Church, 243ff., 247, 279, 283, 286, 289, 298. Meaning of the traditional maxim: "Outside the Church there is no salvation," 418–420

Sanctity (of the Church), as a property of the Church, 436f., and as a distinguishing mark of the true Church, 440f. Sanctity of the Church is taken both passively and actively, that is, the Church is holy in its members and possesses all the means of sanctification, 431

Scripture (Holy). The word "Church" in the Bible, 242, and the Pauline expression "Body of Christ," 244. The Church under the image of sheep and sheepfold, proper to St. John, 263, 307f., and under the title "Spouse of Christ," common to St. John and St. Paul, 263f. Other expressions describing the Church as Kingdom of God, People of God, Temple or House of God, 241, 250, 260–262. St. Paul's doctrine on the Mystical Body, 259f.

The true social character of the Church, 275–277. Authenticity and proper meaning of Matt. 16.18f. and John 21.15–17 on Peter's primacy, 304–308. The biblical basis for the primacy of the Roman Pontiff is the perpetuity of Peter's primacy, 306, 315. Nothing points out the connection of Peter's primacy with the Roman See, footnote 85; there are, however, several allusions to Peter's going to Rome, footnote 100. The infallibility of the Roman Pontiff is based on the same two texts of Matthew and John, 343.

The divine origin of the episcopacy, as power of jurisdiction, is implicitly contained in Scripture, 364–366. It is uncertain whether those who are called bishops or presbyters in the Bible, were real bishops or simple priests, 365, 393. Biblical foundation of the collegiality of episcopacy, 372, and of its monarchical character, 383f. Use of the names bishop, presbyter, and deacon, footnotes 157 and 197. The name "priest" in the proper sense of the Latin word "sacerdos" (performer or worship and sacrifice) is not given to the ministers of the N.T., footnote 198. Divine institution of the three degrees of the hierarchy of Orders, 393–395

Society. Definition of a true and perfect society, 272, 279. The civil society has only the power of jurisdiction, while the Church is endowed also with the powers of Orders and Magisterium, 282, 286, 289. An imperfect society, like the family, has no true jurisdiction, 291, footnote 49. The Church in its external structure is a true and perfect society, in which the Mystical Body is found, 241, 272. Both concepts of external society and Mystical Body must be included in the essential definition of the Church, 244, 256, 263–265. The exterior society is only the visible part of the Mystical Body itself, 265, 292. The Catholic Church as a whole is perfectly equivalent to the Mystical Body, 258, 269, 411–413. *See Church. State*

State (or civil society). The Church is independent from the state and simply superior to it, but the State is also a perfect and independent society in its proper temporal order, 280. In mixed matters or in the case of conflict, the rights of the Church prevail in principle, but the practical policy suggests rather a mutual agreement and a friendly cooperation of the two powers, 280f. *See Church. Forum. Society*

Subdiaconate and Minor Orders, as to their historical origin and development, 405–406. With regard to their true origin and nature, the more common and probable opinion holds that they are not of divine institution

479

nor sacramental, 408. The first to mention one these orders (the lector) is Tertullian at the end of the second century; the first to mention all of them is Pope Cornelius in the middle of the 3rd century, 405f. All these orders have been abolished in the Latin Church by Paul VI (in 1972), 408. *See Orders (Power of)*

Synagogue, being only the embryo of the future Church, 248–250, was *ipso facto* abolished when the Church was instituted, 253f.

Temporal goods are not alien to the spiritual nature and purpose of the Church. Hence the Church has the right to possess temporal goods, to oblige the faithful to furnish them, to have also, if necessary, a civil power or state (as is now the Vatican City), to intervene in temporal and social affairs with its doctrine and influence, 446f., footnote 47

Tertullian, while still a Catholic, affirmed the primacy of the Roman Pontiff and uttered the famous expression: "O happy Rome," but in his heretical montanistic period he denied the papal primacy, teaching that Christ gave the primacy to Peter only as a personal privilege, 318

Theologians vary in opinion about the following questions: Whether the Magisterium obliges directly, or only indirectly as a mere condition of the obligation coming directly from God, 293. Whether the ecclesiastical jurisdiction reaches directly internal acts, footnote 58. Whether the monarchical episcopate, as such, is of divine institution, footnote 191. Whether the three degrees of the power of Orders are of immediate divine institution, footnote 199. Whether the subdiaconate and the minor orders, now abolished, were of divine origin and sacramental, 406–408. Whether the following persons are properly members of the Church: catechumens, those invalidly baptized, internal heretics, material or bona fide heretics, persons solemnly excommunicated, 415f.

Thomas Aquinas (St.) has no distinct treatise on the Church, 241. His doctrine on the Mystical Body does not disagree with the doctrine of Pius XII in his Encyclical "Mystical Body," footnote 33. Long before Pius XII St. Thomas taught that the Holy Spirit is the soul of the Church, footnote 23

Tradition. The social character of the Church, 278–279. St. Peter's primacy 80f. Archaeological monuments on St. Peter's primacy, 309. Some ambiguous expressions of the Fathers in this matter, footnote 78. The primacy of the Roman Pontiff, 315–324, 335. Its negation by Tertullian and its ambiguous expression by St. Cyprian, 318–320. St. Peter's Roman sojourn, episcopacy, and martyrdom, *see Rome*. The Roman Pontiff's infallibility, 345–346. The divine origin of episcopacy, 366–368. Collegiality of the episcopacy, 372f. Divine origin of the monarchical episcopate, 384f. The immediate divine origin of the three degrees of the power of Orders and their historical development, 395–400. *See Fathers (of the Church)*

Unity (of the Church), as to its general notion, 431, as a property of the

Church, 435f., and as a distinctive mark of the true Church, 440

Vatican Council I. The Magisterium or teaching power of the Church, 287f. The Council's infallible definition of St. Peter's primacy, 304, footnote 308, of the primacy of the Roman Pontiff, 314, of the fullness of his power, 334–335, and of his infallibility, 342. The Council affirms the three facts of St. Peter's Roman sojourn, episcopacy, and martyrdom, footnote 99. The full meaning of the Vatican definition on papal infallibility, 338f., 342. Dissent of some Fathers in the Council about this definition, 347, footnote 120. The divine origin of episcopacy, 363. The infallibility of the episcopal body as a whole, footnote 183

Vatican Council II. Ecumenical and eschatological aspects of the Church, 241. History of salvation, 247. The Mystical Body, 258f. Church and State are mutually independent, footnote 44. On the threefold ecclesiastical power of Orders, Magisterium, and jurisdiction, 288. The expression "Ministers of government," used by the Council does not undervalue the true jurisdictional power of the Church, but only emphasizes its ministerial character, as being a service to the people, 293, footnote 54. The Council endorses in full the definitions of Vatican I on St. Peter's primacy, 304, footnote 80, and on the primacy and infallibility of the Roman Pontiff, 304, 334, 342f., footnote 123. The interpretation and valuation of papal documents, footnote 148. A religious submission is due to all pronouncements of the Magisterium, footnote 155.

Divine origin of the episcopacy, 363. The Council completes the doctrine of Trent and Vatican I on episcopacy, 363f., and sets forth the explicit concept of collegiality, *see this entry.* Infallibility of the episcopal college, footnote 183

Immediate divine institution of the three degrees of the power of Orders, 391, 392. The proper functions of bishops, 385, 401, and priests, footnote 209. The Catholic Church and the Mystical Body are the same thing, 412, and consequently the members of the Church and of the Mystical Body are only those who are united to it by Baptism, faith, and government, 413. However, all men without exception belong, in different manners and degrees, to the unity of the Catholic Church, 258, 416–418, 434. The Council's doctrine on the laity, 423. The Council particularly insists on and promotes the manifold activity of the Church in the world at large, namely, the temporal, missionary, ecumenical, and eschatological activities, 448–453, footnotes 273ff.; *see these four entries.* The Council issued no infallible definitions, footnote 152

Wyclif (John) rejected the three powers of Orders, Magisterium, and jurisdiction, 283, 287, and followed the regalistic doctrine, 274, footnote 42; *see Regalism*

BIBLIOGRAPHY

Antón, A., "El tratado 'De Ecclesia' nuevo centro de perspectiva en la enseñanza de la teología," *Gregorianum* 50 (1969) 651–688.

Bouyer, L., *L'Eglise de Dieu, corps du Christ et temple de l'Esprit*, Paris 1970.

Bovis, A. de, *What is the Church?* (tr. R. J. Trevett), New York 1961.

Braun, F. M., *Aspects nouveaux du problème de l'Eglise*, Freiburg (Schweiz) 1944.

Brinktrine, J., *Die Lehre von der Kirche*, Paderborn 1964.

Butler, Chr., *The Idea of the Church*, Baltimore, Md. 1963

Cerfaux, L., *La théologie de l'Eglise suivant Saint Paul*, éd. 3, Paris 1965.

Church (The) Today, Glen Rock, NJ. 1968.

Congar, Y.M.-J., *Vraie et fausse réforme dans l'Eglise*, Paris 1950; éd. 2, 1968; *The Mystery of the Church* (tr. A. V. Littledale), Baltimore, Md. 1960; *L'ecclésiologie du haut moyen âge. De saint Grégoire le Grand à la désunion entre Byzance et Rome*, Paris 1968; *L'Eglise de saint Augustin à l'époque moderne*, Paris 1970; *L'Eglise une, sainte, catholique et apostolique*, Paris 1970.

Coppens, J., "L'Eglise dans l'optique des controverses récentes." *Ephemerides theologicae Lovanienses* 47 (1971) 478–488.

Coppens, J. et al. (eds.), *Ecclesia a Spiritu Sancto Edocta. Mélanges théologiques: Hommage à Mgr Gérard Philips*, Gembloux 1970.

Daniélou, J., *Pourquoi l'Eglise*, Paris 1972.

Di Giorgi, S., *La Chiesa della speranza. La prima trattazione di ecclesiologia biblica*, Torino 1968.

Dirkswager, E. J., *Readings in the Theology of the Church*, Englewood Cliffs, NJ. 1970.

Ecclésiologie (L') au XIXe siècle (collective work), Strasbourg 1959.

Eglise (L') aujourd'hui (collective work, translated from the German by A. Liefooghe), Paris-Tournai 1967.

Ekklesia, Festschrift für Bischof Dr. Matthias Vehr, Trier 1962.

Faynel, P., *L'Eglise*, 2 vols., Paris 1970.

Fries, H., *L'Eglise. Questions actuelles*, Paris 1966.

Garrone, G.-M., *L'Eglise 1965–1972*, Paris 1972.

Gherardini, B., *La Chiesa, Arca dell 'Alleanza. La sua genesi, il suo paradosso, i suoi poteri, il suo servizio*. Rome 1971.

Grabowski, St. J., *The Church*, St. Louis, Mo. 1958.

Hainz, J., *Ekklesia*, Regensburg 1972.

Hamer, J., *The Church Is a Communion* (trans. from the French), New York 1964.

Hasseveldt, R., *The Church, a Divine Mystery* (tr. W. Storry), Chicago 1954.

Jaki, St., *Les tendances nouvelles de l'ecclésiologie*, Rome 1957.

Journet, Ch., *L'Eglise du Verbe Incarné*, vol. 1, Bruges-Paris 1941 (éd. 2, 1955); vol. 2, 1951; vol. 3, 1969. Only the first volume has been translated into English: *The Church and the Word Incarnate* (tr. A. H. C. Downes) New York 1950.

Küng, H., *Die Kirche*, Freiburg i. Br. 1967. French trans., *L'Eglise*, Paris 1968.

English trans., *The Church*, New York 1968. See criticism to Küng's views on the Church in *Nouvelle revue théologique* 89 (1967) 1085–1095; *Revue des sciences philosophiques et théologiques* 53 (1969) 639–706; *Revue thomiste* 70 (1970) 292–310; *Ephemerides theologicae Lovanienses* 46 (1970) 121–130; *Civiltà Cattolica* (1970), vol. 1, pp. 354–366; *Istina* (1970) 389–424.

Latourelle, R., *Christ and the Church: Signs of Salvation* (tr. Sr. D. Parker), Staten Island, N.Y. 1972.

Le Guillon, M. J., *Le Christ et l'Eglise. Théologie du Mystère*, Paris 1963.

Lubac, H. de, *Splendor of the Church* (tr. M. Mason), Glen Rock, N.J. 1956; *The Church: Paradox and Mystery* (tr. J. R. Dunne), Staten Island, N.Y. 1970; *Les églises particulières dans l'Eglise universelle*, Paris 1971.

Maritain J., *De Eglise du Christ. La personne de l'Eglise et son personnel*, Bruges 1970. English trans. by J. W. Evans: *On the Church of Christ*, Notre Dame, Ind. 1973.

Menard, E., *L'ecclésiologie hier et aujourd'hui*, Bruges 1966.

Montecheuil, Y. de, *Aspects of the Church*, Chicago 1955.

Mistero (Il) della Chiesa, 2 vols., Roma 1966.

Mysterium Salutis. Dogmatique de l'histoire du salut (translation of the German collective work), I/3: *L'Eglise et la transmission de la révélation*, Paris, 1969.

Nouvelle (Pour une) image de l'Eglise, Gembloux 1970.

Parente, P., *Saggio di una ecclesiologia alla luce del Vaticano Secondo*, Roma 1968; *Teologia di Cristo, 2: Grazia...La Chiesa...*, Roma 1971.

Paul, R. S., *The Church In Search of Itself*, Grand Rapids 1972.

Philips, G., *L'Eglise et son mystére au Deuxième Concile du Vatican. Histoire, texte et commentaire de la Constitution "Lumen Gentium,"* 2 vols., Tournai-Paris 1966–1968.

Powell, J., *The Mystery of the Church*, Milwaukee, Wis. 1967.

Rahner, K. et al., *The Church: Readings in Theology*, New York 1963.

Rahner, K., *Strukturwandel der Kirche als Aufgabe und Chance*, Freiburg i. Br. 1972.

Ratzinger, J., *Le Nouveau Peuple de Dieu* (trans. from the German), Paris 1971.

Rendtorff, T., *Church and Theology, The Systematic Function of the Church Concept in Modern Theology* (tr. R. H. Fuller), Philadelphia, Pa. 1971.

Rodriguez, P. "Recientes contribuciones a la elaboración de un tratado dogmatico 'De Ecclesia,'" *Scripta theologica* 5 (1973) 881–920.

Schillebeeckx, E., *The Mission of the Church* (tr. N. D. Smith), New York 1973.

Schmaus, M., *Dogma, 4: The Church: Its Origin and Structure* (tr. M. Ledderer), New York 1972.

Scipioni, A. I., "De charactere paedagogiae nostrae 'Docentiae' in tractatu 'De Ecclesia,'" *Angelicum* 43 (1966) 429–444.

Semmelroth, O., *The Church and Christian Belief* (tr. T. R. Milligan), New York 1967.

Vatican II: The Constitution on the Church (ed. K. McNamara), New York 1968.

Vatican II: The Theological Dimensions (ed. A. D. Lee), The Thomist Press, 1963.